The Gospel of Peace and Justice

P6 - Basic needs

MSGR. JOSEPH GREMILLION is among the few North Americans equally at home in both national and international governmental, ecumenical, and Roman Catholic circles involved with the search for global peace and justice. He served from 1960 to 1967 as Director of Development for Catholic Relief Services and was Co-chairman of SODEPAX (joint peace and justice committee of the World Council of Churches and the Vatican) while serving as Secretary of the Pontifical Commission.

For three decades he has been involved in such basic human situations as the resettlement of World War II refugees, the plight of Latin American farmers, the conditions of the Chicano migrant workers, world food production (observer for the Holy See to FAO), and adult education in the Third World (U.S. State Department delegate to UNESCO).

At present Msgr. Gremillion is a Fellow in Theology at the University of Notre Dame and Co-ordinator of the Interreligious Peace Colloquium, an organization which brings together the world's five most influential faiths to plan concerted action on issues of global injustice and threats to peace. In Spring, 1976, he was also appointed Regents' Lecturer at the Law School of the University of California at Berkeley.

The Gospel of Peace and Justice

Catholic Social Teaching since Pope John

Presented by Joseph Gremillion

ORBIS BOOKS

MARYKNOLL, NEW YORK

Nihil Obstat: Daniel V. Flynn, J.C.D.
            Censor Librorum
Imprimatur: + James P. Mahoney, D.D.
            Vicar General, Archdiocese of New York
            November 19, 1975

The nihil obstat and imprimatur are official declarations that a book or pamphlet is free of doctrinal or moral error. No implication is contained therein that those who have granted the nihil obstat and imprimatur agree with the contents, opinions, or statements expressed.

Library of Congress Catalog Card Number: 75-39892
Cloth: ISBN 088344-1659   Paper: ISBN 088344-1667
Manufactured in the United States of America

Fifth Printing, March 1980

Contents

Foreword, by James S. Rausch   ix

Preface   xi

PART ONE
OVERVIEW AND PROSPECTUS

Section I: Evolution of Catholic Social Teaching since Pope John:
The Influence of Secular Currents and World Events   3

Chapter 1
Man's Needs and Aspirations   5

Chapter 2
Unjust Power Structures: Liberation and Reform   15

Chapter 3
Science's Magnification—and Socialization—of Economic Power   23

Chapter 4
Political Power, Ideology, Commitment   39

Chapter 5
Transnational Structures for Justice and Development   47

Chapter 6
The Global Political Community   57

Chapter 7 ✓
Population, Resources, Environment   91

Chapter 8 ✓
The Family's Fate in Technological Society   111

Chapter 9 ✓
Socio-Cultural Effects of Industrialization   113

Section II: The Church as Social Actor   125

Section III: Gospel-and-World Issues: Toward Deeper
Theological Reflection   133

PART TWO
THE DOCUMENTS

Mater et Magistra: Christianity and Social Progress (May 15, 1961)   143

Pacem in Terris: Peace on Earth (April 11, 1963)   201

Gaudium et Spes: Pastoral Constitution on the Church in the Modern
World (Second Vatican Council, December 7, 1965)   243

Dignitatis Humanae: Declaration on Religious Freedom
(Second Vatican Council, December 7, 1965)   337

Message to Humanity (Second Vatican Council, October 20, 1962)   351

Unitatis Redintegratio: Decree on Ecumenism (Second Vatican Council,
November 21, 1964)   355

Nostra Aetate: Declaration on the Relationship of the Church to Non-
Christian Religions (Second Vatican Council, October 28, 1965)   373

Address of His Holiness Paul VI to the General Assembly of the
United Nations (October 4, 1965)   379

Populorum Progressio: On the Development of Peoples
(March 26, 1967)   387

To the Peoples of Africa: Message of His Holiness Paul VI to the Hierarchy
and to All the Peoples of Africa for the Promotion of the
Religious, Civil and Social Good of their Continent
(October 29, 1967) [Excerpts]   417

✓ = see p. xiii

Humanae Vitae: On the Regulation of Birth (July 25, 1968)   427

Medellín Documents: Justice, Peace, Family and Demography, Poverty
    of the Church (September 6, 1968)   445

Message of His Eminence Maurice Cardinal Roy, President of the
    Pontifical Commission "Justice and Peace," on the Occasion of the
    Launching of the Second Development Decade
    (November 19, 1970)   477

Octogesima Adveniens: The Eightieth Anniversary of
    "Rerum Novarum" (May 14, 1971)   485

Justice in the World: Synod of Bishops Second General Assembly
    (November 30, 1971)   513

Reflections by Cardinal Maurice Roy on the Occasion of the Tenth
    Anniversary of the Encyclical "Pacem in Terris" of Pope John XXIII
    (April 11, 1973)   531

Letter of Paul VI to the Federation of Asian Bishops' Conferences,
    First General Assembly, Taipei (April 22–27, 1974)   569

Bull of Indiction of the Holy Year 1975 (May 23, 1974)   573

The Holy See's Intervention at the United Nations Conference on
    Population, Bucharest (August 30, 1974)   589

Evangelization of the Modern World: Synod of Bishops Third General
    Assembly (October 26, 1974)   593

Address of His Holiness Pope Paul VI to the Participants of the
    World Food Conference, Rome (November 9, 1974)   599

Reconciliation—the Way to Peace: Message of His Holiness Pope Paul VI
    for the Celebration of the Day of Peace (January 1, 1975)   607

Index   615
Abbreviations   623

Foreword

The social documents of the aggiornamento reflect something new in the life of the Church, although they are also rooted firmly in the Catholic tradition. The newness is of several kinds.

This body of doctrine articulates the effort of the Church to address the needs and issues of today's world, a world which may indeed be passing through a vast turning point in history. These documents represent, too, a significant breakthrough in Christian thought. Discarding the exaggerated dualism which over the centuries has hampered the attempt of religion to relate to the secular order, they manifest a new awareness that it is an essential part of the Christian mission to humanize and thereby Christianize political, social, economic, cultural, and technological life. The "Church" and the "world" are not identical, but neither are they in irrevocable opposition. For while the "Church" transcends the "world," it also exists *in* the world. Existing there, it has a duty to seek to transform the world according to the mind and message of Christ.

It is neither pietistic nor triumphalistic to believe that the Catholic Church is singularly well-equipped to perform this role. We are, as Monsignor Gremillion remarks, moving into the era of a truly "planetary society." To be sure, this society is often rent by tensions and conflicts which seem to threaten its unity. But in certain respects the unity is already an achieved and irreversible fact. Socioeconomic interdependence on a global scale is a reality of overwhelming importance, as the food and energy crises have forcefully reminded us. The reality of interdependence can operate for good or ill. And the task of the Catholic Church today is to help make interdependence a positive reality. This the Church *can* do precisely because, both in theory and in fact, it is a unique transnational society committed to the highest of human and Christian values.

The social teaching of the aggiornamento Church has special relevance for American Catholics. There are several reasons for this. For one thing, we are citizens of a nation which is one of the dominant superpowers of the world. What the United States does—politically, economically, culturally, militarily—creates waves of influence which circle the globe with dramatic speed and impact. In light of our religious tradition, American Catholics can scarcely be indifferent to the ways in which their country uses its immense power. Furthermore, American Catholicism itself has a long and distinguished history of commitment to social justice. The bicentennial program of the National Conference of Catholic Bishops—a program focused on the theme of "Liberty and Justice for All"—was designed to reaffirm this tradition while simultaneously identifying the new issues and orientations calling for the attention and action of American Catholics today. Close study of the social documents of the aggiornamento remains an indispensable part of this important task.

Joseph Gremillion brings unusual talents and qualifications to this effort. As first secretary of the Vatican's Justice and Peace Commission, he has played a major role on the international scene, both in the development and the practical application of the Church's social doctrine. He is moreover a man of broad scholarship and pastoral sensitivity. A priest of the Diocese of Alexandria, Louisiana, he speaks and writes as a churchman, an American, and, in the best sense, a citizen of the world. I am pleased to commend this timely, intelligent, and thought-provoking work to the attention of Catholics of the United States, especially in connection with the bicentennial, to other Christians and to all men and women of good will who share the belief that the human race can build a more just and happy world. As Monsignor Gremillion says, quoting a passage—also cited by Pope Paul VI—from *Gaudium et Spes* (Pastoral Constitution on the Church in the Modern World): "Perhaps the People of God are discovering a new call and a new way to love and serve God and all His human family. Perhaps they are hearing the Spirit of Christ speaking through Vatican II: 'The expectation of a new earth must not weaken but rather stimulate our concern for cultivating this one. For here grows the body of a new family, a body which even now is able to give some kind of foreshadowing of the new age.' "

THE MOST REV. JAMES S. RAUSCH
GENERAL SECRETARY, U.S. CATHOLIC CONFERENCE

Preface

Recently I was writing an account of the nature, functions, and history of the Pontifical Commission Justice and Peace. It was necessary to refer to a dozen key social documents of the Church since Pope John. These were scattered pell-mell about my desk, most of them only small pamphlets, even leaflets, easily lost and above all without index and cross-reference.

"Why doesn't someone collect these into one volume?" Then—"Why shouldn't I do it?" That is how this book was born.

I decided to add a short commentary, which grew over the months to a more pretentious "Overview and Prospectus," forming Part One. Part Two contains the documents, with an introductory explanation as to why these were chosen and a brief appreciation of their authority and worth. Two separate indexes follow Part Two: of my Overview and of the documents. It is all very straightforward.

I wish to thank Sister Bonita Raine for preparing these indexes, and Mrs. Janice Schilmoeller and Mrs. Barbara Hickey for deciphering my scribble and typing the manuscript.

Above all I express gratitude to the Ford Foundation, which made the grant, affording me the respite from office, cablegrams, and never-ending meetings, necessary for this and other reflection and writing; to the University of Notre Dame, which welcomed me as a Fellow and provided the atmosphere and library facilities which I needed, both for leisure and for work; and finally to my Church superiors, especially Bishop Graves of my home diocese of Alexandria, Louisiana, for permission to pursue this initiative.

This volume deals with the Roman Catholic Church—its social teaching and "conscientization" as a social actor in our fast changing world. The comparable teachings and roles of the other Christian Churches do not figure in this volume, except in passing reference.

This omission is purposeful, first, because a documented account of

Catholic social teaching, even as superficial as this, already presents more material than can be encompassed in a single volume; second, because this renovation of the Catholic Church can be easily and logically surveyed as a unified story by reason of the unity which so marks it as an institution; and third, because this evolution began under the leadership of a specific person, Pope John, with identifiable acts and dates, gathered momentum during a great historical event, Vatican II, was spurred on by other known personalities, and was then led for more than a decade by Pope Paul.

[margin annotation: Summary of Protestants]

The comparable social awakening taking place among the Protestant and Orthodox Churches is more diffuse, less easy to date and document. However, as stated several times in the Overview, their social awakening is as profound and as significant as that among Catholic bodies, particularly through and within the World Council of Churches, which provided communication and stimulation for the national and particular Churches. Of great importance too has been the social consciousness aroused within the world confessional families, notably among the Orthodox, Lutheran, Anglican, and Calvinist bodies; further, Evangelicals and the more fundamental communions show growing awareness, as seen at their Lausanne conference of 1974.

But above all, the World Council of Churches has since 1948 provided a Christian voice and platform for their common statements and actions at the world level. This, it must be remembered, was a role exercised exclusively by the Catholic Church through the Holy See—since Charlemagne in the West, and since 1453 on the global scene.

With the aggiornamento a very fruitful interchange on social issues began among the Churches, and especially between the World Council and the Holy See. In this I have been a privileged participant, particularly through Sodepax, the Committee on Society, Development and Peace, jointly constituted in 1968 by the World Council and the Pontifical Commission Justice and Peace, in close cooperation with the Unity Secretariat of the Holy See.

Naturally, this has resulted in cross-fertilization which could have been noted step-by-step in the Overview. Space precluded this. Also, my express focus here is the Catholic Church, so I have resisted deviation which could have lengthened and complicated an account already long and complex. However, I do wish to acknowledge the telling contribution of the Protestant and Orthodox Churches.

A second obvious shortcoming of this book is that it concentrates on teaching as expressed in documents, making only passing reference to

[margin annotation: this preface is becoming an Apologia]

the social ministry and pastoral praxis which implement this teaching and stimulate the doctrinal pronouncements. Also, it gives only official positions by the most authoritative institutional bodies—the papacy and the College of Bishops. It leaves aside the thousands of movements and voluntary groups, with their manifestos and studies, demonstrations and fasts, marches and petitions.

Consequently, this volume is rather formal and didactic. It does not convey the prophecy and liveliness, the risk and courage and sacrifice, which characterize so much of the Christian story today, especially in the Third World. Again, I plead guilty. I choose to tell about the "institutional" Church and what is going on at its "highest" levels. Many books are now appearing which tell of the freer and more active initiatives. It would seem, however, that a survey of these, with excerpts and summing up of their prophetic statements, praxis and witness, would fill a real need—as a means, above all, of informing and influencing ecclesial institutions and "higher" authorities.

I also find my last two chapters, on Family and on Socio-Cultural Effects, very weak. These are issues in which I am not well grounded. But I realize that they are of such significance, in themselves and in the aggiornamento documents, that they required attention, however inadequate. Nor am I satisfied with the chapter "Population, Resources, Environment." The subject is immensely more grave and complex than I have managed to convey, and its implications for the Church more weighty still.

Finally, in restudying and digesting the documents, and in writing the Overview, I have become aware at a deeper level of the integrated vision needed to grasp the whole—the whole of what is happening within our human family and within our Church. To a pastor or minister or leader, the numberless, ever-changing new elements which must enter policy- and decision-making present a confused, dismaying prospect.

The same is true even for the researcher and experienced professor in academic circles, because a main characteristic of the university is departmentalization. The contents of the simple Overview touch and draw upon many academic disciplines—economics, business, government, politics and law, international and regional studies, sociology, socio-psychology, history and anthropology; and religion, theology, ethics, philosophy, education, and value systems.

How can these specializations, each divisible into many smaller areas, be brought together into some sort of integrated whole—both within research centers and within universities, and in coalitions of these? I raise the possibility of a symbiotic approach for interrelating these several disciplines, so that they illuminate and nourish one another—in a program which might be entitled Justice and Peace Studies: to advance human knowledge and well-being, and to help bearers of the Good News that God cares for all his human family, in the here and now of this world, as well as unto its coming fulfillment.

PART ONE

Overview and Prospectus

In announcing Vatican Council II in 1960, Pope John said he wanted to open up the windows of the Church to let in fresh air from the outside world. This would permit an aggiornamento of the Church, a catching up on the immense societal changes of recent times. In the public mind these fetching and oft-repeated phrases became the hallmark of the Council and of its aftermath.

Looking back on the fifteen years of the aggiornamento—momentous years—one is struck above all by the strong currents of outside influence which have indeed rushed into the Church, and by the degree to which an opening up actually took place almost pell-mell during the decade of the 1960s, and which continues, but with greater discrimination, during the 1970s. This stimulates new ecclesial self-awareness and social consciousness within the Church as it lives amidst and reflects upon the reality of "this-world" in the light of Christ and his Spirit, freshly conceived through Vatican II.

This "conscientization" animates in turn experiments of social ministry striving to meet human needs also freshly perceived. And the resulting pastoral praxis provides new problems to theologians, canonists, biblical and other scholars, challenging them (and the Church as a whole) to deepen and broaden their own reflective grasp of the "whoness" and "whatness" of man and society, of the Church, of Christ and his Spirit breathing amidst this world.

The social documents of the aggiornamento clearly show this evolution of Church teaching and praxis influenced by the rapid transformations taking place in the secular world. Section I of this overview comments on this at some length.

1

Section II briefly points up the degree to which the Church is consciously becoming a transnational, social actor, and the directions in which its social teaching is now moving. Indeed, a signal motif of the aggiornamento documents is movement. This marks a radical departure from status quo models of society which blemished and bemused Catholic social thought since Leo XIII tried to revive medieval guilds and Pius XI and Pius XII espoused a preconceived corporative order. John began the 1960s by praising modernization and socialization; by 1970 the Church took on the *ecclesial* role of promoting deep and rapid change. Paul VI has gone so far as to affirm the value of "utopias." He appreciates their twofold appeal: as critiques of "bureaucratic socialism, technocratic capitalism and authoritarian democracy," and as provoking "the forward-looking imagination . . . to direct itself towards a fresh future" (OA 37*).

From the track of its fifteen-year trajectory I take the risk of projecting some directions in which the Church's teaching and pastoral praxis might move in the future. I also dare to project how the People of God might evolve its ecclesial structures into the next generation or more, so that "the loving, serving Church" implicit in the social documents of the aggiornamento might become more fully lived.

This overview concludes with Section III, which lists a few social issues, current and foreseeable, calling for fresh and future theological reflection. Some perhaps pose new challenges to the faith itself.

---

*OA is the abbreviation for *Octogesima Adveniens*. Similar abbreviations are used throughout, e.g., PT for *Pacem in Terris*, MM for *Mater et Magistra*, etc. The list of abbreviations used is given on page 623. The number given with the abbreviation, here OA 37, refers to the number of the paragraphs given in most papal and episcopal documents. When these are lacking in the original document, I have added numbers for the paragraphs; each such case is indicated by footnotes in Part Two.—J.G.

SECTION I

Evolution of Catholic Social Teaching since Pope John: The Influence of Secular Currents and World Events

(Intro.)

The Christian people and secular society have confronted and cooperated with each other for nineteen hundred years in the West. Their visible communities, especially as structures of Church and State, dominated the historical arena of Europe from Constantine to the French Revolution. Their struggles and reconciliations provide a principal leitmotif for fifteen hundred years of Western history as the two mighty protagonists tried to dominate and to conciliate each other in a constant dialectic of conflict and cooperation. Comparable tension and interchange continues in the wider context of God's people and the world that is both its home and its path of pilgrimage.

Christ himself lived out and foreshadowed this love-hate tension. Sent by the Father who so loved the world, he declared that his kingdom is not from here. Still he was killed, accused of claiming to be a king. Paul of Tarsus and the Christian community of the first century believed the whole secular world would crash into eschatological *kaput* within a decade or two. From the penal island of Patmos, John's followers exulted at this imminent apocalyptic collapse of this world and all its works, personified in the dominant state, the whoring empire of Rome. They saw a new heaven and a new earth coming down from God. They heard the One sitting on the throne, the Alpha and Omega, saying: "Now I am making the whole of creation new" (Rev. 21:2-3).

But Christ did not come again in the expected éclat; the old world lived on. The community of his faithful opposed it, bled, and died; or com-

3

promised, adjusted, and lived on. With Constantine, structures of reconciliation and cooperation were erected and were soon so strongly dominated by the emperor that he insisted on holding an ecumenical council, the first, because controversy about Christ's divinity generated civil strife. Within a hundred years after Nicea, the faith and the world, the Church and the State had become so intertwined that the Christian people, perhaps twenty percent of the population, were blamed for the fall of the Roman Empire. The embrace of otherworld faith was felt to be the kiss of imperial death.

So Saint Augustine wrote his apologia and launched unwittingly the still thriving mental pursuit called philosophy (and theology) of history. His sharp dichotomy between the City of God and the City of Man concretized the mind-set of Western history for over thirteen hundred years: until the secularization process begun in the eighteenth century induced this-world to declare itself adult and emancipated from other-next-world imperatives.

In general the Christian Churches clung to their Augustinian categories of the two empires and the two swords, juridically joined and constantly crossed. They fought rearguard skirmishes to retain a direct role, legally inherited and ethically supported by faith, in temporal affairs—in the political, economic, cultural, social, and scientific fields from throne and parliament to school and laboratory. The Catholic Church, perhaps because it has the longest and richest memory, was foremost in these juridical pretensions a century or so after secularization was on its definitive way.

A goodly version, then, of Western history, both secular and religious, could be written by putting side by side, concordance fashion, the *discords* between Church and society at large.

This is not to endorse a theory that conflict is the inevitable and dominant relation between religion and world. Quite the opposite. To my mind the good news of the aggiornamento is precisely the potential it opens up for reciprocal exchange and fruitful cooperation, *amidst expected tension*. The key to Pope John's window on the world is the Gospel good news that the Creator Father truly cares for man and his needs, and the Redeemer lives on visibly in his Church to the degree that his people love and serve the whole human family—as the Spirit does and enables.

As I read them, this is the general and generous response of the Church to the impact of the Creator's still evolving world, seen through the aggiornamento documents. And I see this secular influence and ecclesial response in a chain of nine causal and reinforcing links which form the basis of the next nine chapters. The first and most basic of these links is the recognition of human needs and aspirations.

CHAPTER 1 (A, B, C)

Man's Needs and Aspirations

(The 1ST & most basic link is the recognition of this)

(A) Welcoming the Welfare State

During the past generation the satisfaction of human needs has increasingly become the conscious goal of economic and political life. The measure of a successful society and a stable government becomes the degree to which man's material and social needs are met.

After World War II the "welfare state" became the model coveted in the West. In the final month of the war, the British—that most mature political people—turned out their hero Churchill, with all his rhetoric of glorious empire and manored history, in favor of self-effacing Clement Atlee, a socialist who promised free medical care, good schools, and cheap housing for all. The Scandinavians embraced this broad welfare goal even before the war and, little affected by its horrors, were the first to attain it. Western Europe united to pull out of the ruins and to pursue abundance for all, even ancient enemies. Japan followed suit, producing another economic miracle even more *wunderbar*.

Roosevelt had offered a New Deal, still spartan compared to Huey Long's "share the wealth" to make "every man a king." Roosevelt, however, did set Americans on the welfare trajectory, which paradoxically benefitted from the accelerating thrust of war production, and which attained the decent levels of Truman's Fair Deal and the heights of supermarket consumerism by the late fifties despite the more conservative economics of Eisenhower.

Entering the 1960s, the First Development Decade, John F. Kennedy found that economic production beyond consumer demand was sufficient to shoot for the moon. There was even enough to start thinking

5

about the aspirations of Blacks and Chicanos, leading to Johnson's Great Society, and to fire up the Indochina War without lowering throw-away waste in suburbia.

Nixon's debut on national television focused on the family dog, fed with more protein than half the world's children. His global debut was the kitchen debate with Khrushchev about dishwashers and detergents. And it was this Soviet leader who began turning the economies of his socialist bloc from heavy machinery to consumer goods, making disarmament and détente discussable.

By 1960 the Northern third of the human family, and particularly the "Christian West," had attained levels of mass abundance quite beyond the expectations of most scientists and socialists since technology launched the Industrial Revolution. Adam Smith's "iron law of wages" (keep the workers hungry to keep them working) was utterly confounded. His dismal economics of laissez-faire gave way to the welfare, full-employment theories of Keynes.

Pope John welcomed this coming of the good life here in this-world. He opens *Mater et Magistra* (Christianity and Social Progress) with the assertion that the Catholic Church was established by Jesus Christ so that all who enter "may find salvation as well as the *fullness of a more excellent life*" (MM 1).* Although the Church has the special task of sanctifying souls and sharing heavenly blessings, "she is also solicitous for the requirements of men in their daily lives, not merely those relating to food and sustenance, but also to their comfort and advancement in various kinds of goods" (MM 3).

In addition to "the minimum necessities of human life," Pope John includes in this "fullness of a more excellent life": health services, education, training in skills, housing, leisure and recreation, press, cinema, radio, television (MM 61). Need for "the goods and services for a better life, . . . the advantages of a more humane way of existence," and "social security," thread throughout John's letter (MM 79, 105). Son and brother of Italian peasants, he wants this abundant life for rural dwellers too: highways, transport and marketing facilities, medical services, schools, housing, pure drinking water, and "finally, furnishings and equipment needed in the modern farm home" (MM 127).

While rejoicing grandfather-like to see this good life reaching the homes of his Western children, John sadly sees the gap between economically advanced nations and those in process of development: "The former enjoy the conveniences of life, . . . a sufficiency and abundance of

*All emphasis within quotations is added to the text by the author, unless it is stated explicitly that the emphasis is part of the original text.

everything." "The latter experience dire poverty" (MM 157). The aggiornamento documents took up this issue of global justice for the development of all peoples; the aspirations of all were fed by the Northern
consumerist image spread by the media; and to the pangs of hunger were
added the fevers of frustration.

Bishops from the "Third World" brought these pastoral worries about
the needs of their people into Vatican II, into St. Peter's Basilica, into the
mainstream of the Church's life. Paul VI made integral development to
meet the human need of all peoples a principal, positive thrust of his
pontificate and "the new name for peace." The College of Bishops,
acquiring self-identity and awareness through their new national and
regional conferences, and a sense of continuing global responsibility
through their synod, declared concern for this-world aspirations to be a
central element of evangelization today:

> Action on behalf of justice and participation in the transformation of the world
> fully appear to us as a constitutive dimension of the preaching of the Gospel,
> or, in other words, of the Church's mission for the redemption of the human
> race and its liberation from every oppressive situation (JW 6).

(B) From Natural Law to Human Fulfillment

Catholic social teaching has been noted for basing itself upon "natural
law," that is, upon the very nature or quality of the human person and
upon the social relationships which flow from the essence or "whatness."
Principal among these relations are those of marriage, economics, and
politics. So Catholic social teaching has hinged heavily upon family,
property, and state, viewed as the "pillars" or structural institutions basic
to every society.

Over the years the natural-law ontology of Catholic social teaching has
been criticized by many brother Christians who believed that human
nature was fundamentally vitiated by the Fall. They appealed to the New
Man, Christ and his revealed law of love, as source and soul of human
community and as providing the fundamental norms of social ethics.

Secular social thinkers were critical of the natural-law base because it
harkened back to the static natural science and ethics of Aristotle. Modern
science, with its evolutionary thrust, and modern philosophy, driven into
perpetual motion by the dialectics of Hegel, then of Marx, at times
belittled and more often ignored the natural-law ethics of Catholicism.
Further, the fount and motives of human acts, solitary and *a fortiori* in
society, were ranged from blind drives to sublimations and repressions
by Freud's probings into the subjective self. The supposedly unchanging

norms of objective natural law were also attacked by humanist liberals and social progressives as supporting the status quo. Then pragmatic technology entered social science to push beyond the organic evolution of Darwin and the class struggle of Lenin to become the social engineering and planning of managerial bureaucracy in so-called socialist and capitalist states alike.

Adequate comment on natural-law ethics is neither fitting nor possible in this overview. Nor can we fully comment on the common good toward which ethics aims, or the principle of subsidiary function which should regulate the balanced relations of individual, family, economic body, and state, together with other communities. As shall be seen briefly at appropriate places below, this inherited teaching is basically reaffirmed in the aggiornamento documents. In fact, Pope John opens the series with the statement: "What the Catholic Church teaches and declares regarding the social life and relationships of men is beyond question for all time valid" (MM 218).

Nevertheless changes do occur. John and the aggiornamento move from a relatively static view of man's nature and reason toward human rights and fulfillment of human capacities, promoted by man's innate worth.

John goes on to repeat that "the cardinal point of this teaching is that individual men are necessarily the foundation, cause, and end of all social institutions. We are referring to human beings, insofar as they are social by nature, and raised to an order of existence that transcends and subdues nature. Beginning with this very basic principle whereby the dignity of the human person is affirmed and defended, Holy Church . . . has arrived at clear social teachings whereby the mutual relationships of men are ordered. . . . Moreover, these norms can be approved by all" (MM 219–220).

Both social order and rights (the stable and the dynamic elements) derive from the *dignity* of the human person, whose "nature is endowed with intelligence and free will. By virtue of this, he has rights and duties of his own, flowing directly and simultaneously from his very nature. These rights are therefore universal, inviolable and inalienable." They include "the means which are necessary and suitable for the proper development of life" (PT 9–11).

Vatican II focused more deeply upon the dignity of the human person as known through and in Christ. But it also stressed the recent scientific knowledge of man (the new anthropology) and the experience of human community in today's technological society (GS 12–32). Then came *Populorum Progressio* (On the Development of Peoples) with its insistence upon the capacity and urge of man to develop integrally, so as to *be* more, rather than merely to *have* more.

Certainly the aggiornamento documents do not view human nature and social order as static entities. Is the term and concept "natural law" still valid and useful for today's social teaching? In his *Reflections on the Tenth Anniversary of Pacem in Terris,* Cardinal Roy raises this question: "For today, this idea of nature is very much questioned, if not rejected." Also, use of the term can erroneously lead to "a strict parallel between man and his morality and biological laws and behavior." In fact the very content of "nature," as forbidding or permitting human acts, presents problems.

> This concept seems too "essentialist" to the people of our time, who challenge, as being a relic of Greek philosophy, the term "Natural Law," which they consider anachronistic, conservative and defensive. They object further that the expression was defined arbitrarily and once and for all in a subjective and Western manner, and is therefore one-sided and lacking in any moral authority for the universal conscience (RR 128).

But Roy goes on to assure that this caricature of nature is not the intended meaning of Pope John; the universal acclaim *Pacem in Terris* (Peace on Earth) received shows this clearly. Although the term "nature" can be misunderstood,

> the reality intended has lost nothing of its forcefulness when it is replaced by modern synonyms (almost all of which moreover are to be found in the Encyclical). Such synonyms are: man, human being, human person, dignity, rights of man or the rights of peoples, conscience, humaneness (in conduct), the struggle for justice, and, more recently "the duty of being," the "quality of life." Could they not all be summarized in the concept of "values," which is very much used today? (RR 129)

Regardless of what words are used, Roy concludes, "in this 'nature,' individuals and peoples all have a common denominator, a 'common good of man.'" This signifies "a basic and existential reality."

> It is a combination of postulates and experiences, ancient and modern, which people do not question, even if they belong to opposed systems, for "men find in it that inalienable part of themselves which links them all: the human in man" (Paul VI to U Thant, 4 October 1970, *AAS* 62, p. 184) (RR 129).

In conclusion, whatsoever may have been the contribution to status quo made by natural-law concepts in the past, current Catholic social teaching is strongly dynamic in its content and rhetoric. Man and his creative attributes, capacities, and initiatives, the upbuilding of a just society, the integral development of every person and of all peoples, the maximizing of responsibility and participation, nourished by experience and community—such are the values and imperatives for man's fulfillment deriving from his dignity, according to the aggiornamento documents. Some may well object that the term "natural law" is inadequate for denoting these. I agree. Other words should be used to avoid misunderstanding.

Still, to use Pope Paul's phrase again, that which is most "human in man" is his natural ability to reflect upon himself and his experience, to acquire self-awareness and personal identity, to know that he is and that he knows and that he wills. This power of consciousness truly separates him from the rest of nature.

It is the deepening and expansion of this capacity of human nature and of human society that now animates Catholic social teaching. Growing self-awareness animates all mankind and the very Church itself. Both John and Paul stated that the first purpose of Vatican II was the examination of the intimate nature of the Church, *her awareness of herself.* This resulted in *Lumen Gentium* (Dogmatic Constitution on the Church) and in *Gaudium et Spes* (Pastoral Constitution on the Church in the Modern World).

These deepened and expanded the Church's self-awareness as a People-in-Community, called together by Christ to love and serve God, each other, and all the human family—a growing family living together on one fragile globe, of many nations, cultures, and social groupings, each freshly aroused to conscious urgent demands for realizing human dignity. In fact, were I to choose one word which best summarizes the root thrust of the aggiornamento documents, it would be "conscientization."

(C) Conscious Demands for Dignity and Rights

Material betterment for all citizens became economically possible through the industrial application of technological advances. It became politically necessary in the West because of the workers' growing awareness of their necessary role in industrial society and of their significant strength when acting in solidarity. Acquiring some degree of class consciousness, they organized into labor unions and political forces to confront employers and the state with their demands for reform.

Or they pressed for a complete overthrow of the capitalist system. It was Marx who perceived and articulated the "conscientization" needed to arouse workers to both goals: reform and revolution.

From *Rerum Novarum* (On the Condition of Workers) in 1891 until the aggiornamento, Catholic social teaching focused precisely on the condition of workers, or at most on industrial relations, to the exclusion of most other societal issues. *The* social question was the welfare of workers(*within* the capitalist system) Credit is due the Church for asserting the moral right of workers to organize into unions over eighty years ago, forty years before such rights became civilly effective in models of democracy like the United States.

Socialist proposals for public ownership of means of production were strongly resisted by Church teaching, partly on philosophical grounds, but especially if they demanded class struggle and dictatorship of the proletariat. Laissez-faire capitalism of the Manchester school was also opposed. In their stead the Church advanced an intermediate corporative system in which the state would play a regulative, common-good role, while workers participated with management in decision-making at various levels from factory to national industrial categories—steel, textiles, transport, etc. This was at the heart of *Quadragesimo Anno* (On the Reconstruction of the Social Order) of 1931, with its *ordines* of industrial corporations.

These proposals, for better or worse, became tainted with similar Fascist experiments in Italy, Spain, and Portugal, and never had a fair trial. Further, they derived from essentialist, natural-law concepts which tended to strengthen the status quo of society's ancient pillars—family, state, and private property. These left insufficient flexibility for experiment in the existential reality in which man lives out his nature and proved nonviable even as ideas in the world of change so speeded up by the technology of World War II.

The Church did espouse social justice, however, through the reform of economic structures to satisfy worker needs and rights. It advanced an ethic of the *social* function of property over that of *individualist* capitalism.

In the aftermath of Nazi racism and genocide and of other ghastly wartime and totalitarian assaults upon man and his social groups, the issue of human rights rose front and center on the world stage. The innate value of man was reasserted; human dignity was extolled. In 1948 the United Nations proclaimed the Universal Declaration of Human Rights, which ranged far beyond industrial relations. Personal, civic, political, and religious rights were proclaimed for all.

Pacem in Terris should be remembered first as a papal declaration of human dignity and rights, then as a program for world peace. It echoes most of the rights stated in the UN declaration fifteen years before and balances these with respective duties. As seen above, Pope John asserts the nature of each person, endowed with intelligence and free will, to be the foundation from which human rights flow—universal, inviolable, and inalienable rights. But the dignity of the human person is esteemed far more highly in the light of revealed truth because: "God also created man in His own image and likeness, endowed him with intelligence and freedom, and made him lord of creation. . . . For men are redeemed by the blood of Jesus Christ. They are by grace the children and friends of God and heirs of eternal glory" (PT 3, 10).

But his dignity, John realizes, becomes meaningful only in the existential situation of real societies. These rights become operative when they are demanded, and the demands arise from growing consciousness collectively experienced by human groups. John deliberately looks for the "distinctive characteristics" of our age, a concept and approach which in Vatican II became "discerning the signs of the times." Among these he places foremost the conscious demands for human dignity and rights:

a) Having begun by claiming their rights in the socio-economic sphere, workers then made claims on the political level and for sharing in the fields of learning and culture (PT 40).

b) "Since women are becoming ever more conscious of their human dignity, they will not tolerate being treated as inanimate objects or mere instruments, but claim, both in domestic and in public life, the rights and duties that befit a human person" (PT 41). (This in 1963!)

c) "Men all over the world have today—or will soon have—the rank of citizens in independent nations. No one wants to feel subject to political power located outside his own country or ethnic group. . . . On the contrary, the conviction that all men are equal by reason of their natural dignity has been generally accepted. Hence, racial discrimination can in no way be justified" (PT 43–44).

d) Modern states organize themselves juridically through a written document called a constitution, which includes "a charter of fundamental human rights." These tendencies "clearly show that the men of our time have become increasingly conscious of their dignity as human persons. This awareness prompts them to claim a share in the public administration of their country, while it also accounts for the demand that their own inalienable and inviolable rights be protected by law" (PT 75–79).

We see here the rhetoric as well as the convictions that dominated the rest of the sixties: Men all over the world—claiming their rights in the socio-economic order—increasingly conscious of their dignity—making claims on the political level—a new awareness prompting them to claim a share in the public administration—women conscious of their human dignity.

This whole process of growing consciousness by peoples and groups now deeply influences the Church. The aggiornamento documents acknowledge and accept this growing "conscientization" of the Church itself by the movement for human dignity in the world. Perhaps the most telling of these is the Declaration on Religious Freedom, which bears the very title *Dignitatis Humanae* (Of Human Dignity). By it the Vatican Council reverses a former stage of Church awareness (or of ecclesiastical amnesia) by declaring the right of man to religious freedom, due to his dignity. "The requirements of this dignity have come to be more adequately known to human reason through *centuries* of experience. What is more, this doctrine of freedom has roots in divine revelation" (DH 9).

Still it took centuries of experience *by and in the world* to awaken the Church to this dignity of man from which arises religious freedom. That is why *Gaudium et Spes*, with its conciliar teaching of human dignity, offers hope that current Catholic concern for man and his future will endure and increase. By listening more attentively to the real world in which it now willingly finds itself, the Church might at least keep up with the continuing creation of God and of man in this-world.

Open to understanding this continuing co-creation, the Church might more fully live out the widespread belief that "all things on earth should be related to man as their center and crown" (GS 12). Loving and serving all the human family, the Church might come indeed to believe in practice that "authentic freedom is an exceptional sign of the divine image within man"—although our contemporaries, in their eager and rightful pursuit of freedom, often "foster it perversely as a license for doing whatever pleases them, even if it is evil" (GS 17).

CHAPTER 2

Unjust Power Structures:
Liberation and Reform
(A,B)

A Growing Criticism of Economic Systems

The conscious claim for human dignity and rights generated in turn another level of conscientization: that their realization is blocked in most countries by existing power structures; that these unjust institutions —economic and political, educational and cultural, military and media—intertwine and reinforce each other; that a small power elite, through inheritance or recruitment, dominates the nation; and that these oppressive national structures combine to forge a transnational system of injustice.

On one hand, many of these charges by the "outs" were oversimplified, while the "ins" often sought justification through self-serving appeals to national security, threatened by internal strife or foreign attack. Charges against the oligarchy at first strengthened the socialist assault from the East against the capitalist West, because it was in keeping with the analysis of capitalist double domination, domestic and colonial, introduced by Marx himself over a century back. But by the sixties, attacks were also directed against leaders inside the "peoples' socialist democracies." They were assailed as *The New Class* by men like Djilas; they were charged with suppressing human rights and building an archipelago of slave prisons by Sakharov and Solzhenitsyn; they were shaken by forlorn uprisings in Hungary, Poland, and Czechoslovakia. The Soviet model now arouses less inner attraction and comes under increasing attack, especially from Mao's new China.

Within Western nations during the 1960s, frustration of minorities and of ethnic and class groups was magnified by the conspicuous affluence of the directing class in their suburban compounds. Often sparked by student and counter-culture dissent, demonstrations raged against the es-

15

tablishment. In the United States, Black Power, Indian and Chicano confrontation at last burst forth against the oppression felt by thirty-five million citizens for three centuries. In Latin America, revolution—violent and nonviolent—gained ground, at times with priest participants and bishop supporters.

Some fifty nations of Africa and Asia, at last politically freed from European empires in the wake of World War II, awakened to their neocolonial bonds forged by the economically advanced mother countries. The latter then formed a "Club of the Rich," a multinational system of technology and trusts, of political and military power, against which the individual "poor nation" was without recourse. Even economic aid and technical assistance became suspect as weapons for continuing domination and dependency. Developmentalism, Western-style, is being replaced by self-reliance and liberation, with each region generating its own style of life and rhythm of growth, based on its own culture and values (GS 86).

Conscientization of the oppressed, communitarian solidarity, and broad-based peoples' participation are now advanced for the transformation of structures and the humanization of daily life. This conscious humanization, Paul VI insists, must not center upon the pursuit of possessions: integral human development means to *be* more, not to *have* more: "Each man can grow in humanity, can enhance his personal worth, can become more a person" (PP 15).

Particularly in Latin America, the Church entered and helped generate this social program. Reflection on the resulting experiments in social ministry led to a "theology of liberation," which largely animated the Latin American Bishops' Conference (CELAM) at Medellín, Colombia, in 1968. While undergoing refinement and fuller articulation, the theology of liberation has already deeply influenced the social thought and pastoral praxis of the Universal Church.

The Medellín school was partially incorporated into the wider body of aggiornamento teaching during the 1971 Synod of Bishops through its document *Justice in the World*. Its scriptural basis and ecclesiology came under some attack during the 1974 Synod on "Evangelization of the Modern World." But certainly its impact was not weakened. Rather, it is now taken seriously, even among the privileged bishops of the North Atlantic and by their beleaguered brothers of Eastern Europe.

The conviction grows that to attain long-term influence a theology of liberation (or its parallels) must deepen and refine, complete and integrate itself in accord with regional situations outside Latin America. Africa and Asia now reflect theologically upon their own traditional cultures and religious values, and their new socio-economic and political processes. A plurality of theological schools, ecclesial communions, and social ministries are sprouting forth.

Liberation and Reform: National and Global

The situation of dependency, from which the liberation school arises, is starkly described and strongly condemned by a litany of social documents. New just structures are needed. The conscientization of the Universal Church proceeds apace, especially concerning the transnational economic system.

John warned in 1961 that "economically developed countries should take particular care lest, in giving aid to poorer countries, they endeavor to turn the prevailing political situation to their own advantage, and seek to dominate them. . . . This clearly would be but another form of colonialism, which, although disguised in name, merely reflects their earlier but outdated dominion" (MM 171–172).

In 1965 Vatican II urged adequate organizations for "harmonizing international trade . . . and for repairing the deficiencies caused by an excessive disproportion in the power possessed by various nations." Suprisingly, however, these measures are viewed as mere "regulatory activity" in the very next sentence, despite later insistence on "a pressing need to reform economic and social structures" (GS 86).

Still the Council wants "the Catholic community to foster progress in needy regions, and social justice on the international scene." For this purpose it urges that "some agency of the universal Church be set up for the world-wide promotion of justice for the poor and of Christ's kind of love for them" (GS 90). This led to the Pontifical Commission Justice and Peace, instituted by Pope Paul as a unit of the Roman Curia in January 1967. The Church Universal now creates its own structures for promoting reform of unjust secular institutions and for upbuilding a more equitable world economic order. Local churches, mission bodies, religious orders, lay organizations, and episcopal conferences launch programs to advance development and justice, which include financial and technical aid among the differing regions of the transnational Church.

In March 1967 came *Populorum Progressio*. Paul VI forthrightly attacks oppressive social structures, "situations whose injustice cries to heaven." These incite grave temptation to violence. A revolutionary uprising however produces new injustices and disasters. Consequently, violent revolution must be avoided—"save where there is manifest, long-standing tyranny which would do great damage to fundamental personal rights and dangerous harm to the common good of the country. . . . A real evil should not be fought against at the cost of greater misery." Still Paul wants "to be clearly understood":

> The present situation must be faced with courage and the injustices linked with it must be fought against and overcome. Development demands bold transformations, innovations that go deep. Urgent reforms should be undertaken without delay (PP 30–32).

A year later, in 1968, Pope Paul was in Colombia for the opening of the Medellín Conference of the Latin American Bishops on "The Church in the Present-Day Transformation of Latin America." He praised the action the Church was undertaking against "systems and structures which cover up and favor grave and oppressive inequalities" ("Opening Address," in Medellín *Conclusions*, p. 31). Initiatives by the bishops' conferences of Bolivia, Brazil, Chile, and Mexico, and by the Jesuit and Salesian societies, were specifically cited. The Medellín documents *Justice* and *Peace* attack the twofold oppression of dominant groups and privileged sectors *within* each country, and *"external* neocolonialism. . . international monopolies and international imperialism of money" (MDP 2–10). Liberation from this double dependency and transformation of the continent are major themes of this historic assembly. The pastors conclude:

> Latin America is obviously under the sign of transformation and development; a transformation that, besides taking place with extraordinary speed, has come to touch and influence every human activity, from the economic to the religious.
>
> This indicates that we are on the threshold of a new epoch in the history of our continent. It appears to be a time full of zeal for full emancipation, of liberation from every form of servitude, of personal maturity and of collective integration. In these signs we perceive the first indications of the painful birth of a new civilization. And we cannot fail to see in this gigantic effort toward a rapid transformation and development an obvious sign of the Spirit who leads the history of man and of peoples toward their vocation ("Introduction" in Medellín *Conclusions*, p. 48).

In 1970 the Second Development Decade began. In a marked departure from past Roman practice, the usual message from the Holy See was not presented to the United Nations by the Pope. Applying Vatican II's principle of collegiality, this duty fell upon the president of the newly created Pontifical Commission Justice and Peace, Cardinal Maurice Roy. This message also criticizes the developmentalist errors of the First Decade which, in less advanced nations, tended "to pile up the riches and consumption of the few and leave a growing mass of 'marginal men' at the base of society" (DD 12). An almost identical process is at work at the planetary level:

> We have now a world economy in which *all* the positions of strength, all the wealth, all the investment, all the commercial services and above all, the whole crucial apparatus of research are concentrated in the small elite of nations which have already achieved modernization (DD 13, emphasis as in original).

Cardinal Roy takes up Medellín's call for double liberation—from both domestic and international systems of injustice which interlock and reinforce each other. New structures are needed in both arenas with full representation and political participation. Among these, "aid flows should be 'institutionalized' and accepted as an incipient world tax system . . . of distributive justice" (DD 17).

And although the Stockholm Conference on Environment and *The Limits to Growth* debate were two years in the future, Cardinal Roy's message introduces these issues into the aggiornamento documents. He urges:

> that a fundamental reconsideration of the planet's resource use and management be undertaken so that the increasingly irrational levels of extravagance, waste and pollution of the "high consumption societies" should not jeopardize the poorer nations' hopes of development and humanity's ultimate hopes of survival (DD 17).

In his apostolic letter of May 1971, *Octogesima Adveniens*, marking the eightieth anniversary of *Rerum Novarum*, Paul VI returns to "situations of injustice," both within national communities and on the international level. These have become so blatant that "many people are reaching the point of questioning the very model of society. . . . The need is felt to pass from economics to politics" (OA 45–46).

Political power is then the express theme of this papal letter. It shows an at-homeness with the realities of this-world power altogether new even to the aggiornamento. It goes beyond lay apostolate categories of the past to stress the commitment of Christian communities, the Church itself, "to bring about the social, political and economic changes seen in many cases to be urgently needed" (OA 4). This key issue of political engagement by the People of God is given direct attention in Chapter 4 below.

By October 1971 the Synod of Bishops, concerned with "Justice in the World," made institutionalized injustice its point of departure and central theme. "Scrutinizing the 'signs of the times' and seeking to detect the meaning of emerging history, while at the same time sharing the aspira-

tions and questionings of all those who want to build a more human
world, we have listened to the Word of God that we might be converted to
the fulfilling of the divine plan for the salvation of the world" (JW 2).
  The Synod discerned:

> • the serious injustices which are building around the world of men a network
> of domination, oppression and abuses which stifle freedom and which keep
> the greater part of humanity from sharing in the building up and the enjoy-
> ment of a more just and more fraternal world (JW 3).

> • the cry of those who suffer violence and are oppressed by unjust systems
> and structures (JW 5).

> • international systems of domination; . . . the unequal distribution which
> places decisions concerning three quarters of income, investment and trade in
> the hands of one third of the human race, namely the more highly developed
> part (JW 13, 12).

> • objective obstacles which social structures place in the way of conversion of
> hearts, or even of the realization of the ideal of charity; . . . the general condi-
> tion of being marginal in society; . . . systematic barriers and vicious circles
> which oppose the collective advance. . . . If the developing nations and re-
> gions do not attain liberation through development, there is a real danger that
> the conditions of life created especially by colonial domination may evolve into
> a new form of colonialism in which the developing nations will be the victims
> of the interplay of international economic forces (JW 16).

> • a set of injustices which constitute the nucleus of today's problems; . . .
> men and nations which because of various forms of oppression and because of
> the present character of our society are silent, indeed voiceless, victims of
> injustice (JW 20).

> • the present-day situation of the world, marked as it is by the grave sin of
> injustice. . . . Such a situation urges us to listen with a humble and open heart
> to the word of God, as he shows us new paths towards action in the cause of
> justice in the world (JW 29).

The bishops then make numerous positive proposals for a new global
economic order, astonishing in their concreteness and detail. These are
reviewed in Chapter 5 below.
  But the Justice document of the 1971 Synod is also earning a special
place in aggiornamento history for advancing two additional levels of
Church consciousness. Besides this awareness of unjust structures, demanding liberation and reform, the Synod insists on "awareness of the
right to development" (JW 15); and that action promoting liberation from
oppression and transformation of the world is "a *constitutive dimension* of

the preaching of the Gospel" (JW 6). This-world awareness clearly stimulates the Church to new levels of consciousness and awakens the People of God to new demands of conscience:

> This aspiring to justice asserts itself in advancing beyond the threshold at which begins a consciousness of enhancement of personal worth with regard both to the whole man and the whole of mankind. This is expressed in an awareness of the right to development. The right to development must be seen as a dynamic interpenetration of all those fundamental human rights upon which the aspirations of individuals and nations are based (JW 15).

> Action on behalf of justice and participation in the transformation of the world fully appear to us as a constitutive dimension of the preaching of the Gospel, or, in other words, of the Church's mission for the redemption of the human race and its liberation from every oppressive situation (JW 6).

In short, through the 1971 Synod the Catholic Church reaches and registers a new peak awareness of unjust structures and of the need for liberation and reform. This assures for *Justice in the World,* so succinct and striking, a unique place among the documents of the aggiornamento. Its moral authority is further strengthened because it is the collegial product of pastors freely selected by their brother bishops from all nations and cultures.

CHAPTER 3

Science's Magnification— and Socialization—of Economic Power

$(A \rightarrow C)$

Industrialization and the Generation of Complex Interdependence

Economic power, the sheer capacity to produce goods and services, has dramatically increased since World War II, in large part a result of the scientific discoveries stimulated by the war. Among these the electronic, nuclear, metallurgical, and pharmaceutical fields stand out. Managerial technique also advanced, aided mightily by computer and allied data systems.

In those thirty years, 1945–1975, the planet's population doubled; instantaneous communications (advertising and aspirations included) engirdled the earth; gargantuan organizations of computerized manpower and their intermeshing skills took shape; massive economic enterprises took hold of man's whole life in most nations.

This increase of human beings, this concentration of magnified economic power, this outpouring of products, this extension of communications, taken together, bring about seven societal mutations which the Church attempts to deal with in the aggiornamento documents. Not with full success, to be sure, but at least with the merit of facing the Monday-morning reality which hundreds of millions must face regularly in factory and field, office and street:

There is (1) accelerating change in the economic process, generated by technology and productive efficiency. This change (2) causes massification of industry and urban living, and (3) industrialization of agriculture,

23

which includes the "urbanization" of rural villages. These factors (4) strengthen, simultaneously, economic structures and the drive toward rapid change, bringing about constant conflict of interest as well as new interdependence and mounting mergers of forces for controlling economic power (with a pervasive dialectic of structure-change, conflict-merger-control, new structure-fresh change, renewing conflict—and so on in continuing process). This development (5) demands far-ranging intervention by public authority, even in so-called "free enterprise, private property, market economies"; this in turn (6) transforms the character of productive property, bringing about the socialization of its control and use, and (7) heightened socialization in the wider totality of human experience, culture, and association, through the multiplication of group relationships into webs of growing complexity.

Pope John opened the aggiornamento by grappling with these issues in *Mater et Magistra*. The documents since have enlarged and updated his approach, and have to some degree balanced the optimism which endeared him to all. No adequate survey is possible here; I select only a few highlights for brief comment.

John sees "the multiplication of social relationships, that is, a daily more complex interdependence of citizens," as a principal characteristic of our time, "introducing into their lives and activities many and varied forms of association." This stems from factors such as "technical and scientific progress, greater productive efficiency, and a higher standard of living among citizens" (MM 59). "Such an advance in social relationships definitely brings numerous services and advantages." These include education and health services, housing, leisure, and recreation. "In addition, through the ever more perfect organization of modern means for the diffusion of thought—press, cinema, radio, television—individuals are enabled to take part in human events on a world-wide scale" (MM 61).

Thus far, Pope John is resolutely affirmative. Then, almost rhetorically, he notes a parallel multiplication of "rules and laws controlling and determining relationships of citizens. . . . As a consequence, opportunity for free action by individuals is restricted within narrower limits. . . . Will men perhaps then become automatons, and cease to be personally responsible, as these social relationships multiply more and more? It is a question which must be answered negatively" (MM 62).

So in 1961 Pope John takes a positive view of the growing complexity of life, of "socialization" with its ever-increasing human relationships and economic benefits—despite dangers to freedom.

A comment is needed here on the meaning of "socialization," because it aroused widespread attention in John's first aggiornamento document.

Newspapers reported that even Prime Minister Nehru perked up his ears. Like many others, the Indian leader appears to have thought that John was praising socialism, that is, the collective or governmental ownership of the means of production and distribution of goods and services. Owing in part to this confusion of meanings, some English translators of the encyclical avoided the word "socialization" and used instead "multiplication of social relationships," an apt rendering of the official Latin text.

However, the Italian version in the official Vatican newspaper, *L'Osservatore Romano,* used *socializzazione* from the very first. Cardinal Amleto Cicognani, Vatican Secretary of State, writing in English to the National Social Action Conference of Canada in 1963, uses the word "socialization" twelve times. He also quotes the word right out of the encyclical. So the Holy See shows no timidity in asserting its own meaning for the English term, which to many sensitive Americans might sound dangerously evocative of socialism. To set all at rest, the Cardinal Secretary of State clarifies the point at the very start of his 1963 letter to the Canadians:

> It is well to emphasize, in the first place, that socialization, as discussed in the encyclical letter *Mater et Magistra,* is in no way to be confused with socialism. Socialization, when freely and prudently actuated, is entirely in conformity with the social nature of man, and is a source of true human progress in every field, economic, social, moral and cultural.

Socialization is then a reality much deeper than the economy. It enwebs the far wider social fabric: *the new human environment* of complex interdependence, made possible (if not inevitable) by industrialization as experienced until now.

In his struggle to know, to control, and to direct his natural environment—earth, water, and air; cold, heat, and energy; plants and animals; distance and time—Western man created, step by accelerating step, a new social environment: from hunting bands, nomadic tribes, farming villages, city-states, nations, and feudal empires he moved to multinational economic and political bodies and blocs; from barter and simple market to commercial partnership, stock company, legal contracts, trade agreements, cooperatives and industrial corporations, banks, insurance and pension funds, stock exchange; from yeomanry and artisan guilds to labor unions, peasant leagues, planters and producers and professional associations, centers for training and education and research; and to groupings for cultural, civic, recreational, humanitarian, secular, and religious purposes—in unimaginable variety.

Soviet style industrial society has multiplied a complexus of bodies which are largely comparable, but with much less variety, spontaneity, and freedom because of the total subjection of every association to economic power, which is in turn completely controlled by political authority and force. The Maoist ethos still seems to draw heavily from the peasant, artisan, and village fabric of China. But where industrial urbanization begins to concentrate, the socialization phenomenon appears. The very purpose of the "cultural revolution" is to remedy some of its effects by doses of peasant and commune experience.

Clearly it is advanced industrialization, as experienced during the past generation or two in both East and West for the first time in human history, which generates socialization. To dramatize this new reality as now experienced in North America, comparison is made with the settler who moved across the frontier in the 1800s. Today's householder no longer wrestles in heroic solitary struggle via windmill, well, and campfire, with water, drought and darkness, cold and heat. He deals rather with the local utility company, which deals with labor unions, environment and planning boards, federal rate and energy commissions; and they in turn with multinational corporations, the Organization of Petroleum Exporting Nations (OPEC), and even eventually with the Arab League and the United Nations.

To get meat and milk, potatoes and transport, the family no longer trails deer and digs the soil, corrals cattle and lassos horses. They drive to the supermarket and call up the airline, which in turn bargain with General Foods and General Motors, the Farm Bureau and Farm Workers, the Federal Aviation Authority, congressional committees, White House staff, and Madison Avenue.

Other associations form to study, to direct, and to coordinate this new social environment at local, state, national, regional, and transnational levels: federations of labor; farmer, industrial, and consumer organizations; technical and professional societies; private and public agencies. Still other centers, staffs, and institutes are formed to analyze, synthesize, and animate the whole complex creation: opinion polls, market research, public relations and lobbying bodies; presidential committees and common-cause sessions; world assemblies on population, food, environment, human values, art, philosophy, and religion—in the thousands upon thousands, webbing into a social fabric of tangled threads a cocoon envelope without the old weave of simple warp and woof.

The constant creation of this new human environment, this "sociosphere" (to adopt a neologism of Teilhard de Chardin), is the continuing consequence of socialization, a process ever weaving and unravelling the social cocoon and weaving anew—as experienced thus far in advanced industrial society.

Property: The Socialization of Its Control and Use

Catholic teaching about property is undergoing basic mutation within this context of socialization. The right to private ownership of the means of production is still asserted. But property management, control, and use are subjected to so many societal directives, purposes, and authorities that the very meaning of "private ownership" has been—and is being further—transformed in societies that still allow it in theory or law. Catholic teaching has evolved in like manner.

Insistence upon the social function and use of property has been a distinguishing mark of the Church's doctrine since the Middle Ages. This provided the basis for condemning acceptance of interest on loans, the usury question which so exercised Thomas Aquinas and other natural-law moralists for some 500 years. It also provided a socio-economic source for conflict with "the Protestant ethic," which, according to Max Weber and other social historians, supported the early capitalist breakaway from the Catholic feudal system and its communitarian property concept.

Any adequate comment on the socialization of property, as a major process during the fifteen-year-old aggiornamento, should first trace the evolution of property-holding systems and of Catholic teaching, as these evolved, from feudalism into the commercial era of the city-states, through the mercantilism of the new nations, then into the Industrial Revolution with its bourgeoisie, tycoon, managerial, and other stages. Such a survey is not possible here. But this centuries-long evolution must be kept in mind, however hazily, in order to grasp what has happened in more recent times.

Fortunately, Pope John in *Mater et Magistra* does review papal teaching on property during the seventy years, 1891–1961, during which the Church became sufficiently conscious of the Industrial Revolution to formulate a coherent doctrinal corpus. The highlights of John's historical sketch in *Mater et Magistra* trace this development of doctrine and also show John's own level of consciousness in 1961 as he launched the aggiornamento:

a) The encyclical of Leo XIII in 1891, *Rerum Novarum*, recognized that the three key factors (or preferably actors) underlying economic life are workers, productive property, and the state. He also showed that their just and equitable *interrelation* is the crucial issue of Catholic social teaching. *Mater et Magistra* summarizes the basic norms of this relationship as given by Leo in 1891:

> • Work, inasmuch as it is an expression of the human person, can by no means be regarded as a mere commodity. For the great majority of mankind, work is the only source from which the means of livelihood are drawn. Hence, its remuneration is not to be thought of in terms of merchandise, but rather according to the laws of justice and equity (MM 18).

> • Private property, including that of productive goods, is a natural right possessed by all, which the State may by no means suppress. However, as there is from nature a social aspect to private property, he who uses his right in this regard must take into account not merely his own welfare but that of others as well (MM 19).

> • The State, whose purpose is the realization of the common good in the temporal order, can by no means disregard the economic activity of its citizens. Indeed, it should be present to promote in a suitable manner the production of a sufficient supply of material goods, . . . safeguard the rights of all citizens, but especially the weaker, such as workers, women and children, . . . contribute actively to the betterment of the living conditions of workers, . . . see to it that labor agreements are entered into according to the norms of justice and equity, and that in the environment of work the dignity of the human being is not violated either in body or spirit (MM 20–21).

Pope John notes approvingly that these principles of Leo XIII have "contributed much to the establishment and promotion of that new section of legal science known as *labor law*," and that modern states have adopted them in their social legislation during the past seventy years. John then recalls two of Leo's elemental teachings on the economic relationship: "The unregulated competition which so-called *liberals* espouse, or the class struggle in the *Marxist sense*, are utterly opposed to Christian teaching and also to the very nature of man" (MM 21–23, emphasis in original). And, of primordial significance to the Church's social commitment since that time and for the future, Pope Leo asserted the right of workers to organize into unions. In 1961 John XXIII recalls that seventy years before:

> in the same Letter moreover, there is affirmed the natural right of workers to enter corporately into associations, whether these be composed of workers only or of workers and management; and also the right to adopt that organizational structure judged more suitable to meet their professional needs. And the workers themselves have the right to act freely and on their own initiative within the above-mentioned associations, without hindrance and as their needs dictate (MM 22).

Commentators on Catholic social teaching have regularly and rightly noted the role of labor unions for creating "worker power," which led to collective bargaining and greater sharing in the economic product and process. But this writer wishes to stress especially that labor organization became a basic cause of the socialization of property and in the formation of today's new type of economic power within the overall sociosphere. By associating into unions, workers began the socialization of the only "productive property" they owned—their own muscle and time and skill. They forged a productive power which counters the raw strength of property and the more recent power of government, subjecting all economic power to a multiple complex of societal relationships. Of late, management, researchers, consumers, the "counter-culture," and other actors have entered the socialization complexus in which economic power is exercised. Here I wish above all to note, and to celebrate with Leo and John, the entry of workers as corporate actors and the erosion of the right of property as "things" pure and simple in the structure and process of society.

b) John then reviews the teaching of Pius XI in *Quadragesimo Anno* (literally "the fortieth year" after Leo's encyclical). Notably, John observes that at that time, 1931:

> some were in doubt as to what should be the judgment of Catholics regarding private property, the wage system, and more especially, a type of moderate socialism. Concerning private property, our predecessor reaffirmed its natural law character. Furthermore, he set forth clearly and emphasized the social character and function of private ownership (MM 29–30).

But, continues John, Pius XI was quite aware that in the past forty years

> historical conditions had profoundly altered. In fact, unrestricted competition, because of its own inherent tendencies, had ended by almost destroying itself. It had caused a great accumulation of wealth and a corresponding concentration of power in the hands of a few who 'are frequently not the owners, but only the trustees and directors of invested funds, who administer them at their good pleasure' (MM 35).

Already in 1931, in short, management had replaced owners in the control of so-called "private property." Therefore, lamented Pius XI:

> economic power has been substituted for the free marketplace. Unbridled ambition for domination has replaced desire for gain; the whole economy has become harsh, cruel, and relentless in frightful measure (MM 36, quoted from *Quadragesimo Anno*).

Since the 1950s, students of modern business management have stressed that today's corporate goals are survival, growth, and power, rather than the simple profit motives of yesterday's owners, who also directed their enterprises. This managerial shift in economic power and purpose, which so worried Pius in 1931, is complicated and worsened because sometimes "it happened that even public authorities were serving the interests of more wealthy men and that concentrations of wealth, to some extent, achieved power over all peoples" (MM 36). John points out the principles invoked by Pius XI in opposing this trend:

1. The wage system is not unjust by its nature, but it must be kept just, equitable, and human; work contracts should "be tempered in certain respects with partnership arrangements, so that 'workers and officials become participants in ownership, or management, or share in some manner in profits' " (MM 32).

2. The organization of economic life must conform to practical morality governed by the laws of justice and charity; competing interests of individuals and of groups, excessive power of wealth, national honor, desire for domination, and similar factors, are not the ultimate criteria in economic life.

3. The varied interests of individuals and especially of social groupings "must be harmonized with the requirements of the common good. This evidently requires . . . the orderly reorganization of society with smaller professional and economic groups existing in their own right, and not prescribed by public authority." This new "juridical order, with appropriate public and private institutions," is a reference to the corporative model, in line with economic categories or *ordines*, cited above in Chapter 1.

4. "Civil authority should reassume its function and not overlook any of the community's interests." This intervention of authority must follow the principle of subsidiary function, which John brings into his own teaching, as seen below.

5. "On a worldwide scale, governments should seek the economic good of all peoples" (MM 37–40).

c) Pius XII did not issue a major encyclical on economic life. But John does refer to his Radio Message of 1941 which commemorated the fiftieth anniversary of *Rerum Novarum*. Pius XII reaffirms "that the right of private property is from natural law itself." However, "the right of every man to use them [material goods] for *his own sustenance* is prior to all other rights in economic life, and hence is prior even to the right of private ownership." He also reasserts the principles of Leo XIII and Pius XI about labor relations and public intervention to safeguard the common good. Turning to the family, Pius XII stresses that private ownership of material goods helps to safeguard and develop family life. "From this arises the right of the family to migrate" (MM 43–45). (We must recall that the uprooting of millions by World War II made migration an acute issue in 1941.)

We see, in John's tracing of Catholic social teaching, that the concept, control, and use of property became increasingly socialized during the seventy years from 1891 to *Mater et Magistra*. John reflects how "contemporary circumstances . . . have changed greatly over the past twenty years." In technology and economics: atomic energy, synthetic products, automation, the agricultural industry, communications, transport, space. In the social field: social security, collective awareness among workers, conveniences, social mobility, decline of class division, imbalances between economic regions within countries and on a world scale. In political affairs: the participation of almost all social strata, much more public intervention in economic and social affairs; "peoples of Asia and Africa, having set aside colonial systems, now govern themselves. . . . As the mutual relationships of peoples increase, they become daily more dependent one upon the other" (MM 46–49).

Therefore, as the aggiornamento begins, socialization reaches new heights of intensity, penetrating all areas of life, and new heights of extension, engirdling all peoples of the planet. John consciously writes *Mater et Magistra* within the context of this "multiplication of social relationships, that is, a daily more complex interdependence of citizens," which he sees as "one of the principal characteristics of our time" (MM 59). After his historical review, John begins his own teaching:

> At the outset it should be affirmed that in economic affairs first place is to be given to the private initiative of individual men who, either working by themselves, or with others in one fashion or another, pursue their common interests (MM 51).

It is noteworthy that John starts from private initiative, not from private property, and he adds immediately: "But in this matter, for reasons pointed out by our predecessors, it is necessary that public authorities take active interest, the better to increase output of goods and to further social progress for the benefit of all citizens" (MM 52). This intervention of public authorities that encourages, stimulates, regulates, supplements, and complements, is based on the *principle of subsidiarity* as set forth by Pius XI in his encyclical *Quadragesimo Anno*:

interesting

> It is a fundamental principle of social philosophy, fixed and unchangeable, that one should not withdraw from individuals and commit to the community what they can accomplish by their own enterprise and industry. So, too, it is an injustice and at the same time a grave evil and a disturbance of right order, to transfer to the larger and higher collectivity functions which can be performed and provided for by lesser and subordinate bodies (MM 53, quoted from *Quadragesimo Anno*).

John goes on immediately to assert that recent developments of science and technology provide additional reasons why, to a greater extent than heretofore, it is within the power of public authorities:

- to reduce imbalances between economic sectors, between regions within the nation, between peoples of the whole world;
- to keep fluctuations of the economy within bounds;
- to provide effective measures for avoiding mass unemployment.

"Consequently, it is requested again and again of public authorities responsible for the common good, that they intervene in a wide variety of economic affairs, and that, in a more extensive and organized way than heretofore, they adapt institutions, tasks, means, and procedures to this end" (MM 54).

After all his insistence on these "precautionary activities of public authorities in the economic field," John returns to the primary rights of private citizens. Notably, John stresses that "experience, in fact, shows that where private initiative of individuals is lacking, political tyranny prevails." Moreover, due to economic stagnation, "all sorts of consumer goods and services, closely connected with needs of the body and more especially of the spirit, are in short supply" (MM 55–57).

> Where, on the other hand, appropriate activity of the State is lacking or defective, commonwealths are apt to experience incurable disorders, and there occurs exploitation of the weak by the unscrupulous strong (MM 58).

John goes on to outline in *Mater et Magistra* the constant dialectic among property, workers, farmers, consumers, professionals, management, stockholders, small owners, and other economic groups and forces in today's complex society. He recognizes that all these changing conditions have occasioned "popular doubt" concerning "the principle whereby it is established that men have from nature a right of privately owning goods, including those of a productive kind" (MM 108). John repeats: "Such a doubt has no foundation, for the rights of private property, including that pertaining to goods devoted to productive enterprises, is permanently valid. . . . It is rooted in the very nature of things. . . . Men are prior to civil society, and hence, . . . civil society is to be directed toward man as its end." And again John appeals finally to the lessons of life actually lived:

> Moreover, experience and history testify that where political regimes do not allow to private individuals the possession also of productive goods, the exercise of human liberty is violated or completely destroyed in matters of primary importance. Thus it becomes clear that in the right of property, the exercise of liberty finds both a safeguard and a stimulus (MM 109).

Two years later, and two months before his death in June 1963, John returns briefly to the question in the litany of human rights with which he opens *Pacem in Terris*. Under the heading "Economic Rights," John lists "the natural right to free initiative in the economic field and the right to work." He reasserts that "the right to private property, even of productive goods, also derives from the nature of man. . . . 'It strengthens and gives serenity to family life, thereby increasing the peace and prosperity of the state.' However, it is opportune to point out that there is a social duty inherent in the right of private property" (PT 18–22).

In summary, John clearly and definitely carries over the Church's inherited teaching on property into the aggiornamento era he is launching. But in doing so he arouses the Church to a reality more basic than the permanency of property: The Church of Vatican II is "inheriting" a society in process of radical transformation, compared with that of the past generation, because of socialization, the multiplying complex of relationships, and interdependence among groups and nations.

National and world society, progressively socialized, requires increasing intervention by public authorities to promote the common good in keeping with the principle of subsidiarity. In Church teaching, *the common good* is not the glib phrase of a political campaign. It forms the bedrock of Catholic social doctrine, more fundamental than property, because its goal and measure is man and his perfection. The common good, Pope John teaches,

> embraces the sum total of those conditions of social living, whereby men are enabled more fully and more readily to achieve their own perfection (MM 65).

To the degree, then, that private property (1) contributes to the total conditions of social living (in the criss-crossing dynamics of the economic, political, social, cultural, familial, and other fields), (2) which enables men (in the plural of all the human family, weak, poor, and oppressed, as well as strong, rich, and dominant) (3) to more fully and more readily achieve their own perfection (in the accelerating thrusts toward human fulfillment through responsible participation)—then, to that degree, private property is justifiable in John's social teaching.

But the aggiornamento moves on. The bishops of Vatican II begin focusing more attention on economic power. Paul VI erodes any primacy of ownership by his development goal of *being* more human rather than *having* more goods. Also, he moves from economics toward the primacy of *political power* for transforming societal structures. The bishops of the synod incorporate justice and transformation of the world into evangelization as a *constitutive dimension* of the Gospel goal. This is directed toward the inner renewal of man as well as the outward upbuilding of just structures, toward the Kingdom of God where all property, indeed *all creation*, is held in common with *all mankind*, in Christ.

This very rush of undigested ideas shows it is time to move this overview beyond the question of property. And so we will. But three quick references to Vatican II must first be made.

a) In *Gaudium et Spes*, the Council Fathers do not reassert the right to private property as deriving from natural law. Nor is it denied. Rather they cite the advantages of "ownership and other forms of private control over material goods," which contribute to the expression of personality, the exercising of roles in society, and the safeguarding of civil liberties. Great importance is given to the access "of both individuals *and communities* to some control over material goods" and to the diversified forms of dominion which include "intangible goods, such as professional skills." Notably, Vatican II insists: "The right of private control, however, is not opposed to the right inherent in various forms of public ownership. . . . By its very nature, private property has a social quality deriving from the law of the communal purpose of earthly goods." Then about half of this entire section entitled "Ownership and Property" is devoted to the reforms needed in consequence of this communal purpose of property, especially agrarian reform (GS 71).

b) Vatican II presents an excellent summary of Catholic teaching on "The Common Purpose of Created Things," which, because of its highest conciliar authority, provides the doctrinal fundament for the subsequent aggiornamento trilogy of justice, development, and peace—national and transnational:

> God intended the earth and all that it contains for the use of every human being and people. Thus, as all men follow justice and unite in charity, created goods should abound for them on a reasonable basis. Whatever the forms of ownership may be, as adapted to the legitimate institutions of people according to diverse and changeable circumstances, attention must always be paid to the universal purpose for which created goods are meant. In using them, there-

fore, a man should regard his lawful possessions not merely as his own but also as common property in the sense that they should accrue to the benefit of not only himself but of others (GS 69).

c) Vatican II shows new awareness of the cultural values and effects resulting from the modern economy: "Industrialization, urbanization, and other causes of community living create new forms of culture (mass-culture), from which arise new ways of thinking, acting, and making use of leisure" (GS 54). These issues will receive attention in Chapter 9 below. The power of economics as such penetrates the inner man, as well as the outer structures of human society.

Many people, especially in economically advanced areas, seem to be hyp-notized, as it were, by economics, so that almost their entire personal and social life is permeated with a certain economic outlook . . . both in nations which favor a collective economy as well as in others (GS 63).

C Regional Adaptations of Economic Power

Before the aggiornamento, Catholic social teaching addressed itself almost exclusively to the North Atlantic region, the nations that first experienced the Industrial Revolution. Indeed, original reflection on the Gospel, Church, and modern economic power was concentrated within a small oblong diamond whose points reach approximately Paris, Brussels, Munich, and Milan. Here, between the mid-1800s and World War II, Catholic teaching took shape in response to pastoral problems raised by bishops such as Von Ketteler, Manning, Gibbons, Lienart, and Cardijn; by laymen such as Harmel, Toniolo, and Powderly; by employers pushed toward laissez-faire capitalism through competition and dominant ideol-ogy; by workers in their millions pulled toward socialism because of misery and a thirst for justice.

The two first charter documents, *Rerum Novarum* of 1891 (a century after the factory system began in Britain) and *Quadragesimo Anno* of 1931 (just in time for the great depression), focused almost entirely on indus-trial relations. Only during World War II did Pius XII begin giving atten-tion to the socio-economic consequences of the colonial states of Africa, of Western imperialism over Asia, and of global interdependence due to new economic technology. Pope John first recognized the industrializa-tion of agriculture a hundred years after the reaper, and fifty after the tractor.

Only during Vatican II did the social ministry pioneers of Latin America begin receiving significant ecclesial support, leading to their own ideologies of people's participation and democratic socialism, and, outstripping any region, leading even to their fledgling theology of liberation. Only under Pope Paul has the Church begun dialogue with Marxism and conversation-negotiation with planned-economy states, an experience which could open Catholic teaching to new property, market, labor, and public authority equations for the common good.

In short, only since the early 1960s has the Church's social doctrine moved outside its Western hearth toward the whole globe *and* the diversities of its regions. Diversities expressed at least in five senses:

a) Regions differing by reason of their millenial religion-cultural values and life styles: For example, tribal customs and community property in Africa, make possible the Ujamaa experiment of Tanzania (under the leadership of a Catholic president); the new *comunidades de base* of Latin America build upon the marked Latin trait of *convivencia*, of human togetherness in living, making possible cooperation and *movimientos populares* less likely to appear among the nuclear-family individualists of the North.

b) Regions differing by reason of their present degree of technological and economic development, and the direction they will now choose to go: They can move toward large economic units and volume production, on the Western and Soviet model which India follows; or toward small-scale technology and communitarian approaches, such as Maoist China attempts in its current stage.

c) Regions and nations differing in the resources of soil, water, oil, and ores available to them: Today it is clear that the economic choices open to petroleum-rich Iran are greater than those of neighboring Pakistan, that the ores of Zaire give it more options than has the Sahel.

d) Regions differing in their political systems, governmental leadership, and organizational ability: It is already clear that countries en route to development will generally choose a planned economy, with public ownership of most productive property and basic services under strong governmental control and direction, because they cannot take the time needed for the gradual growth of a market economy. It is also clear that those advanced nations now having planned, state-controlled economies, such as the Soviet bloc, are unlikely to change to market or "guided" mixed systems in the near future.

e) Regions or nations still retaining so-called market systems based upon so-called private property and contractual relations: These differ considerably among themselves, from the United States, Canadian, and

Australian model, with their many resources and lingering frontier ethos, to socialist-leaning Britain and Italy, and export-minded, high-technology Germany and Japan, both heavily dependent upon outside raw materials and markets. These Northern nations have created the strongest economic power units of the globe, the multinational business corporations now under new scrutiny by the Third World. And the free market region as a whole enters a time of troubles due to inflation, energy crisis, pollution, and internal disorders.

To the extent that the Church of Vatican II becomes conscious of its social ministry within each politico-economic situation, it will evolve a social teaching adapted to that situation. Clear evidence of this role by the local Church appears already in the aggiornamento documents, especially since Medellín, in the recent synods, and in almost every national conference of bishops.

Paul VI encouraged these adaptations in *Populorum Progressio* for economic questions and in *Octogesima Adveniens* from the political perspective. So one unique social teaching, universally applicable to all economic systems, should not be expected from the universal Church. The Churches of each region will constantly reflect on their Gospel role in terms of property, market, workers, and public authority proper to that region. Then the universal Church will probably speak more in universal terms, generally supportive of regional, doctrinal, and pastoral initiatives. It will take on a new transnational role of relating to the regions themselves—regions increasingly interdependent by reason of technology applied to economic power and by reason of Christ and his Church living in the world, serving all God's human family.

CHAPTER 4

Political Power, Ideology, Commitment

From Economic to Political Power

The intervention of public authority. The key role of the state. The power of government and its duty to promote the common good, in season, out of season. Whatever the phrase and context, does any theme loom out more regularly from John's two encyclicals? Does any other refrain so mark the tempo of his forward march for society?

John's image certainly did not emanate from the figure of politician or statesman, ambassador or bureaucratic functionary. "He reminds me of my peasant grandfather," tearfully reported Mrs. Alexei Adzhubei, the daughter of Khrushchev. So thought many of us—somewhat patronizing toward John's rough edges but pleased that he brought "the human" of humor and the common sense of the commonplace into the marble corridors of Vatican palaces, pomp, and power. But preoccupied with the function of political power—that he never appeared to be. Still this quick review of his teaching shows him convinced that public authority must strengthen its central role for governing and directing economic power, grown gargantuan within our technological society.

And still John was not advancing a novel doctrine. Rather, as papal social teaching does most of the time, he was reflecting upon, judging, and ratifying societal reality. Already by 1960 in the industrial North, big business and big labor and mass society had begotten the greatest massification of all—big government.

This is to be expected in socialist nations where, by definition, governmental authority owns and directs the means of production and distribu-

39

tion. Political power dominates economic power by ballot or, to recall Mao's bland boast, by the barrel of a gun. But even in private-property, free-market nations of the West, by a chain of causes as inexorable as the assembly line, technology's magnification of economic power demands massive government action: to regulate relations between management and labor, between enterprises and unions themselves; to collect through taxes an increasing share (around 40 percent in some countries) of production and redistribute it among the people as schools, medicare, social security, welfare; to lace the countryside with superhighways and to rebuild the inner city with parking lots; to generate electric and nuclear energy, dig up mineral resources (in most Western nations subsoil ores and oil are public property) and heal the wounded environment; to own railways, postal services, and airlines; to finance housing and agriculture; to research new technologies for health and economic advance, military plant and power; to serve national security and neoimperial dreams—of both East and West. And all this should be done to promote the common good, to satisfy the human needs for, in John's phrase, "the fullness of a more excellent life" (MM 1).

By 1975 "the government" is the super dominant power in Western society. But it is a paradoxical giant: While it guides or directs the economy, it is in turn manipulated, if not controlled, by economic power. The two form a new societal synergism: the economico-political "field of force," as difficult for careless citizens to conceive as the mathematics of electromagnetism. And it is more difficult yet to control, because decision-making is shrouded under shifting layers of law and impersonal process. It forms a global "it" whose best business model can be appropriately spelled with double letters—as in ITT. Its political symbol has become, with incredible aptness, the key technological invention for regulating the waterpower that irrigated the Sumerian Valley in 4000 B.C.—providing economic power for man's first civilization and completely controlled by a secretive religio-political elite: the Watergate.

And still the economic and the political fields must not be totally confounded and fused together. No matter how closely they interpenetrate, they derive from different sources and should be kept apart, both as concepts and as agents for social control. To comment briefly and very superficially, economics generally revolves around factors *external* to man, usually measurable as quantities of touchable goods and visible services, to satisfy physical needs and sensible appetites. Politics, however, is rooted more deeply inside man, in the *interiority* of awareness and conscience whence derive personal and community relations.

Civil authority may make claims upon interior obedience and loyalty, at least in Christian social ethics and personal morality as traditionally conceived and practiced. But economic power is not permitted entry into this inner sanctum of human will and morality. If civil obedience is not externally expressed, then public authority may impose by force external punishment and sanctions. In cases of national defense, loyalty can be invoked to commandeer life and limb, as well as economic productive power and technology. And *interior* accord is expected, as we see from the appeal made to *conscience* by objectors to military service.

This excursus, banal in its simplicity, is excusable in preparation for the next stage in the aggiornamento momentum, toward political power as the means of directing economic forces to promote, naturally, the common good. If the political is indeed rooted more deeply in human interiority, then the Christian people could undertake a unique role in the coming reordering of human interdependence, national and global. Conscience, community, and commitment are concepts and convictions connate to the Christian soul and spirit.

Consequently, Catholics should not be surprised when Paul VI sees that today's structures of technological, economic, and military power show the radical limitation of economics: "That is why the need is felt to pass from economics to politics" (OA 46).

With these phrases Paul VI moves the social aggiornamento and the Church itself into another phase. The occasion is his apostolic letter, *Octogesima Adveniens,* in observance of the eightieth anniversary of *Rerum Novarum,* by which Leo XIII in 1891 had brought the Church into the world of modern economics and inaugurated its social teaching. Pope Paul's letter of 1971 marks a new departure; it centers on the political engagement of the Church. He sees the risks, as well as the need to take risks:

> It is true that in the term "politics" many confusions are possible and must be clarified, but each man feels that in the social and economic field, both national and international, the ultimate decision rests with *political power* (OA 46).

> The passing to the political dimension also expresses a demand made by the man of today: a greater sharing in responsibility and in decision-making. . . . In order to counterbalance increasing technocracy, modern forms of democracy must be devised, not only making it possible for each man to become informed and to express himself, but also by involving him in a shared responsibility. Thus human groups will gradually begin to share and to live as communities (OA 47).

Ideology and Political Commitment

Pope Paul's letter on politics repeats the oft-heard call that laymen should take up as their own proper task the renewal of the temporal order and that Christian organizations should take collective action "without putting themselves in the place of the institutions of civil society" (OA 51). However, the letter introduces four new elements, which in the context of the aggiornamento could have great significance:

a) Paul recalls approvingly "that the Church has sent on an apostolic mission among the *workers priests* who, by sharing fully the condition of the worker, are at that level the witnesses to the Church's solicitude and seeking" (OA 48). The Pope does not expressly mandate or invite apostolic missions by priests into the political arena. But given the fact that so many *clergy* and *religious*, and even bishops, now engage in political action, as he certainly knows, the Pope appears to encourage these experiments of the aggiornamento.

b) Paul VI stresses the widely varying economico-political situations in the different continents, cultures, and countries. He attempts no unified message, no solution of universal validity. "Such is not our ambition, nor is it our mission. It is up to the *Christian communities* to analyze with objectivity the situation which is proper to their own country." This recognition by the Pope of the local Church's role is a direct result of the Council's teaching on collegiality, and of the new bodies taking shape to implement it: bishops' conferences, priests' senates, pastoral councils (which are dominantly lay), associations of religious, among others. Pope Paul continues:

> It is up to these Christian communities, with the help of the Holy Spirit, in communion with the bishops who hold responsibility and in dialogue with other Christian brethren and all men of goodwill, to discern the options and commitments which are called for in order to bring about the social, political and economic changes seen in many cases to be urgently needed (OA 4).

So Paul urges Christian communities, at all levels and in all places, to discern the options and commitments called for, remaining open to *pluralism*, because "in concrete situations . . . one must recognize a legitimate variety of possible options. The same Christian faith can lead to different commitments" (OA 50; see also GS 43).

c) But can this plurality of possible Christian commitments include *socialism* and, more specifically, *Marxism*?

Pope John had forged an aggiornamento opening of historic dimension when he raised this question in *Pacem in Terris*, after a century of censure within the Church. He drew a clear distinction between philosophical teachings and historical movements: *"False philosophical teachings* regarding the nature, origin and destiny of the universe and of man" cannot be identified "with *historical movements* that have economic, social, cultural or political ends, not even when these movements have originated from these teachings and have drawn and still draw inspiration therefrom." The movements, "working in constantly evolving historical situations," are subject to profound change:

> Besides, who can deny that those movements, insofar as they conform to the dictates of right reason and are interpreters of the lawful aspirations of the human person, contain elements that are positive and deserving of approval? (PT 159).

> It can happen, then, that meetings for the attainment of some practical end, which formerly were deemed inopportune or unproductive, might *now* or in the future be considered opportune or useful (PT 160).

Pope John received general praise for this breakthrough. However, although breaking from the static past toward future dialogue, he does not even mention here the word "socialism," much less "Marxism." John the innovator remains cautious still.

Eight years later, in 1971, Paul VI is much bolder, a measure of the aggiornamento's rapid pace. He quotes approvingly John's distinction between false philosophical teachings and historical movements. Then immediately Paul identifies these movements as "socialist currents and their various developments," to which some Christians are today attracted.

While warning against a tendency to idealize socialism and to forget the limitations of the historical socialist movements, "which remain conditioned by the ideologies from which they originated," Paul makes distinctions

> to guide concrete choices between the various levels of expression of socialism: a generous aspiration and a seeking for a more just society, historical movements with a political organization and aim, and an ideology which claims to give a complete and self-sufficient picture of man (OA 31).

The Pope then points out that these levels are not necessarily separated; in each case concrete links are to be marked out. His discussion on the "attraction of socialist currents" closes with this remark: "This insight will enable Christians to see the degree of commitment possible along these lines, while safeguarding the values, especially those of liberty, responsibility and openness to the spiritual, which guarantee the integral development of man" (OA 31).

Paul VI is much less permissive toward Marxism, but again much bolder than John in discussing the issue openly and at length. In two pages he uses the word ten times, always capitalized, and once hyphenated as Marxism-Leninism. After showing the hydra-headed manifestations of Marxism (he cites half a dozen forms), and having admitted that these distinctions pose questions "for the reflection and activity of Christians," Paul concludes:

> It would be illusory and dangerous . . . to accept the elements of Marxist analysis without recognizing their relationship with ideology, and to enter into the practice of class struggle and its Marxist interpretations, while failing to note the kind of totalitarian and violent society to which this process leads (OA 34).

With seemly impartiality, in the next paragraph the Pope warns against "a renewal of the liberal ideology . . . in the name of economic efficiency, and for the defense of the individual against the increasingly overwhelming hold of organizations, and as a reaction against the totalitarian tendencies of political powers." Certainly, personal initiative must be maintained and developed, but not as derived from philosophical liberalism, which affirms "the autonomy of the individual in his activity, his motivation and the exercise of his liberty." Therefore, the liberal ideology likewise calls for careful discernment by Christians (OA 35).

d) The fourth new element introduced by Paul's letter on political involvement is the most surprising: "Rebirth of Utopias."

The weakness of today's political ideologies is clearly "perceived through the concrete systems in which they are trying to affirm themselves. Bureaucratic socialism, technocratic capitalism and authoritarian democracy are showing how difficult it is to solve the great human problem of living together in justice and equality." This generates protest, a deep-seated social malaise, "while at the same time we are witnessing the rebirth of what it is agreed to call 'utopias.' These claim to resolve the political problem of modern societies better than the ideologies. It would be dangerous to disregard this" (OA 37).

Paul admits that utopias can provide excuses for escaping from concrete tasks to take refuge in an imaginary world, to flee immediate responsibilities. However, he sees more, much more:

But it must clearly be recognized that this kind of criticism of existing society often provokes the forward-looking imagination both to perceive in the present the disregarded possibility hidden within it, and to direct itself towards a fresh future; it thus sustains social dynamism by the confidence that it gives to the inventive powers of the human mind and heart; and, if it refuses no overture, it can also meet the Christian appeal (OA 37).

Here Paul goes beyond the aggiornamento that John began in order to bring the Church up to date and move it from the status quo conservatism of the past into the world of today. Now Paul looks beyond the present. He projects into the future with a confidence and conviction doubly surprising for a man of his position and purported temperament. Here he outdoes the optimism of Pope John. Paul's confidence in the future derives from "the Spirit of the Lord." This Spirit, "who animates man renewed in Christ, continually breaks down the horizons within which his understanding likes to find security and the limits to which his activity would willingly restrict itself; there *dwells within him a power* which urges him to go *beyond every system and every ideology*" (OA 37).

The pastoral praxis of the aggiornamento now evolving demonstrates this power and this urge. Perhaps, too, these experiments of social ministry and political presence, especially in Latin America, prompt Paul's projections and bolster his courage. This is not the place to review these facts and musings, however briefly. I will only add that socio-political engagement by Christian communities, at the service of the human family as distinct from self-serving institutional ends, has risen dramatically these fifteen years and now spreads to all continents and cultures—from California to Korea, from Colombo to Barcelona, from Brazil to Brooklyn—among all Christians and with believers of other living faiths.

Almost everywhere these center around small communities of prayer and social concern. They received considerable attention during the 1974 Synod as witnesses of evangelization. Significantly, that month-long assembly of leading bishops showed that Africa, Asia, and other regions are developing their own models, while the Latin American *comunidades de base* and *movimientos populares* are becoming more politically aware. Among high-consumption nations of the North, comparable coalitions, networks, team ministries, and boycotts form to assert the rights and participation of minorities against the power of big business, labor, and government. Also, social-action and spiritual-life concerns cross-fertilize—for instance, in charismatic, fast, and prayer groups. And all open beyond national borders to world justice and peace.

Perhaps the People of God are discovering a new call and a new way to love and serve God and all his human family. Perhaps they are hearing the Spirit of Christ speaking through Vatican II: "The expectation of a new earth must not weaken but rather stimulate our concern for cultivating this one. For here grows the body of a new human family, a body which even now is able to give some kind of foreshadowing of the new age" (quoted by Pope Paul from GS 39 to conclude his discussion entitled, "Rebirth of Utopias," OA 37).

CHAPTER 5

Transnational Structures
for Justice and Development

Liberation and Building Up a Planetary Society

"Today the principal fact that we must all recognize is that the social question has become world-wide" (PP 3). Here is the new challenge to which Paul VI calls Christians and "all men of good will" in his encyclical *Populorum Progressio* in 1967. Until World War II the Church had addressed itself almost exclusively to workers' rights and social justice within the economy of each nation. After the war transnational social justice becomes the recurring concern.

During the war the Allies projected a successor to the League of Nations which would include social, economic, and agricultural agencies with international goals. These would implement the "freedom from want" article of the Atlantic Charter proclaimed by President Roosevelt and Prime Minister Churchill in 1942. From this was born the United Nations family of agencies, which from the start included the Economic and Social Council (ECOSOC), New York; the Food and Agriculture Organization (FAO), Rome; the UN Educational, Scientific and Cultural Organization (UNESCO), Paris; the World Health Organization (WHO), and the International Labor Organization (ILO), Geneva.

The last named was a vigorous carry-over from the League of Nations, founded in 1919 and due in part to the inspiration of Leo's *Rerum Novarum*. New UN bodies have been formed since 1945 for trade and development, population, environment, human rights, peaceful uses of nuclear energy, and other fields, as the world became conscious of these as global issues.

During World War II, Pius XII also began looking beyond the raging conflict to the task of constructing a better world after the war. He clearly saw that a new global economic system would be needed in the aftermath of the global destruction. Four years before the United Nations was formed, Pius called "for an international order, which, while assuring a just and lasting peace to all peoples, will bring forth well-being and prosperity." He condemned "the so-called absolute autonomy of the state," and insisted that humanity is "linked by moral and juridical bonds into a huge community intended for the good of all peoples and regulated by special laws which safeguard its unity and promote its prosperity."

Pius XII applauded those who "affirmed the necessity that all partake of the goods of the earth, even among those nations which in the realization of this principle would belong to the category of the givers and not of the receivers." Already in 1941 he warned against "narrow egotistical calculations tending to corner sources of economic supply and basic materials to the exclusion of nations less favored by nature" (Radio Message to the World, December 24, 1941, *The Pope Speaks*, Pantheon, pp. 162–66).

The international order did change after the war, but not along the lines hoped for by Pope Pius. Collapse of the old colonial powers made possible the emergence of two blocs, under the hegemony of two superpowers engaged in the Cold War, vying for influence, resources, and markets among the newly independent nations of the Third World. Applying the technologies and mastery of organization which the war had bred, the industrial North began weaving a multinational web of fresh economic bonds. These enveloped the rural, mining South in a new kind of dependency aptly called economic neocolonialism. A goodly dose of neoimperialism, political and military, was added by both East and West.

The principal agent of the West's post-war economic expansion is the multinational business corporation, private in name but usually helped by home government personnel (technical and military), grants, loans, and political leverage (diplomatic and other). The Soviet bloc uses state agencies only, having no private enterprises. Less advanced technically and much less "freewheeling" because of heavy bureaucracy, crasser political drives, and ideological brakes, the Communists have less success in economic penetration. Despite Soviet "investment" of several billion dollars, Cuba and the Aswan Dam have brought economic benefits to the USSR which are marginal at best. What profit, other than politico-ideological, China might reap from the Tanzania-Zambia railway remains to be calculated. Rather than relying on economic penetration, Soviets and Maoists have sought instead political (and military) power by allying with workers' and peasants' movements within each nation.

Therefore, today's world *economic* system is principally a Western creation. Its chief managers and beneficiaries are North America, Western Europe, and Japan. These form OECD, the Organization for Economic Cooperation and Development, and the "Club of Ten" (the ten rich "free market" nations) which determined the world's monetary system until the petroleum producers' unexpected uprising of 1973–1974. Because they provided most of the budget for the UN agencies, the rich nations of the North controlled them also to a large degree until the late 1960s. These offer a trickle of technical aid and a forum of public protest ever more potent.

(The economic power of petroleum began expressing itself as *political* power in the United Nations only during 1974. The consequences of this dramatic shift cannot yet be foreseen, much less adequately treated here. They are now only noted with the expectation that they will affect the basic economic and political constitution of the world order.)

This is the way most Third World peoples— and especially most "conscientized" Christians of Latin America—diagnose the present world economic system, here much simplified and quite caricatured. All the miseries of the South's two billion humans cannot in fact be blamed on today's big business managers and technologists thousands of miles to the North. Much of the gap is due to cultural and historical factors, particularly the technological advance which made possible four centuries of European expansionism. Heavy blame must currently fall on unjust structures controlled by small power elites within developing nations. Critics from the South point out, however, that their own internal oligarchy and system of injustice are kept in place by Northern power—economic, political, and military.

The aggiornamento documents agree with the fundamental position of the South. They urge rapid and deep transformation of this unjust world system, to move from inherited dependency toward the structures of solidarity required by today's interdependence. "But, as *Populorum Progressio* repeatedly underlines, we have now a world economy in which *all* the positions of strength, all the wealth, all the investment, all the commercial services and above all, the whole crucial apparatus of research are concentrated in the small elite of nations which have already achieved modernization" (DD 13—Message of Cardinal Roy to United Nations, November 19, 1970, for Second Development Decade, emphasis in original text).

Such is the lopsided reality, the abysmal gap between the Northern third and the Southern two-thirds which rends the human family into *dominators* and *dependents*. Still, "our technology, our science, our communications all thrust us towards a steadily increasing *interdependence*. A truly planetary society is, as Pope Paul has never ceased to emphasize, the great imperative of our time" (DD 13).

And a truly planetary society requires structures which build and assure planetary social justice. The shaping of these structures is a recurring subject of the aggiornamento documents. It appears prominently in John's two encyclicals and in *Gaudium et Spes*. But it is Paul who makes world justice for development and peace his constant concern, in scores of public statements, in season and out of season. His *Populorum Progressio* lays a foundation of remarkable depth, breadth, and solidity.

In 1971 he assigns to the Synod of Bishops the theme "Justice in the World." These assembled pastors, many themselves engaged directly in human development and the struggle for justice, then produce a most incisive and timely document, which Paul himself thereafter repeatedly uses in his tireless, constant campaign for global justice for all poor and oppressed. Pastorals by episcopal conferences and diocesan ordinaries and programs by religious and laity multiply. A social ministry for justice in the world, with adapted liturgy and spirituality, develops as a "constitutive dimension" of evangelization, as a main current of the regular apostolate, of diocese and parish, school and community. Via normal Church channels and through special groups and coalitions, usually ecumenical, political action is taken. Success is slow and hard to come by, but something does begin to move.

Structures for a New Economic Order

UNCTAD, the United Nations Conference on Trade and Development, was formed in the early sixties at the insistence of the Third World. Its purpose is to provide a forum and fulcrum for forging a countervailing force, so that the economically weak, some two billion humans, can face up to that minority elite of nations who possess almost all the world's technical and economic power—as bemoaned by pope and synod. Since the first UNCTAD Conference in 1963 at Geneva, through the subsequent New Delhi and Santiago sessions in 1968 and 1972, during the patient labors in between, step by minute step, the Church has consistently supported the poor people in their struggle for the structures of a more just world economic system.

During 1973–1974 this goal penetrated the consciousness of the human family to new depths, due to an interconnected series of events and conferences: The sub-Saharan, Indian, and Bangladesh famines; food shortages in the USSR and China; new awareness of rapid population growth despite control efforts in the Third World; formation of the petroleum exporters' bloc; quadrupling of prices and growing nationalization; the use of oil as a political weapon by the Arabs; the Yom Kippur War and subsequent peace efforts; the food and energy crises; worldwide inflation and recession, even in the United States. And in quick succession in 1974: the UN special session on the world economic order in April, and the UN Conferences on the law of the seas, (June, Caracas), population (August, Bucharest), and food (November, Rome).

These events are cause and/or effect of shifts in world consciousness and in economic and political power which could be of historic proportions. These conferences represent first attempts at realigning national and bloc goals, policies, and commitments in view of these changes in world awareness and power structure. (Chapter 6, "The Global Political Community," gives a brief analysis of the system being formed by *blocs* of nations, far beyond the earlier simplicities of East and West, North and South, or the First, Second, and Third Worlds.)

This realignment of nations and their blocs revolves principally around economic issues: the needs of peoples, their productive capacity and distribution systems. Since UNCTAD began in 1963—and with a sudden urgency during 1974—a new economic order has been proposed, based on social justice for all the human family, demanding historic breakthroughs beyond the self-sufficiency of the nation state and its bloc allies. In general, new economic structures are proposed to balance the preponderant power of the rich North—inherited from four centuries of colonial exploitation and its 200-year headstart toward industrialization—and to enable the economically weaker and poorer Southern peoples to participate and to share in their own development, within the wider context of the whole planet.

We shall now survey the new world economic structures advanced by the aggiornamento documents. They correspond closely with the positions of the South, especially with those of the "Fourth World," the poorest quarter of the world's people, having little oil and ore, but with more than a billion humans.

Neither the South nor the Church now has a clear-cut platform, giving its structural "planks" one by one, and tying them into a wholly organized blueprint for building the just society, step by step. Actually the South is now elaborating such a world economic order, but it is still incomplete. In no document does the Church state in consecutive order the changes and structures it promotes. To my mind, nevertheless, these might be grouped into categories outlining the transformation of structures proposed by the aggiornamento as a whole:

TRADE RELATIONS

The raw materials exported by developing countries, mainly the produce of agriculture and mining, should receive better and more secure prices, tariffs, and quotas; their semimanufactures and other products should be allowed access to rich country markets; price ceilings and other adjustments must be made on manufactures imported from rich countries to equalize the enormous differential of labor costs in relation to ability to pay (because Northern workmen often get a wage ten times that of Southerners, making the product's price truly exorbitant; management usually gets excellent remuneration, both North and South) for the South needs the North's products for its development: e.g., locomotives, electrical generators, laboratory apparatus, pharmaceutical plants, machine tools; shipping services, including insurance, now all in hands of the North, must be spread around; commodity stockpiling is needed to create world reserves to prevent shortages and sudden price fluctuations, especially of foods.

Commodity exporting nations should form their own bargaining bodies, that is, for their oil, copper, bauxite, agricultural products, etc. And consumer nations can be expected to form bargaining bodies of their own.

But the 1973–1974 experience of OPEC, Organization of Petroleum Exporting Countries, shows that the impact of such moves can be disastrous for weaker nations and very disturbing for the world economy as a whole if done precipitately. It is probable that no other commodity is as economically and politically potent as petroleum, the price of which quadrupled through sudden bloc action. However, the price of sugar tripled in the same few months, without conspicuous coalitions. New forces seem to have entered today's interdependent world marketplace.

CAPITAL FORMATION VIA GOVERNMENTAL LOANS AND GRANTS

Loans and grants should be via multilateral bodies rather than bilateral arrangements insofar as this does not favor the advanced nation bloc unduly by maintaining an unjust status quo, worldwide and/or within the receiving nation; is not tied to commercial, political, or military conditions; promotes integral human development and the upbuilding of infrastructure, including social and educational services; and does not afflict the weak with excessive indebtedness.

MULTINATIONAL BUSINESSES AND COMPARABLE SOCIALIST CORPORATIONS

Multinational business operations should be regulated by codes of law enforced by multinational juridic bodies, because they possess excessive bargaining power confronting the individual weak country and are usually further supported by the political and military power of their home nation or bloc, whether from North America, Europe, Japan, or the East—and soon probably from the Arab region. They also tend to evade tax payments in their country of origin, so these could be paid at least partially into a world tax fund.

Rapid depletion of a host country's natural resources must be avoided, allowing sufficient lead time for the next stage of its development; close attention should be given to environmental practices, labor relations, and preparation of managers for eventual take-over by local bodies, including the possibility of expropriation and nationalization.

SCIENTIFIC AND TECHNOLOGICAL CAPACITY

Rich-country technology should be generously transferred, via personnel, equipment, and plant, but on a selective basis aimed at meeting priority needs; more important is the advance of research capacity *within* developing regions, favoring intermediate technology which is labor-intensive and appropriate to the culture.

Science and technology should be increasingly regarded as the patrimony of all the human family. Therefore, long-term patents and franchises, which benefit the already rich and powerful, should be modified; transnational regulation of technology's use and abuse should be fostered, for which control of nuclear tests and pollution is a beginning.

MONETARY SYSTEM

Countries with dependent currencies must have a voice in the devaluation and revaluation of dominant currencies; they should also receive greater benefits from the newly created SDR system (Special Drawing Rights) of the International Monetary Fund; debt management, inflation control, and balance of payments—problems of weak-currency countries—demand special consideration in the evolving structures, and not only emergency attention.

REGIONAL INTEGRATION

Neighboring nations, and those of like interests and common culture, should continue drawing together into larger units for trade, production, research, higher education, monetary policy, bargaining power, etc.

WORLD TAX SYSTEM

A world tax system should be promoted as an instrument of distributive justice for all the human family.

Payments of the tax could be graduated to the production and consumption index of each nation, comparable to the graduated income tax paid by individuals within the nation; norms for distribution should include national need, efficacy of use, evidence that social justice is evolving within the nation and that benefits are reaching the lower levels of the needy—the bottom 40 percent of poor-country populations who have until now benefitted little from production increases. Such a tax would in time replace the "foreign aid" programs, which tend to paternalism and to abuse as political weapons. A world and/or regional treasury system should be built up. (*N.B.* This paragraph gives this author's views as to how the graduated world tax proposed in aggiornamento might take shape.)

TRANSNATIONAL AUTHORITY OVER THE SEAS

The new law of the seas now taking shape must go beyond regulation of shipping, fishing, and coastal limits; transnational sovereignty and authority through appropriate bodies must be established also for mining, use of water and polar ice, and pollution control.

A tax could be levied on those who draw products or profits from the seas, e.g., by using shipping lanes or harvesting, and paid into the world treasury mentioned above. Transnational sovereignty and authority should be likewise established over the polar regions, the terrestrial atmosphere, and space. (*N.B.* These are the personal interpretations of this author.)

MIGRATION

New policies and laws of migration must be introduced, particularly for freer entry from crowded regions into nations which still have considerable space, and for entry into highly developed nations, even seasonally or as "guestworkers."

ENVIRONMENT

Programs for safeguarding and improving the planet's environment must be promoted, along the lines projected by the UN Conference at Stockholm in 1972.

Such are the major structures for world justice and development proposed by aggiornamento positions, in the main documents and through hundreds of other statements by the Holy See or its representatives, often at United Nations and other public assemblies. Comparable positions are taken by other bodies of the Catholic Church, including the College of Bishops through its synod and national and regional conferences, and groups of religious through their generalates, provinces, and other associations, and by Protestant and Orthodox bodies, particularly through the World Council of Churches. Often the other Christian Churches take joint positions among themselves, and sometimes with the Catholic Church, particularly through Sodepax, the Committee on Society, Development and Peace, constituted jointly in 1968 by the World Council and by the Pontifical Commission Justice and Peace. In Asia, Christian Churches as a unit are now evolving common programs with followers of the other living transcendental faiths, including the Buddhist, Hindu, Moslem, and Shintoist religio-cultures. Jewish-Christian cooperation has expanded to include also those global structures for justice.

The projected structures for a new planetary order—which some would call utopian—at the service of all the world's peoples are the logical application of a most fundamental and conservative Christian, Jewish, and Moslem conviction: that our one Creator Father has made and destined all his creation—air and ore, soil and sea, as well as human inventiveness and skill—for all his human family, to be shared among all our four billion brothers and sisters—especially the poor and oppressed.

CHAPTER 6

The Global Political Community

Formation of Multinational Blocs

Within this all-embracing technico-economic system which is now engirdling the earth, the individual country loses strength in relation to the total power buildup throughout the planet. Modern transport and communications provide circulatory and nervous systems for voluminous and rapid exchange of goods and information. These tend to bind the nations together into one economic body composed of interdependent parts.

Even the two superpowers with their continental dimensions, the USSR and the USA, must turn abroad for certain necessities: the first for technology and cereals; the second for strategic ores such as tin, copper, bauxite; both for tropical produce. And both seek markets and unhindered transport facilities beyond their national territory. *A fortiori*, the middle and small powers are not economically self-sufficient.

In the political sphere this lack of national sufficiency holds equally true because of the same economic reasons, plus the new global issues of environment and seas, atmosphere and space—and above all because of nuclear warheads and ballistic missiles capable of committing within minutes ten thousand Hiroshimas. All made possible by science.

Ironically, it is the superpowers above all who forge—and force—alliances, spheres of influence, far-flung military bases, webs of espionage. The strongest appear the least self-sufficient. Even their national sovereignty, that absolute value and magnetic pole of vaunted power through which Europeans dominated world history for the past four centuries, has waned beyond recovery. *A fortiori*, the same holds for the 140 other members of the United Nations. Pope John sums it up: "At the present time no political community is able to pursue its own interests and develop itself in isolation, because its prosperity and development are both a reflection and a component part of the prosperity and development of all the other political communities" (PT 131).

Pope Paul bluntly cites nationalism as an obstacle "opposed to the formation of a world which is more just and which is better organized toward a universal solidarity." He understands the attractions of nationalism, both old and new, but the need to pool resources and development efforts outweighs pride of cultural patrimony and history:

> It is only natural that communities which have recently reached their political independence should be jealous of a national unity which is still fragile, and that they should strive to protect it. Likewise, it is to be expected that nations endowed with an ancient culture should be proud of their patrimony which their history has bequeathed to them.
>
> But these legitimate feelings should be ennobled by that universal charity which embraces the entire human family. Nationalism isolates people from their true good. It would be especially harmful where the weakness of national economies demands rather the pooling of efforts, of knowledge and of funds, in order to implement programmes of development and to increase commercial and cultural exchange (PP 62).

Clearly the age of the sovereign nation-state as principal actor on the world scene is over. We now live in an age of blocs and regional groupings which bind together many nations, for purposes and with resources beyond the national unit.

Since World War II, scores of plurinational blocs and regional bodies are taking shape. The active present tense is used purposely, because most should not yet be regarded as set, even for the next decade or two. Nations can adhere to several groupings, and as their policies change, adhesion also shifts at least in the degree of common accord and action. In this post-nationalist era the units are in a state of fusion and split, confusion and flux. Supposed monoliths break apart, as happened between China and the Soviet Union in the early sixties. Cooperation can suddenly replace enmity, as occurred between the Arabs and the United States after the Yom Kippur War.

Still it is instructive to attempt classification to show the variety of blocs and regions. (The stroke signifies opposition or sharp distinction; the hyphen indicates alliance, of some degree.)

West-USA/East-USSR: These two blocs have dominated planetary politics, war, and peace since 1945, under the hegemony of the two superpowers, by persuasion, necessity, or force. Their confrontation has brought the world teetering to the brink of nuclear holocaust—especially during the Berlin Blockade (1948–1950), the Berlin Wall and Cuba Crises (1961–1962), and perhaps again during the Yom Kippur War (1973). The Cold War led to military pacts and the standing armies of the North Atlantic Treaty Organization (NATO) and of the Warsaw Pact. It also contributed significantly to the formation of the European Economic Community (EEC), aided by the Marshall Plan, and its Eastern counterpart, the Council for Mutual Economic Assistance (COMECON). The West is also called the Atlantic bloc; the East, the Soviet or Communist bloc—China being of course excluded since the early 60s.

West Europe's continuing military weakness, probably irremedial because weapon speed so shrivels its size, invites America's military presence to confront Soviet armies. The latter occupy five countries of East Europe—by force, to judge from the uprisings of Hungary, Poland, and Prague (1956–1968). America's economic leadership in West Europe is no longer welcome, and a partnership relationship is now evolving. A policy of détente, rhetorically begun by President De Gaulle in the early 60s, was significantly carried forward by President Nixon, Secretary Brezhnev, and Chancellor Brandt in the early 70s. Economic and technological exchanges gain ground, and mutual disarmament is under discussion after first steps for limiting strategic nuclear arms.

USA bloc/USSR bloc/China bloc: The Eastern bloc included China from 1949, when Chairman Mao Tse-tung wrested control of the world's most populous country from Generalissimo Chiang Kai-shek, until the early 1960s when Maoist China broke violently with the Soviet Union for ideological, nationalist, and geopolitical motives. This substantially weakened Soviet war-making power against the West, and its prestige and truculent self-assertiveness as well—particularly since President Nixon's dramatic visit to China, prepared by Mr. Kissinger, and the ending of open American military operations in Indo-China.

China lacks economic power comparable to the two other blocs. However, the potential of its land mass and population, the distant attraction of its austere ethos and grassroots Communism, its self-identification with the poor South against the rich industrialized North, and its possession of nuclear weapons, all combine to give it extraordinary bargaining power versus East and West. Also, it ably plays upon the two superpowers' fears of each other, thereby weakening both and creating a third power center.

These three contending blocs are here identified closely with the nation states USA/USSR/China, because nationalist motives loom large and each makes decisions quite independently, with little authoritative participation by the other nations that form each bloc. Such relative independence is possible only to countries with large population and territory. This may foreshadow a global movement toward some ten to fifteen blocs and/or regions which cohere around the stronger nations in each, if one or a sufficing combination gives apt and forceful leadership.

North America-Western Europe-Japan have become a trilateral bloc during the last two decades. Of late its business leaders have formed a trilateral commission. Japan's astonishing ascendency to the high status of the world's number three industrial power made possible this improbable alliance, completely unforeseen in 1945. This bloc of Western-style free democracies, with mixed welfare economies, confronts all other blocs and indeed the rest of the world. Its main organizational expression is OECD, the Organization for Economic Cooperation and Development, head-quartered in Paris. Its combined economic and technological power far outweighs that of the USSR-East bloc and is at least tenfold that of the South. But the energy crisis has suddenly revealed its dependency as a bloc upon other regions and the basic fragility of the European and Japanese partners.

North/South: The North is the trilateral group plus the Eastern bloc, i.e., the industrialized third of the globe's people, occupying the temperate zone of the northern hemisphere, more or less north of the 35th parallel. The South embraces the less technically advanced and poorer regions south of the 35th parallel, lying mostly in the tropics: Africa, most of Asia, and Latin America, numbering about two-thirds of the human family. It is noteworthy that from the viewpoint of the South, both East and West are rich oppressors who *together* form the Northern bloc.

The 35th parallel of the northern hemisphere is of course only an approximate dividing line. The so-called frontier wavers south below 30 degrees in the American hemisphere, then veers north more or less along the 35th latitude through the Mediterranean, Black, and Caspian Seas. It then loops farther north along the fateful Soviet-China border and dips sharply south to include Japan among the rich. Still the 35th parallel is a handy average. Other anomalies exist, such as the European transplants in the southern temperate zones: highly industrialized South Africa, Australia and New Zealand, and the burgeoning area extending from São Paulo to Buenos Aires.

"Third World" designates the same majority of peoples as is signified by South. This totals about one hundred nations, most of which gained their independence from European empires after World War II. They then became the object of contest between East and West, led by the USA and

the USSR. During the 1950s the three groups, West, East, and South (the new nations), became designated respectively as the First/Second/Third Worlds. Of late the term "Fourth World" has come into use to designate some forty nations of the Third World (South) who are in economic straits quite worse than the rest of their bloc, a plight dramatically worsened by the oil-energy-food crisis. Among the poor they are marked by the lack of exportable ores and often the lack of enough food for their own needs. This Fourth World includes India, Pakistan, Bangladesh, and the nations of the drought-afflicted southern Sahara. It numbers about one billion humans.

Within UNCTAD, the UN Conference on Trade and Development, member nations have organized themselves into *five categories*, basically along bloc and regional lines: *A*. Africa and Asia; *B*. The West and Japan; *C*. Latin America (except Cuba); *D*. The East, i.e., the USSR and other socialist states (except China and Cuba); *E*. Independents, including China, Cuba, and Israel. These categories are officially recognized in the UNCTAD structure. They hold policy and planning sessions and usually vote solidly as categories. Frequently Category *A* and Category *C*, plus China (i.e. more or less the Third World, or the South) will join forces vis-à-vis the North (i.e. Categories *B* and *D*). Perhaps these categories foreshadow the future formation of political parties within the United Nations system.

Within UN circles this alliance of Categories *A* and *C* is often referred to as *"The 77."* There were originally seventy-seven Southern nations which formed a common front when UNCTAD took shape during the 1960s. The 77, now actually over 100 countries, grows in power and cohesion. They played major roles in the UN Special Assembly, April 1974, held in the wake of the oil-energy-food crisis, and also in the Population and Food Conferences at Bucharest and Rome a few months later. They are steadily wringing concessions from the North along the lines of the structures for world justice proposed above in Chapter 5. To sum up, Third World, South, and The 77 refer to the same bloc of poor nations, but The 77 designates a lobbying, caucusing, and countervailing force acting politically within the UN system. More or less the same nations make up the non-aligned groups, set up at the height of the Cold War in a conference at Bandung, Indonesia, to assert independence from both blocs, East and West.

Since 1970 the *Organization of Petroleum Exporting Countries (OPEC)* has acquired enormous economic power because they control such a large portion of the energy which technology-based societies now require. They began increasing national control and world prices as their organization acquired self-confidence. Within OPEC, the Organization of *Arab* Petroleum Exporting Countries (OAPEC) dominates. To counter the West's pro-Israel policies, the Arab nations suddenly used their massive power as a political-military bloc with astonishing success in late 1973. And with the other OPEC members they combined to quadruple prices and to provoke a global oil-food-energy crisis of new proportions. This has caused a radical shift of world monetary resources of historic consequences for the future alignment of all bloc and regional relations, political and military as well as economic.

It is good to stress the *economic* basis of OPEC, as compared with the religious and cultural identity of the Arab peoples who form its dominant nucleus, OAPEC. These same nations form the Arab League, through which their political and military goals are pursued, backed up by the economic weapon of OAPEC. This economic power is in turn strengthened by the non-Arab members of OPEC, which include Iran, Nigeria, and Venezuela. Iran is Moslem, as are the Arab countries, Nigeria only partly so. All derive from different racial stocks; Nigeria and Venezuela are of different continents and culture. These factors will all play significant parts in the postnational era of the planet's political community.

Following the example of OPEC, *other ore and commodity exporting countries* are forming organizations, regardless of their geographic dispersal and religio-cultural differences. Bauxite and copper exporters are especially advanced in this; the copper market, for example, associates countries from two different continents, cultures, and ethnic origins: Peru and Chile with Zaire and Zambia. Such moves provoke in turn the formation of associations among nations which import these raw materials.

Neighboring nations of a given region or continent, particularly if they share common history, religio-cultural values and/or ideological goals, began associating for economic reasons after World War II. These could lead in turn to political union. The European Economic Community (colloquially the Common Market, formerly the Coal and Steel Community) is the prime exemplar of this move toward the transnational unit, despite centuries of hatred and war for nationalist and religious motives.

While much less advanced, notable experiments at regional integration are afoot in all the continents. East Africa, Central America, and the Andean countries are examples.

The United Nations is constituted by independent member states. But its actual functioning is largely regulated by bloc action, for both political and economic goals. This was already seen within UNCTAD. Additionally, there are *regional UN offices*—e.g., in Bangkok, Nairobi, Santiago,

Beirut, Geneva—which deal with individual nations and with the continental or regional bodies formed by the area's nations—for instance, the
Organization of African Unity, Addis Ababa.

Another most important element is the *regional development fund or bank*,
e.g., the Inter-American Development Bank, Washington; and the Asian
Development Bank, Manila. While juridically separate from the UN system, close working relations are assured through the UN's funding and
monetary bodies: the International Monetary Fund (IMF) and the International Bank for Reconstruction and Development (IBRD), commonly
called the World Bank. Both are headquartered in Washington but have
offices in the different regions.

Religio-Political Implications

This excursus, on plurinational blocs now nascent, is lengthy in the
context of this overview, and still, considering the ground covered, it is
perforce dangerously superficial. Too, it aims more at projecting a prospectus toward the coming generation than at surveying aggiornamento
documents as of 1975. Nevertheless, I inject my personal views at this
point because of the religious, cultural, and political potential of the
bloc-forming process.

a) This movement beyond the nation-state is a principal political happening during the aggiornamento years. It is moving at astonishing
speed; in 1963 *Pacem in Terris* gave scant notice to this regional and bloc
character. Suddenly we become aware that these or similar plurinational
units could provide the shape of world political structure in the future,
with enormous consequence for all the human family, including its
economic structures for justice and its chances for peace.

The domination of all continents by European nations, which began
in the 1600s, is completely ended. Christian identification with this
hegemony has waned notably during the aggiornamento years, which
brought a new awareness of the Church's mission: loving service to all the
human family by promoting justice, development, and peace. Understanding the plurinational pattern is necessary to understanding the
Church's present and coming role of evangelization.

b) This move toward regionalization could also deeply affect the internal organization of the Church itself. Nationalism (e.g., German-
Venetian vs. Hellenic-Slavic) provided essential elements in the
East/West, Byzantine/Roman division of the eleventh century, and even
more in the Protestant/Roman separation of the 1500s. Almost everywhere during the sixteenth and seventeenth centuries, Orthodox and

Protestant churches organized into national bodies, usually in close alliance with the nation-states of Europe then aborning.

The World Council of Churches is today constituted by some 250 member Churches, Orthodox and Protestant, of which over 95 percent are national bodies. But these are now associating into regional or continental councils, especially strong in Africa, Asia, and the Middle East.

Within the Catholic Church comparable regional bodies are being formed by national bishops' conferences, of which CELAM in Latin America is the most advanced. The 1974 Catholic synod showed a marked tendency toward indigenization according to regions, cultures, and plurinational political reality. The Fourth General Assembly of the World Council of Churches, in late 1975 in Nairobi, shows the same orientation in its preparatory documents. Everywhere Orthodox, Protestant, and Catholic bodies work increasingly together within each region. In the Caribbean they have formed a united council.

c) This growing regionalization within the Christian Church, moving beyond fragmentation both national and theological, seems especially indicated in Asia, where other faiths are completely dominant among some two billion humans. There Moslem, Hindu, Buddhist, Confucian, and other religio-cultures experience the double impact of Western-style industrialization with its concomitant welfare materialism, and the awakening to European domination. They also begin their own aggiornamento, in their own way and rhythm.

Christian prosyletism of imperial days from Western power-centers is completely passé. The Church in Asia acquires, too, its own leadership and self-awareness vis-à-vis the Church in Rome and Geneva, Cologne and Paris, London and Chicago. It evolves, too, its own theology within the Asian cultural matrix and societal reality, as does Latin America with its theology of liberation and Black Africa in its moves for Africanization.

d) In several areas leaders of Asian transcendental faiths are now inviting and welcoming Christians to interreligious cooperation for promoting justice, development, and peace. Two bodies largely under Asian leadership especially advance this collaboration: the World Conference on Religion and Peace (WCRP), and the Asian Religio-Cultural Forum on Development (ARCFOD). The first has an office in New York for relations with the United Nations; it has held two major assemblies, in Kyoto (1970) and Louvain (1974). ARCFOD, originally stimulated by Sodepax from Geneva and Rome, is headquartered in Bangkok and Tokyo.

In addition to programs of social ministry and political presence, these are elaborating what might be called "the social documents of the interreligious aggiornamento"—providing Pope John's word and idea are acceptable to Asian believers.

e) Religion and religio-cultural value systems (or ideological equivalents) play significant roles in the collective self-awareness and identity which draw together individuals, families and tribes, villages and provinces toward the national self-consciousness needed to animate a nation-state and to unite it from within. This is now being lived out to some degree in the newly independent states of Africa as they awaken to greater consciousness of nationhood among their coalescing tribes.

This societal function of religion is clearly illustrated from the national histories of Europe, e.g., second-century Rumania, sixth-century France and England, Spain and Portugal from the eighth century onward, Germany's evolution toward united nationhood from Luther to Bismarck. And it is seen in the European experience as a whole until World War II, which by its excesses stirred up revulsion against hypernationalism.

A comparable coalescing role for religion could now be expected within the regional and continental bodies during coming decades. This is eminently clear within the Arab region. As it did from 650 to 1650 A.D., Islam provides again a cohesion of soul beyond geographic national borders; it even offers a unique bond completely outside race and culture, between the Arab and Negroid Moslems of Africa. This Islamic cohesion is strengthened by historic memory of the eleventh-century Crusades and the nineteenth-century Christian missions, closely tied to Western imperial policy. And it is stimulated anew by the young state of Israel, made politically and economically possible by nations of the Christian West, which were Islam's rulers until the past decade or so.

Christian faith and cultural values have filled an obvious function in the ongoing union of Europe since World War II. In the aftermath of Fascist force and Nazi fanaticism, nourished by Caesarian pretentions and Teutonic war-god myths, Europe then faced the still attractive communist ideology. Men who were Christian, by profession or by tradition and basic values, provided outstanding leadership in bringing Europe beyond nationalist enmity: Monnet, Schuman, Adenauer, and Di Gasperi—the last three all "practicing" Christians; Monnet from a traditional Christian family. (His sister, Monique Monnet, was one of only four Catholic laywomen serving as auditors during Vatican II. Monnet's chief executive associate through 1950–1972, Max Kohnstamm, has served with me since 1968 as co-chairman of Sodepax; he was appointed by the World Council of Churches, I by the Holy Father.) The great socialist Spaak of Belgium received significant support for European unity from the Christian Democratic movement of the Benelux countries, from its worker, farmer, and business expressions, as well as from its political parties.

Can—should or will—religion play a comparable role in the reshaping of the world's political structure into plurinational regions and blocs? The aggiornamento documents and praxis to date would favor such an effort.

The universal Church now realizes that "there is of course a wide diversity among the situations in which Christians—willingly or unwillingly—find themselves according to regions, socio-political systems and cultures. . . . It is up to the Christian communities [local, national, regional] . . . to discern the options and commitments which are called for in order to bring about the social, political and economic changes seen in many cases to be urgently needed" (OA 3–4).

The Church of Latin America had anticipated Pope Paul's recognition of regional and cultural self-identity. Already Medellín had condemned "exacerbated nationalism" and urged that all sectors of society should "because of justice and brotherhood. transcend antagonisms in order to become agents of national and continental development. Without this unity, Latin America will not be able to succeed in liberating itself from the neo-colonialism to which it is bound, nor will Latin America be able to realize itself in freedom, with its own cultural, social-political and economic characteristics" (MDP 12; MDJ 13).

In his 1973 *Reflections on the Tenth Anniversary of Pacem in Terris,* Cardinal Roy notes how the world's socio-political map has changed in only ten years:

> *Pacem in Terris* described it as a sum of Nation-States, and linked these different national communities one to another in the manner of the United Nations, as so many totally distinct entities (RR 77, citing PT 42).

> Today, these nations are tending to regroup themselves in *regional or continental systems* and become henceforth international partners. Thus we are witnessing a certain *breaking down of nationalism* (RR 77).

> Let us look at the map of the world. It shows, among other things, a shift towards the Pacific Ocean; the emergence of Latin America; the clear shift also towards the Indian Ocean; the self-affirmation of Africa and the Arab world. As for Europe, it has just gone through a process of enlargement. But *neither Europe nor North America is any longer the centre of the world* (RR 75).

In his 1973 analysis of this regionalization in the decade since *Pacem in Terris,* Roy notes that "the most obvious change is at the level of world politics: the progress from the two-sided system (the 'Atlantic bloc' and the 'Soviet bloc') to many-sidedness." We have seen, too, "a redistribution of roles and a certain removal of the various barriers set up between East and West." However, Roy laments, the greatest and most inhuman moat remains—the abysmal gap between the high-consumption North and the South of *les miserables*:

> We have seen that unfortunately this improvement of East-West relations between countries that are already or almost industrialized is not matched—far from it—in "North-South" relations, that is in the countries of the Third World and, *a fortiori*, of the "Fourth World" (the nations and social categories that are "marginal") (RR 79).

This truly significant shift to the transnational is matched, Roy observes, by another political and socio-psychological movement in the opposite direction. This is typified in Europe by insistence on Flemish, Basque, and Jura self-identity; in North America by Quebec separatism, ethnic awareness, Indian, Black, Hispanic, and Chicano power:

> At the same time we note within each nation the tendency to subnational regroupings on a more human scale, regroupings which answer a need for interpersonal communications. This is a need which is being more and more denied by the growing uniformity of social life.

> This diastolic and systolic movement—of expansion and contraction in relation to the national being—a movement which was already noticeable ten years ago in the time of John XXIII, seems to be a phenomenon typical of today, with the increasing role of "transnational forces" in their different forms: economic (multinational enterprises, monetary systems) and cultural (mass-media; the civilization of the image; ideologies, religions), etc. (RR 78).

The Roman Catholic Church experiences within itself, in its growing self-awareness, and in its restructuring process, a comparable push-pull in two directions: between the Church Universal and the local Church in its various expressions. This provided constant counterpoint within the harmonic ensemble of the 1974 Synod of Bishops. Awareness of responsibility to all the human family, to a planetary order of justice and peace, is balanced and countered with the formation of national and regional episcopal conferences, who take their own initiatives. Even dioceses and parishes are criticized for bigness; smaller communities, ethnic groups, and ad hoc coalitions are formed for prayer, cultural expression, social and political action.

For these reasons this very recent aggiornamento awareness of plurinational blocs and subnational groupings within the evolving socio-political structure needs to be deepened and closely followed within the Church. It must above all become the object of fresh theological reflection. With other aggiornamento processes, this might call for new departures in ecclesiology and in Church law, constitutional as well as canonical, and for more daring experiments in social ministry and further evolution of ecclesial structures—from parish to papacy.

All this is for the purpose of loving and serving God's human family, transforming societal structures toward this goal—drawn by the earthly horizons of utopia opened by Pope Paul and by the fulfilling vision of the Kingdom offered by Christ.

The Catholic Peace Movement

Growing political division into power blocs receives priority attention for another reason: War and the arms race, terrorism and constructing the peace, can only be grasped and grappled with in the context of the new global dynamics of blocs and regions. These issues have become major preoccupations of the aggiornamento.

It was *Pacem in Terris* (Peace on Earth) which won for John and his aggiornamento a universal hearing.

Millions who had never paid the least attention to popes and their jaw-breaker encyclicals suddenly sat up and listened. Here for the first time a pope was addressing himself "to all men of good will." And his message responded to a deep longing shared by all.

Rather, it was clergy and faithful in goodly numbers who were taken aback. Peace had become an object of suspicion in many Catholic circles, especially in the United States, the only Western nation capable of waging war. The "peace offensive" of the communists, identified with their Stockholm conferences of the 1950s and with Picasso's dove, had given the lovely word a bad name. Peace was a dove that went "Boom"!

Pacifism was viewed as a quaint aberration of Quakers and Mennonite sects. US Catholics, on the other hand, were patriots through and through. We fought *just* wars—when our President told us to. Presidential elections in 1952 and 1960 focused on five-star generals and war heroes, who debated rolling back the communists, unleashing Chiang Kai-shek, and closing the missile gap. Many abhorred the United Nations and all its works because it brought real live Russian Reds into New York City. Dorothy Day's forlorn Catholic peace movement was swallowed up among the skyscrapers and cathedrals—until Viet Nam.

European Catholics, on the other hand, had lived through the bombs and concentration camps. They knew that their homes and cities and children would be crushed to oblivion—caught between the two superpowers. And now too, the atom bomb!

The aging Cardinal Suhard, remembered for his aggiornamento pastorals ("Rise or Decline of the Church," "Priest in the World") which helped prepare the aggiornamento during the decade before John, encouraged a young French priest returning from five years in a Nazi stalag. Bernard Lalande's priestly vow was to devote the rest of his life to French and German reconciliation. With a handful of friends, Pax Christi was formed, much assisted by Lalande's leadership and because Suhard chose him to be his personal secretary. They shared residence and daily meals until Suhard's death. Of equal and perhaps greater import, Lalande was in direct frequent contact with Archbishop Roncalli, Papal Nuncio in Paris until 1954, and four years later, John XXIII.

Pax Christi grew, as Europe sought to unite, into the first significant international peace movement under the auspices of Catholic bishops—even of Cardinals: Suhard, Feltin, Doepfner, Frings, Heenan, Suenens, Alfrink, Gouyon, Marty. It prepared the way, and helped prepare Pope John, for launching the peace movement which so marks the aggiornamento era, as compared with pre-World War II Catholic mentality.

Was Pax Christi the first and only international *Catholic* peace movement? Can anyone name another in modern times? Since the Wars of Religion and the Westphalia Treaty of 1648? Since the Peace of God of medieval chivalry on Sundays and holy days? Why have we European Christians so long glorified blood and soil, and the wars to purify and enhance these ultimates? Theology and spirituality, magisterium and liturgy—were they so lacking or ineffective even then over all those centuries? Or so unaware, indifferent, and unworldly that the politics of war was left to political leaders only?

CONSTRUCTING PEACE

With *Pacem in Terris* John launches a planetary Catholic peace movement and an overall program for "constructing peace" which embraces the economic, social, cultural, and political spheres. Vatican II devotes a full chapter of *Gaudium et Spes* to "The Fostering of Peace and the Promotion of a Community of Nations." The two key sections are "Avoidance of War" and "Building Up the International Community." In *Populorum Progressio* Paul propounds that enduring peace is attainable only through the transformation of society's structures for promoting justice and integral human development. In fact, Paul insists, such transformation and development is the new name, the very meaning, of peace.

In this brief review of the new Catholic movement for peace, the last-named element must be listed first: Peace is not the mere absence of war; peace must be built up, perseveringly and progressively, step by painful step.

Peace grows out of just societal structures, particularly economic and political structures in which all citizens participate, deriving from religio-cultural values and convictions deeply rooted in human dignity, rights, and consciousness. Consequently, peace requires the transformation of national structures if these are oppressive. And peace certainly calls for the transformation of global structures because these are now demonstrably oppressive as a world system. This overview has already hurriedly traced the skeleton of these structures and values which upbuild peace.

DEFENSIVE WAR

But the fact of war remains while these structures are under construction, and by reason of the instability of rapid change. And the threat of nuclear catastrophe hangs over the head of all, over human life itself.

Given the present disorganized condition of the world community, with its contending blocs and nations, "governments cannot be denied the right to legitimate defense once every means of peaceful settlement has been exhausted." Therefore, government authorities have "the duty to protect the welfare of the people entrusted to their care and to conduct such grave matters soberly."

"But it is one thing to undertake military action for the just defense of the people, and something else again to seek the subjugation of other nations" (GS 79).

It is noteworthy that "government authorities" are the only actors cited here, and only "other nations" seem subject to subjugation; just defense "of the people" also has a nationalist ring. The much more complex reality of plurinational blocs which now integrate their military power during "peace time" has not yet received adequate attention in aggiornamento documents thus far.

Current negotiations for balanced disarmament and mutual security by the Eastern and Western blocs are being closely followed by the Holy See. Probably more attention to bloc-reality will surface soon in Catholic teaching on war and peace also, gradually replacing the national unit focus of the past five centuries, as well as excessive expectations in the United Nations as now constituted.

TOTAL WAR AND THE BALANCE OF TERROR

It is reliably reported that John's proximate decision to write *Pacem in Terris* grew out of the nuclear confrontation during the Cuban Crisis, October 1962, when Kennedy and Khrushchev drew up "eyeball to eyeball." It appeared six months later (see RR 42).

Strangely, John barely mentions the word "war." Pius XII is twice quoted, already concerned in 1941 with avoiding the calamity of World War III, and desperately crying out, "Nothing is lost by peace; everything is lost by war," in August 1939, six days before the holocaust exploded. Pope John focuses rather on the balance of terror, progressive disarmament, and effective arms control.

The arms race, requiring "a vast outlay of intellectual and economic resources, . . . is allegedly justified on the grounds that in present-day conditions peace cannot be preserved without an equal balance of armaments." So if one country increases its arms strength, others feel the need to match or surpass it. Worst of all:

> If one country is equipped with nuclear weapons, other countries must produce their own, equally destructive.

> Consequently, people live in constant fear lest the storm that threatens every moment should break upon them with dreadful violence. And with good reason, for the arms of war are ready at hand.

> Even though it is difficult to believe that anyone would deliberately take the responsibility for the appalling destruction and sorrow that war would bring in its train, it cannot be denied that the conflagration may be set off by some uncontrollable and unexpected chance.

> And one must bear in mind that, even though the monstrous power of modern weapons acts as a deterrent, it is to be feared that the mere continuance of nuclear tests, undertaken with war in mind, will have fatal consequences for life on earth (PT 109–111).

John concludes "that nuclear weapons should be banned," as urgently demanded by "justice, right reason and humanity" (PT 112). Also demanded are equal and simultaneous reduction of stockpiles and effective methods of arms control. Finally, John's fundamental principle "declares that the true and solid peace of nations can consist, not in equality of arms, but in mutual trust alone" (PT 113). Yes, this is the refreshing directness which Pope John brought into the horrors of nuclear stalemate. Naive? Perhaps. And still he formally repeats "mutual trust" to the powerful heads of nations and blocs, who are constantly accompanied by the little black box that holds the nuclear trigger cocked and ready to hit within minutes:

> In the highest and most authoritative assemblies, let men give serious thought to the problem of a peaceful adjustment of relations between political communities on a world level—an adjustment founded on mutual trust, on sincerity in negotiations and on faithful fulfillment of obligations assumed. . . .
>
> We, for Our part, will not cease to pray God to bless these labors so that they may lead to fruitful results (PT 118–119).

Vatican II treated the issue of total war and the balance of terror much more deeply. The 2,000 bishops showed keen awareness of the fateful character of their debate, which went on for several days. The most salient points:

> The horror and perversity of war are immensely magnified by the multiplication of scientific weapons.
>
> For acts of war involving these weapons can inflict massive and indiscriminate destruction far exceeding the bounds of legitimate defense.
>
> Indeed, if the kind of instruments which can now be found in the armories of great nations were to be employed to their fullest, an almost total and altogether reciprocal slaughter of each side by the other would follow, not to mention the widespread devastation which would take place in the world and the deadly aftereffects which would be spawned by the use of such weapons (GS 80).

It is to be noted that the Council Fathers do not employ the terms "nuclear" or "atomic" arms. The phrases "scientific weapons" or "modern warfare" and "new weapons" are used. So the wider ensemble of technological arms are under consideration and "compel us to undertake an evaluation of war with an entirely new attitude." "With these truths in mind," the Second Vatican Council "makes its own the condemnation of total war already pronounced by recent Popes, and issues the following declaration":

> Any act of war aimed indiscriminately at the destruction of entire cities or of extensive areas along with their population is a crime against God and man himself. It merits unequivocal and unhesitating condemnation (GS 80).

Attempting to grasp the meaning of this condemnation, it seems clear that the Second Vatican Council is saying that Hiroshima and Nagasaki were crimes against God and man himself, because they exceeded the proportional bounds of legitimate defense by destroying entire cities, populations included. Probably the indiscriminate blanket bombing and shelling in Western Europe, of which Coventry, Warsaw, and Dresden are the dread examples, are also condemned, because Vatican II does not refer to nuclear arms only. The solemn form of this declaration is to be noted. Also the use of the words "crime" and "condemnation"; the aggiornamento documents make infrequent use of the ringing anathemas which normally peppered pronouncements of the past.

A footnote in *Gaudium et Spes* identifies the popes who have condemned total war as Pius XII, John XXIII, and Paul VI in his address to the United Nations. It is the definition of total war which is given new precision here by Vatican II: "Any act of war aimed indiscriminately at the destruction of entire cities or of extensive areas with their populations" (GS 80).

During the Council, however, spirited debate in St. Peter's basilica centered mainly not on the actual use of scientific weapons for total war, but rather on their use as a threat in the *balance of terror*: Since use of such arms is criminal, does a nation have a right to manufacture and store nuclear and comparable new weapons, ready and cocked for delivery (perhaps already aboard a flying plane) only *as a threatening deterrent* against the potential enemy's use of similar arms of total war?

To the surprise of some, Vatican II does not condemn such manufacture and possession of scientific weapons, because "many regard this state of affairs as the most effective way by which *peace of a sort* can be maintained between nations at the present time." Peace of a sort, unsure and unauthentic! Under this peace, "the causes of war threaten to grow gradually stronger." In this sort of peace, the arms race, "an utterly treacherous trap for humanity," speeds up and infects all regions of the world. The fear deepens "that if this race persists, it will eventually spawn all the lethal ruin whose path it is now making ready" (GS 81).

Our duty then is to "work for the time when all war can be completely outlawed by international consent. This goal undoubtedly requires the establishment of some universal public authority acknowledged as such by all." But until this hoped-for world authority can be set up,

> everyone must labor to put an end at last to the arms race, and to make a true beginning of disarmament, not indeed a unilateral disarmament, but one proceeding at an equal pace according to agreement, and backed up by authentic and workable safeguards (GS 82).

And while the Council was weighing the balance of terror in Rome, Paul was in New York addressing the United Nations on its twentieth anniversary, October 1965. The drama of his appearance was magnified by worldwide coverage by the media and was solemnized by a simplicity anything but "pontifical" and by a consecration oath liturgical in its penetration of soul. The high point:

> It suffices to remember that the blood of millions of men, that numberless and unheard-of sufferings, useless slaughter and frightful ruin, are the sanction of the past which unites you with an oath which must change the future history of the world: No more war, war never again! Peace, it is peace which must guide the destinies of peoples and of all mankind (UN 19).

CONSCIENTIOUS OBJECTION AND WARTIME SAVAGERY

The frailty of the Catholic peace movement is well illustrated by the Church's negative, or at best feeble, position on objection to military service for reasons of conscience—until the aggiornamento years. Suddenly conscientious objection acquired front-line position among moral, civil, and pastoral issues in the West after 1965—due prominently to the impact of the Vietnam War in North America, to the dissent of youth as a whole in the West, and to the global sympathy aroused by the Third World revolution against the North.

Pacem in Terris in 1963 says nothing about conscientious objection.

Vatican II at least broaches the subject two years later (perhaps another "first" among Church documents at this level). A two-page section devoted to "Curbing the Savagery of War" focuses first on genocide: "actions designed for the methodical extermination of an entire people, nation, or ethnic minority. These actions must be vehemently condemned as horrendous crimes. The courage of those who openly and fearlessly resist men who issue such commands merits supreme commendation" (GS 79).

Next, support is extended to international conventions for "restraining the frightfulness of war," such as "conventions concerning the handling of wounded or captured soldiers, and various similar agreements." Then, an opening appears toward conscientious objection:

> Moreover, it seems right that laws make humane provisions for the case of those who for reasons of conscience refuse to bear arms, provided however, that they accept some other form of service to the human community (GS 79).

The most authoritative English edition of the conciliar documents, whose translation is used in this volume, adds two footnotes which merit attention: Reference to genocide is stimulated by "the post-World War II controversy over responsibility for 'war crimes' and the culpability of subordinates under a corrupt regime. There can be no justification of the conduct of an Eichmann on the score that he simply executed commands from higher authorities" (GS 79, note 255, Abbott edition).

Such observations became much more current for these pastor-bishops of Vatican II five years later, in the wake of the Indo-China War with its My Lai massacres and technological horror inflicted upon a peasant people, witnessed from cozy supper tables in technicolor splendor. This prepared for the sudden turn, among American Catholics in particular, from super-patriotism and prideful soldiering to conscientious objection. In 1965 Vatican II appears still rather unconvinced that the objector has an objective moral basis, as the verb "seems" indicates in the extract above. Translator-commentator Donald R. Campion, S. J., editor of the Jesuit weekly *America*, includes a second footnote in the cited edition. It shows clearly the indecisive state in 1965 of this new doctrinal orientation toward conscientious objection:

> The Constitution is careful in its statement of concern in this passage. The text makes no judgment on the objective moral claim of the conscientious objector. It neither accepts nor rejects the arguments in support of such a position. It simply appeals in the name of equity for humane treatment under the law of those who experience difficulties of conscience with respect to bearing arms (GS 79, note 256).

The 1971 Synod of Bishops returns briefly to genocide, extending its scope to "persecution . . . on tribal grounds" (JW 22); to inhuman treatment of war prisoners, "even after the Geneva Convention"; and to repression "by the political power" and "torture, especially of political prisoners" (JW 24). And most significantly, in addition to disarmament, arbitration, and international police action, the synod urges:

> Let a strategy of non-violence be fostered also, and let conscientious objection be recognized and regulated by law in each nation (JW 65).

Then by 1973, Roy's *Reflections on Pacem in Terris* cites "military conscientious objection" as a new right "which now has legal status in a very large number of countries" (RR 96).

By that date this new right was increasingly admitted for Catholics, as well as for Quakers and Mennonites, in the United States, under the pressures of the Vietnam War. Many pastors and college chaplains, parents and spiritual advisers, whose training and experience went quite the other way, became "conscientized" themselves and counseled draftees to object to service: against war in general, or selectively against this particular war or a designated service branch, e.g., strategic bombing which endangers civilian population or causes ecological devastation of forests and crop lands. Some Catholic draft board members and judges also changed their values and norms.

In Europe, too, Catholics participated in movements to strengthen or initiate legislation permitting conscientious objection, even in Italy and Spain. But simultaneously almost everywhere violence and terrorism increased—nowhere more strikingly than among Catholics and Protestants of faith-blessed Ireland.

VIOLENCE AND TERRORISM

Why have violence and terrorism, outside the "legal" form of warfare, increased during the aggiornamento years (if indeed they have—and we cannot linger here to document what seems daily experience)?

The thirty years since World War II have engendered a world in rapid movement, undergoing a torrent of change: break-up of empires, scores of nations breaking away from old power centers, technological breakthroughs, global communications flow, confrontation of new unstable blocs, fresh power poles, mobility of classes, implosive rush from rural space to urban concentration.

And above all, there occurs conscientization—the interior movement of awakening self-identity as persons and groups, of a new awareness of role, rights, and responsibilities within society. There is a new realization that society must undergo transformation because its inherited structures are themselves unjust and violent, and all the more terrifying because for too long they have functioned so quietly. The society has been well-lubricated by the natural virtues of blind obedience and humble patience—too often well-sublimated with appeals to the moral support of the Church and, most appalling of all, to Christ's free gift of justifying grace.

This torrent of rapid change as the world tries to restructure itself invites violence within nations and the use of terror across national frontiers, by groups not duly constituted as states. ("Not yet!" they would say.) Often these groups act as pawns of legal governments, including the most honorable and peace-loving. They are made mobile by today's jets and lethal by technical advances, such as plastic explosives. Often they are enwebbed in espionage and subversive outbursts engineered by the best brains and financed by the tax billions of superpower citizens.

Violence, almost endemic to modern society even in "peaceful" times, has doggedly worried Paul VI.

Pope John, on the other hand, almost ignored its presence, through innocence or naiveté or choice; this is not to his credit, because mounting violence deserved serious attention from the author of *Peace on Earth*. Vatican II at least broached the issue. It makes passing reference to "the complexity of the modern world and the intricacy of international relations [which] allow guerilla warfare to be drawn out by new methods of deceit and subversion." However, the Council does show insight and foresight in adding, already in 1965, "In many cases the use of terrorism is regarded as a new way to wage war" (GS 79).

Pope Paul bites the bullet. In *Populorum Progressio* he interfaces the plural dilemmas—the imperative of deep and rapid transformation of structures; the danger of haste; the temptation to violence; the new disasters and injustice risked by recourse to revolutionary uprising. Revolution must therefore be avoided—"save where there is a manifest, long-standing tyranny which would do great damage to fundamental personal rights and dangerous harm to the common good of the country. . . . A real evil should not be fought against at the cost of greater misery" (PP 29–31).

And still Paul is not saying "peace at any price"; he immediately adds the key elements of his whole development-liberation message:

> We want to be clearly understood: the present situation must be faced with courage and the injustices linked with it must be fought against and overcome. Development demands bold transformations, innovations that go deep. Urgent reforms should be undertaken without delay (PP 32).

Four years later, in 1971, to bring about these bold and deep transformations, Pope Paul expresses the need "to pass from economics to politics . . . [because] each man feels that in the social and economic field, both national and international, the ultimate decision rests with political power" (OA 46). Oppressed by "economic domination on the social, cultural and even political level, . . . today men yearn to free themselves from need and dependence" (OA 44–45). Understandably, this triggers the struggle for liberation and the temptation to use force. However, "relationships based on force have never in fact established justice in a true and lasting manner. . . ."

> The use of force moreover leads to the setting in motion of opposing forces, and from this springs a climate of struggle which opens the way to situations of extreme violence and to abuses (OA 43; a footnote in the original text refers here to PP 29–32, cited above).

Quite contrary to resorting to external force, "this liberation starts with the interior freedom that men must find again with regard to their goods and their powers; they will never reach it except through a transcendent love for man, and, in consequence, through a genuine readiness to serve."

> Otherwise, as one can see only too clearly, the most revolutionary ideologies lead only to a change of masters; once installed in power in their turn, these new masters surround themselves with privileges, limit freedoms and allow other forms of injustice to become established (OA 45).

And if they dare to protest against *The New Class* and *The Gulag Archipelago*, Djilas goes to jail and Solzhenitsyn into exile. Or their partners in protest find tiger cages and torture chambers in Vietnam and Rhodesia, Korea and Brazil. And Christian ministers are called to become Martin Luther Kings and Helder Camaras and Mother Teresas. While other religious communities beget comparable heroes and saints, amidst the boiling head of violence—which also produced Father Camilo Torres, killed as a *guerrillero* in Colombia, and Father Hector Gallegos, kidnapped and murdered for peacefully conscientizing peasants in nearby Panama.

By 1973, the tenth anniversary of *Pacem in Terris*, the new violence was jetting around the globe at supersonic speed. Roy's *Reflections* notes this "quite recent phenomena of terrorism, anarchical or organized (the taking of hostages, bomb outrages, hijacking of aircraft, assassination of leaders, etc.). The motive behind this terrorism, which has little effect but which mobilizes the mass media, is to draw the attention of the entire world to situations of injustice or oppression hitherto often forgotten by the comity of States" (RR 83).

In fact, Roy goes on, a radical change has taken place in the ten years since *Pacem in Terris*: "Conflict, expressed by violence, is a fact, a new fact, in all its breadth."

> This violence is everywhere, in countries that are not at war and in all social bodies, to the extent that a new chapter would have to be added to the Encyclical: *Bellum in Terris* [War on Earth] (RR 92).

Surveying this conflictual society, Roy wryly concludes that while *Pacem in Terris*, with its society of harmonic assent, has been praised as a symphony, "it is no insult to its memory to say that it was an *unfinished symphony*. John XXIII would have been the first to proceed to an *aggiornamento* of his Letter" (RR 101; emphasis in the original).

EDUCATION AND MINISTRY FOR PEACE

Nevertheless, John's encyclical launched worldwide the new Catholic peace movement, till then barely afloat on the stormy seas of the Cold War. It was delivered to the United Nations by special envoy. *Pacem in Terris* convocations in New York and Geneva, sponsored by secular personalities, drew leaders of all ideologies, religions, and blocs.

But above all, education for peace began penetrating the mainstream of parishes and dioceses, communities and Christian life—through preaching and liturgy, schools and lay organizations. Ministry for peace took on many forms: demonstrations, student marches, fasts, sit-ins, pray-ins, counseling, boycotts, and reconciliation.

It was a peace movement often woefully simplified, without the needed base of justice and liberation, integral development and structures. It especially lacked a grasp of society's complexity, the time required for non-violent change, and the danger inherent in revolutionary upheaval. But on the whole, it was moving in the right direction—and even Church leadership, traditionally conservative, was discreetly applauding. And the Pope himself has opened horizons toward the utopia of justice and peace, and toward the dialogue, cooperation, and loving service such a noble republic demands.

The United Nations and Beyond

NATIONALISM IN EVOLUTION

Around the 1500s the nation-state began taking over the prime role on the global stage. The feudal system crumbled under the impact of the new commerce centering around city-states such as Venice, Bruges, and the Hanse towns, giving birth to the new directing class, the bourgeoisie. These merchantmen joined hands with the rising kings of England, France, and Russia, under an economic political theory aptly called mercantilism.

This national-commercial partnership was directed against landed lords and the remnant Roman Empire, for some reason rendered "holy" by inheritance since Charlemagne. The *national* hearths of the new Catholic empires, Spain and Portugal, benefitted enormously from the first century of exploration and exploitation of Africa, America, and Asia begun during the late 1400s; then they waned under the combined attacks of the city-states and of the young nations and their nascent empires (France, England, and later Russia).

Portugal was the first modern nation, and perhaps the first state ever, to undertake at government expense what would today be called systematic technological research and development for national goals. The Portuguese focused of course on marine technology. Laboratories and experimental vessels perfected the navigational and sailing techniques which made possible within a generation the voyages of Columbus, Vasco da Gama, and Magellan. This research school was financed and directed personally by the king, Henry the Navigator. It is noteworthy that the empire whose keel he laid is only now sinking.

To the East, that other Christian empire, Byzantium, was clawed apart from 650 onward by tribes and dynasties held together by the Islamic Arab national ethos and the Persian imperial experience, reinvigorated by the Moslem movement to form a creative culture. The successor Turkish leadership, beginning from the 1000s, advanced dramatically into Europe, avenging the Crusades. With the capture of Constantinople in 1453, aided by Italian city-states, the Turkomen established their territorial hearth for the Ottoman Empire, which endured until World War I; today's Turkey is the national result.

To the North, the Russian nation took shape, coalescing during the 1200s around trading posts which became the city-states of Novgorod and Muscovy—so culturally and religiously nourished by Byzantium as to become the "Third Rome." From the Baltic they plowed and sledded east through 5000 Siberian miles to Vladivostok on the Pacific, south to the Caucasus and the Himalayas, north to the Arctic, and west to Warsaw. The Leninists wrested this vast empire from the Russian Caesar in the name of the Workers' International. The Stalinists consolidated and extended it westward to Berlin in the wake of World War II. The nation of the Great Russians now commands the world's one remaining territorial empire, an amalgam of some twenty smaller nations, composed of a dozen religio-cultural expressions. This is the Soviet empire that Solzhenitsyn seeks to dissolve into its national components.

The renascent Chinese people, an imperial cauldron of contending invaders and religions for two millennia and more, may be fusing now into a single nation of unique Maoist model. Perhaps they will avoid the temptation of all strong nations to gobble up neighbors, often indigestible. Retaining enough of the mystery of Buddhism and Taoism, of the heavenly order of Confucianism, and of the messianism of Marx to respond to religious needs; molded under the moving austerity and service imperative of their communitarian morality; provided with a good measure of gun-barrel force and fear—the Chinese are far and away the most populous nation of the planet.

They already number some 800 million, eight times their nearest nationalist rivals who dominate the other two super-powers: the Great Russians and the American "Wasps," each counting only about 100 million. And the latter are now notably in decrease because of consumerism and contraception.

This white Anglo-Saxon Protestant plurality, who conquered the North American continent, were pulled by manifest destiny across the Pacific and south to Latin America in the early 1900s, then back to Europe since World War I. In the vacuum of French and English imperial collapse after World War II, the American empire girdled the globe, restrained only by the Great Russians, whom in turn the Wasps strove to contain. "The Best and the Brightest" came to Washington from Wall Street and Harvard as hard-nosed liberals and utopian pragmatists, cool and clear-eyed but lacking depth and "soul," to forge the industrial-military complex as the basic system for building up their empire.

The Wasp nationality, naturalized citizens (non-Anglo names are sometimes prominent) and blue-blood natives alike, is still at it—a bit bloodied now by Vietnam; a bit buffaloed by Soviet arms supremacy; a bit befuddled because ethnics, Blacks, Chicanos, and their Third World relatives are biting back. The Wasps are more than a bit aghast at Arab and Iranian national effrontery, uniting again as they did 1,200 years ago against superior Europeans. They threaten the Wasp modern way-of-waste, so completely opposed to the Puritan austerity which empowered and polarized the American pioneers. And they interfere, worse still, with the monetary system and multinational corporation, twin tools of the world business boom since World War II, tempered too in the blest triangle of Harvard, Wall Street, and Washington.

Adding bad manners to injury, the United Nations is now taken over by "the others." Why, the UN is a Wasp creation! Don't "they" realize that? Churchill and Roosevelt conceived and chartered the United Nations on the wintry waters of the Atlantic in the darkest days of the Nazi nightmare. For that alone they, and their fellow citizens who built up the UN family, deserve the gratitude of all peoples and ethnic groups, religions and cultures. Now Ambassador Moynihan, freshly named delegate from the United States, proposes that his government recognize its minority status and assume a new role of loyal opposition within the world body.

But the United Nations also evolves, as do all living bodies, organisms, nations, religions. Its original format of threescore so-called sovereign states—now mushroomed to 140—controlled through budget, history, and the Security Council by the Five Great Powers, is giving way to the global changes we have so superficially reviewed: eighty new nation members mostly from the Third World, new political structures of blocs, new atomic powers, new technology and communications, new economic powers of the multinationals and the OPECs, new ideologies, religio-cultural renaissance and aggiornamento, continental and global conscientization, fresh futurologies and fears. And new blocs.

The Catholic Church, especially the Holy See, has endorsed the United Nations since it was born. Popes John and Paul have given it exceptionally strong support. But constantly the present UN is seen as a stage in the process toward a much stronger juridico-political world authority system. The United Nations is still based on the principle of sovereign nations acting in solidarity when it suits the interest of each to do so. States' rights remain dominant; transnational rights barely find voice. The United Nations has not yet attained the stage even of a confederation in the metamorphosis of political bodies. Nonetheless, it is a precious youthful beginning, doubly precious precisely because it remains so weak and fragile. And it is the role of the Church to protect and nurture helpless young life, particularly when human civilization, perhaps the very survival of mankind, is at stake.

SOLIDARITY AMONG NATION-STATES

Pacem in Terris presents a concise, coherent teaching on nations and the world community. Throughout, Pope John favors the term "political community," although he does at times use "nation" or "state." His teaching, in summary, on nation-states:

a) The so-called sovereignty of nation-states is relative, because "political communities are reciprocally subjects of rights and duties." Certainly authority is a necessary requirement of the moral order in human society. But it may not be used against that order: "The very instant such an attempt were made, it would cease to be authority, as the Lord has warned us:

> Hear, therefore, kings and understand; learn, you magistrates of the earth's expanse! Harken, you who rule the multitude and lord it over throngs of peoples! Because authority was given you by the Lord and sovereignty by the Most High, who shall probe your works and scrutinize your counsels! (PT 80–83, citing Wisd. 6:1–4).

b) National power is also subject to the moral order "in the regulation of relations between political communities, [because] authority is to be exercised for the achievement of the common good." John quotes Pius XII:

> Order between political communities must be built upon the unshakable and unchangeable rock of the moral law, made manifest in the order of nature by the Creator Himself and by Him engraved on the hearts of men with letters that may never be effaced. . . . Like the rays of a gleaming beacon, its principles must guide the plans and policies of men and nations. These are the signals—of warning, safety and smooth sailing—they will have to heed, if they would not see all their laborious efforts to establish a new order condemned to tempest and shipwreck (PT 84–85, quoted from Radio Message of Pius XII, Christmas Eve 1941, AAS XXXIV (1942) 16; it must be recalled that Pius was actually aiming at the international crimes of World War II, especially those of the totalitarian regimes; note the interlock in these two last quotes of biblical and natural law roots).

c) All nations are equal in dignity: "It is not true that some human beings are by nature superior and others inferior. All men are equal in their natural dignity. Consequently, there are no political communities which are superior by nature, and none which are inferior by nature. All political communities are of equal natural dignity" (PT 89).

d) Consequently, relations between nations are to be regulated by justice: "Political communities have the right to existence, to self-development and to the means necessary for this. They have the right to play the leading part in the process of their own development and the right to their good name and due honors. . . . One state may not develop itself by restricting or oppressing other states. St. Augustine rightly says: 'What are kingdoms without justice but bands of robbers' " (PT 92).

e) Relations between states "also derive great benefits from active solidarity," as well as from the necessary regulation by truth and justice. "This solidarity can be achieved through mutual co-operation on various levels, such as, in our own times, has already taken place with laudable results in the economic, social, political, educational, health and sport spheres." The wider dimensions of national identity are now introduced by John, but still in a negative way:

> We must remember that, of its very nature, civil authority exists, not to confine its people within the boundaries of their nation, but rather to protect, above all else, the common good of that particular civil society, which certainly cannot be divorced from the common good of the entire human family (PT 98).

f) This solidarity must show itself in practical programs, especially concerning urgent issues such as population and resources, migration and political refugees, development aid, war, and disarmament (PT

101–25). It is here that John treats of the balance of terror: "It is hardly possible to imagine that in the atomic era war could be used as an instrument of justice" (PT 127).

Individual nations, at least five of them and perhaps as many as a dozen or so, have the political power to wage war with the nuclear power they possess. Only voluntary acts of "solidarity"—and, of course, the balance of terror—legally restrain them. The same individualism obtains in all other spheres.

TOWARD A PLANETARY POLITICAL AUTHORITY

John now makes a quantum leap beyond national sovereignty to a new qualitative level: "toward the juridico-political organization of the world community." The Universal Declaration of Human Rights, approved by the United Nations Assembly, December 10, 1948, "represents an important step on the path" toward this planetary political organization. The purposes of the United Nations itself, and its intergovernmental agencies, is in keeping with such high goals of peace, equality, and "cooperation in every sector of human endeavor. . . . It is Our earnest prayer that the United Nations—in its structure and in its means—may become ever more equal to the magnitude and nobility of its tasks" (PT 142–45).

This clear teaching constitutes a major happening of the aggiornamento. The mere "solidarity" of separate nations is inadequate in today's new *realpolitik*. John entitles this new chapter: "Relationship of Men and of Political Communities with the World Community." His successive sectional headings form such a perfect outline that these are given as they appear in this key teaching of *Pacem in Terris*:

a) *Interdependence between Political Communities* (PT 130–31): "Recent progress in science and technology has profoundly affected human beings and influenced men to work together and live as one family." This causes greatly increased circulation of ideas, of persons, and of goods from one country to another; it also causes closer relations of private groups and of public authorities from the different nations:

> At the same time the interdependence of national economies has grown deeper, one becoming progressively more closely related to the other, so that they become, as it were, integral parts of the one world economy. Likewise the social progress, order, security and peace of any one country are necessarily connected with the social progress, order, security and peace of all other countries.

At the present time no political community is able to pursue its own interests and develop itself in isolation, because its prosperity and development are both a reflection and a component part of the prosperity and development of all the other political communities.

b) *Insufficiency of Modern States to Insure the Universal Common Good* (PT 132–35): The common good of the entire human family must be objectively promoted because the human family forms a unity, all humans being equal by virtue of their natural dignity. In times past, one could conceive it possible that the authorities of different nations might provide for the universal common good through diplomatic channels or top-level meetings, or by treaties, the law of nations, or international law.

Now however, as "a result of the far-reaching changes which have taken place in the relations of the human family, . . . the public authorities of the individual political communities—placed as they are on a footing of equality one with the other—no matter how much they multiply their meetings or sharpen their wits in efforts to draw up new juridical instruments, are no longer able to face the task of finding an adequate solution to the problems mentioned above."

Now comes the clincher:

> And this is not due to a lack of good will or of a spirit of enterprise, but because of a structural defect which hinders them.

> It can be said, therefore, that at this historical moment the present system of organization and the way its principle of authority operates on a world basis no longer correspond to the objective requirements of the universal common good.

c) *Connection between the Common Good and Political Authority* (PT 136–37): The moral order requires an effective public authority for promoting the common good in human society. The organs through which this authority becomes institutionalized and operative to pursue its ends "must be constituted and act in such manner as to be capable of bringing to realization the new meaning which the common good is taking on in the historical evolution of the human family."

> Today the universal common good poses problems of world-wide dimensions which cannot be adequately tackled or solved except by the efforts of public authorities endowed with a breadth of powers, structures and means of the same proportions: that is, of public authorities which are in a position to act in an effective manner on a world-wide basis.

The moral order itself, therefore, demands that such a form of public authority be established.

d) *Public Authority Instituted by Common Consent, Not Imposed by Force* (PT 138): It is to be feared "that a supranational or world-wide public authority, forcibly imposed by the more powerful communities, might become an instrument of one-sided interests." Despite differences of economic development and military power, all national states value "their juridical equality and their moral dignity. For that reason, they are right in not easily yielding in obedience to an authority imposed by force, or to an authority in whose creation they had no part, or to which they themselves did not decide to submit by conscious and free choice."

e) *The Universal Common Good and Personal Rights* (PT 139): The public authority of the world community "must have as its fundamental objective the recognition, respect, safeguarding and promotion of the rights of the human person . . . by direct action when required, or by creating on a world scale an environment in which the public authorities of the individual political communities can more easily carry out their specific functions."

f) *Principle of Subsidiarity* (PT 140–41): Relations between the respective authorities of each nation and the public authority of the world community must be regulated by the principle of subsidiarity, just as domestic relations are regulated by this principle within each nation among its component groups:

> This means that the public authority of the world community must tackle and solve problems of an economic, social, political or cultural character which are posed by the universal common good. For, because of the vastness, complexity and urgency of those problems, the public authorities of the individual states are not in a position to tackle them with any hope of a positive solution.

At the same time, the transnational authority should not displace nor limit the sphere of the respective national authorities. "On the contrary, its purpose is to create, on a world basis, an environment in which the public authorities of each political community, its citizens and intermediate associations, can carry out their tasks, fulfill their duties and exercise their rights with greater security."

g) *Signs of the Times* (PT 142–45): The United Nations was established in 1945; to it were added "intergovernmental agencies with extensive international tasks in the economic, social, cultural, educational and health fields. The United Nations had as its essential purpose the maintenance and consolidation of peace between peoples, fostering between them friendly relations based on the principles of equality, mutual respect and varied forms of co-operation in every sector of human endeavor. An act of the highest importance performed by the United Nations was the Universal Declaration of Human Rights approved in the General Assembly on December 10, 1948." Some objections and reservations were raised regarding certain points in the Declaration:

> There is no doubt, however, that the document represents an important step on the path toward the juridico-political organization of the world community. . . . It is Our earnest prayer that the United Nations—in its structure and its means—may become ever more equal to the magnitude and nobility of its tasks.

This, John concludes, would provide a safeguard to every human being "for the rights which derive directly from his dignity as a person, and which are therefore universal, inviolable and inalienable." This is all the more to be hoped for because

> all human beings, as they take an ever more active part in the public life of their own political communities, are showing an increasing interest in the affairs of all peoples, and are becoming more consciously aware that they are living members of a world community.

Paul VI's visit to the United Nations, October 4, 1965, was an act of witness to the teaching of Pope John. But it went further; it became "a solemn moral ratification of this lofty institution, . . . convinced as We are that this Organization represents the path that modern civilization and world peace are obliged to take. . . . The peoples of the earth turn to the United Nations as the last hope of concord and peace" (UN 11).

Paul stressed the future evolution of the UN within the historical process. His message, he says, "looks entirely towards the future. The edifice that you have built must never fall; it must be perfected, and made equal to the needs which world history will present. You mark a stage in the development of mankind, from which there must be only advance, no going back" (UN 13).

He insists on its unifying role: "You exist and operate to unite the nations, to bind countries together." Paul intends here a substantial kind of unity embracing all peoples, comparable to that of the Church itself. "We would almost say that your chief characteristic is a reflection, as it were, in the temporal field, of what our Catholic Church aspires to be in the spiritual field: *one and universal.* In the ideological construction of mankind, there is on the natural level nothing superior to this. Your vocation is to make brothers not only of some, but of all peoples. . . .

> Is there anyone who does not see the necessity of coming thus progressively to the establishment of a world authority, able to act efficaciously on the juridical and political levels? (UN 16)

> Once more We reiterate Our good wish: Advance always (UN 17).

As Paul was speaking to the United Nations, the 2,000 bishops of Vatican II were debating and writing along the same lines. "The international agencies, both universal and regional, which already exist assuredly deserve well of the human race. These stand forth as the first attempts to lay international foundations under the whole human community for the solving of the critical problems of our age, the promotion of global progress, and the prevention of any kind of war. The Church rejoices at the spirit of true fraternity flourishing between Christians and non-Christians in all these areas. This spirit strives to see that ever more intense efforts are made for the relief of the world's enormous miseries" (GS 84).

During the decade since Vatican II and the Pope's visit to the United Nations, Paul VI has constantly reaffirmed this teaching. He dramatized his support by a visit to the UN headquarters at Geneva in 1969 on the occasion of the fiftieth anniversary of the ILO, the International Labor Organization. He greatly strengthened the delegations of the Holy See to the UN's numerous conferences, and the permanent missions at New York, Paris, Geneva, and Rome, where the Holy See enjoys special juridic status with the UN bodies.

The 1971 Synod of Bishops became still more concrete in its support while adding the weight of the episcopal college to that of the Pope:

> Let the United Nations Declaration of Human Rights be ratified by all Governments who have not yet adhered to it, and let it be fully observed by all (JW 64).

> Let the United Nations—which because of its unique purpose should promote participation of all nations—and international organizations be supported insofar as they are the beginning of a system capable of restraining the armaments race, discouraging trade in weapons, securing disarmament and settling conflicts by peaceful methods of legal action, arbitration and international police action (JW 65).

Although we recognize that international agencies can be perfected and strengthened, as can any human instrument, we stress also the importance of the specialized agencies of the United Nations, in particular those directly concerned with the immediate and more acute questions of world poverty in the field of agrarian reform and agricultural development, health, education, employment, housing, and rapidly increasing urbanization (JW 68).

CHAPTER 7

Population, Resources, Environment

"The Limits to Growth" Debate

The Limits to Growth (New York: Universe Books, 1972) is a small book, merely 205 pages. It was written by only four persons and published in 1972 after a study of less than two years at a single university, the Massachusetts Institute of Technology. It was sponsored by a four-year-old private association of a hundred individuals called The Club of Rome (without ties to the Church of Rome) and presented as a first report for their modest "Project on the Predicament of Mankind."

But the book raises a timely question involving many disciplines; it uses computer magic to attack basic policy issues; it foresees doomsday disasters and projects answers contrary to the conventional Keynesian economics—extending beyond our generation but appealing to current awareness. So, despite the restrictives, *Limits* has stirred and focused global debate on a vast subject: What, if any, are the limits to the future growth of (1) world population; (2) food production; (3) industrialization (to support production); (4) environmental pollution; and (5) depletion of resources (resulting from pollution)—provided all five factors continue growing at current rates?

The growth of these five factors is studied in a new manner which involves two elements deeply affecting the dynamics of change: (1) as growing *exponentially* in terms of their "doubling time"; and (2) as reinforcing each other through their "feedback loops." This method of understanding the dynamic behavior of interlocking causes and effects upon each other is called Systems Dynamics.

Exponential growth means that a given quantity increases by a constant

91

percentage of the whole in a constant time period. For example, a hundred dollars in a savings account at 7 percent annual interest will double to $200 in ten years. If world food production increases at the rate of 2 percent annually, it will double in thirty-five years. A country like Brazil with 100 million population in 1975, increasing at the rate of 3 percent each year, will reach 200 million in twenty-four years, by 1999.

The same rate of exponential change applies to a decreasing quantity, for instance, the rate of depletion of nonrenewable resources such as oil or mineral ores: If present known reserves of petroleum continue to be used at the present annual rate (static index), this oil supply will be depleted in thirty-one years. But if the annual rate of use continues *to increase* at about 4 percent each year (exponential index), as it is now doing, then petroleum reserves will be exhausted in only twenty years. The projections for depletion are about the same for copper, lead, and natural gas. Aluminum and tungsten reserves will last about thirty years if the present rate of depletion continues to increase exponentially (based on 1970 data).

In systems analysis the *feedback loop* is comparable to the "vicious circle" or spiral of everyday language and life. The wage-price spiral is an example as familiar as the kitchen table—wages increase, causing prices to increase, bringing the demand for higher wages, then higher prices again, and so on. In the feedback loop a chain of reinforcing cause-and-effect relationships closes upon itself, so that increasing any one element in the loop will start a sequence of changes that will result in the originally growing element to increase even more, in a repeating climbing spiral.

The Limits to Growth combines all five growth factors—population, food production, industrialization, pollution, resource depletion—into one super-loop-system enveloping the globe. It shows *positive* feedback: Population increase causes food and industrialization to increase, which provides resources for more population; *increase* of food production, industrialization, and population causes more pollution and depletion, etc. And *negative* feedback: Increasing pollution and resource depletion causes *decreased* food and industrial production rates, which *limits* the possibilities of population growth, etc.

After examining via computer the alternative variables in the world model the study concludes that "under the assumption of no major change in the present system, population and industrial growth will certainly stop within the next century, at the latest" (p. 126). Population will decline because the death rate will rise abruptly due to pollution, lack of food, and decline of health services.

Therefore, the planet cannot maintain the present rate of growth. The earth's carrying capacity is limited. If current growth continues unchecked, collapse of the world's productive system could cause catastrophic suffering within a generation or two. It is wise and humane to foresee this clear danger and to plan now for *a state of global equilibrium*, in which "population and productive capacity are essentially stable, with the forces tending to increase or decrease them in a carefully controlled balance" (p. 171). Birth rate must be brought down to equal death rate. This would require introduction of such policies as:

"1. The population has access to 100 percent effective birth control.

"2. The average desired family size is two children.

"3. The economic system endeavors to maintain average industrial output per capita at about the 1975 level. Excess industrial capability is employed for producing consumption goods rather than increasing the industrial capital investment rate above the depreciation rate" (p. 166).

Such, in brief, are the arguments and proposals of *The Limits to Growth*, an extremely summarized version of a most complex issue, already much simplified by the study itself in its 205 pages.

These views and proposals present a direct confrontation to the well-known views and principles of the Catholic Church concerning population growth, birth control, and to the demographic policy of many governmental bodies, including the United Nations. But before commenting on this new Church-State encounter, which springs up throughout the aggiornamento documents, several secular dimensions of the debate must be noted.

Some criticize *The Limits to Growth* for presenting a mere encore of a tired old scenario. The report itself acknowledges that "a number of philosophers, economists, and biologists have discussed such a state [of equilibrium] and called it by many different names, with as many different meanings." Cited are Plato and Aristotle, 350 and 322 B.C.; Malthus, 1798; J. S. Mill, 1857; Harrison Brown, former executive director of the American Association for the Advancement of Science; and Kenneth Boulding, notable also in this context because he plays a prominent role in this debate within the World Council of Churches (p. 171).

But *Limits* presents an updated scenario by marshalling recent data in novel ways of future projection and interlocking relations. It uses Systems Dynamics, "a new method for understanding the dynamic behavior of systems," evolved at the Massachusetts Institute of Technology during the past thirty years for analysis of industrial dynamics, then adapted to weapons systems, military organization, and the political process.

Limits grips the secular imagination, scientific and popular, because it attains a high visible peak in applying technological method and apparatus (featuring the omnicapable computer) to the social scene, to behaviorial sciences, political policy- and decision-making. This dramatic insertion of technology—its exact measurement and quantification of all factors—into the key areas of human freedom and civil authority, the family and personal privacy, affrights many. Political philosophers and social ethicians, humanists, moralists, and religious leaders question this growing intrusion of the quantifiers into the non-measurable realms of human values and social purpose, community and quality of life, esthetics, emotion, and intimacy. Within Catholic circles, Pope John's question—"Will men perhaps then become automatons?"—is raised afresh (MM 62).

Some technologists criticize *Limits* for ignoring or underrating the exponential growth of technology itself.

Many economists, practitioners of the constant-growth school of Keynes, cannot envision, much less accept, a steady-state economy. Politicians ask how to survive the resulting unemployment, the inevitable recession, then depression or economic stagnation. Guardians of civil rights object to the foreseeable governmental control.

Many nationalists and patriots, minorities and ethnic groups still want as many "of their own kind" as possible. Expansion rather than limitation is a basic aim, a "gut" goal.

Third World leaders are especially suspicious: Planetary application of *Limits* would preserve the status quo dominance of the rich North over the poor South by freezing present economic structures and production levels. It would keep the Third World an agricultural and mining hinterland providing raw materials for Northern factories. They say that they can absorb much more smoke and fumes in exchange for jobs, education, technology; their real pollution is poverty.

A stable population? Several African and Latin American countries want more people in their rural expanses, often sparsely populated by Northern standards. Some see population control as a device of rich-world whites to prevent the liberation and expansion of the South's oppressed poor, who are mostly black and brown and yellow in race. (During the UN Population Year, 1974, Argentina set the doubling of its 50 million population by the year 2000 as a national policy goal; with marked success it led the South's opposition against restrictive policies during the UN Conference on Population at Bucharest in August 1974).

Finally, specialists in statistics and the laws of probability, as applied to societal issues, are professionally critical of the constant extrapolation of figures into the long-range future, upon which *Limits* builds its model. This constant series of projections has too many presumptions. In practice, trends do not remain constant; rather change is *the* constant. The procedure of *Limits* is especially weak because it combines five loops, into each of which several additional trends are projected. Above all, the figures pretend to cover the entire globe, with all its technical and cultural diversity, and its unpredictable possibilities of national decision and human option.

Already anticipating this debate, *Limits* states its own limitations and advantages:

> The model we have constructed is, like every other model, imperfect, over-simplified, and unfinished. We are well aware of its shortcomings, but we believe that it is the most useful model now available for dealing with problems far out on the space-time graph [that is, extending in space beyond the nation and region to include the entire planet, and projecting in time beyond the usual plan for five years or the coming generation into the next 100 years or more]. To our knowledge it is the only formal model in existence that is truly global in scope, that has a time horizon longer than thirty years, and that includes important variables such as population, food production, and pollution, not as independent entities, but as dynamically inter-acting elements, as they are in the real world.

> Since ours is a formal, or mathematical model it also has two important advantages over mental models. First, every assumption we make is written in a precise form so that it is open to inspection and criticism by all. Second, after the assumptions have been scrutinized, discussed, and revised to agree with our best current knowledge, their implications for the future behavior of the world system can be traced without error by a computer, no matter how complicated they become.

> We feel that the advantages listed above make this model unique among all mathematical and mental world models available to us today. But there is no reason to be satisfied with it in its present form. We intend to alter, expand, and improve it as our own knowledge and the world data base gradually improve (pp. 21–22).

The *Limits to Growth* debate is here outlined because it provides the societal setting—*global* in extension as is the universal Church, but secular in character—which is needed to understand a major debate inside the Church during the aggiornamento years. Further, since *Limits* was published in 1972, events—especially the oil-energy-food crisis and worldwide inflation, as well as the UN conferences on population in Bucharest and on food in Rome, August and November 1974—indicate that both debates, secular and ecclesial, will engage Church and State for years to come.

At its annual meeting in October 1974, in West Berlin, the Club of Rome presented a followup study to *Limits*. This is entitled *Mankind at the Turning Point* (M. Mesarovic and E. Pestel). Trying to avoid the well-known deficiencies of *Limits*, this second study presents the world system as composed of interacting regions: the West with Japan and other market economy countries, Eastern Europe, Latin America, North Africa and the Middle East, Tropical Africa, South and Southeast Asia, China and her communist neighbors.

Analyzing concrete current issues such as the North/South gap, the oil crisis, food shortages, inflation, recession, etc., *Turning Point* sees these as reflecting a persistent trend in world historical patterns: "The solution of these crises can be developed only in a global context with full and explicit recognition of the emerging world system and on a long-term basis. This would necessitate, among other changes, a new world economic order and a global resources allocation system" ("A Brief Statement," by Mesarovic and Pestel, p. 4, mimeo paper 111-1T, West Berlin meeting).

Industrial and oil-rich regions should insert some $250 billion annually to help poorer regions. Population must be curbed. "Cancerous growth," which marks present-day one-sided development by individual regions confronting each other, must be replaced by organic relationships in which each region makes its own contribution to the world system in culture, economics, resources, etc. "It is in this sense that mankind is at the turning point in its historical evolution on a global scale: to continue on a path of cancerous growth or to embark on the path of organic growth" (*ibid.*, p. 5).

Almost a year has passed since I heard this presentation of *Turning Point* in Berlin. This second report of the Club of Rome (financed in part by the Volkswagen Foundation) has drawn little attention as compared with *Limits to Growth* two years before. Perhaps the reason is that most of its salient theses now have more prestigious promotors on the highly visible stage of the United Nations. During recent months the debate on "a new world economic order" based on interdependence has been placed at the center of the U.N. agenda by a majority of the planet's peoples, including some eighty nations of the Third and Fourth Worlds.

Birth Regulation and Population Policy

The issue of birth regulation has worried and wracked the interior life of the Catholic Church since 1960 as has no other single issue.

The Church's teaching against the direct use of artificial means to prevent conception was clear and firm when Pius XII died in 1958. It was enforced generally by pastoral practice, family movements, and the pervading spirituality of marriage. As the aggiornamento progressed through the early sixties, perhaps partly because of its ethos of change and openness, the possibilities of amending or updating this teaching were widely discussed. Above all, in many local churches pastoral practice began changing so as to permit birth regulation by periodic or occasional abstinence from intercourse (the rhythm method) for a wide variety of reasons; and by direct use of chemical, mechanical, or pharmaceutical (the pill, newly invented) contraceptive means, for therapeutic and other special cases.

It was among Catholics of North Atlantic regions, Western Europe and North America, that changes were especially marked. Probably this was in part due to ethnic and cultural characteristics and to mass industrialization and urbanization—which replace all prior human experience of economies dominated by agriculture and of rural life with its personal relationships. Northern Catholics were influenced also by social pressure from the views and practices of their neighbors and friends. For the past generation Protestant Churches have, almost unanimously, permitted direct contraception within the marital relationship.

Many Catholics, married faithful as well as clergy, seemed to be moving toward a comparable morality in the first half of the aggiornamento, during which the issue was publicly discussed within the Catholic Church. Under growing pressure for a new examination of this question—of such acute and current concern to them as pastors of living communities—the College of Bishops, gathered for the four years of the Second Vatican Council, were nevertheless forbidden by Pope Paul to discuss it. They merely state that "sons of the Church may not undertake methods of regulating procreation which are found blameworthy by the teaching authority of the Church in its unfolding of the divine law" (GS 51).

A footnote explains:

> Certain questions which need further and more careful investigation have been handed over, at the command of the Supreme Pontiff, to a commission for the study of *population, family, and births,* in order that, after it fulfills its function, the Supreme Pontiff may pass judgment. With the doctrine of the *magisterium in this state,* this holy Synod does not intend to propose immediately concrete solutions (footnote to GS 51).

In July 1968, two and a half years after the Council, Paul VI reaffirmed the teaching of the last three popes in his encyclical *Humanae Vitae* (On the Regulation of Birth): Abortion and sterilization, directly induced, are "absolutely excluded as licit means of regulating birth. . . ."

> Similarly excluded is every action which, either in anticipation of the conjugal act, or in its accomplishment, or in the development of its natural consequences, proposes, whether as an end or as a means, to render procreation impossible (HV 14).

Birth regulation by any means is an issue of personal and family morality, which does not fall directly within the society-wide scope of the social documents as reviewed here. It is brought up (1) because the family is seen as the basic unit of human society in Catholic social teaching; (2) because family size obviously affects population growth, socio-economic development, and quality of life; (3) because in line with governmental penetration into all dimensions of human life as noted above, a large number of nations are adopting policies and plans for reducing population growth for their own citizens and, through the United Nations and other plurinational bodies, for the peoples of other regions, even for the whole human race; and (4) because if future events do indeed lead to some of the dire predictions of *The Limits to Growth*, far-reaching measures will be needed to regulate the conduct of nations, ethnic groups, families, and individuals—by scientific suasion or by political power, subliminal in subtlety or perhaps draconian in force.

The place and role of the family within the changing society and cultural values of the past fifteen years is treated below in Chapter 8. The demographic aspects, more directly concerned with economic development, social well-being, environment, and political engagement, became a constant concern in the aggiornamento documents and must be briefly surveyed.

Already in 1961 Pope John posed the principal points of the *Limits* debate in *Mater et Magistra*. After discussing the North/South gap and the resulting requirement for world justice and aid, John devotes the next fifteen paragraphs to "Population Increase and Economic Development." He summarizes the whole "problematique" of *Limits* eleven years before its appearance in one straightforward sentence:

> More recently, the question often is raised how economic organization and the means of subsistence can be balanced with population increase, whether in the world as a whole or within needy nations (MM 185).

John then sets forth Catholic teaching, updated in terms of the societal setting, but unchanged in its personal and family morality. John puts his

confidence in human dignity, social justice, and technological advance.
His defense brief could be entitled: Limitless Growth through Justice and
Technology. Fifteen years later it remains the most tightly argued and
broad-based presentation of the issue among the major documents. Its
main points are these:

> As regards the world as a whole, some, consequent to statistical reasoning,
> observe that within a matter of decades mankind will become very numerous,
> whereas economic growth will proceed much more slowly. From this some
> conclude that unless procreation is kept within limits, there subsequently will
> develop an even greater imbalance between the number of inhabitants and the
> necessities of life (MM 186).

> It is clearly evident from statistical records of less developed countries that,
> because recent advances in public health and in medicine are there widely
> diffused, the citizens have a longer life expectancy consequent to lowered rates
> of infant mortality. The birth rate, where it has traditionally been high, tends to
> remain at such levels, at least for the immediate future. Thus the birth rate in a
> given year exceeds the death rate. Meanwhile the productive systems in such
> countries do not expand as rapidly as the number of inhabitants. Hence, in
> poorer countries of this sort, the standard of living does not advance and may
> even deteriorate. Wherefore, lest a serious crisis occur, some are of the opinion
> that the conception or birth of humans should be avoided or curbed by every
> possible means (MM 187).

> Now to tell the truth, the interrelationships on a global scale between the
> number of births and available resources are such that we can infer grave
> difficulties in this matter do not arise at present, nor will in the immediate
> future. The arguments advanced in this connection are so inconclusive and
> controversial that nothing certain can be drawn from them (MM 188).

> Besides, God in His goodness and wisdom has, on the one hand, provided
> nature with almost inexhaustible productive capacity; and, on the other hand,
> has endowed man with such ingenuity that, by using suitable means, he can
> apply nature's resources to the needs and requirements of existence. Accord-
> ingly, that the question posed may be clearly resolved, a course of action is not
> indeed to be followed whereby, contrary to the moral law laid down by God,
> procreative function also is violated. Rather, man should, by the use of his
> skills and science of every kind, acquire an intimate knowledge of the forces of
> nature and control them ever more extensively. Moreover, the advances
> hitherto made in science and technology give almost limitless promise for the
> future in this matter (MM 189).

> When it comes to questions of this kind, we are not unaware that in certain
> locales and also in poorer countries, it is often argued that in such an economic
> and social order, difficulties arise because citizens, each year more numerous,
> are unable to acquire sufficient food or sustenance where they live, and

peoples do not show amicable cooperation to the extent they should (MM 190).

But whatever be the situation, we clearly affirm these problems should be posed and resolved in such a way that man does not have recourse to methods and means contrary to his dignity, which are proposed by those persons who think of man and his life solely in material terms (MM 191).

We judge that this question can be resolved only if economic and social advances preserve and augment the genuine welfare of individual citizens and of human society as a whole. Indeed, in a matter of this kind, first place must be accorded everything that pertains to the dignity of man as such, or to the life of individual men, than which nothing can be more precious. Moreover, in this matter, international cooperation is necessary, so that conformably with the welfare of all, information, capital, and men themselves may move about among the peoples in orderly fashion (MM 192).

Obviously, this teaching of Pope John runs counter to the views of *Limits* at almost every point. John is optimistic where *Limits* is pessimistic. John belittles "statistical reasoning" and its arguments, which "are so inconclusive and controversial that nothing certain can be drawn from them." The limiting pessimists propose means contrary to human dignity, because they "think of man and his life solely in material terms." John's superlative confidence in this mundane matter derives from faith in God who has "provided nature with almost inexhaustible productive capacity," and "has endowed man with such ingenuity that . . . science and technology give almost limitless promise for the future in this matter." Moreover, he adds, international cooperation is necessary.

Subsequent aggiornamento documents follow John's basic rebuttal of *Limits'* doomsday prophecies. They do expand on the issues of public policy, world justice, and development. However, since John and *Limits* are both taking all productive capacity and human need within the one worldwide unit, better distribution among nations of the globe offers no basic answer. Only planetary changes of production, consumption, and/or population rates can offer a global solution.

Concerning public policy, Vatican II goes beyond Pope John: "Within the limits of their own competence, government officials have rights and duties with regard to the population problems of their own nation, for instance, in the matter of social legislation as it affects families, of migration to cities, of information relative to the condition and needs of the nation." The Council also expresses the desire that, "especially in universities, Catholic experts in all these aspects should skillfully pursue their studies and projects and give them an ever wider scope," "[because] the minds of men are so powerfully disturbed about this problem" (GS 87).

In fact, perceiving the gathering momentum which was leading to

Limits, the Council recognizes that "many people assert that it is absolutely necessary for population growth to be radically reduced everywhere or at least in certain nations. They say this must be done by every possible means and by every kind of government intervention." Therefore, the Council warns against solutions contradicting moral law, especially if introduced by governments:

> For in view of the inalienable right to marry and beget children, the question of how many children should be born belongs to the honest judgment of parents. The question can in no way be committed to the decision of government (GS 87).

Parents must have "the opportunity to practice upright and truly human responsibility," based upon "a rightly formed conscience." Going beyond John's views, the Council optimistically opens to possible advances in methods of birth regulation:

> Human beings should also be judiciously informed of scientific advances in the exploration of methods by which spouses can be helped in arranging the number of their children. The reliability of these methods should be adequately proven and their harmony with the moral order be clear (GS 87).

By 1967 Pope Paul admits that there is indeed a serious problem. He does not argue directly against "statistical reasoning" as John did. He does not call the arguments "inconclusive and controversial." He does not deny difficulties present and future. Rather, Paul forthrightly states in *Populorum Progressio*:

> It is true that too frequently an accelerated demographic increase adds its own difficulties to the problems of development: the size of the population increases more rapidly than available resources, and things are found to have reached apparently an impasse. From that moment the temptation is great to check demographic increase by means of radical measures (PP 37).

Here Paul follows Vatican II concerning both public policy and parental responsibility: "It is certain that public authorities can intervene, within the limit of their competence." Suitable measures can be adopted by governments, but in conformity with moral law and parental freedom. And Paul does enlarge the factors which enter into decision-making by parents:

> Finally, it is for parents to decide, with full knowledge of the matter, on the number of their children, taking into account their responsibilities towards

God, themselves, and the children they have already brought into the world, and the community to which they belong. In all this they must follow the demands of their own conscience enlightened by God's law authentically interpreted, and sustained by confidence in Him (PP 37).

A year later, in *Humanae Vitae*, Pope Paul clarified the aggiornamento discussion on methods of birth regulation by reaffirming traditional Catholic teaching, as seen above. He returns to the issue because "the recent evolution of society" brings changes and "new questions which the Church could not ignore."

> In the first place, there is the rapid demographic development. Fear is shown by many that world population is growing more rapidly than the available resources, with growing distress to many families and developing countries, so that the temptation for Authorities to counter this danger with radical measures is great (HV 2).

After giving his decision, "calling men back to the observance of the norms of natural law, as interpreted by her [the Church's] constant doctrine" (HV 11), Pope Paul warns of "consequences of methods of artificial birth control." These include the wide and easy road thus "opened up towards conjugal infidelity and the general lowering of morality . . . especially [among] the young, who are so vulnerable on this point." There is also the fear that the man may lose respect for the woman, "to the point of considering her as a mere instrument of selfish enjoyment, and no longer as his respected and beloved companion" (HV 17).

But it is the abuse of *political power* which strongly affrights Paul, because "a dangerous weapon would thus be placed in the hands of those public Authorities who take no heed of moral exigencies."

> Who could blame a Government for applying to the solution of the problems of the community those means acknowledged to be licit for married couples in the solution of a family problem?

> Who will stop rulers from favouring, from even imposing upon their peoples, if they were to consider it necessary, the method of contraception which they judge to be most efficacious?

> In such a way men, willing to avoid individual, family or social difficulties encountered in the observance of the divine law, would reach the point of placing at the mercy of the intervention of public Authorities the most personal and most reserved sector of conjugal intimacy (HV 17).

One month after he issued *Humanae Vitae*, Paul VI inaugurated the Medellín Conference of Latin American Bishops in Colombia. Close to the harsh reality of the continent's teeming slums and struggling peasants, while reaffirming the moral prohibition against artificial means, Paul seems moved to plead for a broad pastoral interpretation:

It [the law which we have reaffirmed] is not a blind race toward over-population, it does not diminish the responsibility or the liberty of husband and wife and does not forbid them a moral and reasonable limitation of birth. It does not hinder any lawful therapy or progress of scientific research ("Opening Address" in Medellín *Conclusions*, p. 32).

The Medellín Conference's third commission and document bear the title *Family and Demography*, "because in Latin America the family suffers heavily from the consequences of the vicious circles of underdevelopment: sub-standard conditions of life and culture, low health level, restricted buying power, etc. In Latin America, as in other areas of the world, the family is feeling the influence of four fundamental social phenomena: a) The transition from a rural to an urban society . . . b) The developmental process . . . c) Rapid demographic growth . . . d) The socialization process" (MDFD 1–2).

The document states the "peculiar complexity and delicacy" of the continent's demographic problem: (1) rapid population growth due to decrease of infant mortality; (2) still, "because the majority of our countries are under-developed, a demographic increase is a prerequisite of development"; (3) however, "the excessively low socio-economic-cultural conditions militate against a pronounced demographic increase" (MDFD 8).

The Latin bishops approach these tangled issues "sensitive to the problems of our people, making ours their sorrows and afflictions. . . ." They condemn any one-sided, simplistic solution, such as the "adoption of a policy of birth control that tends to supplant, substitute, or relegate to oblivion a more demanding, but the only acceptable, policy of development" (MDFD 9). They cite Pope Paul's statement before the United Nations: "The problem, in fact, is not to decrease the number of those who eat, but rather to multiply the bread." Nothing explicit is said about governmental policy. Justice, domestic and worldwide; liberation from foreign domination; integral development—and sympathetic, understanding pastors, who share in the poverty of the "marginalized masses"—are the solutions offered by Latin America's bishops.

UN Conferences on Population and Food, 1974

The United Nations Population Year, 1974, and its world conference at Bucharest, could have presented merely another challenge to the Catholic

Church in this controverted field. The Holy See, however, took the event as a fresh opportunity to reaffirm its teaching on the family, birth regulation, and governmental policy, and to insist that population growth be inserted within the whole context of world justice and development. For the latter approach the Church found many allies, both in the name of a new international economic order and in defense of national sovereignty.

On one hand, the Third World generally opposed the proposals of the West as being too narrowly demographic, avoiding the true causes of massive poverty and unemployment rooted in worldwide economic domination by the rich North. On the other hand the right of each nation to adopt its own demographic policy was asserted against those who urge international programs because, in their view, present population growth threatens resources, taken globally (as *Limits* takes them), and impedes as well the advance of developing regions.

Still the conference did reach consensus on a "World Plan of Action" which, if followed by the 135 individual nations, could substantially reduce by 1985 the current global increase of two percent per year—about 75 million persons now added annually to the human family. The plan is also noteworthy in its concern for consumption patterns and waste, in the name of "international equity":

> Recognizing that per capita use of world resources is much higher in the more developed than in the developing countries, the developed countries are urged to adopt appropriate policies in population, consumption and investment, bearing in mind the need for fundamental improvement in international equity.

> It is imperative that all countries, within them all social sectors, should adapt themselves to more rational utilization of natural resources, without excess, so that some are not deprived of what others waste.

The plan received praise from the Holy See's delegation because of its "affirmation that the problem of population can only be confronted within the more general perspective and overall priority of a global policy of integral human development. To this there must be added the insistence on the fact that policies of development require the setting up of a new socio-economic order in a spirit of international justice and of a new balance in world consumption" (Intervention by Bishop Edouard Gagnon, head of the delegation, at closing session, August 30, 1974; PC 1).

Nevertheless, continues the bishop, "our Delegation considers itself obliged not to associate itself with the consensus" of 135 nations (PC 5). These had unanimously adopted the plan, with some expressing reservations on particular points. The motives of the Holy See for this explicit and lonely dissent are:

a) The plan "remains essentially on the level of a demographic policy, . . . disproportionate emphasis being given to a single one of the demographic variables" [that is, for reducing births] (PC 3).

b) The "feelings" of the Holy See's delegation about "the family, respect for life, and indiscriminate recourse to means of birth prevention" are not adequately met, although, continues Bishop Gagnon, "we gladly recall here that a notable effort to meet our wishes regarding the above-mentioned points was made in the course of the negotiations, which were themselves conducted in an excellent spirit" (PC 4).

c) The formula—followed by some nations—of approving the plan, while publicly stating reservations, is not possible for the Holy See, because it differs from a nation-state. States will defend themselves against unacceptable points "by exercising full sovereignty in the defining of their national population policy." But "from the Holy See people expect a basic stand. . . . We are here dealing with principles concerning which the very nature of the Holy See prohibits any compromise. The Holy See owes this fidelity to Him from whom it receives its mission; equally it owes it to the whole community of man, to which, in a spirit of fraternal service, it offers its teaching" (PC 5, 4).

Therefore, concludes the bishop, "the Holy See's Delegation declares once more that it does not participate in the consensus and requests that the text of the present statement be included in the Conference Report" (PC 6).

We see here a strong, straightforward reaffirmation of the papal position on birth regulation and on population policy.

In several quarters, including some Catholic circles, it was expected that the widespread controversy, theological dissent, and pastoral practice which followed *Humanae Vitae* might give pause to the "Superior Authorities" of Rome, at least in public expressions of its heretofore unambiguous doctrine. It was thought that a "wait and see" attitude, long honored in curial circles, might be advisable: To allow time for pastors of local churches to listen to and understand what their praying, loving, serving communities of married faithful are themselves teaching, by their own belief, practice, and witness, ten years after Vatican II, and also to grasp better some theological and ecclesial implications of new pastoral, scientific, and societal factors.

But such an expectation seems clearly contrary to the mind of Pope Paul, judging by the energy and determination, time and talent devoted by the Holy See to the Bucharest Population Conference and judging too by the actions of its exceptionally large, able, and carefully selected delegation. Publicly the Supreme Pontiff continues to stand by *Humanae Vitae*. At the same time the teaching of *Populorum Progressio* and *Justice in the World* is equally confirmed for the development of all peoples in a new socio-economic order based on transnational equity.

The World Food Conference of the United Nations brought the population-food issue directly to the doorstep of the Holy Father three months later.

The 1,200 delegates from all nations came to the Vatican on November 9, 1974, to hear Paul's views. He expressed the hope that "the perils of the present moment," brought on by the worsening food crisis, now become "this acute crisis of civilization" (FC 5), will bring about "an energetic and binding decision" by the rich to share with the poor. "The wealthy countries or those with international liquid assets" are called to make this decision—"not yet obtained by a sense of solidarity or rather elementary social justice, which consists not only in not 'stealing' but also in knowing how to share" (FC 6). We have here an obvious reference, probably a papal first, to the vast new liquid wealth of the oil-exporting nations.

Paul VI rails against those, many sitting there listening and looking at him, who wage "an irrational and one-sided campaign against demographic growth, rather than get down to the essential point:

> It is inadmissible that those who have control of the wealth and resources of mankind should try to resolve the problem of hunger by forbidding the poor to be born, or by leaving to die of hunger children whose parents do not fit into the framework of theoretical plans based on pure hypotheses about the future of mankind (FC 6).

To this theorizing about famine tomorrow, Paul opposes today's concrete right: "The right to satisfy one's hunger must finally be recognized for everyone, according to the specific requirements of his age and activity" (FC 5). Here the Holy Father is formally proclaiming to the governments of all nations a newly formulated human right from the message of the recent synod: *The Right to Eat* (Message on Human Rights and Reconciliation, Synod of Bishops, October 23, 1974, no. 10. This message was motivated in part by the coming Food Conference and initiated by Cardinal Krol, President of the National Conference of Catholic Bishops).

Paul VI then reaches a dramatic high point:

> In times gone by, in a past that we hope is now finished with, nations used to make war to seize their neighbours' riches. But is it not a new form of warfare to

impose a restrictive demographic policy on nations, to ensure that they will not claim their just share of the earth's goods? (FC 6).

This comparison of injustice to warfare is a striking new note in papal teaching which previously went only as far as "unjust structures." Perhaps this is an incorporation of the Latin American insistence that violence can also be institutionalized through unjust structures. Paul makes a second equivalence of war with famine. He repeats and adapts "the appeal that we made from the tribune of the United Nations: 'No more war, war never again!' And we say to you: 'No more hunger, hunger never again!' " (FC 2). (Two days before, Mr. Kissinger had come to Rome to address the Food Conference. I wonder whether the Pope's reference to war could have been triggered by the public threat of war raised by the same Mr. Kissinger a month previously, as a means of persuading the oil-exporters to reduce prices. This threat, echoed within hours by President Ford, I personally find very disturbing in view of the new power and bloc realities on the global scene, and astonishing in view of the new peace-consciousness within the United States, aroused largely by the comparable "police action" in Vietnam. At least so it seems from this golden-domed, ivory-tower campus of Notre Dame students and social ministry activists. Mr. Kissinger again raised the possibility of war in a press interview in December 1974.)

Besides repeating his pleas for social justice and for increasing development funds, obtainable by decreasing armaments, Pope Paul's most positive points are his urgings "for the rehabilitation of agriculture" and for reducing consumption among the wealthy. "Although the great majority of the population work on the land, agriculture is the most underdeveloped of the sectors of underdevelopment." "The world food crises will not be solved without the participation of the agricultural workers, and this cannot be complete and fruitful without a radical revision of the underestimation by the modern world of the importance of agriculture" (FC 7).

Paul concludes by pleading for "a positive will not to waste thoughtlessly the goods which must be for everyone's benefit." For how given to wastefulness is our age, with its "whole concept of society wherein consumption tends to become an end in itself, with contempt for the needy, and to the detriment, in the end, of those very people who believed themselves to be its beneficiaries, having become incapable of perceiving that man is called to a higher destiny" (FC 9).

Environment and Human Settlements

The environmental issue received little attention in the early aggiornamento documents. As occurred with most world bodies, it burst rather
suddenly upon the scene in the early 1970s. Cardinal Roy gives it specific
mention in his message, presented to the United Nations in November
1970 on the occasion of the launching of the Second Development Decade. He notes that, in addition to the aid, trade, and loan concerns of the
First Development Decade of the sixties, other policies are gaining wider
acceptance as we enter the seventies; these include:

> that a fundamental reconsideration of the planet's resource use and manage-
> ment be undertaken so that the increasingly irrational levels of extravagance,
> waste and pollution of the "high consumption societies" should not jeopardize
> the poor nations' hopes of development and humanity's ultimate hopes of
> survival (RR 17).

A year later the 1971 Synod of Bishops stresses "the new worldwide
preoccupation which will be dealt with for the first time in the conference
on the human environment to be held in Stockholm in June 1972. It is
impossible to see what right the richer nations have to keep up their claim
to increase their own material demands, if the consequence is either that
others remain in misery or that the danger of destroying the very physical
foundations of life on earth is precipitated. Those who are already rich are
bound to accept a less material way of life, with less waste, in order to
avoid the destruction of the heritage which they are obliged by absolute
justice to share with all other members of the human race" (JW 70).

Furthermore, these richer nations, capitalist and socialist alike, dump
such volumes of wastes "in the atmosphere and the sea that irreparable
damage would be done to the essential elements of life on earth, such as
air and water, if their high rates of consumption and pollution, which are
constantly on the increase, were extended to the whole of mankind"
(JW 11).

In his message to the Stockholm Conference, Pope Paul insists also that
use of the "free resources" of the planet—air, water, sun, space, and
natural beauty—are also to be regulated by the social morality of justice:

> No one has the right to take over the environment in an absolute and egotistic
> way. The world man lives in is not a *res nullius*, the property of no one; it is a *res*

omnium, the patrimony of mankind. Those responsible for the environment, both private and public agencies, must regulate the environment for the well-being of all men, for man himself is the first and the greatest wealth of the earth (June 1972).

Paul returns to the issue in *Octogesima Adveniens*, noting that man is suddenly aware "that by an ill-considered exploitation of nature he risks destroying it and becoming in his turn the victim of this degradation" (OA 18).

But it is the problem of *massive urbanization* which dominates in this context: "After long centuries, agrarian civilization is weakening." This causes in rural areas a "miserable economic situation [which] provokes the flight [of country people] to the unhappy crowded conditions of the city outskirts, where neither employment nor housing awaits them" (OA 8).

> This unceasing flight from the land, industrial growth, continual demographic expansion and the attraction of urban centres bring about concentrations of population, the extent of which is difficult to imagine, . . . a 'megalopolis' grouping together tens of millions of persons (OA 8).

> Unlimited competition utilizing the modern means of publicity incessantly launches new products and tries to attract the consumer, while earlier industrial installations which are still capable of functioning become useless (OA 9).

> In this disordered growth, new proletariats are born. They install themselves in the hearts of the cities sometimes abandoned by the rich; they dwell on the outskirts—which become a belt of misery besieging in a still silent protest the luxury which blatantly cries out from centres of consumption and waste (OA 10).

> Urbanization, undoubtedly an irreversible stage in the development of human societies, confronts man with difficult problems. How is he to master its growth, regulate its organization, and successfully accomplish its animation for the good of all? (OA 10).

Paul urges fresh pastoral concern for the massive lonely city, a down-to-the-street urban ministry amidst the crowded slums:

> There is an urgent need to remake at the level of the street, of the neighbourhood or of the great agglomerative dwellings the social fabric whereby man may be able to develop the needs of his personality (OA 11).

> Centres of special interest and of culture must be created or developed at the community and parish levels with different forms of associations, recreational

centres, and spiritual and community gatherings where the individual can escape from isolation and form anew fraternal relationships (OA 11).

To build up the city, the place where men and their expanded communities exist, to create new modes of neighbourliness and relationships, to perceive an original application of social justice and to undertake responsibility for this collective future, which is foreseen as difficult, is a task in which Christians must share (OA 12).

To those who are heaped up in an urban promiscuity which becomes intolerable it is necessary to bring a message of hope. This can be done by brotherhood which is lived and by concrete justice (OA 12).

Let Christians, conscious of this new responsibility, not lose heart in view of the vast and faceless society: let them recall Jonah who traversed Niniveh, the great city, to proclaim therein the good news of God's mercy and was upheld in his weakness by the sole strength of the word of Almighty God (OA 12).

CHAPTER 8

The Family's Fate
in Technological Society

Vatican II strongly reaffirms a—perhaps *the*—basic tenet of Catholic social teaching: "The family is the foundation of society. In it the various generations come together and help one another to grow wise and to harmonize personal rights with the other requirements of social life. All those, therefore, who exercise influence over communities and social groups should work efficiently for the welfare of marriage and the family."

"Public authority," the Council Fathers continue, "should regard it as a sacred duty to recognize, protect, and promote their authentic nature, to shield public morality, and to favor the prosperity of domestic life." Moreover, "the family is a kind of school of deeper humanity." The painstaking cooperation of parents in the education of their children calls for the "active presence of the father" and, especially for younger children, "the care of their mother at home. This domestic role of hers must be safely preserved, though the legitimate social progress of women must not be underrated on that account" (GS 52).

But today "this community of love," which is the foundation of society and a school of deeper humanity, is in many places disfigured and endangered by

> polygamy, the plague of divorce, so-called free love, . . . by excessive self-love, the worship of pleasure, and illicit practices against human generation. Moreover, serious disturbances are caused in families by modern economic conditions, by influences at once social and psychological, and by the demands of civil society. Finally, in certain parts of the world problems resulting from population growth are generating concern (GS 47).

The last-named factor was already reviewed in Chapter 7, in the global context of population growth and socio-economic development, especially in the poorer regions of the Third World. There it becomes an acute social and political issue at national and global levels. But it must be stressed here that regulation by contraception is accepted policy and is practiced in most of the advanced industrial nations of the North. A high level of technical and socio-economic development does not eliminate the question of birth regulation: Rather, it provides social and psychological motivation, plus mechanical, pharmaceutical, and other means for increased practice of direct prevention of conception. Within the West the policy debate is now whether and how to keep population growth at present low levels of less than 1 percent annually. Or to seek "zero population growth." Or even to diminish present levels.

In *Humanae Vitae* Pope Paul shows a broad grasp of the family's fate in technology-based societies:

> Moreover, working and lodging conditions, as well as increased exigencies both in the economic field and in that of education, often make the proper education of an elevated number of children difficult today. A change is also seen both in the manner of considering the person of woman and her place in society, and in the value to be attributed to conjugal love in marriage, and also in the appreciation to be made of the meaning of conjugal acts in relation to that love.

> Finally, and above all, man has made stupendous progress in the domination and rational organization of the forces of nature, such that he tends to extend this domination to his own total being: to the body, to psychical life, to social life and even to the laws which regulate the transmission of life (HV 2).

Since Paul wrote this in 1968 these inroads on traditional Catholic morality, on the family, and on life transmission have accelerated, especially in the "Christian" West. Divorce now wins out even in Italy, despite frontal opposition from the Pope himself. In the United States it increases to such a degree among Catholics that diocesan marriage tribunals simplify procedures to accommodate the overload. Catholic teaching against divorce is now under attack within the Church. Some remarried faithful return to full sacramental communion through decisions arrived at in the private forum of conscience, with or without benefit of clergy.

Trial relationships and temporary liaisons spread, not only among the young. Abortion becomes legally available for numerous reasons—"on demand" in some areas. Sterilization and extracoital fertilization increase. Experiments in the technology of genetics move from laboratory animals to hospital humans.

And these attacks upon the family, the foundation of society and school of humanity, are only part of the much broader impact of technology upon society and humanity as a whole.

CHAPTER 9

Socio-Cultural Effects
of Industrialization

Creativity, Change, Complexity

The new industrial technologies applied to Britain's coal mines and textile mills in the early 1800s spread to the continent and North America by midcentury, and to Japan by the 1880s. The Communist Revolution forced rapid industrialization from Kiev to Vladivostok, and proffered to all peoples an ideology glorifying steel mill, assembly-line worker, and tractor driver. Chemical fumes and factory smoke wafted fresh frankincense from the futurist City of Man up to the old-fashioned Heaven of the Father who had failed. More important still, Marxism exalted the consciousness and culture of industrial workers as a class.

From 1900 onward, Western colonial powers increasingly transferred technology to selected spots of the South, to provide primary commodities—ore, oil, food, and fiber—for Northern factories and populations. After World War II, industrialization acquired the key role in the development plans of some seventy newly independent nations, plus another thirty newly awakened from their milennial agricultural and pastoral patterns.

In 1961, the year Pope John put out the first aggiornamento document, the United Nations launched the First Development Decade. All the planet's peoples proposed industrial advance to satisfy human need through technology-based society as the global, conjoint, and conscious goal of mankind. As we have seen, John and Vatican II embraced the same basic aim, as did the Christian Church in general. Paul VI elevated

113

development to "the new name for peace," and the 1971 Synod of Bishops declared development not only a right, but expressed through justice and transformation of the world even "a constitutive dimension of the preaching of the Gospel, or, in other words, of the Church's mission for the redemption of the human race and its liberation from every oppressive situation" (JW 6).

We have already seen some features and failures of this fifteen years' development thrust in the fields of economic and political power, pollution and population growth—features and failures which are exterior factors, observable, and to a large extent objectively measurable. We have followed the Church's evolving awareness and teaching on these social, economic, and political changes.

However, the technology-based society now engirdling the earth also affects the interior life of man, as well as the family and society in their cultural and qualitative aspects. These impacts upon inner meaning and values, purpose and motives, lie in the subjective realm of socio-psychology rather than the quantifiable area of economics, technology, and power structures. Fifteen years ago, these socio-cultural elements were largely overlooked in the social teaching of the Church. Then, as we have seen, John introduced the dilemma of society's increasing complexity (socialization) and the growing consciousness of human dignity, and Paul went on to urge an integral development which humanizes, permitting man to *be* more rather than merely to *have* more.

But it was Vatican II that brought the profound impact of technology upon human culture into the mainstream of pastoral concern and elevated this to the conciliar heights of the Church's doctrinal corpus. *Gaudium et Spes* opens by asserting that:

> inspired by no earthly ambition, the Church seeks but a solitary goal: to carry forward the work of Christ Himself under the lead of the befriending Spirit. And Christ entered this world to give witness to the truth, to rescue and not to sit in judgement, to serve and not to be served (GS 3).

In the very next sentence, Vatican II, the twenty-first ecumenical council of the Catholic and Apostolic Church, incorporates the biblical concept of "the signs of the times," through which evangelization of the modern world must be constantly updated. We arrive here at the heart of the aggiornamento: "To carry out such a task" [that is, the work of Christ Himself: to give witness, to rescue, to serve]:

> the Church has always had the duty of scrutinizing the signs of the times and of interpreting them in the light of the gospel.

Thus, in language intelligible to each generation, she can respond to the perennial questions which men ask about this present life and the life to come, and about the relationship of the one to the other. We must therefore recognize and understand the world in which we live, its expectations, its longings, and its often dramatic characteristics. Some of the main features of the modern world can be sketched as follows:

Today, the human race is passing through a new stage of its history. Profound and rapid changes are spreading by degrees around the whole world. Triggered by the intelligence and creative energies of man, these changes recoil upon him, upon his decisions and desires, both individual and collective, and upon his manner of thinking and acting with respect to things and to people. Hence we can already speak of a true social and cultural transformation, one which has repercussions on man's religious life as well (GS 4).

The next section details how "today spiritual agitation and changing conditions of life are part of a broader and deeper revolution. As a result of the latter,

intellectual formation is ever increasing based on the mathematical and natural sciences and on those dealing with man himself, while in the practical order the technology which stems from these sciences takes on mounting importance.

This scientific spirit exerts a new kind of impact on the cultural sphere and on modes of thought (GS 5).

This technology now transforms the face of the earth and tries to master outer space. To some extent the scientific intellect extends dominion over time: over the past by history, "over the future by the art of projecting and planning. Advances in biology, psychology, and the social sciences . . . are also helping men to exert direct influence on the life of social groups. At the same time, the human race is giving ever-increasing thought to forecasting and regulating its own population growth." History speeds along at so rapid a pace "that an individual person can scarcely keep abreast of it. . . . Thus, the human race has passed from a rather static concept of reality to a more dynamic, evolutionary one" (GS 5).

The Pastoral Constitution then enumerates a new series of sociocultural problems arising from the impact of science and technology:

Traditional local communities such as father-centered families, clans, tribes, villages. . . experience more thorough changes every day.

The industrial type of society is gradually being spread, . . . radically transforming ideas and social conditions established for centuries.

City living has grown, either because of the multiplication of cities and their inhabitants, or by a transplantation of city life to rural settings.

Media of social communication are contributing to the knowledge of events. By setting off chain reactions, they are giving the swiftest and widest possible circulation to styles of thought and feeling.

Man's ties with his fellows are constantly being multiplied. At the same time "socialization" brings further ties, without, however, always promoting appropriate personal development and truly personal relationships ("personalization").

Change in attitudes and in human structures frequently calls accepted values into question. This is especially true of young people, who have grown impatient on more than one occasion, and indeed become rebels in their distress.

The institutions, laws, and modes of thinking and feeling as handed down from previous generations do not always seem to be well adapted to the contemporary state of affairs.

Finally, these new conditions have their impact upon religion. . . . Growing numbers of people are abandoning religion in practice . . . as requirements of scientific progress or of a certain new humanism (GS 6–7).

Dialectics within the Mass: Conflict/Participation

All these changes, because so rapid and disorderly, beget contradictions, imbalances, discords: within the individual—between practical and theoretical systems of thought, analysis and synthesis, efficacity and the moral conscience, collective conditions and contemplation, specialization and a comprehensive life-view; within the family—from demographic, economic, and social pressures, from the generation gap, from new relationships of men and women; between races, social groups, rich and poor nations, popular desire for peace, and personal ideologies; and because of collective greed. "What results is mutual distrust, enmities, conflicts, and hardships. Of such is man at once the cause and the victim" (GS 8).

And all these imbalances and conflicts "under which the modern world labors are linked with the more basic imbalance rooted in the heart of man." A creature experiencing his multitudinous limitations, he feels also "boundless in his desires and summoned to a higher life" (GS 10).

This inner conflict of multitudinous limitations, boundless desires, and higher summons is harshly accentuated by the outer "living conditions of modern man . . . so profoundly changed in their social and cultural dimensions, that we can speak of a new age in human history." So *Gaudium et Spes* devotes an entire chapter to this new culture produced "by the enormous growth of natural, human, and social sciences, by progress in technology, and by advances in . . . the means by which men communicate with one another. Hence the culture of today possesses particular characteristics:

> For example, the so-called exact sciences sharpen critical judgment to a very fine edge.
>
> Recent psychological research explains human activity more profoundly.
>
> Historical studies make a signal contribution to bringing men to see things in their changeable and evolutionary aspects.
>
> Customs and usages are becoming increasingly uniform.
>
> Industrialization, urbanization, and other causes of community living create new forms of culture (mass-culture), from which arise new ways of thinking, acting, and making use of leisure.
>
> The growth of communication between the various nations and social groups opens more widely to all the treasures of different cultures.
>
> Thus, little by little, a more universal form of human culture is developing, one which will promote and express the unity of the human race to the degree that it preserves the particular features of the different cultures (GS 54).

Within the modest context of this overview only the distinctly societal impact of the new science-based culture can be now summarized.

a) Rapid change—evolutionary, disorderly, and revolutionary—becomes the constant in all societies of our new age. Technology applied to artificial stimulation of wants and aspirations accelerates and universalizes change, from business advertising to political propaganda.

b) Paradoxically, this constant change tends toward uniformity, due to the mass production of culture, economic goods, and social services. Massification is increased by big industry, big government, big labor, big cities—all affected by the advantage claimed for technology applied to large volumes of manufacturing inputs. The bigger has claimed to do the job more efficiently. Quantity and practicality prevail over quality and meaning.

c) But uniformity, massiveness, and mobility generate rootlessness, depersonalization, anomie, frustration. Simultaneously in this uniform mass, particular groups—ethnic, racial, social—retain their identity, or acquire deeper consciousness of their cultural, political, or economic values and advantages. Conflicts arise against uniformizing bigness as a whole, lumped together as the Establishment—among the conscientized power groups and within the groups themselves, splintered by shaded disagreement on goals or methods, by rival leaders, by ideologies.

d) Within the national society, tension and protest, violence and terrorism become daily parallels to the balance of terror accepted as normal between nations and blocs. The conflictual society is also accepted as normal. Social theorists demonstrate that human creativity, collective and individual, is provoked and advanced by conflict. Countervailing force acquires prestige as a basic economic and political principle. Conflict is judged a positive value throughout society—in literature, art, film, politics, even within Church and religion.

Catholic social teaching constantly urged the common good, consensus, cooperation, reconciliation—in the name of Christ, his beatitudes counseled on the mount, his message and his example of love. Even at the height of the Cold War, Pope John presented these Gospel ideals in *Pacem in Terris*. Cardinal Roy in his *Reflections* for that encyclical's tenth anniversary notes that today "the conflicts that can no longer take place between States [because of the balance of terror] are being transferred to the interior of each of these States. There they fester, provoking explosions and crises of extreme gravity" (RR 89).

"It is a different universe from that of John XXIII. Pope John's vision was that of an ordered and hierarchical society, . . . a pyramid of intermediate bodies founded on the 'principle of subsidiarity.' " In John's model, Roy continues, each individual, basic community and group contributes actively, respecting authority and serving the common good: "Society is animated by a common will. It is a *society of participation*, oriented towards 'the *coming* of a collective order'; in short it is a *society of assent*" (RR 90; emphasis in original). Such was the expectation of John the optimist in 1963:

Ten years have passed. A radical change has taken place.

First of all, conflict, expressed by violence, is a fact, a new fact, in all its breadth: this violence is everywhere, in countries that are not at war and in all social bodies, to the extent that a new chapter would have to be added to the Encyclical: *Bellum in Terris* [War on Earth] (RR 91–92).

Cardinal Roy goes on to note the many forms of violence—physical, structural, cultural: an example of the last-named is "the pressure exercised by the audio-visual media, by the timetable and rhythm of work and transport, the numberless constraints imposed by industrial civilization and technology" (RR 92). But what is "specifically new is not so much violence as *awareness of violence*" (RR 93; emphasis in original). In former times, violence was not noticed, was endured as inevitable,

> whereas today it is thought about, analysed and consciously desired. Many people interpret it as a law of history. Society is presented as essentially connected with conflict. The struggle of cultures, classes or ideologies is often relied upon in order to ensure the transformation of social life (RR 93).

More significant still, "this dialectical outlook . . . can also assume a much more radical form—when it brings into question society itself. In this case, it no longer attacks merely a 'system,' but social existence itself. This sort of violence goes much further than street demonstrations or even civil war. It attacks the very fabric of society" (RR 93).

Thus another human right is now finding "a certain juridical existence . . . under the name of 'the right to dissent'. . . . When this civic quality of dissent in the face of unjust oppression refuses to have anything to do with corporal violence, it takes on the name, in some cases at least, of *non-violence.*"

> This is a problem that *Pacem in Terris* did not yet deal with, and is another difference from the present day (RR 96–97).

> One can measure the distance that separates this *society of protest* from the *society of attestation* of which *Pacem in Terris* offers us the model (RR 94; emphasis in original).

Counterculture—Toward Community

For a decade or so the bigness and massiveness, the consumerism, uniformity, and anonymity of the technological society we have known until now, and even technology itself, have faced rising criticism. A counterculture has emerged chorusing quality of life, "small is beautiful," and nonconsumer joys. Simplicity and communitarian living seek to replace modern complexity and its "lonely crowd."

Youth began it. To getting ahead in business like Dad, they countered with a modish poverty bordering on the dirty. They pushed aside time clocks and the rat race for leisurely trips of drag and drug and guitar fests. Usually financed by wealthy parents of the rich North, they demonstrated for peace and urged love, not war, in answer to the conflictual society.

Sometimes their nonviolence shoved people around a bit, ignited riots, and ruined a few libraries or laboratories—if their schools cooperated too closely with the "military-industrial complex." Because most were university students, even dropping out to become a proper hippy required a certain affluence. For that reason, the youth culture and hippydom flourished most richly in North America and northern Europe, sending streams into other continents.

This flood of youthful protest against modern industrial society and its institutions crested in the early seventies. But it leaves its mark, together with other movements, even within the Catholic Church. There, too, protest became quite rampant, accelerating changes of life style and authority structures—changes still underway.

Dialogue and listening; simplicity and directness; concern for others, especially for victims of war, injustice, and oppression; fasts and austerity; self-denying boycotts; and even going to jail—these become new expressions of the evangelical counsels, of Christ's own loving service. The beatitudes and religious vows of old find fresh voice in prayer groups, small communities, and team ministries of wide diversity.

Pushed by the oil-food crisis, the attack upon the North's consumer greed now reaches the floor of the United Nations. The Third World elite are also badgered for their own still more conspicuous consumption. Medium-sized technology and self-reliance, austerity and community effort, bring new energies to their flagging development efforts. Tanzania insists on Ujamaa, community-village cooperation inherited from African culture under the leadership of President Nyerere, a Christian who himself lives in gospel simplicity. China's well-named "cultural revolution" counters simultaneously Confucian classicism, Western consumerism, and Soviet revisionism now aping the West.

Solzhenitsyn urges his brother and sister Russians as a nationality to drop their forced hold upon East Europe and their domination over some dozen other nations, races, and religions now in their empire from the Pacific to the Black Sea. Return, he says, to the ethnic, cultural values of Mother Russia and the Orthodox faith; counter heavy industry, dissolve big cities, and dismantle massive unfeeling bureaucracy with *true soviets*, the basic community councils of Russia before the revolution.

In Latin America, similar *comunidades de base* and people's movements become the main structure and thrust of the Church's apostolate—for pastoral, social, and economico-political goals, for justice and liberation. And indeed these goals become one in the integral development of the full person—children of God, brother and sister of Christ and of every other human.

Renewal and Reconciliation

Amid the protest and conflict within human hearts, families, and groups, inside and outside the Church, Paul VI, during his years as Pope, keeps pleading for renewal and reconciliation. It is no surprise when he makes this the Holy Year theme for 1975:

> For the whole world this call to renewal and reconciliation is in harmony with the most sincere aspirations to liberty, justice, unity and peace that we see present wherever men become aware of their most grave problems and suffer from the mishaps produced by divisions and fratricidal wars (HV 9).

Paul wants this Jubilee Year to strengthen "one of the Church's most pressing concerns, . . . to promote, as far as she can, works of justice and of solidarity in favour of all those in need, of those in the margins of society, of exiles and of the oppressed—in favour of all men, in fact, whether individuals, social groups or peoples" (HY 33). He points out how the ancient origins of the Jubilee:

> in the law and institutions of Israel clearly show that this social dimension is part of its very nature. In fact, as we read in the book of Leviticus, the Jubilee Year, precisely because it was dedicated in a special way to God, involved a new ordering of all things, that were recognized as belonging to God: the land, which was allowed to lie fallow and was given back to its former owners, economic goods, insofar as debts were remitted, and, above all, man, whose dignity and freedom were affirmed in a special way by the manumission of slaves.
>
> The Year of God, then, was also the Year of Man, the Year of the Earth, the Year of the Poor, and upon this view of the whole of human reality there shone a new light which emanated from the clear recognition of the supreme dominion of God over the whole of creation.
>
> In today's world also the problems which most disturb and torment mankind—economic and social questions, the question of ecology and sources of energy, and above all that of the liberation of the oppressed and the uplifting of all men to a new dignity of life—can have light cast on them by the message of the Holy Year (HY 34–35).

Paul goes on to make once more "a particularly strong appeal on behalf of developing countries, and of peoples still afflicted by hunger and by war" (HY 37). Aware also of the value of "the small," he urges the faithful to participate in *micro-realization,* little initiatives "which often find no place in large projects of social reform." In line with the Year's theme, Pope

Paul chose as subject for the 1975 Day of Peace "Reconciliation, the Way to Peace."

So while, as we have seen throughout this chapter, the *outer* mass and force of technology invades the interior life of man, strains and shatters family and the inner cohesion of human communities, the Church calls on inward renewal to bring about exterior reconciliation.

Paul insists that "it is in the depths of the heart that there exists the root of all good and, unfortunately, of all evil. It is in the depths of the heart therefore that there must take place conversion or *metanoia*, that is, a change of direction, of attitude, of option, of one's way of life." In the Holy Year, the Church observes the tenth anniversary of Vatican II and begins "a new phase of building up in the theological, spiritual and pastoral spheres . . . in accordance with the principles of new life in Christ and of the communion of all men in him, who reconciled us to the Father by his blood" (HY 7–8).

Through this message of renewal and reconciliation, the Church herself in process of renewal,

> wishes to indicate to all men of good will the *vertical dimension* of life that ensures the reference of all aspirations and experiences to an absolute and truly *universal value*, without which it is vain to hope that mankind will find once more a point of unification and a guarantee of true freedom. . . . For faith in God is the most powerful safeguard of the human conscience and the solid foundation of those relationships of *justice and brotherhood for which the world yearns* (HY 9).

And What Is Man?

In October 1965, Pope Paul presented himself to the United Nations as "an expert in humanity." He was bringing, too, he said, homage, respect, and prayers of the Second Vatican Council, then concluding its monumental work in Rome.

At that moment the Catholic bishops were writing the final draft of the Pastoral Constitution on the Church in the Modern World, addressed "to the whole of humanity," focusing "on the world of men, the whole human family along with the sum of those realities in the midst of which that family lives" (GS 2).

The followers of Christ form "a community composed of men." "Indeed, nothing genuinely human fails to raise an echo in their hearts." Further, the Good News of Christ "is meant for every man. That is why this community realizes that it is truly and intimately linked with mankind and its history" (GS 1).

By this concentration on man in this world Vatican II inaugurated a new stage and quality of consciousness within the Church. In the ten years since, Catholic theology, liturgy, preaching, and ministry have become much more man-centered—men as individuals and in their billions, in whom Christ through his Spirit lives and loves and acts here and now in human history.

However, this heightened awareness truly awakens but few among Christ's people. And even his nominal followers number but a fraction of the human family. Most men do not accept Christ, much less his followers or his Vicar, as experts in humanity.

And still: Why is the Pope welcomed at the United Nations? Why are his delegates free to disagree with all other nations at Bucharest? Why is he expected to defend the weak and favor the oppressed?

Perhaps this is because "the modern world shows itself at once powerful and weak, capable of the noblest deeds or the foulest. Before it lies the path to freedom or to slavery, to progress or retreat, to brotherhood or hatred. Moreover, man is becoming aware that it is his responsibility to guide aright the forces which he has unleashed and which can enslave him or minister to him. That is why he is putting questions to himself" (GS 9).

In short, technological man has lost his nerve, his self-confidence —with which he was until now well-endowed, from the Renaissance which opened our modern era, through the Enlightenment and the progress promised by reason and science.

Not all are asking fundamental questions. Many serenely "look forward to a genuine and total emancipation of humanity wrought solely by human effort. They are convinced that the future rule of man over the earth will satisfy every desire of his heart." Others, on the contrary, have given up hope; they "despair of any meaning to life and praise the boldness of those who think that human existence is devoid of any inherent significance and who strive to confer a total meaning on it by their own ingenuity alone."

Nevertheless, in the face of modern development of the world, an ever-increasing number of people are raising the most basic questions or recognizing them with a new sharpness:

What is man?

What is this sense of sorrow, of evil, of death, which continues to exist despite so much progress?

What is the purpose of these victories, purchased at so high a cost?

What can man offer to society, what can he expect from it?

What follows this earthly life? (GS 10).

These are the questions which technological man addresses to himself, and even to the Church.

The Church responds that in Christ, in "her most benign Lord and Master can be found the key, the focal point, and the goal of human history. The Church also maintains that beneath all changes there are many realities which do not change and which have their ultimate foundation in Christ, who is the same yesterday and today, yes and forever." This is the Good News about which the Church "wishes to speak to all men in order to illuminate the mystery of man and to cooperate in finding the solution to the outstanding problems of our time" (GS 10).

This is the Gospel of Justice and Peace offered by the social documents of the aggiornamento.

SECTION II

The Church as Social Actor

Section I of this overview traces the *content* of Catholic social teaching as it is evolving since Pope John launched the aggiornamento.

We have also seen, though less explicitly, how the Church becomes more aware of its own role as social teacher, actor, and promotor at all levels of the human community. Section II will advert only briefly to this change which is ongoing within the Church, a transformation of self-awareness, to my mind much more basic than the societal issues already discussed within the content of Church teaching.

In fact, the subject of Section II deserves a whole book unto itself, a book which I have begun writing. Its tentative title: *The Loving, Serving Church: Transforming Its Structures*. Here we can only glimpse this process of transformation in hurried summary.

We have seen that in this thrust for updating the Good News of God's love for all men, Pope John welcomed the welfare state with an open enthusiasm which, in hindsight, is perhaps too uncritical, almost naive. Nevertheless, in *Mater et Magistra*, promotion of "the fullness of a more excellent life" becomes an essential function of the Church. *Pacem in Terris* extends the Church's role into the global political community and the arena of human rights, where it receives a surprising welcome that boosts its self-confidence.

Vatican II takes up from there, surely pressed on by the Holy Spirit. But visibly and vocally the Council became more and more conscious of the Church's universal social role because it was made up of pastors already becoming aware of the Church's social role within the local and national community.

The Council Fathers, in the closing days of the first session, December

1962, heard a moving call for the Vatican Council to turn its pastoral concern *ad extra*, to the world of man, his cares and creations *outside* the Church. It is not surprising that this appeal was made by the pastor of Brussels, the city which begot the Jocist movement, a local Church nourished by the Neo-Thomism of Louvain, the liturgical revival, and the ecumenical movement. Cardinal Suenens's idea received immediate support from two Italian pastors of teeming industrial cities, Cardinals Lercaro of Bologna and Montini of Milan.

Nine months later Montini, opening the Council's second session as Paul VI, returned explicitly to the Suenens proposal. He listed again the three objectives given Vatican II by John XXIII: deeper examination of the Church's nature and awareness, its reform and renewal, and "the bringing together of all Christians in unity." Now Pope Paul added a fourth conciliar objective: "the dialogue of the Church with the contemporary world." And this he did with emphasis. Paul devoted to this fourth goal over eight hundred words of his first address to the Council, September 1963.

This papal leadership assured that "the Active Presence of the Church in Upbuilding the World" would now become a central theme of Vatican II. Such was the tentative title given to "Schema Thirteen" which now grew out of the movement *ad extra* from within St. Peter's Basilica. Undergoing many revisions, this schema became the Pastoral Constitution *Gaudium et Spes*, the only document bearing the word "pastoral" in its title. Because of the flood of concern voiced by Council Fathers from all continents and cultures, because of moving witness by many committed lay men and women summoned posthaste to share their lived experience, and due to wide public interest aroused and instructed by the media, the two thousand bishop-pastors in St. Peter's felt pressed upon them the reality of this world in all its twentieth-century harshness and wonder.

This is a world throbbing with new aspirations and movements for equality and participation, for justice, development, and peace; a world torn too by oppressive structures, protesting an immobility favoring the powerful, breeding hate and violence; a world alive still to the springtime hope of the United Nations, yet burdened with the terror of nuclear balance and with superpower arrogance; a world of young nations, new leaders, and neo-colonialism; of Mao Tse-tung and Gandhi; of apartheid and Martin Luther King; of rapid population growth and choking slums; of 600 million illiterate parents, often without jobs or without schools for their children, burdened with misery, boiling with frustration.

How expect such a world to believe the Good News that God cares? How express Christ's love for all men, especially the miserable and weak?

Many bishops, particularly from the Third World, fired by their daily anxiety as pastors, had brought to the Council their own fatherly concern for workers and *campesinos*, for unemployed parents, malnourished infants, the poor and oppressed of their own dioceses. Outstanding among these voices were Bishop Manuel Larraín of Chile, the president of the Latin American Episcopal Conference (CELAM), and Bishop Helder Camara, general secretary of the Brazilian Conference. Bishops from more affluent countries listened with awakening conscience and added their own pastoral care for "the griefs and anxieties of the men of this age," even among the wealthy. High among these were the fear of nuclear war and a yearning for reconciliation and peace among the older nations of the West.

The College of Bishops also became aware that in today's global village social justice of mere national scope has become obsolete. They were ready to understand Paul's succinct assertion: "Today the principal fact that we must all recognise is that the social question has become worldwide" (PP 3). They began grasping the living relation between diocesan social programs and action for justice on a transnational scale—in the vision of Christ's love for all men and in the hard-nosed facts of modern economic power.

This movement of planetary social awakening within the Catholic Church was matched by comparable experiences within the Protestant and Orthodox Churches. Rising from the post-World War II ruins of rabid nationalism, Protestants and Anglicans formed the World Council of Churches in 1948, which was joined by the Orthodox Churches in the early 1960s. Just as Catholics were becoming aware of their social role during Vatican II, the Orthodox and Protestant Churches began, vigorously and jointly, to voice their international concerns through the World Council of Churches. The ecumenical movement facilitated cross-fertilization which reinforced the burgeoning planetwide commitment of the local churches—Protestant, Orthodox, and Catholic—expressed at the time mainly via Lenten collections for welfare and development aid to the Third World, and through missionaries increasingly engaged in human promotion, literacy programs, and cooperatives.

The presence at Vatican II of some fifty observers from other Churches, whose views were gladly listened to, jet-propelled lecturers on global tours, and the unexpected outburst of coverage by secular media communicated to the Christian faithful everywhere the vision of the whole Church at the service of all the human family. Youth especially, and younger clergy and religious, took the vision seriously in their own exuberant way, often distressing protectors of the status quo.

And above all, we happened to have a pope who was not a protector of the politico-economic status quo. He not only helped Vatican II produce *Gaudium et Spes;* after the Council he took the lead in exploring its bold horizons.

A competent and fair analysis of Paul VI's leadership toward a loving, serving Church consciously becoming a transnational social actor has yet to be made. I shall not essay this here. I do state that his leadership in that direction has been determined and decisive—perhaps even historic, provided that it is not reversed too soon, thereby permitting the penetration of the aggiornamento's seminal convictions for a loving, serving Church into the key structures of ecclesial community and ministry. But this is the subject of my next book; I can say but little more here.

For now a cursory listing of Paul's positive stewardship in this field must suffice: (1) his guidance of Vatican II through three-fourths of its course, including *Gaudium et Spes* and the Declaration on Religious Liberty; (2) his own basic economic and political documents, *Populorum Progressio* and *Octogesima Adveniens* (the latter is still a "sleeper," yet to be discovered and put on trial), which provide bold principles and broad framework for the pastoral experiment and program of the loving, serving Church; (3) his direct support of the transnational politico-economic community now aborning, of which the United Nations is a first phase; (4) his visits to all continents and cultural regions, each distinguished by urgent arousal of local pastors to serve the poor and oppressed; (5) his insistence on *inward* conversion *(metanoia),* the inner renewal of the human heart, as fount and strength for the ministry of external transformation of society; (6) his appreciation of the liturgy's role for bringing about this spiritual conversion of individuals and communities (by the Day of Peace and the Holy Year, for instance, Paul tries to insert the social ministry into the liturgical calendar, an aim whose value some "progressives" do not sufficiently esteem); and (7) his grasp of the secular calendar and of temporal happenings—conferences on population, food, environment, and disarmament, the dramas of catastrophe, terrorism, famine, and conflict, and of reconciliation—as signs of the times and calls by God to social ministry, in season and out of season.

But Paul VI is par excellence a man of the Church, of the institutional Church, the organized People of God with its diverse structures of community and ministry—whose basic corporate institution is the College of Bishops. So in implementing the collegiality stressed by Vatican II, Paul primarily expects and urges the *episcopal bodies* to create the loving, serving Church: (1) Three synods deal with the subject, 1969, 1971, and 1974; (2) he encourages the new national and regional conferences of bishops to give the poor and oppressed central place in their pastoral concern; (3) following the desire of Vatican II, Paul establishes the Pontifical Commission Justice and Peace "to arouse the People of God to full awareness of its role at the present time, . . to promote the development of poor nations and to encourage international social justice" (*Motu proprio*, January 6, 1967).

In *Octogesima Adveniens*, the Pope speaks of the commission's work as an "ecclesial activity in the service of men" (OA 6). Encouraged by Paul, some sixty conferences of bishops have formally established bodies or secretariats comparable to the pontifical commission. These form its global network for promoting justice and development, human rights and peace. But there exist additional hundreds, even thousands, of less formal organizations and movements having national or continental impact, often ecumenical in composition, increasingly interreligious and cooperating with "men of good will."

These are often the creations of lay leaders, or the result of team ministries initiated by members of religious orders. They provide precious feedback of inspiration and openness and flexibility to the formal institutions of the Church—parishes and dioceses, provinces and generalates, welfare and education systems, and especially to episcopal conferences, the papacy, and their curias.

This very positive evaluation of Pope Paul's leadership toward a loving, serving Church should be balanced with "negative critique." I choose to postpone even cursory comment—for reasons of space, but also because criticism of the centuries-old papacy and the Roman Curia, with all their cultural accretions, is so easily formulated in today's fast-changing world that superficiality, and consequently basic error, inevitably accompany cursory appraisal. Besides this book has a different purpose.

I would conclude, however, with a few projections for the continuing transformation of Church structures, as the People of God strive to love and serve all the human family during the coming generation or two. These are not all-inclusive. They are among the major thrusts which I see highlighted by the last two synods as they, representing the transnational College of Bishops, advised their president, Pope Paul, on the themes he addressed to them: Justice in the World, and Evangelization of the Modern World.

First, the Church's role in and relation to the contemporary world obviously preoccupies the papacy and the episcopacy, as we see from bishops, as *national and continental* leaders, taking more initiative in the transnational community, which was the exclusive arena of the pope until Vatican II. Local pastors, closer to the living Christian communities, and to the joys and hopes, griefs and anxieties of the people, will bring their fatherly and brotherly experience into the universal Church, via their conferences and synods.

As the Church's consciousness of its social role increases, it will deepen the meaning of this "constitutive dimension" of the Gospel. And this essential part of its ministry and community experience will penetrate its ecclesial being and action.

Second, small and basic communities will provide the primary unit of God's people in a much more self-conscious way. The formation of community will be seen as a basic task of all ministry—educational, preaching, liturgical, social. The attention given to small groups of Christians during the 1974 Synod, of which the *comunidades de base* of Latin America are but one expression, shows that the secular yearning for community, for interpersonal nourishment and fulfillment, is a sign of the times perceived by the bishops of most regions.

Third, at the other end of the scale, the structures of the universal Church will agglomerate around religio-cultural geopolitical regions. Something has been said about these plurinational units above in Chapter 6, "The Global Political Community," in its treatment of the "Formation of Multinational Blocs" and "Religio-Political Implications."

I foresee the partial transfer of ecclesiastical authority from the papacy "outward and downward," and from diocese and national conference "upward," to gradually form regional ecclesial jurisdictions. Religious orders will do the same. These regional bodies will assume a role comparable to that of the patriarchates of the early centuries in the smaller ecumene of the Mediterranean basin—though its territory was much larger when speed of communication is compared with that in today's planet.

These "regional Churches" would correspond by and large to the multinational political units now in formation—Latin and North America, Western and Eastern Europe, Black Africa, Arabic-Orthodox-Jewish Middle East, South and Southwest and Southeast Asia, China and East Asia, Pacifica. The Successor of Peter would, of course, remain the Chief Pastor and Chairman of the Episcopal College, in overall charge of the whole Church.

Ecumenical councils will meet more often, perhaps about every twenty or thirty years, with triennial and special synods, with growing authority, keeping oversight of the universal Church during the intervals.

Fourth, ecumenical community and ministry among all Christians will increase from "below" in the local Church and its basic groups, to guide and inspire the next stage toward Church unity at national, regional, and global levels.

Fifth, especially in Asia and the Middle East, cooperation will increase markedly between the Christian Church, as one believing, loving, and serving community, and the dominant transcendental faith of each area: Jewish, Moslem, Buddhist, Hindu, Shintoist, and others, and also with this-world "faiths," world-views, and ideologies—Neo-Marxist, Maoist, revised Confucian, Western humanist, etc. Together these will form a "natural-law" (with transcendental insight where appropriate) basis for human dignity and rights, for the common good of the respective regions and of the ethnic-national groups composing them, and for the juridico-political organization of the planetary community of all the human family.

Sixth, religious orders will reorient their apostolates to provide leadership and examples for this ministry and community of loving service. There are now located in Rome the world headquarters (usually called generalates) of ninety-five societies of men religious and two hundred and ten of women. These oversee, direct, and are in turn oriented by the views and work of over 200,000 priests and brothers, and of over 900,000 sisters around the globe.

Particularly stimulated by the 1971 and 1974 Synods, a good portion of these are reexamining themselves. They are probing for justice, or lack of it, within their own communities and in their apostolates in order to transform themselves into conscious social actors of the loving, serving Church, and to advance the transformation of Church structures as a whole. Because most of these religious societies are transnational, because by their vows they embrace the prophecy and austerity of the beatitudes, and because of the solidarity of community which should encourage risk-taking, they should become most open to the horizons of utopia to which Paul VI calls all Christians. And because most of them have "missionary" goals and experience and are mobile among several nations and cultures, they are better able as a group to readjust to these new forms of apostolate.

Seventh, the structures for full participation of the laity in the loving, serving Church are less clear. Pastoral councils remain the principal promise, but the experience is too young to make judgments, especially at diocesan and national levels. (We refer here only to structured participation in ecclesial institutions; individual and group initiatives by laity within the economic, civic, cultural, and social fields will hopefully continue and increase.)

Certainly, laity will take leadership in the formation and direction of the small communities, as is true in Brazil where some 40,000 basic groups have come into being. Also they will function as chairpersons of Christian groups, selected by believers and ratified by the bishop tacitly or expressly; or they will be sent originally as catechist and then evolve into preacher, presider over the liturgy, and community leader, as occurs in Africa.

If this role becomes permanent, they will really become ministers without benefit of sacred orders. Shall we see then a closer convergence of clergy and laity? (The Latin word *clericus* means "set apart.") Or will we see more laypersons as part-time ministers, and vice versa?

At world level there already exist the International Catholic Organizations (the ICOs), grouped according to professional and special interests. A dozen enjoy official consultative status with the United Nations as nongovernmental organizations. Through the Council of the Laity, the ICOs, and a score of lay members offer advice to the pope and his curia. Lay men and women also bring counsel through the *Cor Unum* Council and the Justice and Peace Commission, curial bodies which coordinate and animate the social and service functions of the Church.

Outstanding in the latter body are a dozen men and two lay women, Lady Jackson (Barbara Ward) and Marga Klompe. Both are highly regarded leaders of international political and economic circles. But their very presence and impact raises the question: Why are there not more such leaders among some 200 million Catholic adults? Why is there no adequate structure for fuller lay voice and service "from top to bottom, from periphery to center" within the Church of Rome? It cannot become truly the loving, serving Church unless all God's people are at least invited to participate realistically in community and ministry.

Finally, this tentative prospectus for the loving, serving Church calls for deeper theological reflection and continuing education of Church leaders—and structures to foster this reflection and education. Section III of this overview now touches this challenge ever so briefly.

SECTION III

Gospel-and-World Issues:
Toward Deeper Theological Reflection

A persistent theme of this overview has been that of consciousness, the reflective awareness of self: by the group struggling for liberation and justice; by the nation and the planetary human family; by the individual person to provide the very basis of his dignity and value and rights—for that which is most human in man is this self-awareness; and by the Church itself, which undergoes "conscientization," deliberately examining, reforming, and renewing itself, within the context of the changing world and human history.

The intellectual discipline which reflects upon man and the rest of creation *in their relations to God* is called theology. In a very superficial way I note finally a few issues raised by this overview which especially call for deeper theological reflection. These are chosen because of their relation to the loving, serving Church, consciously becoming a social actor. Therefore, the criteria of choice are not ontological and do not include classic and completely valid themes such as "God Considered in Himself," or "The Relations within the Trinity."

These Gospel-and-World issues are clustered under three focuses: Church, God, Man. I outline these issues as statements and questions, with no pretense at completeness or logical order.

Church

1. The Church is consciously becoming a social actor, promoting justice, development, and peace at local, national, and transnational levels. Is this an aberration? Or is this indeed a "constitutive dimension of the preaching of the Gospel, or, in other words, of the Church's mission for

the redemption of the human race and its liberation from every oppressive situation?" (JW 6)

a) If this role is essential to the Church's mission, what is the status of its social teaching within the larger corpus and role of the magisterium and in its ordinary pastoral ministry—particularly since the social content seems to change substantially on issues such as property, nation, human rights, etc., and since action brings risks to institutional interests?

b) What is the Church's role in the concrete realities of economic and political power, as reflected upon by the recent theologies of politics and of liberation? In view of the various religio-cultural regions, the ethnic-national differences within these, the new technical-communications basis for a transnational economico-political community—and the balance of terror reality which demands that this acquire juridic authority to avoid global human catastrophe?

c) Can a divided Church give Christ-witness as loving and serving all the human family? How unite the Church so it does become the fundamental sacrament for a united world?

d) Do other living religions possess a sufficient transcendental content and vision and conviction, in the judgment of the Christian Church, so that common religious bases for joint interreligious action and for joint theological reflection on the social role of faith groups can be found? Or are present experiments along this line superficial and marginal, without sound prospect?

e) Is the Catholic Church theologically responsible in pursuing a "natural-law" basis for its social teaching, in view of (1) Protestant, Catholic, and secular criticism of this premise; (2) change of terminologies and stress toward revelation sources, notable during the aggiornamento within the Church and important for collaboration with other living faiths and their revelation content; (3) simultaneous resort to ethical foundations very close to "natural law" by the United Nations—e.g., in its Declaration of Human Rights—and by the Eastern and Western blocs at Nuremberg; and (4) secularist, nontranscendental world-views, such as neo-Marxism, humanism, Confucianism, and pragmatism, in applied technics and politics today?

f) Is the loving, serving model of the Church a move away from secularization toward a new sacralization of the temporal—perhaps toward a new Constantinianism and Church-State controversies?

God

According to the Jewish and Christian revelation of Old and New Testaments, as well as of tradition (in the Catholic sense), God is present to and in this world: (1) by his Creator power and providence in all creation; (2) by the incarnation of Christ, the Son; (3) by the continuing Divine Truth-and-Love presence-action through the Spirit; (4) particularly in and through the People of God, the Christian Church, who are "sent" into the world as God's witnesses and agents.

A few questions brought into ecclesial consciousness by the aggiornamento include:

a) Does the "signs of the times" approach to God-world relations introduce another source of "revelation" differing from or adding to the revelation of Scripture and Christian tradition? Is God speaking to man through the awakening mankind experiences as history unfolds (or blacks out) providing new insights to the Church concerning creation and man, God and his Church, his truth and love—in short, elucidating salvation history? Do the "signs of the times" offer true *loci theologici* for theological reflection? Does the Church therefore learn from Galileo, Darwin, Marx, Freud, Einstein, Gandhi?

b) The Jewish, Christian, and Muslim faiths share basic revelation content and sources as "peoples of the Book." Why have they engaged in so much mutual conflict despite this commonality as followers of the one same personal God, the Almighty Creator of all, the All-Merciful and All-Just? Can all they share as believing Jews, Muslims, and Christians provide bases for cooperation on societal issues in the future—within their respective nations and among the regions where one or the other might play significant social roles?

c) In a related way, do the nonbiblical transcendental religions contain truths and values of revelational quality, also providing true *loci theologici*, that is, via Buddhism, Hinduism, Shintoism, Jainism, etc.?

d) To what degree do the first coming of Christ and the New Testament record of his words and deeds provide bases for an evangelization in which concern for the poor and oppressed and the promotion of justice, human development, and peace become indeed a "constitutive dimension" of the loving, serving Church? And to what degree does the Old Testament, especially the prophets, provide such bases?

e) What is the role of the Holy Spirit in begetting communities of loving service, directed "outward" to all the human family as well as "upward" to God and "inward" to the household of the faith? What is the relation between prayer and interpersonal nourishment, social responsibility, and spiritual life within our Christian communities? In the interiority of individuals and as corporate groups? As members whose calling is ecclesial, within the Christian community, or "sent into the world" by the community to witness to the Spirit in a special way?

f) Has the Jewish-Christian-Moslem tradition overstressed the "otherness" of God, leading to an overly radical discontinuity between Creator and his creation? Do the other transcendental faiths, with their primordial monism, call the three biblical religions to new appreciation of the continuum between Absolute and contingent, Eternal and passing, Creator and creature? And reciprocally, will monism open to the horizon of the Other?

g) Do history and science say anything about the discontinuity, or the continuum, between creature and Creator, time and Eternity, energy-matter and Spirit, now and Forever, fate-accident and Providence, predetermined necessity and the Totally Free, chaos and Order, past particulars converging toward Future Fulfillment, individual awareness moving toward the All-Conscious? Are these "signs of the times" in the sense of Vatican II? Do they contribute to revelation in any basic and meaningful sense?

Man

Since Vatican II, several man-focused theologies have begun appearing within the Catholic Church. The political theology of Johannes Metz and the theology of liberation, developed by Gustavo Gutiérrez and colleagues, are the prime examples. Then the theologies of hope and of the Church in the world, within the mainstream of the magisterium, have moved classical other-world theology closer toward the human experience.

Also, Teilhard de Chardin has gained a hearing during the aggiornamento for his creation-centered reflections, in which man and his sociosphere are the by-product of the evolving process of complexity-consciousness. But Teilhard by choice or vocation, gave little attention to man and society as such, on his way toward the fulfilling Omega of the Cosmic Christ.

Deepening and sharper criticism of all these theological approaches is needed. Also, we must seek out their convergences, while remaining relaxed amidst their pluralism—indeed rejoicing over and celebrating it. A few of the points and questions which come to mind:

a) A major point of departure of the theology of liberation is the economic, political, and cultural dependency of Latin America upon North America and Europe. Is such a premise valid sociologically and theologically? And would historians of theology kindly criticize my own proposition: This is the first school of theological thought to arise outside Western Europe since that of the Cappadocians and Eastern Church colleagues of 400–600 A.D.

b) We see now the Church of Latin America becoming sufficiently aware of its ecclesial self-identity, within its regional socio-economic, politico-cultural context, that it reflects upon itself with depth and integrity sufficient to conceive a theological school: (1) Will it survive and mature? (2) Will it continue to affect the Universal Church, and other regions? (3) Will other regional Churches become aware of self and beget appropriate theological schools, e.g., of Black Africa, Middle East, Western and Eastern Europe, North America, Hindu and Buddhist and Confucian and Moslem Asia—always, of course, with cultural-religious cross-fertilization and secular influence, e.g., from Maoism and the sciences, exact and human?

c) Should Church authority (of loving service?) oppose or encourage such a plurality of man-focused schools of theology? Should it favor one or the other? Via the magisterium? By the test of pastoral need and experience?

d) And a few nonecclesial questions will now enter into all theologies if science and industrialization continue to engirdle the earth, questions regarding (1) the discontinuity, or continuum, between man and the rest of nature; (2) man's relation to the microcosm of the subatomic and to the macrocosm of outer space; (3) the significance, or nonmeaning, of man's own creativity, his work (or is all human endeavor absurd *au fond*?); (4) ontological value and moral guidelines for continuing creation (as partnership with God? despite suspected absurdity?) through the conscious upbuilding of society and of human culture, including scientific research.

e) Above all, there is the issue of "man creating himself" through (1) societal planning and engineering; (2) rearranging or manipulating genetic sources; (3) constructing control environments, interior and exterior, along the lines projected by B. F. Skinner in *Beyond Freedom and Dignity* (Knopf, 1971).

f) And a special question arises for the Catholic Church—which relies so heavily upon "natural-law" concepts and principles concerning the biosciences, life-transmission, and life-preservation—regarding its moral positions on such issues as contraception, sterilization, abortion, genetic manipulation, surgery, euthanasia, dying, and death: If society and nature evolve, and if man as part of nature and society changes as well, does the changing nature-base require also openness to basic change in natural law?

A final question which embraces all three focuses, Church-God-Man, lies at the heart of Gospel and Church, central to the meaning of Christ himself: The Kingdom of God, which Christ inaugurated, is already present and yet still to come. What and who, how, where, and when is this Kingdom of God? Is this reign and rule of God deeply related to the teaching and questions above? With what cause and effect? Can man, in or outside the Church, with or without the Spirit, affect its nature and its coming in fullness? May he, and should he consciously try?

These are some of the issues raised by the social teaching of the aggiornamento which call for deeper theological reflection.

PART TWO

The Documents

Only two major documents—Leo's *Rerum Novarum* in 1891 and Pius XI's *Quadragesimo Anno* in 1931—launch and guide the Catholic social apostolate during its first seventy years.

Then suddenly, in the next ten years, five documents of comparable substance and historic significance appear: John's *Mater et Magistra* (1961) and *Pacem in Terris* (1963); *Gaudium et Spes* of Vatican II; and Paul's *Populorum Progressio* (1967) and *Octogesima Adveniens* (1971).

This will to speak forth is itself a measure of the interior consciousness of its social mission which so marks the Church since Pope John. This awareness already showed itself in the allocutions and radio messages of Pius XII, but was never dramatized in a major document, due perhaps to the pressures of the war and its aftermath. But after him other pressures—particularly pastoral needs in the fast changing world—urged forth the deep and rapid stream of teaching reported in this volume.

Another measure of the new elements brought into Church (and salvation) history by the aggiornamento is that *Gaudium et Spes* is the first expressly social and cultural-political document to be proclaimed by an Ecumenical Council of the Catholic and Apostolic Church. The twenty other Councils since Nicea in 325 did enact on occasion decrees and injunctions on specific societal issues. But none even approaches Vatican II in its sweeping horizons and positive teaching, with cautionary guidance where fitting. And of course, the Constitution of an Ecumenical Council composed of the full College of Bishops with the pope carries greater weight in the authority scale of the Catholic Church than does an encyclical issued by a pope alone. Consequently, I want to stress that *Gaudium et Spes* must be accorded preeminent place and authority among our documents.

The five foundation documents of the aggiornamento stand out, so it was easy to select them. But which others should be included, as authoritative and representative founts of the Church's social teaching? Space is limited, so I had to make choices.

I give *Dignitatis Humanae* (The Declaration on Religious Freedom) because it marks such a break with the Church's past teaching *and practice* concerning civic rights and the public expression of religious conscience. In a sense, this document becomes an open witness, and a future test, of the Church's commitment to human rights in general.

Two other documents of Vatican II are also reproduced: *Unitatis Redintegratio* (The Decree on Ecumenism), and *Nostra Aetate* (The Declaration of the Relationship of the Church to Non-Christian Religions). While these last two are not social in content, their socio-cultural and political implications in our transnational community are very profound, as I hope my overview has indicated.

I also include the little known "Message to Humanity," issued by the Council Fathers only nine days after the Council opened in October 1962. This brief address "To All Men," provides the seed for *Gaudium et Spes*, which came forth three years later. The pastoral phrasing of human feeling already appears: "Coming together in unity from every nation under the sun, we carry in our hearts the hardships, the bodily and mental distress, the sorrows, longings and hopes of all the peoples entrusted to us. We urgently turn our thoughts to all the anxieties by which modern man is afflicted" (MH 4). Impelled by the love of Christ, the Fathers cite two substantive issues: peace between peoples and social justice, "so that man's life can become more human according to the standards of the gospel" (MH 5).

Most of the other Council documents contain some reference to the social role of the Church, especially *Apostolicam Actuositatem* (The Decree on the Apostolate of the Laity). But the limit of space prevents their inclusion here. For the complete texts in English I recommend *The Documents of Vatican II*, edited by Walter Abbott, S.J., America Press, New York, and Geoffrey Chapman, London, from which translations used in the present volume are taken. Joseph Gallagher is translation editor of this excellent collection, of which over a million copies have appeared, another index of the aggiornamento's impact. (I wonder how many copies of the decrees of Trent and Vatican I were printed? Any in English?)

Humanae Vitae, Pope Paul's encyclical on the regulation of birth, is also included. Although this is not properly or primarily a social issue, papal teaching on this subject has great consequences for the family as the basic unit of society, for the population-development issue, and for public policy and Church-State relations. All are matters I have touched upon in the Overview.

It was more difficult to select among Paul's other writings, addresses and messages, so numerous and far-ranging. Giving priority to his personally delivered talks to the United Nations, I included those given to the General Assembly, New York, and to the Food Conference, Rome. And recognizing the social, political, and cultural meaning of his extraordinary pastoral journeys to all the continents, I have selected two messages of Paul to regional Churches, "To All the Peoples of Africa" and "To the Federation of Asian Bishops' Conferences." It is noteworthy that the full title of his African Message includes: "For the Promotion of the Religious, Civil, and Social Good of their Continent."

The remaining papal documents quoted here relate to the Holy Year: The Bull of Indiction (i.e., of proclamation), and the annual Day of Peace message for 1975: "Reconciliation—the Way to Peace."

In the Bull of Indiction, Paul sets forth the history and the spiritual and pastoral goals of the Holy Year. He shows how these derive from the Jewish Year of Jubilee and Old Testament views on property, social justice, remission of debt, etc. Reconciliation within the community—of rich and poor, of dominant and oppressed—by renewing the social order was the aim of these practices, which would be deemed extremely radical today. Paul applies these principles to the need and ministry of reconciliation today; the theme of the Holy Year is "Reconciliation and Renewal." Too many have erroneously regarded the Holy Year as concerned mainly with pilgrimages and indulgences.

"Reconciliation—the Way to Peace" commemorates the eighth annual observance of January 1 as opening a special period of teaching and witnessing and praying for peace among men and groups and nations. I wish to record that Paul VI suddenly came up with this idea—his own as far as I could determine—in early December 1967. He saw the need for combining the liturgical and secular calendars on behalf of the burgeoning peace movement. Within a week he had written the first message, in his own neat scribble, with barely a smudge or crossout. Within another week it was translated and printed by the Vatican Polyglot Press in six languages. And by mid-December Cardinal Maurice Roy, as President of the Justice and Peace Commission, dropped all his pre-Christmas pastoral cares in Quebec to make a two day visit to Rome for the press conference announcing Paul's Day of Peace to the World. It could well become a notable event in the civic calendars of most nations and in the liturgical calendars of most faiths.

Then we come to a type of document completely novel to Church history: those issued by the newly instituted Synod of Bishops. Previously the only institutions which spoke to, and on behalf of, the Universal Church were Ecumenical Councils and the Pope. Now the last two Synods have issued major statements in the social field. The juridical authority of the Synod remains only consultative. But the expectations placed in it by the Church as a whole and the hearing it has in fact received give its pronouncements unexpected weight.

This is particularly true of the 1971 document on "Justice in the World," which has gotten major attention in my overview. The message of the 1974 Synod on Human Rights and Reconciliation and its concluding Declaration on "Evangelization of the Modern World" are not as substantial. However, they show how the Church becomes conscious of the essential nature of its social mission, even when this is not the principal theme of this key ecclesial body in its deliberations.

Statements by only one regional bishops' conference are selected—the Medellín Conference of CELAM, the Episcopal Council of Latin America, 1968. The clearly social documents are given: Justice, Peace, Family and Demography, Poverty of the Church. The impact of Medellín on the Catholic Church, and on several Protestant Churches, has been noteworthy. Other regional Churches are beginning now to speak out through their appropriate bodies. This acquiring of self-identity and of awareness of their role in their respective cultural and social situations promises well for the future, as was seen during the 1974 Synod.

Three examples are given of documents or statements coming from members of the Roman Curia, who derive their authority directly from the Pope. The *Reflections* of Cardinal Maurice Roy on the occasion of the tenth anniversary of *Pacem in Terris* is in many ways a significant document, in content and form as well as in its unusual character. It consists of reflections presented to Paul VI by the President of Justice and Peace, a *dicastero* (department) of the Pope's own governing Curia. The subject of the reflections is the ten-year-old encyclical of the preceding Pope.

A second document of Cardinal Roy is given here, his *Message on the Second Development Decade*, presented in person to the Secretary-General (U Thant, a Buddhist) of the United Nations. And, finally, I include the key intervention made at the UN Population Conference, Bucharest, by Bishop Edouard Gagnon, head of the Holy See's delegation. In these two documents we see differing ways in which the Church relates to the United Nations and becomes present in today's world.

Mater et Magistra

Christianity and Social Progress (May 15, 1961)

ENCYCLICAL LETTER OF
HIS HOLINESS, JOHN XXIII
BY DIVINE PROVIDENCE POPE

To Our Venerable Brothers,
the Patriarchs, Primates,
Archbishops, Bishops
and Other Local Ordinaries
in Peace and Communion
with the Holy See,
and to All the Clergy
and Faithful of the Catholic World:

On Recent Developments of the Social Question in the Light of Christian Teaching

Pope John XXIII

VENERABLE BROTHERS AND DEAR SONS:
HEALTH AND APOSTOLIC BENEDICTION

1.   The Catholic Church has been established by Jesus Christ as MOTHER AND TEACHER of nations, so that all who in the course of centuries come to her loving embrace, may find salvation as well as the fullness of a

[The official Latin text is found in *L' Osservatore Romano* of July 15, 1961, and in A.A.S. (*Acta Apostolicae Sedis*) LIII (July 15, 1961), No. 8, pp. 401–464. The English version given here

more excellent life. To this Church, "the pillar and mainstay of the truth,"[1] her most holy Founder has entrusted the double task of begetting sons unto herself, and of educating and governing those whom she begets, guiding with maternal providence the life both of individuals and of peoples. The lofty dignity of this life, she has always held in the highest respect and guarded with watchful care.

2.   For the teaching of Christ joins, as it were, earth with heaven, in that it embraces the whole man, namely, his soul and body, intellect and will, and bids him to lift up his mind from the changing conditions of human existence to that heavenly country where he will one day enjoy unending happiness and peace.

3.   Hence, although Holy Church has the special task of sanctifying souls and of making them sharers of heavenly blessings, she is also solicitous for the requirements of men in their daily lives, not merely those relating to food and sustenance, but also to their comfort and advancement in various kinds of goods and in varying circumstances of time.

4.   Realizing all this, Holy Church implements the commands of her Founder, Christ, who refers primarily to man's eternal salvation when He says, "I am the Way, and the Truth, and the Life"[2] and elsewhere "I am the Light of the World."[3] On other occasions, however, seeing the hungry crowd, He was moved to exclaim sorrowfully, "I have compassion on the crowd,"[4] thereby indicating that He was also concerned about the earthly needs of mankind. The divine Redeemer shows this care not only by His words but also by the actions of His life, as when, to alleviate the hunger of the crowds, He more than once miraculously multiplied bread.

5.   By this bread, given for the nourishment of the body, He wished to foreshadow that heavenly food of the soul which He was to give to men on *the day before He suffered.*

6.   It is no wonder, then, that the Catholic Church, instructed by Christ and fulfilling His commands, has for two thousand years, from the

---

was published by the Paulist Press, Glen Rock, N.J., 1961, by William J. Gibbons, S.J.; he was assisted by Kevin A. Lynch, C.S.P., Urban P. Intondi, Joseph M.F. Marique, S.J., Francis J. Connell, C.S.S.R., John F. Cronin, S.S., and John F.X. Sweeney, S.J. The Prefatory Note of Father Gibbons states: "In the official Latin text no headings or subheadings appear, except Roman numerals for Parts I–IV. Major subdivisions of the encyclical are signified in the A.A.S. by allowing extra space between paragraphs. In our edition, subheads in larger type will be found in such places. In the unofficial translations distributed by the Vatican press office, heads and subheads do appear. It is these, adapted to American usage, which are introduced in the present edition."]

ministry of the early deacons to the present time, tenaciously held aloft
the torch of charity not only by her teaching but also by her widespread
example—that charity which, by combining in a fitting manner the precepts and the practice of mutual love, puts into effect in a wonderful way
this twofold commandment of *giving*, wherein is contained the full social
teaching and action of the Church.

7.   By far the most notable evidence of this social teaching and action,
which the Church has set forth through the centuries, undoubtedly is the
very distinguished Encyclical Letter *Rerum Novarum*,[5] issued seventy
years ago by our predecessor of immortal memory, Leo XIII. Therein he
put forward teachings whereby the question of the workers' condition
would be resolved in conformity with Christian principles.

8.   Seldom have the admonitions of a Pontiff been received with such
universal approbation, as was that Encyclical of Leo XIII, rivaled by few in
the depth and scope of its reasoning and in the forcefulness of its expression. Indeed, the norms and recommendations contained therein were so
momentous that their memory will never fall into oblivion. As a result,
the action of the Catholic Church became more widely known. For its
Supreme Pastor, making his own the problems of weak and harassed
men, their complaints and aspirations, had devoted himself especially to
the defense and restoration of their rights.

9.   Even today, in spite of the long lapse of time since the Letter was
published, much of its effectiveness is still evident. It is indeed evident in
the documents of the Popes who succeeded Leo XIII, and who, when
they discussed economic and social affairs, have always borrowed something from it, either to clarify its application or to stimulate further activity
on the part of Catholics. The efficacy of the document also is evident in the
laws and institutions of many nations. Thus does it become abundantly
clear that the solidly grounded principles, the norms of action, and the
paternal admonitions found in the masterly Letter of our predecessor,
even today retain their original worth. Moreover, from it can be drawn
new and vital criteria, whereby men may judge the nature and extent of
the social question, and determine what their responsibilities are in this
regard.

PART I:

*Teachings of the Encyclical "Rerum Novarum"
and Timely Doctrinal Developments
during the Pontificates of Pius XI and Pius XII*

The Period of the Encyclical, "Rerum Novarum"

10.   The teachings addressed to mankind by this most wise Pontiff undoubtedly shone with greater brilliance because they were published when innumerable difficulties obscured the issue. On the one hand, the economic and political situation was in process of radical change; on the other, numerous clashes were flaring up and civil strife had been provoked.

11.   As is generally known, in those days an opinion widely prevailed and was commonly put into practice, according to which, in economic matters, everything was to be attributed to inescapable, natural forces. Hence, it was held that no connection existed between economic and moral laws. Wherefore, those engaged in economic activity need look no further than their own gain. Consequently, mutual relations between economic agents could be left to the play of free and unregulated competition. Interest on capital, prices of goods and services, profits and wages, were to be determined purely mechanically by the laws of the marketplace. Every precaution was to be taken lest the civil authority intervene in any way in economic affairs. During that era, trade unions, according to circumstances in different countries, were sometimes forbidden, sometimes tolerated, sometimes recognized in private law.

12.   Thus, at that time, not only was the proud rule of the stronger regarded as legitimate, so far as economic affairs were concerned, but it also prevailed in concrete relations between men. Accordingly, the order of economic affairs was, in general, radically disturbed.

13.   While a few accumulated excessive riches, large masses of workingmen daily labored in very acute need. Indeed, wages were insufficient for the necessities of life, and sometimes were at starvation level. For the most part, workers had to find employment under conditions wherein there were dangers to health, moral integrity, and religious faith. Especially inhuman were the working conditions to which children and

women were subjected. The spectre of unemployment was ever present, and the family was exposed to a process of disorganization.

14.   As a natural consequence, workers, indignant at their lot, decided that this state of affairs must be publicly protested. This explains why, among the working classes, extremist theories that propounded remedies worse than the evil to be cured, found widespread favor.

The Way to Reconstruction

15.   Such being the trend of the times, Leo XIII, in his Encyclical Letter *Rerum Novarum*, proclaimed a social message based on the requirements of human nature itself and conforming to the precepts of the Gospel and reason. We recall it as a message which, despite some expected opposition, evoked response on all sides and aroused widespread enthusiasm. However, this was not the first time the Apostolic See, in regard to the affairs of this life, undertook the defense of the needy, since that same predecessor of happy memory, Leo XIII, published other documents which to some extent paved the way for the document mentioned above. But this Letter so effected for the first time an organization of principles, and, as it were, set forth singlemindedly a future course of action, that we may regard it as a summary of Catholic teaching, so far as economic and social matters are concerned.

16.   It can be said with considerable assurance that such proved to be the situation. For while some, confronted with the social question, unashamedly attacked the Church as if she did nothing except preach resignation to the poor and exhort the rich to generosity, Leo XIII did not hesitate to proclaim and defend quite openly the sacred rights of workers. In beginning his exposition of the principles and norms of the Church in social matters, he frankly stated: "We approach the subject with confidence and in the exercise of the rights that belong to us. For no satisfactory solution of this question will ever be found without the assistance of religion and the Church."[6]

17.   Venerable Brothers, you are quite familiar with those basic principles expounded both clearly and authoritatively by the illustrious Pontiff, according to which human society should be renewed in so far as economic and social matters are concerned.

18.   He first and foremost stated that work, inasmuch as it is an expression of the human person, can by no means be regarded as a mere commodity. For the great majority of mankind, work is the only source from which the means of livelihood are drawn. Hence, its remuneration is not to be thought of in terms of merchandise, but rather according to the

laws of justice and equity. Unless this is done, justice is violated in labor agreements, even though they are entered into freely on both sides.

19.   Private property, including that of productive goods, is a natural right possessed by all, which the State may by no means suppress. However, as there is from nature a social aspect to private property, he who uses his right in this regard must take into account not merely his own welfare but that of others as well.

20.   The State, whose purpose is the realization of the common good in the temporal order, can by no means disregard the economic activity of its citizens. Indeed, it should be present to promote in a suitable manner the production of a sufficient supply of material goods, "the use of which is necessary for the practice of virtue."[7] Moreover, it should safeguard the rights of all citizens, but especially the weaker, such as workers, women, and children. Nor may the State ever neglect its duty to contribute actively to the betterment of the living conditions of workers.

21.   In addition, the State should see to it that labor agreements are entered into according to the norms of justice and equity, and that in the environment of work the dignity of the human being is not violated either in body or spirit. On this point, Leo XIII's Letter delineated the broad principles regarding a just and proper human existence. These principles, modern States have adopted in one way or another in their social legislation, and they have—as our predecessor of immortal memory, Pius XI declared, in his Encyclical Letter *Quadragesimo Anno*[8]—contributed much to the establishment and promotion of that new section of legal science known as *labor law*.

22.   In the same Letter, moreover, there is affirmed the natural right to enter corporately into associations, whether these be composed of workers only or of workers and management; and also the right to adopt that organizational structure judged more suitable to meet their professional needs. And workers themselves have the right to act freely and on their own initiative within the above-mentioned associations, without hindrance and as their needs dictate.

23.   Workers and employers should regulate their mutual relations in a spirit of human solidarity and in accordance with the bond of Christian brotherhood. For the unregulated competition which so-called *liberals* espouse, or the class struggle in the *Marxist sense*, are utterly opposed to Christian teaching and also to the very nature of man.

24.   These, Venerable Brothers, are the fundamental principles on which a healthy socio-economic order can be built.

25.   It is not surprising, therefore, that outstanding Catholic men inspired by these appeals began many activities in order to put these

principles to action. Nor were there lacking other men of good will in various parts of the world who, impelled by the needs of human nature, followed a similar course.

26.   For these reasons the Encyclical is known even to the present day as the *Magna Charta*[9] for the reconstruction of the economic and social order.

The Encyclical "Quadragesimo Anno"

27.   Furthermore, after a lapse of forty years since publication of that outstanding corpus, as it were, of directives, our predecessor of happy memory, Pius XI, in his turn decided to publish the Encyclical Letter *Quadragesimo Anno.*[10]

28.   In it the Supreme Pontiff first of all confirmed the right and duty of the Catholic Church to make its special contribution in resolving the more serious problems of society which call for the full cooperation of all. Then he reaffirmed those principles and directives of Leo XIII's Letter related to the conditions of the times. Finally, he took this occasion not only to clarify certain points of doctrine on which even Catholics were in doubt, but he also showed how the principles and directives themselves regarding social affairs should be adapted to the changing times.

29.   For at that time, some were in doubt as to what should be the judgment of Catholics regarding private property, the wage system, and more especially, a type of moderate socialism.

30.   Concerning private property, our predecessor reaffirmed its natural-law character. Furthermore, he set forth clearly and emphasized the social character and function of private ownership.

31.   Turning to the wage system, after having rejected the view that would declare it unjust by its very nature, the Pontiff criticized the inhuman and unjust forms under which it was sometimes found. Moreover, he carefully indicated what norms and conditions were to be observed, lest the wage system stray from justice and equity.

32.   In this connection, it is today advisable as our predecessor clearly pointed out, that work agreements be tempered in certain respects with partnership arrangements, so that "workers and officials become participants in ownership, or management, or share in some manner in profits."[11]

33.   Of great theoretical and practical importance is the affirmation of Pius XI that "if the social and individual character of labor be overlooked, the efficiency of men can neither be justly appraised nor equitably

recompensed."[12] Accordingly, in determining wages, justice definitely requires that, in addition to the needs of the individual worker and his family, regard be had on the one hand for conditions within the productive enterprises wherein the workers labor; on the other hand, for the "public economic good"[13] in general.

34.   Furthermore, the Supreme Bishop emphasized that the views of *communists,* as they are called, and of Christians are radically opposed. Nor may Catholics, in any way, give approbation to the teachings of *socialists* who seemingly profess more moderate views. From their basic outlook it follows that, inasmuch as the order of social life is confined to time, it is directed solely to temporal welfare; that since the social relationships of men pertain merely to the production of goods, human liberty is excessively restricted and the true concept of social authority is overlooked.

35.   Pius XI was not unaware that, in the forty years that had elapsed since the appearance of Leo XIII's Letter, historical conditions had profoundly altered. In fact, unrestricted competition, because of its own inherent tendencies, had ended by almost destroying itself. It had caused a great accumulation of wealth and a corresponding concentration of power in the hands of a few who "are frequently not the owners, but only the trustees and directors of invested funds, who administer them at their good pleasure."[14]

36.   Therefore, as the Supreme Pontiff noted, "economic power has been substituted for the free marketplace. Unbridled ambition for domination has replaced desire for gain; the whole economy has become harsh, cruel, and relentless in frightful measure."[15] Thus it happened that even public authorities were serving the interests of more wealthy men and that concentrations of wealth, to some extent, achieved power over all peoples.

37.   In opposition to this trend, the Supreme Pontiff laid down the following fundamental principles: the organization of economic affairs must be comfortable to practical morality; the interests of individuals or of societies especially must be harmonized with the requirements of the common good. This evidently requires, as the teaching of our predecessor indicated, the orderly reorganization of society with smaller professional and economic groups existing in their own right, and not prescribed by public authority. In the next place, civil authority should reassume its function and not overlook any of the community's interests. Finally, on a world-wide scale, governments should seek the economic good of all peoples.

38.   The two fundamental points that especially characterize the En-

cyclical of Pius XI are these: First, one may not take as the ultimate criteria in economic life the interests of individuals or organized groups, nor unregulated competition, nor excessive power on the part of the wealthy, nor the vain honor of the nation or its desire for domination, nor anything of this sort.

39.   Rather, it is necessary that economic undertakings be governed by justice and charity as the principal laws of social life.

40.   The second point that we consider to be basic to the Letter of Pius XI is that both within individual countries and among nations there be established a juridical order, with appropriate public and private institutions, inspired by social justice, so that those who are involved in economic activities are enabled to carry out their tasks in conformity with the common good.

Radio Broadcast of Pentecost, 1941

41.   In specifying social rights and obligations, our predecessor of immortal memory, Pius XII, made a significant contribution, when on the feast of Pentecost, June 1, 1941, he broadcast to the world community a message: "in order to call to the attention of the Catholic world the memory of an event worthy of being written in letters of gold on the Calendar of the Church: namely, the fiftieth anniversary of the publication of the epoch-making Encyclical of Leo XIII, *Rerum Novarum.*"[16] He broadcast this message, moreover, "to render special thanks to Almighty God that His Vicar on earth, in a Letter such as this, gave to the Church so great a gift, and also to render praise to the eternal Spirit that through this same Letter, He enkindled a fire calculated to rouse the whole human race to new and better effort."[17]

42.   In the message, the great Pontiff claimed for the Church "the indisputable competence" to "decide whether the bases of a given social system are in accord with the unchangeable order which God our Creator and Redeemer has fixed both in the natural law and revelation."[18] He noted that the Letter of Leo XIII is of permanent value and has rich and abiding usefulness. He takes the occasion "to explain in greater detail what the Catholic Church teaches regarding the three principal issues of social life in economic affairs, which are mutually related and connected one with the other, and thus interdependent: namely, the use of material goods, labor, and the family."[19]

43.   Concerning the use of material goods, our predecessor declared that the right of every man to use them for his own sustenance is prior to

all other rights in economic life, and hence is prior even to the right of private ownership. It is certain, however, as our predecessor noted, that the right of private property is from the natural law itself. Nevertheless, it is the will of God the Creator that this right to own property should in no wise obstruct the flow of "material goods created by God to meet the needs of all men, to all equitably, as justice and charity require."[20]

44.   As regards labor, Pius XII repeating what appeared in Leo XIII's Letter, declared it to be both a duty and a right of every human being. Consequently, it is in the first place the responsibility of men themselves to regulate mutual labor relations. Only in the event that the interested parties are unwilling or unable to fulfill their functions, does it "devolve upon the State to intervene and to assign labor equitably, safeguarding the standards and aims that the common good properly understood demands."[21]

45.   Turning to the family, the Supreme Pontiff stresses that private ownership of material goods helps to safeguard and develop family life. Such goods are an apt means "to secure for the father of a family the healthy liberty he needs in order to fulfill the duties assigned him by the Creator, regarding the physical, spiritual, and religious welfare of the family."[22] From this arises the right of the family to migrate. Accordingly, our predecessor reminds governments, both those permitting emigration and those accepting immigrants, that "they never permit anything whereby mutual and sincere understanding between States is diminished or destroyed."[23] If this be mutually accomplished, it will come to pass that benefits are equalized and diffused widely among peoples, as the supply of goods and the arts and crafts are increased and fostered.

Further Changes

46.   But just as contemporary circumstances seemed to Pius XII quite dissimilar from those of the earlier period, so they have changed greatly over the past twenty years. This can be seen not only in the internal situation of each individual country, but also in the mutual relations of countries.

47.   In the fields of science, technology, and economics, these developments are especially worthy of note: the discovery of atomic energy, employed first for military purposes and later increasingly for peaceful ends; the almost limitless possibilities opened up by chemistry in synthetic products; the growth of automation in the sectors of industry

and services; the modernization of agriculture; the nearly complete conquest, especially through radio and television, of the distance separating peoples; the greatly increased speed of all manner of transportation; the initial conquests of outer space.

48.   Turning to the social field, the following contemporary trends are evident: development of systems for social insurance; the introduction of social security systems in some more affluent countries; greater awareness among workers, as members of unions, of the principal issues in economic and social life; a progressive improvement of basic education; wider diffusion among the citizenry of the conveniences of life; increased social mobility and a resulting decline in divisions among the classes; greater interest than heretofore in world affairs on the part of those with average education. Meanwhile, if one considers the social and economic advances made in a growing number of countries, he will quickly discern increasingly pronounced imbalances: first, between agriculture on the one hand and industry and the services on the other; between the more and the less developed regions within countries; and, finally, on a world-wide scale, between countries with differing economic resources and development.

49.   Turning now to political affairs, it is evident that there, too, a number of innovations have occurred. Today, in many communities, citizens from almost all social strata participate in public life. Public authorities intervene more and more in economic and social affairs. The peoples of Asia and Africa, having set aside colonial systems, now govern themselves according to their own laws and institutions. As the mutual relationships of peoples increase, they become daily more dependent one upon the other. Throughout the world, assemblies and councils have become more common, which, being supranational in character, take into account the interests of all peoples. Such bodies are concerned with economic life, or with social affairs, or with culture and education, or, finally, with the mutual relationships of peoples.

Reasons for the New Encyclical

50.   Now, reflecting on all these things, we feel it our duty to keep alive the torch lighted by our great predecessors and to exhort all to draw from their writings light and inspiration, if they wish to resolve the social question in ways more in accord with the needs of the present time. Therefore, we are issuing this present Letter not merely to commemorate

appropriately the Encyclical Letter of Leo XIII, but also, in the light of changed conditions, both to confirm and explain more fully what our predecessors taught, and to set forth the Church's teaching regarding the new and serious problems of our day.

PART II:

Explanation and Development of the Teachings of "Rerum Novarum"

Private Initiative and State Intervention in Economic Life

51.   At the outset it should be affirmed that in economic affairs first place is to be given to the private initiative of individual men who, either working by themselves, or with others in one fashion or another, pursue their common interests.

52.   But in this matter, for reasons pointed out by our predecessors, it is necessary that public authorities take active interest, the better to increase output of goods and to further social progress for the benefit of all citizens.

53.   This intervention of public authorities that encourages, stimulates, regulates, supplements, and complements, is based on the *principle of subsidiarity*[24] as set forth by Pius XI in his Encyclical *Quadragesimo Anno*: "It is a fundamental principle of social philosophy, fixed and unchangeable, that one should not withdraw from individuals and commit to the community what they can accomplish by their own enterprise and industry. So, too, it is an injustice and at the same time a grave evil and a disturbance of right order, to transfer to the larger and higher collectivity functions which can be performed and provided for by lesser and subordinate bodies. Inasmuch as every social activity should, by its very nature, prove a help to members of the body social, it should never destroy or absorb them."[25]

54.   Indeed, as is easily perceived, recent developments of science and technology provide additional reasons why, to a greater extent than heretofore, it is within the power of public authorities to reduce imbalances, whether these be between various sectors of economic life, or between different regions of the same nation, or even between different

peoples of the world as a whole. These same developments make it possible to keep fluctuations in the economy within bounds, and to provide effective measures for avoiding mass unemployment. Consequently, it is requested again and again of public authorities responsible for the common good, that they intervene in a wide variety of economic affairs, and that, in a more extensive and organized way than heretofore, they adapt institutions, tasks, means, and procedures to this end.

55.   Nevertheless, it remains true that precautionary activities of public authorities in the economic field, although widespread and penetrating, should be such that they not only avoid restricting the freedom of private citizens, but also increase it, so long as the basic rights of each individual person are preserved inviolate. Included among these is the right and duty of each individual normally to provide the necessities of life for himself and his dependents. This implies that whatever be the economic system, it allow and facilitate for every individual the opportunity to engage in productive activity.

56.   Furthermore, the course of events thus far makes it clear that there cannot be a prosperous and well-ordered society unless both private citizens and public authorities work together in economic affairs. Their activity should be characterized by mutual and amicable efforts, so that the roles assigned to each fit in with requirements of the common good, as changing times and customs suggest.

57.   Experience, in fact, shows that where private initiative of individuals is lacking, political tyranny prevails. Moreover, much stagnation occurs in various sectors of the economy, and hence all sorts of consumer goods and services, closely connected with needs of the body and more especially of the spirit, are in short supply. Beyond doubt, the attainment of such goods and services provides remarkable opportunity and stimulus for individuals to exercise initiative and industry.

58.   Where, on the other hand, appropriate activity of the State is lacking or defective, commonwealths are apt to experience incurable disorders, and there occurs exploitation of the weak by the unscrupulous strong, who flourish, unfortunately, like cockle among the wheat, in all times and places.

Complexity of Social Structure

DIRECTION OF THE TREND

59.   One of the principal characteristics of our time is the multiplication of social relationships, that is, a daily more complex interdependence

of citizens, introducing into their lives and activities many and varied
forms of association, recognized for the most part in private and even in
public law. This tendency seemingly stems from a number of factors
operative in the present era, among which are technical and scientific
progress, greater productive efficiency, and a higher standard of living
among citizens.

60.   These developments in social living are at once both a symptom
and a cause of the growing intervention of public authorities in matters
which, since they pertain to the more intimate aspects of personal life, are
of serious moment and not without danger. Such, for example, are the
care of health, the instruction and education of youth, the choice of a
personal career, the ways and means of rehabilitating or assisting those
handicapped mentally or physically. But this trend also indicates and in
part follows from that human and natural inclination, scarcely resistible,
whereby men are impelled voluntarily to enter into association in order to
attain objectives which each one desires, but which exceed the capacity of
single individuals. This tendency has given rise, especially in recent
years, to organizations and institutes on both national and international
levels, which relate to economic and social goals, to cultural and recreational activities, to athletics, to various professions, and to political
affairs.

EVALUATION

61.   Such an advance in social relationships definitely brings numerous services and advantages. It makes possible, in fact, the satisfaction of
many personal rights, especially those of economic and social life; these
relate, for example, to the minimum necessities of human life, to health
services, to the broadening and deepening of elementary education, to a
more fitting training in skills, to housing, to labor, to suitable leisure and
recreation. In addition, through the ever more perfect organization of
modern means for the diffusion of thought—press, cinema, radio,
television—individuals are enabled to take part in human events on a
world-wide scale.

62.   But as these various forms of association are multiplied and daily
extended, it also happens that in many areas of activity, rules and laws
controlling and determining relationships of citizens are multiplied. As a
consequence, opportunity for free action by individuals is restricted
within narrower limits. Methods are often used, procedures are adopted,
and such an atmosphere develops wherein it becomes difficult for one to

make decisions independently of outside influences, to do anything on his own initiative, to carry out in a fitting way his rights and duties, and to fully develop and perfect his personality. Will men perhaps then become automatons, and cease to be personally responsible, as these social relationships multiply more and more? It is a question which must be answered negatively.

63.   Actually, increased complexity of social life by no means results from a blind drive of natural forces. Indeed, as stated above, it is the creation of free men who are so disposed to act by nature as to be responsible for what they do. They must, of course, recognize the laws of human progress and the development of economic life and take these into account. Furthermore, men are not altogether free of their milieu.

64.   Accordingly, advances in social organization can and should be so brought about that maximum advantages accrue to citizens while at the same time disadvantages are averted or at least minimized.

65.   That these desired objectives be more readily obtained, it is necessary that public authorities have a correct understanding of the common good. This embraces the sum total of those conditions of social living, whereby men are enabled more fully and more readily to achieve their own perfection. Hence, we regard it as necessary that the various intermediary bodies and the numerous social undertakings wherein an expanded social structure primarily finds expression, be ruled by their own laws, and as the common good itself progresses, pursue this objective in a spirit of sincere concord among themselves. Nor is it less necessary that the above mentioned groups present the form and substance of a true community. This they will do, only if individual members are considered and treated as persons, and are encouraged to participate in the affairs of the group.

66.   Accordingly, as relationships multiply between men, binding them more closely together, commonwealths will more readily and appropriately order their affairs to the extent these two factors are kept in balance: (1) the freedom of individual citizens and groups of citizens to act autonomously, while cooperating one with the other; (2) the activity of the State whereby the undertakings of private individuals and groups are suitably regulated and fostered.

67.   Now if social systems are organized in accordance with the above norms and moral laws, their extension does not necessarily mean that individual citizens will be gravely discriminated against or excessively burdened. Rather, we can hope that this will enable man not only to develop and perfect his natural talents, but also will lead to an appropriate structuring of the human community. Such a structure, as our

predecessor of happy memory, Pius XI, warned in his Encyclical Letter *Quadragesimo Anno,* [26] is absolutely necessary for the adequate fulfillment of the rights and duties of social life.

Remuneration for Work

STANDARDS OF JUSTICE AND EQUITY

68.   Our heart is filled with profound sadness when we observe, as it were, with our own eyes a wretched spectacle indeed—great masses of workers who, in not a few nations, and even in whole continents, receive too small a return from their labor. Hence, they and their families must live in conditions completely out of accord with human dignity. This can be traced, for example, to the fact that in these regions, modern industrial techniques either have only recently been introduced or have made less than satisfactory progress.

69.   It happens in some of these nations that, as compared with the extreme need of the majority, the wealth and conspicuous consumption of a few stand out, and are in open and bold contrast with the lot of the needy. It happens in other places that excessive burdens are placed upon men in order that the commonwealth may achieve within a brief span, an increase of wealth such as can by no means be achieved without violating the laws of justice and equity. Finally, it happens elsewhere that a disproportionate share of the revenue goes toward the building up of national prestige, and that large sums of money are devoted to armaments.

70.   Moreover, in the economically developed countries, it frequently happens that great, or sometimes very great, remuneration is had for the performance of some task of lesser importance or doubtful utility. Meanwhile, the diligent and profitable work that whole classes of decent and hard-working citizens perform, receives too low a payment and one insufficient for the necessities of life, or else, one that does not correspond to the contribution made to the community, or to the revenues of the undertakings in which they are engaged, or to the national income.

71.   Wherefore, we judge it to be our duty to reaffirm once again that just as remuneration for work cannot be left entirely to unregulated competition, neither may it be decided arbitrarily at the will of the more powerful. Rather, in this matter, the norms of justice and equity should be strictly observed. This requires that workers receive a wage sufficient to lead a life worthy of man and to fulfill family responsibilities properly. But in determining what constitutes an appropriate wage, the follow-

ing must necessarily be taken into account: first of all, the contribution of individuals to the economic effort; the economic state of the enterprises within which they work; the requirements of each community, especially as regards over-all employment; finally, what concerns the common good of all peoples, namely, of the various States associated among themselves, but differing in character and extent.

72.   It is clear that the standards of judgment set forth above are binding always and everywhere. However, the measure in which they are to be applied in concrete cases cannot be established unless account is taken of the resources at hand. These resources can and in fact do vary in quantity and quality among different peoples, and may even change within the same country with the passing of time.

BALANCING ECONOMIC DEVELOPMENT
AND SOCIAL PROGRESS

73.   Whereas in our era the economies of various countries are evolving very rapidly, more especially since the last great war, we take this opportunity to draw the attention of all to a strict demand of social justice, which explicitly requires that, with the growth of the economy, there occur a corresponding social development. Thus, all classes of citizens will benefit equitably from an increase in national wealth. Toward this end vigilance should be exercised and effective steps taken that class differences arising from disparity of wealth not be increased, but lessened so far as possible.

74.   "National wealth"—as our predecessor of happy memory, Pius XII, rightfully observed—"inasmuch as it is produced by the common efforts of the citizenry, has no other purpose than to secure without interruption those material conditions in which individuals are enabled to lead a full and perfect life. Where this is consistently the case, then such a people is to be judged truly rich. For the system whereby both the common prosperity is achieved and individuals exercise their right to use material goods, conforms fully to norms laid down by God the Creator."[27] From this it follows that the economic prosperity of any people is to be assessed not so much from the sum total of goods and wealth possessed as from the distribution of goods according to norms of justice, so that everyone in the community can develop and perfect himself. For this, after all, is the end toward which all economic activity of a community is by nature ordered.

75.   We must here call attention to the fact that in many countries today, the economic system is such that large and medium size produc-

tive enterprises achieve rapid growth precisely because they finance replacement and plant expansion from their own revenues. Where this is the case, we believe that such companies should grant to workers some share in the enterprise, especially where they are paid no more than the minimum wage.

76.   In this matter, the principle laid down by our predecessor of happy memory, Pius XI, in the Encyclical Letter *Quadragesimo Anno*, should be borne in mind: "It is totally false to ascribe to a single factor of production what is in fact produced by joint activity; and it is completely unjust for one factor to arrogate to itself what is produced, ignoring what has been contributed by other factors."[28]

77.   The demands of justice referred to, can be met in various ways, as experience shows. Not to mention other ways, it is very desirable that workers gradually acquire some share in the enterprise by such methods as seem more appropriate. For today, more than in the times of our predecessor, "every effort should be made that at least in the future, only an equitable share of the fruits of production accumulate in the hands of the wealthy, and a sufficient and ample portion go to the workingmen."[29]

78.   But we should remember that adjustments between remuneration for work and revenues are to be brought about in conformity with the requirements of the common good, both of one's own community and of the entire human family.

79.   Considering the common good on the national level, the following points are relevant and should not be overlooked: to provide employment for as many workers as possible; to take care lest privileged groups arise even among the workers themselves; to maintain a balance between wages and prices; to make accessible the goods and services for a better life to as many persons as possible; either to eliminate or to keep within bounds the inequalities that exist between different sectors of the economy—that is, between agriculture, industry and services; to balance properly any increases in output with advances in services provided to citizens, especially by public authority; to adjust, as far as possible, the means of production to the progress of science and technology; finally, to ensure that the advantages of a more humane way of existence not merely subserve the present generation but have regard for future generations as well.

80.   As regards the common good of human society as a whole, the following conditions should be fulfilled: that the competitive striving of peoples to increase output be free of bad faith; that harmony in economic affairs and a friendly and beneficial cooperation be fostered; and, finally,

that effective aid be given in developing the economically underdeveloped nations.

81.   It is evident from what has been said that these demands of the common good, on both the national and world levels, should be borne in mind, when there is question of determining the share of earnings assigned to those responsible for directing the productive enterprise, or as interest and dividends to those who have invested capital.

Demands of Justice as Regards Productive Institutions

INSTITUTIONS CONFORMING TO THE DIGNITY OF MAN

82.   Justice is to be observed not merely in the distribution of wealth, but also in regard to the conditions under which men engage in productive activity. There is, in fact, an innate need of human nature requiring that men engaged in productive activity have an opportunity to assume responsibility and to perfect themselves by their efforts.

83.   Consequently, if the organization and structure of economic life be such that the human dignity of workers is compromised, or their sense of responsibility is weakened, or their freedom of action is removed, then we judge such an economic order to be unjust, even though it produces a vast amount of goods, whose distribution conforms to the norms of justice and equity.

REAFFIRMATION OF A DIRECTIVE

84.   Nor is it possible in economic affairs to determine in one formula all the measures that are more comformable to the dignity of man, or are more suitable in developing in him a sense of responsiblity. Nevertheless, our predecessor of happy memory, Pius XII, appropriately laid down certain norms of action: "Small and medium-sized holdings in agriculture, in the arts and crafts, in commerce and industry, should be safeguarded and fostered. Such enterprises should join together in mutual-aid societies in order that the services and benefits of large-scale enterprises will be available to them. So far as these larger enterprises are concerned, work agreements should in some way be modified by partnership arrangements."[30]

ARTISAN ENTERPRISES AND COOPERATIVE ASSOCIATIONS

85.   Wherefore, conformably to requirements of the common good
and the state of technology, artisan and farm enterprises of family type
should be safeguarded and fostered, as should also cooperatives that aim
to complement and perfect such enterprises.

86.   We shall return shortly to the subject of farm enterprises. Here,
we think it appropriate to say something about artisan enterprises and
cooperative associations.

87.   Above all, it must be emphasized that enterprises and bodies of
this sort, in order that they may survive and flourish, should be continuously adapted—both in their productive structure and in their operating
methods—to new conditions of the times. These new conditions constantly arise from advances in science and technology, or from changing
consumer needs and preferences. It is especially appropriate that all this
be done by the craftsmen themselves and by the associates in the cooperatives.

88.   Hence, it is most fitting not only that both these groups be suitably
formed in technical and in spiritual and intellectual matters, but also that
they be joined together professionally. Nor is it less fitting that the State
make special provision for them in regard to instruction, taxes, credit
facilities, social security and insurance.

89.   Moreover, the measures taken by the State on behalf of the
craftsmen and members of cooperatives are also justified by the fact that
these two categories of citizens are producers of genuine wealth, and
contribute to the advance of civilization.

90.   Accordingly, we paternally exhort our beloved sons, craftsmen
and members of cooperatives throughout the world, that they fully
realize the dignity of their role in society, since, by their work, the sense of
responsibility and spirit of mutual aid can be daily more intensified
among the citizenry, and the desire to work with dedication and originality be kept alive.

PARTICIPATION OF WORKERS IN
MEDIUM-SIZE AND LARGE ENTERPRISES

91.   Furthermore, as did our predecessors, we regard as justifiable the
desire of employees to be partners in enterprises with which they are
associated and wherein they work. We do not think it possible, however,
to decide with certain and explicit norms the manner and degree of such

partnership, since this must be determined according to the state of the individual productive enterprises. For the situation is not everywhere the same, and, in fact, it can change suddenly within one and the same enterprise. Nevertheless, we do not doubt that employees should have an active part in the affairs of the enterprise wherein they work, whether these be private or public. But it is of the utmost importance that productive enterprises assume the character of a true human fellowship whose spirit suffuses the dealings, activities, and standing of all its members.

92.   This requires that mutual relations between employers and directors on the one hand and the employees of the enterprise on the other, be marked by mutual respect, esteem, and good will. It also demands that all collaborate sincerely and harmoniously in their joint undertaking, and that they perform their work not merely with the objective of deriving an income, but also of carrying out the role assigned them and of performing a service that results in benefit to others. This means that the workers may have a say in, and may make a contribution toward, the efficient running and development of the enterprise. Thus, our predecessor of happy memory, Pius XII, clearly indicated: "The economic and social functions which everyone aspires to fulfill, require that efforts of individuals be not wholly subjected to the will of others."[31] Beyond doubt, an enterprise truly in accord with human dignity should safeguard the necessary and efficient unity of administration. But it by no means follows that those who work daily in such an enterprise are to be considered merely as servants, whose sole function is to execute orders silently, and who are not allowed to interject their desires and interests, but must conduct themselves as idle standbys when it comes to assignment and direction of their tasks.

93.   Finally, attention is drawn to the fact that the greater amount of responsibility desired today by workers in productive enterprises, not merely accords with the nature of man, but also is in conformity with historical developments in the economic, social, and political fields.

94.   Unfortunately, in our day, there occur in economic and social affairs many imbalances that militate against justice and humanity. Meanwhile, throughout all of economic life, errors are spread that seriously impair its operation, purposes, organization, and the fulfillment of responsibilities. Nevertheless, it is an undeniable fact that the more recent productive systems, thanks to the impulse deriving from advances in technology and science, are becoming more modern and efficient, and are expanding at a faster rate than in the past. This demands of workers greater abilities and professional qualifications. Accordingly, workers

should be provided with additional aids and time to achieve a suitable and more rounded formation, and to carry out more fittingly their duties as regards studies, morals, and religion.

95.   Thus it happens that in our day youths can be allotted additional years to acquire a basic education and necessary skills.

96.   Now if these things be done, a situation will emerge wherein workers are enabled to assume greater responsibilities even within their own enterprises. As regards the commonwealth as such, it is of great importance that all ranks of citizens feel themselves daily more obligated to safeguard the common good.

PARTICIPATION OF WORKERS AT ALL LEVELS

97.   Now, as is evident to all, in our day associations of workers have become widespread, and for the most part have been given legal status within individual countries and even across national boundaries. These bodies no longer recruit workers for purposes of strife, but rather for pursuing a common aim. And this is achieved especially by collective bargaining between associations of workers and those of management. But it should be emphasized how necessary, or at least very appropriate, it is to give workers an opportunity to exert influence outside the limits of the individual productive unit, and indeed within all ranks of the commonwealth.

98.   The reason is that individual productive units, whatever their size, efficiency, or importance within the commonwealth, are closely connected with the over-all economic and social situation in each country, whereon their own prosperity ultimately depends.

99.   Nevertheless, to decide what is more helpful to the overall economic situation is not the prerogative of individual productive enterprises, but pertains to the public authorities and to those institutions which, established either nationally or among a number of countries, function in various sectors of economic life. From this is evident the propriety or necessity of ensuring that not only managers or agents of management are represented before such authorities and institutions, but also workers or those who have the responsibility of safeguarding the rights, needs, and aspirations of workers.

100.   It is fitting, therefore, that our thoughts and paternal affection be directed toward the various professional groups and associations of workers which, in accord with principles of Christian teaching, carry on their activities on several continents. We are aware of the many and great difficulties experienced by these beloved sons of ours, as they effectively

worked in the past and continue to strive, both within their national boundaries and throughout the world, to vindicate the rights of workingmen and to improve their lot and conduct.

101.   Furthermore, we wish to give deserved praise to the work of these our sons. Their accomplishments are not always immediately evident, but nevertheless permeate practically the entire field of labor, spreading correct norms of action and thought, and the beneficial influence of the Christian religion.

102.   And we wish also to praise paternally those dear sons of ours who, imbued with Christian principles, give their special attention to other labor associations and those groups of workingmen that follow the laws of nature and respect the religious and moral liberty of individuals.

103.   Nor can we at this point neglect to congratulate and to express our esteem for the International Labor Organization—variously signified popularly by the letters O.I.L. or I.L.O. or O.I.T.—which, for many years, has done effective and valuable work in adapting the economic and social order everywhere to the norms of justice and humanity. In such an order, the legitimate rights of workers are recognized and preserved.

Private Property

CHANGED CONDITIONS

104.   In recent years, as we are well aware, the role played by the owners of capital in very large productive enterprises has been separated more and more from the role of management. This has occasioned great difficulties for governments, whose duty it is to make certain that directors of the principal enterprises, especially those of greatest influence in the economic life of the entire country, do not depart from the requirements of the common good. These difficulties, as we know from experience, are by no means less, whether it be private citizens or public bodies that make the capital investments requisite for large-scale enterprises.

105.   It is also quite clear that today the number of persons is increasing who, because of recent advances in insurance programs and various systems of social security, are able to look to the future with tranquillity. This sort of tranquillity once was rooted in the ownership of property, albeit modest.

106.   It sometimes happens in our day that men are more inclined to seek some professional skill than possession of goods. Moreover, such

men have greater esteem for income from labor or rights arising from labor, than for that deriving from capital investment or rights associated therewith.

107.   This clearly accords with the inherent characteristics of labor, inasmuch as this proceeds directly from the human person, and hence is to be thought more of than wealth in external goods. These latter, by their very nature, must be regarded as instruments. This trend indicates an advance in civilization.

108.   Economic conditions of this kind have occasioned popular doubt as to whether, under present circumstances, a principle of economic and social life, firmly enunciated and defended by our predecessors, has lost its force or is to be regarded as of lesser moment; namely, the principle whereby it is established that men have from nature a right of privately owning goods, including those of a productive kind.

CONFIRMATION OF THE RIGHT OF PRIVATE PROPERTY

109.   Such a doubt has no foundation. For the right of private property, including that pertaining to goods devoted to productive enterprises, is permanently valid. Indeed, it is rooted in the very nature of things, whereby we learn that individual men are prior to civil society, and hence, that civil society is to be directed toward man as its end. Indeed, the right of private individuals to act freely in economic affairs is recognized in vain, unless they are at the same time given an opportunity of freely selecting and using things necessary for the exercise of this right. Moreover, experience and history testify that where political regimes do not allow to private individuals the possession also of productive goods, the exercise of human liberty is violated or completely destroyed in matters of primary importance. Thus it becomes clear that in the right of property, the exercise of liberty finds both a safeguard and a stimulus.

110.   This explains the fact that socio-political groups and associations which endeavor to reconcile freedom with justice within society, and which until recently did not uphold the right of private property in productive goods, have now, enlightened by the course of social events, modified their views and are disposed actually to approve this right.

111.   Accordingly, we make our own the insistence of our predecessor of happy memory, Pius XII: "In defending the right of private property, the Church has in mind a very important ethical aim in social matters. She does not, of course, strive to uphold the present state of affairs as if it were an expression of the divine will. And even less does she accept the patronage of the affluent and wealthy, while neglecting the rights of the

poor and needy. . . . The Church rather does intend that the institution of private property be such as is required by the plan of divine wisdom and the law of nature."[32] Private ownership should safeguard the rights of the human person, and at the same time make its necessary contribution to the establishment of right order in society.

112.   While recent developments in economic life progress rapidly in a number of countries, as we have noted, and produce goods ever more efficiently, justice and equity require that remuneration for work also be increased within limits allowed by the common good. This enables workers to save more readily and hence to achieve some property status of their own. Wherefore, it is indeed surprising that some reject the natural role of private ownership. For it is a right which continually draws its force and vigor from the fruitfulness of labor, and which, accordingly, is an effective aid in safeguarding the dignity of the human person and the free exercise of responsibility in all fields of endeavor. Finally, it strengthens the stability and tranquillity of family life, thus contributing to the peace and prosperity of the commonwealth.

EFFECTIVE DISTRIBUTION

113.   It is not enough, then, to assert that man has from nature the right of privately possessing goods as his own, including those of productive character, unless, at the same time, a continuing effort is made to spread the use of this right through all ranks of the citizenry.

114.   Our predecessor of happy memory, Pius XII, clearly reminded us that on the one hand the dignity of the human person necessarily "requires the right of using external goods in order to live according to the right norm of nature. And to this right corresponds a most serious obligation, which requires that, so far as possible, there be given to all an opportunity of possessing private property."[33]On the other hand, the nobility inherent in work, besides other requirements, demands "the conservation and perfection of a social order that makes possible a secure, although modest, property to all classes of the people."[34]

115.   It is especially appropriate that today, more than heretofore, widespread private ownership should prevail, since, as noted above, the number of nations increases wherein the economic systems experience daily growth. Therefore, by prudent use of various devices already proven effective, it will not be difficult for the body politic to modify economic and social life so that the way is made easier for widespread private possession of such things as durable goods, homes, gardens, tools requisite for artisan enterprises and family-type farms, investments

in enterprises of medium or large size. All of this has occurred satisfactorily in some nations with developed social and economic systems.

PUBLIC PROPERTY

116.   Obviously, what we have said above does not preclude ownership of goods pertaining to production of wealth by States and public agencies, especially "if these carry with them power too great to be left in private hands, without injury to the community at large."[35]

117.   It seems characteristic of our times to vest more and more ownership of goods in the State and in other public bodies. This is partially explained by the fact that the common good requires public authorities to exercise ever greater responsibilities. However, in this matter, the *principle of subsidiarity*, already mentioned above, is to be strictly observed. For it is lawful for States and public corporations to expand their domain of ownership only when manifest and genuine requirements of the common good so require, and then with safeguards, lest the possession of private citizens be diminished beyond measure, or, what is worse, destroyed.

118.   Finally, we cannot pass over in silence the fact that economic enterprises undertaken by the State or by public corporations should be entrusted to citizens outstanding in skill and integrity, who will carry out their responsibilities to the commonwealth with a deep sense of devotion. Moreover, the activity of these men should be subjected to careful and continuing supervision, lest, in the administration of the State itself, there develop an economic imperialism in the hands of a few. For such a development is in conflict with the highest good of the commonwealth.

SOCIAL FUNCTION OF PROPERTY

119.   Our predecessors have always taught that in the right of private property there is rooted a social responsibility. Indeed, in the wisdom of God the Creator, the over-all supply of goods is assigned, first of all, that all men may lead a decent life. As our predecessor of happy memory, Leo XIII, clearly reminded us in the Encyclical Letter *Rerum Novarum*, "This is the heart of the matter: whoever has received from the divine bounty a larger share of blessings, whether these be corporal or external or gifts of the mind, has received them to use for his own perfection, and, at the same time, as the minister of God's providence, for the benefit of others. 'He who has a talent' [says St. Gregory the Great], 'let him take care that

he hides it not; he who has abundance, let him arouse himself to mercy and generosity; he who has skill in managing affairs, let him make special effort to share the use and utility thereof with his neighbor.' "[36]

120.   Although in our day, the role assigned the State and public bodies has increased more and more, it by no means follows that the social function of private ownership is obsolescent, as some seem to think. For social responsibility in this matter derives its force from the very right of private property. Furthermore, it is quite clear that there always will be a wide range of difficult situations, as well as hidden and grave needs, which the manifold providence of the State leaves untouched, and of which it can in no way take account. Wherefore, there is always wide scope for humane action by private citizens and for Christian charity. Finally, it is evident that in stimulating efforts relating to spiritual welfare, the work done by individual men or by private civic groups has more value than what is done by public authorities.

121.   Moreover, it is well to recall here that the right of private ownership is clearly evident in the Gospels, which reveal Jesus Christ ordering the rich to share their goods with the poor so as to turn them into spiritual possessions: "Do not lay up for yourselves treasures on earth, where rust and moth consume, and where thieves break in and steal; but lay up for yourselves treasures in heaven, where neither rust nor moth consumes nor thieves break in and steal."[37] And the divine Master states that whatever is done for the poor is done for Him: "Amen I say to you, as long as you did it for one of these, the least of My brethen, you did it for Me."[38]

PART III
New Aspects of the Social Question

122.   The progress of events and of time have made it increasingly evident that the relationships between workers and management in productive enterprises must be readjusted according to norms of justice and charity. But the same is also true of the systems whereby various types of economic activity and the differently endowed regions within a country ought to be linked together. Meanwhile, within the over-all human community, many nations with varied endowments have not made identical progress in their economic and social affairs.

Just Requirements in the Matter of Interrelated Productive Sectors

AGRICULTURE: A DEPRESSED SECTOR

123.   First of all, to lay down some norms in regard to agriculture, we would note that the over-all number of rural dwellers seemingly has not diminished. Beyond doubt, however, many farmers have abandoned their rural birthplace, and seek out either the more populous centers or the cities themselves. Now since this is the case in almost all countries, and since it affects large numbers of human beings, problems concerning life and dignity of citizens arise, which are indeed difficult to overcome.

124.   Thus, as economic life progresses and expands, the percentage of rural dwellers diminishes, while the great number of industrial and service workers increases. Yet, we feel that those who transfer from rural activities to other productive enterprises often are motivated by reasons arising from the very evolution of economic affairs. Very often, however, they are caught up by various enticements of which the following are noteworthy: a desire to escape from a confined environment offering no prospect of a more comfortable life; the wish, so common in our age, to undertake new activities and to acquire new experiences; the attraction of quickly acquired goods and fortunes; a longing after a freer life, with the advantages that larger towns and cities usually provide. But there is no doubt about this point: rural dwellers leave the fields because nearly everywhere they see their affairs in a state of depression, both as regards labor productivity and the level of living of farm populations.

125.   Accordingly, in this grave matter, about which enquiries are made in nearly all countries, we should first of all ask what is to be done to prevent so great imbalances between agriculture, industry, and the services in the matter of productive efficiency? Likewise, what can be done to minimize differences between the rural standard of living and that of city dwellers whose money income is derived from industry or some service or other? Finally, how can it be brought about that those engaged in agricultural pursuits no longer regard themselves as inferior to others? Indeed, rural dwellers should be convinced not only that they can strengthen and develop their personalities by their toil, but also that they can look forward to the future vicissitudes with confidence.

126.   Accordingly, we judge it opportune in this connection to lay down some norms of permanent validity; although, as is evident, these

must be adapted as various circumstances of time and place permit, or suggest, or absolutely require.

PROVISION FOR ESSENTIAL PUBLIC SERVICES

127.   First, it is necessary that everyone, and especially public authorities, strive to effect improvements in rural areas as regards the principal services needed by all. Such are, for example: highway construction; transport services; marketing facilities; pure drinking water; housing; medical services; elementary, trade, and professional schools; things requisite for religion and for recreation; finally, furnishings and equipment needed in the modern farm home. Where these requirements for a dignified farm life are lacking to rural dwellers, economic and social progress does not occur at all, or else very slowly. Under such conditions, nothing can be done to keep men from deserting the fields, nor can anyone readily estimate their number.

GRADUAL AND ORDERLY DEVELOPMENT
OF THE ECONOMIC SYSTEM

128.   It is desirable, moreover, that economic development of commonwealths proceed in orderly fashion, meanwhile preserving appropriate balance between the various sectors of the economy. In particular, care must be had that within the agriculture sector innovations are introduced as regards productive technology, whether these relate to productive methods, or to cultivation of the fields, or to equipment for the rural enterprise, as far as the over-all economy allows or requires. And all this should be done as far as possible, in accordance with technical advances in industry and in the various services.

129.   In this way, agriculture not only absorbs a larger share of industrial output, but also demands a higher quality of services. In its turn, agriculture offers to the industrial and service sectors of the economy, as well as to the community as a whole, those products which in kind and in quantity better meet consumer needs. Thus, agriculture contributes to stability of the purchasing power of money, a very positive factor for the orderly development of the entire economic system.

130.   By proceeding in this manner, the following advantages, among others, arise: first of all, it is easier to know the origins and destinations of rural dwellers displaced by modernization of agriculture. Thereupon,

they can be instructed in skills needed for other types of work. Finally, economic aids and helps will not be lacking for their intellectual and cultural development, so that they can fit into new social groups.

APPROPRIATE ECONOMIC POLICY

131.   To achieve orderly progress in various sectors of economic life, it is absolutely necessary that as regards agriculture, public authorities give heed and take action in the following matters: taxes and duties, credit, insurance, prices, the fostering of requisite skills, and, finally, improved equipment for rural enterprises.

TAXATION

132.   As regards taxation, assessment according to ability to pay is fundamental to a just and equitable tax system.
133.   But in determining taxes for rural dwellers, the general welfare requires public authorities to bear in mind that income in a rural economy is both delayed and subject to greater risk. Moreover, there is difficulty in finding capital so as to increase returns.

CAPITAL AT SUITABLE INTEREST

134.   Accordingly, those with money to invest are more inclined to invest it in enterprises other than in the rural economy. And for the same reason, rural dwellers cannot pay high rates of interest. Nor are they generally able to pay prevailing market rates for capital wherewith to carry on and expand their operations. Wherefore, the general welfare requires that public authorities not merely make special provision for agricultural financing, but also for establishment of banks that provide capital to farmers at reasonable rates of interest.

SOCIAL INSURANCE AND SOCIAL SECURITY

135.   It also seems necessary to make provision for a twofold insurance, one covering agricultural output, the other covering farmers and their families. Because, as experience shows, the income of individual farmers is, on the average, less than that of workers in industry and the services, it does not seem to be fully in accord with the norms of social justice and equity to provide farmers with insurance or social security benefits that are inferior to those of other classes of citizens. For those

insurance plans or provisions that are established generally should not differ markedly one from the other, whatever be the economic sector wherein the citizens work, or from which they derive their income.

136. Moreover, since social security and insurance can help appreciably in distributing national income among the citizens according to justice and equity, these systems can be regarded as means whereby imbalances among various classes of citizens are reduced.

PRICE PROTECTION

137. Since agricultural products have special characteristics, it is fitting that their price be protected by methods worked out by economic experts. In this matter, although it is quite helpful that those whose interests are involved take steps to safeguard themselves, setting up, as it were, appropriate goals, public authorities cannot stand entirely aloof from the stabilization procedure.

138. Nor should this be overlooked, that, generally speaking, the price of rural products is more a recompense for farmers' labor than for capital investment.

139. Thus, our predecessor of happy memory, Pius XI, touching on the welfare of the human community, appropriately notes in his Encyclical Letter *Quadragesimo Anno*, that "a reasonable relationship between different wages here enters into consideration." But he immediately adds, "Intimately connected with this is a reasonable relationship between the prices obtained for the products of the various economic groups: agrarian, industrial, and so forth."[39]

140. Inasmuch as agricultural products are destined especially to satisfy the basic needs of men, it is necessary that their price be such that all can afford to buy them. Nevertheless, there is manifest injustice in placing a whole group of citizens, namely, the farmers, in an inferior economic and social status, with less purchasing power than required for a decent livelihood. This, indeed, is clearly contrary to the common good of the country.

STRENGTHENING FARM INCOME

141. In rural areas it is fitting that industries be fostered and common services be developed that are useful in preserving, processing, and finally, in transporting farms products. There is need, moreover, to establish councils and activities relating to various sectors of economic and professional affairs. By such means, suitable opportunity is given

farm families to supplement their incomes, and that within the milieu wherein they live and work.

APPROPRIATE ORGANIZATION OF FARMING ENTERPRISES

142.   Finally, no one person can lay down a universal rule regarding the way in which rural affairs should be definitely organized, since in these matters there exists considerable variation within each country, and the difference is even greater when we consider the various regions of the world. However, those who hold man and the family in proper esteem, whether this be based upon nature alone, or also upon Christian principles, surely look toward some form of agricultural enterprise, and particularly of the family type, which is modeled upon the community of men wherein mutual relationships of members and the organization of the enterprise itself are conformed to norms of justice and Christian teaching. And these men strive mightily that such organization of rural life be realized as far as circumstances permit.

143.   The family farm will be firm and stable only when it yields money income sufficient for decent and humane family living. To bring this about, it is very necessary that farmers generally receive instruction, be kept informed of new developments, and be technically assisted by trained men. It is also necessary that farmers form among themselves mutual-aid societies; that they establish professional associations; that they function efficiently in public life, that is, in various administrative bodies and in political affairs.

Rural Workers: Participants in Improving Conditions

144.   We are of the opinion that in rural affairs, the principal agents and protagonists of economic improvement, of cultural betterment, or of social advance, should be the men personally involved, namely, the farmers themselves. To them it should be quite evident that their work is most noble, because it is undertaken, as it were, in the majestic temple of creation; because it often concerns the life of plants and animals, a life inexhaustible in its expression, inflexible in its laws, rich in allusions to God, Creator and Provider. Moreover, labor in the fields not only produces various foodstuffs wherewith humankind is nourished, but also furnishes an increasing supply of raw materials for industry.

145.   Furthermore, this is a work endowed with a dignity of its own, for it bears a manifold relationship to the mechanical arts, chemistry, and biology: these must be continually adapted to the requirements of emerging situations because scientific and technological advance is of great importance in rural life. Work of this kind, moreover, possesses a special nobility because it requires farmers to understand well the course of the seasons and to adapt themselves to the same; that they await patiently what the future will bring; that they appreciate the importance and seriousness of their duties; that they constantly remain alert and ready for new developments.

SOLIDARITY AND COOPERATION

146.   Nor may it be overlooked that in rural areas, as indeed in every productive sector, farmers should join together in fellowships, especially when the family itself works the farm. Indeed, it is proper for rural workers to have a sense of solidarity. They should strive jointly to set up mutual-aid societies and professional associations. All these are very necessary either to keep rural dwellers abreast of scientific and technical progress, or to protect the prices of goods produced by their labor. Besides, acting in this manner, farmers are put on the same footing as other classes of workers who, for the most part, join together in such fellowships. Finally, by acting thus, farmers will achieve an importance and influence in public affairs proportionate to their own role. For today it is unquestionably true that the solitary voice speaks, as they say, to the winds.

RECOGNIZING DEMANDS OF THE COMMON GOOD

147.   But when rural dwellers, just as other classes of workers, wish to make their influence and importance felt, they should never disregard moral duties or civil law. Rather they should strive to bring their rights and interests into line with the rights and needs of other classes, and to refer the same to the common good. In this connection, farmers who strive vigorously to improve the yield of their farm may rightly demand that their efforts be aided and complemented by public authorities, provided they themselves keep in mind the common needs of all and also relate their own efforts to the fulfillment of these needs.

148.   Wherefore, we wish to honor appropriately those sons of ours who everywhere in the world, either by founding and fostering mutual-

aid societies or some other type of association, watchfully strive that in all civic affairs farmers enjoy not merely economic prosperity but also a status in keeping with justice.

VOCATION AND MISSION

149.   Since everything that makes for man's dignity, perfection, and development seems to be invoked in agricultural labor, it is proper that man regard such work as an assignment from God with a sublime purpose. It is fitting, therefore, that man dedicate work of this kind to the most provident God who directs all events for the salvation of men. Finally, the farmer should take upon himself, in some measure, the task of educating himself and others for the advancement of civilization.

Aid to Less Developed Areas

150.   It often happens that in one and the same country citizens enjoy different degrees of wealth and social advancement. This especially happens because they dwell in areas which, economically speaking, have grown at different rates. Where such is the case, justice and equity demand that the government make efforts either to remove or to minimize imbalances of this sort. Toward this end, efforts should be made, in areas where there has been less economic progress, to supply the principal public services, as indicated by circumstances of time and place and in accord with the general level of living. But in bringing this about, it is necessary to have very competent administration and organization to take careful account of the following: labor supply, internal migration, wages, taxes, interest rates, and investments in industries that foster other skills and developments—all of which will further not merely the useful employment of workers and the stimulation of initiative, but also the exploitation of resources locally available.

151.   But it is precisely the measures for advancement of the general welfare which civil authorities must undertake. Hence, they should take steps, having regard for the needs of the whole community, that progress in agriculture, industry, and services be made at the same time and in a balanced manner so far as possible. They should have this goal in mind, that citizens in less developed countries—in giving attention to economic and social affairs, as well as to cultural matters—feel themselves to be the ones chiefly responsible for their own progress. For a citizen has a sense of his own dignity when he contributes the major share to progress in his own affairs.

152.   Hence, those also who rely on their own resources and initiative should contribute as best they can to the equitable adjustment of economic life in their own community. Nay, more, those in authority should favor and help private enterprise in accordance with the *principle of subsidiarity*, in order to allow private citizens themselves to accomplish as much as is feasible.

IMBALANCES BETWEEN LAND AND POPULATION

153.   It is appropriate to recall at this point that in a number of nations there exists a discrepancy between available agricultural land and the number of rural dwellers. Some nations experience a shortage of citizens, but have rich land resources; others have many citizens but an insufficiency of agricultural land.

154.   Nor are there lacking nations wherein, despite their great resource potential, farmers use such primitive and obsolete methods of cultivation that they are unable to produce what is needed for the entire population. On the other hand, in certain countries, agriculture has so adapted itself to recent advances that farmers produce surpluses which to some extent harm the economy of the entire nation.

155.   It is evident that both the solidarity of the human race and the sense of brotherhood which accords with Christian principles, require that some peoples lend others energetic help in many ways. Not merely would this result in a freer movement of goods, of capital, and of men, but it also would lessen imbalances between nations. We shall treat of this point in more detail below.

156.   Here, however, we cannot fail to express our approval of the efforts of the Institute known as F.A.O. which concerns itself with the feeding of peoples and improvement of agriculture. This Institute has the special goal of promoting mutual accord among peoples, of bringing it about that rural life is modernized in less developed nations, and finally, that help is brought to people experiencing food shortages.

Requirements of Justice as Between Nations Differing in Economic Development

PROBLEM OF THE MODERN WORLD

157.   Perhaps the most pressing question of our day concerns the relationship between economically advanced commonwealths and those

that are in process of development. The former enjoy the conveniences of life; the latter experience dire poverty. Yet, today men are so intimately associated in all parts of the world that they feel, as it were, as if they are members of one and the same household. Therefore, the nations that enjoy a sufficiency and abundance of everything may not overlook the plight of other nations whose citizens experience such domestic problems that they are all but overcome by poverty and hunger, and are not able to enjoy basic human rights. This is all the more so, inasmuch as countries each day seem to become more dependent on each other. Consequently, it is not easy for them to keep the peace advantageously if excessive imbalances exist in their economic and social conditions.

158.   Mindful of our role of universal father, we think it opportune to stress here what we have stated in another connection: "We all share responsibility for the fact that populations are undernourished.[40] [Therefore], it is necessary to arouse a sense of responsibility in individuals and generally, especially among those more blessed with this world's goods."[41]

159.   As can be readily deduced, and as the Church has always seriously warned, it is proper that the duty of helping the poor and unfortunate should especially stir Catholics, since they are members of the Mystical Body of Christ. "In this we have come to know the love of God," said John the Apostle, "that He laid down His life for us; and we likewise ought to lay down our life for the brethren. He who has the goods of this world and sees his brother in need and closes his heart to him, how does the love of God abide in him?"[42]

160.   Wherefore, we note with pleasure that countries with advanced productive systems are lending aid to less privileged countries, so that these latter may the more readily improve their condition.

EMERGENCY ASSISTANCE

161.   It is clear to everyone that some nations have surpluses in foodstuffs, particularly of farm products, while elsewhere large masses of people experience want and hunger. Now justice and humanity require that these richer countries come to the aid of those in need. Accordingly, to destroy entirely or to waste goods necessary for the lives of men, runs counter to our obligations in justice and humanity.

162.   We are quite well aware that to produce surpluses, especially of farm products, in excess of the needs of a country, can occasion harm to various classes of citizens. Nevertheless, it does not therefore follow that nations with surpluses have no obligation to aid the poor and hungry

where some particular emergency arises. Rather, diligent efforts should be made that inconveniences arising from surplus goods be minimized and borne by every citizen on a fair basis.

SCIENTIFIC, TECHNICAL, AND FINANCIAL COOPERATION

163.   However, the underlying causes of poverty and hunger will not be removed in a number of countries by these means alone. For the most part, the causes are to be found in the primitive state of the economy. To effect a remedy, all available avenues should be explored with a view, on the one hand, to instruct citizens fully in necessary skills and in carrying out their responsibilities, and, on the other hand, to enable them to acquire the capital wherewith to promote economic growth by ways and means adapted to our times.

164.   It has not escaped our attention that in recent years there has grown in many minds a deep awareness of their duty to aid poorer countries still lacking suitable economic development, in order that these may more readily make economic and social progress.

165.   Toward this end, we look to councils, either of a number of nations, or within individual nations; we look to private enterprises and societies to exert daily more generous efforts on behalf of such countries, transmitting to them requisite productive skills. For the same reason help is given to as many youths as possible that they may study in the great universities of more developed countries, thus acquiring a knowledge of the arts and sciences in line with the standards of our time. Moreover, international banks, single nations, or private citizens often make loans to these countries that they may initiate various programs calculated to increase production. We gladly take this opportunity to give due praise to such generous activity. It is hoped that in the future the richer countries will make greater and greater efforts to provide developing countries with aid designed to promote sciences, technology, and economic life.

AVOIDANCE OF PAST ERRORS

166.   In this matter we consider it our duty to offer some warnings.

167.   First of all, it seems only prudent for nations which thus far have made little or no progress, to weigh well the principal factor in the advance of nations that enjoy abundance.

168.   Prudent foresight and common need demand that not only more goods be produced, but that this be done more efficiently. Likewise, necessity and justice require that wealth produced be distributed equita-

bly among all citizens of the commonwealth. Accordingly, efforts should be made to ensure that improved social conditions accompany economic advancement. And it is very important that such advances occur simultaneously in the agricultural, industrial, and various service sectors.

RESPECT FOR INDIVIDUAL CHARACTERISTICS OF COUNTRIES

169.   It is indeed clear to all that countries in process of development often have their own individual characteristics, and that these arise from the nature of the locale, or from cultural tradition, or from some special trait of the citizens.

170.   Now when economically developed countries assist the poorer ones, they not only should have regard for these characteristics and respect them, but also should take special care lest, in aiding these nations, they seek to impose their own way of life upon them.

DISINTERESTED AID

171.   Moreover, economically developed countries should take particular care lest, in giving aid to poorer countries, they endeavor to turn the prevailing political situation to their own advantage, and seek to dominate them.

172.   Should perchance such attempts be made, this clearly would be but another form of colonialism, which, although disguised in name, merely reflects their earlier but outdated dominion, now abandoned by many countries. When international relations are thus obstructed, the orderly progress of all peoples is endangered.

173.   Genuine necessity, as well as justice, require that whenever countries give attention to the fostering of skills or commerce, they should aid the less developed nations without thought of domination, so that these latter eventually will be in a position to progress economically and socially on their own initiative.

174.   If this be done, it will help much toward shaping a community of all nations, wherein each one, aware of its rights and duties, will have regard for the prosperity of all.

RESPECT FOR A HIERARCHY OF VALUES

175.   There is no doubt that when a nation makes progress in science, technology, economic life, and the prosperity of its citizens, a great contribution is made to civilization. But all should realize that these things

are not the highest goods, but only instruments for pursuing such goods.
176.   Accordingly, we note with sorrow that in some nations economic
life indeed progresses, but that not a few men are there to be found, who
have no concern at all for the just ordering of goods. No doubt, these men
either completely ignore spiritual values, or put these out of their minds,
or else deny they exist. Nevertheless, while they pursue progress in
science, technology, and economic life, they make so much of external
benefits that for the most part they regard these as the highest goods of
life. Accordingly, there are not lacking grave dangers in the help provided
by more affluent nations for development of the poorer ones. For among
the citizens of these latter nations, there is operative a general awareness
of the higher values on which moral teaching rests—an awareness derived from ancient traditional custom which provides them with motivation.
177.   Thus, those who seek to undermine in some measure the right
instincts of these peoples, assuredly do something immoral. Rather,
those attitudes, besides being held in honor, should be perfected and
refined, since upon them true civilization depends.

CONTRIBUTION OF THE CHURCH

178.   Moreover, the Church by divine right pertains to all nations. This
is confirmed by the fact that she already is everywhere on earth and
strives to embrace all peoples.
179.   Now, those peoples whom the Church has joined to Christ have
always reaped some benefits, whether in economic affairs or in social
organization, as history and contemporary events clearly record. For
everyone who professes Christianity promises and gives assurance that
he will contribute as far as he can to the advancement of civil institutions.
He must also strive with all his might not only that human dignity suffer
no dishonor, but also, by the removal of every kind of obstacle, that all
those forces be promoted which are conducive to moral living and contribute to it.
180.   Moreover, when the Church infuses her energy into the life of a
people, she neither is, nor feels herself to be, an alien institution imposed
upon that people from without. This follows from the fact that wherever
the Church is present, there individual men are reborn or resurrected in
Christ. Those who are thus reborn or who have risen again in Christ feel
themselves oppressed by no external force. Rather, realizing they have
achieved perfect liberty, they freely move toward God. Hence, whatever
is seen by them as good and morally right, that they approve and put into
effect.

181.   "The Church of Jesus Christ," as our predecessor Pius XII clearly stated, "is the faithful guardian of God's gracious wisdom. Hence, she makes no effort to discourage or belittle those characteristics and traits which are proper to particular nations, and which peoples religiously and tenaciously guard, quite justly, as a sacred heritage. She aims indeed at a unity which is profound and in conformity with that heavenly love whereby all are moved in their innermost being. She does not seek a uniformity which is merely external in its effects and calculated to weaken the fibre of the peoples concerned. And all careful rules that contribute to the wise development and growth within bounds of these capacities and forces, which indeed have their deeply rooted ethnic traits, have the Church's approval and maternal prayers, provided they are not in opposition to those duties which spring from the common origin and destiny of all mortal men."[43]

182.   We note with deep satisfaction that Catholic men, citizens of the less developed nations, are for the most part second to no other citizens in furthering efforts of their countries to make progress economically and socially according to their capacity.

183.   Furthermore, we note that Catholic citizens of the richer nations are making extensive efforts to ensure that aid given by their own countries to needy countries is directed increasingly toward economic and social progress. In this connection, it seems specially praiseworthy that appreciable aid in various forms is provided increasingly each year to young people from Africa and Asia, so that they may pursue literary and professional studies in the great universities of Europe and America. The same applies to the great care that has been taken in training for every responsibility of their office men prepared to go to less developed areas, there to carry out their profession and duties.

184.   To those sons of ours who, by promoting solicitously the progress of peoples and by spreading, as it were, a wholesome civilizing influence, everywhere demonstrate the perennial vitality of Holy Church and her effectiveness, we wish to express our paternal praise and gratitude.

Population Increase and Economic Development

185.   More recently, the question often is raised how economic organization and the means of subsistence can be balanced with population increase, whether in the world as a whole or within the needy nations.

IMBALANCE BETWEEN POPULATION
AND MEANS OF SUBSISTENCE

186.   As regards the world as a whole, some, consequent to statistical reasoning, observe that within a matter of decades mankind will become very numerous, whereas economic growth will proceed much more slowly. From this some conclude that unless procreation is kept within limits, there subsequently will develop an even greater imbalance between the number of inhabitants and the necessities of life.

187.   It is clearly evident from statistical records of less developed countries that, because recent advances in public health and in medicine are there widely diffused, the citizens have a longer life expectancy consequent to lowered rates of infant mortality. The birth rate, where it has traditionally been high, tends to remain at such levels, at least for the immediate future. Thus the birth rate in a given year exceeds the death rate. Meanwhile the productive systems in such countries do not expand as rapidly as the number of inhabitants. Hence, in poorer countries of this sort, the standard of living does not advance and may even deteriorate. Wherefore, lest a serious crisis occur, some are of the opinion that the conception or birth of humans should be avoided or curbed by every possible means.

THE TERMS OF THE PROBLEM

188.   Now to tell the truth, the interrelationships on a global scale between the number of births and available resources are such that we can infer grave difficulties in this matter do not arise at present, nor will in the immediate future. The arguments advanced in this connection are so inconclusive and controversial that nothing certain can be drawn from them.

189.   Besides, God in His goodness and wisdom has, on the one hand, provided nature with almost inexhaustible productive capacity; and, on the other hand, has endowed man with such ingenuity that, by using suitable means, he can apply nature's resources to the needs and requirements of existence. Accordingly, that the question posed may be clearly resolved, a course of action is not indeed to be followed whereby, contrary to the moral law laid down by God, procreative function also is violated. Rather, man should, by the use of his skills and science of every kind, acquire an intimate knowledge of the forces of nature and control

them ever more extensively. Moreover, the advances hitherto made in science and technology give almost limitless promise for the future in this matter.

190.   When it comes to questions of this kind, we are not unaware that in certain locales and also in poorer countries, it is often argued that in such an economic and social order, difficulties arise because citizens, each year more numerous, are unable to acquire sufficient food or sustenance where they live, and peoples do not show amicable cooperation to the extent they should.

191.   But whatever be the situation, we clearly affirm these problems should be posed and resolved in such a way that man does not have recourse to methods and means contrary to his dignity, which are proposed by those persons who think of man and his life solely in material terms.

192.   We judge that this question can be resolved only if economic and social advances preserve and augment the genuine welfare of individual citizens and of human society as a whole. Indeed, in a matter of this kind, first place must be accorded everything that pertains to the dignity of man as such, or to the life of individual men, than which nothing can be more precious. Moreover, in this matter, international cooperation is necessary, so that, conformably with the welfare of all, information, capital, and men themselves may move about among the peoples in orderly fashion.

RESPECT FOR THE LAWS OF LIFE

193.   In this connection, we strongly affirm that human life is transmitted and propagated through the instrumentality of the family which rests on marriage, one and indissoluble, and, so far as Christians are concerned, elevated to the dignity of a sacrament. Because the life of man is passed on to other men deliberately and knowingly, it therefore follows that this should be done in accord with the most sacred, permanent, inviolate prescriptions of God. Everyone without exception is bound to recognize and observe these laws. Wherefore, in this matter, no one is permitted to use methods and procedures which may indeed be permissible to check the life of plants and animals.

194.   Indeed, all must regard the life of man as sacred, since from its inception, it requires the action of God the Creator. Those who depart from this plan of God not only offend His divine majesty and dishonor

themselves and the human race, but they also weaken the inner fibre of the commonwealth.

EDUCATION TOWARD A SENSE OF RESPONSIBILITY

195.   In these matters it is of great importance that new offspring, in addition to being very carefully educated in human culture and in religion—which indeed is the right and duty of parents—should also show themselves very conscious of their duties in every action of life. This is especially true when it is a question of establishing a family and of procreating and educating children. Such children should be imbued not only with a firm confidence in the providence of God, but also with a strong and ready will to bear the labors and inconveniences which cannot be lawfully avoided by anyone who undertakes the worthy and serious obligation of associating his own activity with God in transmitting life and in educating offspring. In this most important matter certainly nothing is more relevant than the teachings and supernatural aids provided by the Church. We refer to the Church whose right of freely carrying out her function must be recognized also in this connection.

CREATION FOR MAN'S BENEFIT

196.   When God, as we read in the book of Genesis, imparted human nature to our first parents, He assigned them two tasks, one of which complements the other. For He first directed: "Be fruitful and multiply,"[44] and then immediately added: "Fill the earth and subdue it."[45]
197.   The second of these tasks, far from anticipating a destruction of goods, rather assigns them to the service of human life.
198.   Accordingly, with great sadness we note two conflicting trends: on the one hand, the scarcity of goods is vaguely described as such that the life of men reportedly is in danger of perishing from misery and hunger; on the other hand, the recent discoveries of science, technical advances, and economic productivity are transformed into means whereby the human race is led toward ruin and a horrible death.
199.   Now the provident God has bestowed upon humanity sufficient goods wherewith to bear with dignity the burdens associated with procreation of children. But this task will be difficult or even impossible if men, straying from the right road and with a perverse outlook, use the

means mentioned above in a manner contrary to human reason or to their social nature, and hence, contrary to the directives of God Himself.

International Cooperation

WORLD DIMENSIONS OF IMPORTANT HUMAN PROBLEMS

200.   Since the relationships between countries today are closer in every region of the world, by reason of science and technology, it is proper that peoples become more and more interdependent.

201.   Accordingly, contemporary problems of moment—whether in the fields of science and technology, or of economic and social affairs, or of public administration, or of cultural advancement—these, because they may exceed the capacities of individual States, very often affect a number of nations and at times all the nations of the earth.

202.   As a result, individual countries, although advanced in culture and civilization, in number and industry of citizens, in wealth, in geographical extent, are not able by themselves to resolve satisfactorily their basic problems. Accordingly, because States must on occasion complement or perfect one another, they really consult their own interests only when they take into account at the same time the interests of others. Hence, dire necessity warns commonwealths to cooperate among themselves and provide mutual assistance.

MUTUAL DISTRUST

203.   Although this becomes more and more evident each day to individuals and even to all peoples, men, and especially those with high responsibility in public life, for the most part seem unable to accomplish the two things toward which peoples aspire. This does not happen because peoples lack scientific, technical, or economic means, but rather because they distrust one another. Indeed, men, and hence States, stand in fear of one another. One country fears lest another is contemplating aggression and lest the other seize an opportunity to put such plans into effect. Accordingly, countries customarily prepare defenses for their cities and homeland, namely, armaments designed to deter other countries from aggression.

204.   Consequently, the energies of man and the resources of nature

are very widely directed by peoples to destruction rather than to the advantage of the human family, and both individual men and entire peoples become so deeply solicitous that they are prevented from undertaking more important works.

FAILURE TO ACKNOWLEDGE THE MORAL ORDER

205.   The cause of this state of affairs seems to be that men, more especially leaders of States, have differing philosophies of life. Some even dare to assert that there exists no law of truth and right which transcends external affairs and man himself, which of necessity pertains to everyone, and, finally, which is equitable for all men. Hence, men can agree fully and surely about nothing, since one and the same law of justice is not accepted by all.

206.   Although the word *justice* and the related term *demands of justice* are on everyone's lips, such verbalizations do not have the same meaning for all. Indeed, the opposite frequently is the case. Hence, when leaders invoke *justice* or the *demands of justice*, not only do they disagree as to the meaning of the words, but frequently find in them an occasion of serious contention. And so they conclude that there is no way of achieving their rights or advantages, unless they resort to force, the root of very serious evils.

GOD, THE FOUNDATION OF THE MORAL ORDER

207.   That mutual faith may develop among rulers and nations and may abide more deeply in their minds, the laws of truth and justice first must be acknowledged and preserved on all sides.

208.   However, the guiding principles of morality and virtue can be based only on God; apart from Him, they necessarily collapse. For man is composed not merely of body, but of soul as well, and is endowed with reason and freedom. Now such a composite being absolutely requires a moral law rooted in religion, which, far better than any external force or advantage, can contribute to the resolution of problems affecting the lives of individual citizens or groups of citizens, or with a bearing upon single States or all States together.

209.   Yet, there are today those who assert that, in view of the flourishing state of science and technology, men can achieve the highest civilization even apart from God and by their own unaided powers. Nevertheless, it is because of this very progress in science and technology that men

often find themselves involved in difficulties which affect all peoples, and which can be overcome only if they duly recognize the authority of God, author and ruler of man and of all nature.

210.   That this is true, the advances of science seem to indicate, opening up, as they do, almost limitless horizons. Thus, an opinion is implanted in many minds that inasmuch as mathematical sciences are unable to discern the innermost nature of things and their changes, or express them in suitable terms, they can scarcely draw inferences about them. And when terrified men see with their own eyes that the vast forces deriving from technology and machines can be used for destruction as well as for the advantage of peoples, they rightly conclude that things pertaining to the spirit and to moral life are to be preferred to all else, so that progress in science and technology do not result in destruction of the human race, but prove useful as instruments of civilization.

211.   Meanwhile it comes to pass that in more affluent countries men, less and less satisfied with external goods, put out of their minds the deceptive image of a happy life to be lived here forever. Likewise, not only do men grow daily more conscious that they are fully endowed with all the rights of the human person, but they also strive mightily that relations among themselves become more equitable and more conformed to human dignity. Consequently, men are beginning to recognize that their own capacities are limited, and they seek spiritual things more intensively than heretofore. All of which seems to give some promise that not only individuals, but even peoples may come to an understanding for extensive and extremely useful collaboration.

PART IV:

Reconstruction of Social Relationships in Truth, Justice and Love

Incomplete and Erroneous Philosophies of Life

212.   As in the past, so too in our day, advances in science and technology have greatly multiplied relationships between citizens; it seems necessary, therefore, that the relationships themselves, whether

within a single country or between all countries, be brought into more humane balance.

213.   In this connection many systems of thought have been developed and committed to writing: some of these already have been dissipated as mist by the sun; others remain basically unchanged today; still others now elicit less and less response from men. The reason for this is that these popularized fancies neither encompass man, whole and entire, nor do they affect his inner being. Moreover, they fail to take into account the weaknesses of human nature, such as sickness and suffering: weaknesses that no economic or social system, no matter how advanced, can completely eliminate. Besides, men everywhere are moved by a profound and unconquerable sense of religion, which no force can ever destroy nor shrewdness suppress.

214.   In our day, a very false opinion is popularized which holds that the sense of religion implanted in men by nature is to be regarded as something adventitious or imaginary, and hence, is to be rooted completely from the mind as altogether inconsistent with the spirit of our age and the progress of civilization. Yet, this inward proclivity of man to religion confirms the fact that man himself was created by God, and irrevocably tends to Him. Thus we read in Augustine: "Thou hast made us for Thyself, O Lord, and our hearts are restless until they rest in Thee."[46]

215.   Wherefore, whatever the progress in technology and economic life, there can be neither justice nor peace in the world, so long as men fail to realize how great is their dignity; for they have been created by God and are His children. We speak of God, who must be regarded as the first and final cause of all things He has created. Separated from God, man becomes monstrous to himself and others. Consequently, mutual relationships between men absolutely require a right ordering of the human conscience in relation to God, the source of all truth, justice, and love.

216.   It is well known and recognized by everyone that in a number of countries, some of ancient Christian culture, many of our very dear brothers and sons have been savagely persecuted for a number of years. Now this situation, since it reveals the great dignity of the persecuted, and the refined cruelty of their persecutors, leads many to reflect on the matter, though it has not yet healed the wounds of the persecuted.

217.   However, no folly seems more characteristic of our time than the desire to establish a firm and meaningful temporal order, but without God, its necessary foundation. Likewise, some wish to proclaim the greatness of man, but with the source dried up from which such greatness

flows and receives nourishment: that is, by impeding and, if it were possible, stopping the yearning of souls for God. But the turn of events in our times, whereby the hopes of many are shattered and not a few have come to grief, unquestionably confirm the words of Scripture: "Unless the Lord build the house, they labor in vain who built it."[47]

The Church's Traditional Teaching Regarding Man's Social Life

218.   What the Catholic Church teaches and declares regarding the social life and relationships of men is beyond question for all time valid.

219.   The cardinal point of this teaching is that individual men are necessarily the foundation, cause, and end of all social institutions. We are referring to human beings, insofar as they are social by nature, and raised to an order of existence that transcends and subdues nature.

220.   Beginning with this very basic principle whereby the dignity of the human person is affirmed and defended, Holy Church—especially during the last century and with the assistance of learned priests and laymen, specialists in the field—has arrived at clear social teachings whereby the mutual relationships of men are ordered. Taking general norms into account, these principles are in accord with the nature of things and the changed conditions of man's social life, or with the special genius of our day. Moreover, these norms can be approved by all.

221.   But today, more than ever, principles of this kind must not only be known and understood, but also applied to those systems and methods, which the various situations of time or place either suggest or require. This is indeed a difficult, though lofty, task. Toward its fulfillment we exhort not only our brothers and sons everywhere, but all men of good will.

STUDY OF SOCIAL MATTERS

222.   Above all, we affirm that the social teaching proclaimed by the Catholic Church cannot be separated from her traditional teaching regarding man's life.

223.   Wherefore, it is our earnest wish that more and more attention be given to this branch of learning. First of all, we urge that attention be given to such studies in Catholic schools on all levels, and especially in seminaries, although we are not unaware that in some of these latter institutions this is already being done admirably. Moreover, we desire

that social study of this sort be included among the religious materials used to instruct and inspire the lay apostolate, either in parishes or in associations. Let this diffusion of knowledge be accomplished by every modern means: that is, in journals, whether daily or periodical; in doctrinal books, both for the learned and the general reader; and finally, by means of radio and television.

224.   We judge that our sons among the laity have much to contribute through their work and effort, that this teaching of the Catholic Church regarding the social question be more and more widely diffused. This they can do, not merely by learning it themselves and governing their actions accordingly, but also by taking special care that others also come to know its relevance.

225.   Let them be fully persuaded that in no better way can they show this teaching to be correct and effective, than by demonstrating that present day social difficulties will yield to its application. In this way they will win minds today antagonistic to the teaching because they do not know it. Perhaps it will also happen that such men will find some enlightenment in the teaching.

Application of Social Teaching

226.   But social norms of whatever kind are not only to be explained but also applied. This is especially true of the Church's teaching on social matters, which has truth as its guide, justice as its end, and love as its driving force.

227.   We consider it, therefore, of the greatest importance that our sons, in addition to knowing these social norms, be reared according to them.

228.   To be complete, the education of Christians must relate to the duties of every class. It is therefore necessary that Christians thus inspired, conform their behavior in economic and social affairs to the teachings of the Church.

229.   If it is indeed difficult to apply teaching of any sort to concrete situations, it is even more so when one tries to put into practice the teaching of the Catholic Church regarding social affairs. This is especially true for the following reasons: there is deeply rooted in each man an instinctive and immoderate love of his own interests; today there is widely diffused in society a materialistic philosophy of life; it is difficult at times to discern the demands of justice in a given situation.

230.   Consequently, it is not enough for men to be instructed, accord-

ing to the teachings of the Church, on their obligation to act in a Christian manner in economic and social affairs. They must also be shown ways in which they can properly fulfill their duty in this regard.

231.   We do not regard such instructions as sufficient, unless there be added to the work of instruction that of the formation of man, and unless some action follow upon the teaching, by way of experience.

232.   Just as, proverbially, no one really enjoys liberty unless he uses it, so no one really knows how to act according to Catholic teaching in the economic and social fields, unless he acts according to this teaching in the same area.

A TASK FOR LAY APOSTOLATE

233.   Accordingly, in popular instruction of this kind, it seems proper that considerable attention be paid to groups promoting the lay apostolate, especially those whose aim is to ensure that efforts in our present concern draw their inspiration wholly from Christian law. Seeing that members of such groups can first train themselves by daily practice in these matters, they subsequently will be able the better to instruct young people in fulfilling obligations of this kind.

234.   It is not inappropriate in this connection to remind all, the great no less than the lowly, that the will to preserve moderation and to bear difficulties, by God's grace, can in no wise be separated from the meaning of life handed down to us by Christian wisdom.

235.   But today, unfortunately, very many souls are preoccupied with an inordinate desire for pleasure. Such persons see nothing more important in the whole of life than to seek pleasure, to quench the thirst for pleasure. Beyond doubt, grave ills to both soul and body proceed therefrom. Now in this matter, it must be admitted that one who judges even with the aid of human nature alone, concludes that it is the part of the wise and prudent man to preserve balance and moderation in everything, and to restrain the lower appetites. He who judges matters in the light of divine revelation, assuredly will not overlook the fact that the Gospel of Christ and the Catholic Church, as well as the ascetical tradition handed down to us, all demand that Christians steadfastly mortify themselves and bear the inconveniences of life with singular patience. These virtues, in addition to fostering a firm and moderate rule of mind over body, also present an opportunity of satisfying the punishment due to sin, from which, except for Jesus Christ and His Immaculate Mother, no one is exempt.

PRACTICAL SUGGESTIONS

236.   The teachings in regard to social matters for the most part are put into effect in the following three stages: first, the actual situation is examined; then, the situation is evaluated carefully in relation to these teachings; then only is it decided what can and should be done in order that the traditional norms may be adapted to circumstances of time and place. These three steps are at times expressed by the three words: *observe, judge, act.*

237.   Hence, it seems particularly fitting that youth not merely reflect upon this order of procedure, but also, in the present connection, follow it to the extent feasible, lest what they have learned be regarded merely as something to be thought about but not acted upon.

238.   However, when it comes to reducing these teachings to action, it sometimes happens that even sincere Catholic men have differing views. When this occurs they should take care to have and to show mutual esteem and regard, and to explore the extent to which they can work in cooperation among themselves. Thus they can in good time accomplish what necessity requires. Let them also take great care not to weaken their efforts in constant controversies. Nor should they, under pretext of seeking what they think best, meanwhile, fail to do what they can and hence should do.

239.   But in the exercise of economic and social functions, Catholics often come in contact with men who do not share their view of life. On such occasions, those who profess Catholicism must take special care to be consistent and not compromise in matters wherein the integrity of religion or morals would suffer harm. Likewise, in their conduct they should weigh the opinions of others with fitting courtesy and not measure everything in the light of their own interests. They should be prepared to join sincerely in doing whatever is naturally good or conducive to good. If, indeed, it happens that in these matters sacred authorities have prescribed or decreed anything, it is evident that this judgment is to be obeyed promptly by Catholics. For it is the Church's right and duty not only to safeguard principles relating to the integrity of religion and morals, but also to pronounce authoritatively when it is a matter of putting these principles into effect.

MANIFOLD ACTION AND RESPONSIBILITY

240.   But what we have said about the norms of instruction should indeed be put into practice. This has special relevance for those beloved

sons of ours who are in the ranks of the laity inasmuch as their activity ordinarily centers around temporal affairs and making plans for the same.

241.   To carry out this noble task, it is necessary that laymen not only should be qualified, each in his own profession, and direct their energies in accordance with rules suited to the objective aimed at, but also should conform their activity to the teachings and norms of the Church in social matters. Let them put sincere trust in her wisdom; let them accept her admonitions as sons. Let them reflect that, when in the conduct of life they do not carefully observe principles and norms laid down by the Church in social matters, and which we ourselves reaffirm, then they are negligent in their duty and often injure the rights of others. At times, matters can come to a point where confidence in this teaching is diminished, as if it were indeed excellent but really lacks the force which the conduct of life requires.

A Grave Danger

242.   As we have already noted, in this present age men have searched widely and deeply into the laws of nature. Then they invented instruments whereby they can control the forces of nature; they have perfected and continue to perfect remarkable works worthy of deep admiration. Nevertheless, while they endeavor to master and transform the external world, they are also in danger, lest they become neglectful and weaken the powers of body and mind. This is what our predecessor of happy memory, Pius XI, noted with sorrow of spirit in his Encyclical Letter *Quadragesimo Anno*: "And so bodily labor, which was decreed by divine providence for the good of man's body and soul even after original sin, has too often been changed into an instrument of perversion: for dead matter leaves the factory ennobled and transformed whereas men are there corrupted and degraded."[48]

243.   And our predecessor of happy memory, Pius XII, rightly asserted that our age is distinguished from others precisely by the fact that science and technology have made incalculable progress, while men themselves have departed correspondingly from a sense of dignity. It is a "monstrous masterpiece" of this age "to have transformed man, as it were, into a giant as regards the order of nature, yet in the order of the supernatural and the eternal, to have changed him into a pygmy."[49]

244.   Too often in our day is verified the testimony of the Psalmist concerning worshipers of false gods, namely, human beings in their activity very frequently neglect themselves, but admire their own works

as if these were gods: "Their idols are silver and gold; the handiwork of men."[50]

RESPECT FOR THE HIERARCHY OF VALUES

245.   Wherefore, aroused by the pastoral zeal wherewith we embrace all men, we strongly urge our sons that, in fulfilling their duties and in pursuing their goals, they do not allow their consciousness of responsibilities to grow cool, nor neglect the order of the more important goods.

246.   For it is indeed clear that the Church has always taught and continues to teach that advances in science and technology and the prosperity resulting therefrom, are truly to be counted as good things and regarded as signs of the progress of civilization. But the Church likewise teaches that goods of this kind are to be judged properly in accordance with their natures: they are always to be considered as instruments for man's use, the better to achieve his highest end: that he can the more easily improve himself, in both the natural and supernatural orders.

247.   Wherefore, we ardently desire that our sons should at all times heed the words of the divine Master: "For what does it profit a man, if he gain the whole world, but suffer the loss of his own soul? Or what will a man give in exchange for his soul?"[51]

SANCTIFICATION OF HOLY DAYS

248.   Not unrelated to the above admonitions is the one having to do with rest to be taken on feast days.

249.   In order that the Church may defend the dignity with which man is endowed, because he is created by God and because God has breathed into him a soul to His own image, she has never failed to insist that the third commandment: "Remember to keep holy the Sabbath day,"[52] be carefully observed by all. It is the right of God, and within His power, to order that man put aside a day each week for proper and due worship of the divinity. He should direct his mind to heavenly things, setting aside daily business. He should explore the depths of his conscience in order to know how necessary and inviolable are his relations with God.

250.   In addition, it is right and necessary for man to cease for a time from labor, not merely to relax his body from daily hard work and likewise to refresh himself with decent recreation, but also to foster family unity, for this requires that all its members preserve a community of life and peaceful harmony.

251.   Accordingly, religion, moral teaching, and care of health in turn

require that relaxation be had at regular times. The Catholic Church has decreed for many centuries that Christians observe this day of rest on Sunday, and that they be present on the same day at the Eucharistic Sacrifice because it renews the memory of the divine Redemption and at the same time imparts its fruits to the souls of men.

252.   But we note with deep sorrow, and we cannot but reprove the many who, though they perhaps do not deliberately despise this holy law, yet more and more frequently disregard it. Whence it is that our very dear workingmen almost necessarily suffer harm, both as to the salvation of their souls and to the health of their bodies.

253.   And so, taking into account the needs of soul and body, we exhort, as it were, with the words of God Himself, all men, whether public officials or representatives of management and labor, that they observe this command of God Himself and of the Catholic Church, and judge in their souls that they have a responsibility to God and society in this regard.

Renewed Dedication

254.   From what we have briefly touched upon above, let none of our sons conclude, and especially the laity, that they act prudently if, in regard to the transitory affairs of this life, they become quite remiss in their specific Christian contributions. On the contrary, we reaffirm that they should be daily more zealous in carrying out this role.

255.   Indeed, when Christ our Lord made that solemn prayer for the unity of His Church, He asked this from the Father on behalf of His disciples: "I do not pray that Thou take them out of the world, but that Thou keep them from evil."[53] Let no one imagine that there is any opposition between these two things so that they cannot be properly reconciled: namely, the perfection of one's own soul and the business of this life, as if one had no chance but to abandon the activities of this world in order to strive for Christian perfection, or as if one could not attend to these pursuits without endangering his own dignity as a man and as a Christian.

256.   However, it is in full accord with the designs of God's providence that men develop and perfect themselves by exercise of their daily tasks, for this is the lot of practically everyone in the affairs of this mortal life. Accordingly, the role of the Church in our day is very difficult: to reconcile this modern respect for progress with the norms of humanity

and of the Gospel teaching. Yet, the times call the Church to this role; indeed, we may say, earnestly beseech her, not merely to pursue the higher goals, but also to safeguard her accomplishments without harm to herself. To achieve this, as we have already said, the Church especially asks the cooperation of the laity. For this reason, in their dealings with men, they are bound to exert effort in such a way that while fulfilling their duties to others, they do so in union with God through Christ, for the increase of God's glory. Thus the Apostle Paul asserts: "Whether you eat or drink, or do anything else, do all for the glory of God."[54] And elsewhere: "Whatever you do in word or in work, do all in the name of the Lord Jesus Christ, giving thanks to God the Father through Him."[55]

GREATER EFFECTIVENESS IN TEMPORAL AFFAIRS

257.   As often, therefore, as human activity and institutions having to do with the affairs of this life, help toward spiritual perfection and everlasting beatitude, the more they are to be regarded as an efficacious way of obtaining the immediate end to which they are directed by their very nature. Thus, valid for all times is that noteworthy sentence of the divine Master: "Seek first the kingdom of God and His justice, and all these things shall be given you besides."[56] For he who is, as it were, a *light in the Lord,*[57] and walks as a *son of light,*[58] he perceives more clearly what the requirements of justice are, in the various sectors of human zeal, even in those that involve greater difficulties because of the excessive love which many have for their own interests, or those of their country, or race. It must be added that when one is motivated by Christian charity, he cannot but love others, and regard the needs, sufferings and joys of others as his own. His work, wherever it be, is constant, adaptable, humane, and has concern for the needs of others: For "Charity is patient, is kind; charity does not envy, is not pretentious, is not puffed up, is not ambitious, is not self seeking, is not provoked; thinks no evil, does not rejoice over wickedness, but rejoices with the truth; bears with all things, believes all things, hopes all things, endures all things."[59]

Living Members of the Mystical Body of Christ

258.   But we do not wish to bring this letter of ours to a close, Venerable Brothers, without recalling to your minds that most fundamental and true element of Catholic teaching, whereby we learn that we are living

members of His Mystical Body, which is the Church: "For as the body is one and has many members, and all the members of the body, many as they are, form one body, so also is it with Christ."[60]

259.   Wherefore, we urgently exhort all our sons in every part of the world, whether clergy or laity, that they fully understand how great is the nobility and dignity they derive from being joined to Christ, as branches to the vine, as He Himself said: "I am the vine, you are the branches,"[61] and that they are sharers of His divine life. Whence it is, that if Christians are also joined in mind and heart with the most Holy Redeemer, when they apply themselves to temporal affairs, their work in a way is a continuation of the labor of Jesus Christ Himself, drawing from it strength and redemptive power: "He who abides in Me, and I in him, he bears much fruit."[62] Human labor of this kind is so exalted and ennobled that it leads men engaged in it to spiritual perfection, and can likewise contribute to the diffusion and propagation of the fruits of the Redemption to others. So also it results in the flow of that Gospel leaven, as it were, through the veins of civil society wherein we live and work.

260.   Although it must be admitted that the times in which we live are torn by increasingly serious errors, and are troubled by violent disturbances, yet, it happens that the Church's laborers in this age of ours have access to enormous fields of apostolic endeavor. This inspires us with uncommon hope.

261.   Venerable Brothers and beloved sons, beginning with that marvelous letter of Leo, we have thus far considered with you the varied and serious issues which pertain to the social conditions of our time. From them we have drawn norms and teachings, upon which we especially exhort you not merely to meditate deeply, but also to do what you can to put them into effect. If each one of you does his best courageously, it will necessarily help in no small measure to establish the kingdom of Christ on earth. This is indeed: "A kingdom of truth and of life; a kingdom of holiness and grace; a kingdom of justice, of love and of peace."[63] And this we shall some day leave to go to that heavenly beatitude, for which we were made by God, and which we ask for with most ardent prayers.

262.   For it is a question here of the teaching of the Catholic and Apostolic Church, mother and teacher of all nations, whose light illumines, sets on fire, inflames. Her warning voice, filled with heavenly wisdom, reaches out to every age. Her power always provides efficacious and appropriate remedies for the growing needs of men, for the cares and solicitudes of this mortal life. With this voice, the age-old song of the Psalmist is in marvelous accord, to strengthen at all times and to uplift our souls: "I will hear what God proclaims; the Lord—for He proclaims peace

to His people, and to His faithful ones, and to those who put in Him their hope. Near indeed is His salvation to those who fear Him, glory dwelling in our land. Kindness and truth shall meet; justice and peace shall kiss. Truth shall spring out of the earth, and justice shall look down from heaven. The Lord Himself will give His benefits; our land shall yield its increase. Justice shall walk before Him, and salvation, along the way of His steps."[64]

263.   This is the plea, Venerable Brothers, we make at the close of this Letter, to which we have for a considerable time directed our concern about the Universal Church. We desire that the divine Redeemer of mankind, "who has become for us God-given wisdom, and justice, and sanctification, and redemption"[65] may reign and triumph gloriously in all things and over all things, for centuries on end. We desire that, in a properly organized order of social affairs, all nations will at last enjoy prosperity, and happiness, and peace.

264.   As an evidence of these wishes, and a pledge of our paternal good will, we affectionately bestow in the Lord our apostolic blessing upon you, Venerable Brothers, and upon all the faithful committed to your care, and especially upon those who will reply with generosity to our appeals.

265.   Given at Rome, at Saint Peter's, the fifteenth day of May, in the year 1961, the third year of our Pontificate.

JOHN XXIII, POPE

NOTES

1. Cf. 1 Tim. 3, 15.
2. John 14, 6.
3. John 8, 12.
4. Mark 8, 2.
5. *Acta Leonis XIII*, XI (1891), p. 97–144.
6. *Ibid.*, p. 107.
7. St. Thomas, *De regimine principum*, I, 15.
8. Cf. *Acta Apostolicae Sedis*, XXIII (1931), p. 185.
9. Cf. *Ibid.*, p. 189.
10. *Ibid.*, p. 177–228.
11. Cf. *Ibid.*, p. 199.
12. Cf. *Ibid.*, p. 200.
13. Cf. *Ibid.*, p. 201.
14. Cf. *Ibid.*, p. 210f.
15. Cf. *Ibid.*, p. 211.

200 *Pope John XXIII*

16. Cf. *Acta Apostolicae Sedis*, XXXIII (1941), p. 196.
17. Cf. *Ibid.*, p. 197.
18. Cf. *Ibid.*, p. 196.
19. Cf. *Ibid.*, p. 198f.
20. Cf. *Ibid.*, p. 199.
21. Cf. *Ibid.*, p. 201.
22. Cf. *Ibid.*, p. 202.
23. Cf. *Ibid.*, p. 203.
24. *Acta Apostolicae Sedis*, XXIII (1931), p. 203.
25. *Ibid.*, p. 203.
26. Cf. *Ibid.*, p. 222f.
27. Cf. *Acta Apostolicae Sedis*, XXXIII (1941), p. 200.
28. *Acta Apostolicae Sedis*, XXIII (1931), p. 195.
29. *Ibid.*, p. 198.
30. Radio Broadcast, September 1, 1944; cf. *A.A.S.*, XXXVI (1944), p. 254.
31. Allocution, October 8, 1956; cf. *A.A.S.*, XLVIII (1956), p. 799–800.
32. Radio Broadcast, September 1, 1944; cf. *A.A.S.*, XXXVI (1944), p. 253.
33. Radio Broadcast, December 24, 1942; cf. *A.A.S.*, XXXV (1943), p. 17.
34. Cf. *Ibid.*, p. 20.
35. Encyclical Letter *Quadragesimo Anno; A.A.S.*, XXIII (1931), p. 214.
36. *Acta Leonis XIII*, XI (1891), p. 114.
37. Matt. 6, 19–20.
38. Matt. 25, 40.
39. Cf. *Acta Apostolicae Sedis*, XXIII (1931), p. 202.
40. Allocution, May 3, 1960; cf. *A.A.S.*, LII (1960), p. 465.
41. Cf. *Ibid.*
42. 1 John 3, 16–17.
43. Encyclical Letter *Summi Pontificatus; A.A.S.*, XXXI (1939), p. 428–29.
44. Gen., 1, 28.
45. *Ibid.*
46. *Confessions*, I, 1.
47. Ps. 126, 1.
48. *Acta Apostolicae Sedis*, XXIII (1931), p. 221f.
49. Radio Broadcast, Christmas Eve, 1953; cf. *A.A.S.*, XLVI (1954), p. 10.
50. Ps. 113, 4.
51. Matt. 16, 26.
52. Exod. 20, 8.
53. John 17, 15.
54. I Cor. 10, 31.
55. Col. 3, 17.
56. Matt. 6, 33.
57. Eph. 5, 8.
58. Cf. *Ibid.*
59. I Cor. 13, 4–7.
60. I Cor. 12, 12.
61. John 15, 5.
62. *Ibid.*
63. *Preface of Jesus Christ the King.*
64. Ps. 84, 9ff.
65. I Cor. 1, 30.

Pacem in Terris

Peace on Earth
(April 11, 1963)

To Our Venerable Brothers,
the Patriarchs, Primates,
Archbishops, Bishops
and Other Local Ordinaries
in Peace and Communion
with the Apostolic See,
to the Clergy
and Faithful of the Whole World:

Pope John XXIII
VENERABLE BROTHERS AND BELOVED CHILDREN:
HEALTH AND APOSTOLIC BENEDICTION

Introduction

ORDER IN THE UNIVERSE

1.   Peace on earth, which men of every era have most eagerly yearned for, can be firmly established only if the order laid down by God is dutifully observed.

[The official Latin text is found in A.A.S. LV (April 20, 1963), no. 5, pp. 257–304. The English version given here was published by the America Press, New York, 1963. The editor,

2.   The progress of learning and the inventions of technology clearly show that, both in living things and in the forces of nature, an astonishing order reigns, and they also bear witness to the greatness of man, who can understand that order and create suitable instruments to harness those forces of nature and use them to his benefit.

3.   But the progress of science and the inventions of technology show above all the infinite greatness of God, who created the universe and man himself. He created all things out of nothing, pouring into them the abundance of His wisdom and goodness, so that the holy psalmist praises God in these words: "O Lord, our Lord, how glorious is your name over all the earth."[1] Elsewhere he says: "How manifold are your works, O Lord! In wisdom you have wrought them all."[2]

God also created man in His own "image and likeness,"[3] endowed him with intelligence and freedom, and made him lord of creation, as the same psalmist declares in the words: "You have made him little less than the angels, and crowned him with glory and honor. You have given him rule over the works of your hands, putting all things under his feet."[4]

ORDER IN HUMAN BEINGS

4.   How strongly does the turmoil of individual men and peoples contrast with the perfect order of the universe! It is as if the relationships which bind them together could be controlled only by force.

5.   But the Creator of the world has imprinted in man's heart an order which his conscience reveals to him and enjoins him to obey: "They show the work of the Law written in their hearts. Their conscience bears witness to them."[5]

And how could it be otherwise? For whatever God has made shows forth His infinite wisdom, and it is manifested more clearly in the things which have greater perfection.[6]

6.   But fickleness of opinion often produces this error, that many think that the relationships between men and states can be governed by the same laws as the forces and irrational elements of the universe, whereas the laws governing them are of quite a different kind and are to be sought

Donald R. Campion, S.J., states that this "text of the English version of *Pacem in Terris* is substantially that released by the Vatican Press Office on April 10, 1963. It has been reviewed and collated with the official Latin text. Constant reference to the Italian version proved most helpful in this task. . . . The paragraph numbering conforms to the almost universally adopted practice of basing divisions on the paragraphing in the official Latin text. Section and subsection headings are taken from the modern-language versions furnished by the Vatican."]

elsewhere, namely, where the Father of all things wrote them, that is, in the nature of man.

7.   By these laws, men are most admirably taught, first of all, how they should conduct their mutual dealings among themselves; next, how the relationships between the citizens and the public authorities of each state should be regulated; then, how states should deal with one another; finally, how, on the one hand individual men and states, and on the other hand the community of all peoples, should act toward each other, the establishment of such a world community of peoples being urgently demanded today by the requirements of universal common good.

PART I:

Order Among Men

8.   First of all, it is necessary to speak of the order which should exist among men.

9.   Any human society, if it is to be well-ordered and productive, must lay down as a foundation this principle, namely, that every human being is a person, that is, his nature is endowed with intelligence and free will. By virtue of this, he has rights and duties of his own, flowing directly and simultaneously from his very nature. These rights are therefore universal, inviolable and inalienable.[7]

10.   If we look upon the dignity of the human person in the light of divinely revealed truth, we cannot help but esteem it far more highly. For men are redeemed by the blood of Jesus Christ. They are by grace the children and friends of God and heirs of eternal glory.

Rights

11.   Beginning our discussion of the rights of man, we see that every man has the right to life, to bodily integrity, and to the means which are necessary and suitable for the proper development of life. These means are primarily food, clothing, shelter, rest, medical care, and finally the necessary social services. Therefore, a human being also has the right to security in cases of sickness, inability to work, widowhood, old age, unemployment, or in any other case in which he is deprived of the means of subsistence through no fault of his own.[8]

204 Pope John XXIII

RIGHTS PERTAINING TO MORAL AND CULTURAL VALUES

12.   By the natural law, every human being has the right to respect for his person, to his good reputation, to freedom in searching for truth and—within the limits laid down by the moral order and the common good—in expressing and communicating his opinions, and in pursuit of art. He has the right, finally, to be informed truthfully about public events.

13.   The natural law also gives man the right to share in the benefits of culture, and therefore the right to a basic education or to technical or professional training in keeping with the stage of educational development in the country to which he belongs. Every effort should be made to insure that persons be enabled, on the basis of merit, to go on to higher studies, so that, as far as possible, they may occupy posts and take on responsibilities in human society in accordance with their natural gifts and the skills they have acquired.[9]

RIGHT TO WORSHIP GOD ACCORDING TO CONSCIENCE

14.   Every human being has the right to honor God according to the dictates of an upright conscience, and the right to profess his religion privately and publicly. For, as Lactantius so clearly taught: "We were created for the purpose of showing to the God who bore us the due submission we owe Him, of recognizing Him alone, and of serving Him. We are obliged and bound by this duty to God; from this, religion itself receives its name."[10]

And on this point Our predecessor of immortal memory, Leo XIII, declared: "This genuine, this honorable freedom of the sons of God, which most nobly protects the dignity of the human person, is greater than any violence or injustice; it has always been sought by the Church, and always most dear to her. This was the freedom which the Apostles claimed with intrepid constancy, which the apologists defended with their writings, and which the martyrs in such numbers consecrated with their blood."[11]

RIGHT TO CHOOSE FREELY ONE'S STATE OF LIFE

15.   Human beings have, in addition, the right to choose freely the state of life which they prefer. They therefore have the right to set up a family, with equal rights and duties for man and woman, and also the right to follow a vocation to the priesthood or the religious life.[12]

16.   The family, grounded on marriage freely contracted, monog-

amous and indissoluble, must be considered the first and essential cell of human society. To it must be given, therefore, every consideration of an economic, social, cultural and moral nature which will strengthen its stability and facilitate the fulfillment of its specific mission.

17.   Parents, however, have a prior right in the support and education of their children. [13]

ECONOMIC RIGHTS

18.   When we turn to the economic sphere, it is clear that human beings have the natural right to free initiative in the economic field and the right to work. [14]

19.   Indissolubly linked with those rights is the right to working conditions in which physical health is not endangered, morals are safeguarded and young people's normal development is not impaired. Women have the right to working conditions in accordance with their requirements and their duties as wives and mothers. [15]

20.   From the dignity of the human person there also arises the right to carry on economic activities according to the degree of responsibility of which one is capable. [16] Furthermore—and this must be specially emphasized—there is the worker's right to a wage determined according to criteria of justice. This means, therefore, one sufficient, in proportion to the available resources, to give the worker and his family a standard of living in keeping with human dignity. In this regard, Our predecessor Pius XII said: "To the personal duty to work imposed by nature, there corresponds and follows the natural right of each individual to make of his work the means to provide for his own life and the lives of his children; so profoundly is the empire of nature ordained for the preservation of man." [17]

21.   The right to private property, even of productive goods, also derives from the nature of man. This right, as We have elsewhere declared, "is a suitable means for safeguarding the dignity of the human person and for the exercise of responsibility in all fields; it strengthens and gives serenity to family life, thereby increasing the peace and prosperity of the state." [18]

22.   However, it is opportune to point out that there is a social duty inherent in the right of private property. [19]

RIGHT OF ASSEMBLY AND ASSOCIATION

23.   From the fact that human beings are by nature social, there arises the right of assembly and association. They have also the right to give the

societies of which they are members the form they consider most suitable for the aim they have in view, and to act within such societies on their own initiative and responsibility in order to achieve their desired objectives.[20]

24.   We Ourselves strongly cautioned in the encyclical *Mater et Magistra* that, for the achievement of ends which individual human beings cannot attain except by association, it is necessary and indispensable to set up a great variety of intermediate groups and bodies in order to guarantee the dignity of the human person and safeguard a sufficient sphere of freedom and responsibility.[21]

RIGHT TO EMIGRATE AND IMMIGRATE

25.   Every human being must also have the right to freedom of movement and of residence within the confines of his own country, and, when there are just reasons for it, the right to emigrate to other countries and take up residence there.[22] The fact that one is a citizen of a particular state does not detract in any way from his membership in the human family, nor from his citizenship in the world community and his common tie with all men.

POLITICAL RIGHTS

26.   The dignity of the human person involves, moreover, the right to take an active part in public affairs and to contribute one's part to the common good of the citizens. For, as Our predecessor of happy memory, Pius XII, pointed out: "The human individual, far from being an object and, as it were, a merely passive element in the social order, is in fact, must be and must continue to be, its subject, its foundation and its end."[23]

27.   The human person is also entitled to a juridical protection of his rights, a protection that should be efficacious, impartial and in conformity with true norms of justice.

As Our predecessor Pius XII warns: "That perpetual privilege proper to man, by which every individual has a claim to the protection of his rights, and by which there is assigned to each a definite and particular sphere of rights, immune from all arbitrary attacks, is the logical consequence of the order of justice willed by God."[24]

Duties

RIGHTS AND DUTIES LINKED IN THE ONE PERSON

28.   The natural rights with which We have been dealing are, however, inseparably connected, in the very person who is their subject, with just as many respective duties. And rights as well as duties find their source, their sustenance and their inviolability in the natural law which grants or enjoins them.

29.   For example, the right of every man to life is correlative with the duty to preserve it; his right to a decent standard of living, with the duty of living it becomingly; and his right to investigate the truth freely, with the duty of pursuing it ever more completely and profoundly.

RECIPROCITY OF RIGHTS AND DUTIES BETWEEN PERSONS

30.   Once this is admitted, it is also clear that in human society to one man's natural right there corresponds a duty in other persons: the duty, namely, of acknowledging and respecting the right in question. For every fundamental human right draws its indestructible moral force from the natural law, which, in granting it, imposes a corresponding obligation. Those, therefore, who claim their own rights, yet altogether forget or neglect to carry out their respective duties, are people who build with one hand and destroy with the other.

31.   Since men are social by nature, they are meant to live with others and to work for one another's welfare. Hence, a well-ordered human society requires that men recognize and observe their mutual rights and duties. It also demands that each contribute generously to the establishment of a civic order in which rights and duties are progressively more sincerely and effectively acknowledged and fulfilled.

32.   It is not enough, for example, to acknowledge and respect every man's right to the means of subsistence. One must also strive to insure that he actually has enough in the way of food and nourishment.

33.   The society of men must not only be organized but must also provide them with abundant resources. This, certainly, requires that they recognize and fulfill their mutual rights and duties. It also requires that they all collaborate in the many enterprises that modern civilization either allows or encourages or even demands.

AN ATTITUDE OF RESPONSIBILITY

34.   The dignity of the human person also requires that every man enjoy the right to act freely and responsibly. For this reason, in social relations especially man should exercise his rights, fulfill his obligations and, in the countless forms of collaboration with others, act chiefly on his own responsibility and initiative. This is to be done in such a way that each one acts on his own decision, of set purpose and from a consciousness of his obligation, without being moved by force or pressure brought to bear on him externally.

For any human society that is established on the sole basis of force must be regarded as simply inhuman, inasmuch as the freedom of its members is repressed, when in fact they should be provided with appropriate incentives and means for developing and perfecting themselves.

SOCIAL LIFE IN TRUTH, JUSTICE, CHARITY, FREEDOM

35.   A political society is to be considered well-ordered, beneficial and in keeping with human dignity if it is grounded on truth. As the Apostle Paul exhorts us: "Wherefore, put away lying and speak truth each one with his neighbor, because we are members of one another."[25] This indeed will be the outcome when reciprocal rights and duties are sincerely recognized.

Furthermore, human society will be such as We have just described it, if the citizens, guided by justice, apply themselves seriously to respecting the rights of others and discharging their own duties; if they are moved by such fervor of charity as to make their own the needs of others, and share with others their own goods; if, finally, they everywhere work for a progressively closer fellowship in the world of spiritual values. Moreover, human society is realized in freedom, that is to say, by ways and means in keeping with the dignity of its citizens, who accept the responsibility of their actions precisely because they are by nature rational beings.

36.   Human society, venerable brothers and beloved children, ought to be regarded above all as a spiritual reality; one in which men communicate knowledge to each other in the light of truth; in which they can enjoy their rights and fulfill their duties, and are inspired to strive for goods of the spirit. Society should enable men to share in and enjoy every legitimate expression of beauty. It should encourage them constantly to pass on to others all that is best in themselves, while they strive to make their

own the spiritual achievements of others. These are the values which continually give life and basic orientation to cultural expressions, economic and social institutions, political movements and forms, laws and all other structures by which society is outwardly established and constantly developed.

37.   The order which prevails in society is by nature moral. Grounded as it is in truth, it must function according to the norms of justice, it should be inspired and perfected by mutual love, and finally it should be brought to an ever more refined and human balance in full freedom.

38.   Now an order of this kind, whose principles are universal, absolute and unchangeable, has its ultimate source in the one true God, who is personal and transcends human nature. Inasmuch as God is the first truth and the highest good, He alone is that deepest source from which human society can draw its vitality, if that society is to be well ordered, beneficial and in keeping with human dignity.[26]

As St. Thomas Aquinas says: "Human reason is the norm of the human will, according to which its goodness is measured, because reason derives from the eternal law which is the divine reason itself. . . . It is evident, then, that the goodness of the human will depends much more on the external law than on human reason."[27]

Signs of the Times

39.   Our age has three distinctive characteristics.

40.   First of all, we note that the working classes have gradually gained ground in economic and public affairs. They began by claiming their rights in the socio-economic sphere. They extended their action then to claims on the political level. And, finally, they applied themselves to the acquisition of the benefits of a more refined culture. Today, therefore, workers all over the world bluntly refuse ever to be treated as if they were irrational objects without freedom, to be used at the arbitrary disposition of others. They insist that they be regarded as men with a share in every sector of human society: in the socio-economic sphere and in public life and in the fields of learning and culture.

41.   Secondly, it is obvious to everyone that women are now taking a part in public life. This is happening more rapidly perhaps in nations with a Christian tradition, and more slowly, but broadly, among peoples who have inherited other traditions or cultures. Since women are becoming ever more conscious of their human dignity, they will not tolerate being

treated as inanimate objects or mere instruments, but claim, both in domestic and in public life, the rights and duties that befit a human person.

42.   Finally, the modern world, as compared with the recent past, has taken on an entirely new appearance in the field of social and political life. For since all peoples have either achieved, or are on the way to achieving, independence, there will soon no longer exist a world divided into peoples who rule others and peoples who are subject to others.

43.   Men all over the world have today—or will soon have—the rank of citizens in independent nations. No one wants to feel subject to political power located outside his own country or ethnic group. Thus, in our day, in very many human beings the inferiority complex which endured for hundreds and thousands of years is disappearing, while in others there is an attenuation and gradual fading of the corresponding superiority complex which had its roots in socio-economic privileges, sex or political standing.

44.   On the contrary, the conviction that all men are equal by reason of their natural dignity has been generally accepted. Hence, racial discrimination can in no way be justified, at least doctrinally or in theory. And this is of fundamental importance and significance for the formation of human society according to those principles which We have outlined above. For, if a man becomes conscious of his rights, he must become equally aware of his duties. Thus, he who possesses certain rights has likewise the duty to claim those rights as marks of his dignity, while all others have the obligation to acknowledge those rights and respect them.

45.   When the relations of human society are expressed in terms of rights and duties, men become conscious of spiritual values and understand the meaning and significance of truth, justice, charity and freedom. They become deeply aware that they belong to this world of values. Moreover, when moved by such concerns, they are brought to a better knowledge of the true God, who is personal and transcendent. Thus they make the ties that bind them to God the solid foundation of their lives, both of that life which they live interiorly in the depths of their own souls and of that in which they are united to other men in society.

PART II:

Relations Between Individuals and
Public Authorities Within a Single State

Necessity and Divine Origin of Authority

46.   Human society can be neither well-ordered nor prosperous unless it has some people invested with legitimate authority to preserve its institutions and to devote themselves as far as is necessary to work and care for the good of all.

These, however, derive their authority from God, as St. Paul teaches in the words: "There exists no authority except from God."[28] These words of St. Paul are explained thus by St. John Chrysostom: "What are you saying? Is every ruler appointed by God? I do not say that, he replies, for I am not dealing now with individual rulers, but with authority itself. What I say is, that it is the divine wisdom, and not mere chance, that has ordained that there should be government, that some should command and others obey."[29]

Moreover, since God made men social by nature, and since no society "can hold together unless some one be over all, directing all to strive earnestly for the common good, every civilized community must have a ruling authority, and this authority, no less than society itself, has its source in nature, and has, consequently, God for its author."[30]

47.   But authority is not to be thought of as a force lacking all control. Indeed, since it is the power to command according to right reason, authority must derive its obligatory force from the moral order, which in turn has God for its first source and final end. Wherefore Our predecessor of happy memory, Pius XII, said: "That same absolute order of beings and their ends which presents man as an autonomous person, that is, as the subject of inviolable duties and rights, and as at once the basis of society and the purpose for which it exists, also includes the state as a necessary society invested with the authority without which it could not come into being or live. . . . And since this absolute order—as we learn from sound reason, and especially from the Christian faith—can have no origin save in a personal God who is our Creator, it follows that the dignity of the state's authority is due to its sharing to some extent in the authority of God Himself."[31]

48.　　Where the civil authority uses as its only, or its chief, means either threats and fear of punishment or promises of rewards, it cannot effectively move men to promote the common good of all. Even if it did so move them, this would be altogether opposed to their dignity as men endowed with reason and free will.

Since authority is chiefly concerned with moral force, it follows that civil authority must appeal primarily to the conscience of individual citizens, that is, to each one's duty to collaborate readily for the common good of all. Since by nature all men are equal in human dignity, it follows that no one may be coerced to perform interior acts. That is in the power of God alone, who sees and judges the hidden designs of men's hearts.

49.　　Those, therefore, who have authority in the state may oblige men in conscience only if their authority is intrinsically related with the authority of God and shares in it.[32]

50.　　By this principle the dignity of the citizens is protected. When, in fact, men obey their rulers, it is not at all as men that they obey them. It is God, the provident Creator of all things, whom they reverence through their obedience, since He has decreed that men's dealings with one another should be regulated by an order which He Himself has established. Moreover, in showing this due reverence to God, we not only do not debase ourselves, but rather perfect and ennoble ourselves. For "to serve God is to rule."[33]

51.　　Since the right to command is required by the moral order and has its source in God, it follows that if civil authorities legislate for, or allow, anything that is contrary to that order and therefore contrary to the will of God, neither the laws made nor the authorizations granted can be binding on the consciences of the citizens, since "we must obey God rather than men."[34]

Otherwise, authority breaks down completely and results in shameful abuse. As St. Thomas Aquinas teaches: "Human law has the true nature of law only insofar as it corresponds to right reason, and therefore is derived from the eternal law. Insofar as it falls short of right reason, a law is said to be a wicked law; and so, lacking the true nature of law, it is rather a kind of violence."[35]

52.　　It must not be concluded, however, that, because authority comes from God, men therefore have no right to choose who are to rule the state, to decide the form of government, and to determine both the way in which authority is to be exercised and its limits. It is thus clear that the doctrine which We have set forth is fully consonant with any truly democratic regime.[36]

Attainment of the Common Good

PURPOSE OF THE PUBLIC AUTHORITY

53.   Individual citizens and intermediate groups are obliged to make their specific contributions to the common welfare. One of the chief consequences of this is that they must bring their own interests into harmony with the needs of the community, and must dispose of their goods and services as civil authorities have prescribed, in accord with the norms of justice, in due process, and within the limits of their competence. This they must do by means of formally perfect actions, the content of which must serve the civil good, or at least be capable of being directed toward that good.

54.   Indeed, since the whole reason for the existence of civil authorities is the realization of the common good, it is clearly necessary that in pursuing this objective they should respect its essential elements, and at the same time conform their laws to the needs of a given historical situation.[37]

ESSENTIALS OF THE COMMON GOOD

55.   Assuredly, the ethnic characteristics of the various human groups are to be respected as constituent elements of the common good.[38] But these characteristics by no means exhaust the content of the common good. For the common good is intimately bound up with human nature. It can never exist fully and completely unless, its intimate nature and realization being what they are, the human person is taken into account.[39]

56.   In the second place, the very nature of the common good requires that all members of the political community be entitled to share in it, although in different ways according to each one's tasks, merits and circumstances. For this reason, every civil authority must take pains to promote the common good of all without preference for any single citizen or civic group.

As Our predecessor of immortal memory, Leo XIII, has said: "The civil power must not serve the advantage of any one individual, or of some few persons, inasmuch as it was established for the common good of all."[40]

Considerations of justice and equity, however, can at times demand that those involved in civil government give more attention to the less fortunate members of the community, since they are less able to defend their rights and to assert their legitimate claims.[41]

57.   In this context, We judge that attention should be called to the fact that the common good touches the whole man, the needs both of his body and of his soul. Hence it follows that the civil authorities must undertake to effect the common good by ways and means that are proper to them. That is, while respecting the hierarchy of values, they should promote simultaneously both the material and the spiritual welfare of the citizens.[42]

58.   These principles are clearly contained in the doctrine stated in Our encyclical *Mater et Magistra,* where We emphasized that the common good of all "embraces the sum total of those conditions of social living whereby men are enabled to achieve their own integral perfection more fully and more easily."[43]

59.   Men, however, composed as they are of bodies and immortal souls, can never in this mortal life succeed in satisfying all their needs or in attaining perfect happiness. Therefore all efforts made to promote the common good, far from endangering the eternal salvation of men, ought rather to serve to advance it.[44]

RESPONSIBILITIES OF THE PUBLIC AUTHORITY
AND RIGHTS AND DUTIES OF INDIVIDUALS

60.   It is agreed that in our time the common good is chiefly guaranteed when personal rights and duties are maintained. The chief concern of civil authorities must therefore be to insure that these rights are acknowledged, respected, co-ordinated with other rights, defended and promoted, so that in this way each one may more easily carry out his duties. For "to safeguard the inviolable rights of the human person, and to facilitate the fulfilment of his duties, should be the essential office of every public authority."[45]

61.   This means that if any government does not acknowledge the rights of man or violates them, it not only fails in its duty, but its orders completely lack juridical force.[46]

62.   One of the fundamental duties of civil authorities, therefore, is so to co-ordinate and regulate social relations that the exercise of one man's rights does not threaten others in the exercise of their own rights nor hinder them in the fulfilment of their duties. Finally, the rights of all should be effectively safeguarded and, if they have been violated, completely restored.[47]

DUTY OF PROMOTING THE RIGHTS OF INDIVIDUALS

63.   The common good also demands that civil authorities should make earnest efforts to bring about a situation in which individual citizens can easily exercise their rights and fulfill their duties. For experience has taught us that, unless these authorities take suitable action with regard to economic, political and cultural matters, inequalities between citizens tend, today more than ever, to become more and more widespread; as a result, human rights are denied and the fulfillment of duties is compromised.

64.   It is therefore necessary that the administration give wholehearted and careful attention to the social as well as to the economic progress of citizens, and to the development, in keeping with the development of the productive system, of such essential services as the building of roads, transportation, communications, water supply, housing, public health, education, facilitation of the practice of religion, and recreational facilities. It is necessary also that governments make efforts to see that insurance systems are made available to the citizens, so that, in case of misfortune or increased family responsibilities, no person will be without the necessary means to maintain a decent standard of living.

The government should make similarly effective efforts to see that those who are able to work can find employment in keeping with their aptitudes, and that each worker receives a wage in keeping with the laws of justice and equity. It should be equally the concern of civil authorities to insure that workers be allowed their proper responsibility in the work undertaken in industrial organization, and to facilitate the establishment of intermediate groups which will make social life richer and more effective. Finally, it should be possible for all the citizens to share as far as they are able in their country's cultural advantages.

65.   The common good requires that civil authorities maintain a careful balance between co-ordinating and protecting the rights of the citizens, on the one hand, and promoting them, on the other. It should not happen that certain individuals or social groups derive special advantage from the fact that their rights have received preferential protection. Nor should it happen that governments, in seeking to protect these rights, become obstacles to their full expression and free use.

"For this principle must always be retained: that state activity in the economic field, no matter what its breadth or depth may be, ought not to be exercised in such a way as to curtail an individual's freedom of personal initiative. Rather it should work to expand that freedom as much as possible by the effective protection of the essential personal rights of each and every individual."[48]

66.   The same principle should inspire the various steps which governments take in order to make it possible for citizens more easily to exercise their rights and fulfill their duties in every sector of social life.

Structure and Operation of Public Authority

67.   It is impossible to determine, once and for all, what is the most suitable form of government, or how civil authorities can most effectively fulfill their respective functions, i.e., the legislative, judicial and executive functions of the state.

68.   In determining the structure and operation of government which a state is to have, great weight has to be given to the historical background and circumstances of given political communities, circumstances which will vary at different times and in different places.

We consider, however, that it is in keeping with the innate demands of human nature that the state should take a form which embodies the threefold division of powers corresponding to the three principal functions of public authority. In that type of state, not only the official functions of government but also the mutual relations between citizens and public officials are set down according to law, which in itself affords protection to the citizens both in the enjoyment of rights and in the fulfilment of duties.

69.   If, however, this political and juridical structure is to produce the advantages which may be expected of it, public officials must strive to meet the problems which arise in a way that conforms both to the complexities of the situation and the proper exercise of their function. This requires that, in constantly changing conditions, legislators never forget the norms of morality or constitutional provisions or the objective requirements of the common good.

Moreover, executive authorities must co-ordinate the activities of society with discretion, with a full knowledge of the law and after a careful consideration of circumstances. And the courts must administer justice impartially and without being influenced by favoritism or pressure. The good order of society also demands that individual citizens and intermediate organizations should be effectively protected by law whenever they have rights to be exercised or obligations to be fulfilled. This protection should be granted to citizens both in their dealings with each other and in their relations with government agencies.[49]

LAW AND CONSCIENCE

70.　It is unquestionable that a juridical structure of government in conformity with the moral order and corresponding to the level of development of the political community is of great advantage to achievement of the common good.

71.　And yet, social life in the modern world is so varied, complex and dynamic that even a juridical structure which has been prudently and thoughtfully established seems inadequate again and again for the needs of society.

72.　It is also true that the relations of citizens with each other, of citizens and intermediate groups with public authorities, and finally of the public authorities with one another are often so complex and so sensitive that they cannot be regulated by inflexible legal provisions. Such a situation therefore demands that the civil authorities have clear ideas about the nature and extent of their official duties if they wish to maintain the existing juridical structure in its basic elements and principles, and at the same time meet the exigencies of social life, adapting their legislation to the changing social scene and solving new problems. They must be men of great equilibrium and integrity, competent and courageous enough to see at once what the situation requires and to take necessary action quickly and effectively.[50]

CITIZENS' PARTICIPATION IN PUBLIC LIFE

73.　It is in keeping with their dignity as persons that human beings should take an active part in government, although the manner in which they share in it will depend on the level of development of the political community to which they belong.

74.　Men will find new and extensive advantages in the fact that they are allowed to participate in government. In this situation, those who administer the government come into frequent contact with the citizens, and it is thus easier for them to learn what is really needed for the common good. The fact, too, that ministers of government hold office only for a limited time keeps them from growing stale and allows for their replacement in accordance with the demands of social progress.[51]

Signs of the Times

75.　In modern times, where there is a question of organizing political communities juridically, there is observable first of all the tendency to write in concise and limpid phraseology a character of fundamental human rights, which is, as often as not, inserted in the states' constitutions as an integral part of them.

76.   Secondly, there is also an inclination to determine, by the compilation of a document called the constitution, the procedures through which the governing powers are to be designated, along with their mutual relations, the spheres of their competence, the forms and systems they are obliged to follow in the performance of their office.

77.   The relations between the government and the governed are then set forth in terms of rights and duties. And it is clearly laid down that the paramount task assigned to government officials is that of recognizing, respecting, reconciling, protecting and promoting the rights and duties of citizens.

78.   It is of course impossible to accept the theory which professes to find the original and single source of civic rights and duties, of the binding force of the constitution, and of a government's right to command, in the mere will of human beings, individually or collectively.[52]

79.   The tendencies to which We have referred, however, do clearly show that the men of our time have become increasingly conscious of their dignity as human persons. This awareness prompts them to claim a share in the public administration of their country, while it also accounts for the demand that their own inalienable and inviolable rights be protected by law. It also requires that government officials be chosen in conformity with constitutional procedures and perform their specific functions within the limits of law.

PART III:

Relations Between States

SUBJECTS OF RIGHTS AND DUTIES

80.   Our predecessors have constantly maintained, and We join them in reasserting, that political communities are reciprocally subjects of rights and duties. This means that their relationships also must be harmonized in truth, in justice, in an active solidarity and in freedom. The same moral law which governs relations between individual human

beings serves also to regulate the relations of political communities with one another.

81.   This will be readily understood when one reflects that the individual representatives of political communities cannot put aside their personal dignity while they are acting in the name and interest of their countries; and that they cannot therefore violate the very law of their being, which is the moral law.

82.   It would be absurd, moreover, even to imagine that men could surrender their own human attributes, or be compelled to do so, by the fact of their appointment to public office. On the contrary, they have been given that noble assignment precisely because the wealth of their human endowments has earned them their reputation as outstanding members of the body politic.

83.   Furthermore, authority is a necessary requirement of the moral order in human society. It may not therefore be used against that order; the very instant such an attempt were made, it would cease to be authority, as the Lord has warned us: "Hear, therefore, kings, and understand; learn, you magistrates of the earth's expanse! Hearken, you who rule the multitude and lord it over throngs of peoples! Because authority was given you by the Lord and sovereignty by the Most High, who shall probe your works and scrutinize your counsels!"[53]

84.   Lastly, it is to be borne in mind that also in the regulating of relations between political communities, authority is to be exercised for the achievement of the common good, which constitutes the reason for its existence.

85.   But a fundamental factor of the common good is acknowledgment of the moral order and respect for its prescriptions.

"Order between political communities must be built upon the unshakable and unchangeable rock of the moral law, made manifest in the order of nature by the Creator Himself and by Him engraved on the hearts of men with letters that may never be effaced. . . . Like the rays of a gleaming beacon, its principles must guide the plans and policies of men and nations. These are the signals—of warning, safety and smooth sailing—they will have to heed, if they would not see all their laborious efforts to establish a new order condemned to tempest and shipwreck."[54]

In Truth

86.   First among the rules governing the relations between states is that of truth. This calls, above all, for the elimination of every trace of

racism, and the consequent recognition of the principle that all states are by nature equal in dignity. Each of them, accordingly, is vested with the right to existence, to self-development and the means fitting to its attainment, and to be the one primarily responsible for this self-development. Add to that the right of each to its good name and to the respect which is its due.

87.   Very often, experience has taught us, individuals will be found to differ considerably in knowledge, virtue, talent and wealth. Yet these inequalities must never be held to excuse any man's attempt to lord it over his neighbors. They constitute rather a source of greater responsibility in the contribution which each and every one must make toward mutual improvement.

88.   Similarly, political communities may have reached different levels of culture, civilization or economic development. But that is not a sufficient reason for some to take unjust advantage of their superiority over others. Rather should they see in it an added motive for more serious commitment to the common cause of social progress.

ALL NATIONS EQUAL IN DIGNITY

89.   It is not true that some human beings are by nature superior and others inferior. All men are equal in their natural dignity. Consequently, there are no political communities which are superior by nature, and none which are inferior by nature. All political communities are of equal natural dignity, since they are bodies whose membership is made up of these same human beings. Nor must it be forgotten, in this connection, that peoples can be highly sensitive, and with good reason, in matters touching their dignity and honor.

90.   Truth further demands that the various media of social communications made available by modern progress, which enable nations to know each other better, be used with serene objectivity. That need not, of course, rule out any legitimate emphasis on the positive aspects of their way of life. But those methods of information must be discarded which fall short of meeting the demands of truth and justice and, by the same token, impair the reputation of this people or that.[55]

In Justice

91.   Relations between political communities are, in addition, to be regulated by justice. This implies, over and above recognition of their mutual rights, the fulfillment of their respective duties.

92.   Political communities have the right to existence, to self-development and to the means necessary for this. They have the right to play the leading part in the process of their own development and the right to their good name and due honors. From which it follows that they have also the corresponding duty of respecting these rights in others and of avoiding any act of violation. Just as an individual man may not pursue his own interests to the detriment of other men, so, on the international level, one state may not develop itself by restricting or oppressing other states. St. Augustine rightly says: "What are kingdoms without justice but bands of robbers?"[56]

93.   Not only can it happen, but it actually does happen, that the advantages and conveniences which nations strive to acquire for themselves become objects of contention. Nevertheless, the resulting disagreements must be settled, not by force, nor by deceit or trickery, but rather in the only manner which is worthy of the dignity of man, i.e., by a mutual assessment of the reasons on both sides of the dispute, by a mature and objective investigation of the situation, and by an equitable reconciliation of differences of opinion.

TREATMENT OF MINORITIES

94.   Since the 19th century there has been a rather widespread tendency in historical evolution for political communities to equate themselves with national communities. For various reasons, however, it has not always been possible to make geographical boundaries coincide with ethnic ones. This gives rise to the phenomenon of minorities and to related complex problems.

95.   In the first place, it must be made clear that justice is seriously violated by whatever is done to limit the strength and numerical increase of these minority peoples. The injustice is more serious if such sinful projects are aimed at the very extinction of these groups.

96.   On the other hand, the demands of justice are admirably observed by those civil authorities who promote the natural betterment of those citizens belonging to a minority ethnic group, particularly when that concerns their language, the development of their natural gifts, their ancestral customs, and their accomplishments and endeavors in the economic order.[57]

97.   It should be noted, however, that these minority groups either because of a reaction to their present situation or because of historical difficulties, are often inclined to exalt beyond due measure anything

proper to their own people, so as to place them even above human values, as if that which is proper to humanity were to be at the service of that which is proper to the nation.

Reason rather demands that these very people recognize also the advantages that accrue to them from their peculiar circumstances. For instance, no small contribution is made toward the development of their particular talents and spirit by daily dealings with people who have grown up in a different culture. Through these dealings they can gradually enhance their own vigor and fiber with the good qualities of the others. This, however, will be true only if they know how to act as a bridge, which facilitates the circulation of life in its various expressions among different traditions or civilizations, and not a zone of discord which can cause great damage and choke national development.

In Active Solidarity

98.   Certainly relations between states must be regulated by the norms of truth and justice, but they also derive great benefits from active solidarity. This solidarity can be achieved through mutual co-operation on various levels, such as, in our own times, has already taken place with laudable results in the economic, social, political, educational, health and sport spheres. We must remember that, of its very nature, civil authority exists, not to confine its people within the boundaries of their nation, but rather to protect, above all else, the common good of that particular civil society, which certainly cannot be divorced from the common good of the entire human family.

99.   This entails not only that civil societies should pursue their particular interests without hurting others, but also that they should join forces and plans whenever the efforts of an individual government cannot achieve its desired goals. But in the execution of such common efforts, great care must be taken lest what helps some nations should injure others.

100.   Furthermore, the universal common good requires that in every nation friendly relations be fostered in all fields between the citizens and their intermediate societies.

There are, in many lands, groupings of people of more or less different racial backgrounds. However, the elements which characterize an ethnic group must not be transformed into a water-tight compartment in which human beings are prevented from communicating with their fellow men of other ethnic groups. That would contrast with our contemporary situation, in which the distances separating peoples have been almost wiped out. Nor can one overlook the fact that, even though human beings differ from one another by virtue of their ethnic peculiarities, they all possess certain essential common elements and are inclined by nature to meet each other in the world of spiritual values, whose progressive assimilation opens to them the possibility of perfection without limits. They have the right and duty, therefore, to live in communion with one another.

PROPER BALANCE BETWEEN POPULATION, LAND AND CAPITAL

101.   As everybody knows, there are countries with an abundance of arable land and a scarcity of manpower, while in other countries there is no proportion between natural resources and the capital available. This demands that peoples should set up relationships of mutual collaboration, facilitating the circulation from one to the other of capital, goods and manpower.[58]

102.   Here We deem it opportune to remark that, whenever possible, the work to be done should be taken to the workers, not vice versa.

In this way a possibility of a better future is offered to many persons without their being forced to leave their own environment in order to seek residence elsewhere, which almost always entails the heartache of separation and difficult periods of adjustment and social integration.

PROBLEM OF POLITICAL REFUGEES

103.   The sentiment of universal fatherhood which the Lord has placed in Our heart makes Us feel profound sadness in considering the phenomenon of political refugees, a phenomenon which has assumed large proportions and which always hides numberless and acute sufferings.

104.   Such expatriations show that there are some political regimes which do not guarantee for individual citizens a sufficient sphere of freedom within which their souls are allowed to breathe humanly. In fact, under those regimes even the lawful existence of such a sphere of freedom is either called into question or denied. This undoubtedly is a radical inversion of the order of human society, because the reason for the existence of public authority is to promote the common good, a fundamental element of which is the recognition of that sphere of freedom and the safeguarding of it.

105.   At this point it will not be superfluous to recall that such exiles are persons, and that all their rights as persons must be recognized, since they do not lose those rights on losing the citizenship of the states of which they are former members.

106.   Now among the rights of a human person there must be included the one by which a man may enter a political community where he hopes he can more fittingly provide a future for himself and his dependents. Wherefore, as far as the common good rightly understood permits, it is the duty of that state to accept such immigrants and to help to integrate them as new members.

107.   Wherefore, on this occasion, We publicly approve and commend every undertaking founded on the principles of human solidarity or Christian charity which aims at making the migration of persons from one country to another less painful.

108.   And We will be permitted to single out for the attention and gratitude of all right-minded persons the manifold work which specialized international agencies are carrying out in this very delicate field.

DISARMAMENT

109.   On the other hand, it is with deep sorrow that We note the enormous stocks of armaments that have been and still are being made in the more economically developed countries with a vast outlay of intellectual and economic resources. And so it happens that, while the people of these countries are loaded with heavy burdens, other countries as a result are deprived of the collaboration they need in order to make economic and social progress.

110.   The production of arms is allegedly justified on the grounds that in present-day conditions peace cannot be preserved without an equal balance of armaments. And so, if one country increases its armaments, others feel the need to do the same. And if one country is equipped with nuclear weapons, other countries must produce their own, equally destructive.

111.   Consequently, people live in constant fear lest the storm that threatens every moment should break upon them with dreadful violence. And with good reason, for the arms of war are ready at hand. Even though it is difficult to believe that anyone would deliberately take the responsibility for the appalling destruction and sorrow that war would bring in its train, it cannot be denied that the conflagration may be set off by some uncontrollable and unexpected chance. And one must bear in

mind that, even though the monstrous power of modern weapons acts as a deterrent, it is to be feared that the mere continuance of nuclear tests, undertaken with war in mind, will have fatal consequences for life on earth.

112.   Justice, right reason and humanity, therefore, urgently demand that the arms race should cease; that the stockpiles which exist in various countries should be reduced equally and simultaneously by the parties concerned; that nuclear weapons should be banned; and that a general agreement should eventually be reached about progressive disarmament and an effective method of control.

In the words of Pius XII, Our predecessor of happy memory: "The calamity of a world war, with the economic and social ruin and the moral excesses and dissolution that accompany it, must not be permitted to envelop the human race for a third time."[59]

113.   All must realize that there is no hope of putting an end to the building up of armaments, nor of reducing the present stocks, nor still less of abolishing them altogether, unless the process is complete and thorough and unless it proceeds from inner conviction; unless, that is, everyone sincerely co-operates to banish the fear and anxious expectation of war with which men are oppressed. If this is to come about, the fundamental principle on which our present peace depends must be replaced by another, which declares that the true and solid peace of nations can consist, not in equality of arms, but in mutual trust alone.

We believe that this can be brought to pass, and We consider that it is something which reason requires, that it is eminently desirable in itself and that it will prove to be the source of many benefits.

114.   In the first place, it is an objective demanded by reason. There can be, or at least there should be, no doubt that relations between states, as between individuals, should be regulated, not by the force of arms, but by the light of reason, by the rule, that is, of truth, of justice and of active and sincere co-operation.

115.   Secondly, We say that it is an objective earnestly to be desired in itself. Is there anyone who does not ardently yearn to see war banished, to see peace preserved and daily more firmly established?

116.   And finally, it is an objective which will be a fruitful source of many benefits, for its advantages will be felt everywhere—by individuals, by families, by nations, by the whole human family. The warning of Pius XII still rings in our ears: "Nothing is lost by peace; everything may be lost by war."[60]

117.   Since this is so, We, the Vicar on earth of Jesus Christ, Saviour of the world and author of peace, as interpreter of the profound longing of

the entire human family, following the paternal impulse of Our heart and seized by anxiety for the good of all, feel it Our duty to beseech men, especially those who have the responsibility of public affairs, to spare no labor in order to insure that world events follow a reasonable and human course.

118.   In the highest and most authoritative assemblies, let men give serious thought to the problem of a peaceful adjustment of relations between political communities on a world level—an adjustment founded on mutual trust, on sincerity in negotiations and on faithful fulfillment of obligations assumed. Let them study the problem until they find that point of agreement from which they can commence to go forward toward accords that will be sincere, lasting and fruitful.

119.   We, for Our part, will not cease to pray God to bless these labors so that they may lead to fruitful results.

In Freedom

120.   It has also to be borne in mind that relations between states should be based on freedom. This is to say that no country may unjustly oppress others or unduly meddle in their affairs. On the contrary, all should help to develop in others a sense of responsibility, a spirit of enterprise and an earnest desire to be the first to promote their own advancement in every field.

EVOLUTION OF UNDERDEVELOPED COUNTRIES

121.   Because all men are joined together by reason of their common origin, their redemption by Christ and their supernatural destiny, and are called to form one Christian family, We appealed in the encyclical *Mater et Magistra* to economically developed nations to come to the aid of those which are in the process of development.[61]

122.   We are greatly consoled to see how widely that appeal has been favorably received. And We are confident that even more so in the future it will contribute to the end that the poorer countries, in as short a time as possible, will arrive at that degree of economic development which will enable every citizen to live in conditions more in keeping with his human dignity.

123.   But it can never be sufficiently repeated that this cooperation should be effected with the greatest respect for the liberty of the countries being developed, for these must realize that they are primarily responsi-

ble, and that they are the principal artisans in the promotion of their own economic development and social progress.

124.   Our predecessor Pius XII wisely proclaimed that "in the matter of this new order founded on moral principles, there is no room for violation of freedom, integrity and security of other nations, no matter what may be their territorial extent or their capacity for defense. It is inevitable that the powerful states, by reason of their greater potential and their power, should pave the way in the establishment of economic groups comprising not only themselves but also smaller and weaker states as well. It is nevertheless indispensable that in the interests of the common good they, as all others, should respect the rights of those smaller states to political freedom, to economic development and to the adequate protection, in the case of conflicts between nations, of that neutrality which is theirs according to the natural, as well as international, law. Those states likewise have the right to safeguard their economic development. In this way, and in this way only, will they be able to obtain a fitting share of the common good, and assure the material and spiritual welfare of their people."[62]

125.   It is vitally important, therefore, that the wealthier states, in providing varied forms of assistance to the poorer, should respect the moral heritage and ethnic characteristics peculiar to each, and also that they should avoid any intention of political domination. If this is done, "a precious contribution will be made toward the formation of a world community, a community in which each member, while conscious of its own individual rights and duties, will work in a relationship of equality toward the attainment of the universal common good."[63]

Signs of the Times

126.   Men are becoming more and more convinced that disputes which arise between states should not be resolved by recourse to arms, but rather by negotiation.

127.   It is true that on historical grounds this conviction is based chiefly on the terrible destructive force of modern arms. And it is nourished by the horror aroused in the mind by the very thought of the cruel destruction and the immense suffering which the use of those armaments would bring. And for this reason it is hardly possible to imagine that in the atomic era war could be used as an instrument of justice.

128.   Nevertheless, unfortunately, the law of fear still reigns among peoples, and it forces them to spend fabulous sums for armaments: not

for aggression, they affirm—and there is no reason for not believing them—but to dissuade others from aggression.

129.   There is reason to hope, however, that by meeting and negotiating men may come to discover better the bonds—deriving from the human nature which they have in common—that unite them, and that they may learn also that one of the most profound requirements of their common nature is this: that between them and their respective peoples it is not fear which should reign but love, a love which tends to express itself in a collaboration that is loyal, manifold in form and productive of many benefits.

PART IV:

Relationship of Men and of Political Communities With the World Community

Interdependence Between Political Communities

130.   Recent progress in science and technology has profoundly affected human beings and influenced men to work together and live as one family. There has been a great increase in the circulation of ideas, of persons and of goods from one country to another, so that relations have become closer between individuals, families and intermediate associations belonging to different political communities, and between the public authorities of those communities.

At the same time the interdependence of national economies has grown deeper, one becoming progressively more closely related to the other, so that they become, as it were, integral parts of the one world economy. Likewise the social progress, order, security and peace of any one country are necessarily connected with the social progress, order, security and peace of all other countries.

131.   At the present time no political community is able to pursue its own interests and develop itself in isolation, because its prosperity and development are both a reflection and a component part of the prosperity and development of all the other political communities.

INSUFFICIENCY OF MODERN STATES TO
INSURE THE UNIVERSAL COMMON GOOD

132.   The unity of the human family has always existed because its
members are human beings all equal by virtue of their natural dignity.
Hence there will always exist the objective need to promote in sufficient
measure the universal common good, that is, the common good of the
entire human family.

133.   In times past, one could be justified in feeling that the public
authorities of the different political communities might be in a position to
provide for the universal common good, either through normal diplomatic channels or top-level meetings, or by making use of juridical instruments such as conventions and treaties and other means suggested
by the natural law, or by the law of nations or by international law.

134.   As a result of the far-reaching changes which have taken place in
the relations of the human family, on the one hand the universal common
good gives rise to problems which are complex, very grave and extremely
urgent, especially as regards security and world peace. On the other
hand, the public authorities of the individual political communities
—placed as they are on a footing of equality one with the other—no
matter how much they multiply their meetings or sharpen their wits in
efforts to draw up new juridical instruments, are no longer able to face the
task of finding an adequate solution to the problems mentioned above.
And this is not due to a lack of good will or of a spirit of enterprise, but
because of a structural defect which hinders them.

135.   It can be said, therefore, that at this historical moment the present system of organization and the way its principle of authority operates
on a world basis no longer correspond to the objective requirements of the
universal common good.

CONNECTION BETWEEN THE COMMON GOOD
AND POLITICAL AUTHORITY

136.   There exists an intrinsic connection between the common good
on the one hand and the structure and function of public authority on the
other. The moral order, which needs public authority in order to promote
the common good in human society, requires also that the authority be
effective in attaining that end. This demands that the organs through
which the authority is institutionalized, becomes operative and pursues
its ends, must be constituted and act in such a manner as to be capable of

bringing to realization the new meaning which the common good is taking on in the historical evolution of the human family.

137.   Today the universal common good poses problems of world-wide dimensions which cannot be adequately tackled or solved except by the efforts of public authorities endowed with a breadth of powers, structure and means of the same proportions: that is, of public authorities which are in a position to act in an effective manner on a world-wide basis. The moral order itself, therefore, demands that such a form of public authority be established.

PUBLIC AUTHORITY INSTITUTED BY
COMMON CONSENT, NOT IMPOSED BY FORCE

138.   A public authority, having world-wide power and endowed with the proper means for the efficacious pursuit of its objective, which is the universal common good in concrete form, must be set up by common accord and not imposed by force.

The reason is that such an authority must be in a position to operate effectively, while at the same time its action must be inspired by sincere and real impartiality. In other words, it must be an action aimed at satisfying the objective requirements of the universal common good.

The difficulty is that there would be reason to fear that a supranational or world-wide public authority, forcibly imposed by the more powerful political communities, might become an instrument of one-sided interests. And even should this not happen, it would be difficult for it to avoid all suspicion of partiality in its actions, and this would take away from its effectiveness.

Even though there may be pronounced differences between political communities as regards the degree of their economic development and their military power, they are all very sensitive as regards their juridical equality and their moral dignity. For that reason, they are right in not easily yielding in obedience to an authority imposed by force, or to an authority in whose creation they had no part or to which they themselves did not decide to submit by conscious and free choice.

THE UNIVERSAL COMMON GOOD AND PERSONAL RIGHTS

139.   Like the common good of individual political communities, so too the universal common good cannot be determined except by having regard to the human person. Therefore, the public authority of the world community, too, must have as its fundamental objective the recognition,

respect, safeguarding and promotion of the rights of the human person. This can be done by direct action when required, or by creating on a world scale an environment in which the public authorities of the individual political communities can more easily carry out their specific functions.

PRINCIPLE OF SUBSIDIARITY

140. Just as within each political community the relations between individuals, families, intermediate associations and public authority are governed by the principle of subsidiarity, so too the relations between the public authority of each political community and the public authority of the world community must be regulated by the same principle. This means that the public authority of the world community must tackle and solve problems of an economic, social, political or cultural character which are posed by the universal common good. For, because of the vastness, complexity and urgency of those problems, the public authorities of the individual states are not in a position to tackle them with any hope of a positive solution.

141. The public authority of the world community is not intended to limit the sphere of action of the public authority of the individual political community, much less to take its place. On the contrary, its purpose is to create, on a world basis, an environment in which the public authorities of each political community, its citizens and intermediate associations, can carry out their tasks, fulfill their duties and exercise their rights with greater security.[64]

Signs of the Times

142. As is known, the United Nations (UN) was established on June 26, 1945, and to it there were subsequently added intergovernmental agencies with extensive international tasks in the economic, social, cultural, educational and health fields. The United Nations had as its essential purpose the maintenance and consolidation of peace between peoples, fostering between them friendly relations based on the principles of equality, mutual respect and varied forms of co-operation in every sector of human endeavor.

143. An act of the highest importance performed by the United Nations was the Universal Declaration of Human Rights, approved in the General Assembly on December 10, 1948. In the preamble of that declaration, the recognition and respect of those rights and respective liberties is

proclaimed as an ideal to be pursued by all peoples and all countries.

144.   Some objections and reservations, We observed, were raised regarding certain points in the declaration, and rightly so. There is no doubt, however, that the document represents an important step on the path toward the juridico-political organization of the world community. For in it, in most solemn form, the dignity of a human person is acknowledged in all men. And as a consequence there is proclaimed, as a fundamental right, the right of free movement in the search for truth and in the attainment of moral good and of justice, and also the right to a dignified life, while other rights connected with those mentioned are likewise proclaimed.

145.   It is Our earnest prayer that the United Nations—in its structure and in its means—may become ever more equal to the magnitude and nobility of its tasks. May the day come as quickly as possible when every human being will find therein an effective safeguard for the rights which derive directly from his dignity as a person, and which are therefore universal, inviolable and inalienable rights. This is all the more to be hoped for since all human beings, as they take an ever more active part in the public life of their own political communities, are showing an increasing interest in the affairs of all peoples, and are becoming more consciously aware that they are living members of a world community.

PART V:

Pastoral Exhortations

DUTY OF TAKING PART IN PUBLIC LIFE

146.   Once again We deem it opportune to remind Our children of their duty to take an active part in public life and to contribute toward the attainment of the common good of the entire human family as well as to that of their own political community. They should endeavor, therefore, in the light of their Christian faith and led by love, to insure that the various institutions—whether economic, social, cultural or political in purpose—should be such as not to create obstacles, but rather to facilitate or render less arduous man's perfecting of himself in both the natural order and the supernatural.

SCIENTIFIC COMPETENCE, TECHNICAL CAPACITY
AND PROFESSIONAL EXPERIENCE

147.   Nevertheless, in order to imbue civilization with sound principles and enliven it with the spirit of the gospel, it is not enough to be illumined with the gift of faith and enkindled with the desire of forwarding a good cause; it is also necessary to take an active part in the various organizations and influence them from within.

148.   And since our present age is one of outstanding scientific and technical progress, one cannot enter these organizations and work effectively from within unless he is scientifically competent, technically capable and skilled in the practice of his own profession.

APOSTOLATE OF A TRAINED LAITY

149.   We desire to call attention to the fact that scientific competence, technical capacity and professional experience, although necessary, are not of themselves sufficient to elevate the relationships of society to an order that is genuinely human, that is, to an order whose foundation is truth, whose measure and objective is justice, whose driving force is love, and whose method of attainment is freedom.

150.   For this end it is certainly necessary that human beings carry on their own temporal activities in accordance with the laws governing them and following the methods corresponding to their nature. But it is also necessary that they should carry on those activities as acts within the moral order and, therefore, as the exercise or vindication of a right, as the fulfillment of a duty or the performance of a service, and as a positive answer to the providential design of God directed to our salvation.

In other words, it is necessary that human beings, in the intimacy of their own consciences, should so live and act in their temporal lives as to create a synthesis between scientific, technical and professional elements on the one hand, and spiritual values on the other.

INTEGRATION OF FAITH AND ACTION

151.   It is no less clear that today, in traditionally Christian nations, secular institutions, although demonstrating a high degree of scientific and technical perfection and efficiency in achieving their respective ends, not infrequently are but slightly affected by Christian motivation or inspiration.

152.   It is beyond question that in the creation of those institutions many contributed and contine to contribute who were believed to be and who consider themselves Christians; and without doubt, in part at least, they were and are. How does one explain this? It is Our opinion that the explanation is to be found in an inconsistency in their minds between religious belief and their action in the temporal sphere. It is necessary, therefore, that their interior unity be re-established, and that in their temporal activity faith should be present as a beacon to give light, and charity as a force to give life.

INTEGRAL EDUCATION

153.   It is Our opinion, too, that the above-mentioned inconsistency between the religious faith, in those who believe, and their activities in the temporal sphere, results—in great part if not entirely—from the lack of a solid Christian education. Indeed, it happens in many quarters and too often that there is no proportion between scientific training and religious instruction. The former continues and is extended until it reaches higher degrees, while the latter remains at elementary level.

It is indispensable, therefore, that in the training of youth, education should be complete and without interruption; that is to say, religious values should be cultivated in the minds of the young and their moral conscience refined in a manner to keep pace with the continuous and ever more abundant assimilation of scientific and technical knowledge. And it is indispensable, too, that they be instructed regarding the proper way to carry out their actual tasks.[65]

154.   We deem it opportune to point out how difficult it is to understand clearly the relation between the objective requirements of justice and concrete situations, that is, to perceive the degrees and forms in which doctrinal principles and directives ought to be applied to current human affairs.

155.   And the perception of those degrees and forms is all the more difficult in our times, which require everyone to have regard for the universal common good and which are marked by a pronounced dynamism. For this reason, the problem of bringing social reality into line with the objective requirements of justice is one which will never admit of a definitive solution. Meanwhile, Our children must not take the position that they can relax and feel satisified with objectives already achieved.

156.   In fact, all human beings ought rather to reckon that what has been accomplished is but little in comparison with what remains to be done. This is so because organs of production, trade unions, professional

organizations, insurance systems, legal systems, political regimes, and institutions for cultural, health, recreational or sporting and other similar purposes must all be adjusted to the era of the atom and of the conquest of space, an era in which the human family has already entered on its new advance toward limitless horizons.

RELATIONS BETWEEN CATHOLICS AND NON-CATHOLICS
IN SOCIAL AND ECONOMIC AFFAIRS

157.   The doctrinal principles outlined in this document derive from or are suggested by the requirements of human nature itself, and are, for the most part, dictates of the natural law. They provide Catholics, therefore, with a vast field in which they can meet and come to an understanding both with Christians separated from this Apostolic See, and also with human beings who are not enlightened by faith in Jesus Christ, but who are endowed with the light of reason and with a natural and operative honesty.

"In such relations let the faithful be careful to be always consistent in their actions, so that they may never come to any compromise in matters of religion and morals. At the same time, however, let them be, and show themselves to be, animated by a spirit of understanding and detachment, and disposed to work loyally in the pursuit of objectives which are of their nature good, or conducive to good."[66]

158.   However, one must never confuse error and the person who errs, not even when there is question of error, or inadequate knowledge of truth, in the moral or religious field.

The person who errs is always and above all a human being, and in every case he retains his dignity as a human person. He must always be regarded and treated in accordance with that lofty dignity. Besides, in every human being there is a need that is congenital to his nature and never becomes extinguished, one that compels him to break through the web of error and open his mind to the knowledge of truth. And God will never fail to act on his interior being, with the result that a person, who at a given moment of his life lacks the clarity of faith or even shall have adhered to erroneous doctrines, can at a future date be enlightened and believe the truth.

Meetings and agreements, in the various sectors of daily life, between believers and those who either do not believe or believe insufficiently because they adhere to error, can be occasions for discovering truth and paying homage to it.

159.   It must be borne in mind, furthermore, that neither can false

philosophical teachings regarding the nature, origin and destiny of the universe and of man be identified with historical movements that have economic, social, cultural or political ends, not even when these movements have originated from those teachings and have drawn and still draw inspiration therefrom.

This is so because the teachings, once they are drawn up and defined, remain always the same, while the movements, working in constantly evolving historical situations, cannot but be influenced by these latter and cannot avoid, therefore, being subject to changes, even of a profound nature. Besides, who can deny that those movements, insofar as they conform to the dictates of right reason and are interpreters of the lawful aspirations of the human person, contain elements that are positive and deserving of approval?

160.   It can happen, then, that meetings for the attainment of some practical end, which formerly were deemed inopportune or unproductive, might now or in the future be considered opportune and useful.

But to decide whether this moment has arrived, and also to lay down the ways and degrees in which work in common might be possible for the achievement of economic, social, cultural and political ends which are honorable and useful, are problems which can be solved only with the virtue of prudence, which is the guiding light of the virtues that regulate the moral life, both individual and social.

Therefore, as far as Catholics are concerned, this decision rests primarily with those who live and work in the specific sectors of human society in which those problems arise, always, however, in accordance with the principles of the natural law, with the social doctrine of the Church, and with the directives of ecclesiastical authority. For it must not be forgotten that the Church has the right and the duty not only to safeguard the principles of ethics and religion, but also to intervene authoritatively with her children in the temporal sphere when there is a question of judging the application of those principles to concrete cases.[67]

LITTLE BY LITTLE

161.   There are some souls, particularly endowed with generosity, who, on finding situations where the requirements of justice are not satisfied or not satisfied in full, feel enkindled with the desire to change the state of things, as if they wished to have recourse to something like a revolution.

162.   It must be borne in mind that to proceed gradually is the law of life in all its expressions. Therefore, in human institutions, too, it is not

possible to renovate for the better except by working from within them, gradually. This was also proclaimed by Our predecessor of happy memory, Pius XII, in these terms: "Salvation and justice are not to be found in revolution, but in evolution through concord. Violence has always achieved only destruction, not construction; the kindling of passions, not their pacification; the accumulation of hate and ruin, not the reconciliation of the contending parties. And it has reduced men and parties to the difficult task of rebuilding, after sad experience, on the ruins of discord."[68]

AN IMMENSE TASK

163.　　There is an immense task incumbent on all men of good will, namely, the task of restoring the relations of the human family in truth, in justice, in love and in freedom—the relations between individual human beings; between citizens and their respective political communities; between political communities themselves; between individuals, families, intermediate associations and political communities on the one hand, and the world community on the other. This is a most exalted task, all will agree, for it is the task of bringing about true peace in the order established by God.

164.　　Admittedly, those who are endeavoring to restore the relations of social life according to the criteria mentioned above are not many. To them We express Our paternal appreciation, and We earnestly invite them to persevere in their work with ever greater zeal. At the same time We are comforted by the hope that their number will be increased, especially by those who believe. For it is an imperative of duty; it is a requirement of love.

Every believer in this world of ours must be a spark of light, a center of love, a vivifying leaven amidst his fellow men. And he will be this all the more perfectly, the more closely he lives in communion with God in the intimacy of his own soul.

165.　　In fact, there can be no peace between men unless there is peace within each one of them, unless, that is, each one builds up within himself the order wished by God. Hence St. Augustine asks: "Does your soul desire to overcome your lower inclinations? Let it be subject to Him who is on high and it will conquer the lower self: there will be peace in you; true, secure and well-ordered peace. In what does that order consist? God commands the soul; the soul commands the body; and there is nothing more orderly than this."[69]

THE PRINCE OF PEACE

166.   These words of Ours, which We have wished to dedicate to the problems that most beset the human family today, and on the just solution of which the ordered progress of society depends, are dictated by a profound aspiration which We know is shared by all men of good will: the consolidation of peace in the world.

167.   As the humble and unworthy Vicar of Him whom the prophet announced as the Prince of Peace,[70] We have the duty to expend all Our energies in an effort to protect and strengthen this universal boon. However, peace will be but an empty-sounding word unless it is founded on the order which this present document has outlined in confident hope: an order founded on truth, built according to justice, vivified and integrated by charity, and put into practice in freedom.

168.   This is such a noble and elevated task that human resources, even though inspired by the most praiseworthy good will, cannot bring it to realization alone. In order that human society may reflect as faithfully as possible the Kingdom of God, help from on high is necessary.

169.   For this reason, during these sacred days, Our supplication is raised with greater fervor toward Him who by His painful passion and death overcame sin—the root of discord and the source of sorrows and inequalities—and by His Blood reconciled mankind to the Eternal Father. "For he himself is our peace, he it is who has made both one. . . . And coming, he announced the good tidings of peace to you who were afar off, and of peace to those who were near."[71]

170.   And in the liturgy of these days we hear the announcement: "Our Lord Jesus Christ, after His resurrection, stood in the midst of His disciples and said 'Peace be to you,' alleluia: The disciples rejoiced seeing the Lord."[72]

Thus Christ brings us peace, He leaves us peace. "Peace I leave with you, my peace I give to you; not as the world gives do I give to you."[73]

171.   This is the peace which We implore of Him with the ardent yearning of Our prayer. May He banish from the hearts of men whatever might endanger peace. May He transform them into witnesses of truth, justice and brotherly love. May He enlighten the rulers of peoples so that in addition to their solicitude for the proper welfare of their citizens, they may guarantee and defend the great gift of peace. May He enkindle the wills of all so that they may overcome the barriers that divide, cherish the bonds of mutual charity, understand others, and pardon those who have done them wrong. By virtue of His action, may all peoples of the earth become as brothers, and may the most longed-for peace blossom forth and reign always among them.

172.   As a pledge of this peace, and with the ardent wish that it may shine forth on the Christian communities entrusted to your care, especially for the benefit of those who are most lowly and in the greatest need of help and defense, We are glad to impart to you, Venerable Brothers, to priests both secular and religious, to religious men and women and to all the faithful, particularly to those who make every effort to put these exhortations of Ours into practice, Our apostolic blessings. Finally, upon all men of good will, to whom this encyclical letter is also addressed, We implore from Almighty God health and prosperity.

173.   Given at Rome, at St. Peter's, on Holy Thursday, the eleventh day of April in the year 1963, the fifth of Our Pontificate.

JOHN XXIII

NOTES

1. Ps. 8,1.
2. Ps. 103, 24.
3. Cf. Gen. 1, 26.
4. Ps. 8, 6–8.
5. Rom. 2, 15.
6. Cf. Ps. 18, 8–11.
7. Cf. Radio Message of Pius XII, Christmas Eve, 1942. *Acta Apostolicae Sedis* XXXV (1943), 9–24; and Discourse of John XXIII, Jan. 4, 1963. *Acta Apostolicae Sedis* LV (1963), 89–91.
8. Cf. Encycl. *Divini Redemptoris* of Pius XI. *Acta Apostolicae Sedis* XXIX (1937), 78; and Radio Message of Pius XII, Pentecost, June 1, 1941. *Acta Apostolicae Sedis* XXXIII (1941), 195–205.
9. Cf. Radio Message of Pius XII, Christmas Eve, 1942. *Acta Apostolicae Sedis* XXXV (1943), 9–24.
10. *Divinae Institutiones*, Book IV, ch. 28, 2; Patrologia Latina, 6, 535.
11. Encycl. *Libertas Praestantissimum. Acta Leonis XIII*, VIII (1888), 237–238.
12. Cf. Radio Message of Pius XII, Christmas Eve, 1942. *Acta Apostolicae Sedis* XXXV (1943), 9–24.
13. Cf. Encycl. *Casti Connubii* of Pius XI, *Acta Apostolicae Sedis* XXII (1930), 539–592; and Radio Message of Pius XII, Christmas Eve, 1942. *Acta Apostolicae Sedis* XXXV (1943), 9–24.
14. Cf. Radio Message of Pius XII, Pentecost, June 1, 1941. *Acta Apostolicae Sedis* XXXIII (1941), 201.
15. Cf. Encycl. *Rerum Novarum* of Leo XIII. *Acta Leonis XIII*, XI (1891), 128–129.
16. Cf. Encycl. *Mater et Magistra* of John XXIII. *Acta Apostolicae Sedis* LIII (1961), 422.
17. Cf. Radio Message, Pentecost, June 1, 1941. *Acta Apostolicae Sedis* XXXIII (1941), 201.
18. Encycl. *Mater et Magistra. Acta Apostolicae Sedis* LIII (1961), 428.
19. Cf. *Ibid.*, p. 430.
20. Cf. Encycl. *Rerum Novarum* of Leo XIII. *Acta Leonis XIII*, XI (1891), 134–142; Encycl.

Quadragesimo Anno of Pius XI. *Acta Apostolicae Sedis* XXIII (1931), 199–200; Encycl. *Sertum Laetitiae* of Pius XII. *Acta Apostolicae Sedis* XXXI (1939), 635–644.

21. Cf. *Acta Apostolicae Sedis* LIII (1961), 430.

22. Cf. Radio Message of Pius XII, Christmas Eve, 1952. *Acta Apostolicae Sedis* XLV (1953), 33–46.

23. Cf. Radio Message, Christmas Eve, 1944. *Acta Apostolicae Sedis* XXXVII (1945), 12.

24. Cf. Radio Message, Christmas Eve, 1942. *Acta Apostolicae Sedis* XXXV (1943), 21.

25. Eph. 4, 25.

26. Radio Message of Pius XII, Christmas Eve, 1942. *Acta Apostolicae Sedis* XXXV (1943), 14.

27. Summa Theol., Ia-IIae, q. 19, a. 4; cf. a. 9.

28. Rom. 13, 1.

29. In Epist. ad Rom., c. 13, vv. 1–2, homil. xxiii; Patrologia Graeca, 60, 615.

30. Encycl. *Immortale Dei* of Leo XIII. *Acta Leonis XIII*, V (1885), 120.

31. Cf. Radio Message, Christmas Eve, 1944. *Acta Apostolicae Sedis* XXXVII (1945), 15.

32. Cf. Encycl. *Diuturnum Illud* of Leo XIII. *Acta Leonis XIII*, II (1881), 274.

33. Cf. *Ibid.*, 278; and Encycl. *Immortale Dei* of Leo XIII. *Acta Leonis XIII*, V (1885), 130.

34. Acts 5, 29.

35. Summa Theol., Ia-IIae, q. 93, a. 3 ad 2um: Cf Radio Message of Pius XII, Christmas Eve, 1944. *Acta Apostolicae Sedis* XXXVII (1945), 5–23.

36. Cf. Encycl. *Diuturnum Illud* of Leo XIII. *Acta Leonis XIII*, II (1881), 271–272; and Radio Message of Pius XII, Christmas Eve, 1944. *Acta Apostolicae Sedis* XXXVII (1945), 5–23.

37. Cf. Radio Message of Pius XII, Christmas Eve, 1942. *Acta Apostolicae Sedis* XXXV (1943), 13; and Encycl. *Immortale Dei* of Leo XIII. *Acta Leonis XIII*, V (1885), 120.

38. Cf. Encycl. *Summi Pontificatus* of Pius XII. *Acta Apostolicae Sedis* XXXI (1939), 412–453.

39. Cf. Encycl. *Mit brennender Sorge* of Pius XI. *Acta Apostolicae Sedis* XXIX (1937), 149; and Encycl. *Divini Redemptoris*. *Acta Apostolicae Sedis* XXIX (1937), 65–106.

40. Encycl. *Immortale Dei*, in *Acta Leonis XIII*, V (1885), 121.

41. Cf. Encycl. *Rerum Novarum* of Leo XIII, *Acta Leonis XIII*, XI (1891), 133–134.

42. Cf. Encycl. *Summi Pontificatus* of Pius XII. *Acta Apostolicae Sedis* XXXI (1939), 433.

43. *Acta Apostolicae Sedis* LIII (1961), 19.

44. Cf. Encycl. *Quadragesimo Anno* of Pius XI. *Acta Apostolicae Sedis* XXIII (1931), 215.

45. Cf. Radio Message of Pius XII, Pentecost, June 1, 1941. *Acta Apostolicae Sedis* XXXIII (1941), 200.

46. Cf. Encycl. *Mit brennender Sorge* of Pius XI. *Acta Apostolicae Sedis* XXIX (1937), 149; and Encycl. *Divini Redemptoris*. *Acta Apostolicae Sedis* XXIX (1937), 79; and Radio Message of Pius XII, Christmas Eve, 1942. *Acta Apostolicae Sedis* XXXV (1943), 9–24.

47. Cf. Encycl. *Divini Redemptoris* of Pius XI. *Acta Apostolicae Sedis* XXIX (1937), 81; and Radio Message of Pius XII, Christmas Eve, 1942. *Acta Apostolicae Sedis* XXXV (1943), 9–24.

48. Encycl. *Mater et Magistra*. *Acta Apostolicae Sedis* LIII (1961), 415.

49. Cf. Radio Message of Pius XII, Christmas Eve, 1942. *Acta Apostolicae Sedis* XXXV (1943), 21.

50. Cf. Radio Message of Pius XII, Christmas Eve, 1944. *Acta Aposotlicae Sedis* XXXVII (1945), 15–16.

51. Cf. Radio Message of Pius XII, Christmas Eve, 1942. *Acta Apostolicae Sedis* XXXV (1943), 12.

52. Cf. Apostolic letter *Annum Ingressi* of Leo XIII. *Acta Leonis XIII*, XXII (1902–1903), 52–80.

53. Wis. 6, 1–4.

54. Cf. Radio Message of Pius XII, Christmas Eve, 1941. *Acta Apostolicae Sedis* XXXIV (1942), 16.

55. Cf. Radio Message of Pius XII, Christmas Eve, 1940. *Acta Apostolicae Sedis* XXXIII (1941), 5–14.

56. *De Civitate Dei*, Book IV, ch. 4; Patrologia Latina, 41, 115. Cf. Radio Message of Pius XII, Christmas Eve, 1939. *Acta Apostolicae Sedis* XXXII (1940), 5–13.

57. Cf. Radio Message of Pius XII, Christmas Eve, 1941. *Acta Apostolicae Sedis* XXXIV (1942), 10–21.

58. Cf. Encycl. *Mater et Magistra.* *Acta Apostolicae Sedis* LIII (1961), 439.

59. Cf. Radio Message, Christmas Eve, 1941. *Acta Apostolicae Sedis* XXXIV (1942), 17; and Exhortation of Benedict XV to the rulers of peoples at war, Aug. 1, 1917. *Acta Apostolicae Sedis* IX (1917), 418.

60. Cf. Radio Message, Aug. 24, 1939. *Acta Apostolicae Sedis* XXXI (1939), 334.

61. *Acta Apostolicae Sedis* LIII (1961), 440–441.

62. Cf. Radio Message, Christmas Eve, 1941. *Acta Apostolicae Sedis* XXXIV (1942), 16–17.

63. Encycl. *Mater et Magistra. Acta Apostolicae Sedis* LIII (1961), 443.

64. Cf. Address of Pius XII to youths of Catholic Action from the dioceses of Italy gathered in Rome, Sept. 12, 1948. *Acta Apostolicae Sedis* XL (1948), 412.

65. Cf. Encycl. *Mater et Magistra. Acta Apostolicae Sedis* LIII (1961), 454.

66. Cf. Encycl. *Mater et Magistra. Acta Apostolicae Sedis* LIII (1961), 456.

67. Cf. Encycl. *Mater et Magistra. Acta Apostolicae Sedis* LIII (1961) 456; cf. Encycl. *Immortale Dei* of Leo XIII. *Acta Leonis XIII,* V (1885), 128; Encycl. *Ubi Arcano* of Pius XI. *Acta Apostolicae Sedis* XIV (1922), 698; and Address of Pius XII to Delegates of the International Union of Catholic Women's Leagues gathered in Rome for a joint convention, Sept. 11, 1947. *Acta Apostolicae Sedis* XXXIX (1947), 486.

68. Cf. address to workers from the dioceses of Italy gathered in Rome, Pentecost, June 13, 1943. *Acta Apostolicae Sedis* XXXV (1943), 175.

69. *Miscellanea Augustiniana* . . . Sermones post Maurinos reperti of St. Augustine. Rome, 1930, p. 633.

70. Cf. Is. 9, 5.

71. Eph. 2, 14–17.

72. Responsory at Matins on the Friday after Easter.

73. Jn. 14, 27.

Gaudium et Spes

Pastoral Constitution[1] on the Church in the Modern World (Second Vatican Council, December 7, 1965)

PAUL, BISHOP
SERVANT OF THE SERVANTS OF GOD
TOGETHER WITH THE FATHERS OF THE SACRED COUNCIL
FOR EVERLASTING MEMORY

Preface

THE INTIMATE BOND BETWEEN THE CHURCH AND MANKIND

1.   The joys and the hopes, the griefs and the anxieties of the men of this age, especially those who are poor or in any way afflicted, these too are the joys and hopes, the griefs and anxieties of the followers of Christ.

[Permanent published sources of the official Latin texts of the Second Vatican Council are (1) A.A.S., from February 1964 through December 1966; this Pastoral Constitution appears

Indeed, nothing genuinely human fails to raise an echo in their hearts. For theirs is a community composed of men. United in Christ, they are led by the Holy Spirit in their journey to the kingdom of their Father and they have welcomed the news of salvation which is meant for every man. That is why this community realizes that it is truly and intimately linked with mankind and its history.

FOR WHOM THIS MESSAGE IS INTENDED

2.   Hence this Second Vatican Council, having probed more profoundly into the mystery of the Church, now addresses itself without hesitation, not only to the sons of the Church and to all who invoke the name of Christ, but to the whole of humanity. For the Council yearns to explain to everyone how it conceives of the presence and activity of the Church in the world of today.

---

in A.A.S. LVIII, December 7, 1966, no. 15, pp. 1025–1120; (2) *L'Osservatore Romano*, which printed the Latin texts one at a time, shortly after each document was promulgated; (3) individual booklets printed by the Vatican Polyglot Press, 1964-1966; (4) the collected texts edited by the Secretary General of the Council and published by the Vatican Polyglot Press, 1966. The English version used here, and throughout this volume for all documents of Vatican II, is taken from *The Documents of Vatican II*, pages 199–308 (America Press, New York, and Geoffrey Chapman, London, 1966). Walter M. Abbott, S.J., is General Editor; Msgr. Joseph Gallagher is Translation Editor. The latter states in his Preface: "The translations in this volume are based on the Latin text. . . . All the translations prepared for, and by, the National Catholic Welfare Conference were carefully consulted. . . . I myself prepared for the N.C.W.C. the major part of the translation of the Pastoral Constitution on the Church in the Modern World—whose 23,335 words make it the Council's longest text. The translation has been completely reviewed for this book . . . . While the translation editor accepts final responsibility for the translations, he gladly acknowledges the 'collegiality' of contributions which helped bring about the final product. . . . Special translation help was provided by Rev. Raymond Brown, S.S., Rev. John F. Cronin, S.S., Very Rev. F. Joseph Gossman, Rev. John A. Gray, Rt. Rev. George G. Higgins, Rev. John King, O.M.I., Rev. James A. Laubacher, S.S., Rev. William Leahy, Rev. John T. McGraw, Rt. Rev. John S. Quinn, Rev. Charles K. Riepe, Rev. James R. Schafer, Rev. J. Francis Stafford, Rev. Robert Trisco, Rev. Eugene A. Walsh, S.S., Rt. Rev. Porter J. White, Very Rev. Vincent A. Yzermans, and students at the North American College and the Graduate House of Studies in Rome. Also, in several instances, scholars who serve as commentators in this book made valuable suggestions about the translations."

As editor and author of the present volume, I express admiration for *The Documents of Vatican II* and personal gratitude for permission granted by its publishers to use it extensively herein. I direct this admiration and appreciation in a special way to the General Editor, Father Abbott, who has been for several years a permanent staff member of the Secretariat for Promoting Christian Unity, and therefore my colleague in the Vatican Curia. —J.G.]

Therefore, the Council focuses its attention on the world of men, the whole human family along with the sum of those realities in the midst of which that family lives. It gazes upon that world which is the theater of man's history, and carries the marks of his energies, his tragedies, and his triumphs; that world which the Christian sees as created and sustained by its Maker's love, fallen indeed into the bondage of sin, yet emancipated now by Christ. He was crucified and rose again to break the stranglehold of personified Evil, so that this world might be fashioned anew according to God's design and reach its fulfillment.

THE SERVICE TO BE OFFERED TO HUMANITY

3.   Though mankind today is struck with wonder at its own discoveries and its power, it often raises anxious questions about the current trend of the world, about the place and role of man in the universe, about the meaning of his individual and collective strivings, and about the ultimate destiny of reality and of humanity. Hence, giving witness and voice to the faith of the whole People of God gathered together by Christ, this Council can provide no more eloquent proof of its solidarity with the entire human family with which it is bound up, as well as its respect and love for that family than by engaging with it in conversation about these various problems.

The Council brings to mankind light kindled from the gospel, and puts at its disposal those saving resources which the Church herself, under the guidance of the Holy Spirit, receives from her Founder. For the human person deserves to be preserved; human society deserves to be renewed. Hence the pivotal point of our total presentation will be man himself, whole and entire, body and soul, heart and conscience, mind and will.

Therefore, this sacred Synod proclaims the highest destiny of man and champions the godlike seed which has been sown in him. It offers to mankind the honest assistance of the Church in fostering that brotherhood of all men which corresponds to this destiny of theirs. Inspired by no earthly ambition, the Church seeks but a solitary goal: to carry forward the work of Christ Himself under the lead of the befriending Spirit. And Christ entered this world to give witness to the truth, to rescue and not to sit in judgment, to serve and not to be served.[2]

Introductory Statement

The Situation of Men in the Modern World

HOPE AND ANGUISH

4.   To carry out such a task, the Church has always had the duty of scrutinizing the signs of the times and of interpreting them in the light of the gospel. Thus, in language intelligible to each generation, she can respond to the perennial questions which men ask about this present life and the life to come, and about the relationship of the one to the other. We must therefore recognize and understand the world in which we live, its expectations, its longings, and its often dramatic characteristics. Some of the main features of the modern world can be sketched as follows:

Today, the human race is passing through a new stage of its history. Profound and rapid changes are spreading by degrees around the whole world. Triggered by the intelligence and creative energies of man, these changes recoil upon him, upon his decisions and desires, both individual and collective, and upon his manner of thinking and acting with respect to things and to people. Hence we can already speak of a true social and cultural transformation, one which has repercussions on man's religious life as well.

As happens in any crisis of growth, this transformation has brought serious difficulties in its wake. Thus while man extends his power in every direction, he does not always succeed in subjecting it to his own welfare. Striving to penetrate farther into the deeper recesses of his own mind, he frequently appears more unsure of himself. Gradually and more precisely he lays bare the laws of society, only to be paralyzed by uncertainty about the direction to give it.

Never has the human race enjoyed such an abundance of wealth, resources, and economic power. Yet a huge proportion of the world's citizens is still tormented by hunger and poverty, while countless numbers suffer from total illiteracy. Never before today has man been so keenly aware of freedom, yet at the same time, new forms of social and psychological slavery make their appearance.

Although the world of today has a very vivid sense of its unity and of how one man depends on another in needful solidarity, it is most grievously torn into opposing camps by conflicting forces. For political, social, economic, racial, and ideological disputes still continue bitterly, and with them the peril of a war which would reduce everything to ashes. True, there is a growing exchange of ideas, but the very words by which key concepts are expressed take on quite different meanings in diverse ideological systems. Finally, man painstakingly searches for a better world, without working with equal zeal for the betterment of his own spirit.

Caught up in such numerous complications, very many of our contemporaries are kept from accurately identifying permanent values and adjusting them properly to fresh discoveries. As a result, buffeted between hope and anxiety and pressing one another with questions about the present course of events, they are burdened down with uneasiness. This same course of events leads men to look for answers. Indeed, it forces them to do so.

PROFOUNDLY CHANGED CONDITIONS

5.   Today's spiritual agitation and the changing conditions of life are part of a broader and deeper revolution. As a result of the latter, intellectual formation is ever increasingly based on the mathematical and natural sciences and on those dealing with man himself, while in the practical order the technology which stems from these sciences takes on mounting importance.

This scientific spirit exerts a new kind of impact on the cultural sphere and on modes of thought. Technology is now transforming the face of the earth, and is already trying to master outer space. To a certain extent, the human intellect is also broadening its dominion over time: over the past by means of historical knowledge; over the future by the art of projecting and by planning.

Advances in biology, psychology, and the social sciences not only bring men hope of improved self-knowledge. In conjunction with technical methods, they are also helping men to exert direct influence on the life of social groups. At the same time, the human race is giving ever-increasing thought to forecasting and regulating its own population growth.

History itself speeds along on so rapid a course that an individual person can scarcely keep abreast of it. The destiny of the human community has become all of a piece, where once the various groups of men had a kind of private history of their own. Thus, the human race has passed from a rather static concept of reality to a more dynamic, evolutionary one. In consequence, there has arisen a new series of problems, a series as important as can be, calling for new efforts of analysis and synthesis.

CHANGES IN THE SOCIAL ORDER

6.   By this very circumstance, the traditional local communities such as father-centered families, clans, tribes, villages, various groups and associations stemming from social contacts experience more thorough changes every day.

The industrial type of society is gradually being spread, leading some nations to economic affluence, and radically transforming ideas and social conditions established for centuries. Likewise, the practice and pursuit of city living has grown, either because of multiplication of cities and their inhabitants, or by a transplantation of city life to rural settings.

New and more efficient media of social communication are contributing to the knowledge of events. By setting off chain reactions, they are giving the swiftest and widest possible circulation to styles of thought and feeling.

It is also noteworthy how many men are being induced to migrate on various counts, and are thereby changing their manner of life. Thus a man's ties with his fellows are constantly being multiplied. At the same time "socialization" brings further ties, without, however, always promoting appropriate personal development and truly personal relationships ("personalization").

This kind of evolution can be seen more clearly in those nations which already enjoy the conveniences of economic and technological progress, though it is also astir among peoples still striving for such progress and eager to secure for themselves the advantages of an industrialized and urbanized society. These peoples, especially those among them who are attached to older traditions, are simultaneously undergoing a movement toward more mature and personal exercise of liberty.

PSYCHOLOGICAL, MORAL, AND RELIGIOUS CHANGES

7.   A change in attitudes and in human structures frequently calls accepted values into question. This is especially true of young people, who have grown impatient on more than one occasion, and indeed become rebels in their distress. Aware of their own influence in the life of society, they want to assume a role in it sooner. As a result, parents and educators frequently experience greater difficulties day by day in discharging their tasks.

The institutions, laws, and modes of thinking and feeling as handed down from previous generations do not always seem to be well adapted to the contemporary state of affairs. Hence arises an upheaval in the manner and even the norms of behavior.

Finally, these new conditions have their impact on religion. On the one hand a more critical ability to distinguish religion from a magical view of the world and from the superstitions which still circulate purifies religion and exacts day by day a more personal and explicit adherence to faith. As a result many persons are achieving a more vivid sense of God.

On the other hand, growing numbers of people are abandoning religion in practice. Unlike former days, the denial of God or of religion, or the abandonment of them, are no longer unusual and individual occurrences. For today it is not rare for such decisions to be presented as requirements of scientific progress or of a certain new humanism. In numerous places these views are voiced not only in the teachings of philosophers, but on every side they influence literature, the arts, the interpretation of the humanities and of history, and civil laws themselves. As a consequence, many people are shaken.

IMBALANCES IN THE MODERN WORLD

8.   Because they are coming so rapidly, and often in a disorderly fashion, all these changes beget contradictions and imbalances, or intensify them. Indeed the very fact that men are more conscious than ever of the inequalities in the world has the same effect.

Within the individual person there too often develops imbalance between an intellect which is modern in practical matters, and a theoretical system of thought which can neither master the sum total of its ideas, nor arrange them adequately into a synthesis. Likewise, an imbalance arises between a concern for practicality and efficiency, and the demands of moral conscience; also, very often, between the conditions of collective existence and the requisites of personal thought, and even of contemplation. Specialization in any human activity can at length deprive a man of a comprehensive view of reality.

As for the family, discord results from demographic, economic, and social pressures, or from difficulties which arise between succeeding generations, or from new social relationships between men and women.

Significant differences crop up too between races and between various kinds of social orders; between wealthy nations and those which are less influential or are needy; finally, between international institutions born of the popular desire for peace, and the ambition to propagate one's own ideology, as well as collective greed existing in nations or other groups.

What results is mutual distrust, enmities, conflicts, and hardships. Of such is man at once the cause and the victim.

THE BROADER DESIRES OF MANKIND

9.   Meanwhile, the conviction grows not only that humanity can and should increasingly consolidate its control over creation, but even more, that it devolves on humanity to establish a political, social, and economic order which will to an ever better extent serve man and help individuals as well as groups to affirm and develop the dignity proper to them.

As a result very many persons are quite aggressively demanding those benefits of which with vivid awareness they judge themselves to be deprived either through injustice or unequal distribution. Nations on the road to progress, like those recently made independent, desire to participate in the goods of modern civilization, not only in the political field but also economically, and to play their part freely on the world scene. Still they continually fall behind while very often their dependence on wealthier nations deepens more rapidly, even in the economic sphere.

People hounded by hunger call upon those better off. Where they have not yet won it, women claim for themselves an equity with men before the law and in fact. Laborers and farmers seek not only to provide for the necessities of life but to develop the gifts of the personality by their labors, and indeed to take part in regulating economic, social, political, and cultural life. Now, for the first time in human history, all people are convinced that the benefits of culture ought to be and actually can be extended to everyone.

Still, beneath all these demands lies a deeper and more widespread longing. Persons and societies thirst for a full and free life worthy of man—one in which they can subject to their own welfare all that the modern world can offer them so abundantly. In addition, nations try harder every day to bring about a kind of universal community.

Since all these things are so, the modern world shows itself at once powerful and weak, capable of the noblest deeds or the foulest. Before it lies the path to freedom or to slavery, to progress or retreat, to brotherhood or hatred. Moreover, man is becoming aware that it is his responsibility to guide aright the forces which he has unleashed and which can enslave him or minister to him. That is why he is putting questions to himself.

MAN'S DEEPER QUESTIONINGS

10.   The truth is that the imbalances under which the modern world labors are linked with that more basic imbalance rooted in the heart of

man. For in man himself many elements wrestle with one another. Thus, on the one hand, as a creature he experiences his limitations in a multitude of ways. On the other, he feels himself to be boundless in his desires and summoned to a higher life.

Pulled by manifold attractions, he is constantly forced to choose among them and to renounce some. Indeed, as a weak and sinful being, he often does what he would not, and fails to do what he would.[3] Hence he suffers from internal divisions, and from these flow so many and such great discords in society.

No doubt very many whose lives are infected with a practical materialism are blinded against any sharp insight into this kind of dramatic situation. Or else, weighed down by wretchedness, they are prevented from giving the matter any thought.

Thinking that they have found serenity in an interpretation of reality everywhere proposed these days, many look forward to a genuine and total emancipation of humanity wrought solely by human effort. They are convinced that the future rule of man over the earth will satisfy every desire of his heart.

Nor are there lacking men who despair of any meaning to life and praise the boldness of those who think that human existence is devoid of any inherent significance and who strive to confer a total meaning on it by their own ingenuity alone.

Nevertheless, in the face of the modern development of the world, an ever-increasing number of people are raising the most basic questions or recognizing them with a new sharpness: what is man? What is this sense of sorrow, of evil, of death, which continues to exist despite so much progress? What is the purpose of these victories, purchased at so high a cost? What can man offer to society, what can he expect from it? What follows this earthly life?

The Church believes that Christ, who died and was raised up for all,[4] can through His Spirit offer man the light and the strength to measure up to his supreme destiny. Nor has any other name under heaven been given to man by which it is fitting for him to be saved.[5] She likewise holds that in her most benign Lord and Master can be found the key, the focal point, and the goal of all human history.

The Church also maintains that beneath all changes there are many realities which do not change and which have their ultimate foundation in Christ, who is the same yesterday and today, yes and forever.[6] Hence in the light of Christ, the image of the unseen God, the first born of every creature,[7] the Council wishes to speak to all men in order to illuminate the mystery of man and to cooperate in finding the solution to the outstanding problems of our time.

PART I:
The Church and Man's Calling

THE IMPULSES OF THE SPIRIT DEMAND A RESPONSE

11.　　The People of God believes that it is led by the Spirit of the Lord, who fills the earth. Motivated by this faith, it labors to decipher authentic signs of God's presence and purpose in the happenings, needs, and desires in which this People has a part along with other men of our age. For faith throws a new light on everything, manifests God's design for man's total vocation, and thus directs the mind to solutions which are fully human.

This Council, first of all, wishes to assess in this light those values which are most highly prized today, and to relate them to their divine source. For insofar as they stem from endowments conferred by God on man, these values are exceedingly good. Yet they are often wrenched from their rightful function by the taint in man's heart, and hence stand in need of purification.

What does the Church think of man? What recommendations seem needful for the upbuilding of contemporary society? What is the ultimate significance of human activity throughout the world? People are waiting for an answer to these questions. From the answers it will be increasingly clear that the People of God and the human race in whose midst it lives render service to each other. Thus the mission of the Church will show its religious, and by that very fact, its supremely human character.

CHAPTER I
The Dignity of the Human Person

MAN AS MADE IN GOD'S IMAGE

12.　　According to the almost unanimous opinion of believers and unbelievers alike, all things on earth should be related to man as their center and crown.

But what is man? About himself he has expressed, and continues to express, many divergent and even contradictory opinions. In these he often exalts himself as the absolute measure of all things or debases himself to the point of despair. The result is doubt and anxiety.

The Church understands these problems. Endowed with light from God, she can offer solutions to them so that man's true situation can be portrayed and his defects explained, while at the same time his dignity and destiny are justly acknowledged.

For sacred Scripture teaches that man was created "to the image of God," is capable of knowing and loving his Creator, and was appointed by Him as master of all earthly creatures[8] that he might subdue them and use them to God's glory.[9] "What is man that thou art mindful of him or the son of man that thou visitest him? Thou hast made him a little less than the angels, thou has crowned him with glory and honor: thou hast set him over the works of thy hands, thou hast subjected all things under his feet" (Ps. 8:5–6).

But God did not create man as a solitary. For from the beginning "male and female he created them" (Gen. 1:27). Their companionship produces the primary form of interpersonal communion. For by his innermost nature man is a social being, and unless he relates himself to others he can neither live nor develop his potential.

Therefore, as we read elsewhere in holy Scripture, God saw "all the things that he had made, and they were very good" (Gen. 1:31).

SIN

13.   Although he was made by God in a state of holiness, from the very dawn of history man abused his liberty, at the urging of personified Evil. Man set himself against God and sought to find fulfillment apart from God. Although he knew God, he did not glorify Him as God, but his senseless mind was darkened and he served the creature rather than the Creator.[10]

What divine revelation makes known to us agrees with experience. Examining his heart, man finds that he has inclinations toward evil too, and is engulfed by manifold ills which cannot come from his good Creator. Often refusing to acknowledge God as his beginning, man has disrupted also his proper relationship to his own ultimate goal. At the same time he became out of harmony with himself, with others, and with all created things.

Therefore man is split within himself. As a result, all of human life, whether individual or collective, shows itself to be a dramatic struggle between good and evil, between light and darkness. Indeed, man finds that by himself he is incapable of battling the assaults of evil successfully, so that everyone feels as though he is bound by chains.

But the Lord Himself came to free and strengthen man, renewing him inwardly and casting out that prince of this world (cf. Jn. 12:31) who held him in the bondage of sin.[11] For sin has diminished man, blocking his path to fulfillment.

The call to grandeur and the depths of misery are both a part of human experience. They find their ultimate and simultaneous explanation in the light of God's revelation.

THE MAKE-UP OF MAN

14.   Though made of body and soul, man is one. Through his bodily composition he gathers to himself the elements of the material world. Thus they reach their crown through him, and through him raise their voice in free praise of the Creator.[12]

For this reason man is not allowed to despise his bodily life. Rather, he is obliged to regard his body as good and honorable since God has created it and will raise it up on the last day. Nevertheless, wounded by sin, man experiences rebellious stirrings in his body. But the very dignity of man postulates that man glorify God in his body[13] and forbid it to serve the evil inclinations of his heart.

Now, man is not wrong when he regards himself as superior to bodily concerns, and as more than a speck of nature or a nameless constituent of the city of man. For by his interior qualities he outstrips the whole sum of mere things. He finds re-enforcement in this profound insight whenever he enters into his own heart. God, who probes the heart,[14] awaits him there. There he discerns his proper destiny beneath the eyes of God. Thus, when man recognizes in himself a spiritual and immortal soul, he is not being mocked by a deceptive fantasy springing from mere physical or social influences. On the contrary he is getting to the depths of the very truth of the matter.

THE DIGNITY OF THE MIND; TRUTH; WISDOM

15.   Man judges rightly that by his intellect he surpasses the material universe, for he shares in the light of the divine mind. By relentlessly employing his talents through the ages, he has indeed made progress in the practical sciences, technology, and the liberal arts. In our times he has won superlative victories, especially in his probing of the material world and in subjecting it to himself.

Still he has always searched for more penetrating truths, and finds them. For his intelligence is not confined to observable data alone. It can with genuine certitude attain to reality itself as knowable, though in consequence of sin that certitude is partly obscured and weakened.

The intellectual nature of the human person is perfected by wisdom and needs to be. For wisdom gently attracts the mind of man to a quest and a love for what is true and good. Steeped in wisdom, man passes through visible realities to those which are unseen.

Our era needs such wisdom more than bygone ages if the discoveries made by man are to be further humanized. For the future of the world stands in peril unless wiser men are forthcoming. It should also be pointed out than many nations, poorer in economic goods, are quite rich in wisdom and can offer noteworthy advantages to others.

It is, finally, through the gift of the Holy Spirit that man comes by faith to the contemplation and appreciation of the divine plan.[15]

THE DIGNITY OF THE MORAL CONSCIENCE

16.   In the depths of his conscience, man detects a law which he does not impose upon himself, but which holds him to obedience. Always summoning him to love good and avoid evil, the voice of conscience can when necessary speak to his heart more specifically: do this, shun that. For man has in his heart a law written by God. To obey it is the very dignity of man; according to it he will be judged.[16]

Conscience is the most secret core and sanctuary of a man. There he is alone with God, whose voice echoes in his depths.[17] In a wonderful manner conscience reveals that law which is fulfilled by love of God and neighbor.[18] In fidelity to conscience, Christians are joined with the rest of men in the search for truth, and for the genuine solution to the numerous problems which arise in the life of individuals and from social relationships. Hence the more that a correct conscience holds sway, the more persons and groups turn aside from blind choice and strive to be guided by objective norms of morality.

Conscience frequently errs from invincible ignorance without losing its dignity. The same cannot be said of a man who cares but little for truth and goodness, or of a conscience which by degrees grows practically sightless as a result of habitual sin.

THE EXCELLENCE OF LIBERTY

17.   Only in freedom can man direct himself toward goodness. Our contemporaries make much of this freedom and pursue it eagerly; and

rightly so, to be sure. Often, however, they foster it perversely as a license for doing whatever pleases them, even if it is evil.

For its part, authentic freedom is an exceptional sign of the divine image within man. For God has willed that man be left "in the hand of his own counsel"[19] so that he can seek his Creator spontaneously, and come freely to utter and blissful perfection through loyalty to Him. Hence man's dignity demands that he act according to a knowing and free choice. Such a choice is personally motivated and prompted from within. It does not result from blind internal impulse nor from mere external pressure.

Man achieves such dignity when, emancipating himself from all captivity to passion, he pursues his goal in a spontaneous choice of what is good, and procures for himself, through effective and skillful action, apt means to that end. Since man's freedom has been damaged by sin, only by the help of God's grace can he bring such a relationship with God into full flower. Before the jugment seat of God each man must render an account of his own life, whether he has done good or evil.[20]

THE MYSTERY OF DEATH

18.   It is in the face of death that the riddle of human existence becomes most acute. Not only is man tormented by pain and by the advancing deterioration of his body, but even more so by a dread of perpetual extinction. He rightly follows the intuition of his heart when he abhors and repudiates the absolute ruin and total disappearance of his own person.

Man rebels against death because he bears in himself an eternal seed which cannot be reduced to sheer matter. All the endeavors of technology, though useful in the extreme, cannot calm his anxiety. For a prolongation of biological life is unable to satisfy that desire for a higher life which is inescapably lodged in his breast.

Although the mystery of death utterly beggars the imagination, the Church has been taught by divine revelation, and herself firmly teaches, that man has been created by God for a blissful purpose beyond the reach of earthly misery. In addition, that bodily death from which man would have been immune had he not sinned[21] will be vanquished, according to the Christian faith, when man who was ruined by his own doing is restored to wholeness by an almighty and merciful Savior.

For God has called man and still calls him so that with his entire being he might be joined to Him in an endless sharing of a divine life beyond all corruption. Christ won this victory when He rose to life, since by His death He freed man from death.[22] Hence to every thoughtful man a solidly established faith provides the answer to his anxiety about what the future holds for him. At the same time faith gives him the power to be united in Christ with his loved ones who have already been snatched away by death. Faith arouses the hope that they have found true life with God.

THE FORMS AND ROOTS OF ATHEISM

19.   An outstanding cause of human dignity lies in man's call to communion with God. From the very circumstance of his origin, man is already invited to converse with God. For man would not exist were he not created by God's love and constantly preserved by it. And he cannot live fully according to truth unless he freely acknowledges that love and devotes himself to his Creator.

Still, many of our contemporaries have never recognized this intimate and vital link with God, or have explicitly rejected it. Thus atheism must be accounted among the most serious problems of this age, and is deserving of closer examination.

The word atheism is applied to phenomena which are quite distinct from one another. For while God is expressly denied by some, others believe that man can assert absolutely nothing about Him. Still others use such a method so to scrutinize the question of God as to make it seem devoid of meaning. Many, unduly transgressing the limits of the positive sciences, contend that everything can be explained by this kind of scientific reasoning alone, or, by contrast, they altogether disallow that there is any absolute truth.

Some laud man so extravagantly that their faith in God lapses into a kind of anemia, though they seem more inclined to affirm man than to deny God. Again some form for themselves such a fallacious idea of God that when they repudiate this figment they are by no means rejecting the God of the gospel. Some never get to the point of raising questions about God, since they seem to experience no religious stirrings nor do they see why they should trouble themselves about religion.

Moreover, atheism results not rarely from a violent protest against the evil in this world, or from the absolute character with which certain human values are unduly invested, and which thereby already accords them the stature of God. Modern civilization itself often complicates the approach to God, not for any essential reason, but because it is excessively engrossed in earthly affairs.

Undeniably, those who willfully shut out God from their hearts and try to dodge religious questions are not following the dictates of their consciences. Hence they are not free of blame.

Yet believers themselves frequently bear some responsibility for this situation. For, taken as a whole, atheism is not a spontaneous development but stems from a variety of causes, including a critical reaction against religious beliefs, and in some places against the Christian religion in particular. Hence believers can have more than a little to do with the birth of atheism. To the extent that they neglect their own training in the faith, or teach erroneous doctrine, or are deficient in their religious, moral, or social life, they must be said to conceal rather than reveal the authentic face of God and religion.

SYSTEMATIC ATHEISM

20.   Modern atheism often takes on a systematic expression, which, in addition to other arguments against God, stretches the desire for human independence to such a point that it finds difficulties with any kind of dependence on God. Those who profess atheism of this sort maintain that it gives man freedom to be an end unto himself, the sole artisan and creator of his own history. They claim that this freedom cannot be reconciled with the affirmation of a Lord who is author and purpose of all things, or at least that this freedom makes such an affirmation altogether superfluous. The sense of power which modern technical progress generates in man can give color to such a doctrine.

Not to be overlooked among the forms of modern atheism is that which anticipates the liberation of man especially through his economic and social emancipation. This form argues that by its nature religion thwarts such liberation by arousing man's hope for a deceptive future life, thereby diverting him from the constructing of the earthly city. Consequently, when the proponents of this doctrine gain governmental power they vigorously fight against religion. They promote atheism by using those means of pressure which public power has at its disposal. Such is especially the case in the work of educating the young.

THE CHURCH'S ATTITUDE TOWARD ATHEISM

21.   In her loyal devotion to God and men, the Church has already repudiated[23] and cannot cease repudiating, sorrowfully but as firmly as possible, those poisonous doctrines and actions which contradict reason

and the common experience of humanity, and dethrone man from his native excellence.

Still, she strives to detect in the atheistic mind the hidden causes for the denial of God. Conscious of how weighty are the questions which atheism raises, and motivated by love for all men, she believes these questions ought to be examined seriously and more profoundly.

The Church holds that the recognition of God is in no way hostile to man's dignity, since this dignity is rooted and perfected in God. For man was made an intelligent and free member of society by the God who created him. Even more importantly, man is called as a son to commune with God and to share in His happiness. She further teaches that a hope related to the end of time does not diminish the importance of intervening duties, but rather undergirds the acquittal of them with fresh incentives. By contrast, when a divine substructure and the hope of life eternal are wanting, man's dignity is most grievously lacerated, as current events often attest. The riddles of life and death, of guilt and of grief go unsolved, with the frequent result that men succumb to despair.

Meanwhile, every man remains to himself an unsolved puzzle, however obscurely he may perceive it. For on certain occasions no one can entirely escape the kind of self-questioning mentioned earlier, especially when life's major events take place. To this questioning only God fully and most certainly provides an answer as He summons man to higher knowledge and humbler probing.

The remedy which must be applied to atheism, however, is to be sought in a proper presentation of the Church's teaching as well as in the integral life of the Church and her members. For it is the function of the Church, led by the Holy Spirit who renews and purifies her ceaselessly,[24] to make God the Father and His Incarnate Son present and in a sense visible.

This result is achieved chiefly by the witness of a living and mature faith, namely, one trained to see difficulties clearly and to master them. Very many martyrs have given luminous witness to this faith and continue to do so. This faith needs to prove its fruitfulness by penetrating the believer's entire life, including its worldly dimensions, and by activating him toward justice and love, especially regarding the needy. What does the most to reveal God's presence, however, is the brotherly charity of the faithful who are united in spirit as they work together for the faith of the gospel[25] and who prove themselves a sign of unity.

While rejecting atheism, root and branch, the Church sincerely professes that all men, believers and unbelievers alike, ought to work for the rightful betterment of this world in which all alike live. Such an ideal cannot be realized, however, apart from sincere and prudent dialogue. Hence the Church protests against the distinction which some state authorities unjustly make between believers and unbelievers, thereby ignoring fundamental rights of the human person. The Church calls for the active liberty of believers to build up in this world God's temple too. She courteously invites atheists to examine the gospel of Christ with an open mind.

Above all the Church knows that her message is in harmony with the most secret desires of the human heart when she champions the dignity of the human vocation, restoring hope to those who have already despaired of anything higher than their present lot. Far from diminishing man, her message brings to his development light, life, and freedom. Apart from this message nothing will avail to fill up the heart of man: "Thou hast made us for Thyself," O Lord, "and our hearts are restless till they rest in Thee."[26]

CHRIST AS THE NEW MAN

22.   The truth is that only in the mystery of the incarnate Word does the mystery of man take on light. For Adam, the first man, was a figure of Him who was to come,[27] namely, Christ the Lord. Christ, the final Adam, by the revelation of the mystery of the Father and His love, fully reveals man to man himself and makes his supreme calling clear. It is not surprising, then, that in Him all the aforementioned truths find their root and attain their crown.

He who is "the image of the invisible God" (Col. 1:15),[28] is Himself the perfect man. To the sons of Adam He restores the divine likeness which had been disfigured from the first sin onward. Since human nature as He assumed it was not annulled,[29] by that very fact it has been raised up to a divine dignity in our respect too. For by His incarnation the Son of God has united Himself in some fashion with every man. He worked with human hands, He thought with a human mind, acted by human choice,[30] and loved with a human heart. Born of the Virgin Mary, He has truly been made one of us, like us in all things except sin.[31]

As an innocent lamb He merited life for us by the free shedding of His own blood. In Him God reconciled us[32] to Himself and among ourselves. From bondage to the devil and sin, He delivered us, so that each one of us can say with the Apostle: The Son of God 'loved me and gave himself up for me" (Gal. 2:20). By suffering for us He not only provided us with an example for our imitation.[33] He blazed a trail, and if we follow it, life and death are made holy and take on a new meaning.

The Christian man, conformed to the likeness of that Son who is the firstborn of many brothers,[34] receives "the first-fruits of the Spirit" (Rom. 8:23) by which he becomes capable of discharging the new law of love.[35] Through this Spirit, who is "the pledge of our inheritance" (Eph. 1:14), the whole man is renewed from within, even to the achievement of "the redemption of the body" (Rom. 8:23): "If the Spirit of him who raised Jesus from the death dwells in you, then he who raised Jesus Christ from the dead will also bring to life your mortal bodies because of his Spirit who dwells in you" (Rom. 8:11).[36]

Pressing upon the Christian, to be sure, are the need and the duty to battle against evil through manifold tribulations and even to suffer death. But, linked with the paschal mystery and patterned on the dying Christ, he will hasten forward to resurrection in the strength which comes from hope.[37]

All this holds true not only for Christians, but for all men of good will in whose hearts grace works in an unseen way.[38] For, since Christ died for all men,[39] and since the ultimate vocation of man is in fact one, and divine, we ought to believe that the Holy Spirit in a manner known only to God offers to every man the possibility of being associated with this paschal mystery.

Such is the mystery of man, and it is a great one, as seen by believers in the light of Christian revelation. Through Christ and in Christ, the riddles of sorrow and death grow meaningful. Apart from His gospel, they overwhelm us. Christ has risen, destroying death by His death. He has lavished life upon us[40] so that, as sons in the Son, we can cry out in the Spirit: Abba, Father![41]

CHAPTER II

The Community of Mankind

THE COUNCIL'S INTENTION

23.   One of the salient features of the modern world is the growing interdependence of men one on the other, a development very largely promoted by modern technical advances. Nevertheless, brotherly dialogue among men does not reach its perfection on the level of technical progress, but on the deeper level of interpersonal relationships. These demand a mutual respect for the full spiritual dignity of the person.

Christian revelation contributes greatly to the promotion of this community between persons, and at the same time leads us to a deeper understanding of the laws of social life which the Creator has written into man's spiritual and moral nature.

Since rather recent documents of the Church's teaching authority have dealt at considerable length with Christian doctrine about human society,[42] this Council is merely going to call to mind some of the more basic truths, treating their foundations under the light of revelation. Then it will dwell more at length on certain of their implications having special significance for our day.

GOD'S PLAN GIVES MAN'S VOCATION A COMMUNITARIAN NATURE

24.　　God, who has fatherly concern for everyone, has willed that all men should constitute one family and treat one another in a spirit of brotherhood. For having been created in the image of God, who "from one man has created the whole human race and made them live all over the face of the earth" (Acts 17:26), all men are called to one and the same goal, namely, God Himself.

For this reason, love for God and neighbor is the first and greatest commandment. Sacred Scripture, however, teaches us that the love of God cannot be separated from love of neighbor: "If there is any other commandment, it is summed up in this saying, Thou shalt love thy neighbor as thyself. . . . Love therefore is the fulfillment of the Law" (Rom. 13:9–10; cf. 1 Jn. 4:20). To men growing daily more dependent on one another, and to a world becoming more unified every day, this truth proves to be of paramount importance.

Indeed, the Lord Jesus, when He prayed to the Father, "that all may be one . . . as we are one" (Jn. 17:21–22) opened up vistas closed to human reason. For He implied a certain likeness between the union of the divine Persons, and in the union of God's sons in truth and charity. This likeness reveals that man, who is the only creature on earth which God willed for itself, cannot fully find himself except through a sincere gift of himself.[43]

THE INTERDEPENDENCE OF PERSON AND SOCIETY

25.　　Man's social nature makes it evident that the progress of the human person and the advance of society itself hinge on each other. For the beginning, the subject and the goal of all social institutions is and must be the human person, which for its part and by its very nature stands completely in need of social life.[44] This social life is not something added on to man. Hence, through his dealings with others, through reciprocal duties, and through fraternal dialogue he develops all his gifts and is able to rise to his destiny.

Among those social ties which man needs for his development some, like the family and political community, relate with greater immediacy to his innermost nature. Others originate rather from his free decision. In our era, for various reasons, reciprocal ties and mutual dependencies increase day by day and give rise to a variety of associations and organizations, both public and private. This development, which is called socialization,* while certainly not without its dangers, brings with it many advantages with respect to consolidating and increasing the qualities of the human person, and safeguarding his rights.[45]

But if by this social life the human person is greatly aided in responding to his destiny, even in its religious dimensions, it cannot be denied that men are often diverted from doing good and spurred toward evil by the social circumstances in which they live and are immersed from their birth. To be sure the disturbances which so frequently occur in the social order result in part from the natural tensions of economic, political, and social forms. But at a deeper level they flow from man's pride and selfishness, which contaminate even the social sphere. When the structure of affairs is flawed by the consequences of sin, man, already born with a bent toward evil, finds there new inducements to sin, which cannot be overcome without strenuous efforts and the assistance of grace.

PROMOTING THE COMMON GOOD

26.   Every day human interdependence grows more tightly drawn and spreads by degrees over the whole world. As a result the common good, that is, the sum of those conditions of social life which allow social groups and their individual members relatively thorough and ready access to their own fulfillment, today takes on an increasingly universal complexion and consequently involves rights and duties with respect to the whole human race. Every social group must take account of the needs

---

* The use of "socialization" upset some commentators when John XXIII first employed the term in his *Mater et Magistra*, even though it had previously appeared in letters from the Vatican Secretariat of State. It is true that the Latin text of that encyclical resorted to involved paraphrases of a term that appeared in the several modern-language versions from the Vatican. Here, however, the Council uses the Latin "socializatio" and indicates by paraphrase that it means exactly what John XXIII had in mind back in 1961. [Editor's note in Abbott edition]

and legitimate aspirations of other groups, and even of the general welfare of the entire human family.[46]

At the same time, however, there is a growing awareness of the exalted dignity proper to the human person, since he stands above all things, and his rights and duties are universal and inviolable. Therefore, there must be made available to all men everything necessary for leading a life truly human, such as food, clothing, and shelter; the right to choose a state of life freely and to found a family, the right to education, to employment, to a good reputation, to respect, to appropriate information, to activity in accord with the upright norm of one's own conscience, to protection of privacy and to rightful freedom in matters religious too.

Hence, the social order and its development must unceasingly work to the benefit of the human person if the disposition of affairs is to be subordinate to the personal realm and not contrariwise, as the Lord indicated when He said that the Sabbath was made for man, and not man for the Sabbath.[47]

This social order requires constant improvement. It must be founded on truth, built on justice, and animated by love; in freedom it should grow every day toward a more humane balance.[48] An improvement in attitudes and widespread changes in society will have to take place if these objectives are to be gained.

God's Spirit, who with a marvelous providence directs the unfolding of time and renews the face of the earth, is not absent from this development. The ferment of the gospel, too, has aroused and continues to arouse in man's heart the irresistible requirements of his dignity.

REVERENCE FOR THE HUMAN PERSON

27.   Coming down to practical and particularly urgent consequences, this Council lays stress on reverence for man; everyone must consider his every neighbor without exception as another self, taking into account first of all his life and the means necessary to living it with dignity,[49] so as not to imitate the rich man who had no concern for the poor man Lazarus.[50]

In our times a special obligation binds us to make ourselves the neighbor of absolutely every person, and of actively helping him when he comes across our path, whether he be an old person abandoned by all, a foreign laborer unjustly looked down upon, a refugee, a child born of an unlawful union and wrongly suffering for a sin he did not commit, or a hungry person who disturbs our conscience by recalling the voice of the Lord: "As long as you did it for one of these, the least of my brethren, you did it for me" (Mt. 25:40).

Futhermore, whatever is opposed to life itself, such as any type of murder, genocide, abortion, euthanasia, or willful self-destruction, whatever violates the integrity of the human person, such as mutilation, torments inflicted on body or mind, attempts to coerce the will itself, whatever insults human dignity, such as subhuman living conditions, arbitrary imprisonment, deportation, slavery, prostitution, the selling of women and children; as well as disgraceful working conditions, where men are treated as mere tools for profit, rather than as free and responsible persons; all these things and others of their like are infamies indeed. They poison human society, but they do more harm to those who practice them than those who suffer from the injury. Moreover they are a supreme dishonor to the Creator.

REVERENCE AND LOVE FOR ENEMIES

28.   Respect and love ought to be extended also to those who think or act differently than we do in social, political, and religious matters, too. In fact, the more deeply we come to understand their ways of thinking through such courtesy and love, the more easily will we be able to enter into dialogue with them.

This love and good will, to be sure, must in no way render us indifferent to truth and goodness. Indeed love itself impels the disciples of Christ to speak the saving truth to all men. But it is necessary to distinguish between error, which always merits repudiation, and the person in error, who never loses the dignity of being a person, even when he is flawed by false or inadequate religious notions.[51] God alone is the judge and searcher of hearts; for that reason He forbids us to make judgments about the internal guilt of anyone.[52]

The teaching of Christ even requires that we forgive injuries,[53] and extends the law of love to include every enemy, according to the command of the New Law: "You have heard that it was said, 'Thou shalt love thy neighbor, and shalt hate thy enemy.' But I say to you, love your enemies, do good to those who hate you, and pray for those who persecute and calumniate you" (Mt. 5:43–44).

THE ESSENTIAL EQUALITY OF MEN; AND SOCIAL JUSTICE

29.   Since all men possess a rational soul and are created in God's likeness, since they have the same nature and origin, have been redeemed by Christ, and enjoy the same divine calling and destiny, the basic equality of all must receive increasingly greater recognition.

True, all men are not alike from the point of view of varying physical power and the diversity of intellectual and moral resources. Nevertheless, with respect to the fundamental rights of the person, every type of discrimination, whether social or cultural, whether based on sex, race, color, social condition, language, or religion, is to be overcome and eradicated as contrary to God's intent. For in truth it must still be regretted that fundamental personal rights are not yet being universally honored. Such is the case of a woman who is denied the right and freedom to choose a husband, to embrace a state of life, or to acquire an education or cultural benefits equal to those recognized for men.

Moreover, although rightful differences exist between men, the equal dignity of persons demands that a more humane and just condition of life be brought about. For excessive economic and social differences between the members of the one human family or population groups cause scandal, and militate against social justice, equity, the dignity of the human person, as well as social and international peace.

Human institutions, both private and public, must labor to minister to the dignity and purpose of man. At the same time let them put up a stubborn fight against any kind of slavery, whether social or political, and safeguard the basic rights of man under every political system. Indeed human institutions themselves must be accommodated by degrees to the highest of all realities, spiritual ones, even though meanwhile, a long enough time will be required before they arrive at the desired goal.

MORE THAN AN INDIVIDUALISTIC ETHIC IS REQUIRED

30.   Profound and rapid changes make it particularly urgent that no one, ignoring the trend of events or drugged by laziness, content himself with a merely individualistic morality. It grows increasingly true that the obligations of justice and love are fulfilled only if each person, contributing to the common good, according to his own abilities and the needs of others, also promotes and assists the public and private institutions dedicated to bettering the conditions of human life.

Yet there are those who, while professing grand and rather noble sentiments, nevertheless in reality live always as if they cared nothing for the needs of society. Many in various places even make light of social laws and precepts, and do not hesitate to resort to various frauds and deceptions in avoiding just taxes or other debts due to society. Others think little of certain norms of social life, for example those designed for the protection of health, or laws establishing speed limits. They do not even avert to the fact that by such indifference they imperil their own life and that of others.

Let everyone consider it his sacred obligation to count social necessities among the primary duties of modern man, and to pay heed to them. For the more unified the world becomes, the more plainly do the offices of men extend beyond particular groups and spread by degrees to the whole world. But this challenge cannot be met unless individual men and their associations cultivate in themselves the moral and social virtues, and promote them in society. Thus, with the needed help of divine grace, men who are truly new and artisans of a new humanity can be forthcoming.

RESPONSIBILITY AND PARTICIPATION

31. In order for individual men to discharge with greater exactness the obligations of their conscience toward themselves and the various groups to which they belong, they must be carefully educated to a higher degree of culture through the use of the immense resources available today to the human race. Above all the education of youth from every social background has to be undertaken, so that there can be produced not only men and women of refined talents, but those great-souled persons who are so desperately required by our times.

Now a man can scarcely arrive at the needed sense of responsibility unless his living conditions allow him to become conscious of his dignity, and to rise to his destiny by spending himself for God and for others. But human freedom is often crippled when a man falls into extreme poverty, just as it withers when he indulges in too many of life's comforts and imprisons himself in a kind of splendid isolation. Freedom acquires new strength, by contrast, when a man consents to the unavoidable requirements of social life, takes on the manifold demands of human partnership, and commits himself to the service of the human community.

Hence, the will to play one's role in common endeavors should be everywhere encouraged. Praise is due to those national procedures which allow the largest possible number of citizens to participate in public affairs with genuine freedom. Account must be taken, to be sure, of the actual conditions of each people and the vigor required by public authority.

If every citizen is to feel inclined to take part in the activities of the various groups which make up the social body, these must offer advantages which will attract members and dispose them to serve others. We can justly consider that the future of humanity lies in the hands of those who are strong enough to provide coming generations with reasons for living and hoping.

THE INCARNATE WORD AND HUMAN SOLIDARITY

32.   God did not create man for life in isolation, but for the formation of social unity. So also "it has pleased God to make men holy and save them not merely as individuals, without any mutual bonds, but by making them into a single people, a people which acknowledges Him in truth and serves Him in holiness."[54] So from the beginning of salvation history He has chosen men not just as individuals but as members of a certain community. Revealing His mind to them, God called these chosen ones "His people" (Ex. 3:7–12), and, furthermore, made a covenant with them on Sinai.[55]

This communitarian character is developed and consummated in the work of Jesus Christ. For the very Word made flesh willed to share in the human fellowship. He was present at the wedding of Cana, visited the house of Zacchaeus, ate with publicans and sinners. He revealed the love of the Father and the sublime vocation of man in terms of the most common of social realities and by making use of the speech and the imagery of plain everyday life. Willingly obeying the laws of his country, He sanctified those human ties, especially family ones, from which social relationships arise. He chose to lead the life proper to an artisan of His time and place.

In His preaching He clearly taught the sons of God to treat one another as brothers. In His prayers He pleaded that all His disciples might be "one." Indeed, as the Redeemer of all, He offered Himself for all even to point of death. "Greater love than this no one has, that one lay down his life for his friends" (Jn. 15:13). He commanded His apostles to preach to all peoples the gospel message so that the human race might become the Family of God, in which the fullness of the Law would be love.

As the first-born of many brethren and through the gift of His Spirit, He founded after His death and resurrection a new brotherly community composed of all those who receive Him in faith and in love. This He did through His Body, which is the Church. There everyone, as members one of the other, would render mutual service according to the different gifts bestowed on each.

This solidarity must be constantly increased until that day on which it will be brought to perfection. Then, saved by grace, men will offer flawless glory to God as a family beloved of God and of Christ their Brother.

CHAPTER III
Man's Activity throughout the World

THE PROBLEM DEFINED

33.   Through his labor and his native endowments man has ceaselessly striven to better his life. Today, however, especially with the help of science and technology, he has extended his mastery over nearly the whole of nature and continues to do so. Thanks primarily to increased opportunities for many kinds of interchange among nations, the human family is gradually recognizing that it comprises a single world community and is making itself so. Hence many benefits once looked for, especially from heavenly powers, man has now enterprisingly procured for himself.

In the face of these immense efforts which already preoccupy the whole human race, men raise numerous questions among themselves. What is the meaning and value of this feverish activity? How should all these things be used? To the achievement of what goal are the strivings of individuals and societies heading?

The Church guards the heritage of God's Word and draws from it religious and moral principles, without always having at hand the solution to particular problems. She desires thereby to add the light of revealed truth to mankind's store of experience, so that the path which humanity has taken in recent times will not be a dark one.

THE VALUE OF HUMAN ACTIVITY

34.   Throughout the course of the centuries, men have labored to better the circumstances of their lives through a momumental amount of individual and collective effort. To believers, this point is settled: considered in itself, such human activity accords with God's will. For man, created to God's image, received a mandate to subject to himself the earth and all that it contains, and to govern the world with justice and holiness;[56] a mandate to relate himself and the totality of things to Him who was to be acknowledged as the Lord and Creator of all. Thus, by the subjection of all things to man, the name of God would be wonderful in all the earth.[57]

This mandate concerns even the most ordinary everyday activities. For while providing the substance of life for themselves and their families, men and women are performing their activities in a way which appropriately benefits society. They can justly consider that by their labor they are unfolding the Creator's work, consulting the advantages of their brother men, and contributing by their personal industry to the realization in history of the divine plan.[58]

Thus, far from thinking that works produced by man's own talent and energy are in opposition to God's power, and that the rational creature exists as a kind of rival to the Creator, Christians are convinced that the triumphs of the human race are a sign of God's greatness and the flowering of His own mysterious design. For the greater man's power becomes, the farther his individual and community responsibility extends. Hence it is clear that men are not deterred by the Christian message from building up the world, or impelled to neglect the welfare of their fellows. They are, rather, more stringently bound to do these very things.[59]

THE REGULATION OF HUMAN ACTIVITY

35.   Just as human activity proceeds from man, so it is ordered toward man. For when a man works he not only alters things and society, he develops himself as well. He learns much, he cultivates his resources, he goes outside of himself and beyond himself.

Rightly understood, this kind of growth is of greater value than any external riches which can be garnered. A man is more precious for what he is than for what he has.[60] Similarly, all that men do to obtain greater justice, wider brotherhood, and a more humane ordering of social relationships has greater worth than technical advances. For these advances can supply the material for human progress, but of themselves alone they can never actually bring it about.

Hence, the norm of human activity is this: that in accord with the divine plan and will, it should harmonize with the genuine good of the human race, and allow men as individuals and as members of society to pursue their total vocation and fulfill it.

THE RIGHTFUL INDEPENDENCE OF EARTHLY AFFAIRS

36.   Now, many of our contemporaries seem to fear that a closer bond between human activity and religion will work against the independence of men, of societies, or of the sciences.

If by the autonomy of earthly affairs we mean that created things and societies themselves enjoy their own laws and values which must be gradually deciphered, put to use, and regulated by men, then it is entirely right to demand that autonomy. Such is not merely required by modern man, but harmonizes also with the will of the Creator. For by the very circumstance of their having been created, all things are endowed with their own stability, truth, goodness, proper laws, and order. Man must respect these as he isolates them by the appropriate methods of the individual sciences or arts.

Therefore, if methodical investigation within every branch of learning is carried out in a genuinely scientific manner and in accord with moral norms, it never truly conflicts with faith. For earthly matters and the concerns of faith derive from the same God.[61] Indeed, whoever labors to penetrate the secrets of reality with a humble and steady mind, is, even unawares, being led by the hand of God, who holds all things in existence, and gives them their identity.

Consequently, we cannot but deplore certain habits of mind, sometimes found too among Christians,* which do not sufficiently attend to the rightful independence of science. The arguments and controversies which they spark lead many minds to conclude that faith and science are mutually opposed.[62]

But if the expression, the independence of temporal affairs, is taken to mean that created things do not depend on God, and that man can use them without any reference to their Creator, anyone who acknowledges God will see how false such a meaning is. For without the Creator the creature would disappear. For their part, however, all believers of whatever religion have always heard His revealing voice in the discourse of creatures. But when God is forgotten the creature itself grows unintelligible.

HUMAN ACTIVITY AS INFECTED BY SIN

37.   Sacred Scripture teaches the human family what the experience of the ages confirms: that while human progress is a great advantage to man, it brings with it a strong temptation. For when the order of values is jumbled, and bad is mixed with the good, individuals and groups pay heed solely to their own interests, and not to those of others. Thus it

---

* The official annotation at the close of this sentence is to a recently published study on Galileo. It seems fair to say that the conciliar text intends here to warn against another Galileo affair. Several speakers in the Council had called for some such warning and Bishop Arthur Elchinger had asked for an official rehabilitation and act of amend. It is interesting to note that publication of the two-volume study by Msgr. Pio Paschini had been delayed a number of years and was only finally undertaken at papal urging. [Editor's note in Abbot edition]

happens that the world ceases to be a place of true brotherhood. In our own day, the magnified power of humanity threatens to destroy the race itself.

For a monumental struggle against the powers of darkness pervades the whole history of man. The battle has joined from the very origins of the world and will continue until the last day, as the Lord has attested.[63] Caught in this conflict man is obliged to wrestle constantly if he is to cling to what is good. Nor can he achieve his own integrity without valiant efforts and the help of God's grace.

That is why Christ's Church, trusting in the design of the Creator, acknowledges that human progress can serve man's true happiness. Yet she cannot help echoing the Apostle's warning: "Be not conformed to this world" (Rom. 12:2). By the world is here meant that spirit of vanity and malice which transforms into an instrument of sin those human energies intended for the service of God and man.

Hence if anyone wants to know how this unhappy situation can be overcome, Christians will tell him that all human activity, constantly imperiled by man's pride and deranged self-love, must be purified and perfected by the power of Christ's cross and resurrection. For, redeemed by Christ and made a new creature in the Holy Spirit, man is able to love the things themselves created by God, and ought to do so. He can receive them from God, and respect and reverence them as flowing constantly from the hand of God.

Grateful to his Benefactor for these creatures, using and enjoying them in detachment and liberty of spirit, man is led forward into a true possession of the world, as having nothing, yet possessing all things.[64] "All are yours, and you are Christ's, and Christ is God's" (1 Cor. 3:22–23).

HUMAN ACTIVITY FINDS PERFECTION IN THE PASCHAL MYSTERY

38.   For God's Word, through whom all things were made, was Himself made flesh and dwelt on the earth of men.[65] Thus He entered the world's history as a perfect man, taking that history up into Himself and summarizing it.[66] He Himself revealed to us that "God is love" (1 Jn. 4:8). At the same time He taught us that the new command of love was the basic law of human perfection and hence of the world's transformation.

To those, therefore, who believe in divine love, He gives assurance that the way of love lies open to all men and that the effort to establish a universal brotherhood is not a hopeless one. He cautions them at the same time that this love is not something to be reserved for important matters, but must be pursued chiefly in the ordinary circumstances of life.

Undergoing death itself for all of us sinners,[67] He taught us by example that we too must shoulder that cross which the world and the flesh inflict upon those who search after peace and justice. Appointed Lord by His resurrection and given plenary power in heaven and on earth,[68] Christ is now at work in the hearts of men through the energy of His Spirit. He arouses not only a desire for the age to come, but, by that very fact, He animates, purifies, and strengthens those noble longings too by which the human family strives to make its life more human and to render the whole earth submissive to this goal.

Now, the gifts of the Spirit are diverse. He calls some to give clear witness to the desire for a heavenly home and to keep that desire green among the human family. He summons others to dedicate themselves to the earthly service of men and to make ready the material of the celestial realm by this ministry of theirs. Yet He frees all of them so that by putting aside love of self and bringing all earthly resources into the service of human life they can devote themselves to that future when humanity itself will become an offering accepted by God.[69]

The Lord left behind a pledge of this hope and strength for life's journey in that sacrament of faith where natural elements refined by man are changed into His glorified Body and Blood, providing a meal of brotherly solidarity and a foretaste of the heavenly banquet.

A NEW EARTH AND A NEW HEAVEN

39.   We do not know the time for the consummation of the earth and of humanity.[70] Nor do we know how all things will be transformed. As deformed by sin, the shape of this world will pass away.[71] But we are taught that God is preparing a new dwelling place and a new earth where justice will abide,[72] and whose blessedness will answer and surpass all the longings for peace which spring up in the human heart.[73]

Then, with death overcome, the sons of God will be raised up in Christ. What was sown in weakness and corruption will be clothed with incorruptibility.[74] While charity and its fruits endure,[75] all that creation[76] which God made on man's account will be unchained from the bondage of vanity.

Therefore, while we are warned that it profits a man nothing if he gain the whole world and lose himself,[77] the expectation of a new earth must not weaken but rather stimulate our concern for cultivating this one. For here grows the body of a new human family, a body which even now is able to give some kind of foreshadowing of the new age.

Earthly progress must be carefully distinguished from the growth of

Christ's kingdom. Nevertheless, to the extent that the former can contribute to the better ordering of human society, it is of vital concern to the kingdom of God.[78]

For after we have obeyed the Lord, and in His Spirit nurtured on earth the values of human dignity, brotherhood and freedom, and indeed all the good fruits of our nature and enterprise, we will find them again, but freed of stain, burnished and transfigured. This will be so when Christ hands over to the Father a kingdom eternal and universal: "a kingdom of truth and life, of holiness and grace, of justice, love, and peace."[79] On this earth that kindgom is already present in mystery. When the Lord returns, it will be brought into full flower.

CHAPTER IV

The Role of the Church in the Modern World

THE CHURCH AND THE WORLD AS MUTUALLY RELATED

40.   Everything we have said about the dignity of the human person, and about the human community and the profound meaning of human activity, lays the foundation for the relationship between the Church and the world, and provides the basis for dialogue between them.[80] In this chapter, presupposing everything which has already been said by this Council concerning the mystery of the Church, we must now consider this same Church inasmuch as she exists in the world, living and acting with it.

Coming forth from the eternal Father's love,[81] founded in time by Christ the Redeemer, and made one in the Holy Spirit,[82] the Church has a saving and an eschatological purpose which can be fully attained only in the future world. But she is already present in this world, and is composed of men, that is, of members of the earthly city who have a call to form the family of God's children during the present history of the human race, and to keep increasing it until the Lord returns.

United on behalf of heavenly values and enriched by them, this family has been "constituted and organized in the world as a society"[83] by Christ, and is equipped with "those means which befit it as a visible and social unity."[84] Thus the Church, at once a visible assembly and a spiritual community,[85] goes forward together with humanity and experiences the same earthly lot which the world does. She serves as a leaven and as a kind of soul for human society[86] as it is to be renewed in Christ and transformed into God's family.

That the earthly and the heavenly city penetrate each other is a fact accessible to faith alone. It remains a mystery of human history, which sin will keep in great disarray until the splendor of God's sons is fully revealed. Pursuing the saving purpose which is proper to her, the Church not only communicates divine life to men, but in some way casts the reflected light of that life over the entire earth.

This she does most of all by her healing and elevating impact on the dignity of the person, by the way in which she strengthens the seams of human society and imbues the everyday activity of men with a deeper meaning and importance. Thus, through her individual members and her whole community, the Church believes she can contribute greatly toward making the family of man and its history more human.

In addition, the Catholic Church gladly holds in high esteem the things which other Christian Churches or ecclesial communities have done or are doing cooperatively by way of achieving the same goal. At the same time, she is firmly convinced that she can be abundantly and variously helped by the world in the matter of preparing the ground for the gospel. This help she gains from the talents and industry of individuals and from human society as a whole. The Council now sets forth certain general principles for the proper fostering of this mutual exchange and assistance in concerns which are in some way common to the Church and the world.

THE HELP WHICH THE CHURCH STRIVES TO BRING TO INDIVIDUALS

41.   Modern man is on the road to a more thorough development of his own personality, and to a growing discovery and vindication of his own rights. Since it has been entrusted to the Church to reveal the mystery of God, who is the ultimate goal of man, she opens up to man at the same time the meaning of his own existence, that is, the innermost truth about himself. The Church truly knows that only God, whom she serves, meets the deepest longings of the human heart, which is never fully satisfied by what this world has to offer.

She also knows that man is constantly worked upon by God's Spirit, and hence can never be altogether indifferent to the problems of religion. The experience of past ages proves this, as do numerous indications in our own times. For man will always yearn to know, at least in an obscure way, what is the meaning of his life, of his activity, of his death. The very presence of the Church recalls these problems to his mind.

But only God, who created man to His own image and ransomed him from sin, provides a fully adequate answer to these questions. This He does through what He has revealed in Christ His Son, who became man. Whoever follows after Christ, the perfect man, becomes himself more of a man.

Thanks to this belief, the Church can anchor the dignity of human nature against all tides of opinion, for example, those which undervalue the human body or idolize it. By no human law can the personal dignity and liberty of man be so aptly safeguarded as by the gospel of Christ which has been entrusted to the Church.

For this gospel announces and proclaims the freedom of the sons of God, and repudiates all the bondage which ultimately results from sin.[87] The gospel has a sacred reverence for the dignity of conscience and its freedom of choice, constantly advises that all human talents be employed in God's service and men's, and, finally, commends all to the charity of all.[88]

All this corresponds with the basic law of the Christian dispensation. For though the same God is Savior and Creator, Lord of human history as well as of salvation history, in the divine arrangement itself the rightful autonomy of the creature, and particularly of man, is not withdrawn. Rather it is re-established in its own dignity and strengthened in it.

Therefore, by virtue of the gospel committed to her, the Church proclaims the rights of man. She acknowledges and greatly esteems the dynamic movements of today by which these rights are everywhere fostered. Yet these movements must be penetrated by the spirit of the gospel and protected against any kind of false autonomy. For we are tempted to think that our personal rights are fully ensured only when we are exempt from every requirement of divine law. But this way lies not the maintenance of the dignity of the human person, but its annihilation.

THE HELP WHICH THE CHURCH STRIVES
TO GIVE TO SOCIETY

42.   The union of the human family is greatly fortified and fulfilled by the unity, founded on Christ,[89] of the family of God's sons.

Christ, to be sure, gave His Church no proper mission in the political, economic, or social order. The purpose which He set before her is a religious one.[90] But out of this religious mission itself come a function, a light, and an energy which can serve to structure and consolidate the human community according to the divine law. As a matter of fact, when circumstances of time and place create the need, she can and indeed should initiate activities on behalf of all men. This is particularly true of activities designed for the needy, such as the works of mercy and similar undertakings.

The Church further recognizes that worthy elements are found in today's social movements, especially an evolution toward unity, a process of wholesome socialization and of association in civic and economic realms. For the promotion of unity belongs to the innermost nature of the Church, since she is, "by her relationship with Christ, both a sacramental sign and an instrument of intimate union with God, and of the unity of all mankind."[91]

Thus she shows the world that an authentic union, social and external, results from a union of minds and hearts, namely, from that faith and charity by which her own unity is unbreakably rooted in the Holy Spirit. For the force which the Church can inject into the modern society of man consists in that faith and charity put into vital practice, not in any external dominion exercised by merely human means.

Moreover, in virtue of her mission and nature, she is bound to no particular form of human culture, nor to any political, economic, or social system. Hence the Church by her very universality can be a very close bond between diverse human communities and nations, provided these trust her and truly acknowledge her right to true freedom in fulfilling her mission. For this reason, the Church admonishes her own sons, but also humanity as a whole, to overcome all strife between nations and races in this family spirit of God's children, and in the same way, to give internal strength to human associations which are just.

This Council, therefore, looks with great respect upon all the true, good, and just elements found in the very wide variety of institutions which the human race has established for itself and constantly continues to establish. The Council affirms, moreover, that the Church is willing to assist and promote all these institutions to the extent that such a service depends on her and can be associated with her mission. She has no fiercer desire than that, in pursuit of the welfare of all, she may be able to develop herself freely under any kind of government which grants recognition to the basic rights of person and family and to the demands of the common good.

THE HELP WHICH THE CHURCH STRIVES TO GIVE
TO HUMAN ACTIVITY THROUGH CHRISTIANS

43.   This Council exhorts Christians, as citizens of two cities, to strive to discharge their earthly duties conscientiously and in response to the

gospel spirit. They are mistaken who, knowing that we have here no abiding city but seek one which is to come,[92] think that they may therefore shirk their earthly responsibilities. For they are forgetting that by the faith itself they are more than ever obliged to measure up to these duties, each according to his proper vocation.[93]

Nor, on the contrary, are they any less wide of the mark who think that religion consists in acts of worship alone and in the discharge of certain moral obligations, and who imagine they can plunge themselves into earthly affairs in such a way as to imply that these are altogether divorced from the religious life. This split between the faith which many profess and their daily lives deserves to be counted among the more serious errors of our age. Long since, the prophets of the Old Testament fought vehemently against this scandal[94] and even more so did Jesus Christ Himself in the New Testament threaten it with grave punishments.[95]

Therefore, let there be no false opposition between professional and social activities on the one part, and religious life on the other. The Christian who neglects his temporal duties neglects his duties toward his neighbor and even God, and jeopardizes his eternal salvation. Christians should rather rejoice that they can follow the example of Christ, who worked as an artisan. In the exercise of all their earthly activities, they can thereby gather their humane, domestic, professional, social, and technical enterprises into one vital synthesis with religious values, under whose supreme direction all things are harmonized unto God's glory.

Secular duties and activities belong properly although not exclusively to laymen. Therefore acting as citizens of the world, whether individually or socially, they will observe the laws proper to each discipline, and labor to equip themselves with a genuine expertise in their various fields. They will gladly work with men seeking the same goals. Acknowledging the demands of faith and endowed with its force, they will unhesitatingly devise new enterprises, where they are appropriate, and put them into action.

Laymen should also know that it is generally the function of their well-formed Christian conscience to see that the divine law is inscribed in the life of the earthly city. From priests they may look for spiritual light and nourishment. Let the layman not imagine that his pastors are always such experts, that to every problem which arises, however complicated, they can readily give him a concrete solution, or even that such is their mission. Rather, enlightened by Christian wisdom and giving close attention to the teaching authority of the Church,[96] let the layman take on his own distinctive role.

Often enough the Christian view of things will itself suggest some specific solution in certain circumstances. Yet it happens rather frequently, and legitimately so, that with equal sincerity some of the faithful will disagree with others on a given matter. Even against the intentions of their proponents, however, solutions proposed on one side or another may be easily confused by many people with the gospel message. Hence it is necessary for people to remember that no one is allowed in the aforementioned situations to appropriate the Church's authority for his opinion. They should always try to enlighten one another through honest discussion, preserving mutual charity and caring above all for the common good.

Since they have an active role to play in the whole life of the Church, laymen are not only bound to penetrate the world with a Christian spirit. They are also called to be witnesses to Christ in all things in the midst of human society.

Bishops, to whom is assigned the task of ruling the Church of God, should, together with their priests, so preach the message of Christ that all the earthly activities of the faithful will be bathed in the light of the gospel. All pastors should remember too that by their daily conduct and concern[97] they are revealing the face of the Church to the world. Men will judge the power and truth of the Christian message thereby. By their lives and speech, in union with religious and their faithful, may pastors demonstrate that even now the Church, by her presence alone and by all the gifts which she possesses, is an unspent fountain of those virtues which the modern world most needs.

By unremitting study they should fit themselves to do their part in establishing dialogue with the world and with men of all shades of opinion. Above all let them take to heart the words which this Council has spoken: "Because the human race today is joining more and more in civic, economic, and social unity, it is that much more necessary that priests, united in concern and effort under the leadership of the bishops and the Supreme Pontiff, wipe out every ground of division, so that the whole human race may be brought into the unity of the family of God."[98]

Although by the power of the Holy Spirit the Church has remained the faithful spouse of her Lord and has never ceased to be the sign of salvation of earth, still she is very well aware that among her members,[99] both clerical and lay, some have been unfaithful to the Spirit of God during the course of many centuries. In the present age, too, it does not escape the Church how great a distance lies between the message she offers and the human failings of those to whom the gospel is entrusted.

Whatever be the judgment of history on these defects, we ought to be conscious of them, and struggle against them energetically, lest they inflict harm on the spread of the gospel. The Church also realizes that in working out her relationship with the world she always has great need of the ripening which comes with the experience of the centuries. Led by the Holy Spirit, Mother Church unceasingly exhorts her sons "to purify and renew themselves so that the sign of Christ can shine more brightly on the face of the Church."[100]

THE HELP WHICH THE CHURCH RECEIVES
FROM THE MODERN WORLD

44.   Just as it is in the world's interest to acknowledge the Church as a historical reality, and to recognize her good influence, so the Church herself knows how richly she has profited by the history and development of humanity.

Thanks to the experience of past ages, the progress of the sciences, and the treasures hidden in the various forms of human culture, the nature of man himself is more clearly revealed and new roads to truth are opened. These benefits profit the Church, too. For, from the beginning of her history, she has learned to express the message of Christ with the help of the ideas and terminology of various peoples, and has tried to clarify it with the wisdom of philosophers, too.

Her purpose has been to adapt the gospel to the grasp of all as well as to the needs of the learned, insofar as such was appropriate. Indeed, this accommodated preaching of the revealed Word ought to remain the law of all evangelization. For thus each nation develops the ability to express Christ's message in its own way. At the same time, a living exchange is fostered between the Church and the diverse cultures of people.[101]

To promote such an exchange, the Church requires special help, particularly in our day, when things are changing very rapidly and the ways of thinking are exceedingly various. She must rely on those who live in the world, are versed in different institutions and specialties, and grasp their innermost significance in the eyes of both believers and unbelievers. With the help of the Holy Spirit, it is the task of the entire People of God, especially pastors and theologians, to hear, distinguish, and interpret the many voices of our age, and to judge them in the light of the divine Word. In this way, revealed truth can always be more deeply penetrated, better understood, and set forth to greater advantage.

Since the Church has a visible and social structure as a sign of her unity in Christ, she can and ought to be enriched by the development of human social life. The reason is not that the constitution given her by Christ is defective, but so that she may understand it more penetratingly, express it better, and adjust it more successfully to our times.

She gratefully understands that in her community life no less than in her individual sons, she receives a variety of helps from men of every rank and condition. For whoever promotes the human community at the family level, culturally, in its economic, social, and political dimensions, both nationally and internationally, such a one, according to God's design, is contributing greatly to the Church community as well, to the extent that it depends on things outside itself. Indeed, the Church admits that she has greatly profited and still profits from the antagonism of those who oppose or persecute her.[102]

CHRIST, THE ALPHA AND THE OMEGA

45.   While helping the world and receiving many benefits from it, the Church has a single intention: that God's kingdom may come, and that the salvation of the whole human race may come to pass. For every benefit which the People of God during its earthly pilgrimage can offer to the human family stems fr   the fact that the Church is "the universal sacrament of salvation,"[103] simultaneously manifesting and exercising the mystery of God's love for man.

For God's Word, by whom all things were made, was Himself made flesh so that as perfect man He might save all men and sum up all things in Himself. The Lord is the goal of human history, the focal point of the longings of history and of civilization, the center of the human race, the joy of every heart, and the answer to all its yearnings.[104] He it is whom the Father raised from the dead, lifted on high, and stationed at His right hand, making Him Judge of the living and the dead. Enlivened and united in His Spirit, we journey toward the consummation of human history, one which fully accords with the counsel of God's love: "To re-establish all things in Christ, both those in the heavens and those on the earth" (Eph. 1:10).

The Lord Himself speaks: "Behold, I come quickly! And my reward is with me, to render to each one according to his works. I am the Alpha and the Omega, the first and the last, the beginning and the end" (Apoc. 22:12–13).

PART II:
Some Problems of Special Urgency

PREFACE

46.   This Council has set forth the dignity of the human person and the work which men have been destined to undertake throughout the world both as individuals and as members of society. There are a number of particularly urgent needs characterizing the present age, needs which go to the roots of the human race. To a consideration of these in the light of the gospel and of human experience, the Council would now direct the attention of all.

Of the many subjects arousing universal concern today, it may be helpful to concentrate on these: marriage and the family, human culture, life in its economic, social, and political dimensions, the bonds between the family of nations, and peace. On each of these may there shine the radiant ideals proclaimed by Christ. By these ideals may Christians be led, and all mankind enlightened, as they search for answers to questions of such complexity.

CHAPTER I
Fostering the Nobility of Marriage and the Family

MARRIAGE AND FAMILY IN THE MODERN WORLD

47.   The well-being of the individual person and of human and Christian society is intimately linked with the healthy condition of that community produced by marriage and family. Hence Christians and all men who hold this community in high esteem sincerely rejoice in the various ways by which men today find help in fostering this community of love and perfecting its life, and by which spouses and parents are assisted in their lofty calling. Those who rejoice in such aids look for additional benefits from them and labor to bring them about.

Yet the excellence of this institution is not everywhere reflected with equal brilliance. For polygamy, the plague of divorce, so-called free love, and other disfigurements have an obscuring effect. In addition, married love is too often profaned by excessive self-love, the worship of pleasure, and illicit practices against human generation. Moreover, serious disturbances are caused in families by modern economic conditions, by influences at once social and psychological, and by the demands of civil society. Finally, in certain parts of the world problems resulting from population growth are generating concern.

All these situations have produced anxious consciences. Yet, the power and strength of the institution of marriage and family can also be seen in the fact that time and again, despite the difficulties produced, the profound changes in modern society reveal the true character of this institution in one way or another.

Therefore, by presenting certain* key points of Church doctrine in a clearer light, this Council wishes to offer guidance and support to those Christians and other men who are trying to keep sacred and to foster the natural dignity of the married state and its superlative value.

THE SANCTITY OF MARRIAGE AND THE FAMILY

48.   The intimate partnership of married life and love has been established by the Creator and qualified by His laws. It is rooted in the conjugal covenant of irrevocable personal consent. Hence, by that human act whereby spouses mutually bestow and accept each other, a relationship arises which by divine will and in the eyes of society too is a lasting one. For the good of the spouses and their offspring as well as of society, the existence of this sacred bond no longer depends on human decisions alone.

For God himself is the author of matrimony, endowed as it is with various benefits and purposes.[105] All of these have a very decisive bearing on the continuation of the human race, on the personal development and eternal destiny of the individual members of a family, and on the dignity, stability, peace, and prosperity of the family itself and of human society as a whole. By their very nature, the institution of matrimony itself

---

*It is important to an understanding of the entire section on Christian marriage and family life to realize that the Council intends to discuss "certain" key points only and not to give an exhaustive treatment of all matters in this area. Thus, it clearly intended to leave untouched those aspects of birth control and related themes that are under debate in the special commission set up by Paul VI to study them. [Editor's note in Abbott edition]

and conjugal love are ordained for the procreation and education of children, and find in them their ultimate crown.

Thus a man and a woman, who by the marriage covenant of conjugal love "are no longer two, but one flesh" (Mt. 19:6), render mutual help and service to each other through an intimate union of their persons and of their actions. Through this union they experience the meaning of their oneness and attain to it with growing perfection day by day. As a mutual gift of two persons, this intimate union, as well as the good of the children, imposes total fidelity on the spouses and argues for an unbreakable oneness between them.[106]

Christ the Lord abundantly blessed this many-faceted love, welling up as it does from the fountain of divine love and structured as it is on the model of His union with the Church. For as God of old made Himself present[107] to His people through a covenant of love and fidelity, so now the Savior of men and the Spouse[108] of the Church comes into the lives of married Christians through the sacrament of matrimony. He abides with them thereafter so that, just as He loved the Church and handed Himself over on her behalf,[109] the spouses may love each other with perpetual fidelity through mutual self-bestowal.

Authentic married love is caught up into divine love and is governed and enriched by Christ's redeeming power and the saving activity of the Church. Thus this love can lead the spouses to God with powerful effect and can aid and strengthen them in the sublime office of being a father or a mother.[110]

For this reason, Christian spouses have a special sacrament by which they are fortified and receive a kind of consecration in the duties and dignity of their state.[111] By virtue of this sacrament, as spouses fulfill their conjugal and family obligations, they are penetrated with the spirit of Christ. This spirit suffuses their whole lives with faith, hope, and charity. Thus they increasingly advance their own perfection, as well as their mutual sanctification, and hence contribute jointly to the glory of God.

As a result, with their parents leading the way by example and family prayer, children and indeed everyone gathered around the family hearth will find a readier path to human maturity, salvation, and holiness. Graced with the dignity and office of fatherhood and motherhood, parents will energetically acquit themselves of a duty which devolves primarily on them, namely education, and especially religious education.

As living members of the family, children contribute in their own way to making their parents holy. For they will respond to the kindness of their parents with sentiments of gratitude, with love and trust. They will stand by them as children should when hardships overtake their parents and old age brings its loneliness. Widowhood, accepted bravely as a continuation of the marriage vocation, will be esteemed by all.[112] Families will share their spiritual riches generously with other families too. Thus the Christian family, which springs from marriage as a reflection of the loving covenant uniting Christ with the Church,[113] and as a participation in that covenant, will manifest to all men the Savior's living presence in the world, and the genuine nature of the Church. This the family will do by the mutual love of the spouses, by their generous fruitfulness, their solidarity and faithfulness, and by the loving way in which all members of the family work together.

CONJUGAL LOVE

49.   The biblical Word of God several times urges the betrothed and the married to nourish and develop their wedlock by pure conjugal love and undivided affection.[114] Many men of our own age also highly regard true love between husband and wife as it manifests itself in a variety of ways depending on the worthy customs of various peoples and times.

This love is an eminently human one since it is directed from one person to another through an affection of the will. It involves the good of the whole person. Therefore it can enrich the expressions of body and mind with a unique dignity, ennobling these expressions as special ingredients and signs of the friendship distinctive of marriage. This love the Lord has judged worthy of special gifts, healing, perfecting, and exalting gifts of grace and of charity.

Such love, merging the human with the divine, leads the spouses to a free and mutual gift of themselves, a gift proving itself by gentle affection and by deed. Such love pervades the whole of their lives.[115] Indeed, by generous activity it grows better and grows greater. Therefore it far excels mere erotic inclination, which, selfishly pursued, soon enough fades wretchedly away.

This love is uniquely expressed and perfected through the marital act. The actions within marriage by which the couple are united intimately and chastely are noble and worthy ones. Expressed in a manner which is truly human, these actions signify and promote that mutual self-giving by which spouses enrich each other with a joyful and thankful will.

Sealed by mutual faithfulness and hollowed above all by Christ's sacrament, this love remains steadfastly true in body and in mind, in bright days or dark. It will never be profaned by adultery or divorce. Firmly established by the Lord, the unity of marriage will radiate from the equal personal dignity of wife and husband, a dignity acknowledged by mutual and total love.

The steady fulfillment of the duties of this Christian vocation demands notable virtue. For this reason, strengthened by grace for holiness of life, the couple will painstakingly cultivate and pray for constancy of love, largeheartedness, and the spirit of sacrifice.

Authentic conjugal love will be more highly prized, and wholesome public opinion created regarding it, if Christian couples give outstanding witness to faithfulness and harmony in that same love, and to their concern for educating their children; also, if they do their part in bringing about the needed cultural, psychological, and social renewal on behalf of marriage and the family.

Especially in the heart of their own families, young people should be aptly and seasonably instructed about the dignity, duty, and expression of married love. Trained thus in the cultivation of chastity, they will be able at a suitable age to enter a marriage of their own after an honorable courtship.

THE FRUITFULNESS OF MARRIAGE

50.   Marriage and conjugal love are by their nature ordained toward the begetting and educating of children. Children are really the supreme gift of marriage and contribute very substantially to the welfare of their parents. The God Himself who said, "It is not good for man to be alone" (Gen. 2:18) and "who made man from the beginning male and female" (Mt. 19:4), wished to share with man a certain special participation in His own creative work . Thus He blessed male and female, saying: "Increase and multiply" (Gen. 1:28).

Hence, while not making the other purposes of matrimony of less account, the true practice of conjugal love, and the whole meaning of the family life which results from it, have this aim: that the couple be ready with stout hearts to cooperate with the love of the Creator and the Savior, who through them will enlarge and enrich His own family day by day.

Parents should regard as their proper mission the task of transmitting human life and educating those to whom it has been transmitted. They should realize that they are thereby cooperators with the love of God the Creator, and are, so to speak, the interpreters of that love. Thus they will fulfill their task with human and Christian responsibility. With docile reverence toward God, they will come to the right decision by common counsel and effort.

They will thoughtfully take into account both their own welfare and that of their children, those already born and those which may be foreseen. For this accounting they will reckon with both the material and the spiritual conditions of the times as well as of their state in life. Finally, they will consult the interests of the family group, of temporal society, and of the Church herself.

The parents themselves should ultimately make this judgment, in the sight of God. But in their manner of acting, spouses should be aware that they cannot proceed arbitrarily. They must always be governed according to a conscience dutifully conformed to the divine law itself, and should be submissive toward the Church's teaching office, which authentically interprets that law in the light of the gospel. That divine law reveals and protects the integral meaning of conjugal love, and impels it toward a truly human fulfillment.

Thus, trusting in divine Providence and refining the spirit of sacrifice,[116] married Christians glorify the Creator and strive toward fulfillment in Christ when, with a generous human and Christian sense of responsibility, they acquit themselves of the duty to procreate. Among the couples who fulfill their God-given task in this way, those merit special mention who with wise and common deliberation, and with a gallant heart, undertake to bring up suitably even a relatively large family.[117]

Marriage to be sure is not instituted solely for procreation. Rather, its very nature as an unbreakable compact between persons, and the welfare of the children, both demand that the mutual love of the spouses, too, be embodied in a rightly ordered manner, that it grow and ripen. Therefore, marriage persists as a whole manner and communion of life, and maintains its value and indissolubility, even when offspring are lacking—despite, rather often, the very intense desire of the couple.

HARMONIZING CONJUGAL LOVE
WITH RESPECT FOR HUMAN LIFE

51. This Council realizes that certain modern conditions often keep couples from arranging their married lives harmoniously, and that they find themselves in circumstances where at least temporarily the size of their families should not be increased. As a result, the faithful exercise of love and the full intimacy of their lives are hard to maintain. But where the intimacy of married life is broken off, it is not rare for its faithfulness to be

imperiled and its quality of fruitfulness ruined. For then the upbringing of the children and the courage to accept new ones are both endangered.

To these problems there are those who presume to offer dishonorable solutions. Indeed, they do not recoil from the taking of life. But the Church issues the reminder that a true contradiction cannot exist between the divine laws pertaining to the transmission of life and those pertaining to the fostering of authentic conjugal love.

For God, the Lord of life, has conferred on men the surpassing ministry of safeguarding life—a ministry which must be fulfilled in a manner which is worthy of man. Therefore from the moment of its conception life must be guarded with the greatest care, while abortion and infanticide are unspeakable crimes. The sexual characteristics of man and the human faculty of reproduction wonderfully exceed the dispositions of lower forms of life. Hence the acts themselves which are proper to conjugal love and which are exercised in accord with genuine human dignity must be honored with great reverence.

Therefore when there is question of harmonizing conjugal love with the responsible transmission of life, the moral aspect of any procedure does not depend solely on sincere intentions or on an evaluation of motives. It must be determined by objective standards. These, based on the nature of the human person and his acts, preserve the full sense of mutual self-giving and human procreation in the context of true love. Such a goal cannot be achieved unless the virtue of conjugal chastity is sincerely practiced. Relying on these principles, sons of the Church may not undertake methods of regulating procreation which are found blameworthy by the teaching authority of the Church in its unfolding of the divine law.[118]

Everyone should be persuaded that human life and the task of transmitting it are not realities bound up with this world alone. Hence they cannot be measured or perceived only in terms of it, but always have a bearing on the eternal destiny of men.

ALL MUST PROMOTE THE GOOD ESTATE
OF MARRIAGE AND THE FAMILY

52.   The family is a kind of school of deeper humanity. But if it is to achieve the full flowering of its life and mission, it needs the kindly communion of minds and the joint deliberation of spouses, as well as the painstaking cooperation of parents in the education of their children. The active presence of the father is highly beneficial to their formation. The

children, especially the younger among them, need the care of their mother at home. This domestic role of hers must be safely preserved, though the legitimate social progress of women should not be underrated on that account.

Children should be so educated that as adults they can, with a mature sense of responsibility, follow their vocation, including a religious one, and choose their state of life. If they marry, they can thereby establish their family in favorable moral, social, and economic conditions. Parents or guardians should by prudent advice provide guidance to their young with respect to founding a family, and the young ought to listen gladly. At the same time no pressure, direct or indirect, should be put on the young to make them enter marriage or choose a specific partner.

Thus the family is the foundation of society. In it the various generations come together and help one another to grow wiser and to harmonize personal rights with the other requirements of social life. All those, therefore, who exercise influence over communities and social groups should work efficiently for the welfare of marriage and the family.

Public authority should regard it as a sacred duty to recognize, protect, and promote their authentic nature, to shield public morality, and to favor the prosperity of domestic life. The right of parents to beget and educate their children in the bosom of the family must be safeguarded. Children, too, who unhappily lack the blessing of a family should be protected by prudent legislation and various undertakings, and provided with the help they need.

Redeeming the present time,[119] and distinguishing eternal realities from their changing expressions, Christians should actively promote the values of marriage and the family, both by the example of their own lives and by cooperation with other men of good will. Thus when difficulties arise, Christians will provide, on behalf of family life, those necessities and helps which are suitably modern. To this end, the Christian instincts of the faithful, the upright moral consciences of men, and the wisdom and experience of persons versed in the sacred sciences will have much to contribute.

Those, too, who are skilled in other sciences, notably the medical, biological, social, and psychological, can considerably advance the welfare of marriage and the family, along with peace of conscience, if by pooling their efforts they labor to explain more thoroughly the various conditions favoring a proper regulation of births.

It devolves on priests duly trained about family matters to nurture the vocation of spouses by a variety of pastoral means, by preaching God's

Word, by liturgical worship, and by other spiritual aids to conjugal and family life; to sustain them sympathetically and patiently in difficulties, and to make them courageous through love. Thus families which are truly noble will be formed.

Various organizations, especially family associations, should try by their programs of instruction and action to strengthen young people and spouses themselves, particularly those recently wed, and to train them for family, social, and apostolic life.

Finally, let the spouses themselves, made to the image of the living God and enjoying the authentic dignity of persons, be joined to one another[120] in equal affection, harmony of mind, and the work of mutual sanctification. Thus they will follow Christ who is the principle of life.[121] Thus, too, by the joys and sacrifices of their vocation and through their faithful love, married people will become witnesses of the mystery of that love which the Lord revealed to the world by His dying and His rising up to life again.[122]

CHAPTER II
The Proper Development of Culture

INTRODUCTION

53.   It is a fact bearing on the very person of man that he can come to an authentic and full humanity only through culture, that is, through the cultivation of natural goods and values. Wherever human life is involved, therefore, nature and culture are quite intimately connected.

The word "culture" in its general sense indicates all those factors by which man refines and unfolds his manifold spiritual and bodily qualities. It means his effort to bring the world itself under his control by his knowledge and his labor. It includes the fact that by improving customs and institutions he renders social life more human both within the family and in the civic community. Finally, it is a feature of culture that throughout the course of time man expresses, communicates, and conserves in his works great spiritual experiences and desires, so that these may be of advantage to the progress of many, even of the whole human family.

Hence it follows that human culture necessarily has a historical and social aspect and that the word "culture" often takes on a sociological and ethnological sense.* It is in this sense that we speak of a plurality of cultures.

Various conditions of community living, as well as various patterns for organizing the goods of life, arise from diverse ways of using things, of laboring, of expressing oneself, of practicing religion, of forming customs, of establishing laws and juridical institutions, of advancing the arts and sciences, and of promoting beauty. Thus the customs handed down to it form for each human community its proper patrimony. Thus, too, is fashioned the specific historical environment which enfolds the men of every nation and age and from which they draw the values which permit them to promote human civic culture.

Section 1: The Circumstances of Culture in the World Today

NEW FORMS OF LIVING

54.   The living conditions of modern man have been so profoundly changed in their social and cultural dimensions, that we can speak of a new age in human history.[123] Fresh avenues are open, therefore, for the refinement and the wider diffusion of culture. These avenues have been paved by the enormous growth of natural, human, and social sciences, by progress in technology, and by advances in the development and organization of the means by which men communicate with one another.

Hence the culture of today possesses particular characteristics. For example, the so-called exact sciences sharpen critical judgment to a very fine edge. Recent psychological research explains human activity more profoundly. Historical studies make a signal contribution to bringing men to see things in their changeable and evolutionary aspects. Customs and usages are becoming increasingly uniform. Industrialization, urbanization, and other causes of community living create new forms of culture (mass-culture), from which arise new ways of thinking, acting, and

---

* The concept of "culture" as it is understood by sociologists and anthropologists is a relatively new one. It is not surprising, then, that Vatican II shoud find it necessary to spell out several definitions of the term. [Editor's note in Abbot edition]

making use of leisure. The growth of communication between the various nations and social groups opens more widely to all the treasures of different cultures.

Thus, little by little, a more universal form of human culture is developing, one which will promote and express the unity of the human race to the degree that it preserves the particular features of the different cultures.

MAN THE AUTHOR OF CULTURE

55.   In every group or nation, there is an ever-increasing number of men and women who are conscious that they themselves are the artisans and the authors of the culture of their community. Throughout the world there is a similar growth in the combined sense of independence and responsibility. Such a development is of paramount importance for the spiritual and moral maturity of the human race. This truth grows clearer if we consider how the world is becoming unified and how we have the duty to build a better world based upon truth and justice. Thus we are witnesses of the birth of a new humanism, one in which man is defined first of all by his responsibility toward his brothers and toward history.

PROBLEMS AND DUTIES

56.   In these conditions, it is no wonder that, feeling his responsibility for the progress of culture, man nourishes higher hopes but also looks anxiously upon many contradictions which he will have to resolve:

What must be done to prevent the increased exchanges between cultures, which ought to lead to a true and fruitful dialogue between groups and nations, from disturbing the life of communities, destroying ancestral wisdom, or jeopardizing the uniqueness of each people?

How can the vitality and growth of a new culture be fostered without the loss of living fidelity to the heritage of tradition? This question is especially urgent when a culture resulting from the enormous scientific and technological progress must be harmonized with an education nourished by classical studies as adapted to various traditions.

As special branches of knowledge continue to shoot out so rapidly, how can the necessary synthesis of them be worked out, and how can men preserve the ability to contemplate and to wonder, from which wisdom comes?

What can be done to make all men on earth share in cultural values, when the culture of the more sophisticated grows ever more refined and complex?

Finally, how is the independence which culture claims for itself to be recognized as legitimate without the promotion of a humanism which is merely earth-bound, and even contrary to religion itself?

In the thick of these tensions, human culture must evolve today in such a way that it can develop the whole human person harmoniously and at the same time assist men in those duties which all men, especially Christians, are called to fulfill in the fraternal unity of the one human family.

Section 2: Some Principles of Proper Cultural Development

FAITH AND CULTURE

57.   Christians, on pilgrimage toward the heavenly city, should seek and savor the things which are above.[124] This duty in no way decreases, but rather increases, the weight of their obligation to work with all men in constructing a more human world. In fact, the mystery of the Christian faith furnishes them with excellent incentives and helps toward discharging this duty more energetically and especially toward uncovering the full meaning of this activity, a meaning which gives human culture its eminent place in the integral vocation of man.

For when, by the work of his hands or with the aid of technology, man develops the earth so that it can bear fruit and become a dwelling worthy of the whole human family, and when he consciously takes part in the life of social groups, he carries out the design of God. Manifested at the beginning of time, the divine plan is that man should subdue[125] the earth, bring creation to perfection, and develop himself. When a man so acts he simultaneously obeys the great Christian commandment that he place himself at the service of his brother men.

Futhermore, when a man applies himself to the various disciplines of philosophy, of history, and of mathematical and natural science, and when he cultivates the arts, he can do very much to elevate the human family to a more sublime understanding of truth, goodness, and beauty, and to the formation of judgments which embody universal values. Thus mankind can be more clearly enlightened by that marvelous Wisdom which was with God from all eternity, arranging all things with Him, playing upon the earth, delighting in the sons of men.[126]

In this way, the human spirit grows increasingly free of its bondage to creatures and can be more easily drawn to the worship and contemplation of the Creator. Moreover, under the impulse of grace, man is disposed to acknowledge the Word of God. Before He became flesh in order to save all things and to sum them up in Himself, "He was in the world" already as "the true light that enlightens every man" (Jn.1:9–10).[127]

No doubt today's progress in science and technology can foster a certain exclusive emphasis on observable data, and an agnosticism about everything else. For the methods of investigation which these sciences use can be wrongly considered as the supreme rule for discovering the whole truth. By virtue of their methods, however, these sciences cannot penetrate to the intimate meaning of things. Yet the danger exists that man, confiding too much in modern discoveries, may even think that he is sufficient unto himself and no longer seek any higher realities.

These unfortunate results, however, do not necessarily follow from the culture of today, nor should they lead us into the temptation of not acknowledging its positive values. For among its values are these: scientific study and strict fidelity toward truth in scientific research, the necessity of working together with others in technical groups, a sense of international solidarity, an ever clearer awareness of the responsibility of experts to aid men and even to protect them, the desire to make the conditions of life more favorable for all, especially for those who are deprived of the opportunity to exercise responsibility or who are culturally poor.

All of these values can provide some preparation for the acceptance of the message of the gospel—a preparation which can be animated with divine love by Him who came to save the world.

THE MANY LINKS BETWEEN THE GOSPEL AND CULTURE

58.   There are many links between the message of salvation and human culture. For God, revealing Himself to His people to the extent of a full manifestation of Himself in His Incarnate Son, has spoken according to the culture proper to different ages.

Living in various circumstances during the course of time, the Church, too, has used in her preaching the discoveries of different cultures to spread and explain the message of Christ to all nations, to probe it and more deeply understand it, and to give it better expression in liturgical celebrations in the life of the diversified community of the faithful.

But at the same time, the Church, sent to all peoples of every time and place, is not bound exclusively and indissolubly to any race or nation, nor to any particular way of life or any customary pattern of living, ancient or recent. Faithful to her own tradition and at the same time conscious of her universal mission, she can enter into communion with various cultural modes, to her enrichment and theirs too.

The good news of Christ constantly renews the life and culture of fallen man. It combats and removes the errors and evils resulting from sinful allurements which are a perpetual threat. It never ceases to purify and elevate the morality of peoples. By riches coming from above, it makes fruitful, as it were from within, the spiritual qualities and gifts of every people and of every age. It strengthens, perfects, and restores[128] them in Christ. Thus by the very fulfillment of her own mission[129] the Church stimulates and advances human and civic culture. By her action, even in its liturgical form, she leads men toward interior liberty.

HARMONY BETWEEN THE FORMS OF CULTURE

59.   For the aforementioned reasons, the Church recalls to the mind of all that culture must be made to bear on the integral perfection of the human person, and on the good of the community and the whole of society. Therefore the human spirit must be cultivated in such a way that there results a growth in its ability to wonder, to understand, to contemplate, to make personal judgments, and to develop a religious, moral, and social sense.

Because it flows immediately from man's spiritual and social nature, culture has constant need of a just freedom if it is to develop. It also needs the legitimate possibility of exercising its independence according to its own principles. Rightly, therefore, it demands respect and enjoys a certain inviolability, at least as long as the rights of the individual and of the community, whether particular or universal, are preserved within the context of the common good.

This sacred Synod, therefore, recalling the teaching of the first Vatican Council, declares that there are "two orders of knowledge" which are distinct, namely, faith and reason. It declares that the Church does not indeed forbid that "when the human arts and sciences are practiced they use their own principles and their proper method, each in its own domain." Hence, "acknowledging this just liberty," this sacred Synod affirms the legitimate autonomy of human culture and especially of the sciences.[130]

All these considerations demand too, that, within the limits of morality and general welfare, a man be free to search for the truth, voice his mind, and publicize it; that he be free to practice any art he chooses; and finally that he have appropriate access to information about public affairs.[131]

It is not the function of public authority to determine what the proper nature of forms of human culture should be. It should rather foster the conditions and the means which are capable of promoting cultural life among all citizens and even within the minorities of a nation.[132] Hence in this matter men must insist above all else that culture be not diverted from its own purpose and made to serve political or economic interests.

Section 3: Some Especially Urgent Duties of Christians with Regard to Culture

RECOGNIZING AND IMPLEMENTING THE RIGHT TO CULTURE

60.   The possibility now exists of liberating most men from the misery of ignorance. Hence it is a duty most befitting our times that men, especially Christians, should work strenuously on behalf of certain decisions which must be made in the economic and political fields, both nationally and internationally. By these decisions universal recognition and implementation should be given to the right of all men to a human and civic culture favorable to personal dignity and free from any discrimination on the grounds of race, sex, nationality, religious, or social conditions.

Therefore it is necessary to provide every man with a sufficient abundance of cultural benefits, especially those which constitute so-called basic culture. Otherwise, because of illiteracy and a lack of responsible activity, very many will be prevented from collaborating in a truly human manner for the sake of the common good.

Efforts must be made to see that men who are capable of higher studies can pursue them. In this way, as far as possible, they can be prepared to undertake in society those duties, offices, and services which are in harmony with their natural aptitude and with the competence they will have acquired.[133] Thus all the individuals and the social groups comprising a given people will be able to attain the full development of their culture, a development in accord with their qualities and traditions.

Energetic efforts must also be expended to make everyone conscious of his right to culture and of the duty he has to develop himself culturally and to assist others. For existing conditions of life and of work sometimes thwart the cultural strivings of men and destroy in them the desire for self-improvement. This is especially true of country people and laborers. They need to be provided with working conditions which will not block their human development but rather favor it.

Women are now employed in almost every area of life. It is appropriate that they should be able to assume their full proper role in accordance with their own nature. Everyone should acknowledge and favor the proper and necessary participation of women in cultural life.

CULTURAL EDUCATION

61.   Today it is more difficult than ever for a synthesis to be formed of the various branches of knowledge and the arts. For while the mass and the diversity of cultural factors are increasing, there is a decline in the individual man's ability to grasp and unify these elements. Thus the ideal of the "universal man" is disappearing more and more. Nevertheless, it remains each man's duty to preserve a view of the whole human person, a view in which the values of intellect, will, conscience, and fraternity are pre-eminent. These values are all rooted in God the Creator and have been wonderfully restored and elevated in Christ.

The family is, as it were, the primary mother and nurse of this attitude. There, in an atmosphere of love, children can more easily learn the true structure of reality. There, too, tested forms of human culture impress themselves upon the mind of the developing adolescent in a kind of automatic way.

Opportunities for the same kind of education can also be found in modern society, thanks especially to the increased circulation of books and to the new means of cultural and social communication. All such opportunities can foster a universal culture.

The widespread reduction in working hours, for instance, brings increasing advantages to numerous people. May these leisure hours be properly used for relaxation of spirit and the strengthening of mental and bodily health. Such benefits are available through spontaneous study and activity and through travel, which refines human qualities and enriches men with mutual understanding. These benefits are obtainable too from physical exercise and sports events, which can help to preserve emotional balance, even at the community level, and to establish fraternal relations among men of all conditions, nations, and races.

Hence let Christians work together to animate the cultural expressions and group activities characteristic of our times with a human and a Christian spirit.

All these benefits, however, cannot educate men to a full self-development unless at the same time deep thought is given to what culture and science mean in terms of the human person.

HARMONY BETWEEN CULTURE AND CHRISTIAN FORMATION

62.   Although the Church has contributed much to the development of culture, experience shows that, because of circumstances, it is sometimes difficult to harmonize culture with Christian teaching.

These difficulties do not necessarily harm the life of faith. Indeed they can stimulate the mind to a more accurate and penetrating grasp of the faith. For recent studies and findings of science, history, and philosophy raise new questions which influence life and demand new theological investigations.

Furthermore, while adhering to the methods and requirements proper to theology, theologians are invited to seek continually for more suitable ways of communicating doctrine to the men of their times. For the deposit of faith or revealed truths are one thing; the manner in which they are formulated without violence to their meaning and significance is another.[134]

In pastoral care, appropriate use must be made not only of theological principles, but also of the findings of the secular sciences, especially of psychology and sociology. Thus the faithful can be brought to live the faith in a more thorough and mature way.

Literature and the arts are also, in their own way, of great importance to the life of the Church. For they strive to probe the unique nature of man, his problems, and his experiences as he struggles to know and perfect both himself and the world. They are preoccupied with revealing man's place in history and in the world, with illustrating his miseries and joys, his needs and strengths, and with foreshadowing a better life for him. Thus they are able to elevate human life as it is expressed in manifold forms, depending on time and place.

Efforts must therefore be made so that those who practice these arts can feel that the Church gives recognition to them in their activities, and so that, enjoying an orderly freedom, they can establish smoother relations with the Christian community. Let the Church also acknowledge new forms of art which are adapted to our age and are in keeping with the characteristics of various nations and regions. Adjusted in their mode of expression and conformed to liturgical requirements, they may be introduced into the sanctuary when they raise the mind to God.[135]

In this way the knowledge of God can be better revealed. Also, the preaching of the gospel can become clearer to man's mind and show its relevance to the conditions of human life.

May the faithful, therefore, live in very close union with the men of their time. Let them strive to understand perfectly their way of thinking and feeling, as expressed in their culture. Let them blend modern science and its theories and the understanding of the most recent discoveries with Christian morality and doctrine. Thus their religious practice and morality can keep pace with their scientific knowledge and with an ever-advancing technology. Thus too they will be able to test and interpret all things in a truly Christian spirit.

Through a sharing of resources and points of view, let those who teach in seminaries, colleges, and universities try to collaborate with men well versed in the other sciences. Theological inquiry should seek a profound understanding of revealed truth without neglecting close contact with its own times. As a result, it will be able to help those men skilled in various fields of knowledge to gain a better understanding of the faith.

This common effort will very greatly aid in the formation of priests. It will enable them to present to our contemporaries the doctrine of the Church concerning God, man, and the world in a manner better suited to them, with the result that they will receive it more willingly.[136] Furthermore, it is to be hoped that many laymen will receive an appropriate formation in the sacred sciences, and that some will develop and deepen these studies by their own labors. In order that such persons may fulfill their proper function, let it be recognized that all the faithful, clerical and lay, possess a lawful freedom of inquiry and of thought, and the freedom to express their minds humbly and courageously about those matters in which they enjoy competence.[137]

CHAPTER III
Socio-Economic Life

SOME ASPECTS OF ECONOMIC LIFE

63.   In the socio-economic realm, too, the dignity and total vocation of the human person must be honored and advanced along with the welfare of society as a whole. For man is the source, the center, and the purpose of all socio-economic life.

As in other areas of social life, modern economy is marked by man's increasing domination over nature, by closer and more intense relationships between citizens, groups, and countries and by their mutual dependence, and by more frequent intervention on the part of government. At the same time progress in the methods of production and in the exchange of goods and services has made the economy an apt instrument for meeting the intensified needs of the human family more successfully.

Reasons for anxiety, however, are not lacking. Many people, especially in economically advanced areas, seem to be hypnotized, as it were, by economics, so that almost their entire personal and social life is permeated with a certain economic outlook. These people can be found both in nations which favor a collective economy as well as in others.

Again, we are at a moment in history when the development of economic life could diminish social inequalities if that development were guided and coordinated in a reasonable and human way. Yet all too often it serves only to intensify the inequalities. In some places it even results in a decline in the social status of the weak and in contempt for the poor.

While an enormous mass of people still lack the absolute necessities of life, some, even in less advanced countries, live sumptuously or squander wealth. Luxury and misery rub shoulders. While the few enjoy very great freedom of choice, the many are deprived of almost all possibility of acting on their own initiative and responsibility, and often subsist in living and working conditions unworthy of human beings.

A similar lack of economic and social balance is to be noted between agriculture, industry, and the services, and also between different parts of one and the same country. The contrast between the economically more advanced countries and other countries is becoming more serious day by day, and the very peace of the world can be jeopardized in consequence.

Our contemporaries are coming to feel these inequalities with an ever sharper awareness. For they are thoroughly convinced that the wider technical and economic potential which the modern world enjoys can and should correct this unhappy state of affairs. Hence, numerous reforms are needed at the socio-economic level, along with universal changes in ideas and attitudes.

Now in this area the Church maintains certain principles of justice and equity as they apply to individuals, societies, and international relations. In the course of the centuries and with the light of the gospel she has worked out these principles as right reason demanded. In modern times especially, the Church has enlarged upon them. This sacred Council wishes to re-enforce these principles according to the circumstances of the times and to set forth certain guidelines, primarily with regard to the requirements of economic development.[138]

Section 1: Economic Development

IN THE SERVICE OF MAN

64.   Today, more than ever before, progress in the production of agricultural and industrial goods and in the rendering of services is rightly aimed at making provision for the growth of a people and at meeting the rising expectations of the human race. Therefore, technical progress must be fostered, along with a spirit of initiative, an eagerness to create and expand enterprises, the adaptation of methods of production, and the strenuous efforts of all who engage in production—in a word, all the elements making for such development.

The fundamental purpose of this productivity must not be the mere multiplication of products. It must not be profit or domination. Rather, it must be the service of man, and indeed of the whole man, viewed in terms of his material needs and the demands of his intellectual, moral, spiritual, and religious life. And when we say man, we mean every man whatsoever and every group of men, of whatever race and from whatever part of the world. Consequently, economic activity is to be carried out according to its own methods and laws but within the limits of morality,[139] so that God's plan for mankind can be realized.[140]

UNDER MAN'S CONTROL

65.   Economic development must be kept under the control of mankind. It must not be left to the sole judgment of a few men or groups possessing excessive economic power, or of the political community alone, or of certain especially powerful nations. It is proper, on the contrary, that at every level the largest possible number of people have an active share in directing that development. When it is a question of international developments, all nations should so participate. It is also necessary for the spontaneous activities of individuals and of independent groups to be coordinated with the efforts of public authorities. These activities and these efforts should be aptly and harmoniously interwoven.

Growth must not be allowed merely to follow a kind of automatic course resulting from the economic activity of individuals. Nor must it be entrusted solely to the authority of government. Hence, theories which obstruct the necessary reforms in the name of a false liberty must be branded as erroneous. The same is true of those theories which subordinate the basic rights of individual persons and groups to the collective organization of production.[141]

Citizens, for their part, should remember that they have the right and the duty, which must be recognized by civil authority, to contribute according to their ability to the true progress of their own community. Especially in underdeveloped areas, where all resources must be put to urgent use, those men gravely endanger the public good who allow their resources to remain unproductive or who deprive their community of the material and spiritual aid it needs. The personal right of migration, however, is not to be impugned.

REMOVING HUGE DIFFERENCES

66.   If the demands of justice and equity are to be satisfied, vigorous efforts must be made, without violence to the rights of persons or to the natural characteristics of each country, to remove as quickly as possible the immense economic inequalities which now exist. In many cases, these are worsening and are connected with individual and group discrimination.

In many areas, too, farmers experience special difficulties in raising products or in selling them. In such cases, country people must be helped to increase and to market what they produce, to make the necessary advances and changes, and to obtain a fair return. Otherwise, as too often happens, they will remain in the condition of lower-class citizens. Let farmers, especially young ones, skillfully apply themselves to perfecting their professional competence. Without it, no agricultural progress can take place.[142]

Justice and equity likewise require that the mobility which is necessary in a developing economy be regulated in such a way as to keep the life of individuals and their families from becoming insecure and precarious. Hence, when workers come from another country or district and contribute by their labor to the economic advancement of a nation or region, all discrimination with respect to wages and working conditions must be carefully avoided.

The local people, moreover, especially public authorities, should all treat them not as mere tools of production but as persons, and must help them to arrange for their families to live with them and to provide themselves with decent living quarters. The natives should also see that these workers are introduced into the social life of the country or region which receives them. Employment opportunities, however, should be created in their own areas as far as possible.

In those economic affairs which are today subject to change, as in the new forms of industrial society in which automation, for example, is advancing, care must be taken that sufficient and suitable work can be obtained, along with appropriate technical and professional formation. The livelihood and the human dignity of those especially who are in particularly difficult circumstances because of illness or old age should be safeguarded.

Section 2: Certain Principles Governing Socio-Economic Life as a Whole

LABOR AND LEISURE

67.   Human labor which is expended in the production and exchange of goods or in the performance of economic services is superior to the other elements of economic life. For the latter have only the nature of tools.

Whether it is engaged in independently or paid for by someone else, this labor comes immediately from the person. In a sense, the person stamps the things of nature with his seal and subdues them to his will. It is ordinarily by his labor that a man supports himself and his family, is joined to his fellow men and serves them, and is enabled to exercise genuine charity and be a partner in the work of bringing God's creation to perfection. Indeed, we hold that by offering his labor to God a man becomes associated with the redemptive work itself of Jesus Christ, who conferred an eminent dignity on labor when at Nazareth He worked with His own hands.

From all these considerations there arise every man's duty to labor faithfully and also his right to work. It is the duty of society, moreover, according to the circumstances prevailing in it, and in keeping with its proper role, to help its citizens find opportunities for adequate employment. Finally, payment for labor must be such as to furnish a man with the means to cultivate his own material, social, cultural, and spiritual life worthily, and that of his dependents. What this payment should be will vary according to each man's assignment and productivity, the conditions of his place of employment, and the common good.[143]

Since economic activity is generally exercised through the combined labors of human beings, any way of organizing and directing that activity which would be detrimental to any worker would be wrong and inhuman. It too often happens, however, even in our day, that in one way or another workers are made slaves of their work. This situation can by no means be justified by so-called economic laws. The entire process of productive work, therefore, must be adapted to the needs of the person and to the requirements of his life, above all his domestic life. Such is especially the case with respect to mothers of families, but due consideration must be given to every person's sex and age.

The opportunity should also be afforded to workers to develop their own abilities and personalities through the work they perform. Though they should apply their time and energy to their employment with a due sense of responsibility, all workers should also enjoy sufficient rest and leisure to cultivate their family, cultural, social, and religious life. They should also have the opportunity to develop on their own the resources and potentialities to which, perhaps, their professional work gives but little scope.

ECONOMIC PARTICIPATION AND CONFLICT

68.   In economic enterprises it is persons who work together, that is, free and independent human beings created to the image of God. Therefore the active participation of everyone in the running of an enterprise should be promoted.[144] This participation should be exercised in appropriately determined ways. It should take into account each person's function, whether it be one of ownership, hiring, management, or labor. It should provide for the necessary unity of operations.

However, decisions concerning economic and social conditions, on which the future of the workers and their children depends, are rather often made not within the enterprise itself but by institutions on a higher level. Hence the workers themselves should have a share also in controlling these institutions, either in person or through freely elected delegates.

Among the basic rights of the human person must be counted the right of freely founding labor unions. These unions should be truly able to represent the workers and to contribute to the proper arrangement of economic life. Another such right is that of taking part freely in the activity of these unions without risk of reprisal. Through this sort of orderly participation, joined with an ongoing formation in economic and social matters, all will grow day by day in the awareness of their own function and responsibility. Thus they will be brought to feel that according to their own proper capacities and aptitudes they are associates in the whole task of economic and social development and in the attainment of the universal common good.

When, however, socio-economic disputes arise, efforts must be made to come to a peaceful settlement. Recourse must always be had above all to sincere discussion between the parties. Even in present-day circumstances, however, the strike can still be a necessary, though ultimate, means for the defense of the workers' own rights and the fulfillment of their just demands. As soon as possible, however, ways should be sought to resume negotiations and the discussion of reconciliation.

THE COMMON PURPOSE OF CREATED THINGS

69.   God intended the earth and all that it contains for the use of every human being and people. Thus, as all men follow justice and unite in charity, created goods should abound for them on a reasonable basis.[145] Whatever the forms of ownership may be, as adapted to the legitimate institutions of people according to diverse and changeable circumstances, attention must always be paid to the universal purpose for which created goods are meant. In using them, therefore, a man should regard his lawful possessions not merely as his own but also as common property in the sense that they should accrue to the benefit of not only himself but of others.[146]

For the rest, the right to have a share of earthly goods sufficient for oneself and one's family belongs to everyone. The Fathers and Doctors of the Church held this view, teaching that men are obliged to come to the relief to the poor and to do so not merely out of their superfluous goods.[147] If a person is in extreme necessity, he has the right to take from the riches of others what he himself needs.[148] Since there are so many people in this world afflicted with hunger, this sacred Council urges all, both individuals and governments, to remember the saying of the Fathers: "Feed the man dying of hunger, because if you have not fed him you have killed him."[149] According to their ability, let all individuals and governments undertake a genuine sharing of their goods. Let them use these goods especially to provide individuals and nations with the means for helping and developing themselves.

In economically less advanced societies, it is not rare for the communal purpose of earthly goods to be partially satisfied through the customs and traditions proper to a community. By such means the absolute essentials are furnished to each member. If, however, customs cannot answer the new needs of this age, an effort must be made to avoid regarding them as altogether unchangeable. At the same time, rash action should not be taken against worthy customs which, provided that they are suitably adapted to present-day circumstances, do not cease to be very useful.

Similarly, in highly developed nations a body of social institutions dealing with insurance and security can, for its part, make the common purpose of earthly goods effective. Family and social services, especially those which provide for culture and education, should be further promoted. Still, care must be taken lest, as a result of all these provisions, the citizenry fall into a kind of sluggishness toward society, and reject the burdens of office and of public service.

DISTRIBUTION AND MONEY

70.   The distribution of goods should be directed toward providing employment and sufficient income for the people of today and of the future. Whether individuals, groups, or public authorities make the decisions concerning this distribution and the planning of the economy, they are bound to keep these objectives in mind. They must realize their serious obligation of seeing to it that provision is made for the necessities of a decent life on the part of individuals and of the whole community. They must also look out for the future and establish a proper balance between the needs of present-day consumption, both individual and collective, and the necessity of distributing goods on behalf of the coming generation. They should also bear constantly in mind the urgent needs of underdeveloped countries and regions. In financial transactions they should beware of hurting the welfare of their own country or of other countries. Care should also be taken lest the economically weak countries unjustly suffer loss from a change in the value of money.

OWNERSHIP AND PROPERTY

71.   Ownership and other forms of private control over material goods contribute to the expression of personality. Moreover, they furnish men with an occasion for exercising their role in society and in the economy. Hence it is very important to facilitate the access of both individuals and communities to some control over material goods.

Private ownership or some other kind of dominion over material goods provides everyone with a wholly necessary area of independence, and should be regarded as an extension of human freedom. Finally, since it adds incentives for carrying on one's function and duty, it constitutes a kind of prerequisite for civil liberties. [150]

The forms of such dominion or ownership are varied today and are becoming increasingly diversified. They all remain a source of security not to be underestimated, even in the face of the public funds, rights, and services provided by society. This is true not only of material goods but also of intangible goods, such as professional skills.

The right of private control, however, is not opposed to the right inherent in various forms of public ownership. Still, goods can be transferred to the public domain only by the competent authority, according to the demands and within the limits of the common good, and with fair compensation. It is a further right of public authority to guard against any misuse of private property which injures the common good.[151]

By its very nature, private property has a social quality deriving from the law of the communal purpose of earthly goods.[152] If this social quality is overlooked, property often becomes an occasion of greed and of serious disturbances. Thus, to those who attack the concept of private property, a pretext is given for calling the right itself into question.

In many underdeveloped areas there are large or even gigantic rural estates which are only moderately cultivated or lie completely idle for the sake of profit. At the same time the majority of the people are either without land or have only very small holdings, and there is evident and urgent need to increase land productivity.

It is not rare for those who are hired to work for the landowners, or who till a portion of the land as tenants, to receive a wage or income unworthy of human beings, to lack decent housing, and to be exploited by middlemen. Deprived of all security, they live under such personal servitude that almost every opportunity for acting on their own initiative and responsibility is denied to them, and all advancement in human culture and all sharing in social and political life are ruled out.

Depending on circumstances, therefore, reforms must be instituted if income is to grow, working conditions improve, job security increase, and an incentive to working on one's own initiative be provided. Indeed, insufficiently cultivated estates should be distributed to those who can make these lands fruitful. In this case, the necessary ways and means, especially educational aids and the right facilities for cooperative organization, must be supplied. Still, whenever the common good requires expropriation, compensation must be reckoned in equity after all the circumstances have been weighed.

ECONOMICS AND CHRIST'S KINGDOM

72.   Christians who take an active part in modern socio-economic development and defend justice and charity should be convinced that

they can make a great contribution to the prosperity of mankind and the peace of the world. Whether they do so as individuals or in association, let their example be a shining one. After acquiring whatever skills and experience are absolutely necessary, they should in faithfulness to Christ and His gospel observe the right order of values in their earthly activities. Thus their whole lives, both individual and social, will be permeated with the spirit of the beatitudes, notably with the spirit of poverty.

Whoever in obedience to Christ seeks first the kingdom of God will as a consequence receive a stronger and purer love for helping all his brothers and for perfecting the work of justice under the inspiration of charity. [153]

CHAPTER IV

The Life of the Political Community

MODERN POLITICS

73.   Our times have witnessed profound changes too in the institutions of peoples and in the ways that peoples are joined together. These changes are resulting from the cultural, economic, and social evolution of these same peoples. The changes are having a great impact on the life of the political community, especially with regard to universal rights and duties both in the exercise of civil liberty and in the attainment of the common good, and with regard to the regulation of the relations of citizens among themselves, and with public authority.

From a keener awareness of human dignity there arises in many parts of the world a desire to establish a political-juridical order in which personal rights can gain better protection. These include the rights of free assembly, of common action, of expressing personal opinions, and of professing a religion both privately and publicly. For the protection of personal rights is a necessary condition for the active participation of citizens, whether as individuals or collectively, in the life and government of the state.

Among numerous people, cultural, economic, and social progress has been accompanied by the desire to assume a larger role in organizing the life of the political community. In many consciences there is a growing intent that the rights of national minorities be honored while at the same time these minorities honor their duties towards the political community.

In addition men are learning more every day to respect the opinions and religious beliefs of others. At the same time a broader spirit of cooperation is taking hold. Thus all citizens, and not just a privileged few, are actually able to enjoy personal rights.

Men are voicing disapproval of any kind of government which blocks civil or religious liberty, multiplies the victims of ambition and political crimes, and wrenches the exercise of authority from pursuing the common good to serving the advantage of a certain faction or of the rulers themselves. There are some such governments holding power in the world.

No better way exists for attaining a truly human political life than by fostering an inner sense of justice, benevolence, and service for the common good, and by strengthening basic beliefs about the true nature of the political community, and about the proper exercise and limits of public authority.

NATURE AND GOAL OF POLITICS

74.   Individuals, families, and various groups which compose the civic community are aware of their own insufficiency in the matter of establishing a fully human condition of life. They see the need for that wider community in which each would daily contribute his energies toward the ever better attainment of the common good.[154] It is for this reason that they set up the political community in its manifold expressions.

Hence the political community exists for that common good in which the community finds its full justification and meaning, and from which it derives its pristine and proper right. Now, the common good embraces the sum of those conditions of social life by which individuals, families, and groups can achieve their own fulfillment in a relatively thorough and ready way.[155]

Many different people go to make up the political community, and these can lawfully incline toward diverse ways of doing things. Now, if the political community is not to be torn to pieces as each man follows his own viewpoint, authority is needed. This authority must dispose the energies of the whole citizenry toward the common good, not mechanically or despotically, but primarily as a moral force which depends on freedom and the conscientious discharge of the burdens of any office which has been undertaken.

It is therefore obvious that the political community and public authority are based on human nature and hence belong to an order of things divinely foreordained. At the same time the choice of government and the method of selecting leaders is left to the free will of citizens.[156]

It also follows that political authority, whether in the community as such or in institutions representing the state, must always be exercised within the limits of morality and on behalf of the dynamically conceived common good, according to a juridical order enjoying legal status. When such is the case citizens are conscience-bound to obey.[157] This fact clearly reveals the responsibility, dignity, and importance of those who govern.

Where public authority oversteps its competence and oppresses the people, these people should nevertheless obey to the extent that the objective common good demands. Still it is lawful for them to defend their own rights and those of their fellow citizens against any abuse of this authority, provided that in so doing they observe the limits imposed by natural law and the gospel.

The practical ways in which the political community structures itself and regulates public authority can vary according to the particular character of a people and its historical development. But these methods should always serve to mold men who are civilized, peace-loving, and well disposed toward all—to the advantage of the whole human family.

POLITICAL PARTICIPATION

75.   It is in full accord with human nature that juridical-political structures should, with ever better success and without any discrimination, afford all their citizens the chance to participate freely and actively in establishing the constitutional bases of a political community, governing the state, determining the scope and purpose of various institutions, and choosing leaders.[158] Hence let all citizens be mindful of their simultaneous right and duty to vote freely in the interest of advancing the common good. The Church regards as worthy of praise and consideration the work of those who, as a service to others, dedicate themselves to the welfare of the state and undertake the burdens of this task.

If conscientious cooperation between citizens is to achieve its happy effect in the normal course of public affairs, a positive system of law is required. In it should be established a division of governmental roles and institutions and, at the same time, an effective and independent system for the protection of rights. Let the rights of all persons, families, and associations, along with the exercise of those rights, be recognized, honored, and fostered.[159] The same holds for those duties which bind all citizens. Among the latter should be remembered that of furnishing the commonwealth with the material and spiritual services required for the common good.

Authorities must beware of hindering family, social, or cultural groups, as well as intermediate bodies and institutions. They must not deprive them of their own lawful and effective activity, but should rather strive to promote them willingly and in an orderly fashion. For their part, citizens both as individuals and in association should be on guard against granting government too much authority and inappropriately seeking from it excessive conveniences and advantages, with a consequent weakening of the sense of responsibility on the part of individuals, families, and social groups.

Because of the increased complexity of modern circumstances, government is more often required to intervene in social and economic affairs, by way of bringing about conditions more likely to help citizens and groups freely attain to complete human fulfillment with greater effect. The proper relationship between socialization[160] on the one hand and personal independence and development on the other can be variously interpreted according to the locales in question and the degree of progress achieved by a given people.

When the exercise of rights is temporarily curtailed on behalf of the common good, it should be restored as quickly as possible after the emergency passes. In any case it harms humanity when government takes on totalitarian or dictatorial forms injurious to the rights of persons or social groups.

Citizens should develop a generous and loyal devotion to their country, but without any narrowing of mind. In other words, they must always look simultaneously to the welfare of the whole human family, which is tied together by the manifold bonds linking races, peoples, and nations.

Let all Christians appreciate their special and personal vocation in the political community. This vocation requires that they give conspicuous example of devotion to the sense of duty and of service to the advancement of the common good. Thus they can also show in practice how authority is to be harmonized with freedom, personal initiative with consideration for the bonds uniting the whole social body, and necessary unity with beneficial diversity.

Christians should recognize that various legitimate though conflicting views can be held concerning the regulation of temporal affairs. They should respect their fellow citizens when they promote such views honorably even by group action. Political parties should foster whatever they judge necessary for the common good. But they should never prefer their own advantage over this same common good.

Civic and political education is today supremely necessary for the people, especially young people. Such education should be painstakingly provided, so that all citizens can make their contribution to the political community. Let those who are suited for it, or can become so, prepare themselves for the difficult but most honorable art of politics.[161] Let them work to exercise this art without thought of personal convenience and without benefit of bribery. Prudently and honorably let them fight against injustice and oppression, the arbitrary rule of one man or one party, and lack of tolerance. Let them devote themselves to the welfare of all sincerely and fairly, indeed with charity and political courage.

POLITICS AND THE CHURCH

76.   It is highly important, especially in pluralistic societies, that a proper view exist of the relation between the political community and the Church. Thus the faithful will be able to make a clear distinction between what a Christian conscience leads them to do in their own name as citizens, whether as individuals or in association, and what they do in the name of the Church and in union with her shepherds.

The role and competence of the Church being what it is, she must in no way be confused with the political community, nor bound to any political system. For she is at once a sign and a safeguard of the transcendence of the human person.

In their proper spheres, the political community and the Church are mutually independent and self-governing. Yet, by a different title, each serves the personal and social vocation of the same human beings. This service can be more effectively rendered for the good of all, if each works better for wholesome mutual cooperation, depending on the circumstances of time and place. For man is not restricted to the temporal sphere. While living in history he fully maintains his eternal vocation.

The Church, founded on the Redeemer's love, contributes to the wider application of justice and charity within and between nations. By preaching the truth of the gospel and shedding light on all areas of human activity through her teaching and the example of the faithful, she shows respect for the political freedom and responsibility of citizens and fosters these values.

The apostles, their successors, and those who assist these successors have been sent to announce to men Christ, the Savior of the world. Hence in the exercise of their apostolate they must depend on the power of God, who very often reveals the might of the gospel through the weakness of its witnesses. For those who dedicate themselves to the ministry of God's

Word should use means and helps proper to the gospel. In many respects these differ from the supports of the earthly city.

There are, indeed, close links between earthly affairs and those aspects of man's condition which transcend this world. The Church herself employs the things of time to the degree that her own proper mission demands. Still she does not lodge her hope in privileges conferred by civil authority. Indeed, she stands ready to renounce the exercise of certain legitimately acquired rights if it becomes clear that their use raises doubt about the sincerity of her witness or that new conditions of life demand some other arrangement.

But it is always and everywhere legitimate for her to preach the faith with true freedom, to teach her social doctrine, and to discharge her duty among men without hindrance. She also has the right to pass moral judgments , even on matters touching the political order, whenever basic personal rights or the salvation of souls make such judgments necessary. In so doing, she may use only those helps which accord with the gospel and with the general welfare as it changes according to time and circumstance.

Holding faithfully to the gospel and exercising her mission in the world, the Church consolidates[162] peace among men, to God's glory. For it is her task to uncover, cherish, and ennoble[163] all that is true, good, and beautiful in the human community.

CHAPTER V
The Fostering of Peace and the Promotion of a Community of Nations

INTRODUCTION

77.   In our generation when men continue to be afflicted by acute hardships and anxieties arising from ongoing wars or the threat of them, the whole human family has reached an hour of supreme crisis in its advance toward maturity. Moving gradually together and everywhere more conscious already of its oneness, this family cannot accomplish its task of constructing for all men everywhere a world more genuinely

human unless each person devotes himself with renewed determination to the reality of peace. Thus it happens that the gospel message, which is in harmony with the loftier strivings and aspirations of the human race, takes on a new luster in our day as it declares that the artisans of peace are blessed, "for they shall be called children of God" (Mt. 5:9).

Consequently, as it points out the authentic and most noble meaning of peace and condemns the frightfulness of war, this Council fervently desires to summon Christians to cooperate with all men in making secure among themselves a peace based on justice and love, and in setting up agencies of peace. This Christians should do with the help of Christ, the Author of peace.

THE NATURE OF PEACE

78.   Peace is not merely the absence of war. Nor can it be reduced solely to the maintenance of a balance of power between enemies. Nor is it brought about by dictatorship. Instead, it is rightly and appropriately called "an enterprise of justice" (Is. 32:7). Peace results from that harmony built into human society by its divine Founder, and actualized by men as they thirst after ever greater justice.

The common good of men is in its basic sense determined by the eternal law. Still the concrete demands of this common good are constantly changing as time goes on. Hence peace is never attained once and for all, but must be built up ceaselessly. Moreover, since the human will is unsteady and wounded by sin, the achievement of peace requires that everyone constantly master his passions and that lawful authority keep vigilant.

But such is not enough. This peace cannot be obtained on earth unless personal values are safeguarded and men freely and trustingly share with one another the riches of their inner spirits and their talents. A firm determination to respect other men and peoples and their dignity, as well as the studied practice of brotherhood, are absolutely necessary for the establishment of peace. Hence peace is likewise the fruit of love, which goes beyond what justice can provide.

That earthly peace which arises from love of neighbor symbolizes and results from the peace of Christ who comes forth from God the Father. For by His cross the incarnate Son, the Prince of Peace, reconciled all men with God. By thus restoring the unity of all men in one people and one body, He slew hatred in His own flesh.[164] After being lifted on high by His resurrection, He poured the Spirit of love into the hearts of men.

For this reason, all Christians are urgently summoned "to practice the truth in love" (Eph. 4:15) and to join with all true peacemakers in pleading for peace and bringing it about.

Motivated by this same spirit, we cannot fail to praise those who renounce the use of violence in the vindication of their rights and who resort to methods of defense which are otherwise available to weaker parties too, provided that this can be done without injury to the rights and duties of others or of the community itself.

Insofar as men are sinful, the threat of war hangs over them, and hang over them it will until the return of Christ. But to the extent that men vanquish sin by a union of love, they will vanquish violence as well, and make these words come true: "They shall beat their swords into plowshares and their spears into pruning hooks; one nation shall not raise the sword against another, nor shall they train for war again"(Is.2:4).*

Section 1: The Avoidance of War

CURBING THE SAVAGERY OF WAR

79.   In spite of the fact that recent wars have wrought physical and moral havoc on our world, conflicts still produce their devastating effect day by day somewhere in the world. Indeed, now that every kind of weapon produced by modern science is used in war, the fierce character of warfare threatens to lead the combatants to a savagery far surpassing that of the past. Futhermore, the complexity of the modern world and the intricacy of international relations allow guerrilla warfare to be drawn out by new methods of deceit and subversion. In many cases the use of terrorism is regarded as a new way to wage war.

Contemplating this melancholy state of humanity, the Council wishes to recall first of all the permanent binding force of universal natural law and its all-embracing principles. Man's conscience itself gives ever more emphatic voice to these principles. Therefore, actions which deliberately conflict with these same principles, as well as orders commanding such actions are criminal. Blind obedience cannot excuse those who yield to them. Among such must first be counted those actions designed for the methodical extermination of an entire people, nation, or ethnic minority. These actions must be vehemently condemned as horrendous crimes.

---

*1961 CCD transl. [Editor's note in Abbott edition]

The courage of those who openly and fearlessly resist men who issue such commands merits supreme commendation.

On the subject of war, quite a large number of nations have subscribed to various international agreements aimed at making military activity and its consequences less inhuman. Such are conventions concerning the handling of wounded or captured soldiers, and various similar agreements. Agreements of this sort must be honored. Indeed they should be improved upon so that they can better and more workably lead to restraining the frightfulness of war.

All men, especially government officials and experts in these matters, are bound to do everything they can to effect these improvements. Moreover, it seems right that laws make humane provisions for the case of those who for reasons of conscience refuse to bear arms, provided however, that they accept some other form of service to the human community.

Certainly, war has not been rooted out of human affairs. As long as the danger of war remains and there is no competent and sufficiently powerful authority at the international level, governments cannot be denied the right to legitimate defense once every means of peaceful settlement has been exhausted. Therefore, government authorities and others who share public responsibility have the duty to protect the welfare of the people entrusted to their care and to conduct such grave matters soberly.

But it is one thing to undertake military action for the just defense of the people, and something else again to seek the subjugation of other nations. Nor does the possession of war potential make every military or political use of it lawful. Neither does the mere fact that war has unhappily begun mean that all is fair between the warring parties.

Those who are pledged to the service of their country as members of its armed forces should regard themselves as agents of security and freedom on behalf of their people. As long as they fulfill this role properly, they are making a genuine contribution to the establishment of peace.

TOTAL WAR

80.   The horror and perversity of war are immensely magnified by the multiplication of scientific weapons. For acts of war involving these weapons can inflict massive and indiscriminate destruction far exceeding the bounds of legitimate defense. Indeed, if the kind of instruments which can now be found in the armories of the great nations were to be employed to their fullest, an almost total and altogether reciprocal

slaughter of each side by the other would follow, not to mention the widespread devastation which would take place in the world and the deadly aftereffects which would be spawned by the use of such weapons.

All these considerations compel us to undertake an evaluation of war with an entirely new attitude.[165] The men of our time must realize that they will have to give a somber reckoning for their deeds of war. For the course of the future will depend largely on the decisions they make today.

With these truths in mind, this most holy Synod makes its own the condemnations of total war already pronounced by recent Popes,[166] and issues the following declaration:

Any act of war aimed indiscriminately at the destruction of entire cities or of extensive areas along with their population is a crime against God and man himself. It merits unequivocal and unhesitating condemnation.

The unique hazard of modern warfare consists in this: it provides those who possess modern scientific weapons with a kind of occasion for perpetrating just such abominations. Moreover, through a certain inexorable chain of events, it can urge men on to the most atrocious decisions. That such in fact may never happen in the future, the bishops of the whole world, in unity assembled, beg all men, especially government officials and military leaders, to give unremitting thought to the awesome responsibility which is theirs before God and the entire human race.

THE ARMS RACE

81.   Scientific weapons, to be sure, are not amassed solely for use in war. The defensive strength of any nation is considered to be dependent upon its capacity for immediate retaliation against an adversary. Hence this accumulation of arms, which increases each year, also serves, in a way heretofore unknown, as a deterrent to possible enemy attack. Many regard this state of affairs as the most effective way by which peace of a sort can be maintained between nations at the present time.

Whatever be the case with this method of deterrence, men should be convinced that the arms race in which so many countries are engaged is not a safe way to preserve a steady peace. Nor is the so-called balance resulting from this race a sure and authentic peace. Rather than being eliminated thereby, the causes of war threaten to grow gradually stronger.

While extravagant sums are being spent for the furnishing of ever new weapons, an adequate remedy cannot be provided for the multiple miseries afflicting the whole modern world. Disagreements between nations are not really and radically healed. On the contrary other parts of the world are infected with them. New approaches initiated by reformed attitudes must be adopted to remove this trap and to restore genuine peace by emancipating the world from its crushing anxiety.

Therefore, it must be said again: the arms race is an utterly treacherous trap for humanity, and one which injures the poor to an intolerable degree. It is much to be feared that if this race persists, it will eventually spawn all the lethal ruin whose path it is now making ready.

Warned by the calamities which the human race has made possible, let us make use of the interlude granted us from above and in which we rejoice. In greater awareness of our own responsibility let us find means for resolving our disputes in a manner more worthy of man. Divine Providence urgently demands of us that we free ourselves from the age-old slavery of war. But if we refuse to make this effort, we do not know where the evil road we have ventured upon will lead us.

THE TOTAL BANNING OF WAR, AND
INTERNATIONAL ACTION FOR AVOIDING WAR

82.   It is our clear duty, then, to strain every muscle as we work for the time when all war can be completely outlawed by international consent. This goal undoubtedly requires the establishment of some universal public authority acknowledged as such by all, and endowed with effective power to safeguard, on the behalf of all, security, regard for justice, and respect for rights.

But before this hoped-for authority can be set up, the highest existing international centers must devote themselves vigorously to the pursuit of better means for obtaining common security. Peace must be born of mutual trust between nations rather than imposed on them through fear of one another's weapons. Hence everyone must labor to put an end at last to the arms race, and to make a true beginning of disarmament, not indeed a unilateral disarmament, but one proceeding at an equal pace according to agreement, and backed up by authentic and workable safeguards. [167]

In the meantime, efforts which have already been made and are still under way to eliminate the danger of war are not to be underrated. On the contrary, support should be given to the good will of the very many leaders who work hard to do away with war, which they abominate. Though burdened by the enormous preoccupations of their high office, these men are nonetheless motivated by the very grave peacemaking task to which they are bound, even if they cannot ignore the complexity of matters as they stand.

We should fervently ask God to give these men the strength to go forward perseveringly and to follow through courageously on this work of building peace with vigor. It is a work of supreme love for mankind. Today it most certainly demands that these leaders extend their thoughts and their spirit beyond the confines of their own nation, that they put aside national selfishness and ambition to dominate other nations, and that they nourish a profound reverence for the whole of humanity, which is already making its way so laboriously toward greater unity.

The problems of peace and of disarmament have already been the subject of extensive, strenuous, and relentless examination. Together with international meetings dealing with these problems, such studies should be regarded as the first steps toward solving these serious questions. They should be promoted with even greater urgency in the hope that they will yield practical results in the future.

Nevertheless, men should take heed not to entrust themselves only to the efforts of others, while remaining careless about their own attitudes. For government officials, who must simultaneously guarantee the good of their own people and promote the universal good, depend on public opinion and feeling to the greatest possible extent. It does them no good to work at building peace so long as feelings of hostility, contempt, and distrust, as well as racial hatred and unbending ideologies, continue to divide men and place them in opposing camps.

Hence arises a surpassing need for renewed education of attitudes and for new inspiration in the area of public opinion. Those who are dedicated to the work of education, particularly of the young, or who mold public opinion, should regard as their most weighty task the effort to instruct all in fresh sentiments of peace. Indeed, every one of us should have a change of heart as we regard the entire world and those tasks which we can perform in unison for the betterment of our race.

But we should not let false hope deceive us. For enmities and hatred must be put away and firm, honest agreements concerning world peace reached in the future. Otherwise, for all its marvelous knowledge, humanity, which is already in the middle of a grave crisis, will perhaps be brought to that mournful hour in which it will experience no peace other than the dreadful peace of death.

But, while we say this, the Church of Christ takes her stand in the midst of the anxiety of this age, and does not cease to hope with the utmost confidence. She intends to propose to our age over and over again, in season and out of season, this apostolic message: "Behold, now is the acceptable time" for a change of heart; "behold, now is the day of salvation!"[68]

Section 2: Building Up the
International Community

THE CAUSES AND CURES OF DISCORD

83.   If peace is to be established, the primary requisite is to eradicate the causes of dissension between men. Wars thrive on these, especially on injustice. Many of these causes stem from excessive economic inequalities and from excessive slowness in applying the needed remedies. Other causes spring from a quest for power and from contempt for personal rights. If we are looking for deeper explanations, we can find them in human jealousy, distrust, pride, and other egotistic passions.

Man cannot tolerate so many breakdowns in right order. What results is that the world is ceaselessly infected with arguments between men and acts of violence, even when war is not raging. Moreover, these same evils are found in relationships between nations. Hence, if such evils are to be overcome or prevented, and violence kept from becoming unbridled, it is altogether necessary that international institutions cooperate to a better and surer extent and that they be coordinated. Also, unwearying efforts must be made to create agencies for the promotion of peace.

THE COMMUNITY OF NATIONS
AND INTERNATIONAL ORGANIZATIONS

84.   Today the bonds of mutual dependence become increasingly close between all citizens and all the peoples of the world. The universal common good needs to be intelligently pursued and more effectively achieved. Hence it is now necessary for the family of nations to create for themselves an order which corresponds to modern obligations, particularly with reference to those numerous regions still laboring under intolerable need.

For the attainment of these goals, agencies of the international community should do their part to provide for the various necessities of men. In the field of social life this means food, health, education, and employment. In certain situations which can obtain anywhere, it means the general need to promote the growth of developing nations, to attend to the hardships of refugees scattered throughout the world, or to assist migrants and their families.

The international agencies, both universal and regional, which already exist assuredly deserve well of the human race. These stand forth as the first attempts to lay international foundations under the whole human community for the solving of the critical problems of our age, the promotion of global progress, and the prevention of any kind of war. The Church rejoices at the spirit of true fraternity flourishing between Christians and non-Christians in all these areas. This spirit strives to see that ever more intense efforts are made for the relief of the world's enormous miseries.

INTERNATIONAL COOPERATION
AT THE ECONOMIC LEVEL

85.   The modern interconnection between men also demands the establishment of greater international cooperation in the economic field. For although nearly all peoples have gained their independence, it is still far from true that they are free from excessive inequalities and from every form of undue dependence, or that they have put behind them danger of serious internal difficulties.

The development of any nation depends on human and financial assistance. Through education and professional formation, the citizens of each nation should be prepared to shoulder the various offices of economic and social life. Such preparation needs the help of foreign experts. When they render assistance, these experts should do so not in a lordly fashion, but as helpers and co-workers.

The developing nations will be unable to procure the necessary material assistance unless the practices of the modern business world undergo a profound change. Additional help should be offered by advanced nations, in the form of either grants or investments. These offers should be made generously and without avarice. They should be accepted honorably.

If an economic order is to be created which is genuine and universal, there must be an abolition of excessive desire for profit, nationalistic pretensions, the lust for political domination, militaristic thinking, and intrigues designed to spread and impose ideologies.

Proposals are made in favor of numerous economic and social systems. It is to be hoped that experts in such affairs will find common bases for a healthy world trade. This hope will be more readily realized if individuals put aside their personal prejudices and show that they are prepared to undertake sincere discussions.

SOME USEFUL NORMS

86.   The following norms would seem to be appropriate for this cooperation:

a) Developing nations should strongly desire to seek the complete human fulfillment of their citizens as the explicit and fixed goal of progress. Let them be mindful that progress begins and develops primarily from the efforts and endowments of the people themselves. Hence, instead of depending solely on outside help, they should rely chiefly on the full unfolding of their own resources and the cultivation of their own qualities and tradition. Those who have greater influence on others should be outstanding in this respect.

b) As for the advanced nations, they have a very heavy obligation to help the developing peoples in the discharge of the aforementioned responsibilities. If this world-wide collaboration is to be established, certain psychological and material adjustments will be needed among the advanced nations and should be brought about.

Thus these nations should carefully consider the welfare of weaker and poorer nations when negotiating with them. For such nations need for their own livelihood the income derived from the sale of domestic products.

c) The international community should see to the coordination and stimulation of economic growth. These objectives must be pursued in such a way, however, that the resources organized for this purpose can be shared as effectively and justly as possible. This same community should regulate economic relations throughout the world so that they can unfold in a way which is fair. In so doing, however, the community should honor the principle of subsidiarity.*

Let adequate organizations be established for fostering and harmonizing international trade, especially with respect to the less advanced countries, and for repairing the deficiencies caused by an excessive disproportion in the power possessed by various nations. Such regulatory activity, combined with technical, cultural, and financial help, ought to afford the needed assistance to nations striving for progress, enabling them to achieve economic growth expeditiously.

d) In many instances there exists a pressing need to reform economic and social structures. But nations must beware of technical solutions

---

*The principle of subsidiarity formulated by Pope Pius XI in the encyclical letter *Quadragesimo Anno* reads: "This supremely important principle of social philosophy, one which cannot be set aside or altered, remains firm and unshaken: Just as it is wrong to withdraw from the individual and commit to the community at large what private enterprise and endeavor can accomplish, so it is likewise unjust and a gravely harmful disturbance of right order to turn over to a greater society of higher rank functions and services which can be performed by lesser bodies on a lower plane. For a social undertaking of any sort, by its very nature, ought to aid the members of the body social, but never to destroy and absorb them." AAS 23 (1931), p. 203; quoted by Pope John XXIII in encyclical letter *Mater et Magistra*, AAS 53 (1961), p. 414. [Editor's note in Abbott edition]

immaturely proposed, especially those which offer men material advantages while militating against his spiritual nature and development. For, "Not by bread alone does man live, but by every word that comes forth from the mouth of God" (Mt. 4:4). Each branch of the human family possesses in itself and in its worthier traditions some part of the spiritual treasure entrusted by God to humanity, even though many do not know the source of this treasure.

INTERNATIONAL COOPERATION IN
THE MATTER OF POPULATION

87. International cooperation becomes supremely necessary with respect to those peoples who, in addition to many other problems, are today often enough burdened in a special way with the difficulties stemming from a rapid population growth. There is an urgent need for all nations, especially the richer ones, to cooperate fully and intensely in an exploration as to how there can be prepared and distributed to the human community whatever is required for the livelihood and proper training of men. Some peoples, indeed, would greatly better their conditions of life if they could be duly trained to abandon ancient methods of farming in favor of modern techniques. With necessary prudence they should adapt these techniques to their own situations. In addition they need to establish a better social order and regulate the distribution of land with greater fairness.

Within the limits of their own competence, government officials have rights and duties with regard to the population problems of their own nation, for instance, in the matter of social legislation as it affects families, of migration to cities, of information relative to the condition and needs of the nation. Since the minds of men are so powerfully disturbed about this problem, the Council also desires that, especially in universities, Catholic experts in all these aspects should skillfully pursue their studies and projects and give them an ever wider scope.*

Many people assert that it is absolutely necessary for population growth to be radically reduced everywhere or at least in certain nations. They say this must be done by every possible means and by every kind of

---

* The tone of this passage is clearly different from that of the section in *Mater et Magistra* (188-192), dealing with population problems and birth control. The text admits the reasonableness of formulating an official policy on population growth in a nation. It can be noted that in the United States a small number of Catholic specialists have been at work for some time on the questions raised in this passage. Some systematic investigations have been conducted at Catholic universities, notably Georgetown and Notre Dame. [Editor's note in Abbott edition]

government intervention. Hence this Council exhorts all to beware against solutions contradicting the moral law, solutions which have been promoted publicly or privately, and sometimes actually imposed.

For in view of the inalienable human right to marry and beget children, the question of how many children should be born belongs to the honest judgment of parents. The question can in no way be committed to the decision of government. Now since the judgment of the parents supposes a rightly formed conscience, it is highly important that every one be given the opportunity to practice upright and truly human responsibility. This responsibility respects the divine law and takes account of circumstances and the times. It requires that educational and social conditions in various places be changed for the better, and especially that religious instruction or at least full moral training be provided.

Human beings should also be judiciously informed of scientific advances in the exploration of methods by which spouses can be helped in arranging the number of their children. The reliability of these methods should be adequately proven and their harmony with the moral order should be clear.

THE DUTY OF CHRISTIANS TO
PROVIDE SUPPORT

88.   Christians should collaborate willingly and wholeheartedly in establishing an international order involving genuine respect for all freedoms and amicable brotherhood between all men. This objective is all the more pressing since the greater part of the world is still suffering from so much poverty that it is as if Christ Himself were crying out in these poor to beg the charity of the disciples.

Some nations with a majority of citizens who are counted as Christians have an abundance of this world's goods, while others are deprived of the necessities of life and are tormented with hunger, disease, and every kind of misery. This situation must not be allowed to continue, to the scandal of humanity. For the spirit of poverty and of charity are the glory and authentication of the Church of Christ.

Christians, especially young people, are to be praised and supported, therefore, when they volunteer their services to help other men and nations. Indeed, it is the duty of the whole People of God, following the word and example of the bishops, to do their utmost to alleviate the sufferings of the modern age. As was the ancient custom in the Church, they should meet this obligation out of the substance of their goods, and not only out of what is superfluous.

Without being inflexible and completely uniform, the collection and distribution of aid should be conducted in orderly fashion in dioceses, nations, and throughout the entire world. (Wherever it seems appropriate, this activity of Catholics should be carried on in unison with other Christian brothers.*) For the spirit of charity does not forbid but rather requires that charitable activity be exercised in a provident and orderly manner. Therefore, it is essential for those who intend to dedicate themselves to the service of the developing nations to be properly trained in suitable institutions.

EFFECTIVE PRESENCE OF THE CHURCH ON THE INTERNATIONAL SCENE

89.   In pursuit of her divine mission, the Church preaches the gospel to all men and dispenses the treasures of grace. Thus, by imparting knowledge of the divine and natural law, she everywhere contributes to strengthening peace and to placing brotherly relations between individuals and peoples on solid ground. Therefore, to encourage and stimulate cooperation among men, the Church must be thoroughly present in the midst of the community of nations. She must achieve such a presence both through her public institutions and through the full and sincere collaboration of all Christians, a collaboration motivated solely by the desire to be of service to all.

This goal will come about more effectively if the faithful themselves, conscious of their responsibility as men and as Christians, strive to stir up in their own area of influence a willingness to cooperate readily with the international community. In both religious and civic education, special care must be given to the proper formation of youth in this respect.

THE ROLE OF CHRISTIANS IN INTERNATIONAL INSTITUTIONS

90.   An outstanding form of international activity on the part of Christians undoubtedly consists in the cooperative efforts which, as individuals and in groups, they make to institutes established for the encourage-

---

* The work of Catholic agencies such as the American Catholic Relief Services—NCWC, the German Catholic Misereor program, etc., would be a model for further efforts in this direction. It is a matter of record that in the field some of these agencies have been engaged rather extensively in ecumenical cooperation with other Christian bodies. The World Council of Churches at a meeting in Enugu, in January of 1965, spelled out a positive attitude toward systematic fostering of such cooperation. [Editor's note in Abbott edition]

ment of cooperation among nations. The same is true of their efforts to establish such agencies. There are also various international Catholic associations which can serve in many ways to construct a peaceful and fraternal community of nations. These deserve to be strengthened by an increase in the number of well qualified associates and in the needed resources. Let them be fortified too by a suitable coordination of their energies. For today effective action as well as the need for dialogue demand joint projects.

Moreover, such associations contribute much to the development of a universal outlook—something certainly appropriate for Catholics. They also help to form an awareness of genuine universal solidarity and responsibility.

Finally, this Council desires that by way of fulfilling their role properly in the international community, Catholics should seek to cooperate actively and in a positive manner both with their separated brothers, who together with them profess the gospel of love, and with all men thirsting for true peace.

In view of the immense hardships which still afflict the majority of men today, the Council regards it as most opportune that some agency of the universal Church be set up for the world-wide promotion of justice for the poor and of Christ's kind of love for them. The role of such an organization will be to stimulate the Catholic community to foster progress in needy regions, and social justice on the international scene.*

CONCLUSION

THE ROLE OF INDIVIDUAL BELIEVERS AND DIOCESES

91.   Drawn from the treasures of Church teaching, the proposals of this sacred Synod look to the assistance of every man of our time, whether he believes in God, or does not explicitly recognize Him. Their purpose is to help men gain a sharper insight into their full destiny, so that they can

---

*Much of the initial support for this conciliar recommendation came from a handful of interested parties that included Bishop Edward Swanstrom, Father Arthur MacCormack, and James J. Norris. Mr. Norris, who has been associated for some years with the United States Catholic Relief Services organization, was also a lay auditor at the Council. [Editor's note in Abbott edition]

fashion the world more to man's surpassing dignity, search for a brother-hood which is universal and more deeply rooted, and meet the urgencies of our age with a gallant and unified effort born of love.

Undeniably this conciliar program is but a general one in several of its parts—and deliberately so, given the immense variety of situations and forms of human culture in the world. Indeed, while it presents teaching already accepted in the Church, the program will have to be further pursued and amplified, since it often deals with matters in a constant state of development. Still, we have relied on the Word of God and the spirit of the gospel. Hence we entertain the hope that many of our proposals will be able to bring substantial benefit to everyone, especially after they have been adapted to individual nations and mentalities by the faithful, under the guidance of their pastors.

DIALOGUE BETWEEN ALL MEN

92.　　By virtue of her mission to shed on the whole world the radiance of the gospel message, and to unify under one Spirit all men of whatever nation, race, or culture, the Church stands forth as a sign of that brother-liness which allows honest dialogue and invigorates it.

Such a mission requires in the first place that we foster within the Church herself mutual esteem, reverence, and harmony, through the full recognition of lawful diversity. Thus all those who compose the one People of God, both pastors and the general faithful, can engage in dialogue with ever-abounding fruitfulness. For the bonds which unite the faithful are mightier than anything which divides them. Hence, let there be unity in what is necessary, freedom in what is unsettled, and charity in any case.

Our hearts embrace also those brothers and communities not yet living with us in full communion. To them we are linked nonetheless by our profession of the Father and the Son and the Holy Spirit, and by the bond of charity. We are mindful that the unity of Christians is today awaited and desired by many, too, who do not believe in Christ. For the further it advances toward truth and love under the powerful impulse of the Holy Spirit, the more this unity will be a harbinger of unity and peace for the world at large.

Therefore, by common effort and in ways which are today increasingly appropriate for seeking this splendid goal effectively, let us take pains to pattern ourselves after the gospel more exactly every day, and thus work as brothers in rendering service to the human family. For in Christ Jesus this family is called into the family of the sons of God.

We also turn our thoughts to all who acknowledge God, and who preserve in their traditions precious elements of religion and humanity. We want frank conversation to compel us all to receive the inspirations of the Spirit faithfully and to measure up to them energetically.

For our part, the desire for such dialogue, which can lead to truth through love alone, excludes no one, though an appropriate measure of prudence must undoubtedly be exercised. We include those who cultivate beautiful qualities of the human spirit, but do not yet acknowledge the Source of these qualities.

We include those who oppress the Church and harass her in manifold ways. Since God the Father is the origin and purpose of all men, we are all called to be brothers. Therefore, if we have been summoned to the same destiny, which is both human and divine, we can and we should work together without violence and deceit in order to build up the world in genuine peace.

BUILDING UP THE WORLD AND FULFILLING ITS PURPOSE

93.   Mindful of the Lord's saying: "By this will all men know that you are my disciples, if you have love for one another" (Jn. 13:35), Christians cannot yearn for anything more ardently than to serve the men of the modern world ever more generously and effectively. Therefore, holding faithfully to the gospel and benefiting from its resources, and united with every man who loves and practices justice, Christians have shouldered a gigantic task demanding fulfillment in this world. Concerning this task they must give a reckoning to Him who will judge every man on the last day.

Not everyone who cries, "Lord, Lord," will enter into the kingdom of heaven, but those who do the Father's will and take a strong grip on the work at hand. Now, the Father wills that in all men we recognize Christ our brother and love Him effectively in word and in deed. By thus giving witness to the truth, we will share with others the mystery of the heavenly Father's love. As a consequence, men throughout the world will be aroused to a lively hope—the gift of the Holy Spirit—that they will finally be caught up in peace and utter happiness in that fatherland radiant with the splendor of the Lord.

"Now, to him who is able to accomplish all things in a measure far beyond what we ask or conceive, in keeping with the power that is at work in us—to him be glory in the Church and in Christ Jesus down through all the ages of time without end. Amen" (Eph. 3:20–21).

Each and every one of the things set forth in this Pastoral Constitution has won the consent of the Fathers of this most sacred Council. We too, by the apostolic authority conferred on us by Christ, join with the Venerable Fathers in approving, decreeing, and establishing these things in the Holy Spirit, and we direct that what has thus been enacted in synod be published to God's glory.

Rome, at St. Peter's, December 7, 1965

I, Paul, Bishop of the Catholic Church

There follow the signatures of the Fathers.

NOTES

1. The pastoral constitution *De Ecclesia in Mundo Huius Temporis* is made up of two parts; yet it constitutes an organic unity.

By way of explanation: the constitution is called "pastoral" because, while resting on doctrinal principles, it seeks to express the relation of the Church to the world and modern mankind. The result is that, on the one hand, a pastoral slant is present in the first part, and, on the other hand, a doctrinal slant is present in the second part.

In the first part, the Church develops her teaching on man, on the world which is the enveloping context of man's existence, and on man's relations to his fellow men. In part two, the Church gives closer consideration to various aspects of modern life and human society; special consideration is given to those questions and problems which, in this general area, seem to have a greater urgency in our day. As a result, in part two the subject matter which is viewed in the light of doctrinal principles is made up of diverse elements. Some elements have a permanent value; others, only a transitory one.

Consequently, the Constitution must be interpreted according to the general norms of theological interpretation. Interpreters must bear in mind—especially in part two—the changeable circumstances which the subject matter, by its very nature, involves.

2. Cf. Jn. 18:37; Mt. 20:28; Mk.10:45.
3. Cf. Rom. 7:14 ff.
4. Cf. 2 Cor. 5:15.
5. Cf. Acts 4:12.
6. Cf. Heb. 13:8.
7. Cf. Col. 1:15.
8. Cf. Gen. 1:26; Wis. 2:23.
9. Cf. Eccl. (Sir.) 17:3–10.
10. Cf. Rom. 1:21–25.
11. Cf. Jn. 8:34.
12. Cf. Dan. 3:57–90.
13. Cf. 1 Cor. 6:13–20.
14. Cf. 1 Kg. 16:7; Jer. 17:10.
15. Cf. Eccl. (Sir.) 17:7–8.
16. Cf. Rom. 2:15–16.
17. Cf. Pius XII, radio address on the correct formation of a Christian conscience in the young, Mar. 23, 1952: AAS (1952), p. 271.

18. Cf. Mt. 22:37-40; Gal. 5:14.

19. Cf. Eccl. (Sir.) 15:14.

20. Cf. 2 Cor. 5:10.

21. Cf. Wis. 1:13; 2:23-24; Rom. 5:21; 6:23; Jas. 1:15.

22. Cf. 1 Cor. 15:56-57.

23. Cf. Pius XI, encyclical letter *Divini Redemptoris*, March 19, 1937: AAS 29 (1937), pp. 65-106; Pius XII, encyclical letter *Ad Apostolorum Principis*, June 29, 1958: AAS 50 (1958), pp. 601-614; John XXIII, encyclical letter *Mater et Magistra*, May 15, 1961: AAS 35 (1961), pp. 451-453; Paul VI, encyclical letter *Ecclesiam Suam*, Aug. 6, 1964: AAS 56 (1964), pp.651-653.

24. Cf. Second Vatican Council, dogmatic constitution *Lumen Gentium*, Chap. I, Art. 8: AAS 57 (1965), p. 12.

25. Cf. Phil. 1:27.

26. St. Augustine, *Confessions* I, 1:PL 32, 661.

27. Cf. Rom. 5:14. Cf. Tertullian, *De carnis resurrectione* 6: "The shape that the slime of the earth was given was intended with a view to Christ, the future man.": p. 2, 282; CSEL 47, p. 33, 1. 12-13.

28. Cf. 2 Cor. 4:4.

29. Cf. Second Council of Constantinople, can. 7: "The divine Word was not changed into a human nature, nor was a human nature absorbed by the Word." Denz. 219 (428). Cf. also Third Council of Constantinople: "For just as His most holy and immaculate human nature, though deified, was not destroyed (Theotheisa ouk anerethe), but rather remained in its proper state and mode of being": Denz. 291 (556).Cf. Council of Chalcedon: "to be acknowledged in two natures, without confusion, change, division, or separation." Denz. 148 (302).

30. Cf. Third Council of Constantinople: "and so His human will, though deified, is not destroyed": Denz. 291 (556).

31. Cf. Heb. 4:15.

32. Cf. 2 Cor. 5:18-19; Col. 1:20-22.

33. Cf. 1 Pet. 2:21; Mt. 16:24; Lk. 14:27.

34. Cf. Rom. 8:29; Col. 3:10-14.

35. Cf. Rom. 8:1-11.

36. Cf. 2 Cor. 4:14.

37. Cf. Phil. 3:19; Rom. 8:17.

38. Cf. Second Vatican Council, dogmatic constitution *Lumen Gentium*, Chap. II, Art. 16: AAS 57 (1965), p. 20.

39. Cf. Rom. 8:32.

40. Cf. the Byzantine Easter Liturgy.

41. Cf. Rom. 8:15 and Gal. 4:6; cf. also Jn. 1:22 and Jn. 3:1-2.

42. Cf. John XXIII, encyclical letter *Mater et Magistra*, May 15, 1961: AAS 53 (1961), pp. 401-464, and encyclical letter *Pacem in Terris*, Apr. 11, 1963: AAS 55 (1963), pp. 257—304; Paul VI, encyclical letter *Ecclesiam Suam*, Aug. 6, 1964: AAS 54 (1964), pp. 609-659.

43. Cf. Lk. 17:33.

44. Cf. St. Thomas, 1 Ethica Lect. 1.

45. Cf. John XXIII, encyclical letter *Mater et Magistra*: AAS 53 (1961), p. 418. Cf. also Pius XI, encyclical letter *Quadragesimo Anno*: AAS 23 (1931), p. 222 ff.

46. Cf. John XXIII, encyclical letter *Mater et Magistra*: AAS 53 (1961).

47. Cf. Mk. 2:27.

48. Cf. John XXIII, encyclical letter *Pacem in Terris*: AAS 55 (1963), p. 266.

49. Cf. Jas. 2:15-16.

50. Cf. Lk. 16:18-31.

51. Cf. John XXIII, encyclical letter *Pacem in Terris:* AAS 55 (1963), pp. 299 and 300.

52. Cf. Lk. 6:37–38; Mt. 7:1–2; Rom. 2:1–11; 14:10; 14:10–12.

53. Cf. Mt. 5:43–47.

54. Cf. dogmatic constitution *Lumen Gentium*, Chap. II, Art. 9: AAS 57 (1965), pp.12–13.

55. Cf. Ex. 24:1–8.

56. Cf. Gen. 1:26–27; 9:3; Wis. 9:3.

57. Cf. Ps. 8:7 and 10.

58. Cf. John XXIII, encyclical letter *Pacem in Terris:* AAS 55 (1963), p. 297.

59. Cf. *Message to all Mankind* sent by the Fathers at the beginning of the Second Vatican Council, Oct. 20, 1962: AAS 54 (1962), p. 823.

60. Cf. Paul VI, address to the diplomatic corps, Jan. 7, 1965: AAS 57 (1965), p. 232.

61. Cf. First Vatican Council, *Dogmatic Constitution on the Catholic Faith*, Chap. III: Denz. 1785–1786 (3004-3005).

62. Cf. Msgr. Pio Paschini, *Vita e opere di Galileo Galilei*, 2 volumes, Vatican Press (1964).

63. Cf. Mt. 24:13; 13:24–30 and 36–43.

64. Cf. 2 Cor. 6:10.

65. Cf. Jn. 1:3 and 14.

66. Cf. Eph. 1:10.

67. Cf. Jn. 3:16; Rom. 5:8.

68. Cf. Acts 2:36; Mt. 28:18.

69. Cf. Rom. 15:16.

70. Cf. Acts 1:7.

71. Cf. 1 Cor. 7:31; St. Irenaeus, *Adversus haereses*, V, 36, PG, VIII, 1221.

72. Cf. 2 Cor. 5:2; 2 Pet. 3:13.

73. Cf. 1 Cor. 2:9; Apoc. 21:4–5.

74. Cf. 1 Cor. 15:42 and 53.

75. Cf. 1 Cor. 13:8; 3:14.

76. Cf. Rom. 8:19–21.

77. Cf. Lk. 9:25.

78. Cf. Pius XI, encyclical letter *Quadragesimo Anno:* AAS 23 (1931), p. 207.

79. Preface of the Feast of Christ the King.

80. Cf. Paul VI, encyclical letter *Ecclesiam Suam*, III: AAS 56 (1964), pp. 637–659.

81. Cf. Tit. 3:4: "love of mankind."

82. Cf. Eph. 1:3; 5:6, 13–14, 23.

83. Second Vatican Council, dogmatic constitution *Lumen Gentium*, Chap. I, Art 8: AAS 57 (1965), p. 12.

84. *Ibid.*, Chap. II, Art. 9: AAS 57 (1965), p. 14; cf. Art. 8: AAS loc. cit., p. 11.

85. *Ibid.*, Chap. I, Art 8: AAS 57 (1965), p. 11.

86. Cf. *ibid.*, Chap. IV, Art. 38: AAS 57 (1965), p. 43 with note 120.

87. Cf. Rom. 8:14–17.

88. Cf. Mt. 22:39.

89. Dogmatic constitution *Lumen Gentium*, Chap. II, Art 9: AAS 57 (1956), pp. 12–14.

90. Cf. Pius XII, Address to the International Union of Institutes of Archeology, History and History of Art, Mar. 9, 1956: AAS 48 (1965), p. 212: "Its divine Founder, Jesus Christ, has not given it any mandate or fixed any end of the cultural order. The goal which Christ assigns to it is strictly religious. . . . The Church must lead men to God, in order that they may be given over to him without reserve. . . . The Church can never lose sight of the strictly religious, supernatural goal. The meaning of all its activities, down to the last canon of its code, can only cooperate directly or indirectly in this goal."

91. Dogmatic constitution *Lumen Gentium*, Chap. I, Art. 1: AAS 57 (1965), p. 5.

92. Cf. Heb. 13:14.

93. Cf. 2 Th. 3:6–13; Eph. 4:28.

94. Cf. Is. 58:1–12.

95. Cf. Mt. 23:3–23; Mk. 7:10–13

96. Cf. John XXIII, encyclical letter *Mater et Magistra*, IV: AAS 53 (1961), pp. 456–457; cf. I: AAS loc. cit., pp. 407, 410–411.

97. Cf. dogmatic constitution *Lumen Gentium*, Chapter III, Art. 28: AAS 57 (1965), p. 35.

98. *Ibid.*, Art. 28: AAS loc. cit., pp. 35–36.

99. Cf. St. Ambrose, *De virginitate*, Chapter VIII, Art. 48: ML 16, 278.

100. Cf. dogmatic constitution *Lumen Gentium*, Chap. II, Art. 15: AAS 57 (1965), p. 20.

101. Cf. dogmatic constitution *Lumen Gentium*, Chapter II, Art. 13: AAS 57 (1965), p. 17.

102. Cf. Justin, *Dialogus cum Tryphone*, Chap. 110; MG 6, 729 (ed. Otto), 1897, pp. 391–393: ". . . but the greater the number of persecutions which are inflicted upon us, so much the greater the number of other men who become devout believers through the name of Jesus." Cf. Tertullian *Apologeticus*, Chap. L, 13: "Every time you mow us down like grass, we increase in number: the blood of Christians is a seed!" Cf. dogmatic constitution *Lumen Gentium*, Chap. II, Art. 9: AAS 57 (1965), p. 14.

103. Cf. dogmatic constitution *Lumen Gentium*, Chap. II, Art. 15: AAS 57 (1965), p. 20.

104. Cf. Paul VI, address given on Feb. 3, 1965.

105. Cf. St. Augustine, *De bono coniugii*: PL 40, 375–76 and 394; St. Thomas, *Summa Theol.*, Suppl. Quaest. 49, Art. 3 ad 1; *Decretum pro Armenis*: Denz-Schoen. 1327; Pius XI, encyclical letter *Casti Connubii*: AAS 22 (1930), pp. 547–548; Denz.-Schoen. 3703–3714.

106. Cf. Pius XI, encyclical letter *Casti Connubii*: AAS 22 (1930), pp. 546–547; Denz.-Schoen. 3706.

107. Cf. Os. 2; Jer. 3, 6–13; Ezek. 16 and 23; Is. 54.

108. Cf. Mt. 9:15; Mk. 2:19–20; Lk. 5:34–35; Jn. 3:29; cf. also 2 Cor. 11:2; Eph. 5:27; Apoc. 19:7–8; 21:2 and 9.

109. Cf. Eph. 5:25.

110. Cf. Second Vatican Council, dogmatic constitution *Lumen Gentium*: AAS 57 (1965), pp. 15–16; 40–41; 47.

111. Pius XI, encyclical letter *Casti Connubii*: AAS 22 (1930),p. 583.

112. Cf. 1 Tim. 5:3.

113. Cf. Eph. 5:32.

114. Cf. Gen. 2:22–24; Pr. 5: 15–20; 31:10–31; Tob. 8:4–8; Cant. 1:2–3; 1:16; 4:16; 5:1; 7:8–14; 1 Cor. 7:3–6; Eph. 5:25–33.

115. Cf. Pius XI, encyclical letter *Casti Connubii*: AAS (1930), p. 547 and 548; Denz-Schoen. 3707.

116. Cf. 1 Cor. 7:5.

117. Cf. Pius XII, Address *Tra le visite*, Jan. 20, 1958: AAS 50 (1958), p. 91.

118. Cf. Pius XI, encyclical letter *Casti Connubii*: AAS 22 (1930), Denz-Schoen., 3716–3718; Pius XII, *Allocutio Conventui Unionis Italicae inter Obstetrices*, Oct. 29, 1951: AAS 43 (1951), pp. 835–854; Paul VI, address to a group of cardinals, June 23, 1964: AAS 56 (1964), pp. 581–589. Certain questions which need further and more careful investigation have been handed over, at the command of the supreme Pontiff, to a commission for the study of population, family, and births, in order that, after it fulfills its function, the Supreme Pontiff may pass judgment. With the doctrine of the magisterium in this state, this holy Synod does not intend to propose immediately concrete solutions. [In the Latin text this is footnote 14 of Chap. I, in Part 2 of the document.—Ed.]

119. Cf. Eph. 5:16; Col. 4:5.

120. Cf. *Sacramentarium Gregorianum:* PL 78, 262.

121. Cf. Rom. 5:15 and 18; 6:5–11; Gal. 2:20.

122. Cf. Eph. 5:25–27.

123. Cf. introductory statement of this Constitution, Art. 4 ff.

124. Cf. Col. 3:1–2.

125. Cf. Gen. 1:28.

126. Cf. Pr. 8:30–31.

127. Cf. St. Irenaeus, *Adversus haereses:* III, 11, 8 (ed. Sagnard, p. 200; cf. *ibid.*, 16, 6: pp. 290–292; 21, 10–22: pp. 370–372; 22, 3: p. 378; etc.).

128. Cf. Eph. 1:10.

129. Cf. the words of Pius XI to Father M.D. Roland-Gosselin: " It is necessary never to lose sight of the fact that the objective of the Church is to evangelize, not to civilize. If it civilizes, it is for the sake of evangelization" (Semaines sociales de France, Versailles, 1936, pp. 461–462).

130. First Vatican Council, *Constitution on the Catholic Faith:* Denz. 1795, 1799 (3015, 3019). Cf. Pius XI, encyclical letter *Quadragesimo Anno:* AAS 23 (1931), p. 190.

131. Cf. John XXIII, encyclical letter *Pacem in Terris:* AAS 55 (1963), p. 260.

132. Cf. John XXIII, encyclical letter *Pacem in Terris:* AAS 55 (1963), p. 283; Pius XII, radio address, Dec. 24, 1941: AAS 34 (1942), pp. 16–17.

133. John XXIII, encyclical letter *Pacem in Terris:* AAS 55 (1963), p. 260.

134. Cf. John XXIII, speech delivered on Oct. 11, 1962, at the beginning of the Council: AAS 54 (1962), p. 792.

135. Cf. *Constitution on the Sacred Liturgy,* Art. 123, AAS 56 (1964), p. 131; Paul VI, discourse to the artists of Rome: AAS 56 (1964), pp. 439–442.

136. Cf. Second Vatican Council, *Decree on Priestly Formation and Declaration on Christian Education.*

137. Cf. dogmatic constitution *Lumen Gentium,* Chap. IV, Art. 37: AAS 57 (1965), pp. 42–43.

138. Cf. Pius XII, address on Mar. 23, 1952: AAS 44 (1953), p. 273; John XXIII, allocution to the Catholic Association of Italian Workers, May 1, 1959: AAS 51 (1959), p. 358.

139. Cf. Pius XI, encyclical letter *Quadragesimo Anno:* AAS 23 (1931), p. 190 ff; Pius XII, address of Mar. 23, 1952: AAS 44 (1952), p. 276 ff; John XXIII, encyclical letter *Mater et Magistra:* AAS 53 (1961), p. 450; Vatican Council II, Decree *Inter Mirifica* [on the Instruments of Social Communication], Chapter I, Art. 6: AAS 56 (1964), p. 147.

140. Cf. Mt. 16:26; Lk. 16:1–31; Col. 3:17.

141. Cf. Leo XIII, encyclical letter *Libertas*, in *Acta Leonis XIII,* t. VIII, p. 220ff; Pius XI, encyclical letter *Quadragesimo Anno:* AAS 23 (1931), p. 191 ff; Pius XI, encyclical letter *Divini Redemptoris:* AAS 39 (1937), p. 65 ff; Pius XII, Christmas message, 1941: AAS 34 (1942), p. 10 ff; John XXIII, encyclical letter *Mater et Magistra:* AAS 53 (1961), pp. 401–464.

142. In reference to agricultural problems cf. especially John XXIII, encyclical letter *Mater et Magistra:* AAS 53 (1961), p. 341 ff.

143. Cf. Leo XIII, encyclical letter *Rerum Novarum:* AAS 23 (1890–91), p. 649, p. 662; Pius XI, encyclical letter *Quadragesimo Anno:* AAS 23 (1931), pp. 200–201; Pius XI, encyclical letter *Divini Redemptoris:* AAS 29 (1937), p. 92; Pius XII, radio address on Christmas Eve, 1942: AAS 35 (1943), p. 20; Pius XII, allocution of June 13, 1943: AAS 35 (1943), p. 172; Pius XII, radio address to the workers of Spain, Mar. 11, 1951: AAS 43 (1951), p. 215; John XXIII, encyclical letter *Mater et Magistra:* AAS 53 (1961), p. 419.

144. Cf. John XXIII, encyclical letter *Mater et Magistra:* AAS 53 (1961), pp. 408, 424, 427; however, the word "curatione" has been taken from the Latin text of the encyclical letter

Quadragesimo Anno: AAS 23 (1931), p. 199. Under the aspect of the evolution of the question cf. also: Pius XII, allocution of June 3, 1950: AAS 42 (1950), pp. 485–488; Paul VI, allocution of June 8, 1964: AAS 56 (1964), pp. 574–579.

145. Cf. Pius XII, encyclical *Sertum Laetitiae:* AAS 31 (1939), p. 642; John XXIII, consistorial allocution: AAS 52 (1960), pp. 5–11; John XXIII, encyclical letter *Mater et Magistra:* AAS 53 (1961), p. 411.

146. Cf. St. Thomas, *Summa Theol.:* II–II q. 32, a. 5 ad 2; ibid. q. 66, a. 2; cf. explanation in Leo XIII, encyclical letter *Rerum Novarum:* AAS 23 (1890–91), p. 651; cf. also Pius XII, allocution of June 1, 1941: AAS 33 (1941), p. 199; Pius XII, Christmas radio address 1954: AAS 47 (1955), p. 27.

147. Cf. St. Basil, Hom. in illud Lucae "Destruam horrea mea," Art. 2 (PG 31, 263); Lactantius, Divinarum institutionum, lib. V. on justice (PL 6, 565 B): St. Augustine, In Ioann. Ev. Tr. 50, Art. 6 (PL 35, 1760); St. Augustine, Enarratio in Ps. CXLVII, 12 (PL 37, 192); St. Gregory the Great, Homiliae in Ev., hom. 20 (PL 76, 1165); St. Gregory the Great, Regulae Pastoralis liber, pars III, c. 21 (PL 77, 87); St. Bonaventure, in III Sent. d. 33, dub 1 (ed. Quaracchi III, 728); St. Bonaventure, In IV Sent. d. 15, p. II a.2 q.l (ed. cit. IV, 37lb); q. de superfluo (ms. Assisi, Bibl. Comun. 186, ff. 112a–113a); St. Albert the Great, In III Sent., d. 33, a.3, sol. 1 (ed. Borgnet XXVIII, 611); Id In IV Sent. d. 15, a. 16 (ed. cit. XXIX, 494–497). As for the determination of what is superfluous in our day and age, cf. John XXIII, radio-television message of Sept. 11, 1962: AAS 54 (1962) p. 682: "The obligation of every man, the urgent obligation of the Christian man, is to reckon what is superfluous by the measure of the needs of others, and to see to it that the administration and the distribution of created goods serve the common good."

148. In that case, the old principle holds true: "In extreme necessity all goods are common, that is, all goods are to be shared." On the other hand, for the order, extension, and manner by which the principle is applied in the proposed text, besides the modern authors· cf. St. Thomas, Summa Theol. II-II, q. 66, a. 7. Obviously, for the correct application of the principle, all the conditions that are morally required must be met.

149. Cf. Gratian, Decretum, C. 21, dist. LXXXVI (ed. Friedberg I, 302). This axiom is also found already in PL 54, 591 A (cf. in Antonianum 27 [1952], 349–366).

150. Cf. Leo XIII, encyclical letter *Rerum Novarum:* AAS 23 (1890–91), pp. 643–646; Pius XI, encyclical letter *Quadragesimo Anno:* AAS 23 (1931), p. 191; Pius XII, radio message of June 1, 1941: AAS 33 (1941), p. 199; Pius XII, radio message on Christmas Eve, 1942: AAS 35 (1943), p. 17; Pius XII, radio message of Sept. 1, 1944: AAS 36 (1944), p. 253; John XXIII, encyclical letter *Mater et Magistra:* AAS 53 (1961), pp. 428–429.

151. Cf. Pius XI, encyclical letter *Quadragesimo Anno:* AAS 23 (1931), p. 214; John XXIII, encyclical letter *Mater et Magistra:* AAS 53 (1961), p. 429.

152. Cf. Pius XII, radio message of Pentecost 1941: AAS 44 (1941), p. 199; John XXIII, encyclical letter *Mater et Magistra:* AAS 53 (1961), p. 430.

153. For the right use of goods according to the doctrine of the New Testament, cf. Lk. 3:11; 10:30 ff; 11:41; I Pet. 5:3; Mk. 8:36; 12:39–41; Jas. 5:1–6; 1 Tim. 6:8; Eph. 4:28; 2 Cor. 8:13; 1 Jn. 3:17 ff.

154. Cf. John XXIII, encyclical letter *Mater et Magistra:* AAS 53 (1961), p. 417.

155. Cf. John XXIII, *ibid.*

156. Cf. Rom. 13:1–5.

157. Cf. Rom. 13:5.

158. Cf. Pius XII, radio message, Dec. 24, 1942: AAS 35 (1943), pp. 9–24; Dec. 24, 1944: AAS 37 (1945), pp. 11–17; John XXIII, encyclical letter *Pacem in Terris:* AAS 55 (1963), pp. 263, 271, 277, and 278.

159. Cf. Pius XII, radio message of June 7, 1941: AAS 33 (1941), p. 200; John XXIII, encyclical letter *Pacem in Terris:* 1. c., p. 273 and 274.

160. Cf. John XXIII, encyclical letter *Mater et Magistra:* AAS 53 (1961), p. 416.

161. Pius XI, allocution *Ai dirigenti della Federazione Universitaria Cattolica:* Discorsi di Pio XI, (ed. Bertetto), Turin, vol. 1 (1960), p. 743.

162. Cf. Lk. 2:14.

163. Cf. Second Vatican Council, dogmatic constitution *Lumen Gentium,* Art. 13: AAS 57 (1965), p. 17.

164. Cf. Eph. 2:16; Col. 1:20–22.

165. Cf. John XXIII, encyclical letter *Pacem in Terris*, Apr. 11, 1963: AAS 55 (1963), p. 291: "Therefore in this age of ours which prides itself on its atomic power, it is irrational to believe that war is still an apt means of vindicating violated rights."

166. Cf. Pius XII, allocution of Sept. 30, 1954; AAS 46 (1954),p. 589; radio message of Dec. 24, 1954: AAS 47 (1955), pp. 15ff; John XXIII, encyclical letter *Pacem in Terris:* AAS 55 (1963), pp. 286–291; Paul VI, allocution to the United Nations, Oct. 4, 1965.

167. Cf. John XXIII, encyclical letter *Pacem in Terris* where reduction of arms is mentioned: AAS 55 (1963), p. 287.

168. Cf. 2 Cor. 2:6.

Dignitatis Humanae

Declaration on Religious Freedom (Second Vatican Council, December 7, 1965)

**On the Right of the Person
and of Communities
to Social and Civil Freedom
in Matters Religious**

PAUL, BISHOP

SERVANT OF THE SERVANTS OF GOD

TOGETHER WITH THE FATHERS OF THE SACRED COUNCIL

FOR EVERLASTING MEMORY

1.   A sense of the dignity of the human person has been impressing itself more and more deeply on the consciousness of contemporary man.[1]

[This English version is from *The Documents of Vatican II*, pp. 675–96. Msgr. Joseph Gallagher, Translation Editor of *The Documents of Vatican II*, states in his Preface: "Although these translations are to a major extent my own, there is one exception, and there are several qualifications. The translation of the Declaration on Religious Freedom was chiefly prepared by one of the architects of the Latin original, Father John Courtney Murray, S.J. For this volume, he slightly amended the translation that he had prepared for the National Catholic Welfare Conference. A small number of other changes were made editorially, in favor of consistency of style throughout the book." A.A.S LVIII (November 30, 1966), no. 14, pp. 929–46.]

And the demand is increasingly made that men should act on their own judgment, enjoying and making use of a responsible freedom, not driven by coercion but motivated by a sense of duty. The demand is also made that constitutional limits should be set to the powers of government, in order that there may be no encroachment on the rightful freedom of the person and of associations.

This demand for freedom in human society chiefly regards the quest for the values proper to the human spirit. It regards, in the first place, the free exercise of religion in society.

This Vatican Synod takes careful note of these desires in the minds of men. It proposes to declare them to be greatly in accord with truth and justice. To this end, it searches into the sacred tradition and doctrine of the Church—the treasury out of which the Church continually brings forth new things that are in harmony with the things that are old.

First, this sacred Synod professes its belief that God himself has made known to mankind the way in which men are to serve Him, and thus be saved in Christ and come to blessedness. We believe that this one true religion subsists in the catholic and apostolic Church, to which the Lord Jesus committed the duty of spreading it abroad among all men. Thus He spoke to the apostles: "Go, therefore, and make disciples of all nations, baptizing them in the name of the Father, and of the Son, and of the Holy Spirit, teaching them to observe all that I have commanded you" (Mt. 28:19–20). On their part, all men are bound to seek the truth, especially in what concerns God and His Church, and to embrace the truth they come to know, and to hold fast to it.

This sacred Synod likewise professes its belief that it is upon the human conscience that these obligations fall and exert their binding force. The truth cannot impose itself except by virtue of its own truth, as it makes its entrance into the mind at once quietly and with power. Religious freedom, in turn, which men demand as necessary to fulfill their duty to worship God, has to do with immunity from coercion in civil society. Therefore, it leaves untouched traditional Catholic doctrine on the moral duty of men and societies toward the true religion and toward the one Church of Christ.

Over and above all this, in taking up the matter of religious freedom this sacred Synod intends to develop the doctrine of recent Popes on the inviolable rights of the human person and on the constitutional order of society.

CHAPTER I
General Principle of Religious Freedom

2.   This Vatican Synod declares that the human person has a right to religious freedom. This freedom means that all men are to be immune from coercion on the part of individuals or of social groups and of any human power, in such wise that in matters religious no one is to be forced to act in a manner contrary to his own beliefs. Nor is anyone to be restrained from acting in accordance with his own beliefs, whether privately or publicly, whether alone or in association with others, within due limits.

The Synod further declares that the right to religious freedom has its foundation in the very dignity of the human person, as this dignity is known through the revealed Word of God and by reason itself.[2] This right of the human person to religious freedom is to be recognized in the constitutional law whereby society is governed. Thus it is to become a civil right.

It is in accordance with their dignity as persons—that is, beings endowed with reason and free will and therefore privileged to bear personal responsibility—that all men should be at once impelled by nature and also bound by a moral obligation to seek the truth, especially religious truth. They are also bound to adhere to the truth, once it is known, and to order their whole lives in accord with the demands of truth.

However, men cannot discharge these obligations in a manner in keeping with their own nature unless they enjoy immunity from external coercion as well as psychological freedom. Therefore, the right to religious freedom has its foundation, not in the subjective disposition of the person, but in his very nature. In consequence, the right to this immunity continues to exist even in those who do not live up to their obligation of seeking the truth and adhering to it. Nor is the exercise of this right to be impeded, provided that the just requirements of public order are observed.

3.   Further light is shed on the subject if one considers that the highest norm of human life is the divine law—eternal, objective, and universal—whereby God orders, directs, and governs the entire universe and all the ways of the human community, by a plan conceived in wisdom and love. Man has been made by God to participate in this law, with the result that, under the gentle disposition of divine Providence, he can

come to perceive ever increasingly the unchanging truth. Hence every man has the duty, and therefore the right, to seek the truth in matters religious, in order that he may with prudence form for himself right and true judgments of conscience, with the use of all suitable means.

Truth, however, is to be sought after in a manner proper to the dignity of the human person and his social nature. The inquiry is to be free, carried on with the aid of teaching or instruction, communication, and dialogue. In the course of these, men explain to one another the truth they have discovered, or think they have discovered, in order thus to assist one another in the quest for truth. Moreover, as the truth is discovered, it is by a personal assent that men are to adhere to it.

On his part, man perceives and acknowledges the imperatives of the divine law through the mediation of conscience. In all his activity a man is bound to follow his conscience faithfully, in order that he may come to God, for whom he was created. It follows that he is not to be forced to act in a manner contrary to his conscience. Nor, on the other hand, is he to be restrained from acting in accordance with his conscience, especially in matters religious.

For, of its very nature, the exercise of religion consists before all else in those internal, voluntary, and free acts whereby man sets the course of his life directly toward God. No merely human power can either command or prohibit acts of this kind.[3]

However, the social nature of man itself requires that he should give external expression to his internal acts of religion; that he should participate with others in matters religious; that he should profess his religion in community. Injury, therefore, is done to the human person and to the very order established by God for human life, if the free exercise of religion is denied in society when the just requirements of public order do not so require.

There is a further consideration. The religious acts whereby men, in private and in public and out of a sense of personal conviction, direct their lives to God transcend by their very nature the order of terrestrial and temporal affairs. Government, therefore, ought indeed to take account of the religious life of the people and show it favor, since the function of government is to make provision for the common welfare. However, it would clearly transgress the limits set to its power were it to presume to direct or inhibit acts that are religious.

4.   The freedom or immunity from coercion in matters religious which is the endowment of persons as individuals is also to be recognized as their right when they act in community. Religious bodies are a requirement of the social nature both of man and of religion itself.

Provided the just requirements of public order are observed, religious bodies rightfully claim freedom in order that they may govern themselves according to their own norms, honor the Supreme Being in public worship, assist their members in the practice of the religious life, strengthen them by instruction, and promote institutions in which they may join together for the purpose of ordering their own lives in accordance with their religious principles.

Religious bodies also have the right not to be hindered, either by legal measures or by administrative action on the part of government, in the selection, training, appointment, and transferral of their own ministers, in communicating with religious authorities and communities abroad, in erecting buildings for religious purposes, and in the acquisition and use of suitable funds or properties.

Religious bodies also have the right not to be hindered in their public teaching and witness to their faith, whether by the spoken or by the written word. However, in spreading religious faith and in introducing religious practices, everyone ought at all times to refrain from any manner of action which might seem to carry a hint of coercion or of a kind of persuasion that would be dishonorable or unworthy, especially when dealing with poor or uneducated people. Such a manner of action would have to be considered an abuse of one's own right and a violation of the right of others.

In addition, it comes within the meaning of religious freedom that religious bodies should not be prohibited from freely undertaking to show the special value of their doctrine in what concerns the organization of society and the inspiration of the whole of human activity. Finally, the social nature of man and the very nature of religion afford the foundation of the right of men freely to hold meetings and to establish educational, cultural, charitable, and social organizations, under the impulse of their own religious sense.

5.   Since the family is a society in its own original right, it has the right freely to live its own domestic religious life under the guidance of parents. Parents, moreover, have the right to determine, in accordance with their own religious beliefs, the kind of religious education that their children are to receive.

Government, in consequence, must acknowledge the right of parents to make a genuinely free choice of schools and of other means of education. The use of this freedom of choice is not to be made a reason for imposing unjust burdens on parents, whether directly or indirectly. Besides, the rights of parents are violated if their children are forced to attend lessons or instruction which are not in agreement with their religious beliefs. The same is true if a single system of education, from which all religious formation is excluded, is imposed upon all.

6.   The common welfare of society consists in the entirety of those conditions of social life under which men enjoy the possibility of achieving their own perfection in a certain fullness of measure and also with some relative ease. Hence this welfare consists chiefly in the protection of the rights,[4] and in the performance of the duties, of the human person. Therefore, the care of the right to religious freedom devolves upon the people as a whole, upon social groups, upon government, and upon the Church and other religious Communities, in virtue of the duty of all toward the common welfare, and in the manner proper to each.

The protection and promotion of the inviolable rights of man ranks among the essential duties of government.[5] Therefore, government is to assume the safeguard of the religious freedom of all its citizens, in an effective manner, by just laws and by other appropriate means. Government is also to help create conditions favorable to the fostering of religious life, in order that the people may be truly enabled to exercise their religious rights and to fulfill their religious duties, and also in order that society itself may profit by the moral qualities of justice and peace which have their origin in men's faithfulness to God and to His holy will.[6]

If, in view of peculiar circumstances obtaining among certain peoples, special legal recognition is given in the constitutional order of society to one religious body, it is at the same time imperative that the right of all citizens and religious bodies to religious freedom should be recognized and made effective in practice.

Finally, government is to see to it that the equality of citizens before the law, which is itself an element of the common welfare, is never violated for religious reasons whether openly or covertly. Nor is there to be discrimination among citizens.

It follows that a wrong is done when government imposes upon its people, by force or fear or other means, the profession or repudiation of any religion, or when it hinders men from joining or leaving a religious body. All the more is it a violation of the will of God and of the sacred rights of the person and the family of nations, when force is brought to bear in any way in order to destroy or repress religion, either in the whole of mankind or in a particular country or in a specific community.

7.   The right to religious freedom is exercised in human society; hence its exercise is subject to certain regulatory norms. In the use of all freedoms, the moral principle of personal and social responsibility is to be observed. In the exercise of their rights, individual men and social groups are bound by the moral law to have respect both for the rights of

others and for their own duties toward others and for the common welfare of all. Men are to deal with their fellows in justice and civility.

Furthermore, society has the right to defend itself against possible abuses committed on pretext of freedom of religion. It is the special duty of government to provide this protection. However, government is not to act in arbitrary fashion or in an unfair spirit of partisanship. Its action is to be controlled by juridical norms which are in conformity with the objective moral order.

These norms arise out of the need for effective safeguard of the rights of all citizens and for peaceful settlement of conflicts of rights. They flow from the need for an adequate care of genuine public peace, which comes about when men live together in good order and in true justice. They come, finally, out of the need for a proper guardianship of public morality. These matters constitute the basic component of the common welfare: they are what is meant by public order.

For the rest, the usages of society are to be the usages of freedom in their full range. These require that the freedom of man be respected as far as possible, and curtailed only when and in so far as necessary.

8.   Many pressures are brought to bear upon men of our day, to the point where the danger arises lest they lose the possibility of acting on their own judgment. On the other hand, not a few can be found who seem inclined to use the name of freedom as the pretext for refusing to submit to authority and for making light of the duty of obedience.

Therefore, this Vatican Synod urges everyone, especially those who are charged with the task of educating others, to do their utmost to form men who will respect the moral order and be obedient to lawful authority. Let them form men too who will be lovers of true freedom—men, in other words, who will come to decisions on their own judgment and in the light of truth, govern their activities with a sense of responsibility, and strive after what is true and right, willing always to join with others in cooperative effort.

Religious freedom, therefore, ought to have this further purpose and aim, namely, that men may come to act with greater responsibility in fulfilling their duties in community life.

CHAPTER II
Religious Freedom in the Light of Revelation

9.   The declaration of this Vatican Synod on the right of man to religious freedom has its foundation in the dignity of the person. The requirements of this dignity have come to be more adequately known to human reason through centuries of experience. What is more, this doctrine of freedom has roots in divine revelation, and for this reason Christians are bound to respect it all the more conscientiously.

Revelation does not indeed affirm in so many words the right of man to immunity from external coercion in matters religious. It does, however, disclose the dignity of the human person in its full dimensions. It gives evidence of the respect which Christ showed toward the freedom with which man is to fulfill his duty of belief in the Word of God. It gives us lessons too in the spirit which disciples of such a Master ought to make their own and to follow in every situation.

Thus, further light is cast on the general principles upon which the doctrine of this Declaration on Religious Freedom is based. In particular, religious freedom in society is entirely consonant with the freedom of the act of Christian faith.

10.   It is one of the major tenets of Catholic doctrine that man's response to God in faith must be free. Therefore no one is to be forced to embrace the Christian faith[7] against his own will. This doctrine is contained in the Word of God and it was constantly proclaimed by the Fathers of the Church.[8] The act of faith is of its very nature a free act. Man, redeemed by Christ the Savior and through Christ Jesus called to be God's adopted son,[9] cannot give his adherence to God revealing Himself unless the Father draw him[10] to offer to God the reasonable and free submission of faith.

It is therefore completely in accord with the nature of faith that in matters religious every manner of coercion on the part of men should be excluded. In consequence, the principle of religious freedom makes no small contribution to the creation of an environment in which men can without hindrance be invited to Christian faith, and embrace it of their own free will, and profess it effectively in their whole manner of life.

11.   God calls men to serve Him in spirit and in truth. Hence they are bound in conscience but they stand under no compulsion. God has

regard for the dignity of the human person whom He Himself created; man is to be guided by his own judgment and he is to enjoy freedom.

This truth appears at its height in Christ Jesus, in whom God perfectly manifested Himself and His ways with men. Christ is our Master and our Lord.[11] He is also meek and humble of heart.[12] And in attracting and inviting His disciples He acted patiently.[13] He wrought miracles to shed light on His teaching and to establish its truth. But His intention was to rouse faith in His hearers and to confirm them in faith, not to exert coercion upon them.[14]

He did indeed denounce the unbelief of some who listened to Him; but He left vengeance to God in expectation of the day of judgment.[15] When He sent His apostles into the world, He said to them: "He who believes and is baptized shall be saved, but he who does not believe shall be condemned" (Mk. 16:16); but He Himself, noting that cockle had been sown amid the wheat, gave orders that both should be allowed to grow until the harvest time, which will come at the end of the world.[16]

He refused to be a political Messiah, ruling by force;[17] He preferred to call Himself the Son of Man, who came "to serve and to give his life as a ransom for many" (Mk. 10:45). He showed Himself the perfect Servant of God;[18] "a bruised reed he will not break, and a smoking wick he will not quench" (Mt. 12:20).

He acknowledged the power of government and its rights, when He commanded that tribute be given to Caesar. But He gave clear warning that the higher rights of God are to be kept inviolate: "Render, therefore, to Caesar the things that are Caesar's, and to God the things that are God's" (Mt. 22:21).

In the end, when He completed on the cross the work of redemption whereby He achieved salvation and true freedom for men, He also brought His revelation to completion. He bore witness to the truth,[19] but He refused to impose the truth by force on those who spoke against it. Not by force of blows does His rule assert its claims.[20] Rather, it is established by witnessing to the truth and by hearing the truth, and it extends its dominion by the love whereby Christ, lifted up on the cross, draws all men to Himself.[21]

Taught by the word and example of Christ, the apostles followed the same way. From the very origins of the Church the disciples of Christ strove to convert men to faith in Christ as the Lord—not, however, by the use of coercion or by devices unworthy of the gospel, but by the power, above all, of the Word of God.[22] Steadfastly they proclaimed to all the plan of God our Savior, "who wishes all men to be saved and to come to the knowledge of the truth" (1 Tim. 2:4). At the same time, however, they showed respect for weaker souls even though these persons were in error. Thus they made it plain that "every one of us will render an account of himself to God" (Rom. 14:12),[23] and for this reason is bound to obey his conscience.

Like Christ Himself, the apostles were unceasingly bent upon bearing witness to the truth of God. They showed special courage in speaking "the word of God with boldness" (Acts 4:31)[24] before the people and their rulers. With a firm faith they held that the gospel is indeed the power of God unto salvation for all who believe.[25] Therefore they rejected all "carnal weapons."[26] They followed the example of the gentleness and respectfulness of Christ. And they preached the Word of God in the full confidence that there was resident in this Word itself a divine power able to destroy all the forces arrayed against God[27] and to bring men to faith in Christ and to His service.[28] As the Master, so too the apostles recognized legitimate civil authority. "For there exists no authority except from God," the Apostle teaches, and therefore commands: "Let everyone be subject to the higher authorities . . . : he who resists the authority resists the ordinance of God" (Rom. 13:1–2).[29]

At the same time, however, they did not hesitate to speak out against governing powers which set themselves in opposition to the holy will of God: "We must obey God rather than men" (Acts 5:29).[30] This is the way along which countless martyrs and other believers have walked through all ages and over all the earth.

12.   The Church therefore is being faithful to the truth of the gospel, and is following the way of Christ and the apostles when she recognizes, and gives support to, the principle of religious freedom as befitting the dignity of man and as being in accord with divine revelation. Throughout the ages, the Church has kept safe and handed on the doctrine received from the Master and from the apostles. In the life of the People of God as it has made its pilgrim way through the vicissitudes of human history, there have at times appeared ways of acting which were less in accord with the spirit of the gospel and even opposed to it. Nevertheless, the doctrine of the Church that no one is to be coerced into faith has always stood firm.

Thus the leaven of the gospel has long been about its quiet work in the minds of men. To it is due in great measure the fact that in the course of time men have come more widely to recognize their dignity as persons, and the conviction has grown stronger that in religious matters the person in society is to be kept free from all manner of human coercion.

13.   Among the things which concern the good of the Church and indeed the welfare of society here on earth—things therefore which are always and everywhere to be kept secure and defended against all

injury—this certainly is preeminent, namely, that the Church should enjoy that full measure of freedom which her care for the salvation of men requires.[31] This freedom is sacred, because the only-begotten Son endowed with it the Church which He purchased with His blood. It is so much the property of the Church that to act against it is to act against the will of God. The freedom of the Church is the fundamental principle in what concerns the relations between the Church and governments and the whole civil order.

In human society and in the face of government, the Church claims freedom for herself in her character as a spiritual authority, established by Christ the Lord. Upon this authority there rests, by divine mandate, the duty of going out into the whole world and preaching the gospel to every creature.[32] The Church also claims freedom for herself in her character as a society of men who have the right to live in society in accordance with the precepts of Christian faith.[33]

In turn, where the principle of religious freedom is not only proclaimed in words or simply incorporated in law but also given sincere and practical application, there the Church succeeds in achieving a stable situation of right as well as of fact and the independence which is necessary for the fulfillment of her divine mission. This independence is precisely what the authorities of the Church claim in society.[34]

At the same time, the Christian faithful, in common with all other men, possess the civil right not to be hindered in leading their lives in accordance with their conscience. Therefore, a harmony exists between the freedom of the Church and the religious freedom which is to be recognized as the right of all men and communities and sanctioned by constitutional law.

14.   In order to be faithful to the divine command, "Make disciples of all nations" (Mt. 28:19), the Catholic Church must work with all urgency and concern "that the Word of God may run and be glorified" (2 Th. 3:1). Hence the Church earnestly begs of her children that, first of all, "supplications, prayers, intercessions, and thanksgivings be made for all men. . . . For this is good and agreeable in the sight of God our Savior, who wishes all men to be saved and to come to the knowledge of the truth" (1 Tim. 2:1–4).

In the formation of their consciences, the Christian faithful ought carefully to attend to the sacred and certain doctrine of the Church.[35] The Church is, by the will of Christ, the teacher of the truth. It is her duty to give utterance to, and authoritatively to teach, that Truth which is Christ Himself, and also to declare and confirm by her authority those principles of the moral order which have their origin in human nature itself. Furthermore, let Christians walk in wisdom in the face of those outside, "in the Holy Spirit, in unaffected love, in the word of truth" (2 Cor. 6:6–7). Let them be about their task of spreading the light of life with all confidence[36] and apostolic courage, even to the shedding of their blood.

The disciple is bound by a grave obligation toward Christ his Master ever more adequately to understand the truth received from Him, faithfully to proclaim it, and vigorously to defend it, never—be it understood—having recourse to means that are incompatible with the spirit of the gospel. At the same time, the charity of Christ urges him to act lovingly, prudently and patiently in his dealings with those who are in error or in ignorance with regard to the faith.[37] All is to be taken into account—the Christian duty to Christ, the life-giving Word which must be proclaimed, the rights of the human person, and the measure of grace granted by God through Christ to men, who are invited freely to accept and profess the faith.

15.   The fact is that men of the present day want to be able freely to profess their religion in private and in public. Religious freedom has already been declared to be a civil right in most constitutions, and it is solemnly recognized in international documents.[38] The further fact is that forms of government still exist under which, even though freedom of religious worship receives constitutional recognition, the powers of government are engaged in the effort to deter citizens from the profession of religion and to make life difficult and dangerous for religious Communities.

This sacred Synod greets with joy the first of these two facts, as among the signs of the times. With sorrow, however, it denounces the other fact, as only to be deplored. The Synod exhorts Catholics, and it directs a plea to all men, most carefully to consider how greatly necessary religious freedom is, especially in the present condition of the human family.

All nations are coming into even closer unity. Men of different cultures and religions are being brought together in closer relationships. There is a growing consciousness of the personal responsibility that weighs upon every man. All this is evident.

Consequently, in order that relationships of peace and harmony may be established and maintained within the whole of mankind, it is necessary that religious freedom be everywhere provided with an effective constitutional guarantee, and that respect be shown for the high duty and right of man freely to lead his religious life in society.

May the God and Father of all grant that the human family, through careful observance of the principle of religious freedom in society, may be brought by the grace of Christ and the power of the Holy Spirit to the sublime and unending "freedom of the glory of the sons of God" (Rom. 8:21).

Each and every one of the things set forth in this Declaration has won the consent of the Fathers of this most sacred Council. We too, by the apostolic authority conferred on us by Christ, join with the Venerable Fathers in approving, decreeing, and establishing these things in the Holy Spirit, and we direct that what has thus been enacted in synod be published to God's glory.

Rome, at St. Peter's, December 7, 1965

I, Paul, Bishop of the Catholic Church

There follow the signatures of the Fathers.

NOTES

1. Cf. John XXIII, encyclical *Pacem in Terris*, Apr. 11, 1963: AAS 55 (1963), p. 279; *ibid.*, p. 265; Pius XII, radio message, Dec. 24, 1944: AAS 37 (1945), p. 14.

2. Cf. John XXIII, encyclical *Pacem in Terris*, Apr. 11, 1963: AAS 55 (1963), pp. 260–261; Pius XII, radio message, Dec. 24, 1942: AAS 35 (1943), p. 19; Pius XI, encyclical *Mit Brennender Sorge*, Mar. 14, 1937: AAS 29 (1937), p. 160; Leo XIII, encyclical *Libertas Praestantissimum*, June 20, 1888: Acts of Leo XIII 8 (1888), pp. 237–238.

3. Cf. John XXIII, encyclical *Pacem in Terris*, Apr. 11, 1963: AAS 55 (1963), p. 270; Paul VI, radio message, Dec. 22, 1964: AAS 57 (1965), pp. 181–182.

4. Cf. John XXIII, encyclical *Mater et Magistra*, May 15, 1961: AAS 53 (1961), p. 417; *idem*, encyclical *Pacem in Terris*, Apr. 11, 1963: AAS 55 (1963), p. 273.

5. Cf. John XXIII, encyclical *Pacem in Terris*, Apr. 11, 1963: AAS 55 (1963), pp. 273–274; Pius XII, radio message June 1, 1941: AAS 33 (1941), p. 200.

6. Cf. Leo XIII, encyclical *Immortale Dei*, Nov. 1, 1885: AAS 18 (1885), p. 161.

7. Cf. CIC, c. 1351; Pius XII, allocution to prelate auditors and other officials and administrators of the tribune of the Holy Roman Rota, Oct. 6, 1946: AAS 38 (1946), p. 394; *idem*, encyclical *Mystici Corporis*, June 29, 1943: AAS (1943), p. 243.

8. Cf. Lactantius, *Divinarum Institutionum*, Book V, 19: CSEL 19, pp. 463–464, 465: PL 6, 614 and 616 (ch. 20); St. Ambrose, *Epistola ad Valentianum Imp.*, Letter 21: PL 16, 1005; St. Augustine, *Contra Litteras Petiliani*, Book II, ch. 83: CSEL 52, p. 112: PL 43, 315; cf. C. 23, q. 5, c. 33 (ed. Friedburg, col. 939); *idem*, Letter 23: PL 33, 98; *idem*, Letter 34: PL 33, 132; *idem*, Letter 35: PL 33, 135; St. Gregory the Great, *Epistola ad Virgilium et Theodorum Episcopos Massiliae Galliarum*, Register of Letters I, 45: MGH Ep. 1, p. 72; PL 77, 510–511 (Book I, ep. 47); *idem*, *Epistola ad Johannem Episcopum Constantinopolitanum*, Register of Letters, III, 52: MGH Letter 1, p. 210: PL 77, 649 (Book III, Letter 53); cf. D. 45, c. 1 (ed. Friedberg, col. 160);

Council of Toledo IV, c. 57: Mansi 10, 633; cf. D. 45, c. 5 (ed. Friedberg, col. 161–162); Clement III: X., V. 6, 9: ed. Freidberg, col. 774; Innocent III, *Epistola ad Arelatensem Archiepiscopum*, X., III, 42, 3: ed. Friedberg, col. 646.

9. Cf. Eph. 1:5.
10. Cf. Jn. 6:44.
11. Cf. Jn. 13:13.
12. Cf. Mt. 11:29.
13. Cf. Mt. 11:28–30; Jn. 6:67–68.
14. Cf. Mt. 9:28–29; Mk. 9:23–24; 6, 5–6; Paul VI, encyclical *Ecclesiam Suam*, Aug. 6, 1964: AAS 56 (1964), pp. 642–643.
15. Cf. Mt. 11:20–24; Rom. 12:19–20; 2 Th. 1:8.
16. Cf. Mt. 13:30 and 40–42.
17. Cf. Mt. 4:8–10; Jn. 6:15.
18. Cf. Is. 42:1–4.
19. Cf. Jn. 18:37.
20. Cf. Mt. 26:51–53; Jn. 18:36.
21. Cf. Jn. 12:32.
22. Cf. 1 Cor. 2:3–5; 1 Th. 2:3–5.
23. Cf. Rom. 14:1–23; 1 Cor. 8:9–13; 10:23–33.
24. Cf. Eph. 6:19–20.
25. Cf. Rom. 1:16.
26. Cf. 2 Cor. 10:4; 1 Th. 5:8–9.
27. Cf. Eph. 6:11–17.
28. Cf. 2 Cor. 10:3–5.
29. Cf. 1 Pet. 2:13–17.
30. Cf. Acts 4:19–20.
31. Cf. Leo XIII, letter *Officio Sanctissimo*, Dec. 22, 1887: AAS 20 (1887), p. 269; *idem*, letter *Ex Litteris*, Apr. 7, 1887: AAS 19 (1886), p. 465.
32. Cf. Mk. 16:15; Mt. 28:18–20; Pius XII, encyclical *Summi Pontificatus*, Oct. 20, 1939: AAS 31 (1939), pp. 445–446.
33. Cf. Pius XI, letter *Firmissimam Constantiam*, Mar. 28, 1937: AAS 29 (1937), p. 196.
34. Cf. Pius XII, allocution *Ci Riesce*, Dec. 6, 1953: AAS 45 (1953), p. 802.
35. Cf. Pius XII, radio message, Mar. 23, 1952: AAS 44 (1952), pp. 270–278.
36. Cf. Acts 4:29.
37. Cf. John XXIII, encyclical *Pacem in Terris*, Apr. 11, 1963: AAS 55 (1963), pp. 299–300.
38. Cf. John XXIII, encyclical *Pacem in Terris*, Apr. 11, 1963: AAS 55 (1963), pp. 295–296.

Message to Humanity

(Second Vatican Council,
October 20, 1962)

ISSUED AT THE BEGINNING OF THE
SECOND VATICAN COUNCIL BY ITS
FATHERS, WITH THE ENDORSEMENT
OF THE SUPREME PONTIFF

1.   THE FATHERS OF THE COUNCIL TO ALL MEN

We take great pleasure in sending to all men and nations a message concerning that well-being, love, and peace which were brought into the world by Christ Jesus, the Son of the living God, and entrusted to the Church.

For this is the reason why, at the direction of the most blessed Pope John XXIII, we successors of the apostles have gathered here, joined in singlehearted prayer with Mary the Mother of Jesus, and forming one apostolic body headed by the successor of Peter.

[Vatican II promulgated sixteen official documents. I present here the full text of a seventeenth: a unique and little known Message to Humanity, approved and released October 20, 1962, only nine days after the Council opened. Father Walter Abbott, S.J., General Editor of *The Documents of Vatican II*, notes: "For the first time in the history of Ecumenical Councils, a Council addresses itself to all men, not just members of the Catholic Church. In the following year, Pope John XXIII added, for the first time, the salutation 'and to all men of good will' as the opening of a papal encyclical (*Pacem in Terris*, April 11, 1963)." The numbering of the paragraphs of this Message to Humanity has been added by myself—J.G.]

2.   MAY THE FACE OF CHRIST JESUS SHINE OUT

In this assembly, under the guidance of the Holy Spirit, we wish to inquire how we ought to renew ourselves, so that we may be found increasingly faithful to the gospel of Christ. We shall take pains so to present to the men of this age God's truth in its integrity and purity that they may understand it and gladly assent to it.

Since we are shepherds, we desire that all those may have their longing satisfied who seek God "if perhaps they might find Him as they grope after Him; though indeed He is not far from each of us."[1]

Hence, obeying the will of Christ, who delivered Himself to death "that He might present to Himself the Church, not having spot or wrinkle . . . but that she might be holy and without blemish,"[2] we as pastors devote all our energies and thoughts to the renewal of ourselves and the flocks committed to us, so that there may radiate before all men the lovable features of Jesus Christ, who shines in our hearts "that God's splendor may be revealed."[3]

3.   GOD SO LOVED THE WORLD . . .

We believe that the Father so loved the world that He gave His own Son to save it. Indeed, through this same Son of His He freed us from bondage to sin, reconciling all things unto Himself through Him, "making peace through the blood of his cross,"[4] so that "we might be called sons of God, and truly be such."

The Spirit too has been bestowed on us by the Father, that living the life of God, we might love God and the brethren, who are all of us one in Christ.

It is far from true that because we cling to Christ we are diverted from earthly duties and toils. On the contrary, faith, hope, and the love of Christ impel us to serve our brothers, thereby patterning ourselves after the example of the Divine Teacher, who "came not to be served but to serve."[5] Hence, the Church too was not born to dominate but to serve. He laid down His life for us, and we too ought to lay down our lives for our brothers.[6]

Accordingly, while we hope that the light of faith will shine more clearly and more vigorously as a result of this Council's efforts, we look forward to a spiritual renewal from which will also flow a happy impulse on behalf of human values such as scientific discoveries, technological advances, and a wider diffusion of knowledge.

4.   THE LOVE OF CHRIST IMPELS US

Coming together in unity from every nation under the sun, we carry in our hearts the hardships, the bodily and mental distress, the sorrows, longings, and hopes of all the peoples entrusted to us. We urgently turn our thoughts to all the anxieties by which modern man is afflicted. Hence, let our concern swiftly focus first of all on those who are especially lowly, poor, and weak. Like Christ, we would have pity on the multitude weighed down with hunger, misery, and lack of knowledge. We want to fix a steady gaze on those who still lack the opportune help to achieve a way of life worthy of human beings.

As we undertake our work, therefore, we would emphasize whatever concerns the dignity of man, whatever contributes to a genuine community of peoples. "Christ's love impels us,"[7] for "he who sees his brother in need and closes his heart against him, how does the love of God abide in him?"[8]

5.   TWO ISSUES OF SPECIAL URGENCY CONFRONT US

The Supreme Pontiff, John XXIII, in a radio address delivered on September 11, 1962, stressed two points, especially.

The first dealt with peace between peoples. There is no one who does not hate war, no one who does not strive for peace with burning desire. But the Church desires it most of all, because she is the Mother of all. Through the voice of the Roman Pontiffs, she never ceases to make an open declaration of her love for peace, her desire for peace. She is always ready to lend aid with her whole heart to any sincere effort on behalf of peace. She strives with all her might to bring peoples together and to develop among them a mutual respect for interests and feelings. This very conciliar congress of ours, so impressive in the diversity of the races, nations, and languages it represents, does it not bear witness to a community of brotherly love, and shine as a visible sign of it? We are giving witness that all men are brothers, whatever their race or nation.

The Supreme Pontiff also pleads for social justice. The teaching expounded in his encyclical *Mater et Magistra* clearly shows that the Church is supremely necessary for the modern world if injustices and unworthy inequalities are to be denounced, and if the true order of affairs and of values is to be restored, so that man's life can become more human according to the standards of the gospel.

6.   THE POWER OF THE HOLY SPIRIT

To be sure, we are lacking in human resources and earthly power. Yet we lodge our trust in the power of God's Spirit, who was promised to the Church by the Lord Jesus Christ. Hence we humbly and ardently call for all men to work along with us in building up a more just and brotherly city in this world. We call not only upon our brothers whom we serve as shepherds, but also upon all our brother Christians, and the rest of men of good will, whom God "wills that they be saved and come to the knowledge of the truth."[9] For this is the divine plan, that through love God's kingdom may already shine out on earth in some fashion as a preview of God's eternal kingdom.

The world is still far from the desired peace because of threats arising from the very progress of science, marvelous though it be, but not always responsive to the higher law of morality. Our prayer is that in the midst of this world there may radiate the light of our great hope in Jesus Christ, our only Savior.

NOTES

1. Acts 17:27.
2. Cf. Eph. 5:27.
3. Cf. 2 Cor. 4:6.
4. Cf. Col. 1:20.
5. Mt. 20:28.
6. Cf. 1 Jn. 3:16.
7. 2 Cor. 5:14.
8. 1 Jn. 3:17.
9. Cf. 1 Tim. 2:4.

Unitatis Redintegratio

Decree on Ecumenism
(Second Vatican Council,
November 21, 1964)

PAUL, BISHOP
SERVANT OF THE SERVANTS OF GOD
TOGETHER WITH THE FATHERS OF THE SACRED COUNCIL
FOR EVERLASTING MEMORY

Introduction

1.   Promoting the restoration of unity among all Christians is one of
the chief concerns of the Second Sacred Ecumenical Synod of the Vatican.
The Church established by Christ the Lord is, indeed, one and unique.
Yet many Christian communions present themselves to men as the true
heritage of Jesus Christ. To be sure, all proclaim themselves to be disciples
of the Lord, but their convictions clash and their paths diverge,

---

[Msgr. Joseph Gallagher, Translation Editor of *The Documents of Vatican II*, notes in his
Preface: "The translations of the Decree on Ecumenism and the Declaration on the Relationship of the Church to Non-Christian Religions rely to a notable extent on the informed
version produced by members of the Vatican Secretariat for Promoting Christian Unity."]

as though Christ Himself were divided (cf. 1 Cor. 1:13). Without doubt, this discord openly contradicts the will of Christ, provides a stumbling block to the world, and inflicts damage on the most holy cause of proclaiming the good news to every creature.

Nevertheless, the Lord of Ages wisely and patiently follows out the plan of His grace on behalf of us sinners. In recent times He has begun to bestow more generously upon divided Christians remorse over their divisions and a longing for unity.

Everywhere, large numbers have felt the impulse of this grace, and among our separated brethren also there increases from day to day a movement, fostered by the grace of the Holy Spirit, for the restoration of unity among all Christians. Taking part in this movement, which is called ecumenical, are those who invoke the Triune God and confess Jesus as Lord and Savior. They join in not merely as individuals but also as members of the corporate groups in which they have heard the gospel, and which each regards as his Church and, indeed, God's. And yet, almost everyone, though in different ways, longs that there may be one visible Church of God, a Church truly universal and sent forth to the whole world that the world may be converted to the gospel and so be saved, to the glory of God.

This sacred Synod, therefore, gladly notes all these factors. It has already declared its teaching on the Church, and now, moved by a desire for the restoration of unity among all the followers of Christ, it wishes to set before all Catholics certain helps, pathways, and methods by which they too can respond to this divine summons and grace.

CHAPTER I

Catholic Principles on Ecumenism

2.   What has revealed the love of God among us is that the only-begotten Son of God has been sent by the Father into the world, so that, being made man, the Son might by His redemption of the entire human race give new life to it and unify it (cf. 1 Jn. 4:9; Col. 1:18–20; Jn. 11:52). Before offering Himself up as a spotless victim upon the altar of the cross, He prayed to His Father for those who believe: "That all may be one even as thou, Father, in me, and I in thee; that they also may be one in us, that the world may believe that thou hast sent me" (Jn. 17:21). In His Church

He instituted the wonderful sacrament of the Eucharist by which the unity of the Church is both signified and brought about. He gave His followers a new commandment of mutual love (cf. Jn. 13:34), and promised the Spirit, their Advocate (cf. Jn. 16:7), who, as Lord and life-giver, would abide with them forever.

After being lifted up on the cross and glorified, the Lord Jesus poured forth the Spirit whom He had promised, and through whom He has called and gathered together the people of the New Covenant, who comprise the Church, into a unity of faith, hope, and charity. For, as the apostle teaches, the Church is: "one body and one Spirit, even as you were called in one hope of your calling; one Lord, one faith, one baptism" (Eph. 4:4–5). For "all you who have been baptized into Christ, have put on Christ . . . for you are all one in Christ Jesus" (Gal. 3:27–28). It is the Holy Spirit, dwelling in those who believe, pervading and ruling over the entire Church, who brings about that marvelous communion of the faithful and joins them together so intimately in Christ that He is the principle of the Church's unity. By distributing various kinds of spiritual gifts and ministries (cf. 1 Cor. 12:4–11), He enriches the Church of Jesus Christ with different functions "in order to perfect the saints for a work of ministry, for building up the body of Christ" (Eph. 4:12).

In order to establish this holy Church of His everywhere in the world until the end of time, Christ entrusted to the College of the Twelve the task of teaching, ruling, and sanctifying (cf. Mt. 28:18–20, in conjunction with Jn. 20:21–23). Among their number He chose Peter. After Peter's profession of faith, He decreed that on him He would build His Church; to Peter He promised the keys of the kingdom of heaven (cf. Mt. 16:19, in conjunction with Mt. 18:18). After Peter's profession of love, Christ entrusted all His sheep to him to be confirmed in faith (cf. Lk. 22:32) and shepherded in perfect unity (cf. Jn. 21:15–17). Meanwhile, Christ Jesus Himself forever remains the chief cornerstone (cf. Eph. 2:20) and shepherd of our souls (cf. 1 Pet. 2:25).[1]

It is through the faithful preaching of the gospel by the apostles and their successors—the bishops with Peter's successor at their head—through their administration of the sacraments, and through their loving exercise of authority, that Jesus Christ wishes His people to increase under the influence of the Holy Spirit. Thereby too, He perfects His people's fellowship in unity: in the confession of one faith, in the common celebration of divine worship, and in the fraternal harmony of the family of God.

The Church, then, God's only flock, like a standard lifted high for the nations to see (cf. Is. 11:10–12), ministers the gospel of peace to all mankind (cf. Eph. 2:17–18, in conjunction with Mk. 16:15), as she makes her pilgrim way in hope toward her goal, the fatherland above (cf. 1 Pet. 1:3–9).

This is the sacred mystery of the unity of the Church, in Christ and through Christ, with the Holy Spirit energizing a variety of functions. The highest exemplar and source of this mystery is the unity, in the Trinity of Persons, of one God, the Father and the Son in the Holy Spirit.

3.   From her very beginnings there arose in this one and only Church of God certain rifts (cf. 1 Cor. 11:18–19, Gal. 1:6–9; 1 Jn. 2:18–19), which the apostle strongly censures as damnable (cf. 1 Cor. 1:11 ff.; 11:22). But in subsequent centuries more widespread disagreements appeared and quite large Communities became separated from full communion with the Catholic Church—developments for which, at times, men of both sides were to blame. However, one cannot impute the sin of separation to those who at present are born into these Communities and are instilled therein with Christ's faith. The Catholic Church accepts them with respect and affection as brothers. For men who believe in Christ and have been properly baptized are brought into a certain, though imperfect, communion with the Catholic Church. Undoubtedly, the differences that exist in varying degrees between them and the Catholic Church —whether in doctrine and sometimes in discipline, or concerning the structure of the Church—do indeed create many and sometimes serious obstacles to full ecclesiastical communion. These the ecumenical movement is striving to overcome. Nevertheless, all those justified by faith through baptism are incorporated into Christ.[2] They therefore have a right to be honored by the title of Christian, and are properly regarded as brothers in the Lord by the sons of the Catholic Church.[3]

Moreover some, even very many, of the most significant elements or endowments which together go to build up and give life to the Church herself can exist outside the visible boundaries of the Catholic Church: the written word of God; the life of grace; faith, hope, and charity, along with other interior gifts of the Holy Spirit and visible elements. All of these, which come from Christ and lead back to Him, belong by right to the one Church of Christ.

The brethren divided from us also carry out many of the sacred actions of the Christian religion. Undoubtedly, in ways that vary according to the condition of each Church or Community, these actions can truly engender a life of grace, and can be rightly described as capable of providing access to the community of salvation.

It follows that these separated Churches[4] and Communities, though we believe they suffer from defects already mentioned, have by no means been deprived of significance and importance in the mystery of salvation. For the Spirit of Christ has not refrained from using them as means of salvation which derive their efficacy from the very fullness of grace and truth entrusted to the Catholic Church.

Nevertheless, our separated brethren, whether considered as individuals or as Communities and Churches, are not blessed with that unity which Jesus Christ wished to bestow on all those whom He has regenerated and vivified into one body and newness of life—that unity which the holy Scriptures and the revered tradition of the Church proclaim. For it is through Christ's Catholic Church alone, which is the all-embracing means of salvation, that the fullness of the means of salvation can be obtained. It was to the apostolic college alone, of which Peter is the head, that we believe our Lord entrusted all the blessings of the New Covenant, in order to establish on earth the one Body of Christ into which all those should be fully incorporated who already belong in any way to God's People. During its pilgrimage on earth, this People, though still in its members liable to sin, is growing in Christ and is being gently guided by God, according to His hidden designs, until it happily arrives at the fullness of eternal glory in the heavenly Jerusalem.

4.   Today, in many parts of the world, under the inspiring grace of the Holy Spirit, multiple efforts are being expended through prayer, word, and action to attain that fullness of unity which Jesus Christ desires. This sacred Synod, therefore, exhorts all the Catholic faithful to recognize the signs of the times and to participate skillfully in the work of ecumenism.

The "ecumenical movement" means those activities and enterprises which, according to various needs of the Church and opportune occasions, are started and organized for the fostering of unity among Christians. These are: first, every effort to eliminate words, judgments, and actions which do not respond to the condition of separated brethren with truth and fairness and so make mutual relations between them more difficult; then, "dialogue" between competent experts from different Churches and Communities. In their meetings, which are organized in a religious spirit, each explains the teaching of his Communion in greater depth and brings out clearly its distinctive features. Through such dialogue, everyone gains a truer knowledge and more just appreciation of the teaching and religious life of both Communions. In addition, these Communions cooperate more closely in whatever projects a Christian conscience demands for the common good. They also come together for common prayer, where this is permitted. Finally, all are led to examine their own faithfulness to Christ's will for the Church and, wherever necessary, undertake with vigor the task of renewal and reform.

When such actions are carried out by the Catholic faithful with prudence, patience, and the vigilance of their spiritual shepherds, they contribute to the blessings of justice and truth, of concord and collaboration, as well as of the spirit of brotherly love and unity. The result will be that, little by little, as the obstacles to perfect ecclesiastical communion are overcome, all Christians will be gathered, in a common celebration of the Eucharist, into that unity of the one and only Church which Christ bestowed on His Church from the beginning. This unity, we believe, dwells in the Catholic Church as something she can never lose, and we hope that it will continue to increase until the end of time.

However, it is evident that the work of preparing and reconciling those individuals who wish for full Catholic communion is of its nature distinct from ecumenical action. But there is no opposition between the two, since both proceed from the wondrous providence of God.

In ecumenical work, Catholics must assuredly be concerned for their separated brethren, praying for them, keeping them informed about the Church, making the first approaches towards them. But their primary duty is to make an honest and careful appraisal of whatever needs to be renewed and achieved in the Catholic household itself, in order that its life may bear witness more loyally and luminously to the teachings and ordinances which have been handed down from Christ through the apostles.

For although the Catholic Church has been endowed with all divinely revealed truth and with all means of grace, her members fail to live by them with all the fervor they should. As a result, the radiance of the Church's face shines less brightly in the eyes of our separated brethren and of the world at large, and the growth of God's kingdom is retarded. Every Catholic must therefore aim at Christian perfection (cf. Jas. 1:4; Rom. 12:1–2) and, each according to his station, play his part so that the Church, which bears in her own body the humility and dying of Jesus (cf. 2 Cor. 4:10; Phil. 2:5–8), may daily be more purified and renewed, against the day when Christ will present her to Himself in all her glory, without spot or wrinkle (cf. Eph. 5:27).

While preserving unity in essentials, let all members of the Church, according to the office entrusted to each, preserve a proper freedom in the various forms of spiritual life and discipline, in the variety of liturgical rites, and even in the theological elaborations of revealed truth. In all things let charity be exercised. If the faithful are true to this course of action, they will be giving ever richer expression to the authentic catholicity of the Church, and, at the same time, to her apostolicity.

On the other hand, Catholics must joyfully acknowledge and esteem the truly Christian endowments from our common heritage which are to be found among our separated brethren. It is right and salutary to recognize the riches of Christ and virtuous works in the lives of others who are bearing witness to Christ, sometimes even to the shedding of their blood. For God is always wonderful in His works and worthy of admiration.

Nor should we forget that whatever is wrought by the grace of the Holy Spirit in the hearts of our separated brethren can contribute to our own edification. Whatever is truly Christian never conflicts with the genuine interests of the faith; indeed, it can always result in a more ample realization of the very mystery of Christ and the Church.

Nevertheless, the divisions among Christians prevent the Church from effecting the fullness of catholicity proper to her in those of her sons who, though joined to her by baptism, are yet separated from full communion with her. Furthermore, the Church herself finds it more difficult to express in actual life her full catholicity in all its aspects.

This sacred Synod is gratified to note that participation by the Catholic faithful in ecumenical work is growing daily. It commends this work to bishops everywhere in the world for their skillful promotion and prudent guidance.

CHAPTER II

The Practice of Ecumenism

5.   Concern for restoring unity pertains to the whole Church, faithful and clergy alike. It extends to everyone, according to the potential of each, whether it be exercised in daily Christian living or in theological and historical studies. This very concern already reveals to some extent the bond of brotherhood existing among all Christians, and it leads toward that full and perfect unity which God lovingly desires.

6.   Every renewal of the Church[5] essentially consists in an increase of fidelity to her own calling. Undoubtedly this explains the dynamism of the movement toward unity.

Christ summons the Church, as she goes her pilgrim way, to that continual reformation of which she always has need, insofar as she is an institution of men here on earth. Therefore, if the influence of events or of the times has led to deficiencies in conduct, in Church discipline, or even in the formulation of doctrine (which must be carefully distinguished from the deposit itself of faith), these should be appropriately rectified at the proper moment.

Church renewal therefore has notable ecumenical importance. Already this renewal is taking place in various spheres of the Church's life: the biblical and liturgical movements, the preaching of the word of God, catechetics, the apostolate of the laity, new forms of religious life and the spirituality of married life, and the Church's social teaching and activity. All these should be considered as favorable pledges and signs of ecumenical progress in the future.

7.   There can be no ecumenism worthy of the name without a change of heart. For it is from newness of attitudes (cf. Eph. 4:23), from self-denial and unstinted love, that yearnings for unity take their rise and grow toward maturity. We should therefore pray to the divine Spirit for the grace to be genuinely self-denying, humble, gentle in the service of others, and to have an attitude of brotherly generosity toward them. The Apostle of the Gentiles says: "I, therefore, the prisoner in the Lord, exhort you to walk in a manner worthy of the calling with which you were called, with all humility and meekness, with patience, bearing with one another in love, careful to preserve the unity of the Spirit in the bond of peace" (Eph. 4:1–3). This exhortation applies especially to those who have been raised to sacred orders so that the mission of Christ may be carried on. He came among us "not to be served but to serve" (Mt. 20:28).

St. John has testified: "If we say that we have not sinned, we make him a liar, and his word is not in us" (1 Jn. 1:10). This holds good for sins against unity. Thus, in humble prayer, we beg pardon of God and of our separated brethren, just as we forgive those who trespass against us.

Let all Christ's faithful remember that the more purely they strive to live according to the gospel, the more they are fostering and even practicing Christian unity. For they can achieve depth and ease in strengthening mutual brotherhood to the degree that they enjoy profound communion with the Father, the Word, and the Spirit.

8.   This change of heart and holiness of life, along with public and private prayer for the unity of Christians, should be regarded as the soul of the whole ecumenical movement, and can rightly be called "spiritual ecumenism."

Catholics already have a custom of uniting frequently in that prayer for the unity of the Church with which the Savior Himself, on the eve of His death, appealed so fervently to His Father: "That all may be one" (Jn. 17:21).

In certain special circumstances, such as in prayer services "for unity" and during ecumenical gatherings, it is allowable, indeed desirable, that Catholics should join in prayer with their separated brethren. Such prayers in common are certainly a very effective means of petitioning for the grace of unity, and they are a genuine expression of the ties which even now bind Catholics to their separated brethren. "For where two or three are gathered together for my sake, there am I in the midst of them" (Mt. 18:20).

As for common worship, however, it may not be regarded as a means to be used indiscriminately for the restoration of unity among Christians. Such worship depends chiefly on two principles: it should signify the unity of the Church; it should provide a sharing in the means of grace. The fact that it should signify unity generally rules out common worship. Yet the gaining of a needed grace sometimes commends it.

The practical course to be adopted, after due regard has been given to all the circumstances of time, place, and personage, is left to the prudent decision of the local episcopal authority, unless the Bishops' Conference according to its own statutes, or the Holy See, has determined otherwise.

9.   We must come to understand the outlook of our separated brethren. Study is absolutely required for this, and should be pursued with fidelity to truth and in a spirit of good will. When they are properly prepared for this study, Catholics need to acquire a more adequate understanding of the distinctive doctrines of our separated brethren, as well as of their own history, spiritual and liturgical life, their religious psychology and cultural background. Of great value for this purpose are meetings between the two sides, especially for discussion of theological problems, where each can deal with the other on an equal footing. Such meetings require that those who take part in them under authoritative guidance be truly competent. From dialogue of this sort will emerge still more clearly what the true posture of the Catholic Church is. In this way, too, we will better understand the attitude of our separated brethren and more aptly present our own belief.

10.   Instruction in sacred theology and other branches of knowledge, especially those of a historical nature, must also be presented from an ecumenical point of view, so that at every point they may more accurately correspond with the facts of the case.

For it is highly important that future bishops and priests should have mastered a theology carefully worked out in this way and not polemically, especially in what concerns the relations of separated brethren with the Catholic Church. For it is upon the formation which priests receive that the necessary instruction and spiritual formation of the faithful and of religious depend so very greatly.

Moreover, Catholics engaged in missionary work, in the same territories as other Christians, ought to know, particularly in these times, the problems and the benefits which affect their apostolate because of the ecumenical movement.

11.   The manner and order in which Catholic belief is expressed should in no way become an obstacle to dialogue with our brethren. It is, of course, essential that doctrine be clearly presented in its entirety. Nothing is so foreign to the spirit of ecumenism as a false conciliatory approach which harms the purity of Catholic doctrine and obscures its assured genuine meaning.

At the same time, Catholic belief needs to be explained more profoundly and precisely, in ways and in terminology which our separated brethren too can really understand.

Furthermore, Catholic theologians engaged in ecumenical dialogue, while standing fast by the teaching of the Church and searching together with separated brethren into the divine mysteries, should act with love for truth, with charity, and with humility. When comparing doctrines, they should remember that in Catholic teaching there exists an order or "hierarchy" of truths, since they vary in their relationship to the foundation of the Christian faith. Thus the way will be opened for this kind of fraternal rivalry to incite all to a deeper realization and a clearer expression of the unfathomable riches of Christ (cf. Eph. 3:8).

12.   Before the whole world, let all Christians profess their faith in God, one and three, in the incarnate Son of God, our Redeemer and Lord. United in their efforts, and with mutual respect, let them bear witness to our common hope, which does not play us false. Since in our times cooperation in social matters is very widely practiced, all men without exception are summoned to united effort. Those who believe in God have a stronger summons, but the strongest claims are laid on Christians, since they have been sealed with the name of Christ.

Cooperation among all Christians vividly expresses that bond which already unites them, and it sets in clearer relief the features of Christ the Servant. Such cooperation, which has already begun in many countries, should be ever increasingly developed, particularly in regions where a social and technical evolution is taking place. It should contribute to a just appreciation of the dignity of the human person, the promotion of the blessings of peace, the application of gospel principles to social life, and the advancement of the arts and sciences in a Christian spirit. Christians should also work together in the use of every possible means to relieve the afflictions of our times, such as famine and natural disasters, illiteracy and poverty, lack of housing, and the unequal distribution of wealth. Through such cooperation, all believers in Christ are able to learn easily how they can understand each other better and esteem each other more, and how the road to the unity of Christians may be made smooth.

CHAPTER III

Churches and Ecclesial Communities Separated from the Roman Apostolic See

13.   We now turn our attention to the two main kinds of rending which have damaged the seamless robe of Christ.

The first divisions occurred in the East, either because of disputes over the dogmatic pronouncements of the Councils of Ephesus and Chalcedon, or later by the breakdown of ecclesiastical communion between the Eastern Patriarchates and the Roman See.

Still other divisions arose in the West more than four centuries afterwards. These stemmed from a series of happenings commonly referred to as the Reformation. As a result, many Communions, national or denominational, were separated from the Roman See. Among those in which some Catholic traditions and institutions continue to exist, the Anglican Communion occupies a special place.

These various divisions, however, differ greatly from one another not only by reason of their source, location, and age, but especially in their view of the nature and importance of issues bearing on belief and Church structure. Therefore, neither minimizing the differences between the various Christian bodies, nor overlooking the bonds which continue to exist among them in spite of divisions, this sacred Synod has decided to propose the following considerations for prudent ecumenical action.

The Special Position of the Eastern Churches

14.   For many centuries, the Churches of the East and of the West went their own ways, though a brotherly communion of faith and sacramental life bound them together. If disagreements in belief and discipline arose among them, the Roman See acted by common consent as moderator.

This most sacred Synod gladly reminds all of one highly significant fact among others: in the East there flourish many particular or local Churches; among them the Patriarchal Churches hold first place; and of these, many glory in taking their origins from the apostles themselves. As a result, there prevailed and still prevails among Orientals an eager desire to perpetuate in a communion of faith and charity those family ties which ought to thrive between local Churches, as between sisters. It is equally worthy of note that from their very origins the Churches of the East have had a treasury from which the Church of the West has amply drawn for its liturgy, spiritual tradition, and jurisprudence. Nor must we underestimate the fact that basic dogmas of the Christian faith concerning the Trinity and God's Word made flesh of the Virgin Mary were defined in Ecumenical Councils held in the East. To preserve this faith, these Churches have suffered much, and still do so.

However, the heritage handed down by the apostles was received in different forms and ways, so that from the very beginnings of the Church it has had a varied development in various places, thanks to a similar variety of natural gifts and conditions of life. Added to external causes, and to mutual failures in understanding and charity, all these circumstances set the stage for separations.

Therefore, this sacred Synod urges all, but especially those who plan to devote themselves to the work of restoring the full communion that is desired between the Eastern Churches and the Catholic Church, to give due consideration to these special aspects of the origin and growth of the Churches of the East, and to the character of the relations which obtained between them and the Roman See before the separation, and to form for themselves a correct evaluation of these facts. If these recommendations are carefully carried out, they will make a very great contribution to any proposed dialogues.

15.   Everybody also knows with what love the Eastern Christians enact the sacred liturgy, especially the celebration of the Eucharist, which is the source of the Church's life and the pledge of future glory. In this celebration the faithful, united with their bishop and endowed with an outpouring of the Holy Spirit, gain access to God the Father through the Son, the Word made flesh, who suffered and was glorified. And so, made "partakers of the divine nature" (2 Pet. 1:4), they enter into communion with the most holy Trinity. Hence, through the celebration of the Eucharist of the Lord in each of these Churches, the Church of God is built up and grows in stature,[6] while through the rite of concelebration their bond with one another is made manifest.

In this liturgical worship, the Christians of the East pay high tribute, in very beautiful hymns, to Mary ever Virgin, whom the Ecumenical Synod of Ephesus solemnly proclaimed to be God's most holy Mother so that, in accord with the Scriptures, Christ may be truly and properly acknowledged as Son of God and Son of Man. They also give homage to the saints, including Fathers of the universal Church.

Although these Churches are separated from us, they possess true sacraments, above all—by apostolic succession—the priesthood and the Eucharist, whereby they are still joined to us in a very close relationship. Therefore, given suitable circumstances and the approval of Church authority, some worship in common is not merely possible but is recommended.

Moreover, in the East are to be found the riches of those spiritual traditions to which monasticism gives special expression. From the glorious days of the holy Fathers, there flourished in the East that monastic spirituality which later flowed over into the Western world, and there provided a source from which Latin monastic life took its rise and has often drawn fresh vigor ever since. Therefore Catholics are strongly urged to avail themselves more often of these spiritual riches of the Eastern Fathers, riches which lift up the whole man to the contemplation of divine mysteries.

All should realize that it is of supreme importance to understand, venerate, preserve, and foster the exceedingly rich liturgical and spiritual heritage of the Eastern Churches, in order faithfully to preserve the fullness of Christian tradition, and to bring about reconciliation between Eastern and Western Christians.

16.   From the earliest times, moreover, the Eastern Churches followed their own disciplines, sanctioned by the holy Fathers, by synods, even ecumenical Councils. Far from being an obstacle to the Church's unity, such diversity of customs and observances only adds to her comeliness, and contributes greatly to carrying out her mission, as has already been recalled. To remove any shadow of doubt, then, this sacred Synod solemnly declares that the Churches of the East, while keeping in mind the necessary unity of the whole Church, have the power to govern themselves according to their own disciplines, since these are better suited to the temperament of their faithful and better adapted to foster the good of souls. Although it has not always been honored, the strict observance of this traditional principle is among the prerequisites for any restoration of unity.

17.   What has already been said about legitimate variety we are pleased to apply to differences in theological expressions of doctrine. In the investigation of revealed truth, East and West have used different methods and approaches in understanding and proclaiming divine

things. It is hardly surprising, then, if sometimes one tradition has come nearer than the other to an apt appreciation of certain aspects of a revealed mystery, or has expressed them in a clearer manner. As a result, these various theological formulations are often to be considered as complementary rather than conflicting. With regard to the authentic theological traditions of the Orientals, we must recognize that they are admirably rooted in holy Scripture, fostered and given expression in liturgical life, and nourished by the living tradition of the apostles and by the writings of the Fathers and spiritual authors of the East; they are directed toward a right ordering of life, indeed, toward a full contemplation of Christian truth.

While thanking God that many Eastern sons of the Catholic Church, who are preserving this heritage and wish to express it more faithfully and completely in their lives, are already living in full communion with their brethren who follow the tradition of the West, this sacred Synod declares that this entire heritage of spirituality and liturgy, of discipline and theology, in their various traditions, belongs to the full catholic and apostolic character of the Church.

18.   After taking all these factors into consideration, this sacred Synod confirms what previous Councils and Roman Pontiffs have proclaimed: in order to restore communion and unity or preserve them, one must "impose no burden beyond what is indispensable" (Acts 15:28). It is the Council's urgent desire that every effort should henceforth be made toward the gradual realization of this goal in the various organizations and living activities of the Church, especially by prayer and by fraternal dialogue on points of doctrine and the more pressing pastoral problems of our time. Similarly, to the pastors and faithful of the Catholic Church, it recommends close relationships with those no longer living in the East but far from their homeland, so that friendly collaboration with them may increase in a spirit of love, without quarrelsome rivalry. If this task is carried on wholeheartedly, this sacred Synod hopes that with the removal of the wall dividing the Eastern and Western Church there may at last be but the one dwelling, firmly established on the cornerstone, Christ Jesus, who will make both one.[7]

The Separated Churches
and Ecclesial Communities in the West

19.   The Churches and ecclesial Communities which were separated from the Apostolic See of Rome during the very serious crisis that began in the West at the end of the Middle Ages, or during later times, are bound

to the Catholic Church by a special affinity and close relationship in view of the long span of earlier centuries when the Christian people lived in ecclesiastical communion.

Since in origin, teaching, and spiritual practice, these Churches and ecclesial Communities differ not only from us but also among themselves to a considerable degree,the task of describing them adequately is very difficult; we do not propose to do it here.

Although the ecumenical movement and the desire for reconciliation with the Catholic Church have not yet grown universally strong, it is our hope that the ecumenical spirit and mutual esteem will gradually increase among all men.

At the same time, however, one should recognize that between these Churches and Communities on the one hand, and the Catholic Church on the other, there are very weighty differences not only of a historical, sociological, psychological, and cultural nature, but especially in the interpretation of revealed truth. That ecumenical dialogue may be more easily undertaken, despite these differences, we desire to propose in what follows some considerations which can and ought to serve as a basis and motivation for such dialogue.

20.   Our thoughts are concerned first of all with those Christians who openly confess Jesus Christ as God and Lord and as the sole Mediator between God and man unto the glory of the one God, Father, Son, and Holy Spirit. We are indeed aware that among them views are held considerably different from the doctrine of the Catholic Church even concerning Christ, God's Word made flesh, and the work of redemption, and thus concerning the mystery and ministry of the Church and the role of Mary in the work of salvation. But we rejoice to see our separated brethren looking to Christ as the source and center of ecclesiastical communion. Inspired by longing for union with Christ, they feel compelled to search for unity ever more ardently, and to bear witness to their faith among all the peoples of the earth.

21.   A love, veneration, a near cult of the sacred Scriptures lead our brethren to a constant and expert study of the sacred text. For the gospel "is the power of God unto salvation to everyone who believes, to Jew first and then to Greek" (Rom. 1:16).

Calling upon the Holy Spirit, they seek in these sacred Scriptures God as He speaks to them in Christ, the One whom the prophets foretold, God's Word made flesh for us. In the Scriptures they contemplate the life of Christ, as well as the teachings and the actions of the Divine Master on behalf of men's salvation, in particular the mysteries of His death and resurrection.

But when Christians separated from us affirm the divine authority of the sacred Books, they think differently from us—different ones in different ways—about the relationship between the Scriptures and the Church. In the Church, according to Catholic belief, an authentic teaching office plays a special role in the explanation and proclamation of the written word of God.

Nevertheless, in dialogue itself, the sacred utterances are precious instruments in the mighty hand of God for attaining that unity which the Savior holds out to all men.

22.   By the sacrament of baptism, whenever it is properly conferred in the way the Lord determined, and received with the appropriate dispositions of soul, a man becomes truly incorporated into the crucified and glorified Christ and is reborn to a sharing of the divine life, as the apostle says: "For you were buried together with him in Baptism, and in him also rose again through faith in the working of God who raised him from the dead" (Col. 2:12; cf. Rom. 6:4).

Baptism, therefore, constitutes a sacramental bond of unity linking all who have been reborn by means of it. But baptism, of itself, is only a beginning, a point of departure, for it is wholly directed toward the acquiring of fullness of life in Christ. Baptism is thus oriented toward a complete profession of faith, a complete incorporation into the system of salvation such as Christ Himself willed it to be, and finally, toward a complete participation in Eucharistic communion.

The ecclesial Communities separated from us lack that fullness of unity with us which should flow from baptism, and we believe that especially because of the lack of the sacrament of orders they have not preserved the genuine and total reality of the Eucharistic mystery. Nevertheless, when they commemorate the Lord's death and resurrection in the Holy Supper, they profess that it signifies life in communion with Christ and they await His coming in glory. For these reasons, dialogue should be undertaken concerning the true meaning of the Lord's Supper, the other sacraments, and the Church's worship and ministry.

23.   The Christian way of life of these brethren is nourished by faith in Christ. It is strengthened by the grace of baptism and the hearing of God's Word. This way of life expresses itself in private prayer, in meditation on the Bible, in Christian family life, and in services of worship offered by Communities assembled to praise God. Furthermore, their worship sometimes displays notable features of an ancient, common liturgy.

The faith by which they believe in Christ bears fruit in praise and thanksgiving for the benefits received from the hands of God. Joined to it are a lively sense of justice and a true neighborly charity. This active faith has produced many organizations for the relief of spiritual and bodily distress, the education of youth, the advancement of humane social conditions, and the promotion of peace throughout the world.

And if in moral matters there are many Christians who do not always understand the gospel in the same way as Catholics, and do not admit the same solutions for the more difficult problems of modern society, nevertheless they share our desire to cling to Christ's word as the source of Christian virtue and to obey the apostolic command: "Whatever you do in word or in work, do all in the name of the Lord Jesus, giving thanks to God the Father through him" (Col. 3:17). Hence, the ecumenical dialogue could start with discussions concerning the application of the gospel to moral questions.

24.　　So, after this brief exposition of the circumstances within which ecumenical activity has to operate and of the principles by which it should be guided, we confidently look to the future. This most sacred Synod urges the faithful to abstain from any superficiality or imprudent zeal, for these can cause harm to true progress towards unity. Their ecumenical activity must not be other than fully and sincerely Catholic, that is, loyal to the truth we have received from the apostles and the Fathers, and in harmony with the faith which the Catholic Church has always professed, and at the same time tending toward that fullness with which our Lord wants His body to be endowed in the course of time.

This most sacred Synod urgently desires that the initiatives of the sons of the Catholic Church, joined with those of the separated brethren, go forward without obstructing the ways of divine Providence and without prejudging the future inspiration of the Holy Spirit. Further, this Synod declares its realization that the holy task of reconciling all Christians in the unity of the one and only Church of Christ transcends human energies and abilities. It therefore places its hope entirely in the prayer of Christ for the Church, in the love of the Father for us, and in the power of the Holy Spirit. "And hope does not disappoint, because the charity of God is poured forth in our hearts by the Holy Spirit who has been given to us" (Rom. 5:5).

Each and every one of the things set forth in this Decree has won the consent of the Fathers. We, too, by the apostolic authority conferred on us by Christ, join with the Venerable Fathers in approving, decreeing, and establishing these things in the Holy Spirit, and we direct that what has thus been enacted in synod be published to God's glory.

Rome, at St. Peter's, November 21, 1964

I, Paul, Bishop of the Catholic Church

There follow the signatures of the Fathers.

NOTES

1. I Vatican Council, Sess. IV (1870), the constitution *Pastor Aeternus*: Coll. Lac. 7, 482 a.

2. Cf. Council of Florence, Sess. VIII (1439), the decree *Exultate Deo*: Mansi 31. 1055 A.

3. Cf. St. Augustine, *In Ps. 32*, Enarr. II, 29: PL 36, 299.

4. Cf. IV Lateran Council (1215) Constitution IV: Mansi 22, 990; II Council of Lyons (1274), profession of faith of Michael Palaeologos: Mansi 24, 71 E; Council of Florence, Sess. VI (1439), definition *Laetentur caeli*: Mansi 31, 1026 E.

5. Cf. V Lateran Council, Sess. XII (1517), constitution *Constituti*: Mansi 32, 988 B–C.

6. Cf. St. John Chrysostom, *In Ioannem Homilia XLVI*, PG 59, 260–262.

7. Cf. Council of Florence, Sess. VI (1439), definition *Laetentur caeli*: Mansi 31, 1026 E.

Nostra Aetate

Declaration on the
Relationship of the Church
to Non-Christian Religions
(Second Vatican Council,
October 28, 1965)

PAUL, BISHOP
SERVANT OF THE SERVANTS OF GOD
TOGETHER WITH THE FATHERS OF THE SACRED COUNCIL
FOR EVERLASTING MEMORY

1.   In our times, when every day men are being drawn closer together and the ties between various peoples are being multiplied, the Church is giving deeper study to her relationship with non-Christian religions. In her task of fostering unity and love among men, and even among nations, she gives primary consideration in this document to what human beings have in common and to what promotes fellowship among them.

For all peoples comprise a single community, and have a single origin, since God made the whole race of men dwell over the entire face of the earth (cf. Acts 17:26). One also is their final goal: God. His providence, His manifestations of goodness, and His saving designs extend to all men (cf. Wis. 8:1; Acts 14:17; Rom. 2:6–7; 1 Tim. 2:4) against the day when the elect will be united in that Holy City ablaze with the splendor of God, where the nations will walk in His light (cf. Apoc. 21:23 f.).

Men look to the various religions for answers to those profound mysteries of the human condition which, today even as in olden times, deeply stir the human heart: What is a man? What is the meaning and the purpose of our life? What is goodness and what is sin? What gives rise to our sorrows and to what intent? Where lies the path to true happiness? What is the truth about death, judgment, and retribution beyond the grave? What, finally, is that ultimate and unutterable mystery which engulfs our being, and whence we take our rise, and whither our journey leads us?

2.   From ancient times down to the present, there has existed among diverse peoples a certain perception of that hidden power which hovers over the course of things and over the events of human life; at times, indeed, recognition can be found of a Supreme Divinity and of a Supreme Father too. Such a perception and such recognition instill the lives of these peoples with a profound religious sense. Religions bound up with cultural advancement have struggled to reply to these same questions with more refined concepts and in more highly developed language.

Thus in Hinduism men contemplate the divine mystery and express it through an unspent fruitfulness of myths and through searching philosophical inquiry. They seek release from the anguish of our condition through ascetical practices or deep meditation or a loving, trusting flight toward God.

Buddhism in its multiple forms acknowledges the radical insufficiency of this shifting world. It teaches a path by which men, in a devout and confident spirit, can either reach a state of absolute freedom or attain supreme enlightenment by their own efforts or by higher assistance.

Likewise, other religions to be found everywhere strive variously to answer the restless searchings of the human heart by proposing "ways," which consists of teachings, rules of life, and sacred ceremonies.

The Catholic Church rejects nothing which is true and holy in these religions. She looks with sincere respect upon those ways of conduct and of life, those rules and teachings which, though differing in many particulars from what she holds and sets forth, nevertheless often reflect a ray of that Truth which enlightens all men. Indeed, she proclaims and must ever proclaim Christ, "the way, the truth, and the life" (John 14:6), in whom men find the fullness of religious life, and in whom God has reconciled all things to Himself (cf. 2 Cor. 5:18–19).

The Church therefore has this exhortation for her sons: prudently and lovingly, through dialogue and collaboration with the followers of other religions, and in witness of Christian faith and life, acknowledge, preserve, and promote the spiritual and moral goods found among these men, as well as the values in their society and culture.

3.   Upon the Moslems, too, the Church looks with esteem. They adore one God, living and enduring, merciful and all-powerful, Maker of heaven and earth[1] and Speaker to men. They strive to submit wholeheartedly even to His inscrutable decrees, just as did Abraham, with whom the Islamic faith is pleased to associate itself. Though they do not acknowledge Jesus as God, they revere Him as a prophet. They also honor Mary, His virgin mother; at times they call on her, too, with devotion. In addition they await the day of judgment when God will give each man his due after raising him up. Consequently, they prize the moral life, and give worship to God especially through prayer, almsgiving, and fasting.

Although in the course of the centuries many quarrels and hostilities have arisen between Christians and Moslems, this most sacred Synod urges all to forget the past and to strive sincerely for mutual understanding. On behalf of all mankind, let them make common cause of safeguarding and fostering social justice, moral values, peace, and freedom.

4.   As this sacred Synod searches into the mystery of the Church, it recalls the spiritual bond linking the people of the New Covenant with Abraham's stock.

For the Church of Christ acknowledges that, according to the mystery of God's saving design, the beginnings of her faith and her election are already found among the patriarchs, Moses, and the prophets. She professes that all who believe in Christ, Abraham's sons according to faith (cf. Gal. 3:7), are included in the same patriarch's call, and likewise that the salvation of the Church was mystically foreshadowed by the chosen people's exodus from the land of bondage.

The Church, therefore, cannot forget that she received the revelation of the Old Testament through the people with whom God in his inexpressible mercy deigned to establish the Ancient Covenant. Nor can she forget that she draws sustenance from the root of that good olive tree onto which have been grafted the wild olive branches of the Gentiles (cf. Rom. 11:17–24). Indeed, the Church believes that by His cross Christ, our Peace, reconciled Jew and Gentile, making them both one in Himself (cf. Eph. 2:14–16).

Also, the Church ever keeps in mind the words of the Apostle about his kinsmen, "who have the adoption of sons, and the glory and the covenant and the legislation and the worship and the promises; who have the fathers, and from whom is Christ according to the flesh" (Rom. 9:4–5), the son of the Virgin Mary. The Church recalls too that from the Jewish people sprang the apostles, her foundation stones and pillars, as well as most of the early disciples who proclaimed Christ to the world.

As holy Scripture testifies, Jerusalem did not recognize the time of her visitation (cf. Lk. 19:44), nor did the Jews in large number accept the gospel; indeed, not a few opposed the spreading of it (cf. Rom. 11:28). Nevertheless, according to the Apostle, the Jews still remain most dear to God because of their fathers, for He does not repent of the gifts He makes nor of the calls He issues (cf. Rom. 11:28–29).[2] In company with the prophets and the same Apostle, the Church awaits that day, known to God alone, on which all peoples will address the Lord in a single voice and "serve him with one accord" (Soph. 3:9; cf. Is. 66:23; Ps. 65:4; Rom. 11:11–32).

Since the spiritual patrimony common to Christians and Jews is thus so great, this sacred Synod wishes to foster and recommend that mutual understanding and respect which is the fruit above all of biblical and theological studies, and of brotherly dialogues.

True, authorities of the Jews and those who followed their lead pressed for the death of Christ (cf. Jn. 19:6); still, what happened in His passion cannot be blamed upon all the Jews then living, without distinction, nor upon the Jews of today. Although the Church is the new people of God, the Jews should not be presented as repudiated or cursed by God, as if such views followed from the holy Scriptures. All should take pains, then, lest in catechetical instruction and in the preaching of God's Word they teach anything out of harmony with the truth of the gospel and the spirit of Christ.

The Church repudiates all persecutions against any man. Moreover, mindful of her common patrimony with the Jews, and motivated by the gospel's spiritual love and by no political considerations, she deplores the hatred, persecutions, and displays of anti-Semitism directed against the Jews at any time and from any source.

Besides, as the Church has always held and continues to hold, Christ in His boundless love freely underwent His passion and death because of the sins of all men, so that all might attain salvation. It is, therefore, the duty of the Church's preaching to proclaim the cross of Christ as the sign of God's all-embracing love and as the fountain from which every grace flows.

5.   We cannot in truthfulness call upon that God who is the Father of all if we refuse to act in a brotherly way toward certain men, created though they be to God's image. A man's relationship with God the Father and his relationship with his brother men are so linked together that Scripture says: "He who does not love does not know God" (1 Jn. 4:8).

The ground is therefore removed from every theory or practice which leads to a distinction between men or peoples in the matter of human dignity and the rights which flow from it.

As a consequence, the Church rejects, as foreign to the mind of Christ, any discrimination against men or harassment of them because of their race, color, condition of life, or religion.

Accordingly, following in the footsteps of the holy Apostles Peter and Paul, this sacred Synod ardently implores the Christian faithful to "maintain good fellowship among the nations" (1 Pet. 2:12), and, if possible, as far as in them lies, to keep peace with all men (cf. Rom. 12:18), so that they may truly be sons of the Father who is in heaven (cf. Mt. 5:45).

Each and every one of the things set forth in this Declaration has won the consent of the Fathers of this most sacred Council. We too, by the apostolic authority conferred on us by Christ, join with the Venerable Fathers in approving, decreeing, and establishing these things in the Holy Spirit, and we direct that what has thus been enacted in synod be published to God's glory.

Rome, at St. Peter's, October 28, 1965

I, Paul, Bishop of the Catholic Church

There follow the signatures of the Fathers.

NOTES

1. Cf. St. Gregory VII, letter XXI to Anzir (Nacir), King of Mauretania.
2. Cf. Dogmatic Constitution *Lumen Gentium*, AAS 57, 1965, p. 20.

Address of His Holiness Paul VI to the General Assembly of the United Nations (October 4, 1965)

1.   As We begin to speak to this unique world audience, We wish first of all to express Our profound thanks to your Secretary General, Mr. Thant, for his invitation to visit the United Nations on the occasion of the twentieth anniversary of this world institution for peace and cooperation among all the peoples of the earth.

2.   Our thanks also to the President of the General Assembly, Mr. Amintore Fanfani, who from the beginning of his term has spoken so kindly of Us.

3.   We thank all of you here present for your warm welcome. To each of you, Our cordial and respectful greetings. It was your friendship that invited Us and which now admits Us to this assembly, and it is as a friend that We come before you.

4.   In addition to Our personal homage, We bring you that of the Second Ecumenical Vatican Council, which is now meeting in Rome and which is eminently represented here by the Cardinals accompanying Us.

5.   In their name and in Our own, We greet you all and We pay you Our respects.

[This English version is that published by the Vatican Polyglot Press. The Address was delivered in French. A.A.S. LVII (December 4, 1965), no. 13, pp. 877–85.]

SIMPLICITY AND GREATNESS OF OUR MEETING

6.   This encounter, as you are all well aware, is marked by two characteristics: simplicity and greatness. Simplicity, because he who is speaking to you is a man like you; he is your brother, and indeed one of the smallest among you who represent sovereign states, since he is invested—if you wish to consider Us from this point of view—with but a tiny and quasi-symbolic temporal sovereignty: the minimum necessary to be free to exercise his spiritual mission and to assure all who deal with him that he is independent of any of this world's powers. He has no temporal power, no ambition to compete with you. In fact, We have nothing to ask, no question to raise; at most We have a desire to express, a permission to seek: that of being able to serve you in what is within Our competence, with disinterestedness, humility and love.

7.   This is the first declaration which We have to make. As you see, it is so simple that it can seem insignificant to this Assembly which is used to handling extremely important and difficult affairs.

8.   And yet, as We have told you, and as you know yourselves, this moment is characterised by singular greatness: it is great for Us, it is great for you.

9.   For Us, first of all. You know well who We are. And whatever may be your opinion of the Pontiff of Rome, you know Our mission: We are the bearer of a message for all of mankind. And not only personally in Our own name and in the great Catholic family, but also in the name of those Christian brethren who share the sentiments which We express here, and particularly of those who explicitly bid Us to be their spokesman. And so like a messenger who at the end of a long voyage delivers the letter he had received, so We are conscious of the privileged nature of this moment—brief as it is—in which finally is fulfilled a desire We have carried in Our heart for nearly twenty centuries. You remember it. We have been on the way for a long time, and We carry with Us a long history. We are celebrating here the epilogue of a difficult pilgrimage in search of a dialogue with the whole world, ever since the day on which We were commanded: "Go, bring the Good News to all the nations!" Now, it is you who represent all the nations.

10.   Allow Us to tell you that We have a message for all of you, yes, a happy message to deliver to each of you.

IN THE NAME OF THE DEAD, THE POOR AND THE SUFFERING

11.   (1) We might call Our message a ratification, a solemn moral ratification of this lofty institution. This message comes from our histori-

cal experience. As "an expert in humanity", We bring to this Organisation the prayer of Our recent Predecessors, that of the entire Catholic Episcopate and Our own, convinced as We are that this Organisation represents the path that modern civilisation and world peace are obliged to take. In saying this, We feel We are making Our own the voice of the dead and of the living; of the dead, who fell in the terrible wars of the past; of the living who have survived those wars, bearing in their hearts a condemnation of those who would try to revive wars; and also of those living who are rising fresh and confident, the youth of the present generation, dreaming, as they are fully entitled to do, of a better human race. And We also make Our own the voice of the poor, the disinherited, the suffering, of those who hunger and thirst for justice, for the dignity of life, for freedom, for well-being and progress. The peoples of the earth turn to the United Nations as the last hope of concord and peace; and We presume to present here their tribute of honour and of hope together with Our own.

12. That is why this moment is great for you, also.

JUSTICE, RIGHTS AND NEGOTIATION
IN RELATIONS BETWEEN PEOPLES

13. (2) We feel that you are already aware of this. Listen now to the continuation of Our Message. It looks entirely towards the future. The edifice that you have built must never fall; it must be perfected, and made equal to the needs which world history will present. You mark a stage in the development of mankind, from which there must be only advance, no going back.

14. To the very many States, which can no longer disregard one another, you offer an extremely simple and fruitful formula of coexistence. First of all, you recognise their individual characteristics. You do not confer existence upon sovereign States, but you qualify each single nation as fit to sit in the orderly congress of peoples. That is, you grant recognition, of the highest ethical and juridical value, to each single sovereign national community, guaranteeing it an honoured international citizenship. This in itself is a great service to the cause of humanity, namely, to define clearly and to honour the national subjects of the world community, and to classify them in a juridical condition, worthy thereby of being recognised and respected by all, and from which there may derive an orderly and stable system of international life. You give sanction to the great principle that the relations between peoples should be regulated by reason, justice, law and negotiation; not by force, violence, war, by fear or deceit. So it must be. Allow Us to congratulate you for

having had the wisdom to open this hall to the younger peoples, to those countries which have recently attained independence and national freedom. Their presence is the proof of the universality and magnanimity which inspire the principles of this institution.

15.   Thus it must be. This is Our praise and Our good wish; and, as you can see, We do not attribute these as from outside; We derive them from inside, from the very nature of your Charter.

GENEROUS TRUST, NEVER TREACHERY OR BETRAYAL

16.   (3) Your Charter goes further than this, and Our message of goodwill advances with it. You exist and operate to unite the nations, to bind countries together. Let Us use this second formula: to bring them together. You are an association, a bridge between peoples, a network of relations between nations. We would almost say that your chief characteristic is a reflection, as it were, in the temporal field, of what our Catholic Church aspires to be in the spiritual field: one and universal. In the ideological construction of mankind, there is on the natural level nothing superior to this. Your vocation is to make brothers not only of some, but of all peoples. A difficult undertaking, indeed; but this is what the task, your most noble task, amounts to. Is there anyone who does not see the necessity of coming thus progressively to the establishment of a world authority, able to act efficaciously on the juridical and political levels?

17.   Once more We reiterate Our good wish: Advance always! We will go further, and say: Strive to bring back among you any who have separated themeselves, and study the right method of uniting to your pact of brotherhood, in honour and loyalty, those who do not yet share in it. Act so that those still outside will desire and merit the confidence of all; and then be generous in granting such confidence. You have the good fortune and the honour of sitting in this assembly of peaceful community; hear Us as We say: Ensure that the reciprocal trust which here unites you, and enables you to do good and great things, may never be undermined or betrayed.

PRIDE, THE GREAT OBSTACLE TO NECESSARY HARMONY

18.   (4) The logic of this wish, which might be considered to pertain to the very structure of your Organization, leads Us to complete it with other formulas. Thus, let no one, inasmuch as he is a member of your union, be superior to the others: *Never one above the other*. This is the formula of equality. We are well aware that it must be completed by the evaluation of

other factors besides simple membership in this Institution; but equality, too, belongs to its constitution. You are not equal, but here you make yourselves equal. For several among you, this may be an act of high virtue; allow Us to say this to you, as the representative of a religion which accomplishes salvation through the humility of its divine Founder. Men cannot be brothers if they are not humble. It is pride, no matter how legitimate it may seem to be, which provokes tension and struggles for prestige, for predominance, colonialism, egoism; that is, pride disrupts brotherhood.

LET WEAPONS BE DROPPED AND TOTAL PEACE BUILT UP

19.   (5) And now We come to the most important point of Our message, which is, at first, a negative point. You are expecting Us to utter this sentence, and We are well aware of its gravity and solemnity: *not some peoples against others*, never again, never more! It was principally for this purpose that the Organisation of the United Nations arose: against war, in favour of peace! Listen to the lucid words of a great man, the late John Kennedy who proclaimed four years ago: "Mankind must put an end to war, or war will put an end to mankind". Many words are not needed to proclaim this loftiest aim of your institution. It suffices to remember that the blood of millions of men, that numberless and unheard of sufferings, useless slaughter and frightful ruin, are the sanction of the past which unites you with an oath which must change the future history of the world: No more war, war never again! Peace, it is peace which must guide the destinies of peoples and of all mankind.

20.   Gratitude and high praise are due to you, who for twenty years have laboured for peace; gratitude and praise for the conflicts which you have prevented or have brought to an end. The results of your efforts in recent days in favour of peace, even if not yet proved decisive, are such as to deserve that We, presuming to interpret the sentiments of the whole world, express to you both praise and thanks.

21.   Gentlemen, you have performed and you continue to perform a great work: the education of mankind in the ways of peace. The U.N. is the great school where that education is imparted, and we are today in the assembly hall of that school. Everyone who takes his place here becomes a pupil and also a teacher in the art of building peace. When you leave this hall, the world looks upon you as the architects and constructors of peace.

22.   Peace, as you know, is not built up only by means of politics or the balance of forces and of interests. It is constructed with the mind, with ideas, with works of peace. You are already working in this direction. But

your work is still at the initial stages. Will the world ever succeed in changing that selfish and contentious mentality from which so much of its history has been woven? It is not easy to foresee. On the other hand, it is easy to affirm that we must resolutely march towards a new future, a future of truly human peace, that peace which God has promised to men of good will. The paths that lead to such a peace have already been marked out: the first is that of disarmament.

23.   If you want to be brothers, let the weapons fall from your hands. You cannot love with weapons in your hands. Long before they mete out death and destruction, those terrible arms supplied by modern science foment bad feelings and cause nightmares, distrust, and dark designs. They call for enormous expenditures and hold up projects of human solidarity and of great usefulness. They lead astray the mentality of peoples. As long as man remains that weak, changeable and even wicked being he often shows himself to be, defensive armaments will, alas, be necessary. But you, gentlemen, men of courage and outstanding merit, are seeking means to guarantee the stability of international relations without the need of recourse to arms. This is a goal worthy of your efforts; this is what the peoples of the world expect from you. This is what must be achieved! For that unchallenged confidence in this Organisation must increase; its authority must be strengthened. Then your aim, it may be hoped, will be accomplished. You will thus win the gratitude of all peoples, relieved of an overburdening expenditure on armaments, and freed from the nightmare of ever imminent war.

24.   We are happy to know that many of you have given favourable consideration to the appeal We addressed last December at Bombay to all nations, when We invited them in the interests of peace to apply for the benefit of developing nations a portion at least of the savings that would result from a reduction in armaments. We here renew that invitation, confident of your feelings of humanity and generosity.

BROTHERLY COOPERATION IN ADDITION TO COEXISTENCE

25.   (6) To speak of humanity and generosity is to evoke another basic principle of the United Nations Organisation, and also its noblest aim: for it is not just to avert conflicts between nations that you labour here; you also seek to make it possible for them to work *for one another*. You are not satisfied merely with furthering coexistence between countries; you do something far better, something that deserves Our praise and Our support: you promote the brotherhood of peoples. In this way a system of solidarity is set up, and its lofty civilized aims win the orderly and

unanimous support of all the family of peoples for the common good and for the good of each individual. This aspect of the organisation of the United Nations is the most beautiful; it is its most truly human visage; it is the ideal of mankind in its pilgrimage through time; it is the world's greatest hope; it is, We presume to say, the reflection of the loving and transcendent design of God for the progress of the human family on earth—a reflection in which We see the message of the Gospel which is heavenly become earthly. Indeed, it seems to Us that here We hear the echo of the voice of Our Predecessors, and particularly of that of Pope John XXIII, whose message of "Pacem in Terris" was so honourably and significantly received among you.

26.   You proclaim here the fundamental rights and duties of man, his dignity, his freedom—and above all his religious freedom. We feel that you thus interpret the highest sphere of human wisdom and, We might add, its sacred character. For you deal here above all with human life; and the life of man is sacred; no one may dare offend it. Respect for life, even with regard to the great problem of birth, must find here in your Assembly its highest affirmation and its most reasoned defence. You must strive to multiply bread so that it suffices for the tables of mankind, and not rather favour an artificial control of birth, which would be irrational, in order to diminish the number of guests at the banquet of life.

27.   It does not suffice, however, to feed the hungry; it is necessary also to assure to each man a life conformed to his dignity. This too you strive to perform. We may consider this the fulfilment before Our very eyes, and by your efforts, of that prophetical announcement so applicable to your institution: "They will melt down their swords into ploughshares, their spears into pruning-forks" (Is. II, 4). Are you not using the prodigious energies of the earth and the magnificent inventions of science, no longer as instruments of death but as tools of life for humanity's new era?

28.   We know how intense and ever more efficacious are the efforts of the United Nations and its dependent world agencies to assist those Governments which need help to hasten their economic and social progress.

29.   We know how ardently you labour to overcome illiteracy and to spread good culture throughout the world; to give men adequate modern medical assistance; to employ in man's service the marvellous resources of science, of technology and of organisation—all of this is magnificent, and merits the praise and support of all, including Our own.

30.   We Ourself wish to give the good example, even though our means are so limited that, on the practical, quantitative level, their relevance cannot be measured. We intend to intensify the development of

Our charitable institutions to combat world hunger and fulfil world needs. It is thus, and in no other way, that peace can be built up.

IN ORDER TO SAFEGUARD CIVILIZATION
A PROFOUND RENEWAL OF OUR FAITH IN GOD IS NECESSARY

31.   (7) One more word, Gentlemen, Our final word: this edifice which you are constructing does not rest upon merely material and earthly foundations, for thus it would be a house built upon sand; above all, it is based on our own consciences. The hour has struck for our "conversion", for personal transformation, for interior renewal. We must get used to thinking of man in a new way; and in a new way also of man's life in common; with a new manner too of conceiving the paths of history and the destiny of the world, according to the words of Saint Paul: "You must be clothed in the new self, which is created in God's image, justified and sanctified through the truth" (*Eph.* IV, 23). The hour has struck for a halt, a moment of recollection, of reflection, almost of prayer. A moment to think anew of our common origin, our history, our common destiny. Today as never before, in our era so marked by human progress, there is need for an appeal to the moral conscience of man. For the danger comes, not from progress, nor from science—indeed, if properly utilised, these could rather resolve many of the grave problems which assail mankind. No, the real danger comes from man himself, wielding ever more powerful instruments, which can be employed equally well for destruction or for the loftiest conquests.

32.   In a word, the edifice of modern civilization must be based on spiritual principles capable, not only of sustaining it, but also endowing it with light and life. And because these alone are the indispensable principles of higher wisdom, they can be founded only on faith in God. What of that unknown God of whom Saint Paul spoke to the Athenians in the Areopagus? He was indeed unknown to them although, without realising it, they sought Him and they had Him close to them, as happens also to so many men of our times. To us, in any case, and to all those who accept the ineffable revelation which Christ has given us of Him, He is the living God, the Father of all men.

Populorum Progressio

On the Development of Peoples
(March 26, 1967)

ENCYCLICAL LETTER
OF HIS HOLINESS,
PAUL VI, POPE

To the Bishops,
Priests, Religious,
the Faithful
and to all men of good will:

1.   The development of peoples has the Church's close attention, particularly the development of those peoples who are striving to escape from hunger, misery, endemic diseases and ignorance; of those who are looking for a wider share in the benefits of civilisation and a more active improvement of their human qualities; of those who are aiming purposefully at their complete fulfilment. Following on the Second Vatican Ecumenical Council a renewed consciousness of the demands of the Gospel makes it her duty to put herself at the service of all, to help them grasp their serious problem in all its dimensions, and to convince them that

[This English version is that published by the Vatican Polyglot Press in booklet form, 62 pages. A.A.S. LIX (April 15, 1967), no. 4, pp. 257–99.]

solidarity in action at this turning point in human history is a matter of urgency.

2.   Our predecessors in their great encyclicals, Leo XIII in *Rerum Novarum*,[1] Pius XI in *Quadragesimo Anno*[2] and John XXIII in *Mater et Magistra*[3] and *Pacem in Terris*[4]—not to mention the messages of Pius XII[5] to the world—did not fail in the duty of their office of shedding the light of the Gospel on the social questions of their times.

3.   Today the principal fact that we must all recognise is that the social question has become world-wide. John XXIII stated this in unambiguous terms[6] and the Council echoed him in its Pastoral Constitution on *The Church in the Modern World*.[7] This teaching is important and its application urgent. Today the peoples in hunger are making a dramatic appeal to the peoples blessed with abundance. The Church shudders at this cry of anguish and calls each one to give a loving response of charity to this brother's cry for help.

4.   Before We became Pope, two journeys, to Latin America in 1960 and to Africa in 1962, brought Us into direct contact with the acute problems pressing on continents full of life and hope. Then on becoming Father of all We made further journeys, to the Holy Land and India, and were able to see and virtually touch the very serious difficulties besetting peoples of long-standing civilisations who are at grips with the problem of development. While the Second Vatican Ecumenical Council was being held in Rome, providential circumstances permitted Us to address in person the General Assembly of the United Nations, and We pleaded the cause of poor peoples before this distinguished body.

5.   Then quite recently, in Our desire to carry out the wishes of the Council and give specific expression to the Holy See's contribution to this great cause of peoples in development, We considered it Our duty to set up a Pontifical Commission in the Church's central administration, charged with "bringing to the whole of God's People the full knowledge of the part expected of them at the present time, so as to further the progress of poorer peoples, to encourage social justice among nations, to offer to less developed nations the means whereby they can further their own progress"[8]: its name, which is also its programme, is *Justice and Peace*. We think that this can and should bring together men of good will with our Catholic sons and our Chrisitan brothers. So it is to all that We address this solemn appeal for concrete action towards man's complete development and the development of all mankind.

PART I:
For Man's Complete Development

1. The Data of the Problem

6.   Freedom from misery, the greater assurance of finding subsistence, health and fixed employment; an increased share of responsibility without oppression of any kind and in security from situations that do violence to their dignity as men; better education—in brief, to seek to do more, know more and have more in order to be more: that is what men aspire to now when a greater number of them are condemned to live in conditions that make this lawful desire illusory. Besides, peoples who have recently gained national independence experience the need to add to this political freedom a fitting autonomous growth, social as well as economic, in order to assure their citizens of a full human enhancement and to take their rightful place with other nations.

7.   Though insufficient for the immensity and urgency of the task, the means inherited from the past are not lacking. It must certainly be recognised that colonising powers have often furthered their own interests, power or glory, and that their departure has sometimes left a precarious economy, bound up for instance with the production of one kind of crop whose market prices are subject to sudden and considerable variation. Yet while recognising the damage done by a certain type of colonialism and its consequences, one must at the same time acknowledge the qualities and achievement of colonisers who brought their science and technical knowledge and left beneficial results of their presence in so many underprivileged regions. The structures established by them persist, however incomplete they may be; they diminished ignorance and sickness, brought the benefits of communications and improved living conditions.

8.   Yet once this is admitted, it remains only too true that the resultant situation is manifestly inadequate for facing the hard reality of modern economics. Left to itself it works rather to widen the differences in the world's levels of life, not to diminish them: rich peoples enjoy rapid

growth whereas the poor develop slowly. The imbalance is on the increase: some produce a surplus of foodstuffs, others cruelly lack them and see their exports made uncertain.

9.   At the same time social conflicts have taken on world dimensions. The acute disquiet which has taken hold of the poor classes in countries that are becoming industrialised, is now embracing those whose economy is almost exclusively agrarian: farming people, too, are becoming aware of their "undeserved hardship".[9] There is also the scandal of glaring inequalities not merely in the enjoyment of possessions but even more in the exercise of power. While a small restricted group enjoys a refined civilisation in certain regions, the remainder of the population, poor and scattered, is "deprived of nearly all possibility of personal intiative and of responsibility, and oftentimes even its living and working conditions are unworthy of the human person".[10]

10.   Furthermore, the conflict between traditional civilisations and the new elements of industrial civilisation break down structures which do not adapt themselves to new conditions. Their framework, sometimes rigid, was the indispensable prop to personal and family life; older people remain attached to it, the young escape from it, as from a useless barrier, to turn eagerly to new forms of life in society. The conflict of the generations is made more serious by a tragic dilemma: whether to retain ancestral institutions and convictions and renounce progress, or to admit techniques and civilisations from outside and reject along with the traditions of the past all their human richness. In effect, the moral, spiritual and religious supports of the past too often give way without securing in return any guarantee of a place in the new world.

11.   In this confusion the temptation becomes stronger to risk being swept away towards types of messianism which give promises but create illusions. The resulting dangers are patent: violent popular reactions, agitation towards insurrection, and a drifting towards totalitarian ideologies. Such are the data of the problem. Its seriousness is evident to all.

2.   The Church and Development

12.   True to the teaching and example of her divine Founder, Who cited the preaching of the Gospel to the poor as a sign of His mission,[11] the Church has never failed to foster the human progress of the nations to which she brings faith in Christ. Her missionaries have built, not only churches, but also hostels and hospitals, schools and universities. Teaching the local populations the means of deriving the best advantages from

their natural resources, missionaries have often protected them from the greed of foreigners. Without doubt their work, inasmuch as it was human, was not perfect, and sometimes the announcement of the authentic Gospel message was infiltrated by many ways of thinking and acting which were characteristic of their home country. But the missionaries were also able to develop and foster local institutions. In many a region they were among the pioneers in material progress as well as in cultural advancement. Let it suffice to recall the example of Father Charles de Foucauld, whose charity earned him the title "Universal Brother", and who edited an invaluable dictionary of the Touareg language. We ought to pay tribute to these pioneers who have been too often forgotten, but who were urged on by the love of Christ, just as we honour their imitators and successors who today still continue to put themselves at the generous and unselfish service of those to whom they announce the Gospel.

13.   However, local and individual undertakings are no longer enough. The present situation of the world demands concerted action based on a clear vision of all economic, social, cultural, and spiritual aspects. Experienced in human affairs, the Church, without attempting to interfere in any way in the politics of States, "seeks but a solitary goal: to carry forward the work of Christ Himself under the lead of the befriending Spirit. And Christ entered this world to give witness to the truth, to rescue and not to sit in judgment, to serve and not to be served".[12] Founded to establish on earth the Kingdom of Heaven and not to conquer any earthly power, the Church clearly states that the two realms are distinct, just as the two powers, ecclesiastical and civil, are supreme, each in its own domain.[13] But, since the Church lives in history, she ought to "scrutinize the signs of the times and interpret them in the light of the Gospel".[14] Sharing the noblest aspirations of men and suffering when she sees them not satisified, she wishes to help them attain their full flowering, and that is why she offers men what she possesses as her characteristic attribute: a global vision of man and of the human race.

CHRISTIAN VISION OF DEVELOPMENT

14.   Development cannot be limited to mere economic growth. In order to be authentic, it must be complete: integral, that is, it has to promote the good of every man and of the whole man. As an eminent specialist has very rightly and emphatically declared: "We do not believe in separating the economic from the human, nor development from the civilisations in which it exists. What we hold important is man, each man and each group of men, and we even include the whole of humanity".[15]

15.   In the design of God, every man is called upon to develop and

fulfill himself, for every life is a vocation. At birth, everyone is granted, in germ, a set of aptitudes and qualities for him to bring to fruition. Their coming to maturity, which will be the result of education received from the environment and personal efforts, will allow each man to direct himself toward the destiny intended for him by his Creator. Endowed with intelligence and freedom, he is responsible for his fulfilment as he is for his salvation. He is aided, or sometimes impeded, by those who educate him and those with whom he lives, but each one remains, whatever be these influences affecting him, the principal agent of his own success or failure. By the unaided effort of his own intelligence and his will, each man can grow in humanity, can enhance his personal worth, can become more a person.

16.   However, this self-fulfilment is not something optional. Just as the whole of creation is ordained to its Creator, so spiritual beings should of their own accord orientate their lives to God, the first truth and the supreme good. Thus it is that human fulfilment constitutes, as it were, a summary of our duties. But there is much more: this harmonious enrichment of nature by personal and responsible effort is ordered to a further perfection. By reason of his union with Christ, the source of life, man attains to new fulfilment of himself, to a transcendent humanism which gives him his greatest possible perfection: this is the highest goal of personal development.

17.   But each man is a member of society. He is part of the whole of mankind. It is not just certain individuals, but all men who are called to this fullness of development. Civilisations are born, develop and die. But humanity is advancing along the path of history like the waves of a rising tide encroaching gradually on the shore. We have inherited from past generations, and we have benefitted from the work of our contemporaries: for this reason we have obligations towards all, and we cannot refuse to interest ourselves in those who will come after us to enlarge the human family. The reality of human solidarity, which is a benefit for us, also imposes a duty.

18.   This personal and communal development would be threatened if the true scale of values were undermined. The desire for necessities is legitimate, and work undertaken to obtain them is a duty: "If any man will not work, neither let him eat".[16] But the acquiring of temporal goods can lead to greed, to the insatiable desire for more, and can make increased power a tempting objective. Individuals, families and nations can be overcome by avarice, be they poor or rich, and all can fall victim to a stifling materialism.

19.   Increased possession is not the ultimate goal of nations nor of individuals. All growth is ambivalent. It is essential if man is to develop as

a man, but in a way it imprisons man if he considers it the supreme good, and it restricts his vision. Then we see hearts harden and minds close, and men no longer gather together in friendship but out of self-interest, which soon leads to oppositions and disunity. The exclusive pursuit of possessions thus becomes an obstacle to individual fulfilment and to man's true greatness. Both for nations and for individual men, avarice is the most evident form of moral underdevelopment.

20.   If further development calls for the work of more and more technicians, even more necessary is the deep thought and reflection of wise men in search of a new humanism which will enable modern man to find himself anew by embracing the higher values of love and friendship, of prayer and contemplation.[17] This is what will permit the fullness of authentic development, a development which is for each and all the transition from less human conditions to those which are more human.

21.   Less human conditions: the lack of material necessities for those who are without the minimum essential for life, the moral deficiencies of those who are mutilated by selfishness. Less human conditions: oppressive social structures, whether due to the abuses of ownership or to the abuses of power, to the exploitation of workers or to unjust transactions. Conditions that are more human: the passage from misery towards the possession of necessities, victory over social scourges, the growth of knowledge, the acquisition of culture. Additional conditions that are more human: increased esteem for the dignity of others, the turning toward the spirit of poverty,[18] cooperation for the common good, the will and desire for peace. Conditions that are still more human: the acknowledgement by man of supreme values, and of God their source and their finality. Conditions that, finally and above all, are more human: faith, a gift of God accepted by the good will of man, and unity in the charity of Christ, Who calls us all to share as sons in the life of the living God, the Father of all men.

3. Action to be Undertaken

THE UNIVERSAL PURPOSE OF CREATED THINGS

22.   "Fill the earth and subdue it":[19] the Bible, from the first page on, teaches us that the whole of creation is for man, that it is his responsibility to develop it by intelligent effort and by means of his labour to perfect it, so to speak, for his use. If the world is made to furnish each individual with the means of livelihood and the instruments for his growth and

progress, each man has therefore the right to find in the world what is necessary for himself. The recent Council reminded us of this: "God intended the earth and all that it contains for the use of every human being and people. Thus, as all men follow justice and unite in charity, created goods should abound for them on a reasonable basis".[20] All other rights whatsoever, including those of property and of free commerce, are to be subordinated to this principle. They should not hinder but on the contrary favour its application. It is a grave and urgent social duty to redirect them to their primary finality.

23.   "If someone who has the riches of this world sees his brother in need and closes his heart to him, how does the love of God abide in him?".[21] It is well known how strong were the words used by the Fathers of the Church to describe the proper attitude of persons who possess anything towards persons in need. To quote Saint Ambrose: "You are not making a gift of your possessions to the poor person. You are handing over to him what is his. For what has been given in common for the use of all, you have arrogated to yourself. The world is given to all, and not only to the rich".[22] That is, private property does not constitute for anyone an absolute and unconditioned right. No one is justified in keeping for his exclusive use what he does not need, when others lack necessities. In a word, "according to the traditional doctrine as found in the Fathers of the Church and the great theologians, the right to property must never be exercised to the detriment of the common good." If there should arise a conflict "between acquired private rights and primary community exigencies", it is the responsibility of public authorities "to look for a solution, with the active participation of individuals and social groups".[23]

24.   If certain landed estates impede the general prosperity because they are extensive, unused or poorly used, or because they bring hardship to peoples or are detrimental to the interests of the country, the common good sometimes demands their expropriation. While giving a clear statement on this,[24] the Council recalled no less clearly that the available revenue is not to be used in accordance with mere whim, and that no place must be given to selfish speculation. Consequently it is unacceptable that citizens with abundant incomes from the resources and activity of their country should transfer a considerable part of this income abroad purely for their own advantage, without care for the manifest wrong they inflict on their country by doing this.[25]

INDUSTRIALISATION

25.   The introduction of industry is a necessity for economic growth and human progress; it is also a sign of development and contributes to it.

By persistent work and use of his intelligence man gradually wrests nature's secrets from her and finds a better application for her riches. As his self-mastery increases, he develops a taste for research and discovery, an ability to take a calculated risk, boldness in enterprises, generosity in what he does and a sense of responsibility.

26.   But it is unfortunate that on these new conditions of society a system has been constructed which considers profit as the key motive for economic progress, competition as the supreme law of economics, and private ownership of the means of production as an absolute right that has no limits and carries no corresponding social obligation. This unchecked liberalism leads to dictatorship rightly denounced by Pius XI as producing "the international imperialism of money".[26] One cannot condemn such abuses too strongly by solemnly recalling once again that the economy is at the service of man.[27] But if it is true that a type of capitalism has been the source of excessive suffering, injustices and fratricidal conflicts whose effects still persist, it would also be wrong to attribute to industrialisation itself evils that belong to the woeful system which accompanied it. On the contrary one must recognise in all justice the irreplaceable contribution made by the organisation of labour and of industry to what development has accomplished.

27.   Similarly with work: while it can sometimes be given exaggerated significance, it is for all something willed and blessed by God. Man created to His image "must cooperate with his Creator in the perfecting of creation and communicate to the earth the spiritual imprint he himself has received".[28] God Who has endowed man with intelligence, imagination and sensitivity, has also given him the means of completing His work in a certain way: whether he be artist or craftsman, engaged in management, industry or agriculture, everyone who works is a creator. Bent over a material that resists his efforts, a man by his work gives his imprint to it, acquiring, as he does so, perseverance, skill and a spirit of invention. Further, when work is done in common, when hope, hardship, ambition and joy are shared, it brings together and firmly unites the wills, minds and hearts of men: in its accomplishment, men find themselves to be brothers.[29]

28.   Work of course can have contrary effects, for it promises money, pleasure and power, invites some to selfishness, others to revolt; it also develops professional awareness, sense of duty and charity to one's neighbour. When it is more scientific and better organised, there is a risk of its dehumanising those who perform it, by making them its servants, for work is human only if it remains intelligent and free. John XXIII gave a reminder of the urgency of giving everyone who works his proper dignity by making him a true sharer in the work he does with others:

"every effort should be made that the enterprise become a community of persons in the dealings, activities and standing of all its members".[30] Man's labour means much more still for the Christian: the mission of sharing in the creation of the supernatural world[31] which remains incomplete until we all come to build up together that perfect Man of whom St. Paul speaks "who realises the fulness of Christ".[32]

URGENCY OF THE TASK TO BE DONE

29.   We must make haste: too many are suffering, and the distance is growing that separates the progress of some and the stagnation, not to say the regression, of others. Yet the work required should advance smoothly if there is not to be the risk of losing indispensable equilibrium. A hasty agrarian reform can fail. Industrialisation if introduced suddenly can displace structures still necessary, and produce hardships in society which would be a setback in terms of human values.

30.   There are certainly situations whose injustice cries to heaven. When whole populations destitute of necessities live in a state of dependence barring them from all initiative and responsibility, and all opportunity to advance culturally and share in social and political life, recourse to violence, as a means to right these wrongs to human dignity, is a grave temptation.

31.   We know, however, that a revolutionary uprising—save where there is manifest, long-standing tyranny which would do great damage to fundamental personal rights and dangerous harm to the common good of the country—produces new injustices, throws more elements out of balance and brings on new disasters. A real evil should not be fought against at the cost of greater misery.

32.   We want to be clearly understood: the present situation must be faced with courage and the injustices linked with it must be fought against and overcome. Development demands bold transformations, innovations that go deep. Urgent reforms should be undertaken without delay. It is for each one to take his share in them with generosity, particularly those whose education, position and opportunities afford them wide scope for action. May they show an example, and give of their own possessions as several of Our brothers in the episcopacy have done.[33] In so doing they will live up to men's expectations and be faithful to the Spirit of God, since it is "the ferment of the Gospel which has aroused and continues to arouse in man's heart the irresistible requirements of his dignity".[34]

PROGRAMMES AND PLANNING

33.   Individual initiative alone and the mere free play of competition could never assure successful development. One must avoid the risk of increasing still more the wealth of the rich and the dominion of the strong, whilst leaving the poor in their misery and adding to the servitude of the oppressed. Hence programmes are necessary in order "to encourage, stimulate, coordinate, supplement and integrate"[35] the activity of individuals and of intermediary bodies. It pertains to the public authorities to choose, even to lay down the objectives to be pursued, the ends to be achieved, and the means for attaining these, and it is for them to stimulate all the forces engaged in this common activity. But let them take care to associate private initiative and intermediary bodies with this work. They will thus avoid the danger of complete collectivisation or of arbitrary planning, which, by denying liberty, would prevent the exercise of the fundamental rights of the human person.

34.   This is true since every programme, made to increase production, has, in the last analysis, no other *raison d'être* than the service of man. Such programmes should reduce inequalities, fight discriminations, free man from various types of servitude and enable him to be the instrument of his own material betterment, of his moral progress and of his spiritual growth. To speak of development, is in effect to show as much concern for social progress as for economic growth. It is not sufficient to increase overall wealth for it to be distributed equitably. It is not sufficient to promote technology to render the world a more human place in which to live. The mistakes of their predecessors should warn those on the road to development of the dangers to be avoided in this field. Tomorrow's technocracy can beget evils no less redoubtable than those due to the liberalism of yesterday. Economics and technology have no meaning except from man whom they should serve. And man is only truly man in as far as, master of his own acts and judge of their worth, he is author of his own advancement, in keeping with the nature which was given to him by his Creator and whose possibilities and exigencies he himself freely assumes.

35.   It can even be affirmed that economic growth depends in the very first place upon social progress: thus basic education is the primary object of any plan of development. Indeed hunger for education is no less debasing than hunger for food: an illiterate is a person with an under-nourished mind. To be able to read and write, to acquire a professional formation, means to recover confidence in oneself and to discover that

one can progress along with the others. As We said in Our message to the UNESCO Congress held in 1965 at Teheran, for man literacy is "a fundamental factor of social integration, as well as of personal enrichment, and for society it is a privileged instrument of economic progress and of development".[36] We also rejoice at the good work accomplished in this field by private initiative, by the public authorities and by international organisations: these are the primary agents of development, because they render man capable of acting for himself.

36.   But man finds his true identity only in his social milieu, where the family plays a fundamental role. The family's influence may have been excessive, at some periods of history and in some places, when it was exercised to the detriment of the fundamental rights of the individual. The long-standing social frameworks, often too rigid and badly organised, existing in developing countries, are, nevertheless, still necessary for a time, yet progressively relaxing their excessive hold on the population. But the natural family, monogamous and stable, such as the divine plan conceived it[37] and as Christianity sanctified it, must remain the place where "the various generations come together and help one another to grow wiser and to harmonise personal rights with the other requirements of social life".[38]

37.   It is true that too frequently an accelerated demographic increase adds its own difficulties to the problems of development: the size of the population increases more rapidly than available resources, and things are found to have reached apparently an impasse. From that moment the temptation is great to check the demographic increase by means of radical measures. It is certain that public authorities can intervene, within the limit of their competence, by favouring the availability of appropriate information and by adopting suitable measures, provided that these be in conformity with the moral law and that they respect the rightful freedom of married couples. Where the inalienable right to marriage and procreation is lacking, human dignity has ceased to exist. Finally, it is for the parents to decide, with full knowledge of the matter, on the number of their children, taking into account their responsibilities towards God, themselves, the children they have already brought into the world, and the community to which they belong. In all this they must follow the demands of their own conscience enlightened by God's law authentically interpreted, and sustained by confidence in Him.[39]

38.   In the task of development, man, who finds his life's primary environment in the family, is often aided by professional organisations. If it is their objective to promote the interests of their members, their

responsibility is also great with regard to the educative task which at the same time they can and ought to accomplish. By means of the information they provide and the formation they propose, they can do much to give to all a sense of the common good and of the consequent obligations that fall upon each person.

39.   All social action involves a doctrine. The Christian cannot admit that which is based upon a materialistic and atheistic philosophy, which respects neither the religious orientation of life to its final end, nor human freedom and dignity. But, provided that these values are safeguarded, a pluralism of professional organisations and trade unions is admissible, and from certain points of view useful, if thereby liberty is protected and emulation stimulated. And We most willingly pay homage to all those who labour in them to give unselfish service to their brothers.

40.   In addition to professional organisations, there are also institutions which are at work. Their role is no less important for the success of development. "The future of the world stands in peril", the Council gravely affirms, "unless wiser men are forthcoming". And it adds: "many nations, poorer in economic goods, are quite rich in wisdom and able to offer noteworthy advantages to others".[40] Rich or poor, each country possesses a civilisation handed down by their ancestors: institutions called for by life in this world, and higher manifestations of the life of the spirit, manifestations of an artistic, intellectual and religious character. When the latter possess true human values, it would be grave error to sacrifice them to the former. A people that would act in this way would thereby lose the best of its patrimony; in order to live, it would be sacrificing its reasons for living. Christ's teaching also applies to people: "What does it profit a man to gain the whole world if he suffers the loss of his soul".[41]

41.   Less well-off peoples can never be sufficiently on their guard against this temptation which comes to them from wealthy nations. For these nations all too often set an example of success in a highly technical and culturally developed civilization; they also provide the model for a way of acting that is principally aimed at the conquest of material prosperity. Not that material prosperity of itself precludes the activity of the human spirit. On the contrary, the human spirit, "increasingly free of its bondage to creatures, can be more easily drawn to the worship and contemplation of the Creator".[42] However, "modern civilization itself often complicates the approach to God, not for any essential reason, but because it is excessively engrossed in earthly affairs".[43] Developing nations must know how to discriminate among those things that are held

out to them; they must be able to assess critically, and eliminate those deceptive goods which would only bring about a lowering of the human ideal, and to accept those values that are sound and beneficial, in order to develop them alongside their own, in accordance with their own genius.

42.   What must be aimed at is complete humanism.[44] And what is that if not the fully-rounded development of the whole man and of all men? A humanism closed in on itself, and not open to the values of the spirit and to God Who is their source, could achieve apparent success. True, man can organise the world apart from God, but "without God man can organise it in the end only to man's detriment. An isolated humanism is an inhuman humanism".[45] There is no true humanism but that which is open to the Absolute and is conscious of a vocation which gives human life its true meaning. Far from being the ultimate measure of all things, man can only realise himself by reaching beyond himself. As Pascal has said so well: "Man infinitely surpasses man".[46]

PART II:

The Development of the Human Race in the Spirit of Solidarity

43.   There can be no progress towards the complete development of man without the simultaneous development of all humanity in the spirit of solidarity. As We said at Bombay: "Man must meet man, nation meet nation, as brothers and sisters, as children of God. In this mutual understanding and friendship, in this sacred communion, we must also begin to work together to build the common future of the human race".[47] We also suggested a search for concrete and practical ways of organisation and cooperation, so that all available resources be pooled and thus a true communion among all nations be achieved.

44.   This duty is the concern especially of better-off nations. Their obligations stem from a brotherhood that is at once human and supernatural, and take on a threefold aspect: the duty of human solidarity—the aid that the rich nations must give to developing countries; the duty of social justice—the rectification of inequitable trade relations between powerful nations and weak nations; the duty of universal charity—the effort to bring about a world that is more human towards

all men, where all will be able to give and receive, without one group making progress at the expense of the other. The question is urgent, for on it depends the future of the civilisation of the world.

1. Aid for the Weak

45.   "If a brother or a sister be naked", says Saint James; "if they lack their daily nourishment, and one of you says to them: 'Go in peace, be warmed and be filled', without giving them what is necessary for the body, what good does it do?".[48] Today no one can be ignorant any longer of the fact that in whole continents countless men and women are ravished by hunger, countless numbers of children are undernourished, so that many of them die in infancy, while the physical growth and mental development of many others are retarded and as a result whole regions are condemned to the most depressing despondency.

46.   Anguished appeals have already been sounded in the past: that of John XXIII was warmly received.[49] We Ourselves repeated it in Our Christmas Message of 1963,[50] and again in 1966 on behalf of India.[51] The campaign against hunger being carried on by the Food and Agriculture Organisation (FAO) and encouraged by the Holy See, has been generously supported. Our *Caritas Internationalis* is at work everywhere, and many Catholics, at the urging of Our Brothers in the episcopacy, contribute generously of their means and spend themselves without counting the cost in assisting those who are in want, continually widening the circle of those they look upon as neighbours.

47.   But neither all this nor the private and public funds that have been invested, nor the gifts and loans that have been made, can suffice. It is not just a matter of eliminating hunger, nor even of reducing poverty. The struggle against destitution, though urgent and necessary, is not enough. It is a question, rather, of building a world where every man, no matter what his race, religion or nationality, can live a fully human life, freed from servitude imposed on him by other men or by natural forces over which he has not sufficient control; a world where freedom is not an empty word and where the poor man Lazarus can sit down at the same table with the rich man.[52] This demands great generosity, much sacrifice and unceasing effort on the part of the rich man. Let each one examine his conscience, a conscience that conveys a new message for our times. Is he prepared to support out of his own pocket works and undertakings organised in favour of the most destitute? Is he ready to pay higher taxes so that the public authorities can intensify their efforts in favour of development? Is he ready to pay a higher price for imported goods so that

the producer may be more justly rewarded? Or to leave his country, if necessary and if he is young, in order to assist in this development of the young nations?

48.   The same duty of solidarity that rests on individuals exists also for nations: "Advanced nations have a very heavy obligation to help the developing peoples".[53] It is necessary to put this teaching of the Council into effect. Although it is normal that a nation should be the first to benefit from the gifts that Providence has bestowed on it as the fruit of the labours of its people, still no country can claim on that account to keep its wealth for itself alone. Every nation must produce more and better quality goods to give to all its inhabitants a truly human standard of living, and also to contribute to the common development of the human race. Given the increasing needs of the under-developed countries, it should be considered quite normal for an advanced country to devote a part of its production to meet their needs, and to train teachers, engineers, technicians and scholars prepared to put their knowledge and their skill at the disposal of less fortunate peoples.

49.   We must repeat once more that the superfluous wealth of rich countries should be placed at the service of poor nations. The rule which up to now held good for the benefit of those nearest to us, must today be applied to all the needy of this world. Besides, the rich will be the first to benefit as a result. Otherwise their continued greed will certainly call down upon them the judgement of God and the wrath of the poor, with consequences no one can foretell. If today's flourishing civilisations remain selfishly wrapped up in themselves, they could easily place their highest values in jeopardy, sacrificing their will to be great to the desire to possess more. To them we could apply also the parable of the rich man whose fields yielded an abundant harvest and who did not know where to store his harvest: "God said to him: 'Fool, this night do they demand your soul of you' ".[54]

50.   In order to be fully effective, these efforts ought not remain scattered or isolated, much less be in competition for reasons of power or prestige: the present situation calls for concerted planning. A planned programme is of course better and more effective than occasional aid left to individual goodwill. It presupposes, as We said above, careful study, the selection of ends and the choice of means, as well as a reorganisation of efforts to meet the needs of the present and the demands of the foreseeable future. More important, a concerted plan has advantages that go beyond the field of economic growth and social progress; for in addition it gives significance and value to the work undertaken. While shaping the world it sets a higher value on man.

51.　　But it is necessary to go still further. At Bombay We called for the establishment of a great *World Fund,* to be made up of part of the money spent on arms, to relieve the most destitute of this world.[55] What is true of the immediate struggle against want, holds good also when there is a question of development. Only world-wide collaboration, of which a common fund would be both means and symbol, will succeed in overcoming vain rivalries and in establishing a fruitful and peaceful exchange between peoples.

52.　　There is certainly no need to do away with bilateral and multilateral agreements: they allow ties of dependence and feelings of bitterness, left over from the era of colonialism, to yield place to the happier relationship of friendship, based on a footing of constitutional and political equality. However, if they were to be fitted into the framework of worldwide collaboration, they would be beyond all suspicion, and as a result there would be less distrust on the part of the receiving nations. These would have less cause for fearing that, under the cloak of financial aid or technical assistance, there lurk certain manifestations of what has come to be called neo-colonialism, in the form of political pressures and economic suzerainty aimed at maintaining or acquiring complete dominance.

53.　　Besides, who does not see that such a fund would make it easier to take measures to prevent certain wasteful expenditures, the result of fear or pride? When so many people are hungry, when so many families suffer from destitution, when so many remain steeped in ignorance, when so many schools, hospitals and homes worthy of the name remain to be built, all public or private squandering of wealth, all expenditure prompted by motives of national or personal ostentation, every exhausting armaments race, becomes an intolerable scandal. We are conscious of Our duty to denounce it. Would that those in authority listened to Our words before it is too late!

54.　　This means that it is absolutely necessary to create among all peoples that dialogue for whose establishment We expressed Our hope in Our first Encyclical *Ecclesiam Suam.*[56] This dialogue between those who contribute wealth and those who benefit from it, will provide the possibility of making an assessment of the contribution necessary, not only drawn up in terms of the generosity and the available wealth of the donor nations, but also conditioned by the real needs of the receiving countries and the use to which the financial assistance can be put. Developing countries will thus no longer risk being overwhelmed by debts whose repayment swallows up the greater part of their gains. Rates of interest and time for repayment of the loan could be so arranged as not to be too great a burden on either party, taking into account free gifts, interest-free or low-interest loans, and the time needed for liquidating the debts. Guarantees could be given to those who provide the capital that it will be put to use according to an agreed plan and with a reasonable measure of efficiency, since there is no question of encouraging parasites or the indolent. And the receiving countries could demand that there be no interference in their political life or subversion of their social structures. As sovereign states they have the right to conduct their own affairs, to decide on their policies and to move freely towards the kind of society they choose. What must be brought about, therefore, is a system of cooperation freely undertaken, an effective and mutual sharing, carried out with equal dignity on either side, for the construction of a more human world.

55.   The task might seem impossible in those regions where the cares of day-to-day survival fill the entire existence of families incapable of planning the kind of work which would open the way to a future that is less desperate. These, however, are the men and women who must be helped, who must be persuaded to work for their own betterment and endeavour to acquire gradually the means to that end. This common task will not succeed without concerted, constant and courageous efforts. But let everyone be convinced of this: the very life of poor nations, civil peace in developing countries, and world peace itself are at stake.

2. Equity in Trade Relations

56.   The efforts which are being made to assist developing nations on a financial and technical basis, though considerable, would be illusory if their benefits were to be partially nullified as a consequence of the trade relations existing between rich and poor countries. The confidence of these latter would be severely shaken if they had the impression that what was being given them with one hand was being taken away with the other.

57.   Of course, highly industrialised nations export for the most part manufactured goods, while countries with less developed economies have only food, fibres and other raw materials to sell. As a result of technical progress the value of manufactured goods is rapidly increasing and they can always find an adequate market. On the other hand, raw materials produced by under-developed countries are subject to wide and sudden fluctuations in price, a state of affairs far removed from the progressively increasing value of industrial products. As a result, nations

whose industrialisation is limited are faced with serious difficulties when they have to rely on their exports to balance their economy and to carry out their plans for development. The poor nations remain ever poor while the rich ones become still richer.

58.   In other words, the rule of free trade, taken by itself, is no longer able to govern international relations. Its advantages are certainly evident when the parties involved are not affected by any excessive inequalities of economic power: it is an incentive to progress and a reward for effort. That is why industrially developed countries see in it a law of justice. But the situation is no longer the same when economic conditions differ too widely from country to country: prices which are "freely" set in the market can produce unfair results. One must recognise that it is the fundamental principle of liberalism, as the rule for commercial exchange, which is questioned here.

59.   The teaching of Leo XIII in *Rerum Novarum* is always valid: if the positions of the contracting parties are too unequal, the consent of the parties does not suffice to guarantee the justice of their contract, and the rule of free agreement remains subservient to the demands of the natural law.[57] What was true of the just wage for the individual is also true of international contracts: an economy of exchange can no longer be based solely on the law of free competition, a law which, in its turn, too often creates an economic dictatorship. Freedom of trade is fair only if it is subject to the demands of social justice.

60.   Moreover, this has been understood by the developed nations themselves, which are striving, by means of appropriate measures, to re-establish within their own economies a balance, which competition, if left to itself, tends to compromise. Thus it happens that these nations often support their agriculture at the price of sacrifices imposed on economically more favoured sectors. Similarly, to maintain the commercial relations which are developing among themselves, especially within a common market, the financial, fiscal, and social policy of these nations tries to restore comparable opportunities to competing industries which are not equally prospering.

61.   In this area one cannot employ two systems of weights and measures. What holds for a national economy or among developed countries is valid also in commercial relations between rich nations and poor nations. Without abolishing the competitive market, it should be kept within the limits which make it just and moral, and therefore human. In trade between developed and under-developed economies, conditions are too disparate and the degrees of genuine freedom available too unequal. In order that international trade be human and moral, social justice

requires that it restore to the participants a certain equality of opportunity. This equality is a long-term objective, but to reach it, we must begin now to create true equality in discussions and negotiations. Here again international agreements on a rather wide scale would be helpful: they would establish general norms for regulating certain prices, for guaranteeing certain types of production, for supporting certain new industries. Who is there who does not see that such a common effort aimed at increased justice in business relations between peoples would bestow on developing nations positive assistance, the effects of which would be not only immediate but lasting?

62.   Among still other obstacles which are opposed to the formation of a world which is more just and which is better organised toward a universal solidarity, We wish to speak of nationalism and racism. It is only natural that communities which have recently reached their political independence should be jealous of a national unity which is still fragile, and that they should strive to protect it. Likewise, it is to be expected that nations endowed with an ancient culture should be proud of the patrimony which their history has bequeathed to them. But these legitimate feelings should be ennobled by that universal charity which embraces the entire human family. Nationalism isolates people from their true good. It would be especially harmful where the weakness of national economies demands rather the pooling of efforts, of knowledge and of funds, in order to implement programmes of development and to increase commercial and cultural exchange.

63.   Racism is not the exclusive lot of young nations, where sometimes it hides beneath the rivalries of clans and political parties, with heavy losses for justice and at the risk of civil war. During the colonial period it often flared up between the colonists and the indigenous population, and stood in the way of mutually profitable understanding, often giving rise to bitterness in the wake of genuine injustices. It is still an obstacle to collaboration among disadvantaged nations and a cause of division and hatred within countries whenever individuals and families see the inviolable rights of the human person held in scorn, as they themselves are unjustly subjected to a regime of discrimination because of their race or their colour.

64.   We are deeply distressed by such a situation which is laden with threats for the future. We are, nonetheless, hopeful: a more deeply felt need for collaboration, a heightened sense of unity will finally triumph over misunderstandings and selfishness. We hope that the countries whose development is less advanced will be able to take advantage of their proximity in order to organise among themselves, on a broadened

territorial basis, areas for concerted development: to draw up programmes in common, to coordinate investments, to distribute the means of production, and to organise trade. We hope also that multilateral and international bodies, by means of the reorganisation which is required, will discover the ways that will allow peoples which are still underdeveloped to break through the barriers which seem to enclose them and to discover for themselves, in full fidelity to their own proper genius, the means for their social and human progress.

65.　Such is the goal we must attain. World unity, ever more effective, should allow all peoples to become the artisans of their destiny. The past has too often been characterized by relationships of violence between nations; may the day dawn when international relations will be marked with the stamp of mutual respect and friendship, of interdependence in collaboration, the betterment of all seen as the responsibility of each individual. The younger or weaker nations ask to assume their active part in the construction of a better world, one which shows deeper respect for the rights and the vocation of the individual. This is a legitimate appeal; everyone should hear it and respond to it.

3. Universal Charity

66.　The world is sick. Its illness consists less in the unproductive monopolisation of resources by a small number of men than in the lack of brotherhood among individuals and peoples.

67.　We cannot insist too much on the duty of welcoming others—a duty springing from human solidarity and Christian charity—which is incumbent both on the families and the cultural organisations of the host countries. Centres of welcome and hostels must be multiplied, especially for youth. This must be done first to protect them from loneliness, the feeling of abandonment and distress, which undermine all moral resistance. This is also necessary to protect them from the unhealthy situation in which they find themselves, forced as they are to compare the extreme poverty of their homeland with the luxury and waste which often surround them. It should be done also to protect them against the subversive teachings and temptations to aggression which assail them, as they recall so much "unmerited misery".[58] Finally, and above all, this hospitality should aim to provide them, in the warm atmosphere of a brotherly welcome, with the example of wholesome living, an esteem for genuine and effective Christian charity, an esteem for spiritual values.

68.　It is painful to think of the numerous young people who come to more advanced countries to receive the science, the competence, and the culture which will make them more qualified to serve their homeland, and who certainly acquire there a formation of high quality, but who too often lose the esteem for the spiritual values which often were to be found, as a precious patrimony, in the civilisations where they had grown up.

69.   The same welcome is due to emigrant workers, who live in conditions which are often inhuman, and who economise on what they earn in order to send a little relief to their family living in misery in their native land.

70.   Our second recommendation is for those whose business calls them to countries recently opened to industrialisation: industrialists, merchants, leaders or representatives of larger enterprises. It happens that they are not lacking in social sensitivity in their own country; why then do they return to the inhuman principles of individualism when they operate in less developed countries? Their advantaged situation should on the contrary move them to become the initiators of social progress and of human advancement in the area where their business calls them. Their very sense of organisation should suggest to them the means for making intelligent use of the labour of the indigenous population, of forming qualified workers, of training engineers and staffs, of giving scope to their initiative, of introducing them progressively into higher positions, thus preparing them to share, in the near future, in the responsibilities of management. At least let justice always rule the relations between superiors and their subordinates. Let standard contracts with reciprocal obligations govern these relationships. Finally, let no one, whatever his status, be subjected unjustly to the arbitrariness of others.

71.   We are happy that experts are being sent in larger and larger numbers on development missions by institutions, whether international or bilateral, or by private organisations: "they ought not conduct themselves in a lordly fashion, but as helpers and co-workers".[59] A people quickly perceives whether those who come to help them do so with or without affection, whether they come merely to apply their techniques or to recognise in man his full value.

Their message is in danger of being rejected if it is not presented in the context of brotherly love.

72.   Hence, necessary technical competence must be accompanied by authentic signs of disinterested love. Freed of all nationalistic pride and of every appearance of racism, experts should learn how to work in close collaboration with all. They realise that their competence does not confer on them a superiority in every field. The civilisation which formed them

contains, without doubt, elements of universal humanism, but it is not the only civilisation nor does it enjoy a monopoly of valuable elements. Moreover it cannot be imported without undergoing adaptations. The men on these missions will be intent on discovering, along with its history, the component elements of the cultural riches of the country receiving them. Mutual understanding will be established which will enrich both cultures.

73. Between civilisations, as between persons, sincere dialogue indeed creates brotherhood. The work of development will draw nations together in the attainment of goals pursued with a common effort if all, from governments and their representatives to the last expert, are inspired by brotherly love and moved by the sincere desire to build a civilisation founded on world solidarity. A dialogue based on man, and not on commodities or technical skills, will then begin. It will be fruitful if it brings to the peoples who benefit from it the means of self-betterment and spiritual growth, if the technicians act as educators, and if the instruction imparted is characterised by so lofty a spiritual and moral tone that it guarantees not merely economic, but human development. When aid programmes have terminated, the relationships thus established will endure. Who does not see of what importance they will be for the peace of the world?

74. Many young people have already responded with warmth and enthusiasm to the appeal of Pius XII for lay missionaries.[60] Many also are those who have spontaneously put themselves at the disposition of official or private organisations which are collaborating with developing nations. We are pleased to learn that in certain nations "military service" can be partially accomplished by doing "social service", a "service pure and simple". We bless these undertakings and the good will which inspires them. May all those who wish to belong to Christ hear His appeal: "I was hungry and you gave me to eat, thirsty and you gave me to drink, a stranger and you took me in, naked and you clothed me, sick and you visited me, a prisoner and you came to see me".[61] No one can remain indifferent to the lot of his brothers who are still buried in wretchedness, and victims of insecurity, slaves of ignorance. Like the heart of Christ, the heart of the Christian must sympathise with this misery: "I have pity on this multitude".[62]

75. The prayer of all ought to rise with fervour to the Almighty. Having become aware of such great misfortunes, the human race will apply itself with intelligence and steadfastness to abolish them. This prayer should be matched by the resolute commitment of each individual—according to the measure of his strength and possibilities—to

the struggle against underdevelopment. May individuals, social groups, and nations join hands in brotherly fashion, the strong aiding the weak to grow, exerting all their competence, enthusiasm and disinterested love. More than any other, the individual who is animated by true charity labours skillfully to discover the causes of misery, to find the means to combat it, to overcome it resolutely. A creator of peace, he "will follow his path, lighting the lamps of joy and playing their brilliance and loveliness on the hearts of men across the surface of the globe, leading them to recognise, across all frontiers, the faces of their brothers, the faces of their friends".[63]

4. Development Is the New Name for Peace

76.   Excessive economic, social and cultural inequalities among peoples arouse tensions and conflicts, and are a danger to peace. As We said to the Fathers of the Council when We returned from Our journey of peace to the United Nations: "The condition of the peoples in process of development ought to be the object of our consideration; or better: our charity for the poor in the world—and there are multitudes of them—must become more considerate, more active, more generous".[64] To wage war on misery and to struggle against injustice is to promote, along with improved conditions, the human and spiritual progress of all men, and therefore the common good of humanity. Peace cannot be limited to a mere absence of war, the result of an ever precarious balance of forces. No, peace is something that is built up day after day, in the pursuit of an order intended by God, which implies a more perfect form of justice among men.[65]

77.   The peoples themselves have the prime responsibility to work for their own development. But they will not bring this about in isolation. Regional agreements among weak nations for mutual support, understandings of wider scope entered into for their help, more far-reaching agreements to establish programmes for closer cooperation among groups of nations—these are the milestones on the road to development that leads to peace.

78.   This international collaboration on a world-wide scale requires institutions that will prepare, coordinate and direct it, until finally there is established an order of justice which is universally recognised. With all Our heart, We encourage these organisations which have undertaken this collaboration for the development of the peoples of the world, and Our wish is that they grow in prestige and authority. "Your vocation", as

We said to the representatives of the United Nations in New York, "is to bring not some people but all peoples to treat each other as brothers . . . Who does not see the necessity of thus establishing progressively a world authority, capable of acting effectively in the juridical and political sectors?".[66]

79.   Some would consider such hopes utopian. It may be that these persons are not realistic enough, and that they have not perceived the dynamism of a world which desires to live more fraternally—a world which, in spite of its ignorance, its mistakes and even its sins, its relapses into barbarism and its wanderings far from the road of salvation, is, even unawares, taking slow but sure steps towards its Creator. This road towards a greater humanity requires effort and sacrifice; but suffering itself, accepted for the love of our brethren, favours the progress of the entire human family. Christians know that union with the sacrifice of our Saviour contributes to the building up of the Body of Christ in its plentitude: the assembled people of God.[67]

80.   We are all united in this progress toward God. We have desired to remind all men how crucial is the present moment, how urgent the work to be done. The hour for action has now sounded. At stake are the survival of so many innocent children and, for so many families overcome by misery, the access to conditions fit for human beings; at stake are the peace of the world and the future of civilisation. It is time for all men and all peoples to face up to their responsibilities.

A Final Appeal

81.   First, We appeal to all Our sons. In countries undergoing development no less than in others, the laymen should take up as their own proper task the renewal of the temporal order. If the role of the Hierarchy is to teach and to interpret authentically the norms of morality to be followed in this matter, it belongs to the laymen, without waiting passively for orders and directives, to take the initiative freely and to infuse a Christian spirit into the mentality, customs, laws and structures of the community in which they live.[68] Changes are necessary, basic reforms are indispensable: the laymen should strive resolutely to permeate them with the spirit of the Gospel. We ask Our Catholic sons who belong to the more favoured nations, to bring their talents and give their active partici-

pation to organisations, be they of an official or private nature, civil or religious, which are working to overcome the difficulties of the developing nations. They will certainly desire to be in the first ranks of those who collaborate to establish as fact and reality an international morality based on justice and equity.

82.   We are sure that all Christians, our brethren, will wish to expand their common cooperative effort in order to help mankind vanquish selfishness, pride and rivalries, to overcome ambitions and injustices, to open up to all the road to a more human life, where each man will be loved and helped as his brother, as his neighbour. And, still deeply impressed by the memory of Our unforgettable encounter in Bombay with our non-Christian brethren, We invite them anew to work with all their heart and their intelligence towards this goal, that all the children of men may lead a life worthy of the children of God.

83.   Finally, We turn to all men of good will who believe that the way to peace lies in the area of development. Delegates to international organisations, government officials, gentlemen of the press, educators: all of you, each in your own way, are the builders of a new world. We entreat Almighty God to enlighten your minds and strengthen your determination to alert public opinion and to involve the peoples of the world. Educators, it is your task to awaken in persons, from their earliest years, a love for the peoples who live in misery. Gentlemen of the press, it is up to you to place before our eyes the story of the efforts exerted to promote mutual assistance among peoples, as well as the spectacle of the miseries which men tend to forget in order to quiet their consciences. Thus at least the wealthy will know that the poor stand outside their doors waiting to receive some left-overs from their banquets.

84.   Government officials, it is your concern to mobilise your peoples to form a more effective world solidarity, and above all to make them accept the necessary taxes on their luxuries and their wasteful expenditures, in order to bring about development and to save the peace. Delegates to international organisations, it depends on you to see that the dangerous and futile rivalry of powers should give place to collaboration which is friendly, peaceful and free of vested interests, in order to achieve a responsible development of mankind, in which all men will have an opportunity to find their fulfilment.

85.   If it is true that the world is in trouble because of the lack of thinking, then We call upon men of reflection and of learning, Catholics, Christians, those who hold God in honour, who thirst for an absolute, for justice and for truth: We call upon all men of good will. Following Christ, We make bold to ask you earnestly: "seek and you shall find", [69] open the

paths which lead to mutual assistance among peoples, to a deepening of human knowledge, to an enlargement of heart, to a more brotherly way of living within a truly universal human society.

86.   All of you who have heard the appeal of suffering peoples, all of you who are working to answer their cries, you are the apostles of a development which is good and genuine, which is not wealth that is self-centered and sought for its own sake, but rather an economy which is put at the service of man, the bread which is daily distributed to all, as a source of brotherhood and a sign of Providence.

87.   With a full heart We bless you, and We appeal to all men of good will to join you in a spirit of brotherhood. For, if the new name for peace is development, who would not wish to labour for it with all his powers? Yes, We ask you, all of you, to heed Our cry of anguish, in the name of the Lord.

From the Vatican, on the Feast of Easter, the twenty-sixth day of March in the year one thousand nine hundred and sixty-seven.

PAUL PP. VI

NOTES

1. Cf. *Acta Leonis XIII*, t. XI (1892), pp. 97–148.

2. Cf. *AAS* 23 (1931), pp. 177–228.

3. Cf. *AAS* 53 (1961), pp. 401–64.

4. Cf. *AAS* 55 (1963), pp. 257–304.

5. Cf. in particular the Radio Message of June 1, 1941, for the 50th anniversary of *Rerum Novarum*, in *AAS* 33 (1941), pp. 195–205; Christmas Radio Message of 1942, in *AAS* 35 (1943), pp. 9–24; Address to a group of workers on the anniversary of *Rerum Novarum*, May 14, 1953, in *AAS* 45 (1953), pp. 402–8.

6. Cf. Encyclical *Mater et Magistra*, May 15, 1961: *AAS* 53 (1961), p. 440.

7. *Gaudium et Spes*, nn. 63–72: *AAS* 58 (1966), pp. 1084–94.

8. Motu Proprio *Catholicam Christi Ecclesiam*, Jan. 6, 1967, *AAS* 59 (1967), p. 27.

9. Encyclical *Rerum Novarum*, May 15, 1891: *Acta Leonis XIII*, t. XI (1892), p. 98.

10. *Gaudium et Spes*, n. 63.

11. Cf. Lk 7: 22.

12. *Gaudium et Spes*, n. 3.

13. Cf. Encyclical *Immortale Dei*, Nov. 1, 1885: *Acta Leonis XIII*, t. V (1885), p. 127.

14. *Gaudium et Spes*, n. 4.

15. L.-J. Lebret, O.P., *Dynamique concrète du développement*, Paris: Economie et Humanisme, Les Editions Ouvrières, 1961, p. 28.

16. 2 Thes 3:10.

17. Cf., for example, J. Maritain, *Les conditions spirituelles du progrès et de la paix*, in *Rencontre des cultures à l'UNESCO sous le signe du Concile oecuménique Vatican II*, Paris: Mame, 1966, p. 66.

18. Cf. Mt 5: 3.

19. Gen 1: 28.

20. *Gaudium et Spes*, n. 69.

21. 1 Jn 3: 17.

22. *De Nabuthe*, c. 12, n. 53; (P.L. 14, 747). Cf. J.-R. Palanque, *Saint Ambroise et l'empire romain*, Paris: de Boccard, 1933, pp. 336 f.

23. Letter to the 52nd Session of the French Social Weeks (Brest, 1965), in *L'homme et la révolution urbaine*, Lyons, Chronique sociale, 1965, pp. 8 and 9. Cf. *L'Osservatore Romano*, July 10, 1965; *Documentation catholique*, t. 62, Paris, 1965, col. 1365.

24. *Gaudium et Spes*, n. 71.

25. Cf., *ibid.*, n. 65.

26. Encyclical *Quadragesimo Anno*, May 15, 1931, *AAS* 23 (1931), p. 212.

27. Cf., for example, Colin Clark, *The Conditions of Economic Progress*, 3rd ed., London: Macmillan and Co., and New York: St. Martin's Press, 1960, pp. 3–6.

28. Letter to the 51st Session of the French Social Weeks (Lyons, 1964), in *Le travail et les travailleurs dans la société contemporaine*, Lyons, Chronique sociale, 1965, p. 6. Cf. *L'Osservatore Romano*, July 10, 1964; *Documentation catholique*, t. 61, Paris, 1964, col. 931.

29. Cf., for example, M.-D. Chenu, O.P., *Pour une théologie du travail*, Paris: Editions du Seuil, 1955. Eng. tr.: *The Theology of Work: An Exploration*, Dublin: Gill and Son, 1963.

30. *Mater et Magistra*, *AAS* 53 (1961), n. 423.

31. Cf., for example, O. von Nell–Breuning, S.J., *Wirtschaft und Gesellschaft*, t. 1: *Grundfragen*, Freiburg: Herder, 1956, pp. 183–84.

32. Eph 4: 13.

33. Cf., for example, Bishop Manuel Larrain Errázuriz of Talca, Chile; President of CELAM, "Lettre pastorale sur le développement et la paix", Paris: Pax Christi, 1965.

34. *Gaudium et Spes*, n. 26.

35. *Mater et Magistra*, *AAS* 53 (1961), p. 414.

36. *L'Osservatore Romano*, Sept. 11, 1965; *Documentation catholique*, t. 62, Paris, 1965, col. 1674–75.

37. Mt 19: 16.

38. *Gaudium et Spes*, n. 52.

39. Cf. *ibid.*, n. 50–51 and note 14; and n. 87.

40. *Ibid.*, n. 15.

41. Mt 16: 26.

42. *Gaudium et Spes*, n. 57.

43. *Ibid.*, n. 19.

44. Cf., for example, J. Maritain, *L'humanisme intégral*, Paris: Aubier, 1936. Eng. tr.: *True Humanism*, London: Geoffrey Bles, and New York: Charles Scribner's Sons, 1938.

45. H. de Lubac, S.J., *Le drame de l'humanisme athée*, 3rd ed., Paris: Spes, 1945, p. 10. Eng. tr. *The Drama of Atheistic Humanism*, London: Sheed and Ward, 1949, p. vii.

46. *Pensées*, éd. Brunschvicg, n. 434. Cf. M. Zundel, *L'homme passe l'homme*, Le Caire, Editions du lien, 1944.

47. Address to the Representatives of non-Christian Religions, Dec. 3, 1964, *AAS* 57 (1965), p. 132.

48. Jas 2: 15–16.

49. Cf. *Mater et Magistra*, *AAS* 53 (1961), pp. 440 f.

50. Cf. *AAS* 56 (1964), pp. 57–58.

51. Cf. *Encicliche e Discorsi di Paolo VI*, vol. IX, Roma, ed. Paoline, 1966, pp. 132–36, *Documentation catholique*, t. 43, Paris, 1966, col. 403–6.

52. Cf. Lk 16: 19–31.

53. *Gaudium et Spes*, n. 86.

54. Lk 12: 20.

55. Message to the world, entrusted to Journalists on Dec. 4, 1964. Cf. *AAS* 57 (1965), p. 135.

56. Cf. *AAS* 56 (1964), pp. 639 f.

57. Cf. *Acta Leonis XIII*, t. XI (1892), p. 131.

58. Cf. *ibid.*, p. 98.

59. *Gaudium et Spes*, n. 85.

60. Cf. Encyclical *Fidei Donum*, Apr. 21, 1957, *AAS* 49 (1957), p. 246.

61. Mt 25: 35–36.

62. Mk 8: 2.

63. Address of John XXIII upon Reception of the Balzan Prize for Peace, May 10, 1963, *AAS* 55 (1963), p. 455.

64. *AAS* 57 (1965), p. 896.

65. Cf. Encyclical *Pacem in terris*, Apr. 11, 1963, *AAS* 55 (1963), p. 301.

66. *AAS* 57 (1965), p. 880.

67. Cf. Eph. 4: 12; *Lumen Gentium*, n. 13.

68. Cf. *Apostolicam Actuositatem*, nn. 7, 13 and 24.

69. Lk 11: 9.

To the Peoples of Africa

Message of His Holiness Paul VI
to the Hierarchy
and to All the Peoples of Africa
for the Promotion of the Religious, Civil
and Social Good of their Continent
(October 29, 1967)
[Excerpts]

Introduction

1.   It is still a source of joy for Us to recall the visit We made to some parts of Africa before We were raised to the Supreme Pontificate. We were deeply impressed and moved to admiration by what We saw of the face of the new Africa, as We witnessed at close quarters the beginnings of Christian life in those countries, the peoples' eagerness to learn, their

[This version is that published by the Vatican Polyglot Press in booklet form, 70 pages. The Message covers the whole range of Church and pastoral concerns. Those portions dealing specifically with issues of development and social ministry have been selected for inclusion in this volume. The original numbering of the sections and footnotes has been maintained. Because of the omissions the numbering is consequently not consecutive.]

desire for renewal and their anxiety to find a solution to the complex problems arising from their newly attained political independence. The fervour and vitality of the new Christian communities, in particular, showed Us clearly that Africa was opening itself to the Kingdom of God.

Ever since that visit, We have been conscious of the voice of the peoples of Africa calling out to Us, as the voice called out to St. Paul in his dream at Troas:[1] "Come to our aid. Now is the time. Do not delay, for we are ready to receive you".[2]

Ancient Heritage and Present Situation

5.   We also wish to express Our esteem for all the followers of Islam living in Africa, who have principles in common with Christianity, which give us glad hope of an effective dialogue. Meanwhile We express Our wish that where Muslims and Christians live as neighbours mutual respect will be constantly present in social life also, and common action to promote the acceptance and the defence of man's fundamental rights.
6.   And now We turn to the new nations of Africa. Although they have only recently become nations, they have immediately taken their place with the most ancient nations of the world in the great international assemblies, to cooperate in maintaining and consolidating the peace of humanity.

Nevertheless the present period of Africa's history is one of great delicacy. The first phase of independence is now successfully completed and the new States have entered upon a period of adjustment and consolidation.

The transition to independence was made almost universally in an orderly and peaceful manner. This does honour to all, both the governing and governed, who contributed to it, and continues to give grounds for good hopes. In some countries the internal situation has, unfortunately, not yet been consolidated, and violence has had, or in some cases still has, the upper hand. But this does not justify a general condemnation involving a whole people or a whole nation or, even worse, a whole continent.

Traditional African Values

7.   We have always been glad to see the flourishing state of African studies, and We see with satisfaction that the knowledge of her history and tradition is spreading. This, if done with openness and objectivity, cannot fail to lead to a more exact evaluation of Africa's past and present.

Thus, the more recent ethnic history of the peoples of Africa, though lacking in written documents, is seen to be very complex, yet rich in individuality and spiritual and social experiences, to which specialists are fruitfully directing their analysis and further research. Many customs and rites, once considered to be strange, are seen today, in the light of ethnological science, as integral parts of various social systems, worthy of study and commanding respect.

In this regard, We think it profitable to dwell on some general ideas which typify ancient African religious cultures, because We think their moral and religious values deserving of attentive consideration.

8.   The constant and general foundation of African tradition is the spiritual view of life. Here we have more than the so-called "animistic" concept, in the sense given to this term in the history of religions at the end of last century. We have a deeper, broader and more universal concept which considers all living beings and visible nature itself as linked with the world of the invisible and the spirit. In particular it has never considered man as mere matter limited to earthly life, but recognizes in him the presence and power of another spiritual element, in virtue of which human life is always related to the after-life.

In this spiritual concept, the most important element generally found is the idea of God, as the first or ultimate cause of all things. This concept, perceived rather than analyzed, lived rather than reflected on, is expressed in very different ways from culture to culture, but the fact remains that the presence of God permeates African life, as the presence of a higher being, personal and mysterious.

People have recourse to Him at solemn and more critical moments of life, when they consider the intercession of every other intermediary unavailing. Nearly always fear of God's omnipotence is set aside and He is invoked as Father. Prayers made to Him, whether by individuals or by groups, are spontaneous, at times moving, while among the forms of sacrifice the sacrifice of first fruits stands out because of what it plainly signifies.

9.   Another characteristic common to African tradition is respect for the dignity of man.

It is true that there have been aberrations and also ceremonial rites which are seen to be in violent contrast with the respect due to the human person. But these are aberrations which have brought suffering to the very people who have gone astray, and which, thank God, as in the case of slavery, have completely disappeared or soon will.

Respect for man is seen conspicuously, if not systematically, in the traditional ways of educating within the family, in initiations into society, and in participation in social and political life, in accordance with the traditional pattern of individual nations.

10.   Another characteristic element of African tradition is the sense of family. On this it is significant to note the moral and also the religious value seen in attachment to the family, evidenced further by the bond with ancestors, which finds expression in so many widespread forms of worship.

For Africans the family thus comes to be the natural environment in which man is born and acts, in which he finds the necessary protection and security, and eventually through union with his ancestors has his continuity beyond earthly life.

11.   Then in the family one should note the respect for the part played by the father of the family and the authority he has. Recognition of this is not found everywhere in the same degree but is so extraordinarily widespread and deeply rooted that it is rightly to be considered as a mark of African tradition in general.

Patria potestas is profoundly respected even in the African societies which are governed by matriarchy. There although ownership of goods and the social status of children follow from the mother's family, the father's moral authority in the household remains undiminished.

By reason of the same concept the father of the family in some African cultures has a typically priestly function assigned to him, whereby he acts as a mediator not only between the ancestors and his family, but also between God and his family, performing acts of worship established by custom.

12.   As regards community life—which in African tradition was family life writ large—We note that participation in the life of the community, whether in the circle of one's kinsfolk or in public life, is considered a precise duty and the right of all. But exercise of this right is conceded only after progressive preparation through a series of initiations whose aim is to form the character of the young candidates and to instruct them in the traditions, rules and customs of society.

13.   Today, Africa has met with progress which is taking her onwards to new forms of life made available by science and technology. All this is not in contradiction with the essential values of the moral and religious tradition of the past, which We have briefly described, the values that belong in a way to the natural law which is implanted in the heart of every man and is the foundation for a well-ordered life with his fellow men in every generation.

For this reason, while these values which have been handed down ought to be respected as a cultural legacy from the past, there is no less a duty to give them new meaning and new expression. In the face of modern civilization, however, it is sometimes necessary to "know how to discriminate: to assess critically, and eliminate those deceptive goods which would bring about a lowering of the human ideal, and to accept those values that are sound and beneficial, in order to develop them alongside their own, in accordance with their own genius".[4] New forms of life will thus spring from what is good in the old and the new alike, and will be seen by younger generations as a solid and real inheritance.

14.   The Church views with great respect the moral and religious values of the African tradition, not only because of their meaning, but also because she sees them as providential, as the basis for spreading the Gospel message and beginning the establishment of the new society in Christ. This We Ourselves pointed out at the canonization of the Martyrs of Uganda, who were the first flowering of Christian holiness in the new Africa, sprung from the most vigorous stock of ancient tradition.[5]

The teaching of Jesus Christ and His redemption are, in fact, the complement, the renewal, and the bringing to perfection, of all that is good in human tradition. And that is why the African who becomes a Christian does not disown himself, but takes up the age-old values of tradition "in spirit and in truth".[6]

Counsels and Hopes

15.   But this very positive consideration of the moral and religious values in African tradition does not prevent Us from seeing also the shadows in Africa today which cause Us great grief and concern. We mean the disorders and the violence which have continued to trouble various African countries, causing sufferings and miseries especially to unarmed peoples, as they go peacefully about their occupations. What are We to say, then, when violence, as has unfortunately happened, assumes almost the proportions of genocide, when within the boundaries of the same country different racial groups are pitted against one another? We cannot forget the humiliations, the sufferings and death which have fallen also upon Bishops, priests, religious men and women, and lay people, Catholics and non-Catholics, Africans and non-Africans, who were working for no other end than the spiritual welfare of the local peoples.

Fervent communities of Christians were all of a sudden abandoned and isolated by the forced departure of their priests, and found themselves in a fearful situation.

Yet, in spite of these grave disturbances, hope prevails. With greater confidence Our prayer goes to God, Our Father, to give rest to the victims, to pardon the guilty, to give all a horror of violence and of war, to strengthen their desire for peace, and open the hearts of those who rule to an understanding of the just aspirations of peoples.

16.   What has been achieved with the proclamation of independence requires consolidation by well-ordered legislation and its peaceful implementation. It is therefore necessary both to resist the temptation to violence and to avoid and check the abuse of power.[7]

Peaceful development and stability of institutions are prerequisites for progress in the new African States today, so that all citizens may take an active part in building up the new society, in public bodies and in private associations and enterprises.

This cooperation in the life of the community is now being increased by social planning, the study and implementation of which is the noble task of present-day African governments. In this way by social and economic development which transcends the old, narrow tribal limits, a civic sense is being fostered in all, which puts the common good before restricted sectional interests. If this is to develop, however, everything possible must be done to ensure peace between different States, for this is the indispensable requirement for all progress.

17.   Among the obstacles that impede the full development of the new African States there is also that of racial discrimination. Alas!, in Africa too there are serious manifestations of it on one side and another.

The Second Vatican Council clearly and repeatedly condemned racism in its various forms as being an offence to human dignity, "foreign to the mind of Christ"[8] and "contrary to God's intent".[9] We Ourselves have deplored it in *Populorum Progressio* as an obstacle "to the building up of a juster world, more soundly constructed on the plan of universal solidarity".[10] We draw attention also to the fact that the Catholic bishops have not failed, as recent events have shown, to raise their voices where necessary in the defence of violated rights.

The equality of all men is based, as is well known, on their common origin and destiny as members of the human family: "Since all men possess a rational soul and are created in God's likeness, since they have the same nature and origin, have been redeemed by Christ and enjoy the same divine calling and destiny, the basic equality of all must receive increasingly greater recognition".[11] This equality demands an ever more explicit recognition in civil society of every human being's essential rights, even though this equality does not cancel but rather acknowledges and brings into harmony personal differences and the diversity of function in the community. Consequently, the aspirations of all men desiring to enjoy those rights which flow from their dignity as human persons are wholly legitimate.

Development and Aid

20.   The majority of African states are faced with the difficult problems connected with development. In Our recent appeal to the world, We asked that man's integral development be looked upon by all as an urgent problem of world proportions. In the vast planning entailed, Africa will have to take an important place. But to carry out programmes of development both material resources and men with technical training are required.

Here two main problems come to mind, because they seem to Us particularly pressing in the present situation in Africa. The first is the need for an all-out struggle against illiteracy and continued expansion of school education. "Basic education", We said in Our appeal, "is the primary object of any plan of development. Hunger for education is no less depressing than hunger for food".[13] Also curricula will have to correspond to the actual needs of Africa today, assigning due importance to professional technical training and giving special consideration to the needs of the rural population, which is the most important sector.

The second problem in fact has to do with the agricultural situation, where methods and ways of thinking are often no longer adequate. We fervently hope that this urgent problem will be resolved quickly, along the wise lines pointed out by Our predecessor, John XXIII, in his Encyclical, "Mater et Magistra", [14] repeated and expanded by Us on various occasions.[15]

21.   The mere declaration of independence by the new states has not changed the general conditions for Africa's economic development. Independence has however sometimes led to strained relations with prosperous nations, through fear that financial and technical aid would restrict the liberty and autonomy gained with independence. The African Nations, like every other State in the same situation, are conscious of their needs, but they are also justly and proudly aware of their independence.

To overcome these misgivings and their causes, which come under the heading of neo-colonialism, We appealed for the establishment of a

World Fund as a manifestation and an instrument of world-wide cooperation.[16]

The dignity of people receiving aid must be respected absolutely. They must feel, as Our Predecessor, John XXIII, already declared, "that they are primarily responsible and the principal artisans in the promotion of their economic development and social progress";[17] they should in a word, "become artisans of their own destiny".[18]

When this legitimate need for human worth and responsibility is respected, gratitude and the renewal of friendship will spontaneously follow and, most important, the right use and proper appreciation of aid received.

22.   We have hope and confidence of a well-ordered future for Africa provided it can be faithful to its ancient traditions and at the same time renew itself by its contact with Christianity and modern civilization. In particular, We are confident that Christians, worthy of the name and of the needs of the common good, will not fail to make a significant contribution to the civic development of their nations.

For this reason We wish to address to all sons of Africa and to all men of good will who will live and work there Our words of greeting, advice and encouragement.

To Women

36.   In the realm of the family the position of the woman is brought into greater prominence and is also radically changed, in that there lie open to her new fields of activity in the schoolroom, the hospitals and in the various forms of political and administrative life of the modern state. The reason for this development is to be sought in the Christian teaching and spirit. Hence, "the Church is proud to have glorified and liberated woman, and in the course of centuries, in diversity of characters, to have brought into relief her basic equality with man".[32]

The African woman is asked today to become ever more vividly aware of her dignity as a woman, of her mission as a mother, of her rights to participate in the social life and the progress of the new Africa.

The African woman asks in the first place never to be considered or treated as an instrument. Her dignity is respected in the liberty due to her as a person, whether she enters the married state, in which case she has the right to choose her own partner freely,[33] or whether she prefers to preserve her virginity, consecrating herself to God and devoting her work to the welfare of all.

In fulfilling her principal mission, as a mother, the African woman will give help and affection to her children by being with them as they develop, bringing them to self-awareness and preparing them for their future responsibilities. In professional activities, too, and in all social relationships, she must bring devotion, sweetness and refinement, which are typically feminine and keep alive the proper sense of human proportions in a world dominated by technology.

Women also have the right and the duty to take part in the political and administrative work of society. This participation offers them the possibility of making a direct contribution to the renewal of social institutions, in particular where marriage, the family and the education of children are concerned.

The Church, remaining faithful to her work of education, invites the women of Africa, as she invites women always and everywhere, to imitate Mary, the Mother of God, "whose life", as St. Ambrose says, "was such that it can be a pattern for all".[34]

To Youth

37.   We turn now to you, the youth, the hope of the future. Africa needs you, needs your preparation, your studies, your energy. You are the first to want to know the precise meaning and value of ancient African traditions, and you are also the first to want their renewal and transformation. The fact is that it is your task to overcome the opposition between what is past and the new forms of life and structure of the present. But be on your guard against the easy attraction of materialistic theories which can, unfortunately, lead to erroneous or inadequate conception of humanism and even to the denial of God.

You, in particular, Christian youth, should be conscious of the dignity and of the responsibility that derive from the Christian faith. Live your faith. Give yourselves with enthusiasm to study and to work. Exercise restraint even in your aspirations to do great things for the welfare and progress of your people.

38.   With special affection We next address Ourselves to you, the students, and remind you that the instruction you receive in school should prepare you effectively for your chosen profession, and the tasks which Africa expects of you for its future development. Around you, in your native Africa, there are still those multitudes of people for whom schooling and study are an impossibility. Be prepared and glad to become ministers of learning, by passing on to your brothers, as teachers in schools, the gift which has been given you.

Learn, then, to train yourselves in the spirit of sacrifice and dedication.

Henceforth, the greatest good that you can render to your countries is to prepare yourselves to practise your profession unselfishly and in the spirit of Christian charity.

To those of you who are completing your studies in countries outside of Africa, We say: stay attached to your country; once your preparation is completed, be ready to return to be at the disposal of your countries, making your profession one of service for the progress and welfare of Africa.

NOTES

1. Cf. Acts 16:9.

2. Cf. *Atti della III Settimana Studi Missionari*, Milan, 1962, pp. 2–12.

4. Encyclical *Populorum Progressio*, n. 41: AAS 59, 1967, p. 278.

5. Cf. Homily of Oct. 18, 1964: AAS 56, 1964, p. 907 ff.

6. John 4:24.

7. Cf. Encyclical *Populorum Progressio*, nn. 30–32: AAS 59, 1967, pp. 272 ff.

8. Vatican Council II, *Nostra Aetate*, n. 5: AAS 58, 1966, p. 744; cf. *Ad Gentes*, n. 15: AAS 58, 1966, p. 964.

9. Vatican Council II, *Gaudium et Spes*, n. 29: AAS 58, 1966, p. 1049.

10. N. 62: AAS 59, 1967, p. 287; cf. *ibid.*, n. 63, p. 288.

11. Vatican Council II, *Gaudium et Spes*, n. 29: AAS 58, 1966, pp. 1048–1049.

13. Cf. Encyclical *Populorum Progressio*, n. 35: AAS 59, 1967, p. 274.

14. Cf. AAS 53, 1961, pp. 431–451.

15. Cf. Encyclical *Populorum Progressio*, n. 29: AAS 59, 1967, p. 272.

16. Cf. *ibid.*, nn. 51–54: AAS 59, 1967, pp. 282–284.

17. Encyclical *Pacem in Terris*: AAS 55, 1963, p. 290.

18. Encyclical *Populorum Progressio*, n. 65: AAS 59, 1967, p. 289.

32. Vatican Council II, *Message to Women*, Dec. 8, 1965: AAS 58, 1966, p. 13.

33. Vatican Council II, *Gaudium et Spes*, n. 29: AAS 58, 1966, p. 1049.

34. *De Virginibus*, lib. II, cap. II, n. 15: PL. 16, 22.

Humanae Vitae

On the Regulation of Birth
(July 25, 1968)

ENCYCLICAL LETTER
OF HIS HOLINESS POPE PAUL VI
ON THE REGULATION OF BIRTH

To the Venerable Patriarchs,
Archbishops and Bishops,
and Other Local Ordinaries
in Peace and Communion with the Apostolic See,
to Priests, the Faithful,
and to All Men of Good Will

VENERABLE BROTHERS AND BELOVED SONS:

The Transmission of Life

1.   The most serious duty of transmitting human life, for which married persons are the free and responsible collaborators of God the Creator, has always been a source of great joys to them even if sometimes accompanied by not a few difficulties and by distress.

[This English version is that published by the Vatican Polyglot Press in booklet form, 38 pages. A.A.S. LX (September 30, 1969), no. 9, pp. 481–518.]

At all times the fulfilment of this duty has posed grave problems to the conscience of married persons, but, with the recent evolution of society, changes have taken place that give rise to new questions which the Church could not ignore, having to do with a matter which so closely touches upon the life and happiness of men.

I. New Aspects of the Problem and Competency of the Magisterium

NEW FORMULATION OF THE PROBLEM

2.   The changes which have taken place are in fact noteworthy and of varied kinds. In the first place, there is the rapid demographic development. Fear is shown by many that world population is growing more rapidly than the available resources, with growing distress to many families and developing countries, so that the temptation for Authorities to counter this danger with radical measures is great. Moreover, working and lodging conditions, as well as increased exigencies both in the economic field and in that of education, often make the proper education of an elevated number of children difficult today. A change is also seen both in the manner of considering the person of woman and her place in society, and in the value to be attributed to conjugal love in marriage, and also in the appreciation to be made of the meaning of conjugal acts in relation to that love.

Finally and above all, man has made stupendous progress in the domination and rational organization of the forces of nature, such that he tends to extend this domination to his own total being: to the body, to psychical life, to social life and even to the laws which regulate the transmission of life.

3.   This new state of things gives rise to new questions. Granted the conditions of life today, and granted the meaning which conjugal relations have with respect to the harmony between husband and wife and to their mutual fidelity, would not a revision of the ethical norms in force up to now, seem to be advisable, especially when it is considered that they cannot be observed without sacrifices, sometimes heroic sacrifices?

And again: by extending to this field the application of the so-called "principle of totality", could it not be admitted that the intention of a less abundant but more rationalized fecundity might transform a materially sterilizing intervention into a licit and wise control of birth? Could it not be admitted, that is, that the finality of procreation pertains to the ensemble of conjugal life, rather than to its single acts? It is also asked whether, in view of the increased sense of responsibility of modern man, the moment has not come for him to entrust to his reason and his will, rather than to the biological rhythms of his organism, the task of regulating birth.

COMPETENCY OF THE MAGISTERIUM

4. Such questions required from the teaching authority of the Church a new and deeper reflection upon the principles of the moral teaching on marriage: a teaching founded on the natural law, illuminated and enriched by divine Revelation.

No believer will wish to deny that the teaching authority of the Church is competent to interpret even the natural moral law. It is, in fact, indisputable, as Our Predecessors have many times declared,[1] that Jesus Christ, when communicating to Peter and to the Apostles His divine authority and sending them to teach all nations His commandments,[2] constituted them as guardians and authentic interpreters of all the moral law, not only, that is, of the law of the gospel, but also of the natural law, which is also an expression of the will of God, the faithful fulfilment of which is equally necessary for salvation.[3]

Conformably to this mission of hers, the Church has always provided—and even more amply in recent times—a coherent teaching concerning both the nature of marriage and the correct use of conjugal rights and the duties of husband and wife.[4]

SPECIAL STUDIES

5. The consciousness of that same mission induced Us to confirm and enlarge the Study Commission which Our Predecessor Pope John XXIII of happy memory had instituted in March, 1963. That Commission which included, besides several experts in the various pertinent disciplines, also married couples, had as its scope the gathering of opinions on the new questions regarding conjugal life, and in particular on the regulation of births, and of furnishing opportune elements of information so that the Magisterium could give an adequate reply to the expectation not only of the faithful, but also of world opinion.[5]

The work of these experts, as well as the successive judgements and counsels spontaneously forwarded by or expressly requested from a good number of Our Brothers in the Episcopate, have permitted Us to measure more exactly all the aspects of this complex matter. Hence with all Our heart We express to each of them Our lively gratitude.

REPLY OF THE MAGISTERIUM

6.   The conclusions at which the Commission arrived could not, nevertheless, be considered by Us as definitive, nor dispense Us from a personal examination of this serious question; and this also because, within the Commission itself, no full concordance of judgements concerning the moral norms to be proposed had been reached, and above all because certain criteria of solutions had emerged which departed from the moral teaching on marriage proposed with constant firmness by the teaching authority of the Church.

Therefore, having attentively sifted the documentation laid before Us, after mature reflexion and assiduous prayers, We now intend, by virtue of the mandate entrusted to Us by Christ, to give Our reply to these grave questions.

II. Doctrinal Principles

A TOTAL VISION OF MAN

7.   The problem of birth, like every other problem regarding human life, is to be considered, beyond partial perspectives—whether of the biological or psychological, demographic or sociological orders—in the light of an integral vision of man and of his vocation, not only his natural and earthly, but also his supernatural and eternal vocation. And since, in the attempt to justify artificial methods of birth control, many have appealed to the demands both of conjugal love and of "responsible parenthood", it is good to state very precisely the true concept of these two great realities of married life, referring principally to what was recently set forth in this regard, and in a highly authoritative form, by the Second Vatican Council in its Pastoral Constitution *Gaudium et Spes*.

CONJUGAL LOVE

8.   Conjugal love reveals its true nature and nobility when it is considered in its supreme origin, God, Who is Love,[6] "the Father, from whom every family in heaven and on earth is named".[7]

Marriage is not, then, the effect of chance or the product of evolution of unconscious natural forces; it is the wise institution of the Creator to realize in mankind His design of love. By means of the reciprocal personal gift of self, proper and exclusive to them, husband and wife tend towards the communion of their beings in view of mutual personal perfection, to collaborate with God in the generation and education of new lives.

For baptized persons, moreover, marriage invests the dignity of a sacramental sign of grace, inasmuch as it represents the union of Christ and of the Church.

ITS CHARACTERISTICS

9.   Under this light, there clearly appear the characteristic marks and demands of conjugal love, and it is of supreme importance to have an exact idea of these.

This love is first of all fully *human*, that is to say, of the senses and of the spirit at the same time. It is not, then, a simple transport of instinct and sentiment, but also, and principally, an act of the free will, intended to endure and to grow by means of the joys and sorrows of daily life, in such a way that husband and wife become one only heart and one only soul, and together attain their human perfection.

Then, this love is *total*, that is to say, it is a very special form of personal friendship, in which husband and wife generously share everything, without undue reservations or selfish calculations. Whoever truly loves his marriage partner loves not only for what he receives, but for the partner's self, rejoicing that he can enrich his partner with the gift of himself.

Again, this love is *faithful* and *exclusive* until death. Thus in fact do bride and groom conceive it to be on the day when they freely and in full awareness assume the duty of the marriage bond. A fidelity, this, which can sometimes be difficult, but is always possible, always noble and meritorious, as no one can deny. The example of so many married persons down through the centuries shows, not only that fidelity is according to the nature of marriage, but also that it is a source of profound and lasting happiness.

And finally, this love is *fecund*, for it is not exhausted by the communion between husband and wife, but is destined to continue, raising up new lives. "Marriage and conjugal love are by their nature ordained toward the begetting and educating of children. Children are really the supreme gift of marriage and contribute very substantially to the welfare of their parents".[8]

RESPONSIBLE PARENTHOOD

10.   Hence conjugal love requires in husband and wife an awareness of their mission of "responsible parenthood", which today is rightly much insisted upon, and which also must be exactly understood. Consequently it is to be considered under different aspects which are legitimate and connected with one another.

In relation to the biological processes, responsible parenthood means the knowledge and respect of their functions; human intellect discovers in the power of giving life biological laws which are part of the human person.[9]

In relation to the tendencies of instinct or passion, responsible parenthood means that necessary dominion which reason and will must exercise over them.

In relation to physical, economic, psychological and social conditions, responsible parenthood is exercised, either by the deliberate and generous decision to raise a numerous family, or by the decision, made for grave motives and with due respect for the moral law, to avoid for the time being, or even for an indeterminate period, a new birth.

Responsible parenthood also and above all implies a more profound relationship to the objective moral order established by God, of which a right conscience is the faithful interpreter. The responsible exercise of parenthood implies, therefore, that husband and wife recognize fully their own duties towards God, towards themselves, towards the family and towards society, in a correct hierarchy of values.

In the task of transmitting life, therefore, they are not free to proceed completely at will, as if they could determine in a wholly autonomous way the honest path to follow; but they must conform their activity to the creative intention of God, expressed in the very nature of marriage and of its acts, and manifested by the constant teaching of the Church.[10]

RESPECT FOR THE NATURE
AND PURPOSES OF THE MARRIAGE ACT

11.   These acts, by which husband and wife are united in chaste intimacy, and by means of which human life is transmitted, are, as the Council recalled, "noble and worthy",[11] and they do not cease to be lawful if, for causes independent of the will of husband and wife, they are foreseen to be infecund, since they always remain ordained towards expressing and consolidating their union. In fact, as experience bears witness, not every conjugal act is followed by a new life. God has wisely disposed natural laws and rhythms of fecundity which, of themselves,

cause a separation in the succession of births. Nonetheless the Church, calling men back to the observance of the norms of the natural law, as interpreted by her constant doctrine, teaches that each and every marriage act *(quilibet matrimonii usus)* must remain open to the transmission of life.[12]

TWO INSEPARABLE ASPECTS: UNION AND PROCREATION

12.   That teaching, often set forth by the Magisterium, is founded upon the inseparable connection, willed by God and unable to be broken by man on his own initiative, between the two meanings of the conjugal act: the unitive meaning and the procreative meaning. Indeed, by its intimate structure, the conjugal act, while most closely uniting husband and wife, capacitates them for the generation of new lives, according to laws inscribed in the very being of man and of woman. By safeguarding both these essential aspects, the unitive and the procreative, the conjugal act preserves in its fulness the sense of true mutual love and its ordination towards man's most high calling to parenthood. We believe that the men of our day are particularly capable of seizing the deeply reasonable and human character of this fundamental principle.

FAITHFULNESS TO GOD'S DESIGN

13.   It is in fact justly observed that a conjugal act imposed upon one's partner without regard for his or her condition and lawful desires is not a true act of love, and therefore denies an exigency of right moral order in the relationships between husband and wife. Hence, one who reflects well must also recognize that a reciprocal act of love, which jeopardizes the disponibility to transmit life which God the Creator, according to particular laws, inserted therein, is in contradiction with the design constitutive of marriage, and with the will of the Author of life. To use this divine gift destroying, even if only partially, its meaning and its purpose is to contradict the nature both of man and of woman and of their most intimate relationship, and therefore it is to contradict also the plan of God and His will. On the other hand, to make use of the gift of conjugal love while respecting the laws of the generative process means to acknowledge oneself not to be the arbiter of the sources of human life, but rather the minister of the design established by the Creator. In fact, just as man does not have unlimited dominion over his body in general, so also, with particular reason, he has no such dominion over his generative faculties as such, because of their intrinsic ordination towards raising up life, of

which God is the principle. "Human life is sacred", Pope John XXIII recalled; "from its very inception it reveals the creating hand of God".[13]

ILLICIT WAYS OF REGULATING BIRTH

14.   In conformity with these landmarks in the human and Christian vision of marriage, We must once again declare that the direct interruption of the generative process already begun, and, above all, directly willed and procured abortion, even if for therapeutic reasons, are to be absolutely excluded as licit means of regulating birth.[14]

Equally to be excluded, as the teaching authority of the Church has frequently declared, is direct sterilization, whether perpetual or temporary, whether of the man or of the woman.[15] Similarly excluded is every action which, either in anticipation of the conjugal act, or in its accomplishment, or in the development of its natural consequences, proposes, whether as an end or as a means, to render procreation impossible.[16]

To justify conjugal acts made intentionally infecund, one cannot invoke as valid reasons the lesser evil, or the fact that such acts would constitute a whole together with the fecund acts already performed or to follow later, and hence would share in one and the same moral goodness. In truth, if it is sometimes licit to tolerate a lesser evil in order to avoid a greater evil or to promote a greater good,[17] it is not licit, even for the gravest reasons, to do evil so that good may follow therefrom;[18] that is, to make into the object of a positive act of the will something which is intrinsically disorder, and hence unworthy of the human person, even when the intention is to safeguard or promote individual, family or social well-being. Consequently it is an error to think that a conjugal act which is deliberately made infecund and so is intrinsically dishonest could be made honest and right by the ensemble of a fecund conjugal life.

LICITNESS OF THERAPEUTIC MEANS

15.   The Church, on the contrary, does not at all consider illicit the use of those therapeutic means truly necessary to cure diseases of the organism, even if an impediment to procreation, which may be foreseen, should result therefrom, provided such impediment is not, for whatever motive, directly willed.[19]

LICITNESS OF RECOURSE TO INFECUND PERIODS

16.   To this teaching of the Church on conjugal morals, the objection is made today, as We observed earlier (No. 3), that it is the prerogative of the human intellect to dominate the energies offered by irrational nature and

to orientate them towards an end conformable to the good of man. Now, some may ask: In the present case, is it not reasonable in many circumstances to have recourse to artificial birth control if, thereby, we secure the harmony and peace of the family, and better conditions for the education of the children already born? To this question it is necessary to reply with clarity: The Church is the first to praise and recommend the intervention of intelligence in a function which so closely associates the rational creature with his Creator; but she affirms that this must be done with respect for the order established by God.

If, then, there are serious motives to space out births, which derive from the physical or psychological conditions of husband and wife, or from external conditions, the Church teaches that it is then licit to take into account the natural rhythms immanent in the generative functions, for the use of marriage in the infecund periods only, and in this way to regulate birth without offending the moral principles which have been recalled earlier.[20]

The Church is coherent with herself when she considers recourse to the infecund periods to be licit, while at the same time condemning, as being always illicit, the use of means directly contrary to fecundation, even if such use is inspired by reasons which may appear honest and serious. In reality, there are essential differences between the two cases: in the former, the married couple make legitimate use of a natural disposition; in the latter, they impede the development of natural processes. It is true that, in the one and the other case, the married couple are concordant in the positive will of avoiding children for plausible reasons, seeking the certainty that offspring will not arrive; but it is also true that only in the former case are they able to renounce the use of marriage in the fecund periods when, for just motives, procreation is not desirable, while making use of it during infecund periods to manifest their affection and to safeguard their mutual fidelity. By so doing, they give proof of a truly and integrally honest love.

GRAVE CONSEQUENCES OF METHODS
OF ARTIFICIAL BIRTH CONTROL

17.   Upright men can even better convince themselves of the solid grounds on which the teaching of the Church in this field is based, if they care to reflect upon the consequences of methods of artificial birth control. Let them consider, first of all, how wide and easy a road would thus be opened up towards conjugal infidelity and the general lowering of morality. Not much experience is needed in order to know human weakness, and to understand that men—especially the young, who are so vulnera-

ble on this point—have need of encouragement to be faithful to the moral law, so that they must not be offered some easy means of eluding its observance. It is also to be feared that the man, growing used to the employment of anti-conceptive practices, may finally lose respect for the woman and, no longer caring for her physical and psychological equilibrium, may come to the point of considering her as a mere instrument of selfish enjoyment, and no longer as his respected and beloved companion.

Let it be considered also that a dangerous weapon would thus be placed in the hands of those public Authorities who take no heed of moral exigencies. Who could blame a Government for applying to the solution of the problems of the community those means acknowledged to be licit for married couples in the solution of a family problem? Who will stop rulers from favouring, from even imposing upon their peoples, if they were to consider it necessary, the method of contraception which they judge to be most efficacious? In such a way men, wishing to avoid individual, family, or social difficulties encountered in the observance of the divine law, would reach the point of placing at the mercy of the intervention of public Authorities the most personal and most reserved sector of conjugal intimacy.

Consequently, if the mission of generating life is not to be exposed to the arbitrary will of men, one must necessarily recognize insurmountable limits to the possibility of man's domination over his own body and its functions; limits which no man, whether a private individual or one invested with authority, may licitly surpass. And such limits cannot be determined otherwise than by the respect due to the integrity of the human organism and its functions, according to the principles recalled earlier, and also according to the correct understanding of the "principle of totality" illustrated by Our Predecessor Pope Pius XII.[21]

THE CHURCH GUARANTOR OF TRUE HUMAN VALUES

18.   It can be foreseen that this teaching will perhaps not be easily received by all: too numerous are those voices—amplified by the modern means of propaganda—which are contrary to the voice of the Church. To tell the truth, the Church is not surprised to be made, like her divine Founder, a "sign of contradiction";[22] yet she does not because of this cease to proclaim with humble firmness the entire moral law, both natural and evangelical. Of such laws the Church was not the author, nor consequently can she be their arbiter; she is only their depositary and their interpreter, without ever being able to declare to be licit that which is not

so by reason of its intimate and unchangeable opposition to the true good of man.

In defending conjugal morals in their integral wholeness, the Church knows that she contributes towards the establishment of a truly human civilization; she engages man not to abdicate from his own responsibility in order to rely on technical means; by that very fact she defends the dignity of man and wife. Faithful to both the teaching and the example of the Saviour, she shows herself to be the sincere and disinterested friend of men, whom she wishes to help, even during their earthly sojourn, "to share as sons in the life of the living God, the Father of all men".[23]

III. Pastoral Directives

THE CHURCH MATER ET MAGISTRA

19.   Our words would not be an adequate expression of the thought and solicitude of the Church, Mother and Teacher of all peoples, if, after having recalled men to the observance and respect of the divine law regarding matrimony, We did not strengthen them in the path of honest regulation of birth, even amid the difficult conditions which today afflict families and peoples. The Church, in fact, cannot have a different conduct towards men than that of the Redeemer: she knows their weaknesses, has compassion on the crowd, receives sinners; but she cannot renounce the teaching of the law which is, in reality, that law proper to a human life restored to its original truth and conducted by the Spirit of God.[24] Though We are thinking also of all men of good will, We now address Ourself particularly to Our sons, from whom We expect a prompter and more generous adherence.

POSSIBILITY OF OBSERVING THE DIVINE LAW

20.   The teaching of the Church on the regulation of birth, which promulgates the divine law, will easily appear to many to be difficult or even impossible of actuation. And indeed, like all great beneficent realities, it demands serious engagement and much effort, individual, family and social effort. More than that, it would not be practicable without the help of God, Who upholds and strengthens the good will of men. Yet, to anyone who reflects well, it cannot but be clear that such efforts ennoble man and are beneficial to the human community.

MASTERY OF SELF

21.   The honest practice of regulation of birth demands first of all that husband and wife acquire and possess solid convictions concerning the true values of life and of the family, and that they tend towards securing perfect self-mastery. To dominate instinct by means of one's reason and free will undoubtedly requires ascetical practices, so that the affective manifestations of conjugal life may observe the correct order, in particular with regard to the observance of periodic continence. Yet this discipline which is proper to the purity of married couples, far from harming conjugal love, rather confers on it a higher human value. It demands continual effort yet, thanks to its beneficent influence, husband and wife fully develop their personalities, being enriched with spiritual values. Such discipline bestows upon family life fruits of serenity and peace, and facilitates the solution of other problems; it favours attention for one's partner, helps both parties to drive out selfishness, the enemy of true love; and deepens their sense of responsibility. By its means, parents acquire the capacity of having a deeper and more efficacious influence in the education of their offspring; little children and youths grow up with a just appraisal of human values, and in the serene and harmonious development of their spiritual and sensitive faculties.

CREATING AN ATMOSPHERE FAVOURABLE TO CHASTITY

22.   On this occasion, We wish to draw the attention of educators, and of all who perform duties of responsibility in regard to the common good of human society, to the need of creating an atmosphere favourable to education in chastity, that is, to the triumph of healthy liberty over licence by means of respect for the moral order.

Everything in the modern media of social communications which leads to sense excitation and unbridled customs, as well as every form of pornography and licentious performances, must arouse the frank and unanimous reaction of all those who are solicitous for the progress of civilization and the defence of the supreme good of the human spirit. Vainly would one seek to justify such deprivation with the pretext of artistic or scientific exigencies,[25] or to deduce an argument from the freedom allowed in this sector by the public Authorities.

APPEAL TO PUBLIC AUTHORITIES

23.   To rulers, who are those principally responsible for the common good, and who can do so much to safeguard moral customs, We say: Do

not allow the morality of your peoples to be degraded; do not permit that by legal means practices contrary to the natural and divine law be introduced into that fundamental cell, the family. Quite other is the way in which public Authorities can and must contribute to the solution of the demographic problem: namely, the way of a provident policy for the family, of a wise education of peoples in respect of the moral law and the liberty of citizens.

We are well aware of the serious difficulties experienced by public Authorities in this regard, especially in the developing countries. To their legitimate preoccupations We devoted Our Encyclical Letter "Populorum Progressio". But, with Our Predecessor Pope John XXIII, We repeat: No solution to these difficulties is acceptable "which does violence to man's essential dignity" and is based only "on an utterly materialistic conception of man himself and of his life". The only possible solution to this question is one which envisages the social and economic progress both of individuals and of the whole of human society, and which respects and promotes true human values.[26] Neither can one, without grave injustice, consider divine Providence to be responsible for what depends, instead, on a lack of wisdom in government, on an insufficient sense of social justice, on selfish monopolization, or again on blameworthy indolence in confronting the efforts and the sacrifices necessary to ensure the raising of living standards of a people and of all its sons.[27]

May all responsible public Authorities—as some are already doing so laudably—generously revive their efforts. And may mutual aid between all the members of the great human family never cease to grow: this is an almost limitless field which thus opens up to the activity of the great international organizations.

TO MEN OF SCIENCE

24.   We wish now to express Our encouragement to men of science, who "can considerably advance the welfare of marriage and the family, along with peace of conscience, if by pooling their efforts they labour to explain more thoroughly the various conditions favoring a proper regulation of births".[28] It is particularly desirable that, according to the wish already expressed by Pope Pius XII, medical science succeed in providing a sufficiently secure basis for a regulation of birth, founded on the observance of natural rhythms.[29] In this way, scientists and especially Catholic scientists will contribute to demonstrate in actual fact that, as the Church teaches, "a true contradiction cannot exist between the divine laws pertaining to the transmission of life and those pertaining to the fostering of authentic conjugal love".[30]

TO CHRISTIAN HUSBANDS AND WIVES

25.   And now Our words more directly address Our own children, particularly those whom God calls to serve Him in marriage. The Church, while teaching imprescriptible demands of the divine law, announces the tidings of salvation, and by means of the Sacraments opens up the paths of grace, which makes man a new creature, capable of corresponding with love and true freedom to the design of his Creator and Saviour, and of finding the yoke of Christ to be sweet.[31]

Christian married couples, then, docile to her voice, must remember that their Christian vocation, which began at baptism, is further specified and reinforced by the Sacrament of Matrimony. By it husband and wife are strenghthened and as it were consecrated for the faithful accomplishment of their proper duties, for the carrying out of their proper vocation even to perfection, and the Christian witness which is proper to them before the whole world.[32] To them the Lord entrusts the task of making visible to men the holiness and sweetness of the law which unites the mutual love of husband and wife with their cooperation with the love of God the Author of human life.

We do not at all intend to hide the sometimes serious difficulties inherent in the life of Christian married persons; for them as for everyone else, "the gate is narrow and the way is hard, that leads to life".[33] But the hope of that life must illuminate their way, as with courage they strive to live with wisdom, justice and piety in this present time,[34] knowing that the figure of this world passes away.[35]

Let married couples, then, face up to the efforts needed, supported by the faith and hope which "do not disappoint . . . because God's love has been poured into our hearts through the Holy Spirit, Who has been given to us";[36] let them implore divine assistance by persevering prayer; above all, let them draw from the source of grace and charity in the Eucharist. And if sin should still keep its hold over them, let them not be discouraged, but rather have recourse with humble perseverance to the mercy of God, which is poured forth in the Sacrament of Penance. In this way they will be enabled to achieve the fulness of conjugal life described by the Apostle: "Husbands, love your wives, as Christ loved the Church. . . . Husbands should love their wives as their own bodies. He who loves his wife loves himself. For no man ever hates his own flesh, but nourishes and cherishes it, as Christ does the Church. . . . This is a great mystery, and I mean in reference to Christ and the Church. However, let each one of you love his wife as himself and let the wife see that she respects her husband".[37]

APOSTOLATE IN HOMES

26.   Among the fruits which ripen forth from a generous effort of fidelity to the divine law, one of the most precious is that married couples themselves not infrequently feel the desire to communicate their experience to others. Thus there comes to be included in the vast pattern of the vocation of the laity a new and most noteworthy form of the apostolate of like to like: it is married couples themselves who become apostles and guides to other married couples. This is assuredly, among so many forms of apostolate, one of those which seem most opportune today.[38]

TO DOCTORS AND MEDICAL PERSONNEL

27.   We hold those physicians and medical personnel in the highest esteem who, in the exercise of their profession, value above every human interest the superior demands of their Christian vocation. Let them persevere, therefore, in promoting on every occasion the discovery of solutions inspired by faith and right reason, let them strive to arouse this conviction and this respect in their associates. Let them also consider as their proper professional duty the task of acquiring all the knowledge needed in this delicate sector, so as to be able to give to those married persons who consult them wise counsel and healthy direction, such as they have a right to expect.

TO PRIESTS

28.   Beloved priest sons, by vocation you are the counsellors and spiritual guides of individual persons and of families. We now turn to you with confidence. Your first task—especially in the case of those who teach moral theology—is to expound the Church's teaching on marriage without ambiguity. Be the first to give, in the exercise of your ministry, the example of loyal internal and external obedience to the teaching authority of the Church. That obedience, as you know well, obliges not only because of the reasons adduced, but rather because of the light of the Holy Spirit, which is given in a particular way to the Pastors of the Church in order that they may illustrate the truth.[39] You know, too, that it is of the utmost importance, for peace of consciences and for the unity of the Christian people, that in the field of morals as well as in that of dogma, all should attend to the Magisterium of the Church, and all should speak the same language. Hence, with all Our heart We renew to you the heartfelt plea of the great Apostle Paul: "I appeal to you, brethren, by the name of

our Lord Jesus Christ, that all of you agree and that there be no dissensions among you, but that you be united in the same mind and the same judgement".[40]

29.   To diminish in no way the saving teaching of Christ constitutes an eminent form of charity for souls. But this must ever be accompanied by patience and goodness, such as the Lord Himself gave example of in dealing with men. Having come not to condemn but to save,[41] He was indeed intransigent with evil, but merciful towards individuals.

In their difficulties, may married couples always find, in the words and in the heart of a priest, the echo of the voice and the love of the Redeemer.

TO BISHOPS

30.   Beloved and Venerable Brothers in the Episcopate, with whom We most intimately share the solicitude of the spiritual good of the People of God, at the conclusion of this Encyclical Our reverent and affectionate thoughts turn to you. To all of you we extend an urgent invitation. At the head of the priests, your collaborators, and of your faithful, work ardently and incessantly for the safeguarding and the holiness of marriage, so that it may always be lived in its entire human and Christian fulness. Consider this mission as one of your most urgent responsibilities at the present time. As you know, it implies concerted pastoral action in all the fields of human activity, economic, cultural and social; for, in fact, only a simultaneous improvement in these various sectors will make it possible to render the life of parents and of children within their families not only tolerable, but easier and more joyous, to render the living together in human society more fraternal and peaceful, in faithfulness to God's design for the world.

Final Appeal

31.   Venerable Brothers, most beloved sons, and all men of good will, great indeed is the work of education, of progress and of love to which We call you, upon the foundation of the Church's teaching, of which the Successor of Peter is, together with His Brothers in the Episcopate, the depositary and interpreter. Truly a great work, as We are deeply convinced, both for the world and for the Church, since man cannot find true happiness—towards which he aspires with all his being—other than in respect of the laws written by God in his very nature, laws which he must

observe with intelligence and love. Upon this work, and upon all of you, and especially upon married couples, We invoke the abundant graces of the God of holiness and mercy, and in pledge thereof We impart to you all Our Apostolic Blessing.

Given at Rome, from Saint Peter's, this twenty-fifth day of July, Feast of Saint James the Apostle, in the year nineteen hundred and sixty-eight, the sixth of our Pontificate.

PAULUS PP. VI

NOTES

1. Cf. Pius IX, Encyclical *Qui Pluribus*, Nov. 9, 1846; in Pii IX P. M. Acta, I, pp. 9-10; St. Pius X, Encyc. *Singulari Quadam*, Sept. 24, 1912; in AAS IV (1912), p. 658; Pius XI, Encyc. *Casti Connubii*, Dec. 31, 1930; in AAS XXII (1930), pp. 579–581; Pius XII, Allocution *Magnificate Dominum* to the Episcopate of the Catholic world, Nov. 2, 1954; in AAS XLVI (1954), pp. 671–672; John XXIII, Encyc. *Mater et Magistra*, May 15, 1961; in AAS LIII (1961), p. 457.

2. Cf. Mt. 28, 18–19.

3. Cf. Mt. 7, 21.

4. Cf. *Catechismus Romanus Concilii Tridentini*, Part II, Ch. VIII; Leo XIII, Encyc. *Arcanum*, Feb. 10, 1880; in *Acta Leonis XIII*, II (1881), pp. 26–29; Pius XI, Encyc. *Divini Illius Magistri*, Dec. 31, 1929 in AAS XXII (1930), pp. 58–61; Encyc. *Casti Connubii*, in AAS XXII (1930), pp. 545–546; Pius XII, Alloc. to the Italian Medico-Biological Union of Saint Luke, Nov. 12, 1944, in *Discorsi e Radiomessaggi*, VI, pp. 191–192; to the Italian Catholic Union of Midwives, Oct. 29, 1951, in AAS XLIII (1951), pp. 857–859; to the Seventh Congress of the International Society of Haematology, Sept. 12, 1958, in AAS L (1958), pp. 734–735; John XXIII, Encyc. *Mater et Magistra*, in AAS LIII (1961), pp. 446–447; *Codex Iuris Canonici*, Canon 1067; Can. 1968, par. 1, Can. 1076 pars. 1–2; Second Vatican Council, Pastoral Constitution *Gaudium et Spes*, Nos. 47–52.

5. Cf. Paul VI, Allocution to the Sacred College, June 23, 1964, in AAS LVI (1964), p. 588; to the Commission for Study of Problems of Population, Family and Birth, March 27, 1965, in AAS LVII (1965), p. 388; to the National Congress of the Italian Society of Obstetrics and Gynaecology, Oct. 29, 1966, in AAS LVIII (1966), p. 1168.

6. Cf. I Jn. 4, 8.

7. Cf. Eph. 3, 15.

8. Cf. II Vat. Council, Pastoral Const. *Gaudium et Spes*, No. 50.

9. Cf. St. Thomas, *Summa Theologica*, I–II, Q. 94, Art. 2.

10. Cf. Pastoral Const. *Gaudium et Spes*, Nos. 50, 51.

11. *Ibid.*, No. 49.

12. Cf. Pius XI, Encyc. *Casti Connubii*, in AAS XXII (1930), p. 560; Pius XII, in AAS XLIII (1951), p. 843.

13. Cf. John XXIII, Encyc. *Mater et Magistra*, in AAS LIII (1961), p. 447.

14. Cf. *Catechismus Romanus Concilii Tridentini*, Part II, Ch. VIII; Pius XI, Encyc. *Casti Connubii*, in AAS XXII (1930), pp. 562–564; Pius XII, *Discorsi e Radiomessaggi*, VI (1944), pp.

191–192; AAS XLIII (1951), pp. 842–843; pp. 857–859; John XXIII, Encyc. *Pacem in Terris,* Apr. 11, 1963, in AAS LV (1963), pp. 259–260; *Gaudium et Spes,* No. 51.

15. Cf. Pius XI, Encyc. *Casti Connubii,* in AAS, XXII (1930), p. 565; Decree of the Holy Office, Feb. 22, 1940, in AAS L (1958), pp. 734–735.

16. *Cathechismus Romanus Concilii Tridentini,* Part II, Ch. VIII; Pius XI, Encyc. *Casti Connubii,* in AAS XXII (1930), pp. 559–561; Pius XII, AAS XLIII (1951), p. 843; AAS L (1958), pp. 734–735; John XXIII, Encyc. *Mater et Magistra,* in AAS LIII (1961), p. 447.

17. Cf. Pius XII, Alloc. to the National Congress of the Union of Catholic Jurists, Dec. 6, 1953, in AAS XLV (1953), pp. 798–799.

18. Cf. Rom. 3, 8.

19. Cf. Pius XII, Alloc. to Congress of the Italian Association of Urology, Oct. 8, 1953, in AAS XLV (1953), pp. 674–675; AAS L (1958), pp. 734–735.

20. Cf. Pius XII, AAS XLIII (1951), p. 846.

21. Cf. AAS XLV (1953), pp. 674–675; AAS XLVIII (1956), pp. 461–462.

22. Cf. Lk. 2, 34.

23. Cf. Paul VI, Encyc. *Populorum Progressio,* March 26, 1967, No. 21.

24. Cf. Rom. 8.

25. Cf. II Vatican Council, Decree *Inter Mirifica* on the media of Social Communication, Nos. 6–7.

26. Cf. Encyc. *Mater et Magistra,* in AAS LIII (1961), p. 447.

27. Cf. Encyc. *Populorum Progressio,* Nos. 48–55.

28. Cf. Pastoral Const. *Gaudium et Spes,* No. 52.

29. Cf. AAS XLIII (1951), p. 859.

30. Cf. Pastoral Const. *Gaudium et Spes,* No. 51.

31. Cf. Mt. 11, 30.

32. Cf. Pastoral Const. *Gaudium et Spes,* No. 48; II Vatican Council, Dogmatic Const. *Lumen Gentium,* No. 35.

33. Mt. 7, 14; cf. Hebr. 12, 11.

34. Cf. Tit. 2, 12.

35. Cf. I Cor. 7, 31.

36. Cf. Rom. 5,5.

37. Eph. 5, 25, 28–29, 32–33.

38. Cf. Dogmatic Const. *Lumen Gentium,* Nos. 35 and 41; Pastoral Const. *Gaudium et Spes,* Nos. 48–49; II Vatican Council, Decree *Apostolicam Actuositatem,* No. 11.

39. Cf. Dogmatic Const. *Lumen Gentium,* No. 25.

40. Cf. I Cor. 1, 10.

41. Cf. Jn. 3, 17.

Medellín Documents

Justice
Peace
Family and Demography
Poverty of the Church
(September 6, 1968)

Justice

I. Pertinent Facts

1.   There are in existence many studies of the Latin American people[1]. The misery that besets large masses of human beings in all of our countries is described in all of these studies. That misery, as a collective fact, expresses itself as injustice which cries to the heavens[2].

But what perhaps has not been sufficiently said is that in general the

[This translation is taken from *The Church in the Present-Day Transformation of Latin America in the Light of the Council,* vol. 2, *Conclusions,* the official English edition published by the Latin American Bureau of the United States Catholic Conference and the General Secretariat of the Latin American Episcopal Council (CELAM).The Medellín Conference (Second General Conference of Latin American Bishops) took place August 24–September 6, 1968, in Bogotá and Medellín, Colombia. The English translation appeared in 1970.]

efforts which have been made have not been capable of assuring that justice be honored and realized in every sector of the respective national communities. Often families do not find concrete possibilities for the education of their children. The young demand their right to enter universities or centers of higher learning for both intellectual and technical training; the women, their right to a legitimate equality with men; the peasants, better conditions of life; or if they are workers, better prices and security in buying and selling; the growing middle class feels frustrated by the lack of expectations. There has begun an exodus of professionals and technicians to more developed countries; the small businessmen and industrialists are pressed by greater interests and not a few large Latin American industrialists are gradually coming to be dependent on the international business enterprises. We cannot ignore the phenomenon of this almost universal frustration of legitimate aspirations which creates the climate of collective anguish in which we are already living.

2.   The lack of socio-cultural integration, in the majority of our countries, has given rise to the superimposition of cultures. In the economic sphere systems flourished which consider solely the potential of groups with great earning power. This lack of adaptation to the characteristics and to the potentials of all our people, in turn, gives rise to frequent political instability and the consolidation of purely formal institutions. To all of this must be added the lack of solidarity which, on the individual and social levels, leads to the committing of serious sins, evident in the unjust structures which characterize the Latin American situation.

II.   Doctrinal Bases

3.   The Latin American Church has a message for all men on this continent who "hunger and thirst after justice". The very God who creates men in his image and likeness, creates the "earth and all that is in it for the use of all men and all nations, in such a way that created goods can reach all in a more just manner"[3], and gives them power to transform and perfect the world in solidarity[4]. It is the same God who, in the fullness of time, sends his Son in the flesh, so that He might come to liberate all men from the slavery to which sin has subjected them[5]: hunger, misery, oppression and ignorance, in a word, that injustice and hatred which have their origin in human selfishness.

Thus, for our authentic liberation, all of us need a profound conversion so that "the kingdom of justice, love and peace", might come to us. The origin of all disdain for mankind, of all injustice, should be sought in the internal imbalance of human liberty, which will always need to be rectified in history. The uniqueness of the Christian message does not so much consist in the affirmation of the necessity for structural change, as it does in the insistence on the conversion of men which will in turn bring about this change. We will not have a new continent without new and reformed structures, but, above all, there will be no new continent without new men, who know how to be truly free and responsible according to the light of the Gospel.

4.   Only by the light of Christ is the mystery of man made clear. In the economy of salvation the divine work is an action of integral human development and liberation, which has love for its sole motive. Man is "created in Christ Jesus"[6], fashioned in Him as a " new creature"[7]. By faith and baptism he is transformed, filled with the gift of the Spirit, with a new dynamism, not of selfishness, but of love which compels him to seek out a new, more profound relationship with God, his fellow man, and created things.

Love, "the fundamental law of human perfection, and therefore of the transformation of the world"[8], is not only the greatest commandment of the Lord; it is also the dynamism which ought to motivate Christians to realize justice in the world, having truth as a foundation and liberty as their sign.

5.   This is how the Church desires to serve the world, radiating over it a light and life which heals and elevates the dignity of the human person[9], which consolidates the unity of society[10] and gives a more profound reason and meaning to all human activity.

Doubtless, for the Church, the fullness and perfection of the human vocation will be accomplished with the definitive inclusion of each man in the Passover or Triumph of Christ, but the hope of such a definitive realization, rather than lull, ought to "vivify the concern to perfect this earth. For here grows the body of the new human family, a body which even now is able to give some kind of foreshadowing of the new age"[11]. We do not confuse temporal progress and the Kingdom of Christ; nevertheless, the former, "to the extent that it can contribute to the better ordering of human society, is of vital concern to the Kingdom of God"[12].

The Christian quest for justice is a demand arising from biblical teaching. All men are merely humble stewards of material goods. In the search for salvation we must avoid the dualism which separates temporal tasks from the work of sanctification. Although we are encompassed with imperfections, we are men of hope. We have faith that our love for Christ and our brethren will not only be the great force liberating us from injustice and oppression, but also the inspiration for social justice, understood as a whole of life and as an impulse toward the integral growth of our countries.

III. Projections for Social Pastoral Planning

6.   Our pastoral mission is essentially a service of encouraging and educating the conscience of believers, to help them to perceive the responsibilities of their faith in their personal life and in their social life. This Second Episcopal Conference wishes to point out the most important demands, taking into account the value judgment which the latest Documents of the Magisterium of the Church have already made concerning the economic and social situation of the world of today and which applies fully to the Latin American continent.

DIRECTION OF SOCIAL CHANGE

7.   The Latin American Church encourages the formation of national communities that reflect a global organization, where all of the peoples but more especially the lower classes have, by means of territorial and functional structures, an active and receptive, creative and decisive participation in the construction of a new society. Those intermediary structures—between the person and the state—should be freely organized, without any unwarranted interference from authority or from dominant groups, in view of their development and concrete participation in the accomplishment of the total common good. They constitute the vital network of society. They are also the true expression of the citizens' liberty and unity.

a) The Family

8.   Without ignoring the unique character of the family, as the natural unit of society, we are considering it here as an intermediary structure, inasmuch as the families as a group ought to take up their function in the process of social change. Latin American families ought to organize their economic and cultural potential so that their legitimate needs and hopes be taken into account, on the levels where fundamental decisions are made, which can help or hinder them. In this way they will assume a role of effective representation and participation in the life of the total community.

Besides the dynamism which is generated in each country by the union of families, it is necessary that governments draw up legislation and a healthy and up-to-date policy governing the family.

b) *Professional Organization*

9.   The Second Latin American Episcopal Conference addresses itself to all those who, with daily effort, create the goods and services which favor the existence and development of human life. We refer especially to the millions of Latin American men and women who make up the peasant and working class. They, for the most part, suffer, long for and struggle for a change that will humanize and dignify their work. Without ignoring the totality of the significance of human work, here we refer to it as an intermediary structure, inasmuch as it constitutes the function which gives rise to professional organization in the field of production.

c) *Business Enterprises and the Economy*

10.   In today's world, production finds its concrete expression in business enterprises, the industrial as well as the rural; they constitute the dynamic and fundamental base of the integral economic process. The system of Latin American business enterprises, and through it the current economy, responds to an erroneous conception concerning the right of ownership of the means of production and the very goals of the economy. A business, in an authentically human economy, does not identify itself with the owners of capital, because it is fundamentally a community of persons and a unit of work, which is in need of capital to produce goods. A person or a group of persons cannot be the property of an individual, of a society, or of the state.

The system of liberal capitalism and the temptation of the Marxist system would appear to exhaust the possibilities of transforming the economic structures of our continent. Both systems militate against the dignity of the human person. One takes for granted the primacy of capital, its power and its discriminatory utilization in the function of profit-making. The other, although it ideologically supports a kind of humanism, is more concerned with collective man, and in practice becomes a totalitarian concentration of state power. We must denounce the fact that Latin America sees itself caught between these two options and remains dependent on one or other of the centers of power which control its economy.

Therefore, on behalf of Latin America, we make an urgent appeal to the businessmen, to their organizations and to the political authorities, so that they might radically modify the evaluation, the attitudes and the means regarding the goal, organization and functioning of business. All those financiers deserve encouragement who, individually or through their organizations, make an effort to conduct their business according to the guidelines supplied by the social teaching of the Church. That the social and economic change in Latin America be channeled towards a truly human economy will depend fundamentally on this.

11.   On the other hand this change will be essential in order to liberate the authentic process of Latin American development and integration. Many of our workers, although they gradually become conscious of the necessity for this change, simultaneously experience a situation of dependence on inhuman economic systems and institutions: a situation which, for many of them, borders on slavery, not only physical but also professional, cultural, civic and spiritual.

With the clarity which arises from the knowledge of man and of his hopes, we must reiterate that neither the combined value of capital nor the establishment of the most modern techniques of production, nor economic plans will serve man efficiently if the workers, the "necessary unity of direction" having been safeguarded, are not incorporated with all of the thrust of their humanity, by means of "the active participation of all in the running of the enterprise, according to ways which will have to be determined with care and on a macro-economic level, decisive nationally and internationally"[13].

d) Organization of the Workers

12.   Therefore, in the intermediary professional structure the peasants' and workers' unions, to which the workers have a right, should acquire sufficient strength and power. Their associations will have a unified and responsible strength, to exercise the right of representation and participation on the levels of production and of national, continental and international trade. They ought to exercise their right of being represented, also, on the social, economic and political levels, where decisions are made which touch upon the common good. Therefore, the unions ought to use every means at their disposal to train those who are to carry out these responsibilities in moral, economic, and especially in technical matters.

e) Unity of Action

13.   Socialization understood as a socio-cultural process of personalization and communal growth, leads us to think that all of the sectors of society, but in this case, principally the social-economic sphere, should,

because of justice and brotherhood, transcend antagonisms in order to become agents of national and continental development. Without this unity, Latin America will not be able to succeed in liberating itself from the neo-colonialism to which it is bound, nor will Latin America be able to realize itself in freedom, with its own cultural, socio-political and economic characteristics.

f) Rural Transformation

14.   The Second Episcopal Conference wishes to voice its pastoral concern for the extensive peasant class, which, although included in the above remarks, deserves urgent attention because of its special characteristics. If it is true that one ought to consider the diversity of circumstances and resources in the different countries, there is no doubt that there is a common denominator in all of them: the need for the human promotion of the peasants and Indians. This uplifting will not be viable without an authentic and urgent reform of agrarian structures and policies. This structural change and its political implications go beyond a simple distribution of land. It is indispensable to make an adjudication of such lands, under detailed conditions which legitimize their occupation and insure their productivity for the benefit of the families and the national economy. This will entail, aside from juridical and technical aspects not within our competence, the organization of the peasants into effective intermediate structures, principally in the form of cooperatives; and motivation towards the creation of urban centers in rural areas, which would afford the peasant population the benefits of culture, health, recreation, spiritual growth, participation in local decisions, and in those which have to do with the economy and national politics. This uplifting of the rural areas will contribute to the necessary process of industrialization and to participation in the advantages of urban civilization.

g) Industrialization

15.   There is no doubt that the process of industrialization is irreversible and is a necessary preparation for an independent economy and integration into the modern world-wide economy. Industrialization will be a decisive factor in raising the standard of living of our countries and affording them better conditions for an integral development. Therefore it is indispensable to revise plans and reorganize national macro-economies, preserving the legitimate autonomy of our nation, and allow-

ing for just grievances of the poorer nations and for the desired economic integration of the continent, respecting always the inalienable rights of the person and of intermediary structures, as protagonists of this process.

POLITICAL REFORM

16.   Faced with the need for a total change of Latin American structures, we believe that change has political reform as its pre-requisite.

The exercise of political authority and its decisions have as their only end the common good. In Latin America such authority and decision-making frequently seem to support systems which militate against the common good or which favor privileged groups. By means of legal norms, authority ought effectively and permanently to assure the rights and inalienable liberties of the citizens and the free functioning of inter-mediary structures.

Public authority has the duty of facilitating and supporting the creation of means of participation and legitimate representation of the people, or if necessary the creation of new ways to achieve it. We want to insist on the necessity of vitalizing and strengthening the municipal and communal organization, as a beginning of organizational efforts at the departmental, provincial, regional and national levels.

The lack of political consciousness in our countries makes the educational activity of the Church absolutely essential, for the purpose of bringing Christians to consider their participation in the political life of the nation as a matter of conscience and as the practice of charity in its most noble and meaningful sense for the life of the community.

INFORMATION AND "CONCIENTIZACIÓN"

17.   We wish to affirm that it is indispensable to form a social conscience and a realistic perception of the problems of the community and of social structures. We must awaken the social conscience and communal customs in all strata of society and professional groups regarding such values as dialogue and community living within the same group and relations with wider social groups (workers, peasants, professionals, clergy, religious, administrators, etc.).

This task of *"concientización"* and social education ought to be integrated into joint Pastoral Action at various levels.

18.   The sense of service and realism demands of today's hierarchy a greater social sensitivity and objectivity. In that regard there is a need for direct contact with the different social-professional groups in meetings which provide all with a more complete vision of social dynamics. Such

encounters are to be regarded as instruments which can facilitate a collegial action on the part of the bishops, guaranteeing harmony of thought and activities in the midst of a changing society.

The National Episcopal Conference will implement the organization of courses, meetings, etc., as a means of integrating those responsible for social activities related to pastoral plans. Besides priests and interested religious and laymen, invitations could be extended to heads of national and international development programs within the country. In like manner the institutes organized to prepare foreign apostolic personnel will coordinate their activities of a pastoral-social nature with the corresponding national groups; moreover, opportunities will be sought for promoting study weeks devoted to social issues in order to articulate social doctrine applying to our problems. This will allow us to affect public opinion.

19.   "Key men" deserve special attention; we refer to those persons at a decision-making level whose actions effect changes in the basic structures of national and international life. The Episcopal Conference, therefore, through its Commission on Social Action or Pastoral Service, will support, together with other interested groups, the organization of courses of study for technicians, politicians, labor leaders, peasants, managers and educated men of all levels of society.

20.   It is necessary that small basic communities be developed in order to establish a balance with minority groups, which are the groups in power. This is only possible through vitalization of these very communities by means of the natural innate elements in their environment.

The Church—the People of God—will lend its support to the downtrodden of every social class so that they might come to know their rights and how to make use of them. To this end the Church will utilize its moral strength and will seek to collaborate with competent professionals and institutions.

21.   The Commission of Justice and Peace should be supported in all our countries at least at the national level. It should be composed of persons of a high moral caliber, professionally qualified and representative of different social classes; it should be capable of establishing an effective dialogue with persons and institutions more directly responsible for the decisions which favor the common good and detect everything that can wound justice and endanger the internal and external peace of the national and international communities; it should help to find concrete means to obtain adequate solutions for each situation.

22.   For the implementation of their pastoral mission, the Episcopal Conferences will create Commissions of Social Action or Pastoral Service to develop doctrine and to take the initiative, presenting the Church as a

catalyst in the temporal realm in an authentic attitude of service. The same applies to the diocesan level.

Furthermore, the Episcopal Conferences and Catholic organizations will encourage collaboration on the national and continental scene with non-Catholic Christian Churches and institutions, dedicated to the task of restoring justice in human relations.

"Caritas", which is a Church organization[14] integrated in the joint Pastoral Plan, will not be solely a welfare institution, but rather will become operational in the developmental process of Latin America, as an institution authentically dedicated to its growth.

23.   The Church recognizes that these institutions of temporal activity correspond to the specific sphere of civic society, even though they are established and stimulated by Christians. In actual concrete situations this Second General Conference of Latin American Bishops feels it its duty to offer special encouragement to those organizations which have as their purpose human development and the carrying out of justice. The moral force of the Church will be consecrated, above all, to stimulate them, not acting except in a supplementary capacity and in situations that admit no delay.

Finally, this Second Conference is fully aware that the process of socialization, hastened by the techniques and media of mass communication, makes these means a necessary and proper instrument for social education and for *"concientización"* ordered to changing the structures and the observance of justice. For the same reason this Conference urges all, but especially laymen, to make full use of mass media in their work of human promotion.

NOTES

1. Cf. Synthesis of this situation in the *Work Paper* of the Second Conference of Latin American Bishops, Nos. 1-9.

2. Cf. Paul VI, Enc. *Populorum progressio*, No. 30.

3. Cf. Vatican Council II, pastoral constitution *Gaudium et spes*, No. 69.

4. Cf. Gn 1,26; Vatican Council II, pastoral constitution *Gaudium et spes*, No. 34.

5. Cf. Jn 8,32-35.

6. Cf. Eph 2,10.

7. Cf. 2Cor 5,17.

8. Cf. Vatican Council II, pastoral constitution *Gaudium et spes*, No. 38.

9. Cf. Vatican Council II, pastoral constitution *Gaudium et spes*, No. 41.

10. Cf. Vatican Council II, pastoral constitution *Gaudium et spes*, No. 42.

11. Cf. Vatican Council II, pastoral constitution *Gaudium et spes*, No. 39.

12. Cf. Vatican Council II, pastoral constitution *Gaudium et spes*, ibid.

13. Cf. Vatican Council II, pastoral constitution *Gaudium et spes*, No. 68.

14. Cf. Paul VI, Enc. *Populorum progressio*, No. 46.

Peace

I. The Latin American Situation and Peace

1.   If "development is the new name for peace"[1], Latin American under-development with its own characteristics in the different countries is an unjust situation which promotes tensions that conspire against peace.

We can divide these tensions into three major groups, selecting, in each of these, those variables which constitute a positive menace to the peace of our countries by manifesting an unjust situation.

When speaking of injustice, we refer to those realities that constitute a sinful situation; this does not mean however, that we are overlooking the fact that at times the misery in our countries can have natural causes which are difficult to overcome.

In making this analysis, we do not ignore or fail to give credit to the positive efforts made at every level to build a more just society. We do not include this here because our purpose is to call attention to those aspects which constitute a menace or negation of peace.

TENSIONS BETWEEN CLASSES AND INTERNAL COLONIALISM

2.   *Different forms of marginality:* Socio-economic, cultural, political, racial, religious, in urban as well as rural sectors;

3.   *Extreme inequality among social classes:* Especially, though not exclusively, in those countries which are characterized by a marked bi-classism, where a few have much (culture, wealth, power, prestige) while the majority has very little. The Holy Father describes this situation when directing himself to the Colombian rural workers; " . . . social and economic development has not been equitable in the great continent of Latin America; and while it has favored those who helped establish it in the beginning, it has neglected the masses of native population, which are almost always left at a subsistence level and at times are mistreated and exploited harshly"[2].

4.   *Growing frustrations:* The universal phenomenon of rising expectations assumes a particularly aggressive dimension in Latin America. The reason is obvious: excessive inequalities systematically prevent the satisfaction of the legitimate aspirations of the ignored sectors, and breed increasing frustrations.

The same low morale is obtained in those middle classes which, when confronting grave crises, enter into a process of disintegration and proletarization.

5.   *Forms of oppression of dominant groups and sectors:* Without excluding the eventuality of willful oppression, these forms manifest themselves most frequently in a lamentable insensitivity of the privileged sectors to the misery of the marginated sectors. Thus the words of the Pope to the leaders: "That your ears and heart be sensitive to the voices of those who ask for bread, concern, justice . . . "[3].

It is not unusual to find that these groups, with the exception of some enlightened minorities, characterize as subversive activities all attempts to change the social system which favors the permanence of their privileges.

6.   *Power unjustly exercised by certain dominant sectors:* As a natural consequence of the above-mentioned attitudes, some members of the dominant sectors occasionally resort to the use of force to repress drastically any attempt at opposition. It is easy for them to find apparent ideological justifications (anti-communism) or practical ones (keeping "order") to give their action an honest appearance.

7.   *Growing awareness of the oppressed sectors:* All the above results are even more intolerable as the oppressed sectors become increasingly aware of their situation. The Holy Father referred to them when he said to the rural workers: "But today the problem has worsened because you have become more aware of your needs and suffering, and you cannot tolerate the persistence of these conditions without applying a careful remedy"[4].

The static picture described in the above paragraphs is worsened when it is projected into the future: basic education will increase awareness, and the demographic explosion will multiply problems and tensions. One must not forget the existence of movements of all types interested in taking advantage of and irritating these tensions. Therefore, if today peace seems seriously endangered, the automatic aggravation of the problems will produce explosive consequences.

INTERNATIONAL TENSIONS AND EXTERNAL NEOCOLONIALISM

8.   We refer here, particularly, to the implications for our countries of dependence on a center of economic power, around which they gravitate. For this reason, our nations frequently do not own their goods, or have a say in economic decisions affecting them. It is obvious that this will not

fail to have political consequences given the interdependence of these two fields.

We are interested in emphasizing two aspects of this phenomenon.

9.   *Economic aspect:* We only analyze those factors having greater influence on the global and relative impoverishment of our countries, and which constitute a source of internal and external tensions.

a) *Growing distortion of international commerce:* Because of the relative depreciation of the terms of exchange, the value of raw materials is increasingly less in relation to the cost of manufactured products. This means that the countries which produce raw materials—especially if they are dependent upon one major export—always remain poor, while the industrialized countries enrich themselves. This injustice clearly denounced by *Populorum progressio*[5], nullifies the eventual positive effect of external aid and constitutes a permanent menace against peace, because our countries sense that "one hand takes away what the other hand gives"[6].

b) *Rapid flight of economic and human capital:* The search for security and individual gain leads many members of the more comfortable sectors of our countries to invest their money in foreign countries. The injustice of such procedures has already been denounced categorically by the encyclical *Populorum progressio*[7]. To this can be added the loss of technicians and competent personnel, which is at least as serious and perhaps more so than the loss of capital, because of the high cost of training these people and because of their ability to teach others.

c) *Tax evasion and loss of gains and dividends:* Some foreign companies working in our country (also some national firms) often evade the established tax system by subterfuge. We are also aware that at times they send their profits and dividends abroad, without contributing adequate reinvestments to the progressive development of our countries.

d) *Progressive debt:* It is not surprising to find that in the system of international credits, the true needs and capabilities of our countries are not taken into account. We thus run the risk of encumbering ourselves with debts whose payment absorbs the greater part of our profits[8].

e) *International monopolies and international imperialism of money:* We wish to emphasize that the principal guilt for economic dependence of our countries rests with powers, inspired by uncontrolled desire for gain, which leads to economic dictatorship and the "international imperialism of money"[9] condemned by Pope Pius XI in *Quadragesimo anno* and by Pope Paul VI in *Populorum progressio*.

10.   *Political aspect:* We here denounce the imperialism of any ideolog-

ical bias that is exercised in Latin America either indirectly or through direct intervention.

TENSIONS AMONG THE COUNTRIES OF LATIN AMERICA

11.   We here denounce the particular phenomenon of historico-political origin that continues to disturb cordial relations among some countries and impedes truly constructive collaboration. Nevertheless, the integration process, well understood, presents itself as a commanding necessity for Latin America. Without pretending to set norms of a truly complex, technical nature, governing integration, we deem it opportune to point out its multi-dimensional character. Integration, in effect, is not solely an economic process; it has a broader dimension reflected in the way in which it embraces man in his total situation: social, political, cultural, religious, racial.

Among the factors that increase the tensions among our countries we underline:

12.   An *exacerbated nationalism* in some countries: The Holy Father[10] has already denounced the unwholesomeness of this attitude, especially on a matter where the weakness of the national economies requires a union of efforts.

13.   *Armaments:* In certain countries an arms race is under way that surpasses the limits of reason. It frequently stems from a fictitious need to respond to diverse interests rather than to a true need of the national community. In that respect, a phrase of *Populorum progressio* is particularly pertinent: "When so many communities are hungry, when so many homes suffer misery, when so many men live submerged in ignorance . . . any arms race becomes an intolerable scandal"[11].

II. Doctrinal Reflexion

CHRISTIAN VIEW OF PEACE

14.   The above mentioned Christian viewpoint on peace adds up to a negation of peace such as Christian tradition understands it.

Three factors characterize the Christian concept of peace:

a) Peace is, above all, a work of justice[12]. It presupposes and requires the establishment of a just order[13] in which men can fulfill themselves as men, where their dignity is respected, their legitimate aspirations satisfied, their access to truth recognized, their personal freedom guaranteed;

an order where man is not an object, but an agent of his own history. Therefore, there will be attempts against peace where unjust inequalities among men and nations prevail[14].

Peace in Latin America, therefore, is not the simple absence of violence and bloodshed. Oppression by the power groups may give the impression of maintaining peace and order, but in truth it is nothing but the "continuous and inevitable seed of rebellion and war"[15].

"Peace can only be obtained by creating a new order which carries with it a more perfect justice among men"[16]. It is in this sense that the integral development of a man, the path to more human conditions, becomes the symbol of peace.

b) Secondly, peace is a permanent task[17]. A community becomes a reality in time and is subject to a movement that implies constant change in structures, transformation of attitudes, and conversion of hearts.

The "tranquility of order", according to the Augustinian definition of peace, is neither passivity nor conformity. It is not something that is acquired once and for all. It is the result of continuous effort and adaptation to new circumstances, to new demands and challenges of a changing history. A static and apparent peace may be obtained with the use of force; an authentic peace implies struggle, creative abilities and permanent conquest[18].

Peace is not found, it is built. The Christian man is the artisan of peace[19]. This task, given the above circumstances, has a special character in our continent; thus, the People of God in Latin America, following the example of Christ, must resist personal and collective injustice with v   'fish courage and fearlessness.

    Finally, peace is the fruit of love[20]. It is the expression of true fraternity among men, a fraternity given by Christ, Prince of Peace, in reconciling all men with the Father. Human solidarity cannot truly take effect unless it is done in Christ, who gives Peace that the world cannot give[21]. Love is the soul of justice. The Christian who works for social justice should always cultivate peace and love in his heart.

Peace with God is the basic foundation of internal and social peace. Therefore, where this social peace does not exist there will we find social, political, economic and cultural inequalities, there will we find the rejection of the peace of the Lord, and a rejection of the Lord Himself[22].

THE PROBLEM OF VIOLENCE IN LATIN AMERICA

15.   Violence constitutes one of the gravest problems in Latin America. A decision on which the future of the countries of the continent will depend should not be left to the impulses of emotion and passion. We

would be failing in our pastoral duty if we were not to remind the conscience, caught in this dramatic dilemma, of the criteria derived from the Christian doctrine of evangelical love.

No one should be suprised if we forcefully re-affirm our faith in the productiveness of peace. This is our Christian ideal. "Violence is neither Christian nor evangelical"[23]. The Christian man is peaceful and not ashamed of it. He is not simply a pacifist, for he can fight[24], but he prefers peace to war. He knows that "violent changes in structures would be fallacious, ineffectual in themselves and not conforming to the dignity of man, which demands that the necessary changes take place from within, that is to say, through a fitting awakening of conscience, adequate preparation and effective participation of all, which the ignorance and often inhuman conditions of life make it impossible to assure at this time"[25].

16.   As the Christian believes in the productiveness of peace in order to achieve justice, he also believes that justice is a prerequisite for peace. He recognizes that in many instances Latin America finds itself faced with a situation of injustice that can be called institutionalized violence, when, because of a structural deficiency of industry and agriculture, of national and international economy, of cultural and political life, "whole towns lack necessities, live in such dependence as hinders all initiative and responsibility as well as every possibility for cultural promotion and participation in social and political life"[26], thus violating fundamental rights. This situation demands all-embracing, courageous, urgent and profoundly renovating transformations. We should not be surprised therefore, that the "temptation to violence" is surfacing in Latin America. One should not abuse the patience of a people that for years has borne a situation that would not be acceptable to any one with any degree of awareness of human rights.

Facing a situation which works so seriously against the dignity of man and against peace, we address ourselves, as pastors, to all the members of the Christian community, asking them to assume their responsibility in the promotion of peace in Latin America.

17.   We would like to direct our call in the first place to those who have a greater share of wealth, culture and power. We know that there are leaders in Latin America who are sensitive to the needs of the people and try to remedy them. They recognize that the privileged many times join together, and with all the means at their disposal pressure those who govern, thus obstructing necessary changes. In some instances, this pressure takes on drastic proportions which result in the destruction of life and property.

Therefore, we urge them not to take advantage of the pacifist position of the Church in order to oppose, either actively or passively, the profound transformations that are so necessary. If they jealously retain their privileges and defend them through violence they are responsible to history for provoking "explosive revolutions of despair"[27]. The peaceful future of the countries of Latin America depends to a large extent on their attitude.

18.   Also responsible for injustice are those who remain passive for fear of the sacrifice and personal risk implied by any courageous and effective action. Justice, and therefore peace, conquer by means of a dynamic action of awakening (concientización) and organization of the popular sectors, which are capable of pressing public officials who are often impotent in their social projects without popular support.

19.   We address ourselves finally to those who, in the face of injustice and illegitimate resistance to change, put their hopes in violence. With Paul VI we realize that their attitude "frequently finds its ultimate motivation in noble impulses of justice and solidarity"[28]. Let us not speak here of empty words which do not imply personal responsibility and which isolate from the fruitful non-violent actions that are immediately possible.

If it is true that revolutionary insurrection can be legitimate in the case of evident and prolonged "tyranny that seriously works against the fundamental rights of man, and which damages the common good of the country"[29], whether it proceeds from one person or from clearly unjust structures, it is also certain that violence or "armed revolution" generally "generates new injustices, introduces new imbalances and causes new disasters; one cannot combat a real evil at the price of a greater evil"[30].

If we consider then, the totality of the circumstances of our countries, and if we take into account the Christian preference for peace, the enormous difficulty of a civil war, the logic of violence, the atrocities it engenders, the risk of provoking foreign intervention, illegitimate as it may be, the difficulty of building a regime of justice and freedom while participating in a process of violence, we earnestly desire that the dynamism of the awakened and organized community be put to the service of justice and peace.

Finally, we would like to make ours the words of our Holy Father to the newly ordained priests and deacons in Bogota, when he referred to all the suffering and said to them: "We will be able to understand their afflictions and change them, not into hate and violence, but into the strong and peaceful energy of constructive works"[31].

III. Pastoral Conclusions

20.   In the face of the tensions which conspire against peace, and even present the temptation of violence; in the face of the Christian concept of

peace which has been described, we believe that the Latin American Episcopate cannot avoid assuming very concrete responsibilities; because to create a just social order, without which peace is illusory, is an eminently Christian task.

To us, the Pastors of the Church, belongs the duty to educate the Christian conscience, to inspire, stimulate and help orient all of the initiatives that contribute to the formation of man. It is also up to us to denounce everything which, opposing justice, destroys peace.

In this spirit we feel it opportune to bring up the following pastoral points:

21.   To awaken in individuals and communities, principally through mass media, a living awareness of justice, infusing in them a dynamic sense of responsibility and solidarity.

22.   To defend the rights of the poor and oppressed according to the Gospel commandment, urging our governments and upper classes to eliminate anything which might destroy social peace: injustice, inertia, venality, insensibility.

23.   To favor integration, energetically denouncing the abuses and unjust consequences of the excessive inequalities between poor and rich, weak and powerful.

24.   To be certain that our preaching, liturgy and catechesis take into account the social and community dimensions of Christianity, forming men committed to world peace.

25.   To achieve in our schools, seminaries and universities a healthy critical sense of the social situation and foster the vocation of service. We also consider very efficacious the diocesan and national campaigns that mobilize the faithful and social organizations, leading them to a similar reflection.

26.   To invite various Christian and non-Christian communities to collaborate in this fundamental task of our times.

27.   To encourage and favor the efforts of the people to create and develop their own grass-roots organizations for the redress and consolidation of their rights and the search for true justice.

28.   To request the perfecting of the administration of justice, whose deficiencies often cause serious ills.

29.   To urge a halt and revision in many of our countries of the arms race that at times constitutes a burden excessively disproportionate to the legitimate demands of the common good, to the detriment of desperate social necessities. The struggle against misery is the true war that our nations should face.

30.   To invite the bishops, the leaders of different churches and all

men of good will of the developed nations to promote in their respective
spheres of influence, especially among the political and financial leaders,
a consciousness of greater solidarity facing our underdeveloped nations,
obtaining among other things, just prices for our raw materials.

31.   On the occasion of the twentieth anniversary of the solemn declaration of Human Rights, to interest universities in Latin America to
undertake investigations to verify the degree of its implementation in our
countries.

32.   To denounce the unjust action of world powers that works against
self-determination of weaker nations who must suffer the bloody consequences of war and invasion, and to ask competent international organizations for effective and decisive procedures.

33.   To encourage and praise the initiatives and works of all those who
in the diverse areas of action contribute to the creation of a new order
which will assure peace in our midst.

NOTES

1. Cf. Paul VI, Enc. *Populorum progressio*, No. 87.
2. Cf. Paul VI, *Address to the Peasants*, Mosquera, Colombia, 23 August, 1968.
3. Cf. Paul VI, *Homily of the Mass on Development Day*, Bogotá, 23 August, 1968.
4. Cf. Paul VI, *Address to the Peasants*, Mosquera, Colombia, 23 August, 1968.
5. Cf. Paul VI, Enc. *Populorum progressio*, Nos. 56-61.
6. Cf. Ibid., No. 56.
7. Cf. Ibid., No. 24.
8. Cf. Ibid., No. 54.
9. Cf. Ibid., No. 26.
10. Cf. Ibid., No. 62.
11. Cf. Ibid., No. 53.
12. Cf. Vatican Council II, pastoral constitution *Gaudium et spes*, No. 78.
13. Cf. John XXIII, Enc. *Pacem in terris*, No. 167 and Paul VI, Enc. *Populorum progressio*, No. 76.
14. Cf. Paul VI, *Message of January 1st, 1968*.
15. Cf. Paul VI, *Message of January 1st, 1968*.
16. Cf. Paul VI, Enc. *Populorum progressio*, No. 76.
17. Cf. Vatican Council II, pastoral constitution *Gaudium et spes*, No. 78.
18. Cf. Paul VI, *Christmas Message, 1967*.
19. Cf. Mt 5,9.
20. Cf. Vatican Council II, pastoral constitution *Gaudium et spes*, No. 78.
21. Cf. Jn 14,27.
22. Cf. Mt 25,31-46.
23. Cf. Paul VI, *Homily of the Mass on Development Day*, Bogotá, 23 August, 1968; Cf. Paul VI, *Opening address at the Second General Conference of Latin American Bishops*, Bogotá, 24 August, 1968.

24. Cf. Paul VI, *Message of January 1st, 1968.*
25. Cf. Paul VI, *Homily of the Mass on Development Day*, Bogotá, 23 August, 1968.
26. Cf. Paul VI, Enc. *Populorum progressio*, No. 30.
27. Cf. Paul VI, *Homily of the Mass on Development Day*, Bogotá, 23 August, 1968.
28. Cf. Paul VI, ibid.
29. Cf. Paul VI, Enc. *Populorum progressio*, No. 31.
30. Cf. Paul VI, Enc. *Populorum progressio*, No. 31.
31. Cf. Paul VI, *Address to new priests and deacons*, Bogotá, 22 August, 1968.

Family and Demography

1.   For various reasons it is difficult to reflect on the family in Latin America: because the idea of the family is bound up with extremely diversified sociological realities; because the family has suffered, perhaps more than other institutions, from the impact of social change and transformation, change that cannot always be adequately depicted; because in Latin America the family suffers heavily from the consequences of the vicious circles of underdevelopment: sub-standard conditions of life and culture, low health level, restricted buying power, etc.

I. The Family in Transition in Latin America

2.   In Latin America, as in other areas of the world, the family is feeling the influence of four fundamental social phenomena:

a) The transition from a rural to an urban society which leads patriarchal families to adopt a new life style of greater intimacy, with better distribution of responsibilities and more dependence on other micro-societies.

b) The developmental process brings abundant riches to some families, insecurity to others, and a marginal social existence to the rest.

c) The rapid demographic growth, while it should not be regarded as the only definite demographic variable and much less as the cause of all of Latin America's ills, still does engender various problems, both in the socio-economic and the ethical and religious orders.

d) The socialization process, which deprives the family of some aspects of its social importance and its spheres of influence, but which leaves intact its essential values and its property of being the basic institution of society in general.

3.   These phenomena produce certain repercussions among Latin American families that cause serious problems. Given the impossibility of categorizing them all, we note those that appear to have the greater transcendence, more frequent occurrence, or greater socio-pastoral effects:

a) Extremely low marriage rate; Latin America has the lowest indices of marriage in relation to population. This indicates a high percentage of illegal unions, aleatory and almost without stability, with all the resulting consequences.

b) High percentage of casual unions and illegitimate births, a factor weighing heavily on the demographic explosion.

c) High and increasing rate of family disintegration, by divorce, so widely accepted and legalized, by desertion of the home (almost always on the part of the father), by sexual disorders born of a false concept of masculinity.

d) Stress on hedonism and eroticism as a result of the enervating propaganda put forth by a society of consumption.

e) Disparity between salaries and the real needs of the family.

f) Serious housing problems due to faulty and inadequate policies.

g) Poor distribution of consumer goods and the advantages of civilization, for example, food, clothing, work, means of communication, rest and recreation, culture, etc.

h) Moral and material impossibility of many young people to establish a well-ordered home, which accounts for the presence of many deteriorated family cells.

Our pastoral duty impels us to make an urgent appeal to those who govern and to all who have any responsibility in the matter to acknowledge the importance of the family in the construction of a temporal city worthy of man, and assist in overcoming the grave ills which afflict it and which can prevent the complete fulfillment of its mission.

II. The Role of the Family in Latin America

4.   "The power and strength of the institution of marriage and the family can also be seen in the fact that time and again, despite the difficulties produced, the profound changes in modern society reveal the true character of this institution in one way or another"[1].

It is necessary, therefore, to consider the fundamental values proclaimed by the Church in order to structure a pastoral action which will lead the Latin American family to acquire and preserve the values that enable it to fulfill its mission. We will single out three areas in which the family plays an important role: formation of personalities, education in the faith, promotion of development.

FORMATION OF PERSONALITIES

5.   "The family has received from God its mission to be the first and vital cell of society"[2].

"For it devolves on parents to create a family atmosphere so animated with love and reverence for God and men that a well-rounded personal and social development will be fostered among children"[3].

"It remains each man's duty to preserve a view of the whole human person, a view in which the values of intellect, will, conscience, and fraternity are present . . . The family is, as it were, the primary mother and nurse of this attitude"[4].

This doctrine of Vatican Council II highlights the need for the family to fulfill its commitment of forming complete personalities, for which task it is eminently suited. In fact, the presence and influence of the distinct and complementary masculine and feminine models of the parents, the bond of mutual affection, the atmosphere of trust, intimacy, respect and freedom which permeates the social framework governed by a natural hierarchy, all these elements enable the family to mold strong and balanced personalities for society.

EDUCATION IN THE FAITH

6.   "Christian husbands and wives are cooperators in grace and witnesses of faith on behalf of each other, their children and all others in their household. They are the first to communicate the faith to their children and to educate them . . . "[5]. "They should imbue their offspring, lovingly welcomed from God, with Christian truths and evangelical virtues"[6], and they should do this "by their word and example"[7]. "As a result, with their parents leading the way by example and family prayer, children and indeed everyone gathered around the family hearth will find a readier path to human maturity, salvation and holiness"[8].

We know that many families in Latin America have been incapable of educating in the faith, either because they are not stable or because they have disintegrated, and others because they have imparted this education in purely traditional terms, at times with mythical and superstitious aspects. From this situation springs the necessity of bestowing on today's families the elements which will rebuild their evangelizing capacity in accordance with the doctrine of the Church.

PROMOTION OF DEVELOPMENT

7.   "The family is the first school of those social virtues which every society needs . . . Here too, they (the children) gain their first experience of wholesome human companionship . . . and it is through the family that they are gradually introduced into civic partnership with their fellow men, and into the People of God"[9].

Besides, "the family is a kind of school of deeper humanity"[10] and "the fullest humanism is integral development"[11]. "The family is the foundation of society. In it the various generations come together and help one another to grow wiser and to harmonize personal rights with the other requirements of social life"[12]. "There, in an atmosphere of love, children can more easily learn the true structure of reality. There, too, tested forms of human culture impress themselves upon the mind of the developing adolescent in a kind of automatic way"[13]. "In the family, parents have the task of training their children from childhood to recognize God's love for all men. Especially by example they should teach them little by little to show concern for the material and spiritual needs of their neighbor"[14]. The family will fulfill its mission if it " . . . promotes justice and other good works for the service of all brethren in need"[15]. Hence it follows that "the well-being of the individual person and of human and Christian society is intimately linked with the healthy condition of that community produced by marriage and family"[16], because the family is such an important factor in development.

"All those, therefore, who exercise influence over communities and social groups should work efficiently for the welfare of marriage and the family"[17].

III. Demographic Problems in Latin America

8.   In our continent the demographic problem is characterized by a peculiar complexity and delicacy: speaking in general, it is true that there exists a rapid population growth due more to the falling index of infant mortality and rising index of life expectancy than to an increase in births. But it is likewise certain that because the majority of our countries are under-populated, a demographic increase is a prerequisite of develop-

ment. However, the excessively low socio-economic-cultural conditions militate against a pronounced demographic increase.

9.   As pastors, sensitive to the problems of our people, making ours their sorrows and afflictions we feel it is necessary to discuss some fundamental issues. A one-sided approach, like every simplistic solution to these problems, is incomplete and therefore mistaken. The adoption of a policy of birth control that tends to supplant, substitute, or relegate to oblivion a more demanding, but the only acceptable, policy of development, is particularly harmful. "The problem, in fact, is not to decrease the number of those who eat, but rather to multiply the bread"[18].

10.   The encyclical *Humanae vitae*, which like *Populorum progressio* emphasizes social problems, has special importance for our continent. *Humanae vitae:*

a) Stresses the urgency to confront the challenge of demographic problems with an integral answer focusing on development.

b) Denounces all policies based on indiscriminate birth control advocated at any price and in any way, especially when such a policy is a condition for receiving economic aid.

c) Strongly upholds inalienable values such as: respect for the human person, especially for the poor and the social outcasts; the value of life; and conjugal love.

d) Invites and stimulates couples to achieve their full formation as persons through self-education, learning to exercise self-control, to reject solutions easy but dangerous by virtue of their alienating and deforming qualities, to acknowledge the necessity of God's grace to fulfill the law, to see the faith as giving meaning to existence and to build a new humanism freed from the eroticism of bourgeois civilization.

11.   The application of that part of the encyclical which refers to conjugal ethics, as the Pope himself recognizes, "will surely appear to many to be difficult and even impossible to practice"[19]. Cognizant of those difficulties, and sympathizing with the questions and anguish of all our children, we pledge our support to all without distinction, but we point out the following in a special way to those who listen to the words of the Pope and try to live the ideal they set forth:

a) The teaching of the Magisterium forbidding the voluntary use of artificial means that thwart the conjugal act is clear and unmistakable in the encyclical.

b) But the Holy Father himself reaffirmed on the occasion of the opening of this Conference: "This norm does not solicit a blind race towards over-population; nor does it diminish the responsibility or the freedom of married couples, to whom it does not prohibit honest and reasonable birth control, nor impede the use of legitimate therapeutics or the progress of scientific investigations"[20].

c) The sacramental life, above all as a means towards a progressive growth in human and Christian maturity in marriage, is a right and even a duty, and it is our responsibility as pastors to facilitate that way for Christian couples.

d) The mutual help that couples give each other on coming together, supported by experts in the human sciences and by priests imbued with the pastoral spirit, can be incalculable for those who try to attain the ideal set forth in spite of the difficulties.

e) We state our intention, and we will try to fulfill it. Not only will we, "with the heart of the Good Shepherd . . . lend our service to souls in these great difficulties"[21], but we especially re-affirm our solidarity with the couples who suffer, through the example of our own personal and collective abnegation, in true poverty, in celibacy accepted sincerely and lived seriously and joyfully, in patience and dedication to men, in obedience to the Word of God, and above all in charity carried to heroism.

IV. Guidelines for Pastoral Care of Families

12.   Due to various historical, ethnic, sociological and even regional characteristics, the institution of the family has always enjoyed a tremendous importance in all of Latin America.

It is true that in the large cities it loses some of its preeminence. However, in the rural areas, which still make up the greater part of the continent in spite of all the external changes, the family continues to play a fundamental role in the social, cultural, ethical and religious spheres.

For this reason, and even more in virtue of its primacy in the formation of personalities, education in the faith, and promotion of development, and especially with the purpose of curing all the deficiencies which afflict it and which have grave repercussions, we consider it necessary to give the pastoral care of families priority in the structure of joint pastoral plans. We suggest that policy be determined after securing the advice of married couples, who by their human experience and the divine gifts of the sacrament of matrimony can assist effectively in such planning.

The pastoral care of families ought to be governed by certain fundamental guidelines:

13.   To ensure that adolescents receive a solid education for love that

integrates and at the same time goes beyond simple sex education, inculcating in the young of both sexes sensitivity to and awareness of fundamental values such as love, respect, gift of self.

14.   To encourage and make actually available to all young couples a preparatory marriage course which would include instruction in different aspects: physical, sociological, juridical, moral and spiritual.

15.   To formulate and diffuse a spirituality of marriage based on a clear understanding of the role of the laity in the world and in the Church and on a theology of matrimony as a sacrament.

16.   To inculcate in the young in general and above all in young couples the knowledge and conviction of a really responsible fatherhood.

17.   To awaken in husbands and wives the necessity for conjugal dialogue that leads to profound union with each other and to a spirit of co-responsibility and collaboration.

18.   To facilitate the dialogue between parents and children that will help to overcome the generation gap in the family circle and make of the home "a place where the various generations come together"[22].

19.   To make the family truly a "domestic Church": a community of faith, of prayer, of love, of evangelizing action, a school of catechesis.

20.   To lead all families to a more open relationship with each other, including those of different Christian denominations, and above all with marginal families or families in the process of disintegration; and openness to society, the world and the life of the Church.

21.   We wish, finally, to encourage those married couples who make an effort to live in conjugal sanctity and carry out the family apostolate, and those who, "with wise and common deliberation and with gallant hearts undertake to bring up suitably even a relatively large family"[23].

The pastoral care of families, if well planned and carried out by such meritorious organizations as family movements, can undoubtedly transform our families into a living force (and not, as could well happen, into a dead weight) at the service of the building up of the Church, of the works of development and of the changes our continent needs.

NOTES

1. Cf. Vatican Council II, pastoral constitution *Gaudium et spes*, No. 47.
2. Cf. Vatican Council II, decree *Apostolicam actuositatem*, No. 11.
3. Cf. Vatican Council II, declaration *Gravissimum educationis*, No. 3.
4. Cf. Vatican Council II, pastoral constitution *Gaudium et spes*, No. 61.
5. Cf. Vatican Council II, decree *Apostolicam actuositatem*, No. 11.

6. Cf. Vatican Council II, dogmatic constitution *Lumen gentium*, No. 41.

7. Cf. Ibid., No.11.

8. Cf. Vatican Council II, pastoral constitution *Gaudium et spes*, No. 48.

9. Cf. Vatican Council II, declaration *Gravissimum educationis*, No. 3.

10. Cf. Vatican Council II, pastoral constitution *Gaudium et spes*, No. 52.

11. Cf. Paul VI, Enc. *Populorum progressio*, No. 16.

12. Cf. Vatican Council II, pastoral constitution *Gaudium et spes*, No. 52.

13. Cf. Ibid., No. 61.

14. Cf. Vatican Council II, decree *Apostolicam actuositatem*, No. 30.

15. Cf. Ibid., No. 11.

16. Cf. Vatican Council II, pastoral constitution *Gaudium et spes*, No. 47.

17. Cf. Ibid., No. 52.

18. Cf. Paul VI, *Address to the United Nations*, No. 27, 4 October, 1965.

19. Cf. Paul VI, Enc. *Humanae vitae*, No. 20.

20. Cf. Paul VI, *Opening address at the Second General Conference of Latin American Bishops*, Bogotá, 24 August, 1968.

21. Cf. Ibid.

22. Cf. Vatican Council II, pastoral constitution *Gaudium et spes*, No. 52.

23. Cf. Ibid., No. 50.

Poverty of the Church

I. Latin American Scene

1.   The Latin American bishops cannot remain indifferent in the face of the tremendous social injustices existent in Latin America, which keep the majority of our peoples in dismal poverty, which in many cases becomes inhuman wretchedness.

2.   A deafening cry pours from the throats of millions of men, asking their pastors for a liberation that reaches them from nowhere else. "Now you are listening to us in silence, but we hear the shout which arises from your suffering", the Pope told the "campesinos" in Colombia[1].

And complaints that the hierarchy, the clergy, the religious, are rich and allied with the rich also come to us. On this point we must make it clear that appearance is often confused with reality. Many causes have contributed to create this impression of a rich hierarchical Church. The great buildings, the rectories and religious houses that are better than those of the neighbors, the often luxurious vehicles, the attire, inherited from other eras, have been some of those causes.

The system of taxes and tuition to support clergy and maintain educational endeavors has become discredited and has led to the formation of erroneous opinions about the amount of money received.

To this has been added the exaggerated secrecy in which the finances of high schools, parishes and dioceses have been shrouded, favoring a mysterious atmosphere which magnifies shadows to gigantic proportions and helps to create fictions. Besides, isolated cases of reprehensible opulence have been generalized.

All this has helped substantiate the argument that the Latin American Church is rich.

3.   The reality of the very great number of parishes and dioceses that are extremely poor, and the exceeding number of bishops, priests and religious who live in complete deprivation and give themselves with great abnegation to the service of the poor, generally escapes the appreciation of many and does not succeed in dissipating the prevailing distorted image.

Within the context of the poverty and even of the wretchedness in which the great majority of the Latin American people live, we, bishops, priests and religious, have the necessities of life and a certain security, while the poor lack that which is indispensable and struggle between *anguish* and *uncertainty*. And incidents are not lacking in which the poor feel that their bishops, or pastors and religious, do not really identify themselves with them, with their problems and afflictions, that they do not always support those that work with them or plead their cause.

II. Doctrinal Motivation

4.   We must distinguish:

a) Poverty, as a lack of the goods of this world necessary to live worthily as men, is in itself evil. The prophets denounce it as contrary to the will of the Lord and most of the time as the fruit of the injustice and sin of men.

b) Spiritual poverty is the theme of the poor of Yahweh[2]. Spiritual poverty is the attitude of opening up to God, the ready disposition of one who hopes for everything from the Lord[3]. Although he values the goods of this world, he does not become attached to them and he recognizes the higher value of the riches of the Kingdom[4].

c) Poverty as a commitment, through which one assumes voluntarily and lovingly the conditions of the needy of this world in order to bear witness to the evil which it represents and to spiritual liberty in the face of material goods, follows the example of Christ who took to Himself all the consequences of men's sinful condition[5] and Who "being rich became poor"[6] in order to redeem us.

5.   In this context a poor Church:

—Denounces the unjust lack of this world's goods and the sin that begets it;

—Preaches and lives in spiritual poverty, as an attitude of spiritual childhood and openness to the Lord;

—Is herself bound to material poverty. The poverty of the Church is, in effect, a constant factor in the history of salvation.

6.   All members of the Church are called to live in evangelical poverty, but not all in the same way, as there are diverse vocations to this poverty, that tolerate diverse styles of life and various modes of acting. Among religious themselves, although they all have a special mission to witness within the Church, there will be differences according to personal charisms.

7.   Against this background, it will be necessary to reemphasize strongly that the example and teaching of Jesus, the anguished condition of millions of poor people in Latin America, the urgent exhortations of the Pope and of the Council, place before the Latin American Church a challenge and a mission that she cannot sidestep and to which she must respond with a speed and boldness adequate to the urgency of the times.

Christ, our Savior, not only loved the poor, but rather "being rich He became poor", He lived in poverty. His mission centered on advising the poor of their liberation and He founded His Church as the sign of that poverty among men.

The Church itself has always tried to fulfill that vocation, notwithstanding "very great weaknesses and flaws in the past"[7]. The Latin American Church, given the continent's conditions of poverty and underdevelopment, experiences the urgency of translating that spirit of poverty into actions, attitudes and norms that make it a more lucid and authentic sign of its Lord. The poverty of so many brothers cries out for justice, solidarity, open witness, commitment, strength, and exertion directed to the fulfillment of the redeeming mission to which it is committed by Christ.

The present situation, then, demands from bishops, priests, religious and laymen the spirit of poverty which, "breaking the bonds of the egotistical possession of temporal goods, stimulates the Christian to order organically the power and the finances in favor of the common good"[8].

The poverty of the Church and of its members in Latin America ought to be a sign and a commitment—a sign of the inestimable value of the poor in the eyes of God, an obligation of solidarity with those who suffer.

III. Pastoral Orientations

8.   Because of the foregoing we wish the Latin American Church to be the evangelizer of the poor and one with them, a witness to the value of the riches of the Kingdom, and the humble servant of all our people. Its pastors and the other members of the People of God have to correlate their life and words, their attitudes and actions to the demands of the Gospel and the necessities of the men of Latin America.

PRE-EMINENCE AND SOLIDARITY

9.   The Lord's distinct commandment to "evangelize the poor" ought to bring us to a distribution of resources and apostolic personnel that effectively gives preference to the poorest and most needy sectors and to those segregated for any cause whatsoever, animating and accelerating the initiatives and studies that are already being made with that goal in mind.

We, the bishops, wish to come closer to the poor in sincerity and brotherhood, making ourselves accessible to them.

10.   We ought to sharpen the awareness of our duty of solidarity with the poor, to which charity leads us. This solidarity means that we make ours their problems and their struggles, that we know how to speak with them.

This has to be concretized in criticism of injustice and oppression, in the struggle against the intolerable situation which a poor person often has to tolerate, in the willingness to dialogue with the groups responsible for that situation in order to make them understand their obligations.

11.   We express our desire to be very close always to those who work in the self-denying apostolate with the poor in order that they will always feel our encouragement and know that we will not listen to parties interested in distorting their work.

Human advancement has to be the goal of our action on behalf of the poor man and it must be carried out in such a manner that we respect his personal dignity and teach him to help himself. With that end in mind we recognize the necessity of the rational structuring of our pastoral action and the integration of our efforts with those of other entities.

TESTIMONY

12.   We wish our houses and style of life to be modest, our clothing simple, our works and institutions functional, without show or ostentation.

We ask priests and faithful to treat us in conformity with our mission as fathers and pastors, for we desire to renounce honorable titles belonging to another era.

13.   With the help of all the People of God we hope to overcome the system of fees, replacing it with other forms of financial cooperation not linked to the administration of the sacraments.

The administration of diocesan or parish properties has to be entrusted to competent laymen and put to better use for the welfare of the whole community[9].

14.   In our pastoral work we will trust above all in the strength of God's Word; when we have to employ technical means we will seek those most adequate to the environment in which they will be used and will put them at the disposal of the community[10].

15.   We exhort the priests also to give testimony of poverty and detachment from material goods, as so many do, particularly in rural areas and poor neighborhoods. With great diligence we will procure for them a just though modest sustenance and the necessary social security. To this end we will seek to establish a common fund among all the parishes and the diocese itself; also among the dioceses of the same country[11].

We encourage those who feel themselves called to share the lot of the poor, living with them and even working with their hands, in accord with the Decree *Presbyterorum ordinis*[12].

16.   The religious communities by virtue of their special vocation ought to witness to the poverty of Christ. We encourage those who feel themselves called to form from among their members small communities, truly incarnated in the poor environment; they will be a continual call to evangelical poverty for all the People of God.

We hope also that they (the religious communities) will be able more and more to effect the sharing of their goods with others, especially with the most needy, dividing among them not only superfluities, but also necessities, and disposed to put at the disposal of the human community the buildings and instruments of their work[13].

The distinction between what belongs to the community and what pertains to the work will facilitate this distribution. It will likewise permit the searching for new forms to accomplish those works, in whose administration or ownership other members of the Christian community will participate.

17.   These authentic examples of detachment and freedom of spirit will make the other members of the People of God give a similar witness to poverty. A sincere conversion has to change the individualistic mentality into another one of social awareness and concern for the common good. The education of children and youth at all levels, beginning in the home, ought to include this fundamental aspect of the Christian life.

This feeling of love of neighbor is evinced when one studies and works above all with the intention of performing a service for the community; when one organizes power and wealth for the benefit of the community.

SERVICE

18.   No earthly ambition impels the Church, only her wish to be the humble servant of all men[14].

We need to stress this spirit in Latin America.

We want our Latin American Church to be free from temporalities, from intrigues and from a doubtful reputation; to be "free in spirit as regards the chains of wealth"[15], so that her mission of service will be stronger and clearer. We want her to be present in life and in secular works, reflecting the light of Christ, present in the construction of the world.

We want to recognize all the value and legitimate autonomy of temporal works; aiding them we do not wish to take away their substance nor divert them from their distinctive ends[16]. We desire sincerely to respect all men and to listen to them in order to serve them in their problems and afflictions[17]. Thus, the Church, carrying on the work of Christ, "Who made himself poor for us, being rich in order to enrich us with His poverty"[18], will present before the world a clear and unmistakable sign of the poverty of her Lord.

NOTES

1. Cf. Paul VI, *Address to the peasants*, Mosquera, Colombia, 23 August, 1968.
2. Cf. So 2,3; Lk 1,46-55.
3. Cf. Mt 5,3.
4. Cf. Am 2,6-7; 4,1; Jer 5,28; Mi 6,12-13; Is 10,2 et passim.
5. Cf. Phil 2,5-8.
6. Cf. 2Cor 8,9.
7. Cf. Paul VI, Enc. *Ecclesiam suam*, No. 50.
8. Cf. Paul VI, *Homily of the Mass on Development Day*, Bogotá, 23 August, 1968.
9. Cf. Vatican Council II, decree *Presbyterorum ordinis*, No. 17.
10. Cf. Vatican Council II, pastoral constitution *Gaudium et spes*, No. 69.
11. Cf. Vatican Council II, decree *Presbyterorum ordinis*, No. 21.
12. Cf. Ibid., No. 8.
13. Cf. Vatican Council II, pastoral constitution *Gaudium et spes*, No. 69.
14. Cf. Vatican Council II, pastoral constitution *Gaudium et spes*, No. 3; Paul VI, *Closing address of Vatican Council II*, 7 December, 1965.
15. Cf. Paul VI, *Opening Address to Latin American Bishops' Assembly*, Bogotá, 24 August, 1968.
16. Cf. Vatican Council II, pastoral constitution *Gaudium et spes*. No. 36.
17. Cf. Ibid., Nos 1-3.
18. Cf. 2Cor. 8,9.

Message of His Eminence
Maurice Cardinal Roy
President of the Pontifical Commission
"Justice and Peace,"
on the Occasion of the Launching
of the Second Development Decade
(November 19, 1970)

As President of the Pontifical Commission Justice and Peace,
His Eminence Maurice Cardinal Roy
presented the following message
to U Thant, Secretary General of the United Nations Organization,
in New York on Thursday, November 19, 1970

Christian Commitment
to the Second Development Decade

1.   The world stands at the threshold of the Second Development
Decade. The agonizing question before us is whether it holds more

---

[This original and official English text is from the booklet published by the Vatican Polyglot Press, 18 pages. The historical note is also from the booklet.]

promise than the first for meeting the needs of the poor, the dispossessed, the powerless of our planet. If integral human development must be counted a fundamental right of man, will history record the Seventies as the decade in which, at last, a really serious effort was made to implement this right?

2.   The Pontifical Commission Justice and Peace, of which I have the honour to be President, was created by Pope Paul VI in the wake of the Second Vatican Council precisely to engage the full energies of the Roman Catholic Church in this project of humanity. Ours is the mission of awakening all within the Church to our common responsibilities for peace, international justice and development.

3.   As President of the Commission, therefore, I take the occasion of the United Nations' announcement of the Second Development Decade to appeal for world cooperation toward achieving integral human development for all men.

Crisis in the Seventies

4.   We begin the new Decade of Development with, I believe, deeper insight into the nature of our problems. In the Sixties, both the theory and the practice of development tended to be exclusively economic. Theory drew heavily on the nineteenth century experience of already developed nations and underlined the vital role played by capital accumulation in the process of modernization. In practice, development was judged to be successful if it achieved rates of growth sufficient to provide both for rising population and rising investment. The essential element in economic assistance was believed to lie in a transfer of capital from rich to poor and, as the decade advanced, in wider opportunities for the developing nations in international trade. Given these changes, rapid economic growth would prove both possible and largely sufficient.

5.   These insights of the Sixties—into the need for capital assistance and the necessity of wider opportunities in world trade—are not false. Indeed, the world of the Seventies would be a more stable place if the prime targets of the Sixties had been achieved, in particular the goals of aid equivalent to one per cent of the gross national product of the rich nations, and, for the developing nations, higher export incomes, better access to industrialized markets and more working capital for trade. We do not dismiss or deny such objectives. They must still be achieved. We simply join in the judgement expressed by an increasing number of development experts and practitioners, and indeed embodied in the

international development strategy recently adopted by the General Assembly of the United Nations, that, for truly human societies and a truly peaceful world, these objectives are not enough.

6.   We would suggest two reasons for this change of view. The first came to the fore during the Annual Meeting of the World Bank and the International Monetary Fund in September 1970; the processes of development of the already industrialized nations, which have been taken as the model for contemporary development, contain too many special circumstances for them to be applicable to the wholly altered conditions of today. Within the early, largely Atlantic, developing societies, epidemics and poor sanitation held back population growth, and greater productivity in agriculture, preceding industrialization, released food and manpower to a growing industrial sector where techniques demanded massive supplies of labour and not too much capital. This capital could in any case be secured by the ability of the entrepreneurs to mobilize for investment the whole productive surplus. In these conditions cities grew as a result of industrial expansion, jobs grew with them and by the time technology demanded more skill and more capital, workers had acquired education, built up mass organizations and stabilized family size. The cities were not utopias. But they were dynamic centres of work and life.

7.   In any case, external circumstances eased the strain. The European peoples took over all the remaining temperate land of the globe after 1840. Forty million migrants left Europe in the nineteenth century for new land and jobs in the new world. The Europeans could also complete the colonization of virtually the whole of humanity. Their trade and investment in all the continents gave them—although they made up less that 20 per cent of the world's peoples—80 per cent of the world's resources and trade, 90 per cent of the investment, 100 per cent of the services, banking, shipping, research. These proportions have not changed since 1900 and help to explain the vast elbow-room which was available to the already developed nations when they sought to cross the threshold of modernization.

8.   Today every circumstance in the now developing nations, —internal and external—works in the opposite sense. Public health has preceded modernization. Population grows at twice the nineteenth century pace, the work force, if anything, faster. Capital formation, in the farm and factory, is slowed down by rising numbers of consumers, however marginal, and by the new non-saving high consumption habits of the wealthy elite whose standards are now "western" while their societies are not. Undermodernized agriculture cannot feed its own rising

millions, so its workers move to the cities ahead of any pull of rising industrial employment. Technology today is based on advance models. It demands more capital—which developing countries lack—and fewer workers—which they see increase like a flood. Worklessness rises inexorably in the Third World as the poor of the countryside transfer their misery to the fringes of the cities. As Mr. David Morse, former head of the International Labour Organization, recently pointed out, twenty to twenty-five per cent is a standard rate for contemporary unemployment. Among younger workers, it can be higher still. A more detailed and substantial profile of this process as it works in Latin America can be found in the report "Change and Development" recently prepared by Dr. Raul Prebisch, former Secretary General of the United Nations' Conference on Trade and Development.

9.   There are no external safety valves. The world's free land is occupied, the frontier closed. Political decolonization has not yet altered the overwhelming balance of wealth and power in favour of the already rich. Apart from movements of migrant labour in Europe, the massive migrations today are not across frontiers and oceans to new opportunities. They flow internally, from farm to city, from a rural to an urban misery. And still the numbers rise. Our world will become even more troubled with so great a mass of misery piling up at its base.

10.   This brings us to the second reason for our belief that economic growth is an indispensable but not sufficient cause of full human development. The reason is quite simply, as Pope Paul underlines in his Encyclical *Populorum Progressio,* that the unfettered working of the market, operating between "partners" of grossly unequal strength, does not secure anything like a proper distribution of the fruits of economic development. In the modern economy, with its premium on skill, drive, capacity and investment, it is the intelligent, the tough, the energetic and the already rich that tend to take all the gains, unless strong political and social policies accompany modernization in order to secure greater justice and greater participation.

11.   This is the obvious lesson of the nineteenth century. Even with the vast bounties of new continents to develop and a whole planet to colonize, the industrialized nations were racked with crises of social discontent and class war until they introduced the tax systems, the land reforms, the welfare policies and the extension of the vote needed to liberate the mass of people from total dependence upon the dominant classes, to give them a sense of participation in society and a share in the wealth they worked every day to produce. Even today, whenever undue reliance on the beneficent workings of an uncorrected market economy

persists in developed societies and, as a result, social action is delayed, the weak, the poor, the unskilled, the ethnic minorities tend to fall behind and to relive the squalid miseries of nineteenth century slums and sweatshops.

12.   These are the facts which underlie the international community's growing disenchantment with purely economic development. At the local level, it can be seen ever more clearly that societies in which little or no political and social action ameliorates the lot of the mass of the people and liberates them sufficiently to take a full part in their own development, no amount of economic growth will lead to satisfactory modernization. On the contrary, it will tend to pile up the riches and consumption of the few and leave a growing mass of "marginal men" at the base of society for whom even the most elementary of human needs and decencies—job, home, school, diet, health,—will be almost completely lacking.

13.   At the same time, one can see an almost identical process at work at the planetary level. Our technology, our science, our communications all thrust us towards a steadily increasing interdependence. A truly planetary society is, as Pope Paul has never ceased to emphasize, the great imperative of our time. But, as *Populorum Progressio* repeatedly underlines, we have now a world economy in which *all* the positions of strength, all the wealth, all the investment, all the commercial services and above all, the whole crucial apparatus of research are concentrated in the small elite of nations which have already achieved modernization. It is this extraordinary concentration of wealth, of which industrialized nations themselves are all too often largely unaware, that helps to explain the bitterness and resentment which developing nations sometimes display when aid is offered in terms not much removed from patronage and paternalism and recipients are asked to show gratitude for what to them is not generosity but a marginal act of justice.

14.   To mediate between the wealthy and the developing nations, the international community needs more effective instruments of political responsibility or social good will. The United Nations still lacks the means and support to secure the kind of political participation and commitment required for a truly planetary cooperation. An aid effort which some of the wealthiest nations decreasingly support is not even the beginning, at the world level, of redistributive taxation or a healthy welfare system. In a world of such uneven power, neither justice nor liberation nor cooperation is conceivable, so long as the nations are at one only in their cupidities and their fears, spending 200 billion dollars to defend their so-called security and thirty times less to root out the basic causes of insecurity. Unless the Seventies can reverse the widening gap between rich and poor

both within domestic society and in the world at large, it is all but impossible to believe that mankind can reach, in peace, the end of this troubled century.

Integral Human Development

15.   The nature of our crisis dictates the policies we must try to formulate and carry out in order to counter it. All are not yet accepted. Indeed many still need much more careful research and precise definition. Yet it is possible to see some movement towards a new consensus in which earlier concepts of economic growth are complemented by new ideas of social justice and political participation and the United Nations' international strategy represents the beginning of such a consensus. In short, economic man is beginning to give way a little to the full vision of man as a responsible moral agent, creative in his action, free in his ultimate decisions, united to his fellows in social bonds of respect and friendship and co-partner in the work of building a just and peaceful world.

16.   At the domestic level there is a growing sense that neither internal modernization nor external economic assistance will be effective:

    i) unless the whole of the people are drawn into active participation in their own improvement and in the liberation of their own energies and skills;

    ii) unless the institutions which stultify participation and self-realization are transformed. These include feudal land-holding; non-tax paying, non-saving, wealthy classes; industry without secure wages, opportunity for promotion and wide profit sharing or ownership; education confined to an elite and the acceptance of mass illiteracy; lack of institutions of participation and self-help—workers and peasant organizations, cooperatives; trade unions, saving banks, home loan associations; political systems which allow no play for personal liberty, regionalization and creative experiment;

    iii) unless active social policy, within the framework of a large social sector, deals directly with the worst causes of misery among the 25 per cent of "marginal men" whom the processes of modernization tend to leave behind. Direct action is needed for a full employment policy, housing programs, urban renewal and energetic policies to spread rural employment, cooperatives and land ownership as widely as possible in the wake of the Green Revolution;

    iv) unless population policies are fully adapted to local needs, traditions and values. Policy will vary according to the actual pressure on family well-being, of rising numbers, or speed of growth. But some principles are universal—that the aim of public policy is to enhance the welfare and quality of families, that life-destroying means or artificial means tending to render procreation impossible be excluded, that full respect is given to parents' God-given right to determine in full responsibility their own size of family.

17.   At the international level, in addition to the aims of aid, trade liquidity and debt relief formulated in the Sixties, a number of further policies are gaining wider acceptance:

i) that all aid should be closely linked to those reforms in domestic structure already outlined above;

ii) that international institutions in which the developing nations are fully represented should coordinate and distribute a larger part of the flow of concessionary finance;

iii) that, as Pope Paul suggests in *Populorum Progressio*, the transfer of a much larger flow of finance to development should be achieved by a phased reduction in the intolerable and inflationary burden of armaments;

iv) that aid flows should be "institutionalized" and accepted as an incipient world tax system in such a way as to underline their essential character not of generosity but of distributive justice. As such they would be seen as an integrative element in the coming planetary society;

v) that developing nations, through regional groupings and collective action in the world market, should encourage trade and investment between each other and thus lessen the world economy's imbalance between North and South;

vi) that a fundamental reconsideration of the planet's resource use and management be undertaken so that the increasingly irrational levels of extravagance, waste and pollution of the "high consumption societies" should not jeopardize the poorer nations' hopes of development and humanity's ultimate hopes of survival.

The Christian Commitment

18.   These are the efforts which we seek, with the deepest urgency and sincerity, to assist and pursue. The Catholic Church hopes to work closely in this field with its Christian brothers in ecumenical programs, and indeed with men of all religions and of none, who are concerned with the future of our troubled humanity. It is our hope that some of our Christian insights may be of use in the great efforts of development. It is an even

greater hope that Christian energy and dedication may be mobilized in its service.

19.   It is after all possible to see the planet as an arena in which the fittest survive by virtue of their force or cunning. It is possible to denounce all help to the weak and helpless as a gross interference in the evolutionary process and to proclaim the fitness of conquerors to conquer simply by the fact that they have done so. It may therefore be of assistance to the whole spirit of planetary development in these post-colonial days of vast and deepening inequality if, to the giant disproportions between wealth and poverty, between weak and strong, Christians were to oppose a vision of human responsibility and fraternal love. It is after all the fundamental teaching of the Scriptures that we are our brothers' keeper and that, if we leave the least of our fellow men to misery, hunger and early death, "the blood of Abel will call from the ground" for judgement and brand us with the mark of Cain. We know, too, how strong are the temptations of wealth and power. We know how much of the world's great surplus of careless and accepted wealth is accumulated among the post-Christian peoples. It is possible that they can still be reminded of God's terrible word to those who selfishly fill their barns with an unshared harvest: "Thou fool, this night thy soul is required of thee".

20.   Above all, it takes great energy of soul and great fortitude to undo the injustices of centuries and to rise above the ease of comfort and success. Equally, it demands unparallelled generosity to forgive past insults and present oppressions, and join together in the work of building a planet that can be a home to all its children. We do not say that Christians have this energy and generosity. We say only that if they had it, they could add conviction, dedication and staying power to their part in our world-wide task. We will seek by all means to arouse this energy and put it at the service of our human community. For we do not work without hope. We do not believe that "God has despaired of His children". We believe that, on the contrary, we can "work while it is day", and build together a world which is nearer to our Creator's vision and will for all mankind. And we believe that the Almighty Father of our human family will give us all the help we need and seek.

Vatican City, November 19, 1970

MAURICE Cardinal ROY, *President*
Pontifical Commission "Justice and Peace"

Octogesima Adveniens

The Eighthieth Anniversary of "Rerum Novarum" (May 14, 1971)

APOSTOLIC LETTER
OF HIS HOLINESS POPE PAUL VI
TO CARDINAL MAURICE ROY
PRESIDENT OF THE COUNCIL OF THE LAITY
AND OF THE PONTIFICAL COMMISSION JUSTICE AND PEACE
ON THE OCCASION OF THE EIGHTIETH ANNIVERSARY
OF THE ENCYCLICAL "RERUM NOVARUM"

VENERABLE BROTHER:

1.   The eightieth anniversary of the publication of the encyclical *Rerum Novarum*, the message of which continues to inspire action for social justice, prompts us to take up again and to extend the teaching of our predecessors, in response to the new needs of a changing world. The Church, in fact, travels forward with humanity and shares its lot in the

[This English version is that published by the Vatican Polyglot Press in booklet form, 70 pages. A.A.S. LXIII (June 30, 1971), No. 6, pp. 401-41.]

setting of history. At the same time that she announces to men the Good News of God's love and of salvation in Christ, she clarifies their activity in the light of the Gospel and in this way helps them to correspond to God's plan of love and to realize the fulness of their aspirations.

UNIVERSAL APPEAL FOR MORE JUSTICE

2.   It is with confidence that we see the Spirit of the Lord pursuing his work in the hearts of men and in every place gathering together Christian communities conscious of their responsibilities in society. On all the continents, among all races, nations and cultures, and under all conditions the Lord continues to raise up authentic apostles of the Gospel.

We have had the opportunity to meet these people, to admire them and to give them our encouragement in the course of our recent journeys. We have gone into the crowds and have heard their appeals, cries of distress and at the same time cries of hope. Under these circumstances we have seen in a new perspective the grave problems of our time. These problems of course are particular to each part of the world, but at the same time they are common to all mankind, which is questioning itself about its future and about the tendency and the meaning of the changes taking place. Flagrant inequalities exist in the economic, cultural and political development of the nations: while some regions are heavily industrialized, others are still at the agricultural stage; while some countries enjoy prosperity, others are struggling against starvation; while some peoples have a high standard of culture, others are still engaged in eliminating illiteracy. From all sides there rises a yearning for more justice and a desire for a better guaranteed peace in mutual respect among individuals and peoples.

DIVERSITY OF SITUATIONS

3.   There is of course a wide diversity among the situations in which Christians—willingly or unwillingly—find themselves according to regions, socio-political systems and cultures. In some places they are reduced to silence, regarded with suspicion and as it were kept on the fringe of society, enclosed without freedom in a totalitarian system. In other places they are a weak minority whose voice makes itself heard with difficulty. In some other nations, where the Church sees her place recognized, sometimes officially so, she too finds herself subjected to the repercussions of the crisis which is unsettling society; some of her mem-

bers are tempted by radical and violent solutions from which they believe that they can expect a happier outcome. While some people, unaware of present injustices, strive to prolong the existing situation, others allow themselves to be beguiled by revolutionary ideologies which promise them, not without delusion, a definitively better world.

4.   In the face of such widely varying situations it is difficult for us to utter a unified message and to put forward a solution which has universal validity. Such is not our ambition, nor is it our mission. It is up to the Christian communities to analyze with objectivity the situation which is proper to their own country, to shed on it the light of the Gospel's unalterable words and to draw principles of reflection, norms of judgment and directives for action from the social teaching of the Church. This social teaching has been worked out in the course of history and notably, in this industrial era, since the historic date of the message of Pope Leo XIII on "the condition of the workers", and it is an honour and joy for us to celebrate today the anniversary of that message. It is up to these Christian communities, with the help of the Holy Spirit, in communion with the bishops who hold responsibility and in dialogue with other Christian brethren and all men of goodwill, to discern the options and commitments which are called for in order to bring about the social, political and economic changes seen in many cases to be urgently needed. In this search for the changes which should be promoted, Christians must first of all renew their confidence in the forcefulness and special character of the demands made by the Gospel. The Gospel is not out-of-date because it was proclaimed, written and lived in a different socio-cultural context. Its inspiration, enriched by the living experience of Christian tradition over the centuries, remains ever new for converting men and for advancing the life of society. It is not however to be utilized for the profit of particular temporal options, to the neglect of its universal and eternal message.[1]

SPECIFIC MESSAGE OF THE CHURCH

5.   Amid the disturbances and uncertainties of the present hour, the Church has a specific message to proclaim and a support to give to men in their efforts to take in hand and give direction to their future. Since the period in which the encyclical *Rerum Novarum* denounced in a forceful and imperative manner the scandal of the condition of the workers in the nascent industrial society, historical evolution has led to an awareness of other dimensions and other applications of social justice. The encyclicals

488   *Pope Paul VI*

Quadragesimo Anno[2] and *Mater et Magistra*[3] already noted this fact. The recent Council for its part took care to point them out, in particular in the Pastoral Constitution *Gaudium et Spes*. We ourself have already continued these lines of thought in our encyclical *Populorum Progressio*. "Today", we said, "the principal fact that we must all recognize is that the social question has become worldwide".[4] "A renewed consciousness of the demands of the Gospel makes it the Church's duty to put herself at the service of all, to help them grasp their serious problem in all its dimensions, and to convince them that solidarity in action at this turning point in human history is a matter of urgency".[5]

6.   It will moreover be for the forthcoming Synod of Bishops itself to study more closely and to examine in greater detail the Church's mission in the face of grave issues raised today by the question of justice in the world. But the anniversary of *Rerum Novarum*, venerable brother, gives us the opportunity today to confide our preoccupations and thoughts in the face of this problem to you as President of the Pontifical Commission Justice and Peace and of the Council of Laity. In this way it is also our wish to offer these bodies of the Holy See our encouragement in their ecclesial activity in the service of men.

EXTENT OF PRESENT-DAY CHANGES

7.   In so doing, our purpose—without however forgetting the permanent problems already dealt with by our predecessors—is to draw attention to a number of questions. These are questions which because of their urgency, extent and complexity must in the years to come take first place among the preoccupations of Christians, so that with other men the latter may dedicate themselves to solving the new difficulties which put the very future of man in jeopardy. It is necessary to situate the problems created by the modern economy in the wider context of a new civilization. These problems include human conditions of production, fairness in the exchange of goods and in the division of wealth, the significance of the increased needs of consumption and the sharing of responsibility. In the present changes, which are so profound and so rapid, each day man discovers himself anew, and he questions himself about the meaning of his own being and of his collective survival. Reluctant to gather the lessons of a past that he considers over and done with and too different from the present, man nevertheless needs to have light shed upon his future—a future which he perceives to be as uncertain as it is

changing—by permanent eternal truths. These are truths which are certainly greater than man but, if he so wills, he can himself find their traces.[6]

New Social Problems

URBANIZATION

8.   A major phenomenon draws our attention, as much in the industrialized countries as in those which are developing: urbanization.

After long centuries, agrarian civilization is weakening. Is sufficient attention being devoted to the arrangement and improvement of the life of the country people, whose inferior and at times miserable economic situation provokes the flight to the unhappy crowded conditions of the city outskirts, where neither employment nor housing awaits them?

This unceasing flight from the land, industrial growth, continual demographic expansion and the attraction of urban centres bring about concentrations of population, the extent of which is difficult to imagine, for people are already speaking in terms of a "megalopolis" grouping together tens of millions of persons. Of course there exist medium-sized towns, the dimension of which ensures a better balance in the population. While being able to offer employment to those that progress in agriculture makes available, they permit an adjustment of the human environment which better avoids the proletarianism and crowding of the great built-up areas.

9.   The inordinate growth of these centres accompanies industrial expansion, without being identified with it. Based on technological research and the transformation of nature, industrialization constantly goes forward, giving proof of incessant creativity. While certain enterprises develop and are concentrated, others die or change their location. Thus new social problems are created: professional or regional unemployment, redeployment and mobility of persons, permanent adaptation of workers and disparity of conditions in the different branches of industry. Unlimited competition utilizing the modern means of publicity incessantly launches new products and tries to attract the consumer, while earlier industrial installations which are still capable of functioning become useless. While very large areas of the population are unable to satisfy their primary needs, superfluous needs are ingeniously created. It can thus rightly be asked if, in spite of all his conquests, man is not turning back

against himself the results of his activity. Having rationally endeavoured
to control nature,[7] is he not now becoming the slave of the objects which
he makes?

CHRISTIANS IN THE CITY

10.   Is not the rise of an urban civilization which accompanies the
advance of industrial civilization a true challenge to the wisdom of man,
to his capacity for organization and to his farseeing imagination? Within
industrial society urbanization upsets both the ways of life and the
habitual structures of existence: the family, the neighbourhood, and the
very framework of the Christian community. Man is experiencing a new
loneliness; it is not in the face of a hostile nature which it has taken him
centuries to subdue, but in an anonymous crowd which surrounds him
and in which he feels himself a stranger. Urbanization, undoubtedly an
irreversible stage in the development of human societies, confronts man
with difficult problems. How is he to master its growth, regulate its
organization, and successfully accomplish its animation for the good of
all?

In this disordered growth, new proletariats are born. They install
themselves in the heart of the cities sometimes abandoned by the rich;
they dwell on the outskirts—which become a belt of misery besieging in a
still silent protest the luxury which blatantly cries out from centres of
consumption and waste. Instead of favouring fraternal encounter and
mutual aid, the city fosters discrimination and also indifference. It lends
itself to new forms of exploitation and of domination whereby some
people in speculating of the needs of others derive inadmissible profits.
Behind the facades, much misery is hidden, unsuspected even by the
closest neighbours; other forms of misery spread where human dignity
founders: delinquency, criminality, abuse of drugs and eroticism.

11.   It is in fact the weakest who are the victims of dehumanizing living
conditions, degrading for conscience and harmful for the family institution. The promiscuity of working people's housing makes a minimum of
intimacy impossible; young couples waiting in vain for a decent dwelling
at a price they can afford are demoralized and their union can thereby
even be endangered; youth escape from a home which is too confined and
seek in the streets compensations and companionships which cannot be
supervised. It is the grave duty of those responsible to strive to control
this process and to give it direction.

There is an urgent need to remake at the level of the street, of the
neighbourhood or of the great agglomerative dwellings the social fabric

whereby man may be able to develop the needs of his personality. Centres of special interest and of culture must be created or developed at the community and parish levels with different forms of associations, recreational centres, and spiritual and community gatherings where the individual can escape from isolation and form anew fraternal relationships.

12.   To build up the city, the place where men and their expanded communities exist, to create new modes of neighbourliness and relationships, to perceive an original application of social justice and to undertake responsibility for this collective future, which is foreseen as difficult, is a task in which Christians must share. To those who are heaped up in an urban promiscuity which becomes intolerable it is necessary to bring a message of hope. This can be done by brotherhood which is lived and by concrete justice. Let Christians, conscious of this new responsibility, not lose heart in view of the vast and faceless society; let them recall Jonah who traversed Niniveh, the great city, to proclaim therein the good news of God's mercy and was upheld in his weakness by the sole strength of the word of Almighty God. In the Bible, the city is in fact often the place of sin and pride—the pride of man who feels secure enough to be able to build his life without God and even to affirm that he is powerful against God. But there is also the example of Jerusalem, the Holy City, the place where God is encountered, the promise of the city which comes from on high.[8]

YOUTH

13.   Urban life and industrial change bring strongly to light questions which until now were poorly grasped. What place, for example, in this world being brought to birth, should be given to youth? Everywhere dialogue is proving to be difficult between youth, with its aspirations, renewal and also insecurity for the future, and the adult generations. It is obvious to all that here we have a source of serious conflicts, division and opting out, even within the family, and a questioning of modes of authority, education for freedom and the handing on of values and beliefs, which strikes at the deep roots of society.

THE ROLE OF WOMEN

Similarly, in many countries a charter for women which would put an end to an actual discrimination and would establish relationships of equality in rights and of respect for their dignity is the object of study and at times of lively demands. We do not have in mind that false equality which would deny the distinctions laid down by the Creator himself and which would be in contradiction with woman's proper role, which is of such capital importance, at the heart of the family as well as within society. Developments in legislation should on the contrary be directed to protecting her proper vocation and at the same time recognizing her independence as a person, and her equal rights to participate in cultural, economic, social and political life.

WORKERS

14.   As the Church solemnly reaffirmed in the recent Council, "the beginning, the subject and the goal of all social institutions is and must be the human person".[9] Every man has the right to work, to a chance to develop his qualities and his personality in the exercise of his profession, to equitable remuneration which will enable him and his family "to lead a worthy life on the material, social, cultural and spiritual level"[10] and to assistance in case of need arising from sickness or age.

Although for the defence of these rights democratic societies accept today the principle of labour union rights, they are not always open to their exercise. The important role of union organizations must be admitted: their object is the representation of the various categories of workers, their lawful collaboration in the economic advance of society, and the development of the sense of their responsibility for the realization of the common good. Their activity, however, is not without its difficulties. Here and there the temptation can arise of profiting from a position of force to impose, particularly by strikes—the right to which as a final means of defence remains certainly recognized—conditions which are too burdensome for the overall economy and for the social body, or to desire to obtain in this way demands of a directly political nature. When it is a question of public services, required for the life of an entire nation, it is necessary to be able to assess the limit beyond which the harm caused to society becomes inadmissible.

VICTIMS OF CHANGES

15.   In short, progress has already been made in introducing, in the area of human relationships, greater justice and greater sharing of responsibilities. But in this immense field much remains to be done. Further, reflection, research and experimentation must be actively pursued, unless one is to be late in meeting the legitimate aspirations of the

workers—aspirations which are being increasingly asserted according as their education, their consciousness of their dignity and the strength of their organizations increase.

Egoism and domination are permanent temptations for men. Likewise an ever finer discernment is needed, in order to strike at the roots of newly arising situations of injustice and to establish progressively a justice which will be less and less imperfect. In industrial change, which demands speedy and constant adaptation, those who will find themselves injured will be more numerous and at a greater disadvantage from the point of view of making their voices heard. The Church directs her attention to these new "poor"—the handicapped and the maladjusted, the old, different groups of those on the fringe of society, and so on—in order to recognize them, help them, defend their place and dignity in a society hardened by competition and the attraction of success.

DISCRIMINATION

16. Among the victims of situations of injustice—unfortunately no new phenomenon—must be placed those who are discriminated against, in law or in fact, on account of their race, origin, colour, culture, sex or religion.

Racial discrimination possesses at the moment a character of very great relevance by reason of the tension which it stirs up both within certain countries and on the international level. Men rightly consider unjustifiable and reject as inadmissible the tendency to maintain or introduce legislation or behaviour systematically inspired by racialist prejudice. The members of mankind share the same basic rights and duties, as well as the same supernatural destiny. Within a country which belongs to each one, all should be equal before the law, find equal admittance to economic, cultural, civic and social life and benefit from a fair sharing of the nation's riches.

RIGHT TO EMIGRATE

17. We are thinking also of the precarious situation of a great number of emigrant workers whose condition as foreigners makes it all the more difficult for them to make any sort of social vindication, in spite of their real participation in the economic effort of the country that receives them. It is urgently necessary for people to go beyond a narrowly nationalist attitude in their regard and to give them a charter which will assure them a right to emigrate, favour their integration, facilitate their professional

advancement and give them access to decent housing where, if such is the case, their families can join them.[11]

Linked to this category are the people who, to find work, or to escape a disaster or a hostile climate, leave their regions and find themselves without roots among other people.

It is everyone's duty, but especially that of Christians,[12] to work with energy for the establishment of universal brotherhood, the indispensable basis for authentic justice and the condition for enduring peace: "We cannot in truthfulness call upon that God who is the Father of all if we refuse to act in a brotherly way toward certain men, created to God's image. A man's relationship with God the Father and his relationship with his brother men are so linked together that Scripture says: 'He who does not love does not know God' (1 Jn 4:8)".[13]

CREATING EMPLOYMENT

18.   With demographic growth, which is particularly pronounced in the young nations, the number of those failing to find work and driven to misery or parasitism will grow in the coming years unless the conscience of man rouses itself and gives rise to a general movement of solidarity through an effective policy of investment and of organization of production and trade, as well as of education. We know the attention given to these problems within international organizations, and it is our lively wish that their members will not delay bringing their actions into line with their declarations.

It is disquieting in this regard to note a kind of fatalism which is gaining a hold even on people in positions of responsibility. This feeling sometimes leads to Malthusian solutions inculcated by active propaganda for contraception and abortion. In this critical situation, it must on the contrary be affirmed that the family, without which no society can stand, has a right to the assistance which will assure it of the conditions for a healthy development. "It is certain", we said in our encyclical *Populorum Progressio*, "that public authorities can intervene, within the limit of their competence, by favouring the availability of appropriate information and by adopting suitable measures, provided that these be in conformity with the moral law and that they respect the rightful freedom of married couples. Where the inalienable right to marriage and procreation is lacking, human dignity has ceased to exist".[14]

19.   In no other age has the appeal to the imagination of society been so explicit. To this should be devoted enterprises of invention and capital as important as those invested for armaments or technological achieve-

ments. If man lets himself rush ahead without foreseeing in good time the emergence of new social problems, they will become too grave for a peaceful solution to be hoped for.

MEDIA OF SOCIAL COMMUNICATION

20.   Among the major changes of our times, we do not wish to forget to emphasize the growing role being assumed by the media of social communication and their influence on the transformation of mentalities, of knowledge, or organizations and of society itself. Certainly they have many positive aspects. Thanks to them news from the entire world reaches us practically in an instant, establishing contacts which supersede distances and creating elements of unity among all men. A greater spread of education and culture is becoming possible. Nevertheless, by their very action the media of social communication are reaching the point of representing as it were a new power. One cannot but ask about those who really hold this power, the aims that they pursue and the means they use, and finally, about the effect of their activity on the exercise of individual liberty, both in the political and ideological spheres and in social, economic and cultural life. The men who hold this power have a grave moral responsibility with respect to the truth of the information that they spread, the needs and the reactions that they generate and the values which they put forward. In the case of television, moreover, what is coming into being is an original mode of knowledge and a new civilization: that of the image.

Naturally, the public authorities cannot ignore the growing power and influence of the media of social communication and the advantages and risks which their use involves for the civic community and for its development and real perfecting.

Consequently they are called upon to perform their own positive function for the common good by encouraging every constructive expression, by supporting individual citizens and groups in defending the fundamental values of the person and of human society, and also by taking suitable steps to prevent the spread of what would harm the common heritage of values on which orderly civil progress is based.[15]

THE ENVIRONMENT

21.   While the horizon of man is thus being modified according to the images that are chosen for him, another transformation is making itself felt, one which is the dramatic and unexpected consequence of human

activity. Man is suddenly becoming aware that by an ill-considered exploitation of nature he risks destroying it and becoming in his turn the
victim of this degradation. Not only is the material environment becoming a permanent menace—pollution and refuse, new illnesses and absolute destructive capacity—but the human framework is no longer under
man's control, thus creating an environment for tomorrow which may
well be intolerable. This is a wide-ranging social problem which concerns
the entire human family.

The Christian must turn to these new perceptions in order to take on
responsibility, together with the rest of men, for a destiny which from
now on is shared by all.

Fundamental Aspirations and Currents of Ideas

22.   While scientific and technological progress continues to overturn
man's surroundings, his patterns of knowledge, work, consumption and
relationships, two aspirations persistently make themselves felt in these
new contexts, and they grow stronger to the extent that he becomes better
informed and better educated: the aspiration to equality and the aspiration to participation, two forms of man's dignity and freedom.

ADVANTAGES AND LIMITATIONS OF JURIDICAL RECOGNITION

23.   Through the statement of the rights of man and the seeking for
international agreements for the application of these rights, progress has
been made towards inscribing these two aspirations in deeds and
structures.[16] Nevertheless various forms of discrimination continually
reappear—ethnic, cultural, religious, political and so on. In fact, human
rights are still too often disregarded, if not scoffed at, or else they receive
only formal recognition. In many cases legislation does not keep up with
real situations. Legislation is necessary, but it is not sufficient for setting
up true relationships of justice and equality. In teaching us charity, the
Gospel instructs us in the preferential respect due to the poor and the
special situation they have in society: the more fortunate should renounce
some of their rights so as to place their goods more generously at the
service of others. If, beyond legal rules, there is really no deeper feeling of
respect for and service to others, then even equality before the law can
serve as an alibi for flagrant discrimination, continued exploitation and
actual contempt. Without a renewed education in solidarity, an overem-

phasis of equality can give rise to an individualism in which each one claims his own rights without wishing to be answerable for the common good.

In this field, everyone sees the highly important contribution of the Christian spirit, which moreover answers man's yearning to be loved. "Love for man, the prime value of the earthly order" ensures the conditions for peace, both social peace and international peace, by affirming our universal brotherhood.[17]

THE POLITICAL SOCIETY

24. The two aspirations, to equality and to participation, seek to promote a democratic type of society. Various models are proposed, some are tried out, none of them gives complete satisfaction, and the search goes on between ideological and pragmatic tendencies. The Christian has the duty to take part in this search and in the organization and life of political society. As a social being, man builds his destiny within a series of particular groupings which demand, as their completion and as a necessary condition for their development, a vaster society, one of a universal character, the political society. All particular activity must be placed within that wider society, and thereby it takes on the dimension of the common good.[18]

This indicates the importance of education for life in society, in which there are called to mind, not only information on each one's rights, but also their necessary correlative: the recognition of the duties of each one in regard to others. The sense and practice of duty are themselves conditioned by self-mastery and by the acceptance of responsibility and of the limits placed upon the freedom of the individual or of the group.

25. Political activity—need one remark that we are dealing primarily with an activity, not an ideology?—should be the projection of a plan of society which is consistent in its concrete means and in its inspiration, and which springs from a complete conception of man's vocation and of its differing social expressions. It is not for the State or even for political parties, which would be closed unto themselves, to try to impose an ideology by means that would lead to a dictatorship over minds, the worst kind of all. It is for cultural and religious groupings, in the freedom of acceptance which they presume, to develop in the social body, disinterestedly and in their own ways, those ultimate convictions on the nature, origin and end of man and society.

In this field, it is well to keep in mind the principle proclaimed at the

Second Vatican Council: "The truth cannot impose itself except by virtue of its own truth, and it makes its entrance into the mind at once quietly and with power".[19]

IDEOLOGIES AND HUMAN LIBERTY

26.   Therefore the Christian who wishes to live his faith in a political activity which he thinks of as service cannot without contradicting himself adhere to ideological systems which radically or substantially go against his faith and his concept of man. He cannot adhere to the Marxist ideology, to its atheistic materialism, to its dialectic of violence and to the way it absorbs individual freedom in the collectivity, at the same time denying all transcendence to man and his personal and collective history; nor can he adhere to the liberal ideology which believes it exalts individual freedom by withdrawing it from every limitation, by stimulating it through exclusive seeking of interest and power, and by considering social solidarities as more or less automatic consequences of individual initiatives, not as an aim and a major criterion of the value of the social organization.

27.   Is there need to stress the possible ambiguity of every social ideology? Sometimes it leads political or social activity to be simply the application of an abstract, purely theoretical idea; at other times it is thought which becomes a mere instrument at the service of activity as a simple means of a strategy. In both cases is it not man that risks finding himself alienated? The Christian faith is above and is sometimes opposed to the ideologies, in that it recognizes God, who is transcendent and the Creator, and who, through all the levels of creation, calls on man as endowed with responsibility and freedom.

28.   There would also be the danger of giving adherence to an ideology which does not rest on a true and organic doctrine, to take refuge in it as a final and sufficient explanation of everything, and thus to build a new idol, accepting, at times without being aware of doing so, its totalitarian and coercive character. And people imagine they find in it a justification for their activity, even violent activity, and an adequate response to a generous desire to serve. The desire remains but it allows itself to be consumed by an ideology which, even if it suggests certain paths to man's liberation, ends up by making him a slave.

29.   It has been possible today to speak of a retreat of ideologies. In this respect the present time may be favourable for an openness to the concrete transcendence of Christianity. It may also be a more accentuated sliding towards a new positivism: universalized technology as the

dominant form of activity, as the overwhelming pattern of existence, even as a language, without the question of its meaning being really asked.

HISTORICAL MOVEMENTS

30.   But outside of this positivism which reduces man to a single dimension even if it be an important one today and by so doing mutilates him, the Christian encounters in his activity concrete historical movements sprung from ideologies and in part distinct from them. Our venerated predecessor Pope John XXIII in *Pacem in Terris* already showed that it is possible to make a distinction: "Neither can false philosophical teachings regarding the nature, origin and destiny of the universe and of man be identified with historical movements that have economic, social, cultural or political ends, not even when these movements have originated from those teachings and have drawn and still draw inspiration therefrom. Because the teachings, once they are drawn up and defined, remain always the same, while the movements, being concerned with historical situations in constant evolution, cannot but be influenced by these latter and cannot avoid, therefore, being subject to changes, even of a profound nature. Besides, who can deny that those movements, in so far as they conform to the dictates of right reason and are interpreters of the lawful aspirations of the human person, contain elements that are positive and deserving of approval?".[20]

ATTRACTION OF SOCIALIST CURRENTS

31.   Some Christians are today attracted by socialist currents and their various developments. They try to recognize therein a certain number of aspirations which they carry within themselves in the name of their faith. They feel that they are part of that historical current and wish to play a part within it. Now this historical current takes on, under the same name, different forms according to different continents and cultures, even if it drew its inspiration, and still does in many cases, from ideologies incompatible with faith. Careful judgment is called for. Too often Christians attracted by socialism tend to idealize it in terms which, apart from anything else, are very general: a will for justice, solidarity and equality. They refuse to recognize the limitations of the historical socialist movements, which remain conditioned by the ideologies from which they originated. Distinctions must be made to guide concrete choices between the various levels of expression of socialism: a generous aspiration and a

seeking for a more just society, historical movements with a political organization and aim, and an ideology which claims to give a complete and self-sufficient picture of man. Nevertheless, these distinctions must not lead one to consider such levels as completely separate and independent. The concrete link which, according to circumstances, exists between them must be clearly marked out. This insight will enable Christians to see the degree of commitment possible along these lines, while safeguarding the values, especially those of liberty, responsibility and openness to the spiritual, which guarantee the integral development of man.

HISTORICAL EVOLUTION OF MARXISM

32.   Other Christians even ask whether an historical development of Marxism might not authorize certain concrete rapprochements. They note in fact a certain splintering of Marxism, which until now showed itself to be a unitary ideology which explained in atheistic terms the whole of man and the world since it did not go outside their development process. Apart from the ideological confrontation officially separating the various champions of Marxism-Leninism in their individual interpretations of the thought of its founders, and apart from the open opposition between the political systems which make use of its name today, some people lay down distinctions between Marxism's various levels of expression.

33.   For some, Marxism remains essentially the active practice of class struggle. Experiencing the ever present and continually renewed force of the relationships of domination and exploitation among men, they reduce Marxism to no more than a struggle—at times with no other purpose—to be pursued and even stirred up in permanent fashion. For others, it is first and foremost the collective exercise of political and economic power under the direction of a single party, which would be the sole expression and guarantee of the welfare of all, and would deprive individuals and other groups of any possibility of initiative and choice. At a third level, Marxism, whether in power or not, is viewed as a socialist ideology based on historical materialism and the denial of everything transcendent. At other times, finally, it presents itself in a more attenuated form, one also more attractive to the modern mind: as a scientific activity, as a rigorous method of examining social and political reality, and as the rational link, tested by history, between theoretical knowledge and the practice of revolutionary transformation. Although this type of

analysis gives a privileged position to certain aspects of reality to the detriment of the rest, and interprets them in the light of its ideology, it nevertheless furnishes some people not only with a working tool but also a certitude preliminary to action: the claim to decipher in a scientific manner the mainsprings of the evolution of society.

34.   While, through the concrete existing form of Marxism, one can distinguish these various aspects and the questions they pose for the reflection and activity of Christians, it would be illusory and dangerous to reach a point of forgetting the intimate link which radically binds them together, to accept the elements of Marxist analysis without recognizing their relationships with ideology, and to enter into the practice of class struggle and its Marxist interpretations, while failing to note the kind of totalitarian and violent society to which this process leads.

THE LIBERAL IDEOLOGY

35.   On another side, we are witnessing a renewal of the liberal ideology. This current asserts itself both in the name of economic efficiency, and for the defence of the individual against the increasingly overwhelming hold of organizations, and as a reaction against the totalitarian tendencies of political powers. Certainly, personal initiative must be maintained and developed. But do not Christians who take this path tend to idealize liberalism in their turn, making it a proclamation in favour of freedom? They would like a new model, more adapted to present-day conditions, while easily forgetting that at the very root of philosophical liberalism is an erroneous affirmation of the autonomy of the individual in his activity, his motivation and the exercise of his liberty. Hence, the liberal ideology likewise calls for careful discernment on their part.

CHRISTIAN DISCERNMENT

36.   In this renewed encounter of the various ideologies, the Christian will draw from the sources of his faith and the Church's teaching the necessary principles and suitable criteria to avoid permitting himself to be first attracted by and then imprisoned within a system whose limitations and totalitarianism may well become evident to him too late, if he does not perceive them in their roots. Going beyond every system, without however failing to commit himself concretely to serving his brothers, he will assert, in the very midst of his options, the specific character of the Christian contribution for a positive transformation of society.[21]

REBIRTH OF UTOPIAS

37.   Today moreover the weaknesses of the ideologies are better perceived through the concrete systems in which they are trying to affirm themselves. Bureaucratic socialism, technocratic capitalism and authoritarian democracy are showing how difficult it is to solve the great human problem of living together in justice and equality. How in fact could they escape the materialism, egoism or constraint which inevitably go with them? This is the source of a protest which is springing up more or less everywhere, as a sign of a deep-seated sickness, while at the same time we are witnessing the rebirth of what it is agreed to call "utopias". These claim to resolve the political problem of modern societies better than the ideologies. It would be dangerous to disregard this. The appeal to a utopia is often a convenient excuse for those who wish to escape from concrete tasks in order to take refuge in an imaginary world. To live in a hypothetical future is a facile alibi for rejecting immediate responsibilities. But it must clearly be recognized that this kind of criticism of existing society often provokes the forward-looking imagination both to perceive in the present the disregarded possibility hidden within it, and to direct itself towards a fresh future; it thus sustains social dynamism by the confidence that it gives to the inventive powers of the human mind and heart; and, if it refuses no overture, it can also meet the Christian appeal. The Spirit of the Lord, who animates man renewed in Christ, continually breaks down the horizons within which his understanding likes to find security and the limits to which his activity would willingly restrict itself; there dwells within him a power which urges him to go beyond every system and every ideology. At the heart of the world there dwells the mystery of man discovering himself to be God's son in the course of a historical and psychological process in which constraint and freedom as well as the weight of sin and the breath of the Spirit alternate and struggle for the upper hand.

The dynamism of Christian faith here triumphs over the narrow calculations of egoism. Animated by the power of the Spirit of Jesus Christ, the Saviour of mankind, and upheld by hope, the Christian involves himself in the building up of the human city, one that is to be peaceful, just and fraternal and acceptable as an offering to God.[22] In fact, "the expectation of a new earth must not weaken but rather stimulate our concern for cultivating this one. For here grows the body of a new human family, a body which even now is able to give some kind of foreshadowing of the new age".[23]

THE QUESTIONING OF THE HUMAN SCIENCES

38.   In this world dominated by scientific and technological change, which threatens to drag it towards a new positivism, another more fundamental doubt is raised. Having subdued nature by using his reason, man now finds that he himself is as it were imprisoned within his own rationality; he in turn becomes the object of science. The "human sciences" are today enjoying a significant flowering. On the one hand they are subjecting to critical and radical examination the hitherto accepted knowledge about man, on the grounds that this knowledge seems either too empirical or too theoretical. On the other hand, methodological necessity and ideological presuppositions too often lead the human sciences to isolate, in the various situations, certain aspects of man, and yet to give these an explanation which claims to be complete or at least an interpretation which is meant to be all-embracing from a purely quantitative or phenomenological point of view. This scientific reduction betrays a dangerous presumption. To give a privileged position in this way to such an aspect of analysis is to mutilate man and, under the pretext of a scientific procedure, to make it impossible to understand man in his totality.

39.   One must be no less attentive to the action which the human sciences can instigate, giving rise to the elaboration of models of society to be subsequently imposed on men as scientifically tested types of behaviour. Man can then become the object of manipulations directing his desires and needs and modifying his behaviour and even his system of values. There is no doubt that there exists here a grave danger for the societies of tomorrow and for man himself. For even if all agree to build a new society at the service of men, it is still essential to know what sort of man is in question.

40.   Suspicion of the human sciences affects the Christian more than others, but it does not find him disarmed. For, as we ourself wrote in *Populorum Progressio*, it is here that there is found the specific contribution of the Church to civilizations: "Sharing the noblest aspirations of men and suffering when she sees them not satisfied, she wishes to help them attain their full flowering, and that is why she offers men what she possesses as her characteristic attribute: a global vision of man and of the human race".[24] Should the Church in its turn contest the proceedings of the human sciences, and condemn their pretentions? As in the case of the natural sciences, the Church has confidence in this research also and urges Christians to play an active part in it.[25] Prompted by the same

scientific demands and the desire to know man better, but at the same time enlightened by their faith, Christians who devote themselves to the human sciences will begin a dialogue between the Church and this new field of discovery, a dialogue which promises to be fruitful. Of course, each individual scientific discipline will be able, in its own particular sphere, to grasp only a partial—yet true—aspect of man; the complete picture and the full meaning will escape it. But within these limits the human sciences give promise of a positive function that the Church willingly recognizes. They can even widen the horizons of human liberty to a greater extent than the conditioning circumstances perceived enable one to foresee. They could thus assist Christian social morality, which no doubt will see its field restricted when it comes to suggesting certain models of society, while its function of making a critical judgment and taking an overall view will be strengthened by its showing the relative character of the behaviour and values presented by such and such a society as definitive and inherent in the very nature of man. These sciences are a condition at once indispensable and inadequate for a better discovery of what is human. They are a language which becomes more and more complex, yet one that deepens rather than solves the mystery of the heart of man; nor does it provide the complete and definitive answer to the desire which springs from his innermost being.

AMBIGUOUS NATURE OF PROGRESS

41.   This better knowledge of man makes it possible to pass a better critical judgment upon and to elucidate a fundamental notion that remains at the basis of modern societies as their motive, their measure and their goal: namely, progress. Since the nineteenth century, western societies and, as a result, many others have put their hopes in ceaselessly renewed and indefinite progress. They saw this progress as man's effort to free himself in face of the demands of nature and of social constraints; progress was the condition for and the yardstick of human freedom. Progress, spread by the modern media of information and by the demand for wider knowledge and greater consumption, has become an omnipresent ideology. Yet a doubt arises today regarding both its value and its result. What is the meaning of this never-ending, breathless pursuit of a progress that always eludes one just when one believes one has conquered it sufficiently in order to enjoy it in peace? If it is not attained, it leaves one dissatisfied. Without doubt, there has been just condemnation of the limits and even the misdeeds of a merely quantitative economic growth; there is a desire to attain objectives of a qualitative order also. The

quality and the truth of human relations, the degree of participation and of responsibility, are no less significant and important for the future of society than the quantity and variety of the goods produced and consumed.

Overcoming the temptation to wish to measure everything in terms of efficiency and of trade, and in terms of the interplay of forces and interests, man today wishes to replace these quantitative criteria with the intensity of communication, the spread of knowledge and culture, mutual service and a combining of efforts for a common task. Is not genuine progress to be found in the development of moral consciousness, which will lead man to exercise a wider solidarity and to open himself freely to others and to God? For a Christian, progress necessarily comes up against the eschatological mystery of death. The death of Christ and his resurrection and the outpouring of the Spirit of the Lord help man to place his freedom, in creativity and gratitude, within the context of the truth of all progress and the only hope which does not deceive.[26]

Christians Face to Face with These New Problems

DYNAMISM OF THE CHURCH'S SOCIAL TEACHING

42.   In the face of so many new questions the Church makes an effort to reflect in order to give an answer, in its own sphere, to men's expectations. If today the problems seem original in their breadth and their urgency, is man without the means of solving them? It is with all its dynamism that the social teaching of the Church accompanies men in their search. If it does not intervene to authenticate a given structure or to propose a ready-made model, it does not thereby limit itself to recalling general principles. It develops through reflection applied to the changing situations of this world, under the driving force of the Gospel as the source of renewal when its message is accepted in its totality and with all its demands. It also develops with the sensitivity proper to the Church which is characterized by a disinterested will to serve and by attention to the poorest.

Finally, it draws upon its rich experience of many centuries which enables it, while continuing its permanent preoccupations, to undertake the daring and creative innovations which the present state of the world requires.

FOR GREATER JUSTICE

43.   There is a need to establish a greater justice in the sharing of goods, both within national communities and on the international level. In international exchanges there is a need to go beyond relationships based on force, in order to arrive at agreements reached with the good of all in mind. Relationships based on force have never in fact established justice in a true and lasting manner, even if at certain times the alternation of positions can often make it possible to find easier conditions for dialogue. The use of force moreover leads to the setting in motion of opposing forces, and from this springs a climate of struggle which opens the way to situations of extreme violence and to abuses.[27]

But, as we have often stated, the most important duty in the realm of justice is to allow each country to promote its own development, within the framework of a cooperation free from any spirit of domination, whether economic or political. The complexity of the problems raised is certainly great, in the present intertwining of mutual dependences. Thus it is necessary to have the courage to undertake a revision of the relationships between nations, whether it is a question of the international division of production, the structure of exchanges, the control of profits, the monetary system,—without forgetting the actions of human solidarity—to question the models of growth of the rich nations and change people's outlooks, so that they may realize the prior call of international duty, and to renew international organizations so that they may increase in effectiveness.

44.   Under the driving force of new systems of production, national frontiers are breaking down, and we can see new economic powers emerging, the multinational enterprises, which by the concentration and flexibility of their means can conduct autonomous strategies which are largely independent of the national political powers and therefore not subject to control from the point of view of the common good. By extending their activities, these private organizations can lead to a new and abusive form of economic domination on the social, cultural and even political level. The excessive concentration of means and powers that Pope Pius XI already condemned on the fortieth anniversary of *Rerum Novarum* is taking on a new and very real image.

CHANGE OF ATTITUDES AND STRUCTURES

45.   Today men yearn to free themselves from need and dependence. But this liberation starts with the interior freedom that men must find again with regard to their goods and their powers; they will never reach it

except through a transcendent love for man, and, in consequence, through a genuine readiness to serve. Otherwise, as one can see only too clearly, the most revolutionary ideologies lead only to a change of masters; once installed in power in their turn, these new masters surround themselves with privileges, limit freedoms and allow other forms of injustice to become established.

Thus many people are reaching the point of questioning the very model of society. The ambition of many nations, in the competition that sets them in opposition and which carries them along, is to attain technological, economic and military power. This ambition then stands in the way of setting up structures in which the rhythm of progress would be regulated with a view to greater justice, instead of accentuating inequalities and living in a climate of distrust and struggle which would unceasingly compromise peace.

CHRISTIAN MEANING OF POLITICAL ACTIVITY

46.   Is it not here that there appears a radical limitation to economics? Economic activity is necessary and, if it is at the service of man, it can be "a source of brotherhood and a sign of Providence".[28] It is the occasion of concrete exchanges between man, of rights recognized, of services rendered and of dignity affirmed in work. Though it is often a field of confrontation and domination, it can give rise to dialogue and foster cooperation. Yet it runs the risk of taking up too much strength and freedom.[29] This is why the need is felt to pass from economics to politics. It is true that in the term 'politics' many confusions are possible and must be clarified, but each man feels that in the social and economic field, both national and international, the ultimate decision rests with political power.

Political power, which is the natural and necessary link for ensuring the cohesion of the social body, must have as its aim the achievement of the common good. While respecting the legitimate liberties of individuals, families and subsidiary groups, it acts in such a way as to create, effectively and for the well-being of all, the conditions required for attaining man's true and complete good, including his spiritual end. It acts within the limits of its competence, which can vary from people to people and from country to country. It always intervenes with care for justice and with devotion to the common good, for which it holds final responsibility. It does not, for all that, deprive individuals and intermediary bodies of the field of activity and responsibility which are proper to them and which lead them to collaborate in the attainment of this common good. In fact, "the true aim of all social activity should be to help individual members of the social body, but never to destroy or absorb them".[30] According to the vocation proper to it, the political power must know how to stand aside from particular interests in order to view its responsibility with regard to the good of all men, even going beyond national limits. To take politics seriously at its different levels—local, regional, national and worldwide—is to affirm the duty of man, of every man, to recognize the concrete reality and the value of the freedom of choice that is offered to him to seek to bring about both the good of the city and of the nation and of mankind. Politics are a demanding manner—but not the only one—of living the Christian commitment to the service of others. Without of course solving every problem, it endeavours to apply solutions to the relationships men have with one another. The domain of politics is wide and comprehensive, but it is not exclusive. An attitude of encroachment which would tend to set up politics as an absolute value would bring serious danger. While recognizing the autonomy of the reality of politics, Christians who are invited to take up political activity should try to make their choices consistent with the Gospel and, in the framework of a legitimate plurality, to give both personal and collective witness to the seriousness of their faith by effective and disinterested service of men.

SHARING IN RESPONSIBILITY

47.   The passing to the political dimension also expresses a demand made by the man of today: a greater sharing in responsibility and in decision-making. This legitimate aspiration becomes more evident as the cultural level rises, as the sense of freedom develops and as man becomes more aware of how, in a world facing an uncertain future, the choices of today already condition the life of tomorrow. In *Mater et Magistra*[31] Pope John XXIII stressed how much the admittance to responsibility is a basic demand of man's nature, a concrete exercise of his freedom and a path to his development, and he showed how, in economic life and particularly in enterprise, this sharing in responsibilities should be ensured.[32] Today the field is wider, and extends to the social and political sphere in which a reasonable sharing in responsibility and in decisions must be established and strengthened. Admittedly, it is true that the choices proposed for a decision are more and more complex; the considerations that must be borne in mind are numerous and the foreseeing of the consequences involves risk, even if new sciences strive to enlighten freedom at these important moments. However, although limits are sometimes called for, these obstacles must not slow down the giving of wider participation in working out decisions, making choices and putting them into practice. In

order to counterbalance increasing technocracy, modern forms of democracy must be devised, not only making it possible for each man to become informed and to express himself, but also by involving him in a shared responsibility.

Thus human groups will gradually begin to share and to live as communities. Thus freedom, which too often asserts itself as a claim for autonomy by opposing the freedom of others, will develop in its deepest human reality: to involve itself and to spend itself in building up active and lived solidarity. But, for the Christian, it is by losing himself in God who sets him free that man finds true freedom, renewed in the death and resurrection of the Lord.

Call to Action

NEED TO BECOME INVOLVED IN ACTION

48.   In the social sphere, the Church has always wished to assume a double function: first to enlighten minds in order to assist them to discover the truth and to find the right path to follow amid the different teachings that call for their attention; and secondly to take part in action and to spread, with a real care for service and effectiveness, the energies of the Gospel. Is it not in order to be faithful to this desire that the Church has sent on an apostolic mission among the workers priests who, by sharing fully the condition of the worker, are at that level the witnesses to the Church's solicitude and seeking?

It is to all Christians that we address a fresh and insistent call to action. In our encyclical on the Development of Peoples we urged that all should set themselves to the task: "Laymen should take up as their own proper task the renewal of the temporal order. If the role of the hierarchy is to teach and to interpret authentically the norms of morality to be followed in this matter, it belongs to the laity, without waiting passively for orders and directives, to take the initiative freely and to infuse a Christian spirit into the mentality, customs, laws and structures of the community in which they live".[33] Let each one examine himself, to see what he has done up to now, and what he ought to do. It is not enough to recall principles, state intentions, point to crying injustices and utter prophetic denunciations; these words will lack real weight unless they are accompanied for each individual by a livelier awareness of personal responsibility and by effective action. It is too easy to throw back on others responsibility for injustices, if at the same time one does not realize how each one shares in it personally, and how personal conversion is needed first. This basic humility will rid action of all inflexibility and sectarianism; it will also avoid discouragement in the face of a task which seems limitless in size. The Christian's hope comes primarily from the fact that he knows that the Lord is working with us in the world, continuing in his Body which is the Church—and, through the Church, in the whole of mankind—the Redemption which was accomplished on the Cross and which burst forth in victory on the morning of the Resurrection.[34] This hope springs also from the fact that the Christian knows that other men are at work, to undertake actions of justice and peace working for the same ends. For beneath an outward appearance of indifference, in the heart of every man there is a will to live in brotherhood and a thirst for justice and peace, which is to be expanded.

49.   Thus, amid the diversity of situations, functions and organizations, each one must determine, in his conscience, the actions which he is called to share in. Surrounded by various currents into which, beside legitimate aspirations, there insinuate themselves more ambiguous tendencies, the Christian must make a wise and vigilant choice and avoid involving himself in collaboration without conditions and contrary to the principles of a true humanism, even in the name of a genuinely felt solidarity. If in fact he wishes to play a specific part as a Christian in accordance with his faith—a part that unbelievers themselves expect of him—he must take care in the midst of his active commitment to clarify his motives and to rise above the objectives aimed at, by taking a more all-embracing view which will avoid the danger of selfish particularism and oppressive totalitarianism.

PLURALISM OF OPTIONS

50.   In concrete situations, and taking account of solidarity in each person's life, one must recognize a legitimate variety of possible options. The same Christian faith can lead to different commitments.[35] The Church invites all Christians to take up a double task of inspiring and of innovating, in order to make structures evolve, so as to adapt them to the real needs of today. From Christians who at first sight seem to be in opposition, as a result of starting from differing options, she asks an effort at mutual understanding of the other's positions and motives; a loyal examination of one's behaviour and its correctness will suggest to each one an attitude of more profound charity which, while recognizing the differences, believes nonetheless in the possibility of convergence and

unity. "The bonds which unite the faithful are mightier than anything which divides them".[36]

It is true that many people, in the midst of modern structures and conditioning circumstances, are determined by their habits of thought and their functions, even apart from the safeguarding of material interests. Others feel so deeply the solidarity of classes and cultures that they reach the point of sharing without reserve all the judgments and options of their surroundings.[37] Each one will take great care to examine himself and to bring about that true freedom according to Christ which makes one receptive to the universal in the very midst of the most particular conditions.

51.   It is in this regard too that Christian organizations, under their different forms, have a responsibility for collective action. Without putting themselves in the place of the institutions of civil society, they have to express, in their own way and rising above their particular nature, the concrete demands of the Christian faith for a just, and consequently necessary, transformation of society.[38]

Today more than ever the Word of God will be unable to be proclaimed and heard unless it is accompanied by the witness of the power of the Holy Spirit, working within the action of Christians in the service of their brothers, at the points in which their existence and their future are at stake.

52.   In expressing these reflections to you, venerable brother, we are of course aware that we have not dealt with all the social problems that today face the man of faith and men of goodwill. Our recent declarations—to which has been added your message of a short time ago on the occasion of the launching of the Second Development Decade—particularly concerning the duties of the community of nations in the serious question of the integral and concerted development of man are still fresh in people's minds. We address these present reflections to you with the aim of offering to the Council of the Laity and the Pontifical Commission Justice and Peace some fresh contributions, as well as encouragement, for the pursuit of their task of "awakening the People of God to a full understanding of its role at the present time" and of "promoting the apostolate on the international level".[39]

It is with these sentiments, venerable brother, that we impart to you our Apostolic Blessing.

From the Vatican, 14 May 1971.

PAULUS PP. VI

NOTES

1. *Gaudium et Spes,* 10: *AAS* 58 (1966), p. 1033.
2. *AAS* 23 (1931), p. 209 ff.
3. *AAS* 53 (1961), p. 429.
4. 3: *AAS* 59 (1967), p. 258.
5. *Ibidem,* 1: p. 257.
6. Cf. *2 Cor* 4:17.
7. *Populorum Progressio,* 25: *AAS* 59 (1967), pp. 269-270.
8. Cf. *Rev* 3:12; 21:2.
9. *Gaudium et Spes,* 25: *AAS* 58 (1966), p. 1045.
10. *Ibidem,* 67: p. 1089.
11. *Populorum Progressio,* 69: *AAS* 59 (1967), pp. 290-291.
12. Cf. *Mt* 25:35.
13. *Nostra Aetate,* 5: *AAS* 58 (1966), p. 743.
14. 37: *AAS* 59 (1967), p. 276.
15. *Inter Mirifica,* 12: *AAS* 56 (1964), p. 149.
16. Cf. *Pacem in Terris: AAS* 55 (1963), p. 261 ff.
17. Cf. *Message for the World Day of Peace,* 1971: *AAS* 63 (1971), pp. 5-9.
18. Cf. *Gaudium et Spes,* 74: *AAS* 58 (1966), pp. 1095-1096.
19. *Dignitatis Humanae,* 1: *AAS* 58 (1966), p. 930.
20. *AAS* 55 (1963), p. 300.
21. Cf. *Gaudium et Spes,* 11: *AAS* 58 (1966), p. 1033.
22. Cf. *Rom* 15:16.
23. *Gaudium et Spes,* 39: *AAS* 58 (1966), p. 1057.
24. 13: *Populorum Progressio, AAS* 59 (1967), p. 264.
25. Cf. *Gaudium et Spes,* 36: *AAS* 58 (1966), p. 1054.
26. Cf. *Rom* 5:5.
27. *Populorum Progressio,* 56 ff.: *AAS* 59 (1967), pp. 285 ff.
28. *Ibidem,* 86: p. 299.
29. *Gaudium et Spes,* 63: *AAS* 58 (1966), p. 1085.
30. *Quadragesimo Anno: AAS* 23 (1931), p. 203; cf. *Mater et Magistra: AAS* 53 (1961), pp. 414, 428; *Gaudium et Spes,* 74–76: *AAS* 58 (1966), pp. 1095–1100.
31. *AAS* 53 (1961), pp. 420-422.
32. *Gaudium et Spes,* 68, 75: *AAS* 58 (1966), pp. 1089-1090; 1097.
33. 81: *AAS* 59 (1967), pp. 296-297.
34. Cf. *Mt* 28:30; *Phil* 2:8-11.
35. *Gaudium et Spes,* 43: *AAS* 58 (1966), p. 1061.
36. *Ibidem,* 93: p. 1113.
37. Cf. *1 Thess* 5:21.
38. *Lumen Gentium,* 31: *AAS* 57 (1965), pp. 37-38; *Apostolicam Actuositatem,* 5: *AAS* 58 (1966), p. 842.
39. *Catholicam Christi Ecclesiam, AAS* 59 (1967), pp. 27 and 26.

Justice in the World

Synod of Bishops
Second General Assembly
(November 30, 1971)

Introduction

1.   Gathered from the whole world, in communion with all who believe in Christ and with the entire human family, and opening our hearts to the Spirit who is making the whole of creation new, we have

---

[This English version is that published by the Vatican Polyglot Press in booklet form, 25 pages. The paragraph numbers have been added by me. The Vatican Press booklet includes a Rescript signed by Cardinal John Villot, Secretary of State, dated November 30, 1971. It states as follows: "The Holy Father has carefully examined the two documents containing the proposals by the Second General Assembly of the Synod of Bishops on the themes, 'The Ministerial Priesthood' and 'Justice in the World,' which had been put before the Assembly for study. As he has already announced in his address at the General Audience of 24 November, the Holy Father desires that the aforementioned documents be made public. His Holiness now accepts and confirms all the conclusions in the two documents that conform to the current norms: in particular, he confirms that in the Latin Church there shall continue to be observed in its entirety, with God's help, the present discipline of priestly celibacy. The Holy Father reserves to himself to examine carefully in due course whether the proposals—and which of them—contained in the recommendations of the Synodal Assembly should be convalidated as directive guidelines or practical norms."]

questioned ourselves about the mission of the People of God to further justice in the world.

2.   Scrutinizing the "signs of the times" and seeking to detect the meaning of emerging history, while at the same time sharing the aspirations and questionings of all those who want to build a more human world, we have listened to the Word of God that we might be converted to the fulfilling of the divine plan for the salvation of the world.

3.   Even though it is not for us to elaborate a very profound analysis of the situation of the world, we have nevertheless been able to perceive the serious injustices which are building around the world of men a network of domination, oppression and abuses which stifle freedom and which keep the greater part of humanity from sharing in the building up and enjoyment of a more just and more fraternal world.

4.   At the same time we have noted the inmost stirring moving the world in its depths. There are facts constituting a contribution to the furthering of justice. In associations of men and among peoples themselves there is arising a new awareness which shakes them out of any fatalistic resignation and which spurs them on to liberate themselves and to be responsible for their own destiny. Movements among men are seen which express hope in a better world and a will to change whatever has become intolerable.

5.   Listening to the cry of those who suffer violence and are oppressed by unjust systems and structures, and hearing the appeal of a world that by its perversity contradicts the plan of its Creator, we have shared our awareness of the Church's vocation to be present in the heart of the world by proclaiming the Good News to the poor, freedom to the oppressed, and joy to the afflicted. The hopes and forces which are moving the world in its very foundations are not foreign to the dynamism of the Gospel, which through the power of the Holy Spirit frees men from personal sin and from its consequences in social life.

6.   The uncertainty of history and the painful convergences in the ascending path of the human community direct us to sacred history; there God has revealed himself to us, and made known to us, as it is brought progressively to realization, his plan of liberation and salvation which is once and for all fulfilled in the Paschal Mystery of Christ. Action on behalf of justice and participation in the transformation of the world fully appear to us as a constitutive dimension of the preaching of the Gospel, or, in other words, of the Church's mission for the redemption of the human race and its liberation from every oppressive situation.

I. Justice and World Society

CRISIS OF UNIVERSAL SOLIDARITY

7.   The world in which the Church lives and acts is held captive by a tremendous paradox. Never before have the forces working for bringing about a unified world society appeared so powerful and dynamic; they are rooted in the awareness of the full basic equality as well as of the human dignity of all. Since men are members of the same human family, they are indissolubly linked with one another in the one destiny of the whole world, in the responsibility for which they all share.

8.   The new technological possibilities are based upon the unity of science, on the global and simultaneous character of communications and on the birth of an absolutely interdependent economic world. Moreover, men are beginning to grasp a new and more radical dimension of unity; for they perceive that their resources, as well as the precious treasures of air and water—without which there cannot be life—and the small delicate biosphere of the whole complex of all life on earth, are not infinite, but on the contrary must be saved and preserved as a unique patrimony belonging to all mankind.

9.   The paradox lies in the fact that within this perspective of unity the forces of division and antagonism seem today to be increasing in strength. Ancient divisions between nations and empires, between races and classes, today possess new technological instruments of destruction. The arms race is a threat to man's highest good, which is life; it makes poor peoples and individuals yet more miserable, while making richer those already powerful; it creates a continuous danger of conflagration, and in the case of nuclear arms, it threatens to destroy all life from the face of the earth. At the same time new divisions are being born to separate man from his neighbour. Unless combatted and overcome by social and political action, the influence of the new industrial and technological order favours the concentration of wealth, power and decision-making in the hands of a small public or private controlling group. Economic injustice and lack of social participation keep a man from attaining his basic human and civil rights.

10.   In the last twenty-five years a hope has spread through the human race that economic growth would bring about such a quantity of goods that it would be possible to feed the hungry at least with the crumbs falling from the table, but this has proved a vain hope in underdeveloped

areas and in pockets of poverty in wealthier areas, because of the rapid growth of population and of the labour force, because of rural stagnation and the lack of agrarian reform, and because of the massive migratory flow to the cities, where the industries, even though endowed with huge sums of money, nevertheless provide so few jobs that not infrequently one worker in four is left unemployed. These stifling oppressions constantly give rise to great numbers of "marginal" persons, ill-fed, inhumanly housed, illiterate and deprived of political power as well as of the suitable means of acquiring responsibility and moral dignity.

11.   Furthermore, such is the demand for resources and energy by the richer nations, whether capitalist or socialist, and such are the effects of dumping by them in the atmosphere and the sea that irreparable damage would be done to the essential elements of life on earth, such as air and water, if their high rates of consumption and pollution, which are constantly on the increase, were extended to the whole of mankind.

12.   The strong drive towards global unity, the unequal distribution which places decisions concerning three quarters of income, investment and trade in the hands of one third of the human race, namely the more highly developed part, the insufficiency of a merely economic progress, and the new recognition of the material limits of the biosphere—all this makes us aware of the fact that in today's world new modes of understanding human dignity are arising.

THE RIGHT TO DEVELOPMENT

13.   In the face of international systems of domination, the bringing about of justice depends more and more on the determined will for development.

14.   In the developing nations and in the so-called socialist world, that determined will asserts itself especially in a struggle for forms of claiming one's rights and self-expression, a struggle caused by the evolution of the economic system itself.

15.   This aspiring to justice asserts itself in advancing beyond the threshold at which begins a consciousness of enhancement of personal worth (cf. *Populorum Progressio* 15; A.A.S. 59, 1967, p. 265) with regard both to the whole man and the whole of mankind. This is expressed in an awareness of the right to development. The right to development must be seen as a dynamic interpenetration of all those fundamental human rights upon which the aspirations of individuals and nations are based.

16.   This desire however will not satisfy the expectations of our time if it ignores the objective obstacles which social structures place in the way

of conversion of hearts, or even of the realization of the ideal of charity. It demands on the contrary that the general condition of being marginal in society be overcome, so that an end will be put to the systematic barriers and vicious circles which oppose the collective advance towards enjoyment of adequate remuneration of the factors of production, and which strengthen the situation of discrimination with regard to access to opportunities and collective services from which a great part of the people are now excluded. If the developing nations and regions do not attain liberation through development, there is a real danger that the conditions of life created especially by colonial domination may evolve into a new form of colonialism in which the developing nations will be the victims of the interplay of international economic forces. That right to development is above all a right to hope according to the concrete measure of contemporary humanity. To respond to such a hope, the concept of evolution must be purified of those myths and false convictions which have up to now gone with a thought-pattern subject to a kind of deterministic and automatic notion of progress.

17.   By taking their future into their own hands through a determined will for progress, the developing peoples—even if they do not achieve the final goal—will authentically manifest their own personalization. And in order that they may cope with the unequal relationships within the present world complex, a certain responsible nationalism gives them the impetus needed to acquire an identity of their own. From this basic self-determination can come attempts at putting together new political groupings allowing full development to these peoples; there can also come measures necessary for overcoming the inertia which could render fruitless such an effort—as in some cases population pressure; there can also come new sacrifices which the growth of planning demands of a generation which wants to build its own future.

18.   On the other hand, it is impossible to conceive true progress without recognizing the necessity—within the political system chosen—of a development composed both of economic growth and participation; and the necessity too of an increase in wealth implying as well social progress by the entire community as it overcomes regional imbalance and islands of prosperity. Participation constitutes a right which is to be applied both in the economic and in the social and political field.

19.   While we again affirm the right of people to keep their own identity, we see ever more clearly that the fight against a modernization destructive of the proper characteristics of nations remains quite ineffective as long as it appeals only to sacred historical customs and venerable ways of life. If modernization is accepted with the intention that it serve

the good of the nation, men will be able to create a culture which will constitute a true heritage of their own in the manner of a true social memory, one which is active and formative of authentic creative personality in the assembly of nations.

VOICELESS INJUSTICES

20.   We see in the world a set of injustices which constitute the nucleus of today's problems and whose solution requires the undertaking of tasks and functions in every sector of society, and even on the level of the global society towards which we are speeding in this last quarter of the twentieth century. Therefore we must be prepared to take on new functions and new duties in every sector of human activity and especially in the sector of world society, if justice is really to be put into practice. Our action is to be directed above all at those men and nations which because of various forms of oppression and because of the present character of our society are silent, indeed voiceless, victims of injustice.

21.   Take, for example, the case of migrants. They are often forced to leave their own country to find work, but frequently find the doors closed in their faces because of discriminatory attitudes, or, if they can enter, they are often obliged to lead an insecure life or are treated in an inhuman manner. The same is true of groups that are less well off on the social ladder such as workers and especially farm workers who play a very great part in the process of development.

22.   To be especially lamented is the condition of so many millions of refugees, and of every group of people suffering persecution—sometimes in institutionalized form—for racial or ethnic origin or on tribal grounds. This persecution on tribal grounds can at times take on the characteristics of genocide.

23.   In many areas justice is seriously injured with regard to people who are suffering persecution for their faith, or who are in many ways being ceaselessly subjected by political parties and public authorities to an action of oppressive atheization, or who are deprived of religious liberty either by being kept from honouring God in public worship, or by being prevented from publicly teaching and spreading their faith, or by being prohibited from conducting their temporal affairs according to the principles of their religion.

24.   Justice is also being violated by forms of oppression, both old and new, springing from restriction of the rights of individuals. This is occurring both in the form of repression by the political power and of violence on the part of private reaction, and can reach the extreme of

affecting the basic conditions of personal integrity. There are well known cases of torture, especially of political prisoners, who besides are frequently denied due process or who are subjected to arbitrary procedures in their trial. Nor can we pass over the prisoners of war who even after the Geneva Convention are being treated in an inhuman manner.

25.   The fight against legalized abortion and against the imposition of contraceptives and the pressures exerted against war are significant forms of defending the right to life.

26.   Furthermore, contemporary conciousness demands truth in the communications systems, including the right to the image offered by the media and the opportunity to correct its manipulation. It must be stressed that the right, especially that of children and the young, to education and to morally correct conditions of life and communications media is once again being threatened in our days. The activity of families in social life is rarely and insufficiently recognized by State institutions. Nor should we forget the growing number of persons who are often abandoned by their families and by the community: the old, orphans, the sick and all kinds of people who are rejected.

THE NEED FOR DIALOGUE

27.   To obtain true unity of purpose, as is demanded by the world society of men, a mediatory role is essential to overcome day by day the opposition, obstacles and ingrained privileges which are to be met with in the advance towards a more human society.

28.   But effective mediation involves the creation of a lasting atmosphere of dialogue. A contribution to the progressive realization of this can be made by men unhampered by geo-political, ideological or socioeconomic conditions or by the generation gap. To restore the meaning of life by adherence to authentic values, the participation and witness of the rising generation of youth is as necessary as communication among peoples.

II. The Gospel Message and the Mission of the Church

29.   In the face of the present-day situation of the world, marked as it is by the grave sin of injustice, we recognize both our responsibility and our inability to overcome it by our own strength. Such a situation urges us to listen with a humble and open heart to the word of God, as he shows us new paths towards action in the cause of justice in the world.

THE SAVING JUSTICE OF GOD THROUGH CHRIST

30.   In the Old Testament God reveals himself to us as the liberator of the oppressed and the defender of the poor, demanding from man faith in him and justice towards man's neighbour. It is only in the observance of the duties of justice that God is truly recognized as the liberator of the oppressed.

31.   By his action and teaching Christ united in an indivisible way the relationship of man to God and the relationship of man to other men. Christ lived his life in the world as a total giving of himself to God for the salvation and liberation of men. In his preaching he proclaimed the fatherhood of God towards all men and the intervention of God's justice on behalf of the needy and the oppressed (Lk. 6:21–23). In this way he identified himself with his "least brethren", as he stated: "As you did it to one of the least of these my brethren, you did it to me" (Mt. 25:40).

32.   From the beginning the Church has lived and understood the Death and Resurrection of Christ as a call by God to conversion in the faith of Christ and in fraternal love, perfected in mutual help even to the point of a voluntary sharing of material goods.

33.   Faith in Christ, the Son of God and the Redeemer, and love of neighbour constitute a fundamental theme of the writers of the New Testament. According to St. Paul, the whole of the Christian life is summed up in faith effecting that love and service of neighbour which involve the fulfilment of the demands of justice. The Christian lives under the interior law of liberty, which is a permanent call to man to turn away from self-sufficiency to confidence in God and from concern for self to a sincere love of neighbour. Thus takes place his genuine liberation and the gift of himself for the freedom of others.

34.   According to the Christian message, therefore, man's relationship to his neighbour is bound up with his relationship to God; his response to the love of God, saving us through Christ, is shown to be effective in his love and service of men. Christian love of neighbour and justice cannot be separated. For love implies an absolute demand for justice, namely a recognition of the dignity and rights of one's neighbour. Justice attains its inner fullness only in love. Because every man is truly a visible image of the invisible God and a brother of Christ, the Christian finds in every man God himself and God's absolute demand for justice and love.

35.   The present situation of the world, seen in the light of faith, calls

us back to the very essence of the Christian message, creating in us a deep awareness of its true meaning and of its urgent demands. The mission of preaching the Gospel dictates at the present time that we should dedicate ourselves to the liberation of man even in his present existence in this world. For unless the Christian message of love and justice shows its effectiveness through action in the cause of justice in the world, it will only with difficulty gain credibility with the men of our times.

THE MISSION OF THE CHURCH, HIERARCHY AND CHRISTIANS

36.   The Church has received from Christ the mission of preaching the Gospel message, which contains a call to man to turn away from sin to the love of the Father, universal brotherhood and a consequent demand for justice in the world. This is the reason why the Church has the right, indeed the duty, to proclaim justice on the social, national and international level, and to denounce instances of injustice, when the fundamental rights of man and his very salvation demand it. The Church, indeed, is not alone responsible for justice in the world; however, she has a proper and specific responsibility which is identified with her mission of giving witness before the world of the need for love and justice contained in the Gospel message, a witness to be carried out in Church institutions themselves and in the lives of Christians.

37.   Of itself it does not belong to the Church, insofar as she is a religious and hierarchical community, to offer concrete solutions in the social, economic and political spheres for justice in the world. Her mission involves defending and promoting the dignity and fundamental rights of the human person.

38.   The members of the Church, as members of society, have the same right and duty to promote the common good as do other citizens. Christians ought to fulfil their temporal obligations with fidelity and competence. They should act as a leaven in the world, in their family, professional, social, cultural and political life. They must accept their responsibilities in this entire area under the influence of the Gospel and the teaching of the Church. In this way they testify to the power of the Holy Spirit through their action in the service of men in those things which are decisive for the existence and the future of humanity. While in such activities they generally act on their own initiative without involving the responsibility of the ecclesiastical hierarchy, in a sense they do involve the responsibility of the Church whose members they are.

III. The Practice of Justice

THE CHURCH'S WITNESS

39.   Many Christians are drawn to give authentic witness on behalf of justice by various modes of action for justice, action inspired by love in accordance with the grace which they have received from God. For some of them, this action finds its place in the sphere of social and political conflicts in which Christians bear witness to the Gospel by pointing out that in history there are sources of progress other than conflict, namely love and right. This priority of love in history draws other Christians to prefer the way of non-violent action and work in the area of public opinion.

40.   While the Church is bound to give witness to justice, she recognizes that anyone who ventures to speak to people about justice must first be just in their eyes. Hence we must undertake an examination of the modes of acting and of the possessions and life style found within the Church herself.

41.   Within the Church rights must be preserved. No one should be deprived of his ordinary rights because he is associated with the Church in one way or another. Those who serve the Church by their labour, including priests and religious, should receive a sufficient livelihood and enjoy that social security which is customary in their region. Lay people should be given fair wages and a system for promotion. We reiterate the recommendations that lay people should exercise more important functions with regard to Church property and should share in its administration.

42.   We also urge that women should have their own share of responsibility and participation in the community life of society and likewise of the Church.

43.   We propose that this matter be subjected to a serious study employing adequate means: for instance, a mixed commission of men and women, religious and lay people, of differing situations and competence.

44.   The Church recognizes everyone's right to suitable freedom of expression and thought. This includes the right of everyone to be heard in a spirit of dialogue which preserves a legitimate diversity within the Church.

45.   The form of judicial procedure should give the accused the right to know his accusers and also the right to a proper defence. To be complete,

justice should include speed in its procedure. This is especially necessary in marriage cases.

46.   Finally, the members of the Church should have some share in the drawing up of decisions, in accordance with the rules given by the Second Vatican Ecumenical Council and the Holy See, for instance with regard to the setting up of councils at all levels.

47.   In regard to temporal possessions, whatever be their use, it must never happen that the evangelical witness which the Church is required to give becomes ambiguous. The preservation of certain positions of privilege must constantly be submitted to the test of this principle. Although in general it is difficult to draw a line between what is needed for right use and what is demanded by prophetic witness, we must certainly keep firmly to this principle: our faith demands of us a certain sparingness in use, and the Church is obliged to live and administer its own goods in such a way that the Gospel is proclaimed to the poor. If instead the Church appears to be among the rich and the powerful of this world its credibility is diminished.

48.   Our examination of conscience now comes to the life style of all: bishops, priests, religious and lay people. In the case of needy peoples it must be asked whether belonging to the Church places people on a rich island within an ambient of poverty. In societies enjoying a higher level of consumer spending, it must be asked whether our life style exemplifies that sparingness with regard to consumption which we preach to others as necessary in order that so many millions of hungry people throughout the world may be fed.

EDUCATING TO JUSTICE

49.   Christians' specific contribution to justice is the day-to-day life of the individual believer acting like the leaven of the Gospel in his family, his school, his work and his social and civic life. Included with this are the perspectives and meaning which the faithful can give to human effort. Accordingly, educational method must be such as to teach men to live their lives in its entire reality and in accord with the evangelical principles of personal and social morality which are expressed in the vital Christian witness of one's life.

50.   The obstacles to the progress which we wish for ourselves and for mankind are obvious. The method of education very frequently still in use today encourages narrow individualism. Part of the human family lives immersed in a mentality which exalts possessions. The school and the communications media, which are often obstructed by the established

order, allow the formation only of the man desired by that order, that is to say, man in its image, not a new man but a copy of man as he is.

51.   But education demands a renewal of heart, a renewal based on the recognition of sin in its individual and social manifestations. It will also inculcate a truly and entirely human way of life in justice, love and simplicity. It will likewise awaken a critical sense, which will lead us to reflect on the society in which we live and on its values; it will make men ready to renounce these values when they cease to promote justice for all men. In the developing countries, the principal aim of this education for justice consists in an attempt to awaken consciences to a knowledge of the concrete situation and in a call to secure a total improvement; by these means the transformation of the world has already begun.

52.   Since this education makes men decidedly more human, it will help them to be no longer the object of manipulation by communications media or political forces. It will instead enable them to take in hand their own destinies and bring about communities which are truly human.

53.   Accordingly, this education is deservedly called a continuing education, for it concerns every person and every age. It is also a practical education: it comes through action, participation and vital contact with the reality of injustice.

54.   Education for justice is imparted first in the family. We are well aware that not only Church institutions but also other schools, trade unions and political parties are collaborating in this.

55.   The content of this education necessarily involves respect for the person and for his dignity. Since it is world justice which is in question here, the unity of the human family within which, according to God's plan, a human being is born must first of all be seriously affirmed. Christians find a sign of this solidarity in the fact that all human beings are destined to become in Christ sharers in the divine nature.

56.   The basic principles whereby the influence of the Gospel has made itself felt in contemporary social life are to be found in the body of teaching set out in a gradual and timely way from the encyclical *Rerum Novarum* to the letter *Octogesima Adveniens*. As never before, the Church has, through the Second Vatican Council's constitution *Gaudium et Spes*, better understood the situation in the modern world, in which the Christian works out his salvation by deeds of justice. *Pacem in Terris* gave us an authentic charter of human rights. In *Mater et Magistra* international justice begins to take first place; it finds more elaborate expression in *Populorum Progressio*, in the form of a true and suitable treatise on the right to development, and in *Octogesima Adveniens* is found a summary of guidelines for political action.

57.   Like the apostle Paul, we insist, welcome or unwelcome, that the Word of God should be present in the centre of human situations. Our

interventions are intended to be an expression of that faith which is today binding on our lives and on the lives of the faithful. We all desire that these interventions should always be in conformity with circumstances of place and time. Our mission demands that we should courageously denounce injustice, with charity, prudence and firmness, in sincere dialogue with all parties concerned. We know that our denunciations can secure assent to the extent that they are an expression of our lives and are manifested in continuous action.

58.　　The liturgy, which we preside over and which is the heart of the Church's life, can greatly serve education for justice. For it is a thanksgiving to the Father in Christ, which through its communitarian form places before our eyes the bonds of our brotherhood and again and again reminds us of the Church's mission. The liturgy of the word, catechesis and the celebration of the sacraments have the power to help us to discover the teaching of the prophets, the Lord and the Apostles on the subject of justice. The preparation for baptism is the beginning of the formation of the Christian conscience. The practice of penance should emphasize the social dimension of sin and of the sacrament. Finally, the Eucharist forms the community and places it at the service of men.

COOPERATION BETWEEN LOCAL CHURCHES

59.　　That the Church may really be the sign of that solidarity which the family of nations desires, it should show in its own life greater cooperation between the Churches of rich and poor regions through spiritual communion and division of human and material resources. The present generous arrangements for assistance between Churches could be made more effective by real coordination (Sacred Congregation for the Evangelization of Peoples and the Pontifical Council "Cor Unum"), through their overall view in regard to the common administration of the gifts of God, and through fraternal solidarity, which would always encourage autonomy and responsibility on the part of the beneficiaries in the determination of criteria and the choice of concrete programmes and their realization.

60.　　This planning must in no way be restricted to economic programmes; it should instead stimulate activities capable of developing that human and spiritual formation which will serve as the leaven needed for the integral development of the human being.

ECUMENICAL COLLABORATION

61.　　Well aware of what has already been done in this field, together with the Second Vatican Ecumenical Council we very highly commend cooperation with our separated Christian brethren for the promotion of justice in the world, for bringing about development of peoples and for establishing peace. This cooperation concerns first and foremost activities for securing human dignity and man's fundamental rights, especially the right to religious liberty. This is the source of our common efforts against discrimination on the grounds of differences of religion, race and colour, culture and the like. Collaboration extends also to the study of the teaching of the Gospel insofar as it is the source of inspiration for all Christian activity. Let the Secretariat for Promoting Christian Unity and the Pontifical Commission Justice and Peace devote themselves in common counsel to developing effectively this ecumenical collaboration.

62.   In the same spirit we likewise commend collaboration with all believers in God in the fostering of social justice, peace and freedom; indeed we commend collaboration also with those who, even though they do not recognize the Author of the world, nevertheless, in their esteem for human values, seek justice sincerely and by honourable means.

INTERNATIONAL ACTION

63.   Since the Synod is of a universal character, it is dealing with those questions of justice which directly concern the entire human family. Hence, recognizing the importance of international cooperation for social and economic development, we praise above all else the inestimable work which has been done among the poorer peoples by the local Churches, the missionaries and the organizations supporting them; and we intend to foster those initiatives and institutions which are working for peace, international justice and the development of man. We therefore urge Catholics to consider well the following propositions:

64.   (1) Let recognition be given to the fact that international order is rooted in the inalienable rights and dignity of the human being. Let the United Nations Declaration of Human Rights be ratified by all Governments who have not yet adhered to it, and let it be fully observed by all.

65.   (2) Let the United Nations—which because of its unique purpose should promote participation by all nations—and international organizations be supported insofar as they are the beginning of a system capable of restraining the armaments race, discouraging trade in weapons, securing disarmament and settling conflicts by peaceful methods of legal action, arbitration and international police action. It is absolutely necessary that international conflicts should not be settled by war, but that other methods better befitting human nature should be found. Let a strategy of

non-violence be fostered also, and let conscientious objection be recognized and regulated by law in each nation.

66.   (3) Let the aims of the Second Development Decade be fostered. These include the transfer of a precise percentage of the annual income of the richer countries to the developing nations, fairer prices for raw materials, the opening of the markets of the richer nations and, in some fields, preferential treatment for exports of manufactured goods from the developing nations. These aims represent first guidelines for a graduated taxation of income as well as for an economic and social plan for the entire world. We grieve whenever richer nations turn their backs on this ideal goal of world wide sharing and responsibility. We hope that no such weakening of international solidarity will take away their force from the trade discussions being prepared by the United Nations Conference on Trade and Development (UNCTAD).

67.   (4) The concentration of power which consists in almost total domination of economics, research, investment, freight charges, sea transport and insurance* should be progressively balanced by institutional arrangements for strengthening power and opportunities with regard to responsible decision by the developing nations and by full and equal participation in international organizations concerned with development. Their recent *de facto* exclusion from discussions on world trade and also the monetary arrangements which vitally affect their destiny are an example of lack of power which is inadmissible in a just and responsible world order.

68.   (5) Although we recognize that international agencies can be perfected and strengthened, as can any human instrument, we stress also the importance of the specialized agencies of the United Nations, in particular those directly concerned with the immediate and more acute questions of world poverty in the field of agrarian reform and agricultural development, health, education, employment, housing, and rapidly increasing urbanization. We feel we must point out in a special way the need for some fund to provide sufficient food and protein for the real mental and physical development of children. In the face of the population explosion we repeat the words by which Pope Paul VI defined the function of public authority in his encyclical *Populorum Progressio:* "There is no doubt that public authorities can intervene, within the limit of their competence, by favouring the availability of appropriate information

---

*The Vatican Press edition, from which this English text is taken, gives here the word "securities" for the original French word "assurance". I have changed this translation to "insurance" This is the correct rendering of "assurance" here.—J.G.

and by adopting suitable measures, provided that these be in conformity with the moral law and that they absolutely respect the rightful freedom of married couples" (37; A.A.S. 59, 1967, p. 276).

69.   (6) Let governments continue with their individual contributions to a development fund, but let them also look for a way whereby most of their endeavours may follow multilateral channels, fully preserving the responsibility of the developing nations, which must be associated in decision-making concerning priorities and investments.

70.   (7) We consider that we must also stress the new worldwide preoccupation which will be dealt with for the first time in the conference on the human environment to be held in Stockholm in June 1972. It is impossible to see what right the richer nations have to keep up their claim to increase their own material demands, if the consequence is either that others remain in misery or that the danger of destroying the very physical foundations of life on earth is precipitated. Those who are already rich are bound to accept a less material way of life, with less waste, in order to avoid the destruction of the heritage which they are obliged by absolute justice to share with all other members of the human race.

71.   (8) In order that the right to development may be fulfilled by action:

   a) people should not be hindered from attaining development in accordance with their own culture;

   b) through mutual cooperation, all peoples should be able to become the principal architects of their own economic and social development;

   c) every people, as active and responsible members of human society, should be able to cooperate for the attainment of the common good on an equal footing with other peoples.

RECOMMENDATIONS OF THE SYNOD

72.   The examination of conscience which we have made together, regarding the Church's involvement in action for justice, will remain ineffective if it is not given flesh in the life of our local Churches at all their levels. We also ask the episcopal conferences to continue to pursue the perspectives which we have had in view during the days of this meeting and to put our recommendations into practice, for instance by setting up centres of social and theological research.

73.   We also ask that there be recommended to the Pontifical Commission Justice and Peace, the Council of the Secretariat of the Synod and to competent authorities, the description, consideration and deeper study of the wishes and desires of our assembly, and that these bodies should bring to a successful conclusion what we have begun.

IV. A Word of Hope

74.   The power of the Spirit, who raised Christ from the dead, is continuously at work in the world. Through the generous sons and daughters of the Church likewise, the People of God is present in the midst of the poor and of those who suffer oppression and persecution; it lives in its own flesh and its own heart the Passion of Christ and bears witness to his resurrection.

75.   The entire creation has been groaning till now in an act of giving birth, as it waits for the glory of the children of God to be revealed (cf. Rom. 8:22). Let Christians therefore be convinced that they will yet find the fruits of their own nature and effort cleansed of all impurities in the new earth which God is now preparing for them, and in which there will be the kingdom of justice and love, a kingdom which will be fully perfected when the Lord will come himself.

76.   Hope in the coming kingdom is already beginning to take root in the hearts of men. The radical transformation of the world in the Paschal Mystery of the Lord gives full meaning to the efforts of men, and in particular of the young, to lessen injustice, violence and hatred and to advance all together in justice, freedom, brotherhood and love.

77.   At the same time as it proclaims the Gospel of the Lord, its Redeemer and Saviour, the Church calls on all, especially the poor, the oppressed and the afflicted, to cooperate with God to bring about liberation from every sin and to build a world which will reach the fullness of creation only when it becomes the work of man for man.

Reflections by Cardinal Maurice Roy
on the Occasion of the Tenth Anniversary
of the Encyclical "Pacem in Terris"
# of Pope John XXIII
(April 11, 1973)

Most Holy Father,

Ten years ago, in his Encyclical Letter Pacem in Terris *Pope John XXIII addressed to all men of good will a message of peace and hope. In its essence this message exhorted them to profound and practical commitment, in order that all men's efforts in favour of peace might become an ever more living reality in the conscience of each one and within the whole human family.*

In recalling today the tenth anniversary of the Encyclical, as President of the Pontifical Commission Justice and Peace I feel impelled to gather together the echoes that for ten years the inspired voice of Pope John XXIII has awakened in the hearts of Catholics and non-Catholics, in the most diverse lands and in the most widely differing cultures.

It is not my intention to compose a "triumphalistic" eulogy of the Encyclical. My desire is rather to present to Your Holiness a series of simple and practical reflections, in order to highlight the living and enduring relevance of the message of John XXIII, during the ten years that have passed, in the rapid and profound transformations of the present day and for the unfolding of the history of tomorrow.

The Magisterium of the Church during the past ten years has not ceased to draw attention to the urgent need to make peace an effective dimension of reality. It has done this by teaching us to read, interpret and extend the message of Pacem in Terris.

The Encyclical Ecclesiam Suam, *the Constitution* Gaudium et Spes, *the speech which Your Holiness gave at the headquarters of the United Nations, the Encyclical* Populorum Progressio, *the institution of the World Day of Peace and the Apostolic Letter* Octogesima Adveniens *which Your Holiness was pleased to address to me—all these represent some of the most notable testimonies of the pastoral solicitude already evident in the Encyclical.*

These various acts of the Magisterium of the Church enable us to see still more clearly the message of Pacem in Terris *through the repeated acts and teachings of the pontificate of Your Holiness with regard to peace.*

Moreover, the many changes undergone by society impel us to be ever more watchful and alert to the "signs of the times," and to concentrate our study and efforts upon certain fundamental aspects of the Encyclical.

In analyzing, after the elapse of ten years, this profound evolution in the light of the "facts" and "signs" of contemporary reality and in the light of my experience of several years in the Pontifical Commission Justice and Peace, I have been led to gather together a number of considerations in a document which I have the honour to present very humbly to Your Holiness.

This document is intended as a modest contribution to the reflection of the People of God and as an echo of Your Holiness's great desire to make men of good will more sensitive, more aware and more responsible with regard to that conviction which is becoming ever more deeply rooted: "Peace is possible."

In presenting these reflections to Your Holiness on the occasion of the tenth anniversary of Pacem in Terris, *I would like to make myself the spokesman of all those who are working to build up peace and of all those who are suffering for the sake of peace. In their name, and with sentiments of profound veneration, I ask your paternal Apostolic Blessing.*

7 April 1973.

MAURICE CARD. ROY

INTRODUCTION
Purpose of this Anniversary

1.   We are celebrating today the tenth anniversary of *Pacem in Terris*. That the Holy Father himself has taken this initiative shows what importance he attaches to this commemoration, which also recalls his great predecessor John XXIII. It is also a response to the desire of the Christian People and of all men of good will. The Encyclical was addressed to them and they have not forgotten it.

2.   The purpose of this "celebration" is not only filial devotion. It is not meant to be "triumphalistic"; were it so, how could it respect the humility of Pope John and his desire for a Church which serves and which is poor? This celebration is a commemoration not only of the Encyclical but of its accomplishment. It has been said that *Pacem in Terris* was the testament of Pope John. This is true in a twofold sense. The Encyclical was—in his own words—"the Easter gift" of the living Pope (John XXIII, Message of 12 April 1963, *AAS* 55 [1963], p. 400). At Pentecost it was to become the last offering of the Pope as he lay dying.

3.   We are all called upon to put into practice, at our different levels, this first and last desire of Pope John.

4.   On the occasion of this anniversary I have assembled certain reflections within the Pontifical Commission Justice and Peace of which I am President. These are in the context of the daily reflection which the Commission makes and gathers from its constant dialogue with the most diverse persons and communities, whether Catholic or not. I have done this in response to the desire expressed by the Holy Father and in conjunction with this new organization for justice, peace and development, established by Pope Paul VI after the Council and in accordance with its desire.

5.   What sense and what content is to be given to this anniversary in order to capture all its potential?

6.   After reflection, it seems that we can concentrate on a double purpose.

7.   The *purpose of continuity*. We have received *Pacem in Terris* as a

---

[This English version is that published by the Vatican Polyglot Press in booklet form, 93 pages.]

legacy. We have to make an inventory and an examination of conscience. In other words, we should ask three questions:
— what has *Pacem in Terris* done?
— what have we done with *Pacem in Terris*?
— what remains to be done in this field with regard to the new situation of today?

8.   The *operational purpose:* to renew our action for peace and to arouse new interest for the objectives which this Encyclical proposed and still proposes to Christians and all men of good will.

9.   Having recalled its impact on public opinion, I would therefore like:
— to outline an analysis, a brief synthesis of today's main problems in regard to peace;
— to point out certain lines of research and action, so that we may not remain stationary with the peace of yesterday but prepare ourselves without delay for the peace of tomorrow.

10.   I need hardly say that these reflections are only suggestions, meant as a starting-point for work by individuals and organizations able to undertake such work, and which I put forward as President of the Pontifical Commission Justice and Peace.

PART ONE:

Echoes and Impact of "Pacem in Terris"

1. What has "Pacem in Terris" Done?

I. FIRST READING: ORIGINALITY OF THE ENCYCLICAL

11.   As soon as it appeared on Holy Thursday, 11 April 1963, the Encyclical aroused great interest.

12.   From East to West, from the man in the street to heads of state, from the agnostic to the committed Christian, it finds in all milieux, countries, blocs and religions an almost unanimous approval. In the press and on the radio each one underlines what the Encyclical means to him and the support that he promises in return.

13.   Words are followed by action. The text of *Pacem in Terris* is sol-

emnly received from the Pope's envoy by the Secretary-General of the United Nations Organization. Two years later, from 17 to 20 February 1965, in this same hall of the General Assembly, there is held an important "Symposium on the world problems of peace in the light of the teaching of John XXIII in the Encyclical *Pacem in Terris."*

14.   Finally, numerous organizations, institutes and centres of study and encounter for peace or development are born from the Encyclical or take its name; at the same time it gives rise to numberless publications.

15.   How can such an impact upon public opinion be explained? The reason is that there was agreement between the world's expectations and the response given by this message.

16.   Let us go back to the written or audio-visual commentaries of this springtime of 1963. What did people read in this document and remember?

What made this document an event?

17.   It was the *originality of this "Letter to the World,"* whether one considers it in its readers or in its content.

A. *Its author.*

18.   The personality of John XXIII was an important element.

19.   On every page is found his simplicity, his common sense, his psychological penetration. But, as has been mentioned, the Encyclical is also considered as his testament. It is inseparable from his death, which was offered for peace. It sets the seal on a series of teachings and initiatives, of which history will especially remember the Second Vatican Council, and all of which were directed towards openness to the world.

B. *Its readers.*

20.   The originality of the Encyclical is what one sees—what was immediately seen—in considering those to whom the Letter was addressed. The Pope addresses it not only to the Episcopate of the Universal Church, to the clergy and faithful, but *to all men of good will.* John XXIII himself gives an explanation. Although the Encyclical is inspired "by the light of divine Revelation, its doctrinal lines . . . belong especially to the domain of natural law. Universal peace is indeed a good that concerns all men; . . . this explains the novelty that is proper to this document" (9 April 1963).

This novelty inspires all the rest.

21.   First of all, *dialogue.* This follows from the simple fact that peace is the right and duty of all men without exception, since they "form one and

the same human family" (*Pacem in Terris,* 25; the numbers correspond to the order of paragraphs in the edition of the *Acta Apostolicae Sedis*). The rule that guides them is not war—cold or hot—nor division, but peaceful coexistence and finally harmonious life together. This dialogue and cooperation between individuals and nations, which are indispensable for peace, are often called into question by ideologies. What then must be done? In the last pages of his Letter John XXIII has answered this question. And it was this which, indisputably, was seen and felt at the time as the most novel point of the Encyclical. When Catholics are to collaborate "with Christians separated from this Apostolic See or with those who are not Christians but who are faithful . . . to the natural law" (157), it is necessary in justice to make *a double distinction.* On the one hand, between the man and his error (158); and on the other hand, between "false philosophical theories" and "historical movements" flowing from them but which in the course of the years have evolved into principles conforming "to the dictates of right reason and are an expression of man's lawful aspirations" (159).

22.   Reason. Person. These two terms serve as points of reference for the entire body of the Encyclical. The scope of this pastoral approach to peace was immediately considered extraordinary. It was seen to be—and it can still be seen to be—a "programme of ecumenism and reconciliation," a "breaking with the tone and the habits of thought of the cold war," and even—as we shall presently see—a "turning," a "decisive revision," a "new phase" and even a "new era" in the Church world relationship.

C. *Its content.*

23.   The entire content of the message flows from these postulates.

24.   The first reading of *Pacem in Terris,* practically speaking, involved only the following points: human rights—those of individuals and groups—with the whole problem of underdevelopment and decolonization; the discrediting of war, anachronistic and useless for the restoration of justice, with the imperative of disarmament, especially nuclear disarmament; the desire and programme for a world authority suited to the new community of nations.

II. SECOND READING: FIRST BALANCE

25.   It was necessary to let some years pass in order to be able to gauge, with the test of time and from a critical point of view, the impact of *Pacem in Terris* not only on public opinion (the fidelity of which nevertheless also

constitutes a test) but on thought and action in the area of peace, both inside and outside the Church.

26.   As we shall see, in the final analysis it is the method and approach of John XXIII which gained for his last encyclical the greatest audience and the most enduring influence.

A. *Impact on thought.*

27.   1. *Within the Church.* A long study would be required in order to discern in the evolution of the social and international thought of the Church during the last ten years what flows directly from *Pacem in Terris.* Its influence has been exercised by osmosis. But it is possible to verify its exact consequences, notably on the Council.

28.   *The Council.* Within the context and orientations of the first session of the Council (October 1962), the Encyclical found a favourable climate for its advent. In return, it made an impact on the entire further development of Vatican II.

29.   One sees its mark in the Dogmatic Constitution *Lumen Gentium* (21 November 1964). For example in paragraph 36, on the value of the creation and finality of universal progress in freedom, based on an equitable distribution of goods among all men.

30.   One discerns the influence of *Pacem in Terris* in the Decree *Ad Gentes* (7 December 1965), which shows that "the missionary activity of the Church . . . has an intimate connection with human nature and its aspirations" (8); by preaching Christ, the Church brings to men "the Gospel . . . which presents itself always as a leaven of brotherhood, unity and peace" (*ibid.*).

31.   In the Decree on Ecumenism (*Unitatis Redintegratio*, 21 November 1964), is found the appeal for dialogue (*op. cit.*, 4) and for collaboration (12) between separated brothers as "a sign of the times" (4).

32.   It is the same with the Declaration on Religious Liberty. Its title *Dignitatis Humanae* and its first lines take up and make explicit reference to the fundamental affirmation of the nobility and freedom of the human person, an affirmation which opens the first chapter of *Pacem in Terris* on the Rights of Man (8-9).

33.   *Gaudium et Spes.* It is on *Gaudium et Spes* that the Encyclical exercised an undeniable influence. This is evident in the chapter devoted to war and peace (part II, chapter 5); but it is equally clear in the very inspiration and structure of this "pastoral constitution." In these two documents peace is not equated with the absence of war or with the techniques of coexistence or of development. It goes much further than the suppression of the causes of conflicts. It is an anthropology, a total

vision of the human condition in the world of today; it is a reflection on the personal and collective action of humanity that considers the paschal mystery and eschatology as the origin and end of peace.

34.   *Its posterity. Pacem in Terris* is not something complete in itself, an isolated absolute. It takes its place within a whole; it is situated in a living tradition.

35.   *Before being a legacy, it is something that has itself inherited from the past.* John XXIII was careful to say this in his presentation. "The new document which is linked with *Mater et Magistra* summarizes on the theme of peace the teaching of our predecessors from Leo XIII to Pius XII" (Radio Message of 13 April 1963). The Encyclical received as much as it gave. And because of this patrimony it can make progress and become in its turn a legacy. One recognizes its influence *in the great documents that came after it* and which go further than itself along the ways which it had opened up, or which concern problems which *Pacem in Terris* could do no more than vaguely glimpse. Hence we have *Ecclesiam Suam* on Dialogue and *Populorum Progressio* on the Development of Peoples; later on, though less directly, the Letter *Octogesima Adveniens* and the document "Justice in the World" of the recent Synod of Bishops.

36.   But side by side with these great acts of the Apostolic See or of the assembled episcopate, who could ever adequately show the decisive influence of *Pacem in Terris* on the teaching and doctrinal orientations *of the episcopal conferences or of bishops* in their own dioceses?

37.   Its influence has been equally decisive in regard to the changes introduced in the fields of the social sciences and of theology, in the reflections of lay apostolate movements, in the catechesis of the young and of adults, or in the themes of preaching and in the teaching given in seminaries and educational institutions.

38.   2. *Outside the Church.* One would have to make a similar study of non-Christian literature and intellectual activities in order to see the often radical change brought about by the Encyclical. It is the very image of the Church that finds itself transformed by it. But here too we must await the work of historians before we can evaluate in detail and in its entirety the impact of *Pacem in Terris* on contemporary thought.

B. *Impact on socio-political activities.*

39.   (1) *War and disarmament.* In the face of the threat of nuclear suicide, John XXIII asks two things from "all men and especially those who govern" (117):

—not to have recourse to war, which is no longer a possible means of obtaining justice when rights have been violated (127);

—to undertake disarmament (112).

40.   On the first point he has certainly contributed to a change of attitude on the part of a very large number of Christians, and by this very fact he has helped to reinforce this "conviction . . . *that possible conflicts among peoples must not be regulated by recourse to arms, but by negotiation"* (126).

41.   His solemn exhortation to "the highest authorities . . . to study thoroughly the problem of an international balance which is truly human" (118) and to obtain a *progressive and controlled disarmament*—a theme solemnly taken up by Paul VI before the General Assembly of the United Nations on 4 October 1965—has certainly brought an element of ideological strengthening to the great negotiations of recent years: the SALT negotiations (Strategic Arms Limitation Talks, taking place since 1969); the Treaty on the Non-Proliferation of Nuclear Weapons (in force since 5 March 1970) to which the Holy See itself has given its support; the agreements signed in Moscow between the United States and the Soviet Union (May 1972).

42.   The various declarations of the Catholic hierarchy and the campaigns waged in favour of those declarations by different Christian movements or organizations have carried great weight with public opinion and, through the latter, have influenced those responsible for political and military orientations in this matter. One recalls the reverberations caused in the world by the appeal of John XXIII on 25 October 1962 at the time of the dramatic incident of Cuba, which would not have been unconnected with the Pope's decision to write this Letter *Pacem in Terris*.

43.   It is also this passage of the Encyclical (part III, 109-119 and 126-129) that was taken as a point of reference by a large number of movements or initiatives aimed at calling into question war, recourse to military action or the sale of arms.

44.   It served and still serves as a basis, together with the already quoted chapter V of *Gaudium et Spes* (79, 3), for movements or legal statutes in favour of conscientious objection.

45.   (2) *Human rights. Human rights are the foundation of peace;* they form part of the definition of peace, and peace is false or impossible without them: these statements have won the Encyclical both an audience and lasting results. In regard to the latter, although they are difficult to discern they are certain, especially in the case of groups and collectivities. In this field the Encyclical takes a visible and special interest: the lot of national, ethnic, religious, cultural and political minorities. It is greatly concerned with the millions of migrants (25, 106) and with population movements (101). This has aroused attention, led to the setting up of enquiries and organizations and given rise to studies and campaigns directed at public authorities and enterprises (102). It has led to political concern and the

consideration of racial discrimination (89, 86, 44), by situating the problem on the level of justice and of legislation and not only on that of humanitarian assistance. Hence the precise and juridical character which John XXIII wished to give to his *Charter of the Rights of Man* (8-27) and his encouragement of the *Universal Declaration of the United Nations* (142-144).

46.   Above all, by recalling that the "same moral law that rules the life of men must also rule that of states" (80) and immediately applying this fundamental principle to the "development of peoples recently colonized" (42-44) and, more generally, to all "political communities" (42, 86, 88, 125), *Pacem in Terris*, following the path laid down by *Mater et Magistra*, paved the way for *Populorum Progressio*, which was to become the *Magna Charta* of the development of peoples.

47.   To base peace on the rights of man is to base it on justice: *Opus justitiae pax*. And here once more is seen *what the second synodal theme "Justice in the World" owes to Pacem in Terris*.

48.   But there is more to be said. To these rights—the Encyclical insists on this point—there correspond the same number of reciprocal duties (28-30). And in this way the *dynamics of peace are introduced*. Peace is not a mere absence of war nor a juridical order of equal consumption; "it is an exchange, a communion, a permanent readiness to share with others the best of oneself" (33, 36). It has an element of cooperation and love. It demands a political morality on the part of nations—whose guiding principle has habitually been sacred selfishness—as on the part of individuals. It gives a soul to this great body of humanity of which the international institutions constitute the bone structure. Thus when John XXIII devotes part IV of his Letter to the project of a "public authority of universal competence" (133-137), he assigns it a role of "economic, social and cultural" animation (142) and not only of collective security. For him, *peace is the indivisible life of the "human family"* (132; 129). *It is the state of health of that family. Peace is successful society.*

49.   (3) *Dialogue and openness.* It is in this context that one must now place the third impact of *Pacem in Terris*—or, in the eyes of many, perhaps the first: the impact on socio-political activities, that is, dialogue and openness between nations, blocs or ideologies as an essential condition for security and coexistence. Suffice it to mention here the thaw quickly noted in many sectors: the lifting of numerous exclusions; the progress of ecumenism and of contacts with other religions; the change of tone and of practical attitudes at the professional and civic levels; the resumption of diplomatic relations; the increased number of meetings, etc. Obviously one does not claim that results of such amplitude are all due to the Encyclical. But is it not of great importance that the Encyclical has so well

understood, foreseen and accompanied this current and this aspiration to unity?

C. *Impact of the method of* Pacem in Terris.

50.   As Pope John recognized with his customary simplicity, "the Encyclical has provoked an echo without precedent. It has moved the very stones themselves" (8 May 1963).

51.   Among the causes of such an effect is cited, above all, its method. For John XXIII has a method and he takes care to make it known. We have already met it, in the case of the audience to which the Encyclical is addressed and the document's appeal for dialogue. But it is not without value to see the method now in its entirety and in its theological and pastoral motivations and, above all, *in its intention, which is essentially missionary and universalist.* "Today as yesterday, the Church . . . calls men to unity in charity. It is this that the Encyclical has wished to say again in language which—we hope—will be understood by all" (John XXIII, 11 April 1963, *AAS* 55 [1963], p. 393).

This language has certain key expressions.

52.   *Nature.* To be understood by all, such language could not be —by definition—the expression of faith but that of reason and of nature. John XXIII knows well that this human nature needs "help from on high" (168) for its peace. But this fact does not prevent him from admiring it (3-6). He has confidence in it. Man is capable, if he so desires, of making peace. Peace is possible. And we recognize here—and it is not accidental—a total harmony with the theme of the last World Day of Peace and of the year 1973. Is not *Pacem in Terris* the Encyclical on the possibility of peace? Nature has not been totally corrupted by sin; redeemed by Jesus Christ, it is, with his grace, capable of good, and especially of this higher good which is peace.

53.   *Order.* Peace is not the effect of chaos. It is the sign and the fruit of order, with everything that this word implies: permanence, stability and identity. The rights of the human person are "inviolable and inalienable" (9). They are also universal: man is everywhere man, throughout the entire earth, "of equal nobility and dignity" (86, 89). Hence there can be no racialism, no segregation (44, 86).

54.   This order manifests itself objectively by four essential criteria: *truth, justice, love and freedom,* which are "the four pillars of the house of peace" open to all (John XXIII, 11 April 1963). By the fact that peace is order, it comes under the control of the intellect and the will of man, who is able by science and technical skill to overcome physical or social obsta-

cles and above all to control himself, conforming his conduct to the eternal law of God, of which the natural law is the expression.

55.   *History.* Peace according to *Pacem in Terris* is not static. One must not see in history a conservative immobility. For order, of which it is a sign, is not a ready-made order: it is an order to be constructed, a history to be successfully acomplished. *Pacem in Terris* establishes the dynamics of peace. "Peace on earth . . . the object of the.desire of mankind of every age . . . " (1). A natural desire so universal in space and time could not be in vain. In fact, in spite of blood and ruin, human beings—individuals or groups—are constantly impelled to hope and to transform the universe. The bond between peace and development, just recently discovered, is one sign among others.

56.   *Signs of the times.* John XXIII examines and analyses. He creates the phenomenology of peace. His method is not deductive but *inductive;* he speaks of that which he has seen and discovered. He makes a certain number of statements about society, and he expounds them at the end of each of the four parts of his Letter. To these he attaches great importance, especially when he notes "consensus" and collective convictions. These convergences take on in his eyes the value of indications or of psychosociological laws, then that of moral obligations in so far as they denote the common good.

57.   But the originality of his method is something more than this. It is *comparative.* It brings these relevant events—or these well-established invariables—face to face with Christian Revelation and the doctrinal tradition or teaching of the Church. And it seeks to find, under the surface of the collective phenomenon observed, a certain searching for God.

58.   Although barely outlined in *Pacem in Terris*, this theology of the "signs of the times," a theology born of the Gospel, which John XXIII himself quotes in this regard (*Matt* 16:4), has been taken up and ably synthesized in *Gaudium et Spes* (4, 10-11, 42, 44 etc.), which gives it a decisive spiritual and methodological importance.

2. What Have We Done With "Pacem in Terris"?

59.   After this brief survey of what *Pacem in Terris* has achieved, "let us now make our inventory . . . as at the end of an exercise in accounting"—in the words of Paul VI spoken last February 10th. We, that is the world—civil society, of which we are a part—and we, that is Christians—the People of God. Not for sterile remorse but for a new *aggiornamento.*

60.   Let us briefly review the principal points and appeals of the Encyclical:

61.   *What have we done in regard to war?* Total war has not broken out. Dissuasion and the balance of terror have strangely played a regulating role. But will this continue for ever? And the world has easily become accustomed—as to an abscess-like fixation—to local conflicts, even such very long and bloody ones as that in Vietnam.

62.   At the same time violence spreads, as a substitute for total war and as a collective phenomenon and concept in search of meaning.

63.   *Decolonization?* Since 1963 it has not made as much progress as had been hoped. In certain States, only a minority colonial population enjoys full political and social rights.

64.   Has *cooperation* with countries with poor technical development been successfully entered into? I take the liberty of repeating this question, which has already been directed at the highest international authorities, in September 1970, at the beginning of the Second Decade of Development. As for the dependence of States, it has changed its form: *an economic neo-colonialism* has often succeeded the former political colonization. It prepares a future which is heavy with menace. The same is true of racial discrimination, in which psychological opposition hardens into political institutions.

65.   *Human rights?* Charters have a reverse side: their non-ratification; their non-application. How many human rights which were so clearly vindicated by the Encyclical are still a dead letter! Again, how many of them have been won through the democratic procedures described by John XXIII? And how many have no hope of being won except through violent revolution?

66.   *Worldwide solidarity?* Here also these last ten years have not realized the hope of the Encyclical (130-132). Interdependence plays its part—but among the rich nations, whose economies have less and less need of the countries technically far removed from them and which make these countries feel deeply this "marginalization." Can we say without lying that "our humanity . . . presents a social and political organization profoundly transformed" or "that one no longer distinguishes between peoples who dominate and those who are dominated" (42)?

67.   We could continue for a long time this "general confession" of our omissions and collective faults, admitting the partial or biased exegesis which we have often made of this Letter at the risk of altering the nature of its purpose or content, the pages which we have not read, the values entrusted to us which we have buried, the appeals which we have not listened to and the legacy which we have refused.

68.   But rather than weep over the past, let us try to see what has changed, by comparing the present state of the world and the Church with that of 1963. In this way perhaps we shall better be able to understand what there remains for us to do in order to bring to realization, extend and complete *Pacem in Terris* in relation to the new context of today.

PART TWO
Today's Problems

69.   It is a question therefore of attempting an analysis, which might be termed an "analysis of difference," in order to measure the changes which ten years have brought to the problem and to attitudes. The second task will be to indicate roughly a few suggestions regarding the future, suggestions aimed at defining a few major priorities in the search for peace and action for peace in the coming years. Once this has been done, it will be possible to see that John XXIII's method, enriched and completed by various acts and documents of Paul VI, retains its fundamental value, both within the Church and outside the Church, for the building up of peace.

1. An Analysis of Difference

70.   In view of the vast list of contents and the different ideas of peace, I must obviously make a choice, and in the first place reject almost entirely one of the two aspects of the problem: that of Development. *Mater et Magistra* having already tackled this aspect, *Pacem in Terris* is content to meet it along the way. The theme of *Pacem in Terris* is thereby at the same time lightened and given extra weight, if it is true that henceforth peace has society as its name and its yardstick.

71.   It is possible, it seems (and it is to this that I shall limit myself), to reduce these differences of the two contexts to the three following points:

I. A WORLDWIDE REMODELLING

72.   The context in which John XXIII found himself when he wrote his Letter was dominated by the following four elements: a two-sided sys-

tem, based upon the balance of terror, accompanied by a general inequality of the nations in relation to the two Great Powers and in which the Third World served as a pawn, each bloc striving to cause it to fall into its own camp, without the United Nations being able to intervene in any other way.

73.   The framework presented by the Encyclical is, on the contrary, a system of equality between States, the balance of trust, aid for the Third World linked with respect for its independence, and an effective world authority over and above the Nation-States.

74.   Ten years later, things have changed a great deal.

75.   Let us first look at the *map of the world*. It shows, among other things, a shift towards the Pacific Ocean; the emergence of Latin America; the clear shift also towards the Indian Ocean; the self-affirmation of Africa and the Arab world. As for Europe, it has just gone through a process of enlargement. But neither Europe nor North America is any longer the centre of the world.

76.   Upon this physical map we must superimpose demography, an immense problem which by itself would form the subject of a long study.

77.   *The socio-political map* has also changed considerably. *Pacem in Terris* described it as a sum of Nation-States, and linked these different national communities one to another in the manner of the United Nations, as so many totally distinct entities (*Pacem in Terris*, 42). Today, these nations are tending to regroup themselves in regional or continental systems and become henceforth international partners. Thus we are witnessing a certain breaking down of nationalism.

78.   At the same time we note within each nation the tendency to subnational regroupings on a more human scale, regroupings which answer a need for interpersonal communications. This is a need which is being more and more denied by the growing uniformity of social life. This diastolic and systolic movement—of expansion and contraction in relation to the national being—a movement which was already noticeable ten years ago in the time of John XXIII, seems to be a phenomenon typical of today, with the increasing role of "transnational forces" in their different forms: economic (multinational enterprises, monetary systems) and cultural (mass-media; the civilization of the image; ideologies, religions), etc.

From the two-sided to the many-sided.

79.   But the most obvious change is at the level of world politics: the progress from the two-sided system (the "Atlantic bloc" and the "Soviet bloc") to many-sidedness. This latter entails a redistribution of roles and a certain removal of the various barriers set up between East and West. As everyone knows, it is the risk of a frontal atomic clash which has largely

led to this thaw and mutual neutralization on the military level. But it has also been caused by the accession of new countries to the ranks of the Great Powers, and likewise by the urgent need for technical and commercial exchanges. We have seen that unfortunately this improvement of East-West relations between countries that are already or almost industrialized is not matched—far from it—in "North-South" relations, that is in the countries of the Third World and, *a fortiori*, of the "Fourth World" (the nations and social categories that are "marginal").

II. WAR

80.   "We are now in a post-war period." Can we apply to war as a whole this judgment of Paul VI (28 January 1973), expressed on the occasion of the ending of the conflict in Vietnam?

81.   The answer is yes, from a certain point of view. As everyone is vaguely aware, it seems as though a page has been turned: that of nuclear terror. We are emerging from the war of nerves. Total war is not probable at the present time. This is a radical difference distinguishing our time from that of John XXIII. As analyses show us, *it is war itself, by reason of its stalemates, that prevents war*. The determinism which quite recently led peoples to a trial of strength are now in a way secreting their own "antibodies." Each of the camps feels itself, so to speak, condemned to peace. For war no longer seems only a crime, but an absurdity as well. It reveals for all to see "its disastrous irrationality" (Paul VI, *ibid*.). It appears as nonsense, as an end which is self-destructive. It is no longer a solution. It no longer finds a place among political aims.

82.   But to conclude from this that we are beginning a new and definitive phase of the human race, that of non-war, would be pure sophistry. In fact, we still remain at the mercy of an error of judgement or a breakdown of equilibrium, from the very fact of the possible entry of new members into the exclusive club of the nuclear Powers.

83.   Whatever we may think of the hypothetical use on a world scale of atomic weapons, *local conflicts* remain and are doubtless going to remain an existing reality. Institutes of warfare, that is to say for the scientific study of war, have drawn up a list of such conflicts and classified them into families. It will suffice to mention one or two: wars waged by interposed States, lightning wars, the blockading of sea routes, intimidatory manoeuvres, conflicts of intervention, ethnic and tribal struggles, separatist struggles, civil wars, racial revolts, genocide, tribal massacres. Then, we have the quite recent phenomena of terrorism, anarchical or organized (the taking of hostages, bomb outrages, hijacking of

aircraft, assassination of leaders, etc.). The motive behind this terrorism, which has little effect but which mobilizes the mass media, is to draw the attention of the entire world to situations of injustice or oppression hitherto often forgotten by the comity of States.

But, at the same time, the arms race.

84.   To these various open conflicts, which daily make up the international news in our newspapers and on our television screens, we must add the arms race, for it carries the germs of war.

85.   Of the trilogy of arms—A.B.C.—usually only the atomic weapon is retained. And yet the two others, biological and chemical, are not just something out of science fiction. In 1973 just as in 1963, the two latter are no more immune to malice or to an error of use than the atomic bomb. Their manufacture, their stockpiling and their transportation are a danger to our human environment. But—and this it seems is new by comparison with the time at which the Encyclical was written—*trading in arms* has enormously increased and today takes on the aspect of a "contagious epidemic" (Paul VI, 9 January 1972). For this very reason it is a standing provocation to war.

86.   Mention should also be made of psychological arms, barbaric penal procedures (concentration camps, arbitrary arrest, torture), which cause as many victims by slow death as do wars which are openly declared.

87.   In the face of such an arsenal and such a scourge, even if the risk of total war is receding can we truly speak of peace? This, of course, does not bring into question the reality and the immense hope (as yet unknown by the Encyclical) of the post-war period we have entered.

III. VIOLENCE AND PROTEST

88.   In the opinion of the best experts, we are witnessing a double transition:

    —*from the military to the economic:* the impossible confrontation by means of arms is changing into economic competition. This latter is taking over from cold war, hot war and military colonization. It is creating new distances and divisions between nations, phenomena which are far removed from the descriptions and hopes spoken of by *Pacem in Terris* with regard to "the natural equality of all political communities and their right . . . to development" (89, 88, 138). For this very reason it is introducing new tensions and oppositions and new barriers.

89.   —*from the international to the national:* because of opposed posi-

tions, relations between States are tending to become stabilized, to the point that international society is becoming a blockaded society. The conflicts that can no longer take place between States are being transferred to the interior of each of these States. There they fester, provoking explosions and crises of extreme gravity.

90.   It is a different universe from that of John XXIII. Pope John's vision was that of an ordered and hierarchical society, with a place for each nation and each nation in its place. From the bottom to the top, from the individual to the "public authority of universal competence" (137), society forms a pyramid of intermediate bodies (53) founded on the "principle of subsidiarity" (141-142). Each one—individual, basic community or State—makes its active contribution, with respect for authority and in the service of the common good. Governed by a bill of rights and mutual duties, society is animated by a common will. It is a *society of participation* (31, 40, 53, 73, 146), oriented towards "the *coming* of a collective order" (31); in short it is a *society of assent*.

91.   Ten years have passed. A radical change has taken place.

92.   First of all, conflict, expressed by violence, is a fact, a new fact, in all its breadth: this violence is everywhere, in countries that are not at war and in all social bodies, to the extent that a new chapter would have to be added to the Encyclical: *Bellum in Terris*. It takes many forms. One notes today *physical violence*, which places at risk the life or material liberty of individuals or groups. But, and this is new, one also notes almost everywhere *structural violence*: violence which stems from institutions, regimes and systems of law. Then there is *cultural violence*, for example the pressure exercised by the audio-visual media, by the timetable and rhythm of work and transport, the numberless constraints imposed by industrial civilization and technology, the constraints connected with knowledge and power.

93.   However, what should be noted as specifically new is not so much violence as *awareness of violence*. In former times violence was not noticed, or was endured as something inevitable, whereas today it is thought about, analysed and consciously desired. Many people interpret it as a law of history. Society is presented as essentially connected with conflict. The struggle of cultures, classes or ideologies is often relied upon in order to ensure the transformation of social life. This dialectical outlook normally pursues concrete and limited aims, for example a change of regime. But it can also assume a much more radical form—when it brings into question society itself. In this case, it no longer attacks merely a "system," but social existence itself. This sort of violence goes much further than street demonstrations or even civil war. It attacks the very fabric of society.

94.   One can measure the distance that separates this *society of protest* from the *society of attestation* of which *Pacem in Terris* offers us the model.

95.   For John XXIII, leaving aside the case of an unjust law justifying or even demanding either civil disobedience or revolt (48-52), the duty of every citizen and every collective body, from the democratic viewpoint, is civic consciousness, that is to say the making of a positive contribution to the political, social, economic and cultural wellbeing of the community to which one belongs, with respect for other communities.

96.   Today, there are appearing (is it a "fact of the times" or a "sign of the times?") a certain number of behavioural patterns which aspire to become new rights to be written into laws and constitutions (*Pacem in Terris*, 75, 77). This is the case with military conscientious objection, which now has legal status in a very large number of countries. But one notices after a while a civil variety of conscientious objection. This is also tending to find a certain juridical existence and to be invoked in different places under the name of "the right to dissent" as a part of the right to freedom of opinion, which is recognized in the Universal Declaration of Human Rights (article 19). We shall meet this problem again a little later.

97.   When this civic quality of dissent in the face of unjust oppression refuses to have anything to do with corporal violence, it takes on the name, in some cases at least, of *non-violence*. This is a problem that *Pacem in Terris* did not yet deal with, and is another difference from the present day, when the spirit and strategies of non-violence are becoming more and more widespread.

98.   It is not the aim here to enlarge upon problems of such wide scope, but merely to mention them as a fresh problem connected with peace.

2. Orientations

99.   "In the face of such widely varying situations it is difficult for us to utter a unified message and to put forward a solution which has universal validity. Such is not our ambition, nor is it our mission." How could I not take to heart these words of the Holy Father in the Letter *Octogesima Adveniens* which he graciously addressed to me on 15 May 1971 (*op. cit.*, 4)?

100.   *First Remark.* I do not forget that "it is up to the Christian community to analyse . . . the situation" (*ibid.*), and that it is up to all men of good will and all those in positions of responsibility to face the problems connected with it. My intention on this anniversary is not to say everything but to pick out a few priorities that stand out from recent study and

action in this vast field. Moreover, it is much more a matter of asking questions and encouraging research than of putting forward clearly defined solutions. And this is to be done as a sort of extension and completion of the Encyclical of John XXIII.

101.   It has been said of *Pacem in Terris*, in fact, that it was a symphony. This is true. But it is no insult to its memory to say that it was an *unfinished symphony*. John XXIII would have been the first to proceed to an *aggiornamento* of his Letter, of which the care for topicality has been so unanimously praised. Nowadays, in our changing world, the present moment changes with great rapidity. When we have asked ourselves what we have done about *Pacem in Terris*, it remains for us to see how we are going to *apply it to the present moment by extending it*, in the light of the differences that this rapid analysis has tried to sketch.

102.   *Second Remark.* The study of the problem of peace runs the risk of being radically false if it is not placed in a double dimension: the "things" of peace and the "subjects" of peace. If one keeps exclusively to the things, that is to say to the determinisms, structures, modes of behaviour and the balance of forces facing one another, peace escapes man's grasp and one ends up in a state of immobility. On the other hand, if one keeps only to the psychological, affective and spiritual sources within man, leaving out the mediation of economic, monetary and diplomatic laws, one condemns oneself to the good intentions of a sentimental pacifism which once again risks discrediting the cause of peace by robbing it of its scientific and sociological roots.

103.   *Third Remark.* The effectiveness of the study of the problems that Christians propose to deal with therefore rests in the *method of John XXIII*, with its further developments, rather than in a table of contents.

104.   Finally, just as is the case with the Encyclical itself, these few anniversary reflections are to be applied to the peace of all and by all, but with constant reference to the mission and the *specific part to be played by Christians within this common task*. I shall envisage them under two aspects: that of the "realizations" or the "objects" of peace, and that of the "subject" of peace, in other words man himself.

I. THE THINGS OF PEACE

A. *Eliminating war.*

105.   "We are now in a post-war period, and we cannot fail to take an interest in it, both as citizens of the world and especially as Christians" (Paul VI, 28 January 1973). But it is *a post-war period which is still full of wars,*

which are to be stopped or prevented. The appeals of the last three Popes against war: "Wage war on war", "War never again" seem to imply the following *two objectives:*

106.   (1) *Stopping the arms race.* The arms race is in fact a *danger,* a permanent temptation to use arms or to intimidate (dissuasion going as far as blackmail), an *injustice* and a theft: the unbelievable budgets involved constitute a veritable diversion of funds and wastage by the rich countries, which in itself represents an aggression against the less favoured countries or social categories: "The arms race . . . hurts the poor in an intolerable way . . . " (*Gaudium et Spes,* 8, 3), " . . . it is a scandal . . ." (8,12). It is *madness:* it does not ensure security; it creates extra risks, by causing an instability which is capable of upsetting the balance of terror. It is a *danger:* whether it is a question of nuclear arms or conventional weapons, of great or small Powers, the arms race has become a dynamic process with its own momentum, independent of feelings of aggression, which escapes the control of States. It is a machine gone mad. It is a *mistake,* when it is asserted that disarmament would lead to the ruin of States and to the unemployment of the workers. On the contrary, history shows that industrial societies have prospered in spite of constant alterations. The conversion of the manufacture and sale of military products into the manufacture and sale of "civil" products is seen to be quite possible, if a persevering political will foresees it and makes timely plans for it. "As though it were admissible that it is not possible to find work for hundreds of thousands of workers except by employing them to make instruments of death!" (Paul VI, Address to the Diplomatic Corps, 9 January 1972, *AAS* 64 [1972], p. 54).

107.   Finally, and perhaps especially, the arms race or the possession of massive quantities of weapons by a certain number of States is the sign and the *cause of a hegemony in intention or in fact.* To arm oneself, even for the purpose of not using these arms, is to lay down or maintain an imperialistic concept of the world by substituting the primacy of force for the primacy of right.

108.   (2) *Combatting economic imperialism.* Since the economic aspect is taking over from the military aspect, the transposition is obligatory. *The imperative "War never again" must be applied to the whole economic sphere* in order to combat the aggression and oppression exercised by the heavy infrastructures and the new "Powers"—financial, industrial and commercial—in their race for a monopoly or for domination on land, on the seabed and in space. The right to legitimate self-defence and to national or regional identity must be safeguarded and defended henceforth in international dealings and foreign policies with as much firmness

and courage as in the matter of military national security. Peace, without becoming identified solely with economic development, must constantly concern itself with this.

B. *Replacing war with the dynamism of peace.*

109.   (1) *The Power of right.* It is a matter of a reverse success. "Let the moral force of right be substituted for the material force of arms" (Benedict XV). It is a matter of giving right a chance, and in the first place of establishing it, making it a part of legal systems and institutions that conform to justice. These latter are meant to lay down and guarantee the rights of man and the rights of peoples.

110.   *The Charter of Human Rights* (the twenty-fifth anniversary of which—10 December 1948—we are celebrating this year) and *Pacem in Terris* are to be supplemented by a certain number of new rights (at least at the stage of aspirations or projects), in order that at every moment justice may coincide with the evolution of situations and of modes of behaviour.

111.   The image that *Pacem in Terris* outlined for us was that of a peaceful society, linked to the juridical concept of a democracy based on assent. Many people at the present time, and not only among the young, would seem to be more sensitive to the tension of societies torn and disrupted from within by the refusal, on the part of the citizens or of a part of them, to accept the national destiny that is proposed to them.

112.   *The notion of authority* presented by the Encyclical equally seems to some people too vertical and extrinsic. These people would like to develop paragraphs 48 to 51 by replacing the concept of a civic quality of acceptance with concepts of social life that are both more dialectic and more anarchical. They would like to find in these paragraphs clearer references to the struggle for justice and to the notion of liberation. The description of "peace within each political community" (*Pacem in Terris*, part 2) seems to them too "law-abiding." In their eyes, it does not give enough *space to the irrational, to instinct, to initiative or to adventure.* To them it seems too far from "utopia" in the sense that *Octogesima Adveniens* spoke of it and described it (*op. cit.*, 37).

113.   It is in this spirit and with reference to these cultural currents of today that one may quote here and there certain formulations of new rights, to be ratified by laws: the *right to dissent*, that is, the theoretical and practical ability of the citizen to practise conscientious objection of the civil type. Military conscientious objection invokes the Ten Commandments ("Thou shall not kill"); social dissent, on the other hand, invokes the right and duty not to agree with the totalitarian ideology of one's group, and also, when all recourse to legal means has been exhausted, to

practise civil disobedience to certain laws by invoking the principle which has always been recognized: "It is better to obey God than men". This right to dissent is the right to "non-alignment" with the teaching and the acts of a totalitarian regime; it is a right determined by a physical or ideological abuse of power; it is moral resistance to unjust and qualified oppression, such as religious, moral, civic or racial intolerance. It is not the undetermined or unlimited right of an individual or group systematically to reject any society—*a fortiori,* if there is a refusal at the same time to substitute the rejected "pattern" with some other. It would no longer be a case of opposition or dissent, but of nihilism, which is so contrary to reason and to the common good.

114.   Among the new rights proposed today, an appeal is also made along the same lines, the *right to a vision of the world* and to *freedom of education.* The same is true again of the *right to the image*—in other words, the right of any person or group to be presented to public opinion as he or they really are, and not under the stereotyped form too often put out by the mass media, without any right or possibility of reply or correction being given to the victims of this distortion. Then there is the *right to privacy:* the protection of the interior or family environment of the individual, the home, etc.

115.   These are but a few examples. Their common characteristics reveal at the same time their novelty. They constitute a *transition from freedom understood as non-domination to freedom understood as a greater degree of being.* They reflect and introduce a cultural current, a contemporary assertion of rights, that is probably going to permeate more and more all spheres of existence: *the quality of life (and so the quality of peace).* Previously there had been a great emphasis upon prosperity (in the nineteenth century) and upon growth (in the twentieth century) as signs of an advanced civilization and factors governing an equitable distribution of goods. Today, there is a greater realization of the fact that growth or quantitative development that does not go as far as changing life is condemned in its very principle, *a fortiori* in its satiety. Such growth even creates the imminent risk of creating poverty, through the uncontrolled consumption of the natural physical resources essential for life. For wealthy countries and social categories, therefore, the moderation of consumption is not only a sign of self-control and of the virtue of temperance; it is an objective condition for ensuring collective survival in the coming decades.

116.   (2) *The role of International Institutions* (which can only be hinted at in such a brief exposé) must be constantly examined and re-examined from this aspect of *being more rather than having more,* as *Populorum*

Progressio so vigorously states (6). It is exercised in two ways: the defence of human rights, and the promotion of human rights.

117.   *Pacem in Terris* had magnificently stressed this active role of International Institutions, and had proposed the setting up of a "public authority of universal competence" (137-145).

118.   While awaiting the appearance of this world authority (which at the present time remains more a hope than an imminent reality), *John XXIII strongly encouraged the United Nations Organization as a first attempt at this Great Design.* It is well known how strongly *Paul VI* later assured the Organization of his confidence and trust, both when he paid it a historic visit on 4 October 1965 and when he expounded his thoughts on the role and first balance-sheet of the Institution, on the occasion of its twenty-fifth anniversary in 1970. It "represents the essential path of modern civilization, of world peace" (Speech of Paul VI to the United Nations, 4 October 1965). It constitutes a "privileged forum" in spite of its limitations and deficiencies, of which the nations are aware and for which they are responsible: "Where else . . . could these governments and peoples better find a bridge to link them, a table round which they can gather, and a tribunal where they may plead the cause of justice and peace?" (Message to U Thant for the 25th Anniversary of the United Nations Organization, 4 October 1970, *AAS* 62 [1970], p. 683).

119.   It would seem that great importance should be attached to international or supranational structures if one is to understand and resolve what may be called "globalities," already existing or still to come into being, that is to say a combination of realities that henceforth impose themselves as a fact upon the existence and culture of all human beings and all nations, and which neither individual nations nor all of them taken together are capable of resolving. Examples of such realities are social communications, demography, ecology, the civilization of the image, etc. Only a concerted effort by the Nation-States, the international institutions and the human community as such can ensure control of the future.

II. THE SUBJECT OF PEACE

120.   What we have seen up to now fell above all into the category of the "things of peace." We now turn to the "subject of peace," that is to say, the situation of modern man in relation to these objective realities, how he sees them and how he sees himself in the construction of peace. Everything depends on this. From this point of view, it is true to say that "man is the measure of all things." This is as true of peace as of everything

else. The "machines" of peace must not enslave him; nor must its structures alienate him by becoming ends in themselves. *Peace is in the subject.* It is his work. Saying this is to deliver peace from chance and physical determinism. If peace is no more a matter of fate than war, it is possible for man, if he wants it.

121.   But does he want it? And can he achieve it? In 1973, the answer is no longer that of 1963; at the very least it is ambiguous. Since our future depends on it, we shall have to search among our orientations: to discover what prevents man from being the subject; on the other hand, what means should be used to help him to become it, over and above the difficulties met on the way.

A. *At the level of the individual person.*

122.   Is it possible to be the subject, amid the universal and rapid change of today, in the sweeping aside of the person, who is divided within himself, and in face of the calling into question of social forms or being?

123.   Without ceasing, of course, along the lines of the last Synod, to attack the *objective causes* of conflicts and of general dissatisfaction, it seems essential also to discover *their subjective and psychological sources.* Among these sources, reference is made to the traditional conflicts between the generations and the sexes, the Oedipus complex, the absence of great causes that arouse incentive, the projection on to the collective body of individual ills and resentments, the intensification of distrust, etc. In addition, the list of the *frustrations that are at the root of social explosions* grows longer every day: inequality of chances of obtaining education, the lack of participation, by right and in fact, in economic or political power, the need for consideration and for identity: being known and recognized by society, the thirst for human warmth, love and "relaxation." Since coexistence and cooperation are hindered or lessened by them, none of these things, should seem "insignificant" or secondary in our study of the problem. On the contrary: it is a question of studying and supporting the sciences of man—biology, psychology, psycho-sociology, etc., in order to explain conflicts, but especially in order to solve them and use them positively. *This psychological method must be accompanied by a spiritual transformation. In order to be an "agent of peace,"* one must achieve peace within oneself. The *peace of the world depends upon the conversion of the subject.*

B. *The collective subject.*

124.   It will never again be possible to establish this peace unless it becomes the act of a collective subject: the whole human race. Peace is for

all; peace is attained through the efforts of all. There are many ways of imagining peace and creating it historically. It is manysided, a combination of different sorts of peace rather than a monolithic entity. It presupposes many separate approaches.

125.   But at the same time and without contradiction, peace, since it is the peace of all, must be indivisible: as we have seen, *the "globalities" of the great present objectives demand a "globality," realized and accepted, of the subject:* a humanity consciously gathered together. The *phenomenon of the masses,* noted everywhere today, is a sign of this. It is also a hopeful sign; "achievement of awareness" by the masses, their power as "consumers" and "economic, cultural and political agents" may obtain, for example, that "disarmament of minds" without which "the disarmament of weapons" is a snare (113). What is meant for everybody can only be created and guaranteed by everybody.

126.   In our orientations we must therefore include, as a capital priority, *education for peace,* and this in the widest sense: the transformation of public opinion, *the metamorphosis of the world mentality,* in order to enter the "new era" evoked by Paul VI at the United Nations (4 October 1965).

3. A Method for Our Times

127.   The first step of the method of *Pacem in Terris* consists, as we know, in *the appeal to men of good will.* This appeal has the avowed purpose of inspiring action: *peace needs men. But how is one to gather men together in one same workshop? In whose name? And for what purpose? What can their common reference be?*

I. HUMAN NATURE

128.   *The answer is nature, the Encyclical says. Is this answer still valid, ten years later?* For today, this idea of nature is very much questioned, if not rejected. There is argument concerning the word itself, which could lead one to suppose that there is a strict parallel between man and his morality and biological laws and behaviour. There is argument also about its content, negative (what nature forbids) or positive (what nature permits). This concept seems too "essentialist" to the people of our time, who challenge, as being a relic of Greek philosophy, the term "Natural Law," which they consider anachronistic, conservative and defensive. They object further that the expression was defined arbitrarily and once and for

all in a subjective and Western manner, and is therefore one-sided and lacking in any moral authority for the universal conscience.

129.   The context of *Pacem in Terris* shows sufficiently clearly, as does its success, that it was not to this caricature of nature that John XXIII was referring. Although the term "nature" does in fact lend itself to serious misunderstandings, the reality intended has lost nothing of its forcefulness when it is replaced by modern synonyms (almost all of which moreover are to be found in the Encyclical). Such synonyms are: man, human being, human person, dignity, the rights of man or the rights of peoples, conscience, humaneness (in conduct), the struggle for justice, and, more recently, "the duty of being," the "quality of life." Could they not all be summarized in the concept of "values," which is very much used today? (33, 35, 36). This concept lends a qualitative character to the notions of "common good" and "common denominator," which might at first sight lead one to think of a material heritage, a legacy or a code, whereas it is essentially a matter of the harmonization of wills and "ideals" with the image of society itself which the Encyclical presents as "a reality of the spiritual order" (45). Thus, leaving aside what words are used, the important point is this: in this "nature," individuals and peoples all have a common denominator, a "common good of man," which is neither a simple label nor a mere compromise but a basic and existential reality. It is a combination of postulates and experiences, ancient and modern, which people do not question, even if they belong to opposed systems, for "men find in it that inalienable part of themselves which links them all: the human in man" (Paul VI to U Thant, 4 October 1970, *AAS* 62 [1970], p. 684).

130.   The consequences that follow are clear. *Dialogue,* to be begun or begun again; *cooperation,* to be extended to the greatest number of spheres; and especially a persevering *search for common ground:* all those similar or identical elements that all ideologies, cultures or anticultures bear within themselves, hidden under the most striking and provocative differences. All this demands very serious intellectual research in the years ahead. It likewise demands many meetings, and patience in cultural relations at all levels, for these will more and more decide the fate and the quality of peace.

A. *Nature and order.*

131.   For John XXIII, reference to nature also means defining peace as "absolute respect for the order laid down by God" (*Pacem in Terris,* 1). *But here again, this word jars the modern mentality,* as does, even more, the idea that it summons up: a sort of complicated organic scheme or gigantic

genealogical tree, in which each being and group has its predetermined place. In other words, a *static peace*, one that is mathematical and governed by determinism and a code of external moral ordinances. *A peace without freedom or movement.* And a peace *without hope,* for its immobility seems to conceal a firmly entrenched disorder.

132.   Since this clearly is not what John XXIII wishes to say to us, *how does he picture this order?* To find out, we have only to open *Pacem in Terris.* Order is not confused with the "laws that the irrational elements of the universe obey. . . . Man's norms of conduct are of a different essence: they must be sought where God has inscribed them, namely in human nature . . . in the conscience of man, whom the Creator has made, in his own image, intelligent and free" (*Pacem in Terris, 3-6).*

133.   Thus, *peace is first of all a given order,* "the fruit of an order inscribed in human society by its Divine Founder" (*Gaudium et Spes,* 78, 1). Human nature does not change. Man is and will remain man till the end of time. And this is what guarantees the continuity and security of his personal and collective identity. Man does not create peace out of nothing. He has responsibility for the civilization, the nation, and the society of which at his birth he is the co-heir. He is responsible for these things to his contemporaries and his descendants. He has a certain duty to manage, with others, this human patrimony. He must contribute to the moral rectitude of his community or country, for example, in the matter of its foreign policy. He exercises a certain *critical power,* by his action upon opinion. *But he also shares* (at least in democratic regimes) *in legislative and executive power. The right to dissent, as we have seen above, does not therefore dispense one from the duty of taking part: each complements the other.*

B. *Nature and history.*

134.   However, while man must respect that which is true order in society, *he must be creative, he must achieve the creation of society.* This flows simply from the fact, spelled out by the Encyclical, that man is living, intelligent and free. *Because order, for a living being, is growth and change: "progress is the law of all life"* (162). For an intelligent being, order means thinking and inventing. For a free being, order means willing and acting. *Peace therefore is also an order to be created,* a future to be brought into being. This dynamic concept of peace, as we know, is already present in *Pacem in Terris* (progress: 64, 130, 166; promotion: 31, 40, 41, etc.). John XXIII takes as his starting-point the aspirations of the person and of communities. He tells us so in the first line of his Encyclical, when he presents "peace on earth" as the "object of the deep desire of mankind" (1). Peace is therefore not just the fruit of reason, but also the satisfaction of a certain number of

affective and instinctive needs. *Thus it plays a dynamic part;* it exercises an attraction; it is the driving force of each human being, each society.

135.   We find here once more the dynamic and historical character of nature, which does not exist in the pure state, but in living and identifiable persons. Hence we can understand better why John XXIII takes it as a point of support. Beginning with the human subject and with his community needs, he discovers in each man a tendency and availability for action for peace. *Is not history a remedy for the ills of societies, a far better one than war?*

136.   In view of the ever more rapid changes of the last ten years, this idea of a history to be brought to successful realization according to the pace of the present time presents itself with ever increasing urgency. *It is a question of successfully accomplishing the transformation and so to speak the cultural revolution of these decisive years.*

137.   According to the nature of the problems and of countries, this successful development has taken or could take the form of *evolution.* Elsewhere, circumstances have imposed more abrupt *changes,* and perhaps will do so again. But in any hypothesis, the success of history and therefore of peace must be situated *at two levels: the level of the "plan",* that is, the management of the present and the future, *and the level of the event,* that is, the ability to respond as well as possible to the unforeseen demands of the actual moment.

138.   The first series of efforts demands vision and foresight of things as a whole, as well as organization. The present popularity of "forecasting", or "futurology", is revealing. At the time of the Encyclical this science was not yet fully developed. Its present expansion is a sufficient indication that it is demanded by the vast transformations of recent times. It likewise indicates, as a consequence, the close attention that the various "actors" of peace must give it. On condition, of course, that it is not considered as a universal panacea or, still less, as an escape from the present; on the contrary, it must sink its roots deeply into the present. Another condition is that it must not be reduced to pure technocracy. The final condition is that *the expectations and forecasts of this new science must be followed with an accompanying and proportionate effort of thought and spirituality.* We find here a new viewpoint, one noted by *Octogesima Adveniens: the meaning of "utopia",* in the sense in which the word is understood today (*op. cit.,* 37).

139.   The foregoing leads us also, as a major imperative, to *introduce skilfully anthropology and theology into all our attempts to study the problem.*

140.   Here it is clearly not a question of entering into this vast mass of intellectual, political and pastoral research, but simply of inserting a

recommendation: anthropology and theology, in their indispensable development, *must constantly preserve the twofold dimensions of being and
becoming, identity and renewal.*

A new criterion.

141.   *"Pacem in Terris" had set forth four criteria* for a peaceful society:
truth, justice, love and liberty. It is a question here of four values which
are so essential that they constitute not only the signs by which one can
recognize a successful society but "the four principles which sustain the
house of peace" (John XXIII, Address on the occasion of his reception of
the Balsan Prize, *AAS* 55 [1963], p. 452). John XXIII returns frequently to
this idea of "foundations" or of "bases for life in society" (163), of
"norms" and of "the order which defines true peace" (167). He compares
them to four "pillars". These are all images that evoke the idea of permanence in regard to peace. It is necessary to state that it was not suggested
that the idea of progress was introduced here in order to call this permanence into question. For progress does not destroy identity; on the
contrary, it presupposes it. Change is the coming into being or the
evolution of a clearly-defined being which remains fully the same at each
phase of its transformation. The adult is not a different being from the
infant that he was, or from the elderly person that he will become. It is the
same with human society. In order to emphasize the fact more clearly to
our contemporaries, who are very sensitive to this idea and to this reality,
it would seem well to point out also, as a component of peace, this idea of
evolution from the beginning to the conclusion. For a society which did
not progress would not be an ordered and living society. It would have
within itself a strange and disquieting element, especially in a universe
which is in such rapid and universal transformation. *Gaudium et Spes*
already noted this: "The human race is passing from a more or less static
notion of the order of things to a more dynamic and evolutionary concept.
Hence there arises a vast new problem which calls for new analyses and
new syntheses" (*op. cit.*, 5, 3).

142.   But here it is necessary to make an important observation. It is
not a question of change for change's sake or of thinking that every
change is good. For if it is true that life is defined by movement, there are
changes which are evidently neither the sign nor the cause of the living
body: sickness, and death which destroys the body. It is the same with the
"body" of society. Side by side with the changes which one could qualify,
at least morally speaking, as indifferent or secondary, as for example the
evolution of a language in the course of centuries, there are others which
must be rejected because they violate justice or the good; others, on the

contrary, must be thought out, put forward, proposed and promoted: changes which represent something better, a value or progress.

143.   And we find here the affirmation so forcefully emphasized that "development is the new name for peace". Of course, this is true only on condition that development is not equated with merely economic growth but is really and fully human in all its dimensions and constitutes an authentic liberation and development "of the whole man and of every man."

144.   Paul VI insists on this constantly, especially in *Populorum Progressio:*

145.   "In God's plan, each man is called to develop himself . . . each man can grow in humanity, increase in value and in being. But each man is a member of society: he belongs to the whole of mankind. It is not just this or that man, but all men who are called to this full development. Civilizations are born, grow and die. But, as the waves of the rising tide advance, each one further than the last, up the shore, *so humanity is advancing along the path of history"* (*op. cit.,* 15-17).

146.   In the light of this judgment of the Council and of *Populorum Progressio,* cannot and should not one see in this "constant" of change a new "sign of the times?"

II. SIGNS OF THE TIMES

147.   As we have seen in connection with the impact of the Encyclical, the most widely-noted novelty of its method is the recourse to the idea of the "signs of the times."

148.   John XXIII is content to enunciate this approach to reality by practising it, in all simplicity. It is *Gaudium et Spes that worked out the theory of it, as well* as its own proper methodology. In an audience of 16 April 1966, Paul VI pointed out *the originality of this integration of the "signs of the times" into the anthropology of Gaudium et Spes.* This document described it as a "theological interpretation of contemporary history" (*op. cit.,* 42-44), "stating that it is not merely a matter of a posthumous reading of the past" but of an effort "to discover, in time, signs . . . indications of a relationship with the kingdom of God . . . ".

149.   But in the name of what is this comparison made? And who is endowed with the ability to undertake this discernment of history? And in what way?

150.   *Pacem in Terris* does not answer these questions. Its method remained to be completed on the theoretical level. Since 1964, this work of completion has been accomplished by the Encyclical *Ecclesiam Suam* of

Paul VI, which provided its theological and pastoral elaboration, while a year later *Gaudium et Spes* continued this work, which was finally completed in 1971 by the Letter *Octogesima Adveniens*, which, following the lines laid down by *Ecclesiam Suam*, provided the final completion.

A. *Some observations.*

151.   *In the light of these important documents*, it seems possible now to make *a few observations;* I repeat that my intention is not to make elaborate theses out of them.

152.   (1) It is *the right and duty of every man and of all men* to carry out *this discernment* between events and the moral good that they know through their consciences (5). In the words of St. Paul, "they are a law to themselves, even though they do not have the law" (*Rom* 2:14). Thus, *the theory of the signs of the times* concerns all men of good will; it is *not a monopoly of Christians. Gaudium et Spes* (44) notes with insistence all that the Church receives from the world, how she recognizes and affirms the presence of the Holy Spirit and of redemptive grace in all men, and not only in the baptized.

153.   (2) *Christians however have something specific to say and do in the interpretation and accomplishment of history.* For Christians, in fact, interpreting history through the signs of the times means asking themselves whether events, accomplishments and currents of opinion that make themselves felt represent or not an enrichment of human nature, which is always perfectible and which completes itself by developing in time. Since human nature is created by God, the question arises in this form for Christians: is the new event the image or the caricature of human nature? The method of the signs of the times, therefore, consists *in the first place in discovering correspondences and resemblances.*

154.   But it also consists (since we are dealing with nature in motion) in asking *whether the unfolding of this history is really in conformity* with the divine plan, in short, with sacred history, *biblical and messianic history,* which, according to the New Testament, continues from the Resurrection of Christ until his second coming, the Parousia.

155.   (3) The Christian can certainly not make this comparison with the aid of his own *individual conscience* alone. *His conscience needs to be assisted* and enlightened, for one person cannot know all the data relating to situations that demand a moral judgment. Moreover, even given an equal knowledge of the facts, the moral judgments made by Christians are seen to differ very widely. As *Octogesima Adveniens* emphasizes, "One must recognize a legitimate variety of possible options. The same Christian faith can lead to different commitments" (*op. cit.*, 50). The interpreta-

tion of the signs of the times can therefore lead to very different attitudes. For Christians the temptation is very great to identify their own Christian interpretation of history with that of God and of his entire Church, and this temptation is the greater in proportion to the individual's faith in the Gospel and to his generosity. Thus there is *a whole field of theological and pastoral research to be studied* (fortunately this task is already being widely undertaken) *on the idea of "prophetism."* The duty of speaking in the name of God and of his "Book," the Bible, is more pressing than ever. *Peace calls for a minister of the Word.* But this Word of God is passed on and given to us in the Church and by the Church. It is therefore within the People of God that there are to be found the individual and collective criteria of a Christian affirmation or action in the matter of peace.

156.   (4) *The clarification that the Apostolic Letter of Paul VI brings to Pacem in Terris* is precisely this: it indicates the *conditions* in which Christian communities will be able to exercise this discernment. These communities will be able to carry out this task with "the help of the Holy Spirit, in communion with the bishops, who hold responsibility, and in dialogue with other Christian brethren and all men of good will" (*Octogesima Adveniens*, 4). The Letter states that they will have to do so "without putting themselves in the place of the institutions of civil society . . . and rising above their particular nature" (*ibid.*, 51). This is what saves the Christian interpretation of the signs of the times from the *temptation to pseudoprophetism and neoclericalism,* which consist in wishing to derive directly from Scripture a political system (and one only) at the whim of individual exegesis.

157.   (5) The above clarification equally protects the Christian interpretation and commitment from *another risk,* one no less serious and real—*that of the ghetto and intolerance.* However paradoxical it may seem, the very value that one attributes to the Gospel creates the danger of building a dividing wall between the Gospel and those who do not accept it, or, while admitting its value, do not make it their guiding principle in human and political matters. There is a good and a bad use of the Gospel. The good use consists in making the Gospel the constant inspiration of our "vision" of the world and our commitments, and not a code of political techniques. On the other hand, there is a certain way of misusing the Gospel which cuts off all communication and which is in direct contradiction with the respect that one professes to have for nonbelievers. If this respect is genuine, one must have trust in non-believers' motives as men of good will, motives which are based precisely on reason, the heart and a right conscience. Otherwise, one returns to the point of *replacing this much vaunted dialogue by a confessional political*

monologue. And so the Encyclical retains all its immediacy when it demands that one should have confidence in man, quite apart from motives drawn from Revelation. It retains at the same time all its specific Christian nature, since it asks Christians to bring the riches of Revelation into their common action with all their non-Christian brethren.

158.   The conclusion seems obvious. *The approach which uses the "signs of the times" must therefore be combined with the approach of "man of good will".* In this way the following will be avoided: on the one hand, the danger of Christianity becoming swallowed up by a totally atheistic concept of peace; on the other hand, the absorption of non-believers by the People of God, which would thus regain (unconsciously no doubt, but in fact) the triumphalism that it rejects today. At the same time, *dialogue with the world would become, by a strange twist, a Christian monologue,* if not a new crusade, which would once more bring into question the inestimably valuable acquisition of a just separation of Church and State, of the spiritual power from the temporal.

B. *Peace of the Church, peace in the Church.*

159.   (1) *Specifically Christian character.* Here a place should be found for a profound and extended reflection *upon the specifically Christian contribution* in the matter of peace, upon the theological and pastoral meaning of expressions such as the peace of Christ, Christian peace, peace of the Church. A study should also be made on the question of how the Church is a "subject of peace," in what way, through what pedagogy, at the price of what investments in thought, research and relations with the other bodies devoted to peace. The same goes for *peace in the Church*: this would call for important development. I will limit myself to a brief allusion.

160.   If the Church, as is her vocation, wishes to be the sign and "sacrament" of peace in the world and for the world, she must exercise that "discernment of spirits" to which the approach using the signs of the times invites us. It is this purification with regard to political activity which will constitute its most certain effectiveness.

161.   But the Church will also (and perhaps above all) have to fulfil another condition: *restore peace within herself.* Can we say, in strict Christian truth, that we are giving an example of this at the present time and living its reality?

162.   The tensions making themselves felt within the People of God are certainly not without causes. Far from hiding these causes, we must seek them out and look them in the face. But this examination must not become an alibi reproducing in our New Testament age the dialectic of the

scapegoat. John XXIII insists strongly upon this *unity of exterior witness and reality lived within* (*Pacem in Terris*, 151-153). Numerous documents of Paul VI have similarly underlined this point.

163.   Peace in the Church is not an affair of compromise, with the denial of real problems. Peace must be truth, which is one of the criteria of a successful society. But John XXIII, by also including love among the criteria of this successful society, obliges us in conscience and *a fortiori* to apply it to the ecclesial society.

164.   For these tensions become unjustifiable when they turn into sectarianism. *The same ardour with which Christians struggle against all racial, ethnic, national or ideological discrimination must inspire their own relationships within the People of God.* We know unfortunately that it is not so. Mutual intolerance and excommunication too often rage within the People of God, as well as the practical and systematic refusal of communion with other Catholic brethren who do not have the same political views or who do not belong to the same social or cultural category. This *de facto* contradiction between Catholics' inner and outward behaviour must be eliminated, under penalty of lying, counter-witness and ineffectiveness. "By this love you have for one another, everyone will know that you are my disciples" (*Jn* 13: 35).

165.   In the study of the problem of peace, the place of love must not only be foreseen; it must be given pride of place.

166.   (2) *Love as the driving-force of history.* The Synod's document, "Justice in the World," comes back several times to this point, in speaking of the relationship between justice and charity (part II) and in the assertion "that in history there are sources of progress other than conflict, namely love and right" (part III, p. 17). The Synod then alludes clearly to a path chosen by an ever increasing number of Christians—and non-Christians: "This priority of love in history draws other Christians to prefer *the way of non-violent action*" (*ibid*).

167.   Here again we are faced with a great problem, one into which I cannot enter but which I was anxious to mention, as a very important path for the promotion of peace.

168.   We would find a great number of categorical affirmations of the prime motive role of love in society if we re-read the documents of Vatican II, especially of course *Gaudium et Spes*. "The further (the unity of Christians) advances towards truth and love under the powerful impulse of the Holy Spirit, the more this unity will be a harbinger of unity and peace for the world at large" (*op. cit.*, 92). This idea returns again and again in the words and writings of *Paul VI. Notably on the occasion of the World Day of Peace*, an initiative which of itself constitutes a witness to this confidence

in human communion, reconciliation and friendship as a factor of worldwide peace. It will suffice to quote one of the recent allusions of the Holy Father on this subject: "True peace is based on human hearts, not on the victory of arms, not on political arrogance. . . . *It is based on love. . .* " (Paul VI, 28 January 1973, on the occasion of the ceasefire in Vietnam).

169.   Finally, *John XXIII* presented his Encyclical *Pacem in Terris* as nothing other than *"the echo of Christ's testament of love,* on the evening of Holy Thursday" (11 April 1963, Address to the Diplomatic Corps).

CONCLUSION

170.   On this tenth anniversary of *Pacem in Terris,* we feel that the Church and the world cannot and do not wish to forget it. At the same time, we are aware that *this Word that the Church addressed to herself and to the world has been enriched during these past ten years.* We no longer take the Encyclical by itself or read it in isolation, as when it appeared. *It comes to us in a whole body of documents,* of which it now forms part and which completes it harmoniously. In other words *Pacem in Terris* is set within a context, a living collection of interventions, actions and messages which confirm and extend it.

171.   In the midst of these prophetic testimonies of the People of God and its magisterium, *Pacem in Terris* retains all its originality: love and confidence in man, realistic optimism, the reading of the signs of the times, unlimited dialogue and communion.

172.   The way in which we can best be faithful to the Encyclical is by putting it into practice.

173.   *Paul VI* has unceasingly told us this and exhorted us to carry it out. Here, chosen from many others, are a few testimonies of it:

174.   *"Today, Pope John's appeal is more topical than ever.* We have ourself adopted it as one of the most valuable elements of his heritage . . . " (Paul VI, Message to the Second *Pacem in Terris* Conference, Geneva, 28 May 1967, *AAS 59* [1967], p. 541).

175.   Again quite recently, in his Message for the World Day of Peace, 1 January 1973, the Holy Father asks all those who are active and aware to undertake every possible effort to make peace possible. He says to them: "Establish and build up in truth, in love and in freedom peace for the

coming centuries. . . . This was the programme which our predecessor John XXIII traced out in his Encyclical *Pacem in Terris,* the tenth anniversary of which will fall in April 1973. And just as ten years ago you listened with respect and gratitude to his paternal voice, so we trust that the memory of that great flame which he kindled in the world will strengthen hearts to new and firmer resolutions for peace" (1 January 1973, *AAS* 64 [1972], p. 758).

176.   In conclusion, how could I not make my own the words that his future successor spoke after the death of John XXIII, when, as Cardinal Montini, he was still Archbishop of Milan? He addressed to all an appeal, to remain faithful "to his heritage, which the tomb cannot swallow up; to the spirit which he infused into our age, and which death cannot stifle," and, " . . . looking now to the horizon which he opened up for the forward march of the Church and of history," to gaze resolutely "at the future which is born from him" (Cardinal Montini, Panegyric of John XXIII, Milan, 24 June 1963).

Letter of Paul VI
to the Federation of
Asian Bishops' Conferences,
First General Assembly, Taipei
(April 22-27, 1974)

To Our Venerable Brothers
the Bishops of Asia

1.   On the occasion of the First General Assembly of the Federation of Asian Bishops' Conferences we gladly send you our fraternal greetings. You have chosen to discuss during this Assembly the question of Evangelization. You will examine how best you can proclaim Christ, "the way, the truth and the life" (Jn 14:6), to the peoples of Asia—to more than half of mankind.

2.   The immensity of this Evangelization is both a challenge and a consolation. It constitutes a burden which in human terms may seem unbearable, but which you know can easily be borne, because it was given to you by Christ, whose yoke is easy and whose burden is light (cf. Mt 11:30).

3.   At the same time the very vastness of your task gives you a special position and the results of your present deliberations can prove to be of great help to your brother bishops and to the whole Church during the forthcoming Synod.

[This original English text is that published by *L'Osservatore Romano* of April 21, 1974, page 1. Paragraph numbers have been added.]

4.   You know of our personal affection for you and for all the peoples of Asia, both those who have already received the Message of Christ, and those to whom it has still to be proclaimed, not by force or by imposition, but in an open and friendly approach which demonstrates Christian love. We have given testimony to this affection in the visits which we were privileged to make to Asia.

5.   Dear Brothers in Christ, because of this love which we have for the peoples of Asia, because of the importance of Evangelization in your countries, and because of the value which we attach to your discussions, we now take this opportunity to share with you some of our thoughts, and to reiterate some of the things we said when we stood in your midst on Asian soil in 1970.

6.   You have the consolation and the inspiration of going forth to sow the seed of Christ's Message in fertile ground. The persuasion of spiritual values, the high degree of ascetical discipline, the family-oriented sense of filial devotion and the thirst for spiritual culture shown by your nations through their different religions—all these things are indisputable pointers to the primacy among your peoples of the things of the spirit. The propagation of the Christian Message must in no way cancel out or lessen these cultural and spiritual values, which constitute a priceless heritage. The Church must make herself in her fullest expression native to your countries, your cultures, your races. Let the seed, which is the word of God, put down deep roots in the fertile soil of Asia. Let the Church draw nourishment from the genuine values of venerable Asian religions and cultures. Her own contribution to Asia will surely be welcomed by your peoples, who are accustomed by centuries of spiritual formation to recognize and acknowledge what is good in others. Let the Church be seen, therefore, as a community of brethren, distinguished by their love for one another and for all men, imitating their founder who went about doing good (cf. Acts 10:39).

7.   It is our earnest and constant prayer that the increasing pace of Evangelization may help to preserve your peoples from the danger of materialism. Let it do so, not by ignoring material needs, but by responding to the hunger for bread, for responsibility, for freedom and for justice. Let Evangelization respond to these needs by demonstrating that practical and all-embracing brotherly solidarity with one another under the common fatherhood of God which typifies our Christian Religion (cf. Message to the Peoples of Asia, 29 November, 1970, AAS LXIII [1971], 35–40).

8.   Finally, we hope and pray that the Evangelization of Asia will give

great glory to God in heaven and bring peace on earth, peace of heart, peace within families, peace among nations. Blessed indeed are those who spread the Gospel of peace.

Beloved Brothers, in pledge of our enduring spiritual affection we gladly impart our Apostolic Blessing.

PAULUS PP. VI

Bull of Indiction
of the Holy Year 1975
(May 23, 1974)

Paul
Servant of the Servants of God,

TO ALL THE FAITHFUL:

HEALTH AND APOSTOLIC BENEDICTION

1.   The memorials of the Apostles, the holy places of Rome where there are worthily preserved and religiously venerated the tombs of the Apostles Peter and Paul, those "holy fathers" through whom the City became not only the "disciple of truth" but also the teacher of truth[1] and the centre of Catholic unity, now—as the universal Jubilee to be celebrated there approaches—shine forth more brightly to the minds of the faithful as the goal of pilgrimage.

2.   Down the centuries, these memorials have always impelled the Christian people to be fervent in their faith and to testify to ecclesial communion. This is so because the Church recognizes her identity and the cause of her unity in the foundation laid by Jesus Christ, namely, the Apostles.[2] From as early as the second century the faithful came to Rome to see and venerate the "trophies" of the Apostles Peter and Paul in those very places where they are preserved;[3] and they made pilgrimages to the Church of Rome to contemplate her "regal dignity".[4] In the fourth century the pilgrimage to Rome became the principal form in the West of that kind of religious journey. It was similar to, and had the same religious purpose as, the pilgrimage which was made in the East to Jerusalem

---

[This English version is that published by the Vatican Polyglot Press in booklet form, 30 pages. Paragraph numbers have been added.]

where the Lord's sepulchre is found.[5] In the early Middle Ages there came on pilgrimage to Rome from various parts of Europe and even from the East, especially monks, those who were "linked to the Chair of Peter"[6] and who wished to make a profession of their orthodox faith at the tombs of the Apostles.[7]

3.   The idea of a pilgrimage increased further from the twelfth to the thirteenth century, becoming all the more common by reason of a renewal of spirituality and popular piety which spread throughout Europe at that time. This renewal served to enrich the ancient notion which the Church received from tradition and which was equally to be found in other religions, namely, the concept of a "pilgrimage undertaken for the love of God".[8] In this way the Jubilee Year originated: it was as it were the result of a process of maturing in the doctrinal, biblical and theological fields.[9] It emerged plainly for the first time in the year 1220, when our predecessor Honorius III proclaimed a Jubilee Year for the pilgrimage to the tomb of Saint Thomas Becket.[10] Later, as is well known, pilgrims came to Rome to the Basilicas of Saint Peter and Saint Paul, in the great popular and penitential movement of the year 1300, a movement confirmed by our predecessor Boniface VIII,[11] and which was marked by a longing to obtain pardon from God and peace among men. This movement was directed to this very lofty motive: "the glory of God and the exaltation of the faith".[12]

4.   The Roman Jubilee of 1300 was the beginning and the pattern of those which have followed (every twenty-five years from the fifteenth century onwards, except when the series was interrupted by extraneous circumstances). This is an indication of the continuity and vitality which have always confirmed the relevance of this venerable institution for every age.

5.   It is correct to say that the Jubilees celebrated in recent times have preserved this outstanding value, whereby the unity and renewal of the Church are affirmed in a special way and all men encouraged to recognize one another as brothers and to walk in the path of peace. Such a desire manifested itself at the beginning of this century, when our predecessor Leo XIII proclaimed the Jubilee Year in 1900. The human family was filled with the same hopes and expectations when, a quarter of a century later, afflicted by grave dangers and contention, it awaited the Holy Year of 1925. These were proposed for the special Holy Year of 1933 on the occasion of the nineteenth centenary of the Redemption. It was the same noble aspirations for justice and peaceful coexistence among men that Pius XII put forward in the last Jubilee, in the year 1950.

I

6.   It seems to us that in the present Holy Year all the principal and important motives of the previous Jubilees are present and expressed in summary form in the themes that we ourself laid down in our discourse of 9 May 1973 when we first announced the Holy Year: renewal and reconciliation.[13] We have offered these themes for the reflection of the pastors and faithful, particularly during the anticipated celebration of the Jubilee in the local Churches, and we have added to them our exhortations and our catechesis. But the aspirations that the two themes enunciate and the lofty ideals that they express will find a more complete realization in Rome, where the pilgrims to the Tombs of the Apostles Peter and Paul and to the memorials of the other martyrs will come more easily into contact with the ancient sources of the Church's faith and life, in order to be converted by repentance, strengthened in charity and united more closely with their brethren by the grace of God.

7.   This renewal and reconciliation pertain in the first place to the interior life, above all because it is in the depths of the heart that there exists the root of all good, and, unfortunately, of all evil. It is in the depths of the heart therefore that there must take place conversion or *metanoia*, that is, a change of direction, of attitude, of option, of one's way of life.

8.   But also for the Church as a whole, at a distance of ten years from the end of the Second Vatican Council we view the Holy Year as the ending of a period of reflection and reform and the beginning of a new phase of building up in the theological, spiritual and pastoral spheres, which will develop upon the foundations laboriously laid down and consolidated during the past years, in accordance with the principles of new life in Christ and of the communion of all men in him, who reconciled us to the Father by his blood.[14]

9.   For the whole world this call to renewal and reconciliation is in harmony with the most sincere aspirations to liberty, justice, unity and peace that we see present wherever men become aware of their most grave problems and suffer from the mishaps produced by divisions and fratricidal wars. With the message of the Holy Year, therefore, the Church wishes to indicate to all men of good will the vertical dimension of life that ensures the reference of all aspirations and experiences to an absolute and truly universal value, without which it is vain to hope that mankind will find once more a point of unification and a guarantee of true freedom. Even though it is characteristic of many sectors of modern society to

assume secular forms, the Church, without interfering in matters which do not come within her competence, nevertheless wishes to impress on men the need of being converted to God, who alone is necessary,[15] and of imbuing all their actions with fear and love of him. For faith in God is the most powerful safeguard of the human conscience and the solid foundation of those relationships of justice and brotherhood for which the world yearns.

10.   The pilgrimage to Rome by representatives of all the local Churches, both pastors and people, will therefore be a sign of a new process of conversion and brotherly reconciliation.

11.   As the minister of the word and of the grace of reconciliation, we respond to this sign of the interior dispositions of the pilgrims and of the renewed resolve of the Christian people whom they represent, by imparting the gift of the Jubilee Indulgence, insofar as we are able, to all the pilgrims who come to Rome and to all those who, though prevented from making the journey, accompany them in spirit.

II

12.   It is well known from the Church's very ancient custom that the indulgence attached to many penitential practices was granted as a gift in a special way on the occasion of pilgrimages to the places sanctified by the life, Passion and Resurrection of our Saviour Jesus Christ and by the confession of the Apostles. Today too we associate ourself with that venerable tradition, according to the principles and norms that we have ourself laid down in the Apostolic Constitution *Indulgentiarum Doctrina*[16] and which we wish at this point briefly to recall.

13.   Since Christ is our "Justice" and, as has been fittingly said, our "Indulgence", we, as the humble minister of Christ the Redeemer, willingly extend a share in the gift of indulgence—in accordance with the Church's tradition—to all the faithful who, through a profound conversion of the heart to God, through works of penance, piety and brotherly solidarity, sincerely and fervently attest to their desire to remain united in charity with God and their brethren and to make progress in that charity.[17] In fact, this sharing comes from the fullness of the treasury of salvation which is primarily found in Christ the Redeemer himself, "in whom subsist in all their value the satisfactions and merits of his

Redemption".[18] In this fullness in Christ, of which we have all received,[19] there shines forth "the most ancient dogma of the Communion of Saints, whereby, in Christ and through Christ, the lives of the individual sons of God are linked with the lives of all the other Christian brethren by a marvellous bond in the supernatural unity of the Mystical Body of Christ, as in one mystical person".[20]

14.   For, "by the hidden and benevolent mystery of the divine will, men are linked together in a supernatural relationship, whereby just as the sin of one also harms the others, so also the holiness of one is beneficial to the others".[21] By means of the indulgence, the Church, making use of her power as the minister of the Redemption of Christ the Lord, communicates to the faithful a sharing in this fullness of Christ in the Communion of Saints,[22] providing them with the ample means of salvation.

15.   Thus the Church, aiding and embracing them like a mother, sustains her weak and infirm children, who find a firm support in the Mystical Body of Christ, which in its entirety works for their conversion through charity, example and prayer. Thus penitents find in this singular form of ecclesial charity a powerful aid to help them to put off the old man and put on the new, and conversion and renewal consist precisely in this.[23] In fact, the Church's aim in granting indulgences is not only that of helping the faithful to expiate the punishment they have deserved but also that of stimulating them to carry out works of piety, penance and charity, and in particular works that serve to favour the growth of faith and the common good.[24]

III

16.   For this reason, interpreting as it were the Church's maternal sentiments, we impart the gift of the Plenary Indulgence to all the faithful who are properly disposed, and who, after confessing their sins and receiving Holy Communion, pray for the intentions of the Supreme Pontiff and the College of Bishops:

17.   1) if they undertake a sacred pilgrimage to one of the Patriarchal Basilicas (the Basilica of Saint Peter's in the Vatican, Saint Paul's Outside-the-Walls, the Lateran Archbasilica of the Most Holy Saviour, or Saint Mary Major's), or to some other church or place of the City of Rome

designated by the competent authority, and there devoutly take part in a liturgical celebration, especially the Sacrifice of the Mass, or some exercise of piety (e.g. the Way of the Cross, the Rosary);

18.   2) if they visit, in a group or individually, one of the four Patriarchal Basilicas and there spend some time in devout recollection concluding with the Our Father, the Profession of Faith in any approved form and a prayer to the Blessed Virgin Mary;

19.   3) if, being prevented by illness or some other grave reason from going on a pilgrimage to Rome, they unite themselves spiritually with this pilgrimage and offer their prayers and sufferings to God;

20.   4) if, being prevented while in Rome by illness or some other grave reason from taking part in a liturgical celebration or exercise of piety or visit made by their group (ecclesial, family or social, as mentioned in 1) and 2) above), they unite themselves spiritually with the group and offer their prayers and sufferings to God.

21.   During the Holy Year moreover there remain in force the other concessions of indulgences, with the proviso as before that a plenary indulgence can be gained only once a day;[25] however, all indulgences can always by applied to the dead *in mundum suffragii.*[26]

22.   For the same reasons, namely, in order that the faithful be provided with every possible aid to salvation, and to help priests, especially confessors, we lay down that confessors taking part in the Jubilee pilgrimage may use the faculties they have been given in their own dioceses by the legitimate authority,[27] so that both on the journey and in Rome they may hear the confessions of the faithful accompanying them on the pilgrimage, and also the confessions of others who, together with the members of their own group, may approach them. The right of the Penitentiaries of the Patriarchal Basilicas regarding the confessionals reserved to them is maintained,[28] and special faculties will be granted by the Sacred Apostolic Penitentiary to the Penitentiaries.

IV

23.   We have stated above that the following two principal purposes have been laid down for the Holy Year: spiritual renewal in Christ and reconciliation with God, and we have said that these aims concern not only the interior life of each individual but the whole Church, and also in a

certain sense the whole of human society. For this reason we earnestly exhort all concerned to consider these proposals, to undertake initiatives and to coordinate programmes, so that during the Holy Year real progress may be made in the renewal of the Church and also in the pursuit of certain goals which we have especially at heart, in accordance with the farsighted spirit of the Second Vatican Ecumenical Council. Repentance, the purification of the heart and conversion to God must consequently bring about an increase in the apostolic activities of the Church.

24.   During the Holy Year therefore generous efforts must be made to further evangelization, which is certainly the first of all the activities to be promoted. For the pilgrim Church "has been divinely sent to all nations that she might be 'the universal sacrament of salvation' "[29] and she "is by her very nature missionary",[30] and in her historical course is renewed to the extent that she shows herself ready to accept and to deepen through faith the Gospel of Jesus Christ the Son of God, and to proclaim his saving message to men by word and the witness of her life.

25.   The coming assembly of the Synod of Bishops does not have a merely extrinsic and fortuitous connection with the Holy Year. On the contrary, as we have already stated, "a zealous effort must be made to coordinate and link closely together both these ecclesial events".[31] In this regard the Synod will propose directives and suggestions for the reflection of the Pastors, gathered about the Supreme Pontiff, so that they may carefully consider in the light to faith "the evangelization of the modern world", taking into account, in the light of the charity of Christ, the wishes of the whole Church and the more urgent needs of our time.

26.   Therefore devout attention to the Word of God together with catechetical instruction given to the faithful of every state and of all ages must lead Christians to a purifying of their way of living and to a higher knowledge of faith; it must dispel doubts, and stimulate the negligent to activate joyfully in their lives the Gospel message; it must impel everyone towards a conscious and fruitful sharing in the Sacraments; it must encourage communities and individuals to give witness to the faith by the uprightness and strength of their lives, so that the world may see the reason for the hope that is in us.[32]

27.   Now that ten years have passed since the Second Vatican Council began the great and salutary work of renewal in the fields of the pastoral ministry, the practice of penance and the sacred liturgy, we consider it altogether fitting that this work should be reviewed and carried further. If what the Church has clearly approved is kept in mind, it will be possible to recognize the valid and legitimate elements to be found in the many and varied experiments that have been carried out everywhere. Similarly,

these same elements can, by a more earnest effort, be put into practice in accordance with the norms and principles suggested by pastoral prudence and a sense of true piety.

28.   The presence of large numbers of pilgrims, both pastors and people, from Christian communities throughout the world, brought together in Rome by a fraternal desire to gain the true benefits of the grace and love of Christ, will undoubtedly afford excellent opportunities for putting forward, comparing and evaluating studies and viewpoints of various kinds. This will most certainly be the case if congresses and meetings are held at different levels in the ecclesial community and by varied groups of experts, and provided that prayer and a ready willingness to carry out the apostolate are joined together.

29.   At this point we wish to draw particular attention to the need to find a just and proper balance between the different demands of the pastoral ministry today, a balance similar to that which has been admirably achieved in the sacred liturgy. We refer to the balance between tradition and renewal, between the necessarily religious nature of the Christian apostolate and its effectiveness as a force in all fields of social living, between free and spontaneous activity—which some are accustomed to call charismatic—in this apostolate and fidelity to laws based on the commands of Christ and of the pastors of the Church. For these laws, laid down by the Church and continually brought up to date, make allowance for individual experiments within the Christian community, in such a way that they are a help to the building up the Body of Christ, which is the Church, and not a hindrance.[33]

30.   We wish likewise to draw attention to the ever increasing need to promote the kind of apostolate which, without damaging the Church's necessary and traditional institutions, namely dioceses and parishes, takes special account of particular local circumstances and categories of people. Such an apostolate must ensure that the leaven of the Gospel permeates those forms of modern social living which often differ from traditional forms of ecclesial life and seem foreign to the communities in which the faithful gather together and are linked in prayer, faith and charity. The forms we are thinking of are principally those of workers, members of the academic world and young people.

31.   It will also be necessary to examine with care methods of teaching religion and of preaching the sacred word of God, to ensure that they meet the needs of our time. This must be done with the aim of finding effective methods. Special care must be taken to ensure that the media of social communications promote the human and Christian progress both of individuals and of communities.

32.   These are questions of the greatest seriousness and importance. We must face up to them, and with humble prayer seek the grace of the Holy Year in order to solve them.

V

33.   As is well known, in recent years one of the Church's most pressing concerns has been to disseminate everywhere a message of charity, of social awareness and of peace, and to promote, as far as she can, works of justice and of solidarity in favour of all those in need, of those on the margins of society, of exiles and of the oppressed—in favour of all men, in fact, whether individuals, social groups or peoples. We earnestly desire therefore that the Holy Year, through the works of charity which it suggests to the faithful and which it asks of them, should be an opportune time for strengthening and supporting the moral consciousness of all the faithful and of that wider community of all men which the message of the Church can reach if an earnest effort is made.

34.   The ancient origins of the Jubilee as seen in the laws and institutions of Israel clearly show that this social dimension is part of its very nature. In fact, as we read in the book of Leviticus,[34] the Jubilee Year, precisely because it was dedicated in a special way to God, involved a new ordering of all things that were recognized as belonging to God: the land, which was allowed to lie fallow and was given back to its former owners, economic goods, insofar as debts were remitted, and, above all, man, whose dignity and freedom were reaffirmed in a special way by the manumission of slaves. The Year of God, then, was also the Year of Man, the Year of the Earth, the Year of the Poor, and upon this view of the whole of human reality there shone a new light which emanated from the clear recognition of the supreme dominion of God over the whole of creation.

35.   In today's world also the problems which most disturb and torment mankind—economic and social questions, the question of ecology and sources of energy, and above all that of the liberation of the oppressed and the uplifting of all men to a new dignity of life—can have light cast on them by the message of the Holy Year.

36.   We wish, however, to invite all the sons and daughters of the Church, and especially the pilgrims coming to Rome, to undertake certain

definite tasks which, as successor of Peter and head of that Church "which presides over the universal gathering of charity"[35] we now publicly propose and commend to all. We refer to the carrying out of works of faith and charity for the benefit of our needy brethren in Rome and in other Churches of the world. These works will not necessarily be grandiose ones, although such are in no way to be excluded. In many cases what are today called "micro-realizations" will be sufficient, corresponding as they do to the Gospel spirit of charity. In this field the Church, in view of the modest resources at her disposal, will perhaps have to limit herself more and more to giving men nothing more than the widow's mite.[36] But she knows and teaches that the good which counts most is that which, in humble and very often unknown ways, manages to give help where there is a little need and to heal small wounds—things which often find no place in large projects of social reform.

37.   Nevertheless, the Church feels that it is necessary to give encouragement also to these larger programmes for promoting justice and the progress of peoples. She renews her call to all those who have the power and the duty to build up in the world a more perfect order of social and human relations, that they should not give up because of the difficulties of the present times, and that they should not be won over by selfish interests. Once more we make a particularly strong appeal on behalf of developing countries, and of peoples still afflicted by hunger and by war. Let special attention be given to the many needs which oppress man today, to the finding of employment by which men can provide for the needs of life, to housing which so many lack, to schools which need much assistance, to social and medical aid, and to the development and safeguarding of decent public moral standards.

38.   We should like also to express the humble and sincere desire that in this present Holy Year too, in accordance with the tradition of previous Jubilees, the proper authorities of the different nations should consider the possibility of wisely granting an amnesty to prisoners, as a witness to clemency and equity, especially to those who have given sufficient proof of moral and civic rehabilitation, or who may have been caught up in political and social upheavals too immense for them to be held fully responsible.

39.   We express in anticipation our gratitude and invoke the Lord's abundant blessings on all those who will strive to ensure that this message of charity, of social awareness and of freedom, which the Church addresses to all men in the lively hope that she may be understood and listened to, is accepted and translated into reality in the political and social

order. In expressing this hope we are conscious of following a wonderful tradition which began with the law of Israel and found its fullest expression in our Lord Jesus Christ, who from the very beginning of his ministry presented himself as the fulfilment of the ancient promises and figures connected with the Jubilee Year: "The Spirit of the Lord is upon me, because he has anointed me to preach good news to the poor. He has sent me to proclaim release to the captives and recovering of sight to the blind, to set at liberty those who are oppressed, to proclaim the acceptable year of the Lord".[37]

VI

40.   If there is one spiritual advantage which we especially desire will come about from the celebration of the Holy Year, it is an increase in the number of those who devote their lives to serving the Church, especially priests and religious. For in order that the paths of grace and the means of salvation which the Holy Year indicates and offers to all the faithful may be properly explained and made available there will always be a need of those sacred ministers and witnesses of Christ's Gospel who by completely following the Lord show their fellowmen, namely the men of this and subsequent ages, the way of penance and of holiness.

41.   Thus the voice of God must be listened to diligently. He never ceases to stir up and invite chosen individuals to dedicate themselves generously to the service of the Church and of the whole human race by the exercise of the priestly ministry and by the faithful witness of the religious life. Some will be called by God to offer themselves to him through obedience and sacred celibacy and as priests of Christ to teach and sanctify and lead the faithful wherever they may be. Others, men and women of various ages and conditions, will be attracted to the religious life, so that by fulfilling their baptismal promises through a higher way of life they may fully live in the Spirit and truly benefit the Church and society. We desire strongly that the multitude of these especially dear members of the Church may increase and flourish more and more, so that through their priesthood and the activity of their religious life they may bear the joyful message of Christ to the ends of the earth and all give glory to the heavenly Father.

VII

42.   Finally we wish to proclaim and preach that the reconciliation of Christians is one of the principal aims of the Holy Year. However, before all men can be brought together and restored to the grace of God our Father, communion must be reestablished between those who by faith have acknowledged and accepted Jesus Christ as the Lord of mercy who sets men free and unites them in the Spirit of love and truth. For this reason the Jubilee Year, which the Catholic Church has accepted as part of her own custom and tradition, can serve as a most opportune period for spiritual renewal and for the promotion of Christian unity.

43.   We would moreover point out that the Second Vatican Council has taught that every effort and undertaking directed towards the reconciliation of Christians and all true ecumenism must necessarily start from an inner conversion of the heart, since the desire for Christian communion springs and grows from spiritual renewal, self-denial, the full exercise of charity and fidelity to revealed truth.[38]

44.   It is here that there is to be found the full and proper realization of the whole ecumenical movement, to which the Catholic Church adheres as far as she is able, and through which Churches and Communities not yet fully in communion with the Apostolic See seek and desire the perfect unity willed by Christ. It is in fact the task and duty of the whole Church to reestablish this unity in full ecclesial communion.[39] The Year of Grace, in this sense, provides an opportunity for doing special penance for the divisions which exist among Christians; it offers an occasion for renewal in the sense of a heightened experience of holiness of life in Christ; it allows progress towards that hoped-for reconciliation by intensified dialogue and concrete Christian collaboration for the salvation of the world: "that they also may be one in us, so that the world may believe".[40]

45.   We have expressed once more our intentions and our desires concerning the celebration of the Holy Year in this City of Rome. We now invite our brothers in the episcopate and all the pastors and faithful of the Churches throughout the world, of those Churches also which are not in full communion with the Roman Church, and indeed all who believe in God, to participate at least spiritually in this feast of grace and redemption, in which Christ offers himself as the teacher of life. Together with the pastors and faithful on pilgrimage to the tombs of the Apostles and the early martyrs, we desire to profess faith in God the almighty and merciful Father and in Jesus Christ our Redeemer.

46.   For our part we would hope that all who come to Rome to see Peter[41] may through us experience in the Holy Year the truth of the words of Saint Leo the Great: "For in the whole Church Peter repeats each day, 'You are Christ the Son of the Living God', and every tongue which confesses the Lord is inspired by the teaching of this voice".[42]

47.   We would wish also that through our ministry and that of our brother priests a huge multitude of faithful may come to the sources of salvation.[43] May the Holy Door which we shall open on the night of Christmas Eve be a sure sign of this new approach to Christ, who alone is the Way[44] and the Door.[45] It will be a sure sign too of the paternal affection with which, filled with love and desiring peace, we open our heart to all.

48.   We implore the Blessed Virgin Mary, the Holy Mother of the Redeemer and of the Church, Mother of grace and of mercy, collaborator of reconciliation and shining example of the new life, to ask her Son to grant to all our brethren and sons and daughters the grace of his Holy Year, to renew and preserve them. To her hands and to her maternal heart we commend the beginning, the development and the conclusion of this most important matter.

49.   We wish this our Letter to take full and immediate effect, in such a manner that whatsoever has been laid down and decreed in it be religiously observed by all concerned, and come into force, all things to the contrary notwithstanding. If anyone knowingly or unknowingly shall act other than in accordance with what we have laid down, we order that such action be considered altogether null and void.

50.   Given in Rome, at Saint Peter's, on the twenty-third day of May, the Solemnity of the Ascension of the Lord, in the Year one thousand nine hundred and seventy-four, the eleventh of our Pontificate.

I PAUL

BISHOP OF THE CATHOLIC CHURCH

NOTES

1. Cf. St Leo the Great, *Sermo* LXXXII, 1: PL 54, 422.

2. Cf. Rev. 21:14.

3. Cf. the testimony of Gaius, an ecclesiastic of the time of Pope Zephyrinus, in Eusebius, *Historia Ecclesiastica*, II, 25, 7.

4. Cf. the inscription of Abercius, Bishop of Hierapolis in Phrygia at the end of the second century: text and translation in M. Guarducci, *L'iscrizione di Abercio*, "Ancient Society" 2 (1971), pp. 176–177.

5. Cf. St Maximus of Turin, *Homilia* 72: PL 57, 405 B.

6. The expression is found in a letter of St Columban to Pope Boniface IV in 613: *Sancti Columbani Opera*, ed. G.S.M. Walker, Dublin 1957, p. 48.

7. Concerning this custom cf. F.M. Mignanti, *Istoria della sacrosanta basilica Vaticana* . . . , Rome-Turin 1867, p. 180.

8. Cf. in general B. Kötting, *Peregrinatio religiosa. Wallfahrten in der Antike und das Pilgerwesen in der alten Kirche*, Regensburg 1950.

9. R. Foreville, *L'idée de Jubilé chez les théologiens et les canonistes (XII-XIII s.) avant l'institution du Jubilé romain (1300)*: "Revue d'Histoire Ecclésiastique" LVI (1961), pp. 401–423.

10. P. Pressuti, *Regesta Honorii III*, Roma 1888–95, 1840; text in R. Foreville, *Le Jubilé de Saint Thomas Becket du XIII au XV siècle (1220–1470). Etudes et documents*, Paris 1958, pp. 163–164.

11. Bull *Antiquorum habet fida relatio*, dated 22 February 1300: Extravagantes comm. V, IX, 1.

12. Cf. the *Glossa* of Cardinal Giovanni Monaco on the same Bull.

13. Cf. Paul VI, *Allocutio qua christifidelibus in Basilica Vaticana coram admissis nuntiat Se universalem Iubilaeum in annum MCMLXXV indictum*, d. 9 m. Maii a. 1973: AAS 65 (1973), pp. 322–325.

14. Cf. 2 Cor 5:18–20; Rom 5:10.

15. Cf. Lk 10:42; Mt 6:33.

16. Apostolic Constitution *Indulgentiarum Doctrina:* AAS 59 (1967), pp. 5–24.

17. Cf. Paul VI, Epist. ad E.mum P.D. Maximilianum S.R.E. Cardinalem de Fürstenberg ob indictum universale maximumque iubilaeum in annum MCMLXXV, *Iniziandosi ufficialmente*, d. 31m. Maii a. 1973: AAS 65 (1973), pp. 357–360.

18. Apost. Const. *Indulgentiarum Doctrina*, 5: AAS 59 (1967), p. 11.

19. Cf. Jn 1:16.

20. Apost. Const. *Indulgentiarum Doctrina*, 5: AAS 59 (1967), pp. 10–11; cf. St. Thomas Aquinas *Summa Theologiae*, III, q. 48, a. 2 ad 1 and q. 49, a. 1.

21. Apost. Const. *Indulgentiarum Doctrina*, 4: AAS 59 (1967), p. 9.

22. Cf. Apost. Const. *Indulgentiarum Doctrina*, 8: AAS 59 (1967), p. 16.

23. Cf. Paul VI, Epist. ad Rev. P. Constantinum Koser, Ordinis Fratrum Minorum Vicarium Generalem, septingentesimo quinquagesimo anno volvente ab "Indulgentia Portiunculae" per Honorium Pp. III Sancto Francisco concessa, *Sacrosancta Portiunculae ecclesia*, d. 14 m. Iulii a. 1966: AAS 58 (1966), pp. 631–634.

24. Cf. Apost. Const. *Indulgentiarum Doctrina*, 8: AAS 59 (1967), p. 17.

25. Cf. *Enchiridion Indulgentiarum*, norma 24, para. 1.

26. *Ibid.*, norma 4.

27. Cf. Paul VI, Motu Proprio *Pastorale Munus*, I, 14: AAS 56 (1964), p. 8.

28. Cf. First Synod of Rome, 1960, art. 63.

29. Second Vatican Ecumenical Council. Decree on the missionary activity of the Church *Ad Gentes Divinitus*, 1: AAS 58 (1966), p. 947.

30. *Ibid.*, 2: AAS 58 (1966), p. 948.

31. Discourse to the General Secretariat of the Synod of Bishops: *L'Osservatore Romano* of 6 April 1974, p. 4.

32. Cf. 1 Peter 3:15.

33. Cf. Rom 15:2; 1 Cor 14:3; Eph 4:12.

34. Lev 25:8ff.

35. Cf. St Ignatius of Antioch, *Epist. ad Romanos*, Inscr.: Funk 1, 252.

36. Cf. Lk 21:2; Mk 12:42.

37. Lk 4:18–19.
38. Cf. Decree on Ecumenism *Unitatis Redintegratio*, 7: AAS 57 (1965), p. 97.
39. Cf. *ibid.*, 5: AAS 57 (1965), p. 96.
40. Jn 17:21.
41. Cf. Gal 1:18.
42. *Sermo* III: *PL* 54, 146.
43. Cf. Is 12:3.
44. Cf. Jn 14:6.
45. Cf. Jn 10:7, 9.

The Holy See's Intervention at the United Nations Conference on Population, Bucharest (August 30, 1974)

INTERVENTION BY THE HEAD OF THE HOLY SEE'S DELEGATION
DURING THE DEBATE ON THE WORLD PLAN OF ACTION

Mr. President,

1.   The text of the World Plan of Action which has been submitted for the approval of the Conference represents a substantial improvement on the draft presented to the delegates at the beginning of our work. This is the result of some hard work, the quality of which has in part made up for the procedural difficulties and for the shortness of time available for drawing up a text charged with political and ethical implications for the public life of nations and for the private life of families and of every individual. Some of the changes which have been made constitute a notable correction of the previous situation. Thus, above all else, there is the affirmation that the problem of population can only be confronted within the more general perspective and overall priority of a global policy of integral human development. To this there must be added the insistence on the fact that policies of development require the setting up of a

---

[This English version was given out by the Vatican Press Office, in mimeographed form, 2 pages. The paragraph numbers have been added. The head of the Holy See's Delegation was Bishop Edouard Gagnon, President of the Committee for the Family of the Roman Curia. He delivered the talk in French; Bishop Gagnon is Canadian.]

new socio-economic order in a spirit of international justice and of a new balance in world consumption.

2.   The Holy See's Delegation has not ceased during the course of this Conference to defend these same theses, and congratulates those whose initiative has made it possible for them to be stated so expressly in the Plan. May all who make use of the Plan find inspiration in these points.

3.   We regret however that even in this new perspective the Plan, rather than embracing the breadth of a true population policy, remains essentially on the level of a demographic policy. We explained this during our intervention in the general debate. Such a wider approach would have avoided the disproportionate emphasis given to a single one of the demographic variables. It would have allowed some qualification to be given to references made in some passages to facts and hypotheses which, in our view, are presented in a manner which is too absolute for a document of this kind.

4.   Mr. President, if the Holy See's Delegation does express its satisfaction with this re-orientation of the World Plan of Action, it nevertheless has grave preoccupations about other points which are at stake in the Plan as a whole. The Delegation has never hidden its feelings about them: the family, respect for life, and indiscriminate recourse to means of birth prevention. We gladly recall here that a notable effort to meet our wishes regarding the above-mentioned points was made in the course of the negotiations, which were themselves conducted in an excellent spirit. It was because of a desire to work with our colleagues in a spirit of loyalty that we tabled precise amendments formulating our positions. Thus we were able to find out just how far agreement was possible. We also recognized the point at which our propositions did not meet with the assent of the majority. Furthermore, some proposals or expressions retained from the original text, some changes introduced during the session, and the result of some of the voting create, in regard to these sectors of capital importance, ambiguities to which our Delegation is not able to give its assent. Everyone will understand that we are here dealing with principles concerning which the very nature of the Holy See prohibits any compromise. The Holy See owes this fidelity to Him from whom it receives its mission; equally it owes it to the whole community of man, to which, in a spirit of fraternal service, it offers its teaching.

5.   In these circumstances, our Delegation considers itself obliged not to associate itself with the consensus regarding the adoption of the Conference's World Plan of Action. Another formula of agreement, that of approval with reservations, would undoubtedly seem more appro-

priate to many people, especially after two weeks of stimulating collaboration. It is not, however, possible for us to use this formula. States will defend themselves against what seems to them inacceptable in the plan, thanks to their recognized right of exercising full sovereignty in the defining of their national population policy. From the Holy See people expect a basic stand. It is known that recourse to distinctions about what in the plan has been accepted and what has not been accepted scarcely retains any meaning for those who accept a doctrine or ask for advice. We recognize that the persistence of ambiguities, the introduction of unfortunate expressions, the omission also of certain essential elements, are subject to too many interpretations and harmful consequences to allow us to approve as a whole the plan which embodies them and which logically could inspire them.

6.   It is in these circumstances, Mr. President, while not failing to recognize the value of some of the changes incorporated into the Plan, that the Holy See's Delegation declares once more that it does not participate in the consensus and requests that the text of the present statement be included in the Conference Report.

Thank you, Mr. President.

Evangelization of the Modern World

Synod of Bishops
Third General Assembly
(October 26, 1974)

DECLARATION OF THE SYNODAL FATHERS
APPROVED AT THE CONCLUSION
OF THE 1974 ASSEMBLY OF THE SYNOD

1.   We are consoled in the Holy Spirit at what the Lord allowed us to accomplish at this Synod and wish to share that consolation with the entire People of God, beginning with our brothers in the Episcopate whom we have represented, and with all those as well who in any way feel themselves tested by the Gospel of Christ.

2.   In the fraternal communication of our experiences, carried out in confident attachment to Paul VI, the Successor of Peter, we have had occasion to verify the close and vigorous unity which the Holy Spirit works in such a variety of conditions wherein the Church's life is nourished.

[This English version is that distributed by the Vatican Press Office, Bulletin no. 25, October 26, 1974. This mimeographed bulletin says that this is "a free translation of the integral Latin text."]

At the same time we experienced the richness contained in variety. It expressed itself in our attempts to radicalise the Gospel in its entirety among peoples of differing cultures, promulgating in some way the method of the incarnation which God wishes to use in his work of salvation through Christ. In that way the Good News of the Saviour shines forth more effectively.

3.   The copious riches which we have found in such reciprocal communication could not be easily unified without jeopardising its integrity. Having certainly become the richer through this experience, we have preferred to offer the integral fruits of our exchange to the Holy Father with great confidence and simplicity, and to await new impetus from him. In our own particular Churches at the same time, we want to pursue the rich experiences which we encountered at the Synod. This we will do in a spirit of dialogue, especially with priests and religious, with theologians and with all the faithful in general. Now, however, with this declaration of ours, we would simply like to manifest some fundamental convictions and a few of the more urgent guidelines to further promote and deepen the work we began.

4.   Sustained by our faith in Christ who died and rose again to save us, and fortified in the Church by our paschal experience, we wish to confirm anew that the mandate to evangelise all men constitutes the essential mission of the Church. Indeed, the deeper and more widespread that current changes appear to us—be they in the field of religion, ideology, culture or mores, the more evident and urgent becomes the necessity to proclaim the Gospel to all nations and to every individual man. It is evident and urgent especially for those to whom the announcement of the Good News of Christ has not yet been brought, wherever they might be on the face of the earth, so that the evangelisation and the foundation of the Church might take root in all peoples and places.

5.   Christ's love and His Mandate urge all the faithful to dispense to others the gifts received freely from Him. Therefore, the duty to proclaim the Gospel belongs to the whole People of God, gathered by the Holy Spirit in the Church through the Word of God and the Eucharist. No real Christian may absent himself from this duty which he must carry out in keeping with his state and in communion with his pastors. We hope that this Synod, together with the Supreme Pontiff's insistent exhortation for world missionary day will have offered to all the sons of the Church a new opportunity to renew the intimate and efficacious conviction of their rightful participation in the task of evangelisation. In a special way we address young people whom we do not consider only as a subject to be

evangelised, but also as particularly suited to evangelise others, especially their own age group. Furthermore, we are convinced that young people to the extent that they are searching for the fundamental values of the Gospel and demanding true authenticity in conceiving and witnessing the faith, challenge us adults and compel us to renew unceasingly the new commitment to evangelise.

6.　　At the same time, we are profoundly convinced that without the grace of God, which is spread by the Father in our hearts through the Holy Spirit, we would be completely incapable of carrying out this mission as it should be done (cf. Rom 5:5). In fact, this work demands incessant interior conversion on the part of individual Christians and continual renewal of our communities and institutions. In this way, faith will become stronger, purer and more intimate and we will become better fit and more credible as witnesses of the faith through the coherence of our individual and social life with the Gospel which we must preach. We will acquire the ability to discover and discern the signs of the times and to recognise and respect the action of the Spirit of Christ who is always at work in the life of the Church itself and in all human history so that everyone may have the fullness of a better life.

7.　　From this, one can clearly see the need for intimate union with God, through assiduous prayer, meditation of the Word of God, contemplation, all strengthened and sustained by frequent participation in the sacraments. In this way the People of God may render more efficacious the testimony of a real brotherly community, diligent to respond speedily to the expectations of men of goodwill, in evangelical solidarity with their more distressing problems. In this way, the Church will be a more credible witness to the joyful announcement of the Saviour of humankind; she will be a more suitable instrument of the Holy Spirit in the ministry to proclaim the Gospel.

8.　　In our discussions we did not ignore either old or new difficulties and obstacles which seem to hinder the work of evangelisation. In fact, some phenomena of our time have been given careful examination. Secularisation is one of them. Although it presents some positive aspects, it nevertheless inclines to the ideology of secularism, which completely excludes God from the horizon of human life and therefore from the profound meaning of existence. Another is atheism in its manifold forms which is widespread in many countries. Such phenomena should be examined carefully and their causes sought more deeply so that the appeal of God—which demands greater purity in the confession and testimony of our faith—be discovered. Another major difficulty has not escaped us, a difficulty which is used with astuteness and often with violence, that is, impeding religious liberty and the life of the Church and even to reducing it to silence.

We did not forget those who are oppressed, especially all those who suffer persecution for the Gospel. Bearing in themselves the good news of the Cross, they are performing excellent work of evangelisation and are of great assistance to the whole Church in the fulfilment of its mission.

9.   We are also convinced of the difficulties which arise from such a rapid and radical change in the conditions of our times, with regard to making the evangelical message more intelligible to today's men. But we also know that communication of the Gospel is a dynamic process. This communication takes place through word, work and life, each closely connected and is determined by various almost constitutive elements of the hearers of the Word of God: that is, their needs and desires, their way of speaking, hearing, thinking, judging and entering into contact with others. All these conditions which differ widely according to different places and times, impel the particular churches towards an appropriate "translation" of the evangelical message. According to the principle of incarnation, they must devise new but faithful "ways to take root". Furthermore, the development of the means of social communication has opened new ways to evangelisation, in keeping with the ways today's people think and act. At the same time, we firmly believe that the Holy Spirit works unceasingly in Christ's Church, through the work of those who give witness of a holy life, through the pastoral experience of those whom God has called to govern the Church and of all their collaborators in the ecclesial ministries, and through the fruitful collaboration between pastors and theologians.

10.   In carrying out these things we intend to collaborate more diligently with those of our Christian brothers with whom we are not yet in the union of a perfect communion, basing ourselves on the foundation of Baptism and on the patrimony which we hold in common. Thus we can henceforth render to the world a much broader common witness of Christ, while at the same time working to obtain full union in the Lord. Christ's command impels us to do so; the work of preaching and rendering witness to the Gospel demands it.

11.   Confident in the Holy Spirit's action which overflows the bounds of the Christian community, we wish to further dialogue with other religions which are not Christian, thus to achieve a deeper understanding of the Gospel's newness and of the fullness of Revelation, and to be able to show them thereby the salvific truth of God's love which fulfills itself in Christ.

We intend furthermore to seek the collaboration of all men of good will who for reasons which are undoubtedly diverse but sincere, are in search of a deeper meaning to life or are committed to gaining more human conditions of life for their brothers.

12.   Among the many subjects dealt with by the Synod, special attention was drawn to the mutual relationship between evangelisation and integral salvation or the complete liberation of man and of peoples.

In a matter of such importance we experienced profound unity in reaffirming the intimate connexion between evangelisation and liberation. Stimulating us to do this were not only the close relations with our faithful and with other men, whose life and common fate we share in, but primarily the Gospel, mercifully entrusted to us, which constitutes for all men and society the Good News of salvation. That Good News is to be initiated and made manifest on earth from now on, although it is only beyond the confines of this present life that it can achieve its complete fulfillment. Prompted by the love of Christ and illumined by the light of the Gospel, let us nurture the hope that the Church, in more faithfully fulfilling the work of evangelisation, will announce the total salvation of man or rather his complete liberation, and from now on will start to bring this about. The Church, in fact, as a community totally involved in evangelisation, must conform to Christ who explained His own mission in these words: "The spirit of the Lord is upon Me, for this He consecrated Me with anointing and sent Me to announce glad tidings to the poor, to give the prisoners their freedom, the blind their sight, to set the oppressed free" (Lk. 4:18).

Faithful to her evangelising mission, the Church as a truly poor, praying and fraternal community can do much to bring about the integral salvation or the full liberation of men. She can draw from the Gospel the most profound reasons and ever new incentives to promote generous dedication to the service of all men—the poor especially, the weak and the oppressed—and to eliminate the social consequences of sin which are translated into unjust social and political structures. But the Church, supported by Christ's Gospel and fortified by His grace can harness such dedication to the elimination of deviations. And so the Church does not remain within merely political, social and political limits (elements which she must certainly take into account) but leads towards freedom under all its forms—liberation from sin, from individual or collective selfishness—and to full communion with God and with men who are like brothers. In this way the Church, in her evangelical way, promotes the true and complete liberation of all men, groups and peoples.

In this spirit of human and evangelical solidarity, throughout these days we have wished to send the world a message on human rights and reconciliation.

13.   By our mission we have the duty to be present among the men of our times to bring the presence of Christ, the Incarnate Word among them. Therefore, in returning to our particular Churches, we, as disciples comforted by the experience of the Risen Christ, will discover new opportunities to more effectively foster the evangelisation of the whole world and its authentic liberation.

Certainly, we are aware that we must face numerous difficulties. However, we journey towards the future with great hope. This hope springs from our profound union with the Crucified Christ who leads us to participate in an effective way in His Resurrection.

Thus, it will come about that, more deeply rooted in the perennial actuality of Pentecost, the Church will know new times of evangelisation. While trying to be faithful to its mission in today's world, the Church commits itself completely to the service of the future world. In fact, even if the destinies of this future world are unknown to us, Christ the Lord and Centre of human history, stimulates us so that we can progress more and more. The time which occurs between Easter and the Parusia is the time of tension and aspiration towards the world which must come.

In such a period of time it is the task of the Church to prefigure and prepare the final actuation of the Kingdom of God. We know that the Lord helps His Church continuously and accompanies us on our pilgrimage. He will be with us all days (cf. Mt 28:30), comforting us with the gifts of His grace, gradually leading us to the whole truth through the action of His Holy Spirit (cf. Jn 16:13), confirming our word with signs (cf. Mk 16:20), while we confess that Jesus Christ is the Lord to the glory of God the father (cf. Phil. 2:11).

On the eve of Holy Year which is about to be celebrated in Rome, let us nurture the hope that all the People of God, profiting from this special occasion of grace, through the conversion of heart, complete renewal and interior reconciliation, can better fulfill their duty to evangelise, and the Church can more clearly appear as having been sent to the peoples to be the universal sign of salvation.

Concluding our work in the Synod, let us raise our eyes and our hearts to the Blessed Virgin Mary, the Mother of the Church, to receive, following her example, the Word of God with an open mind and a docile spirit, to offer it to the world after having meditated upon it and faithfully translated it into daily life.

Address of His Holiness Pope Paul VI to the Participants of the World Food Conference, Rome (November 9, 1974)

Mr. President,
Mr. Secretary General,
Ladies and Gentlemen,

We are happy to greet you, the participants at the World Food Conference assembled in Rome under the auspices of the United Nations. There is no need to tell you that we share intensely in your preoccupations, for our mission is to carry on the teaching and activity of the Master from whom the sight of a hungry crowd prompted the moving exclamation: "I feel sorry for all these people; they . . . have nothing to eat. I do not want to send them off hungry, they might collapse on the way" (Mt 15:32).

1.   In the course of recent years the situation that we described in the Encyclical *Populorum Progressio* has reached still more alarming proportions, and what we said at that time has gained in relevance: "Today no one can be ignorant any longer of the fact that in whole continents countless men and women are ravished by hunger, countless numbers of children are undernourished, so that many of them die in infancy, while the physical growth and mental development of many others are retarded and as a result whole regions are condemned to the most depressing despondency" (45). The documentation prepared by your Conference

[This English version is from that published by the Vatican Polyglot Press in leaflet form, 4 pages.]

describes the various aspects of hunger and of malnutrition, uncovers their causes and attempts to foresee their consequences, by recourse to statistics, market research and indices of production and consumption. In their accuracy, these indications take on a tragic eloquence: but what is it like then to come face to face, on the spot, with the realities that they represent? Recent disasters of every kind—drought, floods, wars—immediately give rise to pathetic cases of food scarcity. In a less spectacular but equally painful way, all are faced by the hardship created in the deprived classes by the rise in the cost of foodstuffs, which is a sign of their impending scarcity, and by the ever more marked lessening of international aid—given in the form of foodstuffs—which had powerfully contributed to the rehabilitation and progress of peoples after the last war.

Lack of proper nourishment has long-term and sometimes unforeseeable effects. It has serious consequences on future generations and presents ecological and health hazards which cause damage to populations, more deep-seated than the maladies immediately apparent. It is truly painful to come to such a realization and to admit that, up to now, society seems incapable of tackling world hunger, although unprecedented technical progress has been achieved in all spheres of production. This is the case, for example, in regard to fertilizers and mechanization, and in regard to distribution and transport. A very few years ago, in fact, it was hoped that in one way or another the rapidity of the transmission of information and of goods, as well as the technological advances achieved, would be able speedily to eliminate the dangers of the ancient scourge of famine afflicting for a long period a nation or a whole region. That these hopes have not been realized explains the grave atmosphere surrounding your work. Hence also comes the hope mingled with anxiety with which the peoples of the world are watching your work. To use once again the words that we addressed in 1965 to the World Assembly of Youth gathered under the standard of the world campaign against hunger: "It is a drama of life or death for mankind, which must unite in order to survive and therefore must first learn to share the daily bread", which the Lord teaches us is ours, that is, for each and for all (Allocution of 15 October 1965: AAS 57 (1965), p. 910).

2.   To you who are engaged in a task at once so difficult yet so rich in promise, we put forward two principles to guide your work: on the one hand, to face up to the data of the problem without allowing yourselves to become bewildered in your evaluation of them through panic or through excessive timidity; and on the other hand to feel yourselves sufficiently stimulated by the absolute urgency and priority of the needs in question so that you will not be satisfied in any single case by delays or by

half-measures. This Conference will not resolve everything on its own; it is not in its nature to do so. However, through the clarity and energy of its conclusions it will give the impetus to a series of effective and sincerely accepted commitments; or, contrary to the expectations placed in it and in spite of the good will of its members, it will have been held in vain. In order to beg you to avoid such a result, we do not hesitate to repeat, and adapt, the appeal that we made from the tribune of the United Nations: "No more war, war never again!" And we say to you: "No more hunger, hunger never again!"

3.   Ladies and gentlemen, this objective can be attained. The threat of hunger and the burden of malnutrition are not an inevitable destiny. In this crisis nature is not unfaithful to man. Its productive capacity, on land and in the seas remains immense and is still largely unexploited. While on the one hand fifty percent of arable land has, according to the generally accepted view, not yet been put to use, on the other hand we are faced by the scandal of enormous surpluses of foodstuffs that certain countries periodically destroy, because of the lack of a wise economy which would have guaranteed the useful employment of these surpluses. Here we have merely illustrations of a fact which no one challenges in its stark reality, even if some doubt whether it is possible to draw quickly enough from this potential what is needed to allay the hunger of expanding mankind. And when we speak of "allaying hunger" we are all in agreement that it is a question of more than just prolonging a minimal and subhuman biological existence. What is in question is "to provide each man with enough to live—to live a truly human life, to be capable by his own work of guaranteeing the upkeep of his family and to be able through the exercise of his intelligence to share in the common goods of society by a commitment freely agreed to and by an activity voluntarily assumed" (Speech to FAO, 16 November 1970: AAS 62 (1970), p. 831). It is of course with a view to this level of life that you have drawn up the calculations of your reports, according to which a campaign capable of feeding expanding mankind is possible on a technical level, but demands considerable effort.

4.   The present crisis appears in fact above all to be a crisis of civilization and of solidarity. A crisis of civilization and of method, which shows itself when the development of life in society is faced from a onesided point of view, and when only the model of society that leads to an industrialized civilization is considered, that is to say, when too much confidence is placed in the automatic nature of purely technical solutions, while fundamental human values are forgotten. It is a crisis that shows itself when the accent is placed on the quest for mere economic success

deriving from the large profits of industry, with a consequential almost total abandonment of the agricultural sector, and the accompanying neglect of its highest human and spiritual values. It is also a crisis of solidarity, a crisis that sustains and sometimes accelerates the imbalances between individuals, groups and peoples, a crisis that is unfortunately the result—as is increasingly evident—of the insufficient willingness to contribute to a better distribution of available resources, especially to the countries that are less well provided for and to the sections of mankind that live essentially on an agriculture which is still primitive.

We thus touch upon the paradox of the present situation: mankind has at its disposal an unequalled mastery of the universe. It has means capable of making the resources of the universe yield their full potential. Will those who possess these means remain as though struck by paralysis when confronted with the absurdity of a situation in which the wealth of some can tolerate the enduring poverty of so many? Or a situation in which the highly enriched and diversified food consumption of some peoples can be satisfied at seeing the minimum necessary for existence doled out to all the others? Or a situation in which human intelligence could come to the aid of so many people afflicted by sickness, and yet evade the task of ensuring an adequate nourishment for the most defenceless sectors of mankind?

5.   One could not have arrived at that point without having committed serious errors of orientation, even if sometimes only through negligence or omission. It is indeed time to find out where the mechanisms have broken down, so that the situation can be corrected, or rather reordered from beginning to end. The right to satisfy one's hunger must finally be recognized for everyone, according to the specific requirements of his age and activity. This right is based on the fact that all the goods of the earth are destined primarily for universal use and for the subsistence of all men, before any individual appropriation. Christ based the judgment of each human being on respect for this right (cf. Mt 25:31 ff.). In examining the data of the problem, some facts are immediately evident. One of the most obvious causes of the present confusion is to be found in the increased prices of foodstuffs and of the materials needed for their production. An example is fertilizers. Their high price and scarcity are perhaps watering down the beneficial effects that were rightly hoped for from the "Green Revolution". Is not this a case intimately bound up with the fluctuations of a production based more on the calculations of profits to be gained than on satisfying the needs of mankind? The reduction of food supplies, which is also at the root of present worries, is at least partially due to certain commercial decisions which result in the lack of available reserves

for victims of sudden and unforeseen shortages. A general food crisis is apparent and it is foreseen that it will worsen, while in some regions which are particularly well situated to ensure a surplus and emergency reserves the arable acreage has been reduced in an astonishing degree. Here we are face to face with the contradictions which characterize this acute crisis of civilization. At least when these phenomena are the result of ill-advised actions it must be possible to correct them and to put them right, provided that one employs the necessary wisdom and courage.

We have spoken of the quantity of food necessary for the life of each and every man. But the problem of quality is equally important and also depends on an economic choice. In this matter the more industrialized nations are particularly concerned. In an atmosphere which is becoming polluted and in the face of the frenzied rush to create artificial substitutes, capable of quicker production, how shall we manage prudently to safeguard healthy nourishment with no serious risk for the health of the consumers, especially children and young people? And how, in these same nations, can we break with a consumption which is excessive because of the rich abundance of foodstuffs, which proves to be damaging to those concerned and which leaves others unprovided for? In this field too the situation calls for vigilance and courage.

6.   Other observations concern the flow of the resources which would allow the present situation to be remedied. All are agreed that multilateral and bilateral aid to the agricultural sector has been notoriously insufficient. In preparation for your Conference great care has been taken to list the requirements which would be entailed by the intensification of food production in the developing countries, by the drawing up of policies and programmes aimed at improving nutrition, and by measures for strengthening world food security. The sums arrived at by these calculations for the next ten years undoubtedly far surpass the effort so far made. But they are still quite modest in relation to the national budgets of the wealthy countries or those with international liquid assets. A recent crisis has modified the balance of these liquid assets but it has not reduced their volume. As far back as 1964, on the occasion of our journey to India, we launched an appeal to the nations, asking that, by a truly substantial commitment—the result mainly of a reduction in expenditure on arms—there be set up a Fund with the aim of giving a decisive impulse to the integral advancement of the less well-endowed sectors of mankind. Today the time has come for an energetic and binding decision along the same lines. Will such a decision—not yet obtained by a sense of solidarity or rather elementary social justice, which consists not only in not "stealing" but also in knowing how to share—finally be imposed by the perils of

the present moment? Or will men obstinately close their eyes to their own fate and look for alibis, for instance an irrational and onesided campaign against demographic growth, rather than get down to the essential point?

It is inadmissible that those who have control of the wealth and resources of mankind should try to resolve the problem of hunger by forbidding the poor to be born, or by leaving to die of hunger children whose parents do not fit into the framework of theoretical plans based on pure hypotheses about the future of mankind. In times gone by, in a past that we hope is now finished with, nations used to make war to seize their neighbours' riches. But is it not a new form of warfare to impose a restrictive demographic policy on nations, to ensure that they will not claim their just share of the earth's goods?

We renew our full moral support for those who have repeatedly declared at international gatherings that they are not only ready to recognize the right of every man to enjoy the goods necessary for life but are equally ready, by agreeing voluntarily to a proportionate sacrifice of the resources and potential to place these goods effectively at the disposal of the individuals and peoples who need them, without any exclusion or discrimination. Thus we have the prospect of courageous reforms aimed at eliminating the obstacles and imbalances stemming also from out-of-date structures, which perpetuate inacceptable injustices or impede the dynamism of production and the impetus needed for an adequate circulation of the goods necessary for life.

7.   But the most widespread international aid, the increased tempo of research and of the application of agrarian technology and the most detailed planning of food production will have little effect unless one of the most serious gaps in technical civilization is filled as quickly as possible. The world food crises will not be solved without the participation of the agricultural workers, and this cannot be complete and fruitful without a radical revision of the underestimation by the modern world of the importance of agriculture. For agriculture is easily subordinated to the immediate interests of other sectors of the economy, even in countries which at present are trying to initiate the process of growth and economic autonomy.

Our predecessor John XXIII, who devoted a chapter of his Encyclical *Mater et Magistra* to agriculture, spoke of it in these terms: "The farming sector, almost everywhere, is a depressed area, whether as regards the index of productivity or of the labour force, or as regards the standard of living of the agricultural rural populations" (AAS 53 [1961], p. 432). From this depression we shall only note two indices: first, the drop in the number of agricultural workers and sometimes also the reduction of cultivated land in the industrialized countries; secondly, the fact that in the developing nations of the world, although the great majority of the population work on the land, agriculture is the most underdeveloped of the sectors of underdevelopment. Whatever may be the value of the technical means employed, nothing will be achieved without the true reform represented by the rehabilitation of agriculture and the reversal of present attitudes towards it.

It is the dignity of those who work on the land and of all those engaged in different levels of research and action in the field of agricultural development which must be unceasingly proclaimed and promoted. We said as much when we received the FAO Conference in 1971: "It is no longer sufficient to stem the growing distortion of the situation of the members of the rural community in the modern world; it is necessary to make them an integral part of it in such a way that coming generations will no longer experience this debilitating feeling of being left aside, of being on the sidelines of modern progress where improvement is concerned " (AAS 63 [1971], p. 877).

This will be achieved through a worldwide and balanced process of development supported by a political desire on the part of governments to give agriculture its rightful place. It is a question of putting an end to the pressure of the stronger economic sectors—a pressure which is stripping the countryside of those very energies which would be able to ensure high productivity agriculture. There must be established a policy which will guarantee to the young people of rural areas the fundamental personal right to a deliberate choice of a worthwhile profession, equal both in conditions and advantages to what only the exodus to the city and industry seems able to guarantee them today.

8.   Without any doubt, here again the reforms will have value only if individuals adapt themselves to them. That is why education and training have a fundamental role to play, by ensuring that proper preparation is not lacking. "The collaboration of the rural population is necessary; . . . agricultural workers must be faithful to the profession which they have chosen and which they value; . . . let them follow the programmes of cultural improvement which are essential if agriculture is to break out of its rooted and empirical immobility and adopt new forms of work, new machines, new methods" (Address to Italian Agricultural Workers, 13 November 1966: *L'Osservatore Romano*, 14-15 November 1966).

What is especially important therefore to those afflicted with hunger is that governments should offer all agricultural workers the chance to learn how to cultivate the land, how to improve soils, how to avoid diseases in farm animals and how to increase yield. It is also important finally that, within the framework of an adequate preparation, agricultural workers should be granted the credit they need. In a word, it is necessary to give to the members of the farming community responsibility in their production and progress. Thus we find ourselves brought back to the notion of integral development embracing the whole man and all men. For our part we have never ceased to exhort humanity to work towards this goal.

9.   These are the thoughts which we offer you as our contribution to your work. They come from the awareness that we have of our pastoral duty and they are inspired by confidence in God who neglects none of his children, and by confidence in man, created in God's image and capable of accomplishing wonders of intelligence and of goodness. Faced with the hungry crowds, the Lord did not content himself with expressing his compassion. He gave his disciples a command: "Give them something to eat yourselves" (Mt 14:16), and his power came to the aid only of their helplessness, not of their selfishness. This episode of the multiplication of the loaves, then, contains many lessons that are applicable in view of the grave needs of the present moment. Today we wish primarily to re-echo this call to effective action. We must envisage the creation, on a long-term basis, of the possibility, for each people, of accurately ensuring its subsistence in the most suitable way. Nor must we forget in the immediate future to remedy, by sharing, the urgent needs that are experienced by a great part of mankind. Action must be united to charity.

This progressive reorientation of production and distribution also involves an effort which must not be simply a constraint imposed by fear of want, but also a positive will not to waste thoughtlessly the goods which must be for everyone's benefit. After freely feeding the crowds, the Lord told his disciples—the Gospel relates—to gather up what was left over, lest anything should be lost (cf. Jn 6:12). What an excellent lesson in thrift—in the finest and fullest meaning of the term—for our age, given as it is to wastefulness! It carries with it the condemnation of a whole concept of society wherein consumption tends to become an end in itself, with contempt for the needy, and to the detriment, in the end, of those very people who believed themselves to be its beneficiaries, having become incapable of perceiving that man is called to a higher destiny. May our appeal then be clear and may it reach men's hearts. If the potential of nature is immense, if that of the mastery of the human genius over the universe seems almost unlimited, what is it that is too often missing—in order that we should act with equity and with a desire for the well-being of all our brothers and sisters in the human race—except that generosity, that anxiety which is stimulated by the sight of the sufferings and the miseries of the poor, that deep conviction that the whole family suffers when one of its members is in distress? It is this solidarity which we hope to see inspiring your work and, above all, your decisions. And we implore the Father of all light to grant you his grace.

Reconciliation— the Way to Peace

Message of His Holiness Pope Paul VI for the Celebration of the Day of Peace (January 1, 1975)

To all men of good will.

Here is our Message for the year 1975!
You know it already, nor could it be any different:
Brethren! Let us make Peace!

1.   Our message is very simple, but at the same time it is so serious and so demanding as to seem offensive: does not Peace yet exist? What else and what more can be done for Peace than what has already been done and is still being done? Is the history of mankind not travelling, under its own power, towards worldwide Peace?
2.   Yes, it is; or rather it seems to be. But Peace has to be "made". It has to be continually generated and produced. It results from a balance of forces that is unstable and that can only be maintained by movement in

---

[This English version is that published by the Vatican Polyglot Press in booklet form, 17 pages. Paragraph numbers have been added.]

proportion to its speed. The very institutions that in the juridical order and in international society have the task and merit of proclaiming and preserving Peace reach their opportune aim if they are continually active, if they know how to generate Peace, make Peace, at every moment.

3.   This necessity results mainly from the human phenomenon of becoming, from the ceaseless evolutionary process of mankind. Men succeed men, generations succeed generations. Even if no changes took place in the existing juridical and historical situations, there would still be a need for an effort, continually "in fieri", to educate mankind to stay faithful to the fundamental laws of society. These laws must remain, and they will guide history for an indefinite period, but only on condition that changeable men, and the young people taking the place of those passed on, are unceasingly educated in the discipline of order for the common good and in the ideal of Peace. From this point of view, making Peace means educating to Peace. And it is not a small undertaking, nor an easy one.

4.   But we all know that it is not just men that change on the stage of history. Things change too. This is to say, the questions on the balanced solution of which depends men's peaceful life together in society. No one can maintain that the organization of civil society and of the international context is perfect. Many, very many problems still remain potentially open. The problems of yesterday remain; the problems of today are arising; tomorrow others will arise. And they are all awaiting a solution. This solution, we declare, cannot and must not ever again spring from selfish and violent conflicts, still less from murderous wars between men. As has been said by wise men, learned in the history of peoples and experts in the economy of nations, and as we too, defenceless as we are in the midst of the world's strife, yet strong in the divine Word, have said: all men are brothers. And at last the whole of civilization has admitted this fundamental principle. Therefore: if men are brothers, but there still exist and spring up among them causes of conflict, then Peace must become operative and wise. Peace must be made; Peace must be produced; Peace must be invented. It must be created through an ever watchful disposition, with a will ever fresh and untiring. Thus we are all persuaded of the principle that animates modern society: Peace can be neither passive nor oppressive; it must be inventive, preventive and operative.

5.   We are glad to note that these guiding criteria of social living in the world are today universally accepted, at least in the main. And we feel it is our duty to thank, to praise and to encourage the leaders and the institutions destined today to promote Peace on earth, for having chosen,

as the first article of their activity, this basic axiom: only Peace generates Peace.

6.   Allow us to repeat in a prophetic way to the farthest boundaries of the globe the message of the recent Ecumenical Council: "It is our clear duty, then, to strain every muscle as we work for the time when all war can be completely outlawed by international consent. . . . Peace must be born of mutual trust between the nations rather than imposed on them through fear of one another's weapons. . . . For government officials, who must simultaneously guarantee the good of all their own people and promote the universal good, depend on public opinion and feeling to the greatest possible extent. It does them no good to work at building peace so long as feelings of hostility, contempt and distrust, as well as racial hatred and unbending ideologies, continue to divide men and place them in opposing camps.

7.   "Hence arises a surpassing need for renewed education of attitudes and for new inspiration in the area of public opinion. Those who are dedicated to the work of education, particularly of the young, or who mould public opinion, should regard as their most weighty task the effort to instruct all in fresh sentiments of Peace. Indeed, every one of us should have a change of heart as we regard the entire world and those tasks which we can perform in unison for the betterment of our race" (Pastoral Constitution *Gaudium et Spes,* 82).

8.   And it is in this regard that our message centres on its characteristic and inspiring point, affirming that Peace only has value to the extent that it seeks first to be interior before becoming exterior. Minds must be disarmed if we wish effectively to stop the recourse to arms which strike bodies. It is necessary to give to Peace, that is to say to all men, the spiritual roots of a common form of thought and love. Saint Augustine, designer of a new City, writes that the identity of men's nature is not sufficient to bring them together among themselves. They must be taught to speak the same language, that is to say to understand one another, to possess a common culture, to share the same sentiments, otherwise "man will prefer to be with his dog rather than with a man who is a stranger" (cf. *De Civ. Dei,* XIX, VII; PL 41, 634).

9.   This interiorization of Peace is true humanism, true civilization. Fortunately it has already begun. It is maturing as the world develops. It finds its persuasive strength in the universal dimensions of the relations of every kind which men are establishing among themselves. It is a slow and complicated work, but one which, to a great extent, is happening spontaneously: the world is progressing towards its unity. Nevertheless

we cannot delude ourselves, and while peaceful concord among men is spreading, through the progressive discovery of the complementarity and interdependence of countries, through commercial exchanges, through the diffusion of an identical vision of man, always however respectful of the original and specific nature of the various civilizations, through the ease of travel and social communications, and so on, we must take note that today new forms of jealous nationalism are being affirmed, enclosed in manifestations of touchy rivalries based on race, language and traditions; there remain sad situations of poverty and hunger. Powerful economic multinational expressions are arising, full of selfish antagonisms. Exclusive and arrogant ideologies are being organized into social systems. Territorial conflicts break out with frightening ease. And above all, there is an increase in the number and the power of murderous weapons for possible catastrophic destruction, such as to stamp terror with the name of Peace. Yes, the world is progressing towards its unity, but even as it does so there increase the terrifying hypotheses which envisage more possible, more easy and more terrible fatal clashes—clashes which are considered, in certain circumstances, inevitable and necessary, and called for, as it were, by justice. Will justice be one day the sister no longer of peace but of wars? (cf. Saint Augustine, *ibid.*).

10.   We are not playing at utopias, either optimistic ones or pessimistic. We want to remain in the realms of reality—a reality which, with its phenomenology of illusory hope and deplorable desperation, warns us once more that there is something not functioning properly in the monumental machine of our civilization. This machine could explode in an indescribable conflagration because of a defect in its construction. We say a defect, not a lack. The defect, that is, of the spiritual element, though we admit that this element is already present and at work in the general process of the peaceful development of contemporary history, and worthy of every favourable recognition and encouragement. Have we not awarded to UNESCO our prize named after Pope John XXIII, the author of the Encyclical *Pacem in Terris?*

11.   But we dare to say that more must be done. We have to make use of and apply the spiritual element in order to make it capable not only of impeding conflicts among men and predisposing them to peaceful and civilized sentiments, but also of producing reconciliation among those same men, that is of generating Peace. It is not enough to contain wars, to suspend conflicts, to impose truces and armistices, to define boundaries and relationships, to create sources of common interest; it is not enough to paralyze the possibility of radical strife through the terror of unheard-of destruction and suffering. An imposed Peace, a utilitarian and provisional Peace is not enough. Progress must be made towards a Peace

which is loved, free and brotherly, founded, that is, on a reconciliation of hearts.

12.   We know that it is difficult, more difficult than any other method. But it is not impossible, it is not a fantasy. We have faith in a fundamental goodness of individuals and of peoples: God has made the generations wholesome (cf. Wis 1:14). The intelligent and persevering effort for the mutual understanding of men, of social classes, of cities, of peoples and of civilizations is not sterile.

13.   We rejoice, especially on the eve of International Women's Year, proclaimed by the United Nations, at the ever wider participation of women in the life of society, to which they bring a specific contribution of great value, thanks to the qualities that God has given them. These qualities, of intuition, creativity, sensibility, a sense of piety and compassion, a profound capacity for understanding and love, enable women to be in a very particular way the creators of reconciliation in families and in society.

14.   It is equally a source of special satisfaction to be able to note that the education of young people to a new universal mentality of human oneness, a mentality which is not sceptical, not vile, not inept, not oblivious of justice, but generous, and loving, has already started and has already made progress. It possesses unforeseeable resources for reconciliation. This can signpost the road of Peace, in truth, in honour, in justice, in love, and thus in the stability and in the new history of mankind.

15.   Reconciliation! Young men and women, strong men and women, responsible men and women, free men and women, good men and women—will you think of it? Could not this magic word find a place in the dictionary of your hopes and of your successes?

16.   This then is our message of good wishes for you: reconciliation is the way to Peace.

> *For you, men and women of the Church!*
> *Brothers in the Episcopate,*
>   *priests and men and women religious!*
> *For you, the members of our militant Catholic laity,*
>   *and all the faithful!*

17.   The message on Reconciliation as the way to Peace demands a complement, even if it is already known and present to you.

18.   This is not only an integral part of our message, but an essential one, as you know. For it reminds us all that the first and indispensable

reconciliation to be achieved is reconciliation with God. For us believers there can be no other way to Peace than this. Indeed, in the definition of our salvation, reconciliation with God and our Peace coincide; one is the cause of the other. This is the work of Christ. He has repaired the break which sin produces in our vital relationship with God. We recall, among many, one of the phrases of Saint Paul in this regard: "It is all God's work. It was God who reconciled us to himself through Christ" (2 Cor 5:18).

19.   The Holy Year which we are about to begin wishes to involve us in this first and happy reconciliation: Christ is our Peace; he is the principle of reconciliation in the unity of his Mystical Body (cf. Eph 2:14-16). Ten years after the close of the Second Vatican Council we shall do well to meditate more deeply on the theological and ecclesiological sense of these basic truths of our faith and of our Christian life.

20.   Hence a logical and necessary consequence—one that is also easy if we are truly in Christ: we must perfect the sense of our unity—unity *in* the Church, unity *of* the Church. Mystical, constitutive communion, the former (cf. 1 Cor 1:10; 12: 12–27); ecumenical restoration of the unity of all Christians, the latter (cf. Conciliar Decree *Unitatis Redintegratio*). One and the other demand their own proper reconciliation, which must bring to the Christian collectivity that Peace which is the fruit of the Spirit, following upon love and its joy (cf. Gal 5:22).

21.   In these spheres too we must "make Peace"! There will certainly come to your attention the text of our "Exhortation on Reconciliation within the Church", published at this time. We exhort you in the name of Jesus Christ to meditate on this document and to try to draw therefrom resolves of reconciliation and of Peace. Let no one think that he can escape these inevitable demands of communion with Christ—reconciliation and Peace—by clinging to long familiar positions which are in conflict with Christ's Church. Let us rather aim at this: that each and every one may make a new and sincere contribution to the filial, humble and positive building up of this Church. Shall we not perhaps recall the last words of the Lord in explanation of his Gospel: " . . . may they be so completely one that the world will realize that it was you who sent me" (Jn 17:23)? Shall we not have the joy of seeing brethren who are loved and far away come back once more to the old and happy harmony?

22.   We shall have to pray that this Holy Year will give the Catholic Church the inexpressible experience of the restoration of the unity of some groups of brethren, already so near to the one fold but still hesitant to cross its threshold. And we shall pray also for the sincere followers of other religions, so that there may develop the friendly dialogue that we

have begun with them, and so that, together, we may collaborate for world Peace.

23.   And above all we must ask God to give us that humility and love which will endow the clear and constant profession of our faith with the attracting power of reconciliation and the strengthening and joyous charism of Peace.

24.   And with our greeting and blessing: " . . . that peace of God, which is so much greater than we can understand, will guard your hearts and your thoughts in Christ Jesus" (Phil 4:7).

From the Vatican, 8 December 1974.

PAULUS PP. VI

Index

(Numerals in italics refer to pages within Msgr. Gremillion's preliminary sections.)

Ad Gentes, 537

✓*Aggiornamento*, *ix*, *1–2*, *4*, *8–11*, *13*, *16*, *19*, *20*, *21*, *23–24*, *27*, *31*, *33*, *35*, *37*, *41–44*, *45*, *49*, *51*, *54*, *55*, *63–65*, *67–69*, *74*, *76*, *78*, *82*, *84*, *93*, *97*, *100*, *102*, *108*, *113*, *114*, *124*, *125*, *128*, *134*, *135*, *136*, *139*, 140

Agricultural development, 162, 170–77, 302, 390, 396, 423, 451, 518, 527, 602, 604–6

Agriculture, *23–24*, *31*, *89*

Aid to less developed areas, 176–88, 226–27, 250, 301–2, 305–6, 321–23, 384, 385, 388, 400–01, 402–7, 423–24, 527, 582, 604–5

Amnesty, 582

Aquinas, Saint Thomas, *27*, 209, 212

Armaments, 158, 186–87, 224–25, 227–28, 403, 458, 462, 483, 515, 526–27, 547, 551, 609–10

Asian Religio-Cultural Forum on Development (ARCFOD), *64*

Atheism, 257–60, 399, 498, 518, 595

Atlee, Clement, *5*

Augustine, Saint, *4*, *83*, 221, 237, 459, 609, 610

Authority
criticism of *Pacem in Terris'* concept of, 552
origins of, 211–12, 230
planning for change by, 397
purpose of, 213
refusal to obey, 345–46, 549, 552–53
relationship of church to civil, 380
and relation to the common good, 229–30, 308–9, 438–39, 452
responsibilities of, 214, 309–10, 394, 412, 452
structure and operation of, 216, 548
and world order, *82–89*, 102

Bicentennial Program, *x*

Birth control, *see* Contraception, Regulation of birth

Brandt, Willy, *59*

Brezhnev, Leonid, *59*

Camara, Dom Helder, *78*, *127*

Campion, Donald R., *75*

Capital, *52–54*

Capitalism, 2, *10–11*, *15*, *16*, *35*, *44–45*, 395

Cardijn, Bishop, *35*

CELAM, *16*, *64*, *127*

Chiang Kai-shek, *59*, *68*

Christian Democratic Movement, *65–66*

Chrysostom, Saint John, 211

Church, Catholic
aggiornamento of, *ix*, *1*, *45*
call to be poor, 471–76, 523
changes in social teaching of, 152–54, 169–88, 506–7
conscientization of, *133*
dialogue with Marxism, *36*, *44*
in the Empire, *3–4*
evolution of, *1*
in Latin America, *16*, *36*, *45*, *66*
law of, *68*
lay persons within, *42*, *130–32*
Limits to Growth debate in, *91–96*
local, *42*, *67*, *97*, *126*, *130–32*, 525, 528
ministry of, 595
mission of, *6–7*, *42*, *125–34*, 281, 312–13, 380, 390–93, 473, 476, 485–86, 488, 509–10, 514, 519–21, 524–25, 537, 564, 594, 595–96, 598, 599
natural law and, *7–11*, *27*, 102, *131*, *134*, *137*
nature of, *7*, *10*, *128*, 579
non-Christians and, *55*, *64–65*, *130–31*, *134–36*, *137*
policy on birth regulation and population, *96–103*
political engagement of, *see* Political engagement of the church
relationship to the world, *see* Relationship of church to world
relations with the state, *3–4*
secularization and, *3–4*, *135*
as a social actor, *1–2*, *17*, *37–38*, *55*, *125–32*, *133–34*
social change and, *1–3*
social consciousness within, *1*, *125*
social responsibility of, 143–45, 147, 149, 151, 178, 190, 191, 453, 473, 513–14, 519–23, 524–25, 528, 597–98
social teaching of, *ix–x*, *7*, *9–13*, *27–29*, *31*, *34*, *35–37*, *47–48*, *51*, *97–102*, *111*, *118*, *125–26*, *134*, *137*, 144–88, 190–99, 236, 300–01, 312–13, 316–17, 344, 388, 487–88, 505, 524, 537–38, 562–64, 566

teaching authority, *see* Teaching authority of the church
transformation of structures of, *129–32*
United Nations and, *82*
Churches, Christian, *4, 55, 63–66, 113, 127, 131, 134, 135, 137*
Churchill, Sir Winston, *5, 81*
Cigognani, Cardinal Amleto, *25*
Civil disobedience, *see* Authority, refusal to obey
Class consciousness, *11*
Club of Rome, *91*
"Club of Ten," *49*
"Club of the Rich," *16*
Collective bargaining, *29*
Colonialism, *180, 383, 389, 403, 451, 456–58, 517, 536, 543*
Common good, *8, 9, 11, 30, 32, 33, 39, 83, 85, 86, 118, 131, 148, 150, 151, 155, 157, 159, 160–61, 162, 164, 173, 175–76, 203, 206, 211, 212, 213–16, 219, 222, 223, 224, 227, 229–30, 234, 263–64, 295–97, 305, 306–7, 308–9, 314–15, 359–61, 393, 394, 398–99, 424, 448, 453, 461, 462, 473, 475–76, 492, 507–8, 521, 528, 542, 548, 553*
Communications, *153, 495, 519*
  growth of, *23–24, 31*
Community, *10, 41, 67, 78, 97, 102–3, 105, 110, 111, 119–20, 129, 130*
  Christian, *3–4, 10, 19, 42, 45, 66, 122, 129, 135*
  comunidades de base, 36, 45, 120, 130
  formation of, *130–32*
  human, *6–8, 74, 125*
  political, *57–63, 66, 70, 73, 82–89, 125, 130, 131*
  structures of, *129, 134*
Conference of Bishops, promotion of justice by, *528*
Conjugal love, *285–90, 431–33, 468, 470*
Conscience, *202, 212, 217, 249, 255, 258, 264, 267, 276, 324, 338, 340, 346, 347, 359, 386, 401, 448, 452, 460, 462, 525, 557, 562*
Conscientious objection, *74–76, 527, 539, 549, 552*
Conscientization, *1, 10, 11, 13, 15, 16, 17, 76, 82, 133, 452–54, 456, 461 493, 514, 516, 524*
Constantine, *4*
Constantinianism, *134*
Consumerism, *5–6, 7, 18–19, 32, 81, 100, 119, 120*
Consumption patterns, *479, 481, 483, 488, 489, 516, 523, 528, 553, 599–600, 602, 606*

Contraception, *81, 96–107, 111–12, 135, 137, see also* Regulation of birth
Cooperatives, *see* Unions and cooperatives
Corporative system, *2, 11, 30*
Cor Unum Council, *132*
Council for Mutual Economic Assistance (COMECON), *59*
Council of the Laity, *132*
Counterculture, *119–20*
Culture, *250, 267, 290–99, 308, 374–75, 399, 446*

Darwin, Charles, *8, 135*
Day, Dorothy, *68*
Day of Peace, *122, 128*
Death, *256–57, 261, 273*
Debt, *457*
De Chardin, Teilhard, *26, 136*
Declaration on Religious Liberty, 128
De Gaulle, Charles, *59*
Demographic growth, *see* Population
Dependence, *456–58, 460, 464*
Dependency, *16, 17, 48, 51, 53, 136*
Developing nations, *49, 51, 53, 120*
Development, *7, 10, 16, 17, 36, 47, 49, 50, 52, 55, 86, 98, 102–3, 107, 108, 109, 111, 114, 129, 144, 157, 158, 159–61, 176–90, 215, 226–27, 228, 270, 280–81, 290–93, 296–97, 301–8, 321–23, 381, 384, 387–415, 422–24, 447, 450, 451, 453–54, 455, 456–58, 459, 464, 467–68, 469, 477–84, 506, 515–18, 527–28, 536, 537, 540, 544, 547, 559, 561, 589, 603–5*
  in social documents, *9–10, 18, 20–21, 49–50, 55, 69, 77, 83–84, 100, 124, 126*
Development Decade
  First, *5, 18, 108, 113*
  Second, *18, 108*
Development programs, criteria for, *397, 402, 406–7, 408*
Dignitatis Humanae, 13, 537
Disarmament, *71–76, 83–84, 88, 107, 224–26, 315–20, 383–84, 526, 536, 538–39, 551, 556, 603–4*
Discrimination, *210, 265–66, 302–3, 376–77, 490, 493, 565, 603–4, see also* Racial discrimination
Distribution of goods, *158, 159–61, 163, 167, 170, 176, 177–82, 215, 223, 250, 300, 302, 305–6, 320, 322, 324–25, 364, 389–90, 397, 402, 405, 410, 446–47, 465, 473, 480–81, 484, 486, 488, 506, 515, 516, 537, 553*
Divine law, *325, 339, 437*
Djilas, Milovan, *78*

Economic and Social Council (ECOSOC), 47
Economic and social institutions, criteria for, 161, 322, 393
Economic life, private initiative in, 154–55, 215
Economic organization, criteria for, 150–51, 161, 205, 449–50
Economic rights, 205, 299–308, 321
Economic systems, 12–13, 15–16, 17, 23–24, 48–55
Ecumenical movement, 127, 130–32, 135–36
Education, 246, 297, 385, 397, 423, 452, 456, 466, 469–70, 519, 527, 605, 609, 611
Education for justice and peace, 191–92, 234, 325, 383, 397, 412, 460, 462, 497, 523–25, 556, 609, 611
Einstein, Albert, 135
Emergency relief, 178–79, 324
Emigration rights, 152, 206, 493–94
Environment, 25, 55, 57, 108–9, 495–96, 515, 516, 528
Equality, 220, 231, 265–66, 308, 342, 376–77, 382–83, 405–6, 422–23, 493, 515, 545
Ethnic rights, 213, 221, 222–23, 227, 418–19, 539
European Economic Community (EEC), 59, 62
Evangelization, 280, 466–67, 470, 474, 569, 570–71, 579, 590–91, 593–98
Evangelization of the Modern World, 129

Family, 5, 6, 7, 10, 12, 13, 15, 25, 31, 33, 96–103, 111–12, 151, 152, 204–5, 249, 264, 268, 282–90, 297, 341, 398, 420, 424–25, 448, 464–71, 490, 570
Fascism, 11, 65
Food and Agricultural Organization (FAO), 47
Food production, 91–96, 103–7, *see also* Hunger
Fourth World, 51, 61, 67
Freedom, 13, 16, 20, 77, 208, 209, 226, 255–56, 258, 264, 267, 276, 295, 298–99, 306–7, 338, 342–43, 345, 522, 537, 553, 570, 575, 596, 597
Free enterprise, 23–24
Freewill, 9
Freud, Sigmund, 7, 135

Gagnon, Bishop, 104–5
Galileo, 135
Gallegos, Hector, 78
Gandhi, 126, 135
Gaudium et Spes, x, 10, 122–24, 126, 128, 388, 488, 524, 537, 539, 542, 560, 561, 562, 565, 609

on balance of power among nations, 17
on conscientious objection, 74–75
on development, 16
on dignity of the human person, 10, 13
on family, 111
on international agencies, 88
on peace, 70, 72–75, 77
on private property, 34–35
on progress, 114–16, 122–23
as quoted in *Octogesima Adveniens*, 45
on the regulation of birth, 97, 100–01
on relationship of church to the world, 114–16, 126
on renewal of social structures, 17, 50
on social justice, 17
on violence and terrorism, 77
on women, 111
Genocide, 421, 518
Gibbons, Bishop, 35
Government intervention
  in economic life, 146, 148, 150, 152, 154–55, 157, 162, 164, 168, 176, 301–2, 306–7, 310–12
  limitations of, 215, 310–12
  in regulating communications, 495
"Green Revolution," 482, 602
Gutiérrez, Gustavo, 135

Harmel, 35
Hegel, 7
Holy days, 195–96
Holy Year, 128, 573–87, 598, 612
Human dignity, 8, 9–13, 131, 133, 147, 148, 158, 161, 163, 181, 189, 196, 202, 203, 205, 206, 208, 209, 210, 212, 218, 226, 229, 232, 235, 245, 251, 252–61, 262, 264, 265, 269, 274–76, 282, 290, 300, 303, 308, 314, 337–40, 344, 346, 364, 377, 389, 396, 419, 422, 424, 447, 449, 458–60, 474, 490, 494, 515, 516, 520, 521, 524, 526, 581
Human nature, 202–3, 209, 211, 216, 276, 289, 537, 541, 556–61
Human needs, 1, 5–6,11
Human rights, 9, 10–13, 17–21, 129, 131, 133, 155, 178, 203–7, 210, 215–16, 218–19, 230–32, 266, 276, 300, 302, 307, 308, 324, 377, 385, 460, 463, 516, 520, 521, 526, 536, 537, 539–40, 543, 552, 553, 554
Hunger, 144, 177–79, 185, 207, 246, 250, 263–64, 338, 340, 342–43, 353, 364, 385, 386, 387, 388, 401–2, 403, 478, 484, 515–16, 570, 582, 597, 599–606, 610

Indigenization, 64
Individual differences, 138, 180, 222–23, 227, 266, 309–11, 399, 486–87, 517, 544, 596

Industrialization, 6, 11, 23–26, 27, 35–37, 64, 91–96, 97, 108–9, 113–24, 248, 301, 390, 394–96, 451, 489–90, 493

Interdependence, 228–32, 261, 262–63, 481, 515, 543, 610

International Affairs, moral order in, 187–88, 219, 354, 540, 551, 552, 558

International Catholic Organizations (ICO), 132

International cooperation, 186–88, 228, 269, 301–2, 313–26, 381–82, 384–85, 402, 463, 526–28

International Labor Organization (ILO), 47, 88

International Monetary Fund, 54, 63, 479

International relations, criteria for, 218–28, 381

Intervention of Head of the Holy See's Delegation at Closing Session, U.N. Population Conference, 104–6

Investment, 161, 165–66, 167, 172, 173, 176, 306, 321, 468, 478, 479, 516, 528

Jubilee, 573, 575, 581, 582, 583, see also Holy Year

Justice, 1–2, 5–7, 9, 12, 17–21, 27, 30, 31, 35, 47–55, 71, 73, 104, 109, 120, 121, 126, 129, 133, 136–37

action on behalf of, 193–94, 234, 375, 410, 507–11, 514, 519, 522, 528, 529, 599

quest for, 445–54, 518–19, 520–21

unequal distribution of, 404–7, 445–47, 455–56, 458–59, 471, 486, 515, 527

see also Transnational social justice

Justice and Peace, see Pontifical Commission Justice and Peace

Justice in the World, 106, 538, 565

action on behalf of justice in, 7, 21, 114, 133–34

ecclesiology of, 16

on environment, 108

on institutionalized injustice, 20–21

on the right to development, 20–21

on the United Nations, 88–89

Just Wage, 147, 149, 158–59, 160, 174, 205, 215, 302–4, 492, 522

Kennedy, John F., 5

Keynes, John Maynard, 6

Khrushchev, Nikita, 6, 39

King, Martin Luther, Jr., 78, 126

Kingdom of God, 34, 68, 137, 138

Kissinger, Henry, 59, 107

Klompe, Marga, 132

Krol, Cardinal, 106

Labor, 148, 149–50, 151, 152, 165, 166, 167, 303–4, 395

Labor unions, 10–11, 27–28

Laissez-faire economics, 6, 11, 35, 150–51, 395, 405

Laland, Bernard, 69

Larraín, Bishop Manuel, 127

Law of the seas, 51, 54

Lay apostolate, 191, 192, 197, 233, 279–80, 411

Lay person, see Church, lay persons within

League of Nations, 47

Lenin, 8, 44

Liberalism, 395, 405, 449, 498, 501

Liberation, 17, 19, 21, 47–55, 77, 78, 94, 103, 120, 446–47, 450, 471, 473, 481, 482, 514, 517, 520, 521, 529, 552, 561, 597–98, see also Theology of liberation

Lienart, Bishop, 35

Limits to Growth debate, 19, 91–96, 98, 100–01, 104

Long, Huey, 5

Lumen Gentium, 10, 537

Manning, Bishop, 35

Mao Tse-tung, 15, 26, 37, 40, 59, 80, 126, 137

Marginality, 455, 456, 464–65, 493, 516, 517, 543, 546

Marx, Karl, 7, 10–11, 15, 80, 135

Marxism, 28, 36, 42–44, 113, 134, 148, 449, 498, 500–01

Mater et Magistra, 206, 214, 353, 388, 423, 488, 508, 524, 538, 540, 544, 604

on aspiration toward the fullness of life, 6–7, 8, 40, 125

on authority of Catholic teaching, 8

on common good, 33

on contemporary change, 31

on dignity of the human person, 8

on neo-colonialism, 17

on organization of economic life, 29–30

on population increase and economic development, 98–100

on private initiative, 31

on property, 27–28, 29, 30–33

on public intervention in economic life, 31–33

on rural life, 6

on socialism, 24–25, 31

Materialism, 251, 399, 402, 425, 498, 570

Medellín documents, 16, 18, 19, 37, 66, 102–3

Mercantilism, 27

Message of Cardinal Roy to the United Nations, 49–50

Metz, Johannes, 136

Migrants, 408, 518, 539

Ministry, see Pastoral ministry, Social ministry

Minorities, 221–22, 539
Money, imperialism of, 395, 457, 551
Moynihan, Daniel, *81*
Multinational blocs, *50–51, 52, 57–63, 65–66, 71, 82–84, 129*
Multinational corporations, *26, 48, 50, 53, 82*
Mystical Body of Christ, 197–99

Nationalism, *51, 58–63, 64–67, 79–84,* 214, 318–19, 321, 381–82, 406, 458, 517, 545, 610
Nation states, inadequacy of modern, 229, 389
Natural law, 147, 148, 149, 152, 204, 207, 229, 235, 236, 309–10, 315–16, 325, 535–36, 556–57, *see also* Church, Catholic, natural law and
Natural resources, *91–92, 108–9*
Nazism, *11, 65, 68–69*
Nehru, 25
Nixon, Richard, *6, 59*
Nonviolence, 522, 526, 565
North Atlantic Treaty Organization (NATO), *59*
Nuclear weapons, *71–74, 84, 126*
Nyerere, Julius, *120*

Octogesima Adveniens, 128, 524, 538, 549, 552, 559, 562
  on economic systems, *37*
  on growth and urbanization, *109*
  on pluralism concerning change, *43–45*
  on political engagement of the church, *42*
  on Pontifical Commission Justice and Peace, *129*
  on regionalization, *66*
  on revolution and violence, *77–78*
  on situations of injustice, *19*
  on socialism, *43–45*
  on utopias, *2, 44*
OECD, *49, 60*
On the Regulation of Birth, 97–98, 102, 112
OPEC, *26, 51, 52, 61–62, 82, 106*
Oppressed, *see* Poor and oppressed
Order in created things, 201–3, 250, 255, 288, 305, 309, 394, 403, 433–34

Pacem in Terris, 119, 385, 388, 524, 533–67, 610
  as declaration of human dignity, *11–12*
  on economic rights, *33*
  on historical movements, *43*
  on interdependence of nations, *58, 84–85*
  on multinational blocs, *63*
  on nations and the world community, *82–87, 125*

on peace, *69–72*
on rights and duties, *9, 125*
on solidarity, *83–84*
on women's rights, *12*
Participation in public life, 206, 207, 217, 232, 267, 278–79, 308–9, 310–12, 325–26, 411–12, 424–25, 481, 482, 507–8, 517, 521–22, 528, 558–59, *see also* Workers' participation
Pastoral ministry, *1, 2, 16, 45, 137, 448,* 453–54, 579–80
Paul, Saint, 211, 396, 520, 524, 562
Pax Christi, *69*
Peace, *6, 12, 47, 68–79, 88, 113–14, 126, 128–29,* 225–26, 229, 237–39, 308, 312–19, 352, 353–54, 377, 381, 383–84, 410–11, 418, 422, 453, 455–63, 486, 494, 536, 537–38, 539, 540, 541–42, 544, 546, 547, 549, 550–56, 557–59, 560, 561, 563, 564–67, 571, 575, 581, 607–13
Peasant class, 451
People of God, *2, 19, 21, 46, 128, 129, 130, 135*
Philosophies of life, 188–90, 194–95, 235–36, 257–60, 302, 498–501, 535, 609–10
Political engagement of the church, 276–77, 312–13, 507–9
Political freedom, 206
Political organization, 217–18, 497–502
Political power, *39–45*
Political prisoners, 223–24, 519
Political refugees, 518
Politics, nature and goals of, 309–10, 507–9
Pollution, *91–96, 108–10*
Pontifical Commission Justice and Peace, 17, *18, 55, 129, 132,* 388, 478, 488, 511, 526, 528, 533, 534
Poor and oppressed, preference for, 145, 213, 243–44, 310–11, 322, 353, 381, 388, 453, 462, 468, 474, 496, 581, 582, 597
Pope John XXIII, *1, 4, 6–7, 8, 9, 10, 12, 17, 24, 25, 27–35, 39, 42, 43, 45, 50, 58, 65, 68, 69, 71, 73, 77, 78, 82–87, 98–100,* 113, 118, 125, 126, 385, 395, 401, 423, 508, 533, 535–46, 548, 549, 550, 554, 557, 558, 560, 561, 565, 566, 567, 588, 604, 610
Pope Leo XIII, *2,* 27, 28, 29, 41, 47, 145–52, 154, 168, 204, 213, 405, 487, 538
Pope Paul VI, *7, 10, 17, 18, 19, 34, 36, 37, 41–47, 50, 58, 73, 77, 82, 87–88, 97–98, 101–3, 105–10, 112, 113, 114, 121–23, 126, 128–29, 131,* 457, 461, 478, 480, 481, 483, 527, 533, 539, 542, 544, 546, 554, 556, 561, 562, 563, 565, 566, 593
Address to U.N. on Twentieth Anniversary, *73, 87–88*
Address to U.N. Conference on Food, Rome, *106–7*

Bull of Indiction of Holy Year, *121–22*
Message to Stockholm Conference on the Environment, 108–9
Pope Pius XI, *29, 30–31,* 148, 149, 151, 154, 158, 160, 173, 194, 395, 457, 506
Pope Pius XII, *31, 35, 48, 71, 73, 83, 97,* 151, 152, 159, 161, 163, 166, 167, 182, 194, 205, 206, 211, 225, 227, 237, 388, 409, 538
Population, *23, 51, 83, 91–106, 108–9, 111–12, 115, 127,* 177, *182–86,* 223, 247, *323–24,* 385, 398, 439, 456, *464–65, 467–68,* 479, *482–83, 515–16,* 517, *527–28,* 545, *589–91,* 604
Populorum Progressio, 106, 128, 422, 457, 458, 468, 480, 481, 483, 488, 494, 503, 509, 524, 527, 538, 540, *553–54,* 561, 599
  on economic systems, *37, 49*
  on integral development, *8–9, 17*
  on oppressive social structures, *17*
  on peace, *69–70*
  on population growth and regulation, *101*
  on revolution, *77*
  on transnational social justice, *128*
Poverty, *7, 17, 19, 55, 99, 109, 116, 126–27, 178–79,* 183, 185, 246, 267, 364, 381, 390, 401, 404, 410, 412, 457, *471–76,* 484, *515–16,* 523, 527, 553, 597, 602, 610
Powderly, *35*
Power structures, *15–21*
Praxis, *see* Pastoral ministry, Social ministry
Price stabilization of agricultural products, *173–74*
Prisoners of war, 519
Private property, 148, 149, 152, *165–69,* 205, *306–7, 393–94,* 395
Profits, regulation of, *159–61,* 395, *449–50*
Progress, 157, 158, 194, 195, 202, 217, 220, 228, 233, 238, *246–49,* 255, 270, 272, *291–92,* 300, 308, 322, 364, 385, 386, 393, 394, 396, *397–98, 400–01,* 402, 410, 420, 422, 424, 447, 492, *504–5,* 516, 517, 522, 523, 558, *560–61,* 565, 582, 605, 610
Property, *7, 11, 24, 27–35, 36, 37, 40, see also* Private property, Public property
Protest, 549, *552–53*
Protestant ethic, 27
Public life, *see* Participation in public life
Public property, 168, *306–7*

Quadragesimo Anno, 148, *149–51,* 154, 158, 160, 173, 194, 388, 457, 488
  on industrial relations, *35*
  on private property, *29*
  on state's participation in economy, *11*
  on subsidiarity, *31–32*

Racial discrimination, *12,* 210, 220, 377, 406, 421, 422, 493, 518, 540, 609
Reconciliation, *3, 121–22, 127,* 265, 352, 536, *565–66, 575–76,* 579, *597–98, 607–13*
Reflections on Pacem in Terris
  on conscientious objection, *75*
  on natural law, *9*
  on peace, *71–72*
  on regionalization, *66–67*
  on violence and terrorism, *77*
Reform of social and economic structures, *396–97, 401–2, 404–7, 446–47,* 448, 452, 456, 460, 480, *482–83,* 487, 507, 517, 527, 582, 597
Regionalism, *35–37, 54, 57–59, 63–64, 66–68*
Regulation of birth, 184, 185, 286, 289, *323–24,* 385, 398, *434–36, 468–69, 482–83,* 519, *603–4*
Relationship between faith and social action, 177, 399, 462, *520–21, 524–25*
Relationship of church to world, *ix, 37, 114, 125–26, 127, 129–30, 133–34, 181–82,* 243–45, 252, *270–71, 274–81, 294–95, 312–13, 325–28, 346–47,* 380, 391, *411–12, 453–54,* 576, *485–86,* 501, *509–10,* 514, *519–23, 524–25,* 528, 529, 536, *562–64,* 597
Religions, non-Christian, *55, 64, 130–31, 135,* 137
Religious liberty, 204, *337–49,* 518
Rerum Novarum, 11, 19, 27–28, 30, 35, 41, 47, 145–49, 150, 151, 152, 154, 168, 388, 405, 485, 487, 488, 506, 524
Responsible parenthood, 185, 205, *283–85, 286–90,* 432, *440–41, 466–67,* 470
Revolution and violence, *236–37, 314–16,* 381, 390, 396, 418, *421–22, 458–62,* 498, *506–7, 518–19,* 543, *547–48, 586–87,* 595, 608
Right to life, 519
Roosevelt, Franklin D., *5, 81*

Sakharov, Andrei, *15*
Second Development Decade, Message of Cardinal Roy on, *8–19, 49, 108*
Secularization, *575–76,* 595
Self-determination, *226–27,* 322, *403–4,* 407, 517, 524, 527, 528
Self-development, 220, 221, 305, 322, *391–92*
"Signs of the times," *12, 86–87, 130, 135,* 209–10, *217–18, 227–28, 231–32,* 246, 347, 359, 514, 537, 542, 549, *561–66,* 595
Sin, *253–54,* 256, 263, *271–76,* 295, *314–15,* 376, 446, 455, *472–73,* 514, 519, 521, 524, 529, 541, 597, 612
Skinner, B.F., *137*
Smith, Adam, *6*
Social ethics, *7–8*

Social insurance, 162, 165, 172–73, 203, 215
Socialism, *2, 5, 8, 11, 15, 25, 35, 36, 37, 39–40, 42–45,* 149, 150, *499–500,* 516
Socialization, *2, 24–29, 31, 33, 114,* 155–57, 248, 262–63, 310–12, 450–51, 454, 464
Social ministry, *1–2, 16, 17, 37, 45, 50, 64, 130, 131, 137*
Social responsibility, 155–58, 162, 168–69, 178, 207–09, 215–19, 222, 263–64, 266–67, 277–80, 309–12, 343, 388, 392, 408, 411–12, 507–11, 515, 521
Sociosphere, *26–27, 29*
SODEPAX, *55, 64, 65*
Solzhenitsyn, Aleksandr, *78*
Special Drawing Rights (SDR) System, *53–54*
State, purpose of, 148
Structure of government, criteria for, 216
Structures, *see* Reform of social and economic structures
Subsidiarity, principle of, *30, 31, 33, 86, 118,* 154, 168, 177, 231, 322
Synod of Bishops, *7, 16, 19–21, 34, 37, 45, 50, 55, 67, 75, 88, 108, 114, 129, 130, 131*
Systems dynamics, *93*

Taxation, 229, 233, 456–57, 472, 480, 481, 527
Teaching authority of the church, 143, 151, 190, 236, 262, 280, 428–30, 436–37, 441–42, 521, 566
Technological advancement, 152, 154, 156, 160, 163, 179, 185, 186, 187–88, 189, 194, 195, 202, 228, 233, 247, 248, 254, 261, 291, 294, 299, 301, 353, 385, 408, 420, 439, 479–80, 515, 600, 604–5
Technology, *2, 6, 8, 10, 16, 23, 31, 36, 37, 39, 40, 48, 53, 57, 59, 80, 94, 99–100, 112, 113–24*
Teresa, Mother, *78.*
Terrorism, 315–16, 546–47
Theological reflection, *2, 133–38*
Theology of liberation, *16, 36, 64, 134, 136, see also* Liberation
Third World, *37, 48–51, 60–61, 67, 81–82, 94, 104, 111–12, 120, 127*
bishops of, *7,* 127
Toniolo, *35*
Torres, Camilo, *78*
Trade relations, *52,* 321, 404–5, 463, 483, 527
Transnational social justice, *47–55, 67,* 177–78, 220–21, 226–27, 325–26, 388, 405–6, 518–19, 526–28
Truman, Harry, *5*

Ujamaa, *36, 120*
UNCTAD, *see* United Nations, Conference on Trade and Development

Unemployment, 155, 160, 203, 480, 489, 494, 516
UNESCO, *see* United Nations, Educational, Scientific, and Cultural Organization
Unions and cooperatives, 146, 148, 153, 162, 164–65, 174, 175, 303–4, 398–99, 450, 451, 492
Unitatis Redintegratio, 537
United Nations, *12, 18, 26, 48, 50, 51, 55, 61, 66, 70, 73–74, 78–89, 93, 98, 120, 122, 123, 126, 128, 132, 134,* 231, 232, 379–86, 388, 410, 411, 478–81, 526, 527, 535, 540, 545, 554, 556, 599, 611
agencies, 47
Bucharest Conference on Population, *51, 94, 95, 103–6, 589–91*
Conference on Trade and Development (UNCTAD), *50–51, 95,* 480, 527
Declaration of Human Rights, *11, 84, 87, 88, 134*
Educational, Scientific, and Cultural Organization (UNESCO), 47, 610
Rome Conference on Food, *54, 95, 106–7,* 599–606
Stockholm Conference on Environment, *19, 55, 108*
Urbanization, 248, 451, 464, 489–91, 516, 527
Utopias, *2, 43–45, 55, 68, 79, 81, 131,* 502, 552, 559, 610

Values, 248, 252, 290–91, 292, 297, 388, 392, 399, 402, 420–21, 519, 526, 557, 560, 670
Vatican Council II, *1, 7, 8, 10, 12, 13, 17, 18, 33–35, 46, 65, 72–74, 75, 88, 97, 100–02, 111, 113–16, 122–23, 125–28, 136*
Violence, *17, 20, 76–78, 118–19, 126*
institutionalized, 460, 548, *see also* Revolution and violence
Von Ketteler, Bishop, *35*

War, *70–74, 83–84, 88, 107, 187,* 224–25, 227–28, 313–21, 353, 381, 383, 422, 463, 519, 526, 536, 537, 538–39, 543, 546–47, 550–51, 575, 582, 600, 601, 604, 608, 610
Ward, Barbara, *132*
Watergate, *40*
Weber, Max, *27*
Welfare state, *5–7*
Women's rights, 204, 205, 209–10, 266, 288–90, 296–97, 424–25, 446, 491, 522, 611
Women's Year, International, 611
Worker priests, *42*
Workers
participation in industry by, 149, 159–60, 162–65, 304–5

rights of, 146–48, 149–50, 158, 205, 264–65, 303–5, 408, 449, 492, 494

World authority, establishment of, 230, 231–32, 318–19, 410–11, 536, 553–54, 582, 584

World Bank, 479

World Conference on Religion and Peace (WCRP), 64

World Council of Churches, 55, 64, 65, 93, 127

World Fund, 403, 423–24

World Health Organization (WHO), 47

"World Plan of Action," 104–5

Youth, 248–49, 324, 381, 407–8, 409, 425–26, 446, 469–70, 492, 519, 594–95, 608

Abbreviations

AFR	To the Peoples of Africa: Message of Pope Paul VI to the Hierarchy and to All the Peoples of Africa
DD	Message of Maurice Cardinal Roy on the Occasion of the Launching of the Second Development Decade
DH	Dignitatis Humanae: Declaration on Religious Freedom (Second Vatican Council)
EMW	Evangelization of the Modern World: Synod of Bishops Third General Assembly
FABC	Letter of Paul VI to the Federation of Asian Bishops' Conferences, First General Assembly, Taipei
FC	Address of Pope Paul VI to the Participants of the World Food Conference, Rome
GS	Gaudium et Spes: Pastoral Constitution on the Church in the Modern World (Second Vatican Council)
HV	Humanae Vitae: On the Regulation of Birth
HY	Bull of Indiction of the Holy Year 1975
JW	Justice in the World: Synod of Bishops Second General Assembly
MDFD	Medellín Document, Family and Demography
MDJ	Medellín Document, Justice
MDP	Medellín Document, Peace
MDPC	Medellín Document, Poverty of the Church
MH	Message to Humanity (Second Vatican Council)
MM	Mater et Magistra: Christianity and Social Progress
NA	Nostra Aetate: Declaration on the Relationship of the Church to Non-Christian Religions (Second Vatican Council)
OA	Octogesima Adveniens: The Eightieth Anniversary of "Rerum Novarum"
PC	The Holy See's Intervention at the United Nations Conference on Population, Bucharest
PP	Populorum Progressio: On the Development of Peoples
PT	Pacem in Terris: Peace on Earth
RR	Reflections by Cardinal Roy on the Occasion of the Tenth Anniversary of the Encyclical "Pacem in Terris"
RWP	Reconciliation—the Way to Peace: Message of His Holiness Pope Paul VI for the Celebration of the Day of Peace
UR	Unitatis Redintegratio: Decree on Ecumenism (Second Vatican Council)
UN	Address of Pope Paul VI to the General Assembly of the United Nations